THE SUN AT MIDNIGHT

THE REVEALED MYSTERIES
OF THE AHLUL BAYT SUFIS

LAURENCE GALIAN

QUIDDITY
INC.

Library of Congress Control Number: 00-092962

ISBN: 0-9679458-0-1

Typesetting and Design by JM Press, Brentwood, Tennessee (JMpress.com)

Quiddity , Inc.

PRINTED IN THE UNITED STATES OF AMERICA

Bismillah ir Rahman ir Rahim
(In the name of the Infinite Reality, Compassionate and Merciful)

"Stories about the Green Man Khidr, and stories Khidr himself told come back. We thought they were lost."

-Jelaluddin Rumi [1]

ALSO BY LAURENCE GALIAN :

BEYOND DUALITY: THE ART OF TRANSCENDENCE
New Falcon Publications 1995

THE ART OF DANCE ACCOMPANYING
Blackwell Distributors 1988

MEMORIAL

To the memory of my beloved Father, Laurence Hyacinth Dermit Gagliano.

September 11, 1920 - April 25, 1996.

". . . that's the glory of love."

TABLE OF CONTENTS

ا

ب

ت

ث

ج

ح

خ

ل

ن

ر

ز

س

ط

ظ

ع

غ

ف

ق

ك

ل

م

ن

ه

و

ع

ى

لا

"The true direction of life is pointing towards our heart, the only place where man will find his unity with God."

- Habiba [2]

"The Kingdom of God is within you."

- Prophet Isa ('Alaihi Assalam),
Luke 17:21

ACKNOWLEDGMENTS

Specifically we want to thank certain people for their gracious and generous help in making our manuscript manifest as a book. For his editorial and proofreading assistance, we want to thank the late author and poet, Robert Johnston. Special acknowledgments go to Mary Woodward for her always-insightful suggestions, as well as to Aaron Vlek and Walter Alter. We are grateful to Julianne Sullivan of the Hofstra University Academic Computing Faculty who has so generously helped us in our endeavors, and to Rosann Kelly, Acting Director of the Hofstra University College of Continuing Education. We express our appreciation to the University of Haifa. Acknowledgments also go out to the people at the "Cyber-Café," "Garden of Delight" and "Trinity College," in Dublin, Ireland.

TA'WIL[3] OF SURA FATIHA FROM THE QUR'AN

In the Resonance of the Ultimate Reality, the Opening of Love

First Appearing as Balance and Measure,

We offer Praise to the Essence of Essences, the Radiance of all Domains of

Existence,

The Primary Equilibrium and Destiny.

Wielder of the Apotheosis of Karma.

Thee we serve as Image of Unity, and through Thee, we find Awareness.

Your Reality Guides us on the razor sharp Way of Symmetry,

The Balanced Way of the Living Truth known to the Few.

The Few that do not feel disconnected from the Living World

In spite of distressing experiences.

The Few whose Universal Selves are reflections of the Unitary Being.

PRAYER

O Lord! All praise belongs to You as much as befits Your Glory and Sublime Majesty.[4] Glory to Allah and praise Him to the number of His creation and to the extent of His pleasure and to the extent of the weight of His Throne and to the extent of the ink used in recording words for His Praise.[5] *Subhan Allah wa bi hamdihi* - Glorified is Allah with all praise to Him.[6] We beg forgiveness of our sins from you, O Allah, *ya Tawwab.*

We ask the blessings of *"one of Our servants unto whom We had given mercy from Us, and whom We had taught knowledge proceeding from Us,"* upon all who read this book.

We beseech the blessings of the Ahlul Bayt (the five "Companions of the Mantle"): Muhammad Mustafa - The Seal of the Prophets (Peace be upon him), Imam Ali Haydar ('Alaihi Assalam), Lady Fatima tul Zehra ('Alaiha Assalam), Imam Hassan ('Alaihi Assalam) and Imam Hussain ('Alaihi Assalam), and the sixth, upon this book.[7]

*"Out beyond duality,
we have a home, and it is Majesty."*

- Jelaluddin Rumi [8]

A REQUEST

Before you begin to read this book, please put it down and meditate for five minutes on your inner self.

1

"Do not seek to follow in the footsteps of the men of old; seek what they sought."

> *- Matsuo Basho*

"Through all the Western politeia
Religion withers to the roots."

> *- Iqbal*

"Proclaim the truth."

> *- Imam Ali Ibn Abi Talib*
> *('Alaihi Assalam)*

"O Lord, remove the dryness of our cities with Thy watering."
> *- Imam Zain al-Abidin*
> *('Aalaihi Aaslam)*

"Attributeless and predicateless though the divine Being is, the mystics nevertheless make their inexplicable journey to IT, and gaze upon ITS face."
> *- Der Islam*

". . . how can this Unknowable, Unimaginable, and Inconceivable be nevertheless 'reached' by mystic souls?"
> *- W. H. T. Gairdner*

THE SUBLIME UNITY

One. The Clear. The Obvious. The Infinitely Pre-Existent. The Living. The Reality. The Mighty Splendor. The Knower of the Most Subtle Mysteries. We put our trust only in Allah. IT's Essence is unknowable, as IT IS. They asked Abu 'l-'Abbas al-Dinawari, *"How did you know God?"* He replied, *"By the fact that I do not know Him."* No book, speech, wisdom, or religion can fully explain Allah. For Allah is Endless and Fathomless. IT is the beginning and the end. However, there is no beginning to IT's beginning and no end to IT's end.

   "(God is) . . . an Existent who transcends ALL that is comprehensible by human Sight or human Insight,"[9] describes Al-Ghazali. Elsewhere he writes, *"And God's knowledge is absolutely unlike that of His creatures."*[10] Finally, Ghazali makes this astonishing pronouncement to his Lord; *"I do not count praises unto Thee as Thou hast praised Thyself."*[11] All the praise from time immemorial until the Final Day of Reckoning is inadequate to proclaim Allah's praiseworthiness.

   If God is unknowable, how does the Sufi *know* God? Al-Siddiq offers this insight, *"Glory be to Him Who has not appointed for creatures any way to know him, save by incapacity to know Him.*" The Murid must divest him or herself from any preconception of God and any hope of intellectually knowing God. All we can say is, *"May Allah forgive us our sins,"* and then hope for Allah's Mercy. This One Living Being cannot be said to be located anywhere or in any particular place, for that would be a restriction and limitation. There is no place that exists that is not filled with Allah, for Allah is Omniscient and Omnipresent.

Yet, the Sufis know the mystery. The means to the direct experience of the Ultimate Reality is found within the Human Heart. *"The heart is the place where the Forgiver casts his gaze, and the seat of belief, and the receptacle of secrets, and the source of lights."*[12] The Infinite Reality that cannot be contained in all the universes upon universes can fit into the heart of the believer. The Holy Prophet of the Divine Reality, Muhammad (Peace be upon him) made it clear to us that if the heart is healthy, the whole body is healthy; and if it is unhealthy, the whole body is unhealthy.

"Do you not see that the heart lies between the two fingers of the All-merciful?"[13] The fluctuation of the heart is caused only by the All Merciful, that is, whether it follows the straight path or swerves from the path. It is important to remember that *"mercy is the heart's fundamental reality. It cannot but return to the divine mercy in the end."*[14] Ibn 'Arabi amplifies this sacred insight. *"The heart is His Throne and not delimited by any specific attribute. On the contrary, it brings together all the divine names and attributes, just as the All-merciful possesses all the Most Beautiful Names."*[15]

Ghazali was a staunch defender of Allah's uniqueness, though at times he bestowed glimpses of ways to experience Allah directly. *"There is no veil between you and Him except your preoccupation with aught else."*[16] In other words, you separate yourself from Allah, thereby preventing a direct experience of Allah. If you clean the mirror of your soul, then Allah sees Allah. If you are preoccupied with the drama of your lives, Allah will forever remain to you - *ya Batin*, The Hidden. Nonetheless, there is a way to approach in an intimate manner, this Essence. *"There is only one way of approach – simply **being** Essence."*[17]

"It is not a sin to question traditional doctrines. It is a sin to be afraid to."
- Bill Donahue

"Pure truth, like pure gold, has been found unfit for circulation because men have discovered that it is far more convenient to adulterate the truth than to refine themselves."
- Charles Caleb Colton

RADICAL SPIRITUALITY
(REGAINING THE TREASURE STOLEN FROM US)

In this book, this poorest of Allah's creatures, a lover, *muhip*, of the Family of the Mantle, endeavors to pass from his heart to the heart of the reader the spontaneous words of Divine Light uttered by the Sheikhs of the *Alevi*. Alevi is a general term applied to those who recognize Imam Ali ('Alaihi Assalam) as the rightful Imam following the Prophet and to those who recognize a special attachment to Ali ('Alaihi Assalam). Other Sufi orders trace themselves back to one or another of the companions of the Prophet Muhammad (Peace be upon him), such as the Naqshi and Mevlevi Orders which go back in tradition to Abu Bakr. We believe our Way came from Imam Ali ('Alaihi Assalam).

We write this book in the spirit of Hazreti Khezr ('Alaihi Assalam) and therefore we may be sometimes irreverent, surprising, controversial, outrageous, and perhaps misunderstood by those who can only see the outward form. Many *tekkes* have turned into stagnant ponds. The perceptive one sees that a body of water, lacking movement and a fresh influx of water, fills with silt and dies. Mathematicians are now revealing the wonder of "chaos theory" - the beauty and infinite designs resident in weather patterns, coastlines, galaxies, seashells, and so forth. The world is not a gigantic clock where everything happens in an ordered and predictable manner. The real world is disordered, free. Chaos reigns over predictability. The perceptive one knows that many people do not like chaos entering their lives. Hermann Hesse realized this verity and wrote: *"Chaos demands to be recognized and experienced before letting itself be converted into a new order."* This very "chaos," this infinitely coiled and uncoiling ever-new creation, must be a part of any system (be it a pond or a *tekke*) in order for that system to be vital and alive. Balance must be struck between Tradition and the Fresh Vision.[18] Laws govern the Universe, but the laws are of a different kind than previously thought. Like the common law system, the Laws of Wisdom are inherently flexible.

The new discoveries of the Science of Chaos, and the scientists in this field - "Chaosticians" are revolutionizing the world of science. The Science of Chaos began to appear in the last part of this century, although Khezr ('Alaihi Assalam) was teaching these mysteries from time immemorial to those who would listen. The Chaosticians' close measurements revealed that the unpredictable appeared in what scientists previously believed to be the most ordered and predictable of systems, the swinging of a simple pendulum - the very heart of a clock. As James Gleick's book "Chaos"[19] shows, the brave early explorers of Chaos found that Science had been fooling itself for centuries by ignoring tiny deviations in its data and experiments If a number was slightly off what the causal laws predicted, the pre-chaos scientists simply assumed there was an error in measurement in order to uphold the sanctity of the law itself. The Chaos lurking behind all order, would not be denied. Khezr ('Alaihi Assalam) cannot be denied. The charade of perfect order and fudged experimental data could not last forever. Nor could the traditional ways of the Turkish tekkes continue as they had been. Sheikh Muzaffer Ashki-al Jerrahi al-Halveti, appeared in America, and forever set tradition on its ear. By the nineteen seventies the pre-chaos world view began to crumble, the conceptual blinders were falling from the eyes of more and more scientists. By the nineteen eighties the fly in the ointment, the unpredictable results in what should have been perfect predictability, could no longer be denied. The Science of Chaos was born. Our understanding of the world will never be the same. After nearly two decades now of work by Chaosticians made up of the leading scientists and mathematicians in a wide variety of fields, the evidence is overwhelming. Simple, linear systems which are causal and predictable are the exception in the Universe, not the rule. Most of the Universe works in jumps, in a nonlinear fashion that cannot be exactly predicted. It is infinitely complex.[20]

It is time for Sufism to experience a quantum metamorphosis. It is time for a dawn of splendor on the path of Reality to occur. This is happening as we write this, for in this book, we present several chapters about the lives of the Prophet Muhammad (Peace be upon him) and certain members of the Prophet's family, together known as the Ahlul Bayt. Reliable information about the Ahlul Bayt is lacking in the west, and there is little written about the Ahlul Bayt from a Sufi perspective in English. Why will historical information about the lives of these excellent people change the face of Sufism?

Before we began following the Sufi Way in 1981, we first became a Sunni Muslim. The Sunni sect is the largest sect in Islam. It was only during our research for this present book did we uncover the most vile conspiracy that commenced just before the death of the Holy Prophet of Islam - Muhammad (Peace be upon him) and continues to this day. The purpose of this conspiracy was to obscure and thwart the Holy Prophet's clear instructions to the Islamic community as to what should happen after his death. This conspiracy has robbed Islam and hence Sufism, of its full richness and its true soul. Therefore, for the purpose of uncovering this conspiracy, and revealing the beauty that it has hidden, this book describes in detail the lives of Ahlul Bayt, so that the mirror of Islam may be cleaned and polished. The truth, no matter how painful, is always better than ignorance or denial. There was much pain in the lives of these lofty spiritual beings. Some Sufis would prefer to read a book on Sufism that did not include any harsh realities. They would prefer a book that makes them feel good. Our goal is not to make the reader "feel good," but to help the reader find *Haqiqat* (The Level of Truth). *"Then as for those who believe in Allah and hold fast by Him, He will cause them to enter into His mercy and grace and guide them to Himself on a right path."*[21] This right path is the Ahlul Bayt. Love and acknowledgment of the Ahlul Bayt by the Sufis will create a new dimension and expansion of consciousness. The time has come for America and the rest of the Western World to know the facts about this beautiful and fragrant bouquet of persons who make up what is known as the Ahlul Bayt.

We ask you to read this book with an open and clear mind, free of judgement. Allow yourself to experience the lives of these holy persons. Then, after reading the book, assess what you have read about the Ahlul Bayt in an unbiased manner, allowing your heart to answer all questions. *"This is a clear statement for men, and a guidance and an admonition to those who guard (against evil)."*[22]

"The Province that casts this spell
And speaks so many tongues to tell,
Transcends the earth, heaven and hell,
But is contained in this cast.
The yearning tormented my mind:
I searched the heavens and the ground;
I looked and looked, but failed to find.
I found Him inside man at last."

-Yunus Emre

WE ARE SPIRITUAL BEINGS
HAVING A HUMAN EXPERIENCE

All humanity is an aspect of Divinity, having its existence within the Omniconscious Unicity known as God. This state of Unity is Abundantly Compassionate and It exists in a state of Transcendent Awareness that encompasses all the polarities that the manifest world possesses. Everything proceeds from that Point of Transcendence and Glory. Oh, our brothers and sisters of the Way, Sufism is the most delicate and dangerous of paths, for the dervish dares to storm the gates of heaven itself. The dervish must be careful and watchful, always to guard against pride, despair, apathy, and intellectualism. Find where your true existence is. It lies in the center of your soul. Concentrate your attention there. We live in chaotic times. We are seeing vastly sweeping changes in our society, country and the world. We are a culture in crisis. The repercussions of war, violence, crime, and terrorism are constantly affecting us. Our mundane lives have changed in various ways to adapt to these changes in our world. All stores now have metal gratings over their doors and windows. Each new car has several anti-theft devices installed. "Road Rage" explodes over the nation's highways as ordinary people get behind the wheel and impulsively let out their pent-up frustrations by driving in a belligerent, hostile and an aggressive manner. There have been several incidents when a traffic dispute has erupted into gunfire and death. Fear is sweeping America.

Negative advertising, drug laundering, media manipulation, censorship, confiscatory tax rates, the threat of international chemical, biological, and nuclear terrorism, and partisan politics beset us from all directions. Financial interests are pitted against health interests in hospitals; profit is given priority over education in universities. Wealthy campaign contributors and powerful lobbyists determine public policy. *"People seek to turn away from the world with its disappointments and seek refuge in a life of devotion and faith trying to overcome the world."*[23] However, this is not the way of the Sufi. Americans hold the key to the word's spiritual future. America is a kind of spiritual lynchpin – if America falls, the world falls, if America becomes spiritual, the world is saved.

The world is shrinking. The Internet, FAX machines, cellular telephones, and the World Wide Web, bring the world community closer together. Spirituality has to adapt to the times, it must provide some sort of passage through the labyrinth, and afford people some measure of context. Unfortunately, contemporary society is not finding spiritual fulfillment in the mainstream religions of today. The old Patriarchal-Dualistic paradigm failed us miserably in the 20th Century. Therefore, we are offering spiritual knowledge *(ilm a la dun)* to be of help to people during these difficult times, *"the oldest love in new shapes"* [24] as Rumi declares. We soundly base this approach on the wisdom of the greatest Sufi Saints and Sheikhs.

The world is undergoing a kind of nervous breakdown. The reason the world is coming apart is that it needs an openhearted and truthful concept of Divinity. *"All things appear different, depending on the angle from which they are considered, being only true to a certain extent in comparison to ultimate truth, which is beyond all speculative theory,"* states Pir-o-Murshid Inayat Khan.[25] Humanity is crying out for a fresh way to relate to the Divine. We are offering a Way in this book.

While all across the globe, humanity is going through a spiritual crisis; spiritual energy is streaming toward the Earth. Humanity is at a spiritual turning point. The human race has the opportunity to channel this Divine energy to bring forth a new way of experiencing the Living World. It is time to reveal the esoteric secrets held by the Ahlul Bayt Sufis, so that the world may survive the present crisis. Through this book, we hope to facilitate the rebirth of spirituality in society. We can experience the Absolute Existence in the 21st Century, as IT has no time constraints, and because IT is Eternal.

All proceeds from the Sublime One even what we humanly term "good" and "bad." Explaining rationally the problem of personal suffering, the suffering of ethnic groups and the suffering of nations is impossible. Schopenhauer eloquently says, *"If we were to conduct the most hardened and callous optimist through hospitals, infirmaries, operating theaters, through prisons, torture-chambers, and slave hovels, over battlefields and to places of execution; if we were to open to him all the dark abodes of misery, where it shuns the gaze of cold curiosity, and finally were to allow him to glance into the dungeon of Ugolino where prisoners starved to death, he too would certainly see in the end what kind of a world is this 'meilleur des mondes possible'."* [26] Kelley L. Ross, Ph.D. adds, *"Where 'Ugolino' is just a name to us, we can only imagine how today Schopenhauer might replace it with Verdun, Auschwitz, Hiroshima, Cambodia, Bosnia, Rwanda, or any of the many other stupefying horrors of the 20th century."* [27] No one can understand Allah's justice.

"We all lose and we all gain.
Dark crowds the light.
Light fills the pain . . .
It is a conversation with no end
a dance with no steps
a song with no words
a reason too big for any mind . . ." [28]

Nevertheless, certain glimpses of the Divine Premeasurement, which governs all created beings, can be gleaned, and will be discussed in this book.

Sufis and Muslims have believed in the coming of the Imam Mahdi ('Alaihi Asslam). This exalted being would mark the last era, and would make the inner doctrine public and inaugurate an era of pure spiritual knowledge. When human beings free themselves from the dust of the traditions and enter the clean space, they will see the brilliant face of the friend of God and benefit from his presence without any obstruction, in public. At that time ordinances of religion will become something else, and religion will attain its original form and everything will be different. The Mahdi ('Alaihi Asslam) speaks to the hearts of all true Lovers of God. May Allah permit us to speak the inner doctrine. There is a term in Sufism known as *tafsir* that the Sheikhs define as an exploration of the deeper and hidden meanings of the Qur'an. This is accomplished through intuitive awareness for the purposes of economic, social, moral, political, and esoteric education of all people. Everything has a hidden or esoteric side to it. A music composition, a tree and the Qur'an, all have an external face and an internal face. The Prophet Muhammad (Peace be upon him) said, *"The Qur'an has its external meaning, zahir, and its hidden meaning, batin, and in its hidden meaning are other hidden meanings even to the seventh and the seventieth hidden meaning."* Referring to the Sufi's understanding of the hidden meaning of things, Jami writes, *"God has granted them a revealing light to show them things as they really are. This light appears within at the appearance of a level beyond the level of the intellect."* [29] This present work can be considered a tafsir work.

Through stories and tales, we can bypass the egoistic conscious mind and see through the veil of our Limited Selves to a larger view of reality. Therefore, throughout this book we have woven a golden thread of Sufi tales transmitted "heart-to-heart" from teacher to student over the centuries. To make these tales immediate to the reader, we have updated them into a modern context and interlaced them into an agreeable story line about two individuals.

We ask you, in the words of Yakov Leib Frank, *"only to listen and do and go on until we come to a certain hidden place."*

"As long as there is duality, [one's] relationship is with Adam and Eve. But when duality departs, the one [reality] is God. When the path of Lordship (rububiyat) appears, the dust of humanness departs."
- *Jabir Bin Abdullah Ansari*

"I form the light and create darkness. I make peace and create evil. I the Lord do all these things."
- *Isaiah 45:7*

THE VEILING OF TRUTH

The various schools, *dergahs*, *ashrams*, tekkes, organizations, and holistic centers that purportedly teach paths to "enlightenment" have some poor track records of late. To cover up their students' widespread lack of enlightenment, the teachers of these schools portray enlightenment as something that is infrequent, unusual and difficult to achieve. Ibn Ata'allah of Alexandria states, *"One should distrust the shaykh who tells you that enlightenment is 'far off,' and trust the one who assures you that it is 'near'."* Shaykh Nur al-Anwar al-Jerrahi illuminates, *"Radical non-dualistic masters state that all conscious beings are already awake and that wakefulness is the very nature of consciousness. If you raise your hand before your face and hold up three fingers, you will know with absolute clarity and certainty, without any ambiguity, those are three fingers, not four fingers or five fingers. That kind of clarity is the natural, innate awakeness of consciousness."*[30]

The traditional approaches toward spirituality are failing us during these difficult times. These schools turn out people who dress in "spiritual garments," who can regurgitate an endless amount of aphorisms and spiritual-sounding jargon, yet these schools have failed truly to introduce these students to the All-Pervasive Reality of Existence. What perplexes us is the number of Sufi Sheikhs that give lip service to Rumi, al-Hallaj, al-Ghazali, and Ibn al-'Arabi, yet do not heed these saints' advice to transcend religion! These "lip-service" Sheikhs insist on emphasizing disciplinary religion and *shariat* over the World Encompassing Spiritual message that these saints exhorted. As the distinguished dancer-choreographer, Robin Becker who is deeply involved in Sufi studies, points out, *"Breath cannot move through tension."* Certain Sufi Sheikhs, steeped in the traditions of their homeland, forget the fact that, *"The Tradition offers us its ritual, culture, and wisdom, but we must apply these under new and always changing circumstances . . . we are dealing with a society that has different economic structure, gender relationships, and social norms."*[31]

Contemporary spirituality has fallen into a great error! Specifically, we are referring to the error of focusing exclusively on Love and Light. We object to the "white light" view of the spirit world because this depiction overlooks the robustness, color, texture, strength, passion, fullness, and depth that the spirit world possesses. The spirit world of the "white lighters" is a thin, insipid and one-dimensional place. These people are existing in an unreasonable state of happiness. "Dark" spirituality is not encouraged nor acknowledged as a valid spiritual way by various contemporary spiritual commentators. We recommend that the spiritually inclined heed the wisdom of Rumi on the subject:

> *"The inhaling-exhaling is from spirit,*
> *now angry, now peaceful.*
> *Wind destroys, and wind protects."*[32]

Because Western religion has created this image of the "God of Good in Whom there is no Darkness," a grand enantiodrama is occurring around the globe. The "Light" has been over emphasized in religion, and they have sentenced its opposite characteristic to the dungeon of society's collective unconscious. Sometimes the repressed characteristic bursts forth wildly into daylight with a lethal force. We are witnessing this enantiodrama enacted daily as we watch the Evening News.

Tekkes, spiritual centers, and dergahs, are not immune from this process either. Michael Rogge writes, *"Man in a herd may not show the best side of his nature. Unconscious drives may reign his behavior. This is applicable especially in circumstances that man strives for the spiritual. He may tend to show split-personality behavior. On one hand the spiritual personality which is supposed to have come to terms with his animal nature. It is wise, friendly and compassionate on the outside. In the shadows lurks the personality that has been forced into the background, still ridden with all the expulsed human frailties. In moments of weakness, it will see its chance to play hideous tricks. It will do so without being noticed by the person involved. The result being: uncharitable behavior, envy, malicious gossip, harsh words, insensitivity, unfounded criticism and even worse, not expected from such charismatic figure. It is one of the main reasons for people leaving a particular group in great disappointment."*[33]

The Sufi poet Kabir informs us that,

> *"Between the conscious and the unconscious,*
> *the mind has put up a swing;*
> *all earth creatures, even the supernovas, sway*
> *between these two trees,*
> *and it never winds down."*[34]

The followers of the "Good God" often denigrate the use of dark imagery. Yet, they miss an essential point. Certain aspects of our being exist in the evening twilight and night. The seed grows in the darkness of the earth. The fetus develops in the darkness of the womb, and the soul awaits rebirth in the darkness of death. Black also represents the feminine aspect of the Divine, an aspect overlooked by Western culture for too long.

Another aspect of the Divine of which Western culture is frightened is Death. Western society is conditioned to avoid death. We do not wash, dress and bury our dead - we give the job to funeral directors. One hundred years ago death was still a personal phenomenon. Black represents Death. Clarissa Pinkola Estes, Ph.D.[35] states, *"Without death there is no dark for the diamond to shine from."* The Sufi does not fear Death. He or she sees it as part of a sacred integral cycle. Death is the greatest gift of Allah. In his commentary on the Forty Traditions, Ibn Kamal says, *"When you are confused, seek the help of the people of the tombs."*

Some modern day Sufis would have us distance ourselves from Islam and its matrix – Judaism and Christianity. These contemporary Sufis are uncomfortable with certain aspects of the above-mentioned religions' holy books and histories, for example, the wars of Yahweh and Israel mentioned in the Torah, or the battles of the Prophet as he spread Islam recorded in the Qur'an. While these aspects are indeed unpleasant, life contains wars, murders and terrible bloodshed. We are not asking the reader to embrace orthodox religion, but we are asking the reader to seriously consider accepting that spirituality is not a way to distance oneself from life's unpleasantness. Spirituality is lived every day by every human on the face of the earth. As Shaykh Nur al-Anwar al-Jerrahi insightfully observed, *"Let's not talk about 'spiritual' life. This sounds as if there are a few people living a spiritual life and the rest of humanity is not. This period of testing, of feeling everything is lost, happens with regularity to all human beings. They must get through it and that's the way they grow. Human life itself is spiritual life."* [36]

Life is not lived in "weekend retreats," but through watching our parents die, earning our livelihood, the sweat and tears of raising children, and the daily interactions with everyone with whom we come in contact. This author gently warns the reader that if he or she prefers spiritual pleasantries and platitudes to the harsh realities of life, then we have not written this book for this type of person. People experience anxiety attacks, depression, nervous breakdowns, divorces, illnesses and frightening experiences. People do fight; they argue all the time. Some contemporary spiritual people believe that a truly spiritual person should be so "advanced" that these events do not occur to him or her. This is hogwash. We must nurture and develop each part of us.

We point out the fact that a child that does not eat properly will not physically and mentally develop correctly. A child that is not given love by his or her parents will not emotionally develop correctly. Food but no love, love but no food, will not make a mature adult. Humans have physical, etheric, emotional, mental, and spiritual aspects. Each must be cared for and appropriately nurtured.

The great spiritual initiate and Sufi, Gurdjieff, would not teach prospective students whom he thought were psychologically immature. Kabir Helminski, servant of Mevlana, defines maturity as follows, *"By maturity we mean that overall development of character and virtue, including the ability to express oneself and participate effectively in the life around us."* First, Gurdjieff would send the "psychologically immature" to a psychiatrist with whose work he was familiar, who, in turn, would send them back to Gurdjieff when the psychotherapy had developed and steadied their emotions.

Besides the aforementioned aspects, each human being (except for the Prophet Muhammad – Peace be upon him), no matter how beautiful, walks around with a shadow at their feet. The journey to *marifat* (becoming the mirror of Allah) may be long or it may occur at your next breath, but in the meanwhile, we must encounter duality. Duality is as "Divine" as non-duality. The light and the dark must be regarded as sacred so we do not fall into faulting Allah for the thorns on the rosebush. Completeness, *al-insān al-kāmil*, comes in stages, and one instruction of those stages is to be nonjudgmental and to embrace all parts of your being and life. There are no shortcuts. Do not try to take shortcuts.

At the beginning levels, the *Murid* prays for marifat, and sincerely tries to live as though this was a reality. At the intermediate levels, the Murid only praises Allah and only sees Allah. At the advanced levels, the Dervish returns to the sacred garden of duality as the Gardener.

We hold that pretending to be living in a state of marifat is dangerous for the inexperienced Murid. It is dangerous because the Murid often puts him or herself into the mind-set of denial, pretending he or she is a perfect spiritual being without a fault. Believing oneself to be perfect is often the sign of a delusional mind. We feel that this attempt to be "perfect" is psychologically dangerous and a red-carpet invitation to the ego to run amok. Or else, the Murid will take the other tack, which is thinking him or herself to be a worthless and sinful nobody. During your lifetime many events will happen, events that are not pleasant and that are painful. Often Allah sends these experiences to us for our spiritual development. In that sense, they can in no wise be construed as faults of the person or of the universe. Human experience is sacred – from the pain of childbirth, to the joy of seeing your newborn child. Spirituality is NOT about escaping unpleasant aspects of human existence. It is about Remembering our Source.

"Yea the darkness hideth not from Thee; but the night shineth as the day: the darkness and the light are both alike to Thee."
- The Prophet Daud
(Peace be upon him)

THE EXPRESSION OF EVERYTHING

Allah created the day and the night, the light and the dark. It is foolishness to say that because there is an absence of sunlight during the nighttime that therefore the night does not exist. The Qur'an tells us to, *"Reflect upon God's creation . . . "* The dark holds mystical secrets. Sufism has discerning perspectives regarding darkness: the Sheikhs have said that when you close your eyes, you think you see darkness, but in actuality this darkness is a curtain that shields you from a light so powerful and luminescent that most people could not bear Its intensity. Aleister Crowley writes, *"There is a light so strenuous that it is not perceived as light."* The Hidden Light of the Night softens the wheat and the fruit, making it sweet. The reader should also remember that the Prophets made their ascensions during the night. 'Ain al-Qudat al-Hamadhani describes it thus, *"He is veiled from created beings because of the extreme luminosity of His Light."*[37] The worldly sunlight seems black in comparison to the Inner Light within the heart of the dervish.

You cannot grow spiritually by repressing the "dark" side. To grow as a person and so as a Sufi, it is imperative that you respect both poles of the psyche. The unity of the self encompasses light and dark poles. Shaykh Nur al-Anwar al-Jerrahi addresses the issue of spiritual communities that create a tremendous dualistic pull by over-emphasizing the "white light" over the full spectrum, *"The spiritual trips are all setting up romantic attractions. How about a teaching that is plain and profound?"*[38]

There is a rhythm to the natural world as seen in expansion and contraction. The Divine manifests a plant, and then returns the plant to the condition of non-manifestation. People pray and defecate, sing and pass gas. Even the mightiest of kings must sit on the toilet every day. Yet, people chronically hide their shadows. They feel shame. It is terrible that most people feel such a strong need to hide aspects of their humanity. That is why truly spiritual persons may be at odds with society and religion for they are scientists of the balance. They perform marriages each day, the marriages of the poles of existence. *"God unites the polarity of qualities only in Adam, to confer a distinction on him."*[39] However, to do this the Sufis must often go against the grain of society's mores, and this ruffles feathers.

A large portion of humanity suffers from this dichotomized spirituality. Western religious values and ways of viewing the world strongly influence people on a subconscious level. This spiritual value system teaches you to reject the Shadow and call it evil. Since the Shadow is an inherent and necessary part of the human being, the Western religious standard causes individuals to be split from their selves. It is essential for those on the spiritual way to integrate the shadow. By definition, the Shadow is that which is Hidden or Occulted. Allah has an Unmanifest Mystery that He veils to us. The Shadow represents the forces within us of which we have been afraid, ashamed, or have ignored. The Shadow needs to be understood and united into consciousness. Allah Most High does permit certain people of those who love Him and who are Beloved of Him, to see into the dark. *"Thus thy Lord will prefer thee and will teach thee the interpretation of events, and will perfect His grace upon thee and upon the family of Jacob as He perfected it upon thy forefathers, Abraham and Isaac. Lo! thy Lord is Knower, Wise."* [40]

This book is only the finger pointing at the moon. It is not the Moon. IT cannot be pointed out. We are not worthy to write about such things, so we beg for the Sublime Reality's Mercy on our soul. *Insha-Allah,* through this book, we hope to open a door to the integration of Sufi wisdom and the contemporary world.

One of our goals is to bring the wisdom of the Sufi Masters into the present in a form that is accessible by the spiritual Aspirant of today. Westerners have based their spiritual beliefs upon false presumptions. Therefore, Westerners have built their houses on sand. The Way of the Heart is not about dogma, evil spirits, rules, and restrictions. It is about responsibility. The true Murid must search for, and hunt down all of his or her spiritual assumptions, and carefully analyze these beliefs. No Teacher or Guru can make you into a spiritual person unless you clearly assume responsibility for your spiritual growth. Use your Guide to work on yourself, not to run away from yourself. We cannot stress enough the role of personal responsibility in spiritual development. The Japanese Puppeteers have a saying, *"To surpass your master pays the debt for what he gave you."*

There are many false "teachers" in the spiritual community that are surface effect and no depth. Talking the talk is the easiest part. Walking the walk can be hard, lonely, exhausting, and filled with fear. It takes courage to embrace the Shadow. Not many have the motivation or the inclination for that journey. We all know of various famous teachers who, while they outwardly seem masterful, all the unacknowledged shadow aspects of their characters privately overwhelm them. The True Teacher does not advertise his or her spiritual station.

"For some time I would seek Him yet would find my self. Now I seek my self and find Him."

- Jabir Bin Abdullah Ansari

"In the depth of winter, I finally learned that within me there lay an invincible summer."

- Albert Camus

"We ourselves feel that what we are doing is just a drop in the ocean. But the ocean would be less because of that missing drop."
- Mother Teresa

THE INTEGRAL SUFI

The Sufis say, *"All wisdom is the believer's lost camel."* We have always had one goal: first-hand gnosis. To this purpose, starting in 1971, we practiced with Christian mystics, Gnostics, Hermeticists, Qabalists, and Anthroposophists. Later, we spent years with various wise Wiccans, Ceremonial and Chaos Magickians and practiced Qabalah with a student of a famous Rabbi from Chenobyl. Beginning in 1981, we lived the way of the Sufi, studying with the Halveti-Jerrahi Order of Sufi Dervishes from Istanbul, Turkey, and more recently, the Rifa'i Ma'rufi Order. Ultimately, the concepts contained in this book are what Allah Most Gracious has permitted us to glimpse of the Universe at this point in life.

We explore the essential nature of reality. We do not speak the language of academic scholastic philosophy. A person knows nothing, save by Allah's (May His Name be Exalted) permission. By Allah's permission a person who is illiterate and uneducated can become the wisest of saints. We have been on a long pilgrimage into the mystical realm of the unconscious. Oriental religions have recommended this journey for thousands of years. We have invested in our self-discovery, exploring the essence of what it is to be Human. We have wrestled with our inner demons. We have looked inside ourselves with brutal honesty and searched our soul. We have consciously decided to be frank about what our struggles and internal evolution have inspired us to understand about the spiritual way.

Essentially, our practice derives from the non-dualistic schools of thought, in the tradition of certain Sufi Traditions such as the Bektashi Dervishes in Turkey. We hold that "light" and "dark" are complementary poles of life that cannot exist apart from each other. We also wish to point out that humor and the "unexpected" play an important role in spiritual development.

Intellectual congruency is not a *sine qua non* element of spiritual legitimacy. As the poet Iqbal writes, *"Go beyond Reason's light: her's is the lamp that shows the road, not marks the destination."* Go beyond reasoning if you want to get at the Deep Mysteries.

During the past years, we have been exploring what we do not know. We are seeking out the spaces *between* our knowledge, in other words, the pregnant silence. We are seeking the Essence hidden behind spiritual beliefs, societal conditioning and philosophy. We are coming to know the emptiness of all religious thought and pursuit and the obviousness of the Radiant Expression of Everything. Ultimately, spirituality is not about seeking. It is about transcending seeking. The mystic can never be satisfied with words and ideas. Just as music has nothing to do with musical notes in its ultimate manifestation, also spirituality has nothing to do with religion.

We are, through this book, attempting to reform the Sufi consciousness of Allah. We seek to recall (by exploring the Qur'an, the writings and sayings of the Ahlul Bayt, and the writings and sayings of the great Sufi Saints) the Real identity of Allah. We seek to deliver modern day Sufism from its state of petrification. If our writings are considered an apostasy, then so be it. Although this apostasy was a traumatic breakdown experience for us, nonetheless we perceive it as a necessary phase in the process of restoring the Real Form of Sufism. For we do not seek to reveal a new understanding of Allah, but to remind the Sufi community of the roots of our belief that have been already revealed to us. Many writers are fond of quoting such poets as Rumi, yet these same writers shy away from the explosive and controversial sections of his work. These controversial sections are precisely those that need exploring, for they are controversial because they challenge contemporary Sufi teachings. This work requires psychological transfiguration. Our antinomian, anti-Law approach, is the Way to free Sufism from its prison of petrification. We address the mystery of the opposition and polarity within the Godhead. Only by traveling the route of apostasy can we travel around the Circle of the Divine to return to an understanding of the Mother Source of the Qur'an. We seek to jolt perception awake from robotic sleep and into seeing the world in a new, fresh way that is nonlinear and multidimensional. The human in his or her ordinary state of consciousness is literally asleep (*"and when he dies he wakes,"* as Mohammad, Peace be upon him said). He or she lives in a dream, whether of enjoyment or suffering - a phenomenal, illusory existence. This disruption of the reality-complex of Sufism will break it up and release some of the primordial spiritual fuel that ignited Sufism. We seek to reach the flow of waters that the Prophet Musa (Peace be upon him) sought. This mixture of the two waters will create a state of fluidity in Sufism that will dissolve all borders and boundaries and create new, dynamic relationships.

True spirituality is at once elusive and yet supremely obvious. Then in what way can true spirituality be experienced? It can be experienced by understanding the concept that it is not what a person knows, it is his or her ability to find genuine impulses and connect with honest responses that makes the person spiritually mature. Experience the Obvious.

In this present book, we have decided to use a variety of names for THAT which calls ITSELF "Allah." In the Qur'an (the Book of Unitary Knowledge), Allah has chosen to reveal Himself partially, through Ninety-Nine Names, concealing One Name. The *Ismi Azam* or greatest Name of Allah, is even said to be "Man." The Sheikhs teach that a human being can know the Essence through the Divine Names. Some of these Names are used in this book. We feel that the traditional word "God" is filled with highly charged emotional and intellectual connotations for most people. Allah is One without being "One." It is therefore our hope that by offering a variety of names for the Divine, the reader may begin to experience the Divine in an unspoiled and fresh way and with an immediate orientation. Joseph Chazan, a Rabbi in Manchester, England writes, *"The Name of God has great hidden mysteries, these teachings open the search to His Name Essence."*

However, the name ALLAH is most sacred. Riaz Ahmed Gohar Shahi states that, *"The name 'ALLAH' predates Islam and is not confined to the Muslims or to the Holy Qur'an. This Name existed well before the time of the Prophet Mohammed (Peace be upon him) and his father's name was Abd'Allah. 'Allah' is the name of the 'Essence' of God and has been so since the beginning of time and is found in the scriptures revealed to the Prophets David, Moses and Jesus (Peace be upon them)."*

We regard the universe as One. This One, in the state of manifestation, known as Reality, exhibits two poles that we commonly call the Yang and Yin. As a divine theater that contains a stage whose curtains go up and down, the cosmos can at times seem dualistic. Yet, ultimately the theater of ecstasy exhibits an apparent duality contained within a Sublime Unity. When the Unicity manifests as the Physical World, it does so as a bipolar phenomena. Ultimately, the Essence of the Omniconscious Unicity subsumes and is beyond the Yang and the Yin.

We experience the power of Spirit - of Spirit not over, but in integral partnership with the Universe.

This present book is, in fact, four books in one. It consists of,

1. A series of spiritual practices designed to manifest the Complete Human,

2. A story about Sam - a homeless person, and a Mr. Khadir - an enigmatic figure,

3. Commentary on topics directly and indirectly influencing and factoring in the spiritual development of the Murid.

4. Historical accounts of the Prophet Muhammad (Peace be upon him) and his family (the Ahlul Bayt).

In addition, we have included several quotations at the beginning of each chapter. We have done this to inspire the reader and to confirm that we have soundly based our intuitions and writings on Sufi concepts and exegesis. Finally, we have added a useful glossary for those who may not be fully acquainted with Sufi terminology.

Some people once came up to the Prophet of Islam, Muhammad (Peace be upon him), and asked him, *"What is the spirit?"* He replied, *"The spirit - its knowledge is with my Lord. And of knowledge you (humankind) have been given only a little."*

What we offer you is a little knowledge of a little knowledge. Allah Most High willing, it will be helpful to you in your spiritual quest. Our goal is that the inner knowing of divulgence formerly taught only to the chosen will become the outer path available to all.[41] This book is written on the level of haqiqat (truth), not shariat or tariqat. Responsibility for all the faults and failings in this work rest with us alone.

Please consider us a traveling companion as we walk along the road for a time together. May we not be so much of a teacher as a flame that lights others on fire, a smile that causes others to smile, and a song that makes people break into song. We have only one request. Please suspend all judgment as you read this book. Judgment throws the mind into a state of duality. Do not expect foolish consistency from us. Joseph Campbell wrote, *"The Cosmic Dancer does not rest heavily in a single spot, but gaily, lightly turns and leaps from one position to another."* We therefore invite all aspiring Sufis who are reading this book to dance with us into the "Theater of Ecstasy." May we all dance the mystic dance together!

"Life is either a daring adventure or nothing."

           - Helen Keller

"A beggar's purse is bottomless."

           - Pythagoras

TALES FROM UNDER THE OVERPASS

Extending eastward from New York City lies an elongated island. The island is roughly in the shape of a fish, about one hundred miles long, and is named "Long Island," the one time Xanadu of returning soldiers from World War II, offering them a piece of the American Dream. Previously, Long Island was only home to potato farms. Yet, after the war, the United States government had no place to house the numerous returning soldiers. Small homes in places called "Levittown" and "Hicksville" sprang up. At first, the public said that these communities would never last, and that they would turn into ghettos. However, they flourished.

Each day, hundreds of thousands of commuters from Long Island make the pilgrimage into and out of the city by navigating the Long Island Expressway. Since at rush hour, the expressway barely moves faster than five miles per hour, it has been dubbed the "longest parking lot in the world."

Exit number 24, Kissena Boulevard, marks the Long Island - New York border. It is at this junction of those two worlds that our story begins. Sam is forty-four. He is a short man with a rather long beard. He does not smile but his blue eyes express a curious light that seems to radiate softly about his head. Beneath the westbound ramp for Kissena Boulevard, Sam built his home, a makeshift shanty of broken palettes and sundry wooden planks lashed together with string and strips of cloth covered with sheets of plastic he found in a dumpster. There was nothing romantic about Sam's situation. Life was not pleasant. There was no end to the trash flung from the windows of passing motorists or to the winds that scattered it about. The air was thick with the smell of stale urine, excrement and rotting garbage.

Sam had no status in the world. He lived in squalor among the other homeless and outcasts, smelled from lack of bathing, and had to endure unimaginable privations. Sam survived torrential rainstorms that flooded his shanty and winter storms that blew deadly cold snow through the shack and through his bones. He had neither hope nor desire of gaining rank or position.

Sam did not want a job; he could barely find a reason to get up in the morning. Each day Sam went out and rummaged through garbage cans to harvest things to eat, wear and sell. Although to the world, Sam does not amount to much, he does have one jewel of great price: Sam is free of self-importance. Life was not always like this for Sam.

There was a time when love filled his heart, but no more. Once Sam had sought enlightenment and thought he'd found its path on an Ashram outside Los Angeles. Once Sam had a teacher in whom he believed without reservation, who had helped him discover the inner resonances of the divine within himself. Sam had read that one could become a completely God-realized being and was awed and inspired by this perfection he saw in his teacher. As Sam progressed, his guru became more than his teacher, he became his beloved friend. Sam grew in stature and recognition in the community of spiritual seekers gathered about the guru. Sam's utter admiration made the truth more painful still when he discovered that advancement within the order was not by merit alone but that several of the higher ranking members had been conferred their status in exchange for sexual favors and that the donations made to the center went first and foremost toward the material enrichment of the leader.

Life for Sam then lost its reason. He had no faith in any human being not even himself. He certainly had no faith left for the merciful and benevolent God that allowed his loving devotee to fall into the hands of such a charlatan. Sam was deeply disillusioned and heartbroken. He walked out of the center that day with no possessions, no money, no beliefs. His great spiritual quest had brought him here to New York, a homeless man living in a makeshift shanty under the overpass of the Long Island Expressway.

Sam was numb inside. He did not think about his guru; he could not bear to think about the guru. Therefore, he hid his great pain deep inside himself.

"We all are lions, but lions on a banner;
because of the wind they are rushing onward from moment to moment.
Their onward rush is visible, and the wind is unseen:
may that which is unseen not fail from us!
Our wind whereby we are moved and have our being are of Thy gift;
our whole existence is from Thy bringing into being."
                                        - Jelaluddin Rumi

"The Fabric of You, not away from You
Not inside of You, but
of the Matrix.
Here is a singing bird, all leaves tremble Here.
Here is a great Exhaling, and in linkage, radiating."

                                        -Şirin Kaye

THE LIMITED SELF

The dissolution or training of the human "ego" is a major focus of most spiritual disciplines. When the Sheiks of Sufism speak about "ego," they are referring to the great delusion that results in a sense of separateness from the Creator. These Sheiks do not experience separateness from the rest of Reality, but exist in a state of Unitary Consciousness.

We must draw some distinctions in our discussion of the "ego." In one understanding, some spiritual denotations of "ego" are egotism, self-centeredness, vanity and conceit. To others, "ego" means mind, logic, rationality, and reasoning. There is also the understanding of "ego" as psychological entity. Finally, some teachers define "ego" in a spiritual sense as the "divine sentient seed" implanted in the matrix of earth, air, fire, and water known as the human body.

Therefore, we must be careful when using this term, as it means different things to different people. *"One of the great ideals of a Sufi is the awakening of the heart qualities, resulting in a broader outlook,"* writes Pir-o-Murshid Inayat Khan. Therefore, we propose a fresh term: the Limited Self, or what Kabir Helminski calls the "false self." Since childhood, parents, society, and the educational system have taught you nonsense about Reality, limiting your experience of Reality. Television is an awful culprit, manipulating people into forgetting that they are spiritual beings, brainwashing people into false views of Reality, and causing people to develop ego identities in which they feel disconnected from the Living World. *"There can be no justice in our present state, no justice in prison. The only thing one can seriously think about*

22

when one realizes that one is in prison is how to escape, not sit and cry about injustice in prison. "[42] Most people are asleep to the wholeness of their being. All they are aware of are their biases, that is, what they like and what they do not like. Their selves are narrow and superficial. *"Die before you die, "* mystically utters the Prophet of the Ultimate Reality. In other words, allow your caterpillar self to die so your butterfly self may live! "Die before you die" means to give up your phony and counterfeit self that you learned from your parents and society. Surrender your "victim's story," your mask, and your persona.

The Limited Self is like a flower bud. It is within itself. It exists for itself and lives for itself. However, when it blossoms, it joins the circle of beauty, radiating its unique loveliness for the upliftment of all.

"Each creature is a word (kalima) of God. "[43]

"Though all the trees in the earth were pens, and the sea – seven seas after it to replenish it – [were ink,] yet would the words of God not be spent. "[44]

Therefore, the art we refer to consists of taking the shackles off the self to manifest - the Sufi! There is an "I," the Limitless Self, inside of "i," the Limited Self. Your little will disappears in the All Powerful. There are eighteen thousand universes contained in that one little dot above the "i." This dot is a Hidden Treasure inside of you that you must discover to manifest the Divine "I." When you discover this, your horizon opens and you become a unique configuration of the Divine Attributes. You have melted into the Heart of Hearts. We may also call the Limitless Self the Transconscious or True Self. The vertical line of the "I" symbolically represents *"the One who Alone is, of Him no being precedeth. "*[45] It is not that the person actually disappears, the person still walks the face of the earth, but the person now becomes part of an intricate web of Radiant Being. [46]

A wise dervish once told us that *"There is a You inside of you. "* There is a great message here, and a transformative stimulus, for those who meditate on his words. Each being, including minerals, plants, animals, and humans is a kind of lens through which Allah experiences Allah. There is only Allah. However, Allah experiences ITSELF through the uniqueness of each creature.

The poet Eliza Scudder writes,

"Thou life within my life, than self more near,
Thou veiled Presence infinitely clear,
From all my nameless weariness I flee
To find my center and rest in Thee. "

After the transformation, the foot of the Sufi remains a foot, but it is part of the Whole. So too the Sufi's eye, it is still an eye; it does not somehow become this amorphous, shapeless entity. Just so with the ego, or what we call the Limited Self, it does not disappear, it just changes context. Some say that it dissolves. It is no longer the little dictator. You become a conscious expression of the Infinite Web of Reality. The Limited Self is Consciousness in a static, dense, or "frozen" state. The Limitless Self is Consciousness in a dynamic, mobile, or "fluid" state.

The Limited Self is not bad; it just sees part of the picture and tends to want to preserve its hard won analysis of the picture. The Limited Self thinks it needs to preserve its viewpoint to stave off confusion and despair. Avatar Adi Da observes, *"You are perceiving reality out of fear."*[47] The Limited Self's view is an obstacle to transformation. The Limited Self thinks and presumes it is separate. Its limited view prevents you from achieving your full potential. We propose that you activate your Totality! Become the Complete Human. The You inside of you is a clap of thunder about to sound.

It is difficult for a five-year-old child to leave his or her mother and go off to kindergarten. Often the child will cry and sob for his or her mother. So too, it is difficult to leave the familiar kindergarten and go off to start Grade School.

When it is time to go to Junior and Senior High School similar problems present themselves. Always the familiar must be left for new and different surroundings. Friends must be left behind and new social groups explored.

Entering the university may be the most difficult transformation in that the student will often move out of his or her home to a different state. Not only must he or she make new friends, but also he or she must learn new roads, the location of restaurants, laundromats, bus stops, and the whole collection of buildings that comprise the university.

The above examination of student life is akin to the experiences of the Limited Self as it begins to expand. It is painful to the ego to expand its boundaries, just as it is painful for the five-year-old to leave its Mama. The Murid must be willing to endure the process of transformation. This process involves sacrifice. Bubba Free John declares, *"Sacrifice is God."* [48]

Gradually, the Murshid helps the Murid to see wider horizons, leading the ego to open its petals and flower, embracing a greater totality of being. As Dhû-l-Nûn stated, *"Whatever you imagine, God is the opposite of that."*[49] These words are worth pondering, if you are first starting out on the Sufi Way or if you have followed the Way for untold years. Avatar Adi Da Samraj also has some clear-sighted words to say on the subject. *"The Reality of the Cosmic Domain and so forth, is not what you're now perceiving it to be. It's not that way. I tell you quite frankly and directly, it is not at all what you are thinking and perceiving it to be."*[50]

As the Grade School student must experience the death of his or her Kindergarten self, so in addition, must the ego experience the death of the

Limited Self!

Learning always involves pain. Sometimes, it is only a little pain, like when you study a subject that you enjoy. For example, if we give you fifty pounds of rocks to carry up a hill on your back, you will be grunting, groaning and complaining the whole way. However, if we tell you we will give you fifteen thousand gold coins for doing the task, you will sprint up the hill with a smile on your face and hardly remember the weight on your back. Just so, having the love of the Divine Reality in your heart makes the trials and difficulties of life more bearable.

Love the God inside you. Love the Beloved who dwells fully and completely within your heart.

PRACTICE

This book contains a series of spiritual exercises designed to liberate your Limited Self eventually revealing the Limitless Self. Ultimately, we devise these exercises to enable the Murid to see the Ultimate Reality with the inner eye.

We must say one thing from the start. Ultimately, spiritual development does not depend on what you do and what you do not do. For spiritual development only depends on the Will of the Ultimate One. We pray that Allah Most High, the Primordial Source of the Universe, will bless each of you with inner spiritual development.

If it is the Will of the Divine Reality, these exercises will be of use to you in expanding your awareness of whom you are. Nevertheless, your intention and level of sincerity is important to achieve success in this area.

For too long, spiritual Murids have had to rely on faith alone. We design these exercises to give the Murid spiritual knowledge. The time for faith is over; the new millennium brings with it a monumental need on the part of humanity for direct spiritual experience.

We will put a special emphasis on the following practice in this book: the Murid must broaden his or her horizons and pass through the narrow and superficial aspects of what he or she likes and does not like. There is a great chance for growth in embracing the things the Murid does not like; there is a validity and power to be experienced in the shadow aspect of one's preferences. The Murid must go beyond intellectual understanding to grow spiritually.

"Tyger, tyger, burning bright,
In the forests of the night
What immortal hand or eye,
Could frame thy fearful symmetry?"

- William Blake

" 'Catastrophe Theory' in science deals with sudden and drastic changes in
some feature of a system, such as the earth's crust, or human society. In
popular usage the word catastrophe has 'bad' connotations, but some sud-
den changes may well be experienced as positive. Revelation itself might be
called a catastrophe. Mystical insight or Wisdom (hikmah) can also work
catastrophically on the system known as human consciousness."

- Peter Lamborn Wilson [51]

"The divine is a threatening chaos."

- Georg Feuerstein

"Your whole life can change in a second, and you never even know when
its coming."

- *"Before and After"*

THE SACRED MATRIX

Do not dare to pretend that you know Who God is! An awakened One asks the question: do you know what anything is?

To develop spiritually, the aspiring Sufi needs to acknowledge that humanity acts and interacts within the natural environment. The Murid must realize that he or she is part of the vast Ecosystem. Francis Bacon wrote: *"In nature things move violently to their place and calmly to their place."* Many well-intentioned spiritual seekers look for the Exalted Truth in spiritual books or through contemplating in a quiet corner of their room. They do not realize that spiritual development is intimately connected to entering into a sacred relationship with Nature. *"Whoever pretends he can hear, yet cannot hear the glorification of birds, trees and the wind, is a liar,"* so said Abu Ali al-Farmadi at-Tusi.

The next error the Murid often makes is that he or she selectively focuses on only certain aspects of nature, and chooses to avoid facing its more unpleasant guises. *"One cannot stop the natural course of life with either mate-rial or spiritual powers . . . ,"* wrote Pir-o-Murshid Inayat Khan.[52] The Murid understands that tornadoes, polar shifts, earthquakes, mud slides, tidal waves, icebergs, avalanches, and comets that strike the ground, are all facts of Allah's Creation. *". . .whatever is in the heavens and the earth is His; all are obedient to Him."*[53] This is the law of the earth: humanity and the earth echo together. Natural disasters are no respecters of class, rank, privilege or church, temple, and mosque. All can be leveled in an instant. The perceptive ones understand that there is a destructive and entropic element infused into Nature. However, Allah is the final Arbiter. The Murid has to accept Reality. *"And that infinite meaningfulness, or God, comes to us in various ways and unexpectedly speaks to us or turns us around right in the middle of what appears meaningless."* [54]

The Sufi is a person of rare courage. He or she looks into the naked face of Reality and does not flinch. While it may be difficult to face the facts of physical existence so honestly, half the battle is won once you acknowledge your place in the natural world. There is a "fearful symmetry" to the face of nature. All of creation contains infinity within it. A harmonious relation can be achieved with the facts of existence, but this can only be discovered through an honest appraisal of your physical existence on the Earth, for *"the Reality never withdraws from the forms of the Cosmos."*[55]

The Prophet (Peace be upon him) said that if you come into a town of unbelievers, and if they are poor and hungry, do not teach them how to pray. Instead, he (Peace be upon him) instructs us to build a grinding stone so the people may eat, for people cannot focus on affairs of the spirit while their stomachs are empty.

As children of the Earth, let your beings arise in harmony and attunement with your natural physiological origins. Allah tells us in the Qur'an He has made us caretakers of the Earth.

The Sufi must feed daily at the waters of the Original Wholeness. We are completely dependent upon Allah. There is no existence but the Ultimate Reality, nor does anything exist other than the Ultimate Reality, *"in that you are His Form and He is your Spirit."*[56]

Murids must acknowledge the forces that surround them, whether they are the forces of Nature or of Spirit. They must face the fact that they are entering a world more vast than the world to which they are accustomed, allowing their hardened world-views to dissolve in the dance of Nature and Spirit. Robin Becker suggests that the student *"explore the two directions of the breath, the two realms of Infinity."*[57]

We are not teaching a method to achieve perfection, but a method to BE. We want to help you to be completely human, not perfect, for society has forgotten the meaning of the word "perfection." Socrates said that the perfect human being is all human beings put together. So, therefore, focus on being human.

"Chaos demands to be recognized and experienced before letting itself be converted into a new order."
> *- Hermann Hesse*

"Don't take a script from anyone; do your own thinking."
> *- Sean Tracey*

"The timid and inhibited will fear what they see."
> *- James Gerard DeMartini*

"There can be no sense of security in your existence when it depends upon outside factors, for the unpredictable changes of reality can never be controlled."
> *- Deepak Chopra*

SHELTER FROM THE STORM

Let us contemplate on the world and the people in it. Nearly all mortals live in terror or despair. Economic studies show that most individuals are only two paychecks from being out in the street. Thunderclaps reverberate and the earth shakes. No wonder people go running to anything that seems to provide shelter from the chaos. Yet, the Sufi does not run away from the Condition of Reality. The Holy Prophet of Universal Islam said, *"Revile not the world, for God – He is the world."* This saying points to the fact that the existence of the world is God's existence without partner or like or equal,[58] and therefore the Murid needs to encounter the world directly, and not hide from it within forms and paradigms. We seek the deconstruction of the socially constructed mind.

Yet, humans fear the chaos that surrounds them. Who can control the wind and the rain? Folks hide behind all sorts of comfortable conventions so that they do not have to face the truth of their situation. Consider how people spend so much time manicuring their lawns. If someone in the neighborhood prefers to let his or her grass and shrubs grow to a natural height, the neighbors are dismayed and alarmed. Humans desperately try to check nature, to reign her in. Nature herself is one of the most visible and present reminders of how utterly powerless humanity is, in the face of the cosmos, in the face of the Almighty.

Our physical organisms are dependent upon the most particular of climatic environmental factors. The weather on Earth cannot be too hot or too cold because human beings can only survive in a narrow temperature range. Internally also, all our bodily processes take place within a small temperature range. A few degrees above or below our normal state are all that separates the human being from death.

People are forever organizing themselves to stave off chaos. Community identities are developed out of our fear of nature. People want things to be the same every day with the result that they have imprisoned themselves within their routines. They do not realize that vulnerability and letting go of their desire to control nature makes them stronger. *"But when the ego (or self-contraction) is understood and transcended, then Nature is seen from the point of view of Wisdom. And, in that case, the egoic struggle in Nature or against Nature is also understood and transcended,"* writes Da Free John.

The entire fashion industry is based on people's desire to fit in with the rest of society. If an individual dresses differently than is socially acceptable, that little bit of chaotic behavior on his or her part will earn plenty of censure from friends, co-workers and even strangers.

People flock into churches to have the world explained to them in a neat little package. For most people, religion is chaos insurance. Religion lays down a template on the world so that people can try to make some sense of it. The problem is that people end up living in the template and shutting out reality altogether.

Individuals, who become political activists, are locked into viewing their world in political terms. Their existence and the people around them are explained in terms of political interactions. Religious fundamentalists tend to see the world in terms of fundamentalism. Psychologists see the world in terms of psychology. Sports fans see the world in terms of sports. All this is a deliberate (although unconscious) need on an individual's part to have some system that he or she can follow that explains the world.

Groups are not bad, we only want you to become aware that each group has an inherently limited world view, some groups being relative prisons of consciousness, while others are much more expansive and palatial. Nonetheless, the group world-view is not to be preferred over direct experience with the Supreme Reality.

The human race reminds us of ostriches with their heads in the sands. People run from work to their cable television, and dare not let anything spontaneous enter their worlds. They eat the same foods and drive the same route to work each week. They drink the same drink. They wear the same clothes everyone else wears and cut their hair the way everyone else cuts their hair. When they vacation, they stay in hotels, and sightsee in hermetically sealed tour buses.

The Sufi does not run away from the world's duties, pains and sorrows, unlike the ascetics of other religions who do not face the world and take to seclusion for good.[59] Shaykh Ahmadu Bamba holds that *"The ascetic who is secluded in the desert and receives his food from the hands of the caravaneers, has less merit in the face of Allah, than the donors who deprived themselves of something that they have earned with much difficulty."* [60]

The famous Sufi Rabi'a wrote,

O Lord, if I worship You out of fear of Hell,
burn me in Hell,
and if I worship You in hope of Paradise,
exclude me from Paradise;
but if I worship You for Your own sake,
do not deny me Your beauty."[61]

Let us ponder her words in the light of beauty. In the first stanza, Rabi'a speaks about the fear of Hell. Here she is referring to those people who want to escape the pains of the world through spirituality. Once when Rabi'a was sick a person visited her named 'Abd al-Wahid' Amr, along with her constant visitor Sufyán. The former relates, *"I and Sufyán Thawri visited Rabi'a when she was sick, and from awe I was not able to begin to speak, and I said to Sufyán, 'Say something.' He said (to Rabi'a) 'If you would utter a prayer, (God) would relieve your suffering.' She turned her face to him and said, 'O Sufyán, do you not know who it is that wills this suffering for me, is it not God who wills it?' He said, 'Yes.' She said, 'When you know this, why do you bid me ask for what is contrary to His will? It is not well to oppose one's Beloved.'"*

In the second stanza, she points to those individuals who desire to get a "high" from their spirituality. *"The ecstasy that is sought for the purposes of escaping the burden of egoism cannot emancipate us from that egoism because it is a direct expression of it,"* writes Kabir Helminski, adding, *"We live in a time when ecstatic experience is compulsively sought."*[62] What we teach is to resist yearning for ecstasy. Become aware of the All-Pervasive Reality of Existence as It is manifesting to you now. In the last stanza, this great woman is teaching us to focus on what transcends pleasure and pain and is prior to all conditions.

Dr. J. Nurbakhsh, the Master of the Nimatullahi Order of Sufis offers a further intensification of this concept, *"No longer does the cell of seclusion or the assembly of the Sufis, being alone or being in a crowd, have any meaning for him. In every place, in every state, he sees only the manifestation of Divine Beauty and hears only the harmonious sounds of the Beloved."* He goes on to say, *"Sufis . . . are not paying attention to either this world or the next."*[63]

PRACTICE

The goal of this practice is to open your perspective from an individual context to a cosmological context. Contemplate on the vastness of the universe. Ponder the myriads of stars, galaxies and nebulas that exist. Then consider how inconsequential your individual problems and concerns are, and how inconsequential is the mask that you wear every day.

Visualize the immense breadth of the ocean, with all its intensity, gradually dissolving mountains, turning them to dust and carrying them away. [64]

*"Relinquish attachment
to the known. Step into
the unknown, and you will
step into the field of all possibilities."*

- Anonymous

"Lucky are fools."

- Russian saying

"The poor man needs neither himself nor his Lord."
- Junayd

"For me the poor man has neither heart nor Lord."
- Sheikh Ali al-Jurayri

*"One does not discover new lands without consenting to lose sight of the
shore for a very long time."*
- André Gide

"A good traveler has no fixed plans, and is not intent on arriving."
- Lao Tzu (570-490 B.C.E.)

TALES FROM UNDER THE OVERPASS

*O*ne warm June morning, during rush hour, a man appeared at the entrance
to the rag picker's shack.

"I am intruding," the mysterious man said, startling the rag picker.

The first thing Sam noticed was the green tie. Sam had seen green ties
before certainly, it was just that Sam wasn't sure that he had ever seen that particular shade of green. It made him think of the green in a rainbow he had once
seen, sparkling and brilliant, or a flash of green he once saw in a botanical
garden. Sam wasn't sure, but the essence of the color resonated deep inside
Sam. The tie was paired with shoes the shade and shine of the wax red lips children sometimes wear at Halloween. With the conservative black suit and shirt,
the outfit should have looked ridiculous. On this man it did not.

Sam tried to collect his wits. "O my soul. Who are you?" he asked
more in wonder at the visitor than in fear. Sam was no longer used to people.
He didn't give many people the time of day. Nevertheless, there was something
about this one that was fascinating. It was as if he exuded life from every pore
in his body.

"My name is Mr. Khadir. I am from the Middle East."

Sam thought the stranger was referring to a town on the East End of

Long Island. He figured the man was a commuter whose car had probably overheated on the Expressway.

"I am a stranger" Mr. Khadir continued, "and so are you; come with me in these deserts so that you may seek God."

Sam scrutinized Mr. Khadir's face. It expressed kindliness and gentleness, as well as mischievousness and fierceness. He stood about five feet ten inches with a pale-skinned complexion. His long softly curly hair, slightly graying at the temples, was parted in the middle, and went to the bottom of his neck. He had a hooked nose over which rose a prominent brow ridge. His eyes were penetrating like an eagle's. He held a single rose in his hand. Although, Sam couldn't see it, a drop of green blood lay on his hand where one of the thorns had pierced his skin. A hint of a smile was on his face and he seemed restless. He said nothing but looked at Sam expectantly.

"I'm tired of seeking. My life is empty, and that's just fine with me," Sam declared emphatically.

"If you feel with all your being that you are empty, then I advise you to try once more," Mr. Khadir gently replied.

Mr. Khadir wore a jewel around his neck, a large emerald. It was remarkably similar to a jewel Sam's mother used to wear. Something about the sight of the emerald touched Sam deeply within his soul. Sam took it as a sign that he should take Mr. Khadir up on his invitation. Sam knew there was no such thing as coincidence.

Finally, the homeless man answered his enigmatic visitor, "I will follow you if you will teach me the Right Way."

"You will not be able to bear patiently with me, for how can you experience true patience concerning events about which you lack full knowledge?" Mr. Khadir answered turning away.

The panic Sam felt that the stranger might leave him behind surprised him. He was already following Khadir toward the service road as he replied, "You will find me, if God wills, patient and obedient to your mystic teaching."

Mr. Khadir said softly, "Then yes, I will teach you. When your poverty is complete, you will be God. But I must warn you: even if you see me doing strange things, acting foolishly, childishly — you must bear with me and attend to it all. Woe to you if you turn away."

"Where are we going?" Sam wanted to know.

"Allah knows best," Mr. Khadir replied.

"O Allah, make me one who often cries out 'ah' to you."

*- The Prophet Muhammad (Peace
be upon him)* [65]

*"Allah says: 'I am to my servant as he expects of Me, I am with him when
he remembers Me. If he remembers Me in his heart, I remember him to
Myself, and if he remembers me in an assembly, I mention him in an
assembly better than his . . .' "*

- Hadith Qudsi

"To Allah belong the most beautiful names, so call Him by them."

- Qur'an 7:180

CALLING OUT TO ALLAH

Sufis repeat the Name(s) of Allah infinitely throughout their lives. They do this either alone or in gatherings. The gatherings may be informal, spontaneous events, or traditional Sufi ceremony and ritual. Wherever, whenever and however the Sufi remembers the Name(s) of Allah is not important; what is essential is that he or she not fail in continuously remembering Allah through His Name(s).

The Murshid gives to his or her Murid certain Names of Allah to repeat on a daily basis, and a certain precise number of times to say each Name. This remembrance of Allah through His Name(s) is known as Zikr, Zikruallah, or Dhikr. It can be done privately or publicly, in silence or aloud. However, as the Love for the Beloved grows in the Heart, the Heart cannot help but utter the Beloved's Name(s) at all times of the day and night. Some people will tell you that you must be given an *'esma* by your Sheikh. However, the fact that many Sheikhs and Evliyas have written books on the Ninety-Nine Names of Allah (such as Sheikh Muzaffer Ozak al-Jerrahi al-Halveti and His Holiness M. R. Bawa Muhaiyaddeen) proves that these Sheikhs want the Murid to contemplate on these names, and what is contemplation if not Zikr? Especially noted is Sheikh Muzaffer's book that offers specific relief and blessings conferred upon those who repeat various Names, including the precise number of times to repeat these Names for various purposes.

Umar bin al-Khattab reported that the Prophet said, *"When you pass by the gardens of Paradise, avail yourselves of them."* The companions asked, *"What are the gardens of Paradise, O Messenger of Allah?"* He replied, *"The circles of dhikr. There are roaming angels of Allah who go about looking for the circles of dhikr, and when they find them they surround them closely."* [66]

The Prophet (Peace be upon him) praised a man who was *awwah* - literally, one who says ah, ah! - that is, loud in his Zikr, even when others censured him. Ahmad narrated with a good chain in his "Musnad" (4:159) from 'Uqba ibn Amir, *"The Prophet said of a man named Dhu al-bijadayn: 'innahu awwah'. ('He is a man who says "ah" a lot.') This is because he was a man abundant in his Zikr of Allah in Qur'an recitation, and he would raise his voice high when supplicating)."*

The Absolute Reality reveals to us *"Remember me, I shall remember you."*[67] The Murid should immerse him or herself in the vibration of Zikr perpetually. Imam Ghazali reports, *"I heard that Abul Hassan al-Farmadhi said, 'the Ninety-Nine Attributes of Allah will become attributes and descriptions of the seeker of the way of Allah.'"* The Prophet Muhammad (Peace be upon him) taught us that Zikr is the best of all acts of piety in the eyes of Allah; Zikr will elevate our status in the Hereafter, and carries more virtue than the spending of gold and silver in the service of Allah.[68] Zikr polishes the heart of the Murid.

According to As-Sayyid Shaykh Muhammad Hisham Kabbani[69], the word dhikr has many meanings. It means,

1. Allah's Book and its recitation
2. Prayer
3. Learning and teaching (Qurtubi said, *"Gatherings of dhikr are the gatherings for knowledge and admonition, those in which the Word of Allah and the sunnah of His Messenger, accounts of our righteous predecessors, and sayings of the righteous scholars are learned and practiced without any addition or innovation, and without any ulterior motives or greed."*)
4. Invocation of Allah with the tongue according to one of the formulas taught by the Prophet or any other formula
5. Remembrance of Allah in the heart, or in both the heart and the tongue.

For the Murid, all these aspects of Zikruallah are important. However, in this chapter we will focus on the last two meanings. The Prophet (Peace be upon him) has said, *"The best dhikr is La ilaha illallah."*[70] This saying can be translated directly as "There is no god, but God." It is the first part of the Islamic profession of faith. The Sufi subtly understands this to mean "There is no reality, except the Supreme Reality."

Ibn Hajar Asqalani shares valuable insight into the science of Zikruallah in his Fath al-Bari, [71]

"Dhikr can take place with the tongue, for which the one who utters it receives reward, and it is not necessary for this that he understand or recalls its meaning, on condition that he not mean other than its meaning but its utterance; and if, in addition to its utterance, there is dhikr in the heart, then it is more complete; and if there is, added to that, the recollection of the meaning of the dhikr and what it entails such as magnifying Allah and exalting Him above defect or need, it is even more complete; and if all this takes place inside

a good deed, whether an obligatory prayer, or jihad, or other than that, it is even more complete; and if one perfects one's turning to Allah and purifies one's sincerity towards Him: then that is the farthest perfection."

What are two of the most intimate Names? "Hu" and "Hayy" are a pronoun and name of Allah Almighty in the Qur'an according to the ayat al-Kursi, *"Allahu la ilaha illa HU AL-HAYY al-Qayyum."*[72] *(Allah! There is no god except HE, the LIVING the Self-Subsistent).*

PRACTICE

We suggest you read two particular types of books. We recommend those books written by Sufi Sheikhs and *Evliyas* (Saints). Do not read analytical and academic books about Sufism and the spirit world. Read books written by Sheikhs and Evliyas who have directly experienced the spontaneous revelation of the Divine.

The Holy Prophet of Islam Muhammad (Peace be upon him) said,

"Knowledge is of two kinds: formal knowledge which does not go beyond verbal profession. It is the evidence of God against those people who profess such knowledge, and according to it, God will judge them; and, genuine knowledge, which is deep-rooted in the heart - this is the knowledge which is most useful." [73]

We suggest you read writings of the great Sufis because their writings are actual living powers. These writings are culled from the Living World and as such are alive with energy and spirit.

"Art is the clothing of a revelation."
                                    - Joseph Campbell

"Seek out the fastness of some glowing heart!"
                                    - Iqbal

"Was music once a proof of God's existence?"
                                    - Seamus Heaney

*"The measure of a man is in the image of his creation; immortal because
of his inheritance – vulnerable as the awkward arrogance of a sun flower."*
                                    - James Gerard DeMartini

*"He who splashed a thousand worlds with color
How can He buy the paint of 'I and thou'?
Colors, colors – nothing but whim and fantasy;
HE is colorless, and one must adopt His hue."*
                                    - 'Ayn al-Qozat Hamadani

*"Of all that is lawful or forbidden, nothing is more commendable than
singing and the tambourine at a wedding."*
                                    - The Prophet Muhammad [74]

CONTRASTING TEXTURES - THE SUBCONSCIOUS "BRAILLE" FOR ALL LIVING THINGS

Feriduddin Attar relates in his "Mantiku'l-Tayr" how Muhammad (Peace be upon him) one day confided a secret to his son-in-law Ali ('Alaihi Assalam), who then repeated it into a well. Allah created a long reed in the well, and a passing shepherd cut off the end to make himself a reed-flute. One day Muhammad (Peace be upon him) encountered the shepherd and heard the secret he had told Ali ('Alaihi Assalam) coming from the shepherd's pipe. Ali ('Alaihi Assalam) was moved by the miracle and thankful that his love and loyalty to the Prophet had prevented him revealing the secret to another person. For Sufis, as this story indicates, music has great religious and mystic significance.

At age six we began our musical training at the piano. James Gerard DeMartini, Professor of Music at the Brooklyn Conservatory of Music and noted abstract artist, taught us classical piano technique for ten years. It was a fascinating experience to go to his studio each week. We would sit at his grand piano and gaze all around us when he was not in the room. What first caught our eye was Mr. DeMartini's library that took up an entire wall of the studio.

On the bookshelves, he also displayed his collection of African figure sculpture in ebony wood. These long and lean body shapes endlessly bewitched us.

Taking up the majority of the space in the room were various art works and sculptures in various degrees of completion. Near us at the piano were many of Mr. DeMartini's art supplies: brushes, color pencils, oils, and the rest. During our lesson, he would sit behind his easel and call out if we played a wrong note, and without missing a brush stroke tell us what note we should be playing or what we were doing wrong.

If we were lost in a musical section of a piece Mr. DeMartini would get up and come over to the piano. At those times, we were fearful of his impatience and occasional harsh tone with us. On a few occasions he honored us and took us by surprise by asking our opinion and advice concerning his work. We were much affected that he would often listen attentively to what we had to say and that he showed respect for our opinions.

Mr. DeMartini used to say that it is the imperfections in an orchestral rendition of a piece that render the performance so interesting. James Gerard DeMartini had a deep insight into the nature of reality. Each human being exhibits a unique texture. Our blemishes make each of us a Divine Revelation.

Resistance is manifested through texture. The word "texture" has to do with the characteristic look and feel of woven threads in a fabric. As you run your hands over textured cloth you feel some resistance, the bumps and weave of the cloth, as opposed to, for instance, the smooth feel of running your hands over silk. You are all the fabric of the earth. Earth covers earth. Texture is an important element in artistic composition, arising from the artist's blending of elements, such as the timbre in music and the pigment and brushwork in painting.

James Gerard DeMartini writes, *"The symphysis of all wisdom reveals the contrasting textures or patterns of behavior. The measurement of this texture is the subconscious "braille" for all living things. The texture of color, not merely its reflection, is the architecture of the environment of our atmosphere – an ever-changing and expanding dimension."*

Texture lends a distinctive dimensional quality to objects. Brick walls give a room texture. The nap and grain of life can be used to enhance any activity in life. A romantic date that contains adventurous moments is much more memorable than the usual dinner and a movie. Consequently, you see that there is a beneficial aspect hidden inside the concept of resistance. Resistance can be used to create texture, a thing highly desirable in the Arts, in life and in Spirituality.

There are many seemingly wise individuals who base their faith on the two ideas of order and perfection. It may come as a surprise to them, but the necessary inherent contradiction inside "order" is chaos, and inside "perfection", imperfection.

Consider the lilies of the field. No two flowers are alike, and they grow at random, scattered haphazardly by the wind. Consider those people of the past who sought to create the "perfect" human being, and an entire race of "perfect" human beings. If society imposed the rational mind's idea of order and perfection on the natural world, it would create a monstrous place. Ponder on the "order" imposed by a military state or by a dictator.

The truth of perfection is imperfection. Each person is beautiful in his or her own right. It is through our differences, our human imperfections, that our true majesty is revealed.

Do not let perfection and order become your masters! These are the two most dangerous traps set for the spiritual Murid. True spirituality proceeds from an honoring and awareness of chaos and imperfection. Who would dare untangle a rainforest? Destructive events such as a forest-fire are a necessary way that Nature recycles and renews Herself. To quote from James Gerard DeMartini, *". . . an intuitive creativeness at once both primitive and sophisticated, becomes the mirror of man. His reflection is best equated by a pendulum that swings between happiness and despair. This is the common denominator."*

Journey to the Heart of Beauty; do not be obsessed with mental and egoic ideas of form and perfection. Get your hands and feet dirty, dance in the rain, and rejoice in the Life that is Living Itself through the Uniqueness of You!

Again, DeMartini, *"Color alone is not enough. Rather it is its specific density which communicates."* There is no black and white. There are different tones from light to dark. Tones suggest the shadow and shape of things. We see because there exist dark tones and light tones. A painter will mix his or her colors with either black or white.

The Prophet used to tell people to eat *balah* or green dates together with *tamr* or dried ripe dates for when the sons of Adam eat them Shaitan is angry and says, *"The sons of Adam are eating the new together with the old!"* This is because green dates are cold and dry while dried ripe ones are hot and moist, and each possesses benefits that complement those of the other. The Prophet would join together cucumbers, *rutab* or fresh ripe dates, *sha`ir* or barley bread, and *tamr* or dry ripe dates, as well as mix cold water with honey and drink it on an empty stomach. All this makes for lasting good health, because good health endures when foods of hot and cold elements are joined.

Blend the waters of chaos and order carefully, creating a fluid that is not too volatile, not too inactive. However, let there always be the sense that the chaos of ecstasy could erupt at any moment. Pour from one flask perfection, and from the other flask imperfection. Your drink should taste sweet, but also contain subtle hints of various sour and bitter herbs and spices. *"For waters are variously flavored and weather changes, and the character of the people at every place where one stops differs from their character at the next."* [75]

Trees are gnarled and twisted in beautiful ways. Allow yourself to be a weather beaten, gnarly old oak in your spirituality and rejoice in your Divine twists and turns.

"How can I see what is not visible but I know is sensible?"
- Flora Edwards

"First, any human soul, by reflecting deeply, will in the long run be unable to disregard the fact that its most important questions concerning the meaning and significance of life must remain unanswered if there be no access to supersensible worlds."
- Rudolf Steiner

"Lo! Verily the friends of Allah are those on whom fear comes not, nor do they grieve."
- Qur'an 10:62

"The human power of cognition can be strengthened and enhanced, just as the faculty of eyesight can be strengthened. The means, however, for strengthening cognition are of an entirely spiritual nature; they are purely inner soul functions."
- Rudolf Steiner

"Fear the clairvoyance of the believer. For he sees by the light of God."
- Muhammad
(Peace be upon him) [76]

THE AWLIYA'S KASHF - UNVEILING OF THE UNSEEN

What exactly is the subtle knowledge that some fortunate ones obtain? In Sufism, it is known as *Kashf*, or the Unveiling of the Unseen. This knowledge is bestowed by Allah upon His most Intimate Friends.

First, people are familiar with the five known senses: touch, taste, hearing, seeing, and smell. However, all humans are heirs to more than five senses. They are inheritors of senses that can perceive the spirit realms. In ancient times, these "super" senses were accepted as normal and the heritage of every human being. However, over the centuries, these senses have been increasingly ignored and fallen into disuse. Presently, they exist in most people as only slumbering powers. They lie dormant.

Therefore, supersensible knowledge is spirit knowledge that is obtained with senses other than the known five senses. Al-Sharif al-Jurjani defines it as, *"apprehending beyond the veil of ordinary phenomena, whether by vision or experience, the meanings and realities that pertain to the unseen."* [77] This knowledge is neither illusion nor fantasy; supersensible knowledge is obtained through senses that have eluded scientific detection thus far.

Rudolf Steiner spoke and wrote extensively that the scientific method can be applied to mystic experience as it can to experiences in the laboratory. Ken Wilber, in "Eye to Eye: The Quest for the New Paradigm"[78] states that observations made with the "third eye" are as valid as those made with the ordinary eyes, though third eye observations are as subject to illusions, as are all observations. 'Ain al-Qudat al-Hamadhani affirms, *"The science of Sufism is the noblest and most obscure of all sciences; none but Sufis know its manifest and hidden meanings."*[79]

Supersensible awareness is the awareness of that which supports life to such an extent that if its transmission were to be interrupted for three days the kernel of the individual dies, just as someone would die if he or she were deprived of food. Such knowledge, therefore, is something that continually pours into human beings.

Ordinarily, the mind is limited to the knowledge that it harvests from the perceptual screens of its sense organs. We know there are limitations to the information these sense organs can gather. Consequently, human beings have sought through the ages ways to augment these five senses. The Master Abū Madyan Shu'ayb said: *"Spiritual insight confirms usefulness."* For instance, most people are aware that we cannot see infrared and ultraviolet with the unaided eye. Therefore, we have developed special binoculars, camera film, satellites, and other instrumental sensors to enable us to "see" infrared and ultraviolet light. Much is going on in the universe of which our five senses and all our scientific instruments are unaware.

Scientists demand objective verification for claims of supersensible perception, in other words, we both have to see planet X through our telescopes. They insist on double-blind studies written up in peer review journals. Ironically, those scientists whom most vociferously argue that there is nothing that exists besides the physical world do so through the power of their conscious minds. All their thinking takes place in the imaginal realm. It is truly ironic that through consciousness, they argue for the exclusion of anything beyond the physical!

For as long as humanity has walked the face of this earth, there have been persistent reports of the existence of realms that are not perceptible to the five senses but that are subjectively perceived. Verification of these realms through scientific testing has been difficult. However, today increasing recognition and legitimacy is being given to the reality of inner existence, or the noumenal realm. It has been advanced that the inner worlds are just as necessary to the foundation of existence as are the outer worlds.

Many traditionalist Sufis tell us that only the saints can experience these supersensible realities, *"By the stage of sainthood we mean that it is pos-*

sible for a saint to have revealed to him truths which the man of reason cannot be conceived of as attaining or stumbling upon by means of his natural equipment."[80] Nevertheless, Allah Most High instructs us in the Qur'an to request this knowledge. *"Pray with your entire being, My beloved, 'O precious Lord, increase and advance me in spiritual states and mystic knowledge.'* "[81]

Awakening these slumbering senses, requires spiritual discipline, and so the discerning Sufi may say that these "super" senses are both a natural human birthright and a gift of Allah. Riaz Ahmed Gohar Shahi sheds light on this subtlety, *"You cannot love God by simply saying that 'I love God' with your tongue. To truly love God is to have the heart say it. To achieve this it is important to awaken it. The love of God is created, found, contained and received in the human heart and there is a spiritual method and practice by which the heart can be awakened and taught to receive the Love of God."* Therefore, in one meaning, these supersensible organs exist in potential in every human being, but only those who strive to become Complete Human beings develop these sense organs. Sometimes, these organs begin functioning spontaneously, and in other cases, much work and discipline is required for their unfolding.

Nonetheless, it is the solemn responsibility for the Murid to attain Supersensible or Theophanic Vision. The freer the Murid is of "ego" the more he or she can discern the meaning hidden within every form, and thus see things as they truly are. For by gaining an intimation of what things symbolize on a spiritual level, the Murid *spiritualizes* these material things. This is part of humanity's work as Allah's Stewards of this Planet Earth. The Murid must not simply process sensory data, rather he or she must see through things. This Vision is mediated by *himma*, the power of the heart.[82]

Although, you may not yet have had direct experience of the spirit world, you can still be confident that it is feasible for you to perceive these realities. *"It is possible for a man possessed of reason, to reach by way of reason, belief in the existence of a stage which he has not yet attained personally. Thus, a man may be deprived of the taste for poetry, and yet he may come to recognize the existence of something in the man possessing such taste, whilst at the same time he must confess total ignorance of the nature of that thing."*[83]

This ability to experience the invisible realms is known among the masters of spiritual states and stations. *"The truthful, righteous Muslim (al-muslim al-sadiq al-salih) is he whose state matches that of Prophets and thereby is bestowed (ukrima) some of the same kind of gift they were, and that is to behold the unseen (wa huwa al-ittila' 'ala al-gayb)."*[84] Ruzbihan offers this discernment, *"For the oceans of sainthood and prophethood interpenetrate each other."*[85] Clearly, the Way to gain these gifts is not an easy Way. The Murid must rid him or herself of the *"rust of screens"* and to perfect his or her *"inner detachment."*[86]

Many people seek this knowledge. Unfortunately, numerous Murids have been tricked by mistaken Murshids into thinking that rigid adherence to the Shariat (rules and discipline of Islam) is an essential aspect of the Sufi Way to knowledge. A Murshid should make you think, not believe. This knowledge is so much more advanced a thing than belief (what people call faith) that in the words of Ghazali, *"those who really know are seven hundred degrees in rank about those who only believe."*

Yet, Allah alone *"knows best about the states of His Intimate Friends whom He has raised with His most excellent upbringing, and the mirrors of whose hearts He has polished with His most excellent polish, until they witnessed the Station of Divine Presences and Abiding (maqam al-hudr wa al-baqa')."* [87]

The knowledge, bestowed by Allah, of hidden realities may attain higher levels than that of any other knowledge of humankind and jinn including in certain cases even the knowledge of Prophets. For example, a Friend of Allah was with the Prophet Solomon and brought him the throne of Balqis faster than the blink of an eye. He was characterized as *"one who had knowledge of the Book."* As Allah stated, *"One with whom was knowledge of the Scripture said, I will bring it thee (O Solomon) before thy gaze returneth unto thee. . ."*[88] This Friend was the Prophet Solomon's scribe Asif Ibn Barkhya.

It is evident from the definition of the term kashf that it refers to a hidden knowledge of a tremendous nature, and that is what Ibn al-'Arabi meant by saying *"the secrets of Allah Most High,"* as is alluded to in the hadith of Abu Huraira, *"I have stored up from the Prophet two large vessels of knowledge. One I have disseminated among the people; if I were to disseminate the other, they would cut my throat."* [89]

PRACTICE 90

All the roads that go to Allah pass through the roads of humanity.
Each morning, before leaving the house, say the following prayer:

*"O Lord, make me come into contact with beautiful people today. The work
that I am going to do, let me do it with love. Make me strong, courageous,
self-sacrificing, in doing the work. You are the only being to be loved. All of
my service is for you, ya Wadud (The Loving One)."*

Say this prayer with sincerity and with passion.

"Thou must first comprehend thine original Nature in every Point, as it was before thou was forced to bow before the Gods of Wood and Stone that Men have made.
> *- Aleister Crowley*

"The heart of a rich man is always weary."
> *- Arabic Proverb*

"Since the whole world
Cannot buy
A single spring day, Of what avail
To seek yellow gold?"

> *- His Pei Lan*
> *(Ch'ing Dynasty poet)*

"Behold, We have created you all out of a male and a female,
and have made you into nations and tribes,
so that you might come to know one another . . .
This community of yours is one single community,
Since I am the Sustainer of you all: remain, then, conscious of me."
> *- Qur'an 49:13, 23:52*

"We are prone to judge success by the index of our salaries or the size of our automobiles rather than by the quality of our service and relationship to humanity."
> *- Martin Luther King*

TALES FROM UNDER THE OVERPASS

*W*here there is no hope there is no expectation or disillusionment and as the cars sped by on the Expressway, Sam began to miss his little shack. Even the westbound direction in which they walked pointed toward Los Angeles and reminded him of his foolishness in trusting in another for guidance on a spiritual path. Sam resolved that he would take the adventure with both eyes open this time and find out what he could about his new-found comrade in travel.

Sam asked Mr. Khadir where he lived. Mr. Khadir replied, *"I lived in a house on an island, but it may well have been destroyed."*

"You don't know if you have a house?" Sam was surprised at Mr. Khadir's answer.

"I'm busy with something more important than a house," replied Mr. Khadir, *"even though my home may be destroyed I would gain something*

vaster than a house. By giving up everything, one gains everything. The open road is not expensive in return for a few yards of land."

They stopped at a gas station for a soda. A well groomed man in an impeccable suit was screaming at the mechanic who worked on the new Mercedes in the garage. He was an affluent Wall Street type fellow with a great deal of toys and obviously used to getting his way.

Mr. Khadir said to Sam, "He or she who is seeking the world is in reality seeking a spiritual one, but he or she is unaware of it!" Mr. Khadir walked into the repair bay and said to the owner of the car: "Were you born for this?"

The man turned, surprised by Mr. Khadir's voice. At first a flush of anger crossed his face, but then his face turned part sheepish, part defensive, "I paid six figures for that damned car and pay a whole lot more for some mechanic to take half the day to fix it," the mechanic turned and shot him a look. The man continued without hesitating: "I'm three hours late for a board meeting. This doesn't make me happy."

Mr. Khadir responded by asking the man, "Why do you seek happiness?"

The man was confused. He started to say something, but stopped. Then he said with some reflection: "Isn't that what all human beings seek?"

"Peace doesn't equal comfort. Truth," Mr. Khadir said, "is infinitely more important than happiness. You can become a prisoner of happiness, as you can of woe. You have all but wasted your life because you have been a liar. Your lie has been in seeking happiness when you could have been seeking Truth.

"And so you have met me," Mr. Khadir continued, "because you had sufficient sincerity to want Truth for its own sake, if just for an instant. It was that sincerity, in that single instant, which made me answer your call. However, my friend, your new knowledge calls to be acted upon. If not satisfied, it will depart."

Seeing how overwhelmed the rich man looked, Khadir patted his arm gently and said, "Delve into your soul and there seek out life's buried tracks. Until now you have imagined that happiness must be the same as Truth, but happiness flows from a life of Truth. It is not something that can be artificially induced. The more involved a person is in the world, the more he hides from the Spirit. To separate oneself from things of time and to connect oneself with things of eternity is highest wisdom."

The sound of a cell phone ringing turned the man's attention from Khadir. The man laughed gruffly, "I'm just not the type to keep all the laws and regulations of religion."

Mr. Khadir knew the best of all deeds in the eyes of his Lord, and so spoke, "I understand. I advise you in two things: keep your tongue always *moist with mentioning the Name of Allah, and second, now that you have found Truth, beautify your actions."*

"The Baal Shem Tov himself, the originator of Hasidism, is said to have viewed music as among the most direct ways that we all can experience the splendors of the universe."
> *- Edward Hoffman*

"In the rhythm of music a secret is hidden. If I were to divulge it; it would overturn the world."
> *- Jelaluddin Rumi*

"Listen to music religiously as if it were the last strain you might hear."
> *- Henry D. Thoreau*

"Often Love conquers the ear before the eye."
> *- Fakhruddin 'Iraqi*

"Music is something you listen to while you're listening to the music."
> *- Philip Glass*

"Music is the voice of Allah."

> *- Sheikh el-Hajj Şerif Çatalkaya er-Rıfa'i er-Marufi*

MUSICAL AWAKENING

At the age of seventeen, during a visit to the Hicksville Public Library, we decided to listen to some record albums. Until that time playing the piano was something that we did well, it was a source of pride and accomplishment, and was physically pleasurable in a tactile way. That is, we would enjoy feeling our fingers properly execute the musical passages. We were only dimly aware that music could have a connection to our heart. While at that time we enjoyed listening to classical music, we did not enjoy listening to opera. However, we had been a fan of the great conductor Arturo Toscanini. It was for that reason we ventured into unknown territory that day and chose a selection from the operatic repertoire conducted by the maestro.

Before we played the record we suggested to ourselves that we would suspend all judgment as we listened to the work, suspend all thoughts and give our complete attention to the music. For some mysterious reason we also suggested to ourselves that we pay attention to the music as if we were listening to a speaker give a lecture, following his or her train of thought and awaiting understanding.

While listening to the Toscanini recording of the "Prelude and Libestod" of Richard Wagner's "Tristan und Isolde" we experienced a music-heart-love awakening. Within moments of placing the needle on the record, we found ourselves drawn into the music. Our soul was in new territory. There we sat in the middle of the Hicksville Library, listening to this old scratchy record, on an old turntable, with cheap plastic headphones, but with tears unashamedly streaming down our cheeks as the music soared to ecstatic and soul shaking heights of passion and love. *"Some are deeply moved by beauty in music, poetry and art, whereas others are as dull as stone if something subtle is not yet awakened in their hearts."*[91] From that moment on, our life was transformed. We knew the meaning of love and the power of music.

"Until music builds us a house
our home is where the music
touches us." [92]

Music has the power to "model" emotions and states, that is, to create a blueprint of an emotion or state in the listener that the listener can decode. Music is a method to transmit mystical revelation over vast distances in time and space. When the listener decodes the message of the music, the listener unlocks primeval and forgotten feeling-memories from deep within his or her being.

That is what happened that day in the Hicksville Public Library - our soul was suddenly awakened and shown various mysteries and wonders it had forgotten.

PRACTICE

The purpose of this exercise is to know and remember the fact that Allah Most High alone is the single Light of Truth that reveals both heavenly and earthly planes of being.

Imagine in your mind's eye, a lamp. Inside this lamp is a mystic flame. This flame has a transparent glass covering it. The glass is radiant and sparkles – effulgent as a brilliant star. Inside burns a fire with a bright light.

This spiritual lamp is enshrined in a high prayer niche. This fire is kindled from oil from a Transcendent Tree. This oil itself is luminant, although no flame has kindled it! This tree is not found in the east OR the west.

Light upon Light. Light here! Light there! This is the Light of the Soul, shining forth with Divine Light.[93]

Through such profound meditations, Allah Most High guides whomever He wills into His most intimate Light.

"Love is fire, love is fire."

- Ahmed er Rifa'i

AHMED ER RIFA'I (1118-1181)

Ahmed er Rifa'i was related to our Prophet (Peace be upon him) from his father's and mother's side by blood. Before Ahmed er Rifa'i's birth, his maternal uncle, a famous Sheikh, Mansur Rabbani, had seen the Prophet Muhammad (Peace be upon him) and was told that his sister would have a male child who would be famous and be known by the name "Rifa'i." When the child reached the proper age for Sufism, he should be sent to Sheikh Aleyyul Vasiti for education and training.

Ahmed er Rifa'i's father passed away when he was seven years old in 519 A.H.; he is buried in Baghdad. So Ahmed er Rifa'i's maternal uncle started taking care of little Ahmed er Rifa'i. After a while he was sent to Sheikh Vasiti in accordance with his uncle's vision. Sheikh Mansur has said that as long as Ahmed er Rifa'i stayed with him, he saw many miracles come through Ahmed er Rifa'i and that many blessings came through him for everyone.

Ahmed er Rifa'i showed ability and wisdom beyond his age when he started his education under Sheikh Vasiti. He acquired a high *makam* by explaining the book of the *Shafee* school called "Tenbih."

In the year 555 A.H. Ahmed er Rifa'i went on pilgrimage, and in Medina (al-Munawwarah) he went to see our Prophet (Peace be upon him). The guard did not want to let him in because he was not traveling in his Sayyid clothes that would have shown that he was a blood relative of the Prophet. When the guard didn't let him in, he was sad and yelled towards our Prophet's tomb and said *"Eselamu-aleyke ya jeddi"* (*"Peace be on you, my ancestor"*) and then our Prophet answered saying *"Aleykesselam ya veledi"* (*"And peace be on you, my son"*) and our Prophet's hand came out of the tomb and Ahmed er Rifa'i kissed our Prophet's hand. When the people nearby saw this miracle, they went into a state of *vejd* (ecstasy) and began stabbing themselves with their swords and knives. When the ecstasy moment passed, there were people lying wounded all over the floor with lots of blood. So Ahmed er Rifa'i went around and healed them all back to their normal health. After that, Ahmed er Rifa'i was known to have this gift and this is known as a Rifa'i miracle.

One day somebody asked Abdul Qadir Geylani (who was Ahmed er Rifa'i's cousin) *"Ya Hazret, what is love?"* Abdul Qadir Geylani told the guy to go ask this question to Sayyid Ahmed er Rifa'i, so the person went to Ahmed er Rifa'i and after saying Abdul Qadir Geylani sent his salaams he asked, *"What is love?"* When Ahmed er Rifa'i heard the question, he stood up and started saying *"Love is fire, love is fire."* He started whirling and then he passed into the unseen and disappeared. When the person saw this, he became abashed, he did not know what was happening. He had asked the question and suddenly the one he asked was gone. At that moment, the spiritual presence of Abdul Qadir Geylani appeared and said, *"Look at the last place he stepped on and pour rose water on the spot where my brother Ahmed er Rifa'i disappeared."* The person did this and in a couple of moments, Sayyid Ahmed er Rifa'i appeared, whirling in the exact same place. When this person went back to Baghdad, he visited Abdul Qadir al Geylani and the master asked him, *"Did you see love? My brother Sayyid Rifa'i has reached stations that many walis have not been able to reach."*

One day, Hadrat Abdul Qadir al Geylani, Sayyid Ahmad Rifa'i, and several of Ahmad Rifa'i's disciples were siting by the Tigris River. As they talked, Abdul Qadir displayed such *karamats* (miracles) as bewildered the audience. When one of them, entirely dazed with admiration, inadvertently let slip a laudatory remark, Hadrat Abdul Qadir al Geylani humiliated his self and woke the others from oblivion with the following modest reply, *"I do not presume there could be a Muslim on earth lower than I am."*

Sayyid Ahmed er Rifa'i really loved and respected Abdul Qadir al Geylani and told his students that whoever visited Baghdad and did not visit Abdul Qadir al Geylani's tomb would not be welcomed by Allah or them.

Abu Musa el-Haddadi said that in the town of Haddahiye there was a woman whose children were always stillborn. This lady said, if I have a child, I will give this child in the service of Ahmed er Rifa'i. A couple of years later she had a daughter who was hunchback and lame. Because of this, the other children in the village always made fun of her. One day, Ahmed er Rifa'i was visiting this town and all the people got on the road to see him. The little girl threw herself at Ahmed er Rifai's feet and said *"You are my mother's Sheikh, please heal me from these problems"* and cried. When Ahmed er Rifa'i saw her situation, he cried as well, and he started praying over her, and he put his hand on her back and on her head. The girl's back and leg were both healed. This is why Ahmed er Rifa'i is called Beynennas *(Sheikh ul Ureja)*.

Kamil Mustafa al-Shaiba, in his "Sufism and Shi'sm," quotes al-Wasiti saying that Ahmad al-Rifa'i was considered to be "a Mahdi, renewing the Qur'an, disposing of heaven and earth," and was considered to have reached a station just below that of the twelve Imams.

"Perceive the secrets of thy soul
In the countenance
The wide world turns toward thee.
Perceive the living essence of the World
In the countenance
Imprinted by it on thine inmost soul."
                                        - Rudolf Steiner

"The color of mountains is Buddha's pure body,
The sound of running water is his great speech."
                                        - Dogen Zenji

"The planting of one tree is worth the prayers of a whole year."
                                        - Turkish Proverb

WE ARE BEAUTIFUL

When we were nineteen, we were engrossed in the study of the Japanese martial art Aikido. One autumn the dojo went on a retreat to the mountains of New Hampshire.

The view from our condominium was spectacular. A mountain reared up next to us, exposing its entire tree-filled side. All the leaves had changed. The awesome beauty of nature was evident all around us.

One evening we stood on our porch looking out at the spectacle with a fellow Aikido practitioner. He happened to be a psychologist. We were shy as a young man, yet we felt comfortable amongst these nice people. We turned to him and uncharacteristically expressed our thoughts.

"Why is it that we can look at this gorgeous sight and without hesitation, pronounce it beautiful? We see an eagle fly by and we know it is splendid. A bear appears and the episode is a revelation. Yet, when we look at human beings we say, 'this one is attractive, that one is unattractive'. We never say, 'this bear is a lot more beautiful than that bear.' On the other hand, if we look at a tree, although we notice the knots in the wood and dead branches we still think it is beautiful. Why is this?"

The psychologist answered, *"You have a good point. It is a shame that we don't see ourselves so."* Still, he did not have an answer to our question, although we could tell he was in tune with our contemplations.

Consider the possibility of ceasing your struggle with yourself. You are a beautiful, splendid, revelation of the Presence of Life. Work on regarding yourself with the same Total Acceptance that you offer to an Elephant, a Tiger and an Owl. Leave all artificial human-made dualities (attractive and unattractive, worthy and unworthy, cool and loser) behind. *"Basically, non-duality is a continual correction of dualistic conceptions as they arise. It's a spontaneous process which, without judgement, playfully erases lines of division as they arise,"* confirmed Shaykh Nur al-Anwar al-Jerrahi. [94]

Everything in nature is precious. The tiniest pebble in a stream is important. Even a weather-beaten old tree is spectacular. You are a pure manifestation of the Infinite Field of Being. Cease struggling with yourself. Treat yourself with the utmost respect. Know that you are just as majestic and magnificent as a poppy flower. Let your wholeness and beauty radiate and bless all around you.

PRACTICE

When meeting a person, notice their strengths, instead of their weaknesses. *"Shall I not inform you about a better act than fasting, charity and prayer? - - - making peace between one another. Enmity and malice tear up heavenly rewards by the roots,"* disclosed the Prophet Muhammad (Peace be upon him). Observe a person's merits, what is worthwhile about a person, what recommends him or her to you. *"Deal gently with people and be not harsh; cheer them and do not condemn them,"* the compassionate Mercy to the World, Muhammad (Peace be upon him) taught us. The reason the Divine has given us eyelids is so that we can close our eyes to our friends' mistakes. The Prophet (Peace be upon him) also warned, *"Don't count your friend's mouthfuls."* [95]

No one should see a fault in anyone. Bayazid al Bistami said that a man asked him, *"Show me the shortest way to reach Allah Most High."* Bayazid said, *"Love the beloved of Allah and make yourself lovable to them that they love you, because Allah looks into the hearts of those whom he loves seventy times a day. Perchance he will find your name in the heart of the one he loves, then he will love you too and he will forgive your wrongdoings."* [96]

The path to Allah is through human beings. Kabir wrote,

"I said to the wanting-creature inside me:
What is this river you want to cross?
There are no travelers on the river-road, and no road. Do you see anyone moving about on that bank, or
resting?
There is no river at all, and no boat, and no
Boatman. There is no tow rope either, and no one to pull it.
There is no ground, no sky, no time, no bank, no
ford!" [97]

Everything you are searching for is in the human being. People who have compassion toward humanity are worthy of respect. The beautiful human being is the one who lives in beautiful understanding with people. *"Do not belittle others,"* warns Allah Most High in the Qur'an. [98]

The Islamic sect, the Khawarij refuse to judge human actions because that privilege is reserved to God. Tradition has it that the Prophet had foreseen Islam having seventy-three sects, but that in the end only one would remain. [99]

Ibrahim Ad'ham has said, *"You see all the faults of your brothers and sisters in religion, yet you fail to look at your own faults."*[100]

"To affirm that the sun . . . is at the center of the universe and only rotates on its axis without going from east to west, is a very dangerous attitude and one calculated not only to arouse all scholastic philosophers and theologians but also to injure our holy faith by contradicting the scriptures."

> *- Cardinal Bellarmino,*
> *17th Century church master*
> *Collegio Romano, who imprisoned*
> *and tortured Galileo*
> *for his astronomical works*

"Nature is always hinting at us.
It hints over and over again.
And suddenly we take the hint."

> *- Robert Frost*

TALES FROM UNDER THE OVERPASS

*S*am and Mr. Khadir continued walking along the service road of the "L.I.E." (as native Long Islanders refer to the expressway). The heat of the June morning was becoming intense.

Sam asked, *"Where are we going?"*

"He is not a friend who asks 'Whither?' when you say to him 'Come along with us!'" Mr. Khadir replied.

They continued to walk on in silence for a while.

"Would you like to hear a story?" Mr. Khadir asked Sam.

"Okay," Sam answered.

"There was an old frog who lived all his life in a muggy and dark well. One day a frog from the ocean paid him a visit. This frog from the ocean had lived past the age of four thousand years. It never rested from glorifying Allah saying 'O Praiser of Thyself with every tongue, O remembered One in every place!'.

'Where do you come from?' asked the frog in the well.

'From the great sea,' he replied.

'How big is your sea?'

'It's enormous.'

'You mean about a quarter the dimensions of my well here?'

'Bigger.'

'Bigger? You mean half as big?'

'No, even bigger.'

'Is it . . . as enormous as this well?'

'There's no comparison.'

'That's impossible! I've got to see this for myself.'

They set off together. When the frog from the well saw the sea, it was such a shock that his head just exploded into pieces.

The old frog declared, 'Glory to the One Who is worshiped in the abysses of the sea!'

Sam shook with the fear of Allah. [101]

"We are adjured constantly to study and make ourselves familiar with the lives, doings and sayings of the wise because a link of understanding exists between these factors and the potentiality in ourselves."
> *- Bahaudin the Designer*
> *(Naqshband)*

"There's more in life than money, sir."
> *- Charles Dickens*

"Words let water from an unseen, infinite ocean
Come into this place as energy for the dying and even the dead."
> *- Jelaluddin Rumi* [102]

THE FAVORABLE DISPOSITION

A certain attitude is required to develop spiritually. Emotions such as awe, veneration and reverence, trigger the release of subtle vibrations in the body that open the psychic centers.

Criticalness is a dangerous attitude. The more critical or cynical a person is, the less open to the unknown that person becomes. Focusing the conscious mind in a critical way on something, forces the event through the sieve of the restrictions of the conscious mind, thereby reducing the event to a set of dualistic possibilities. The critical mind bursts the bubble of divine revelation. It shines a cold and critical spotlight onto the event, thereby obstructing the light of the event from being seen, replacing it with the critical cast of mind.

Wonder is the one soul-quality that takes us furthest into the Spirit World. The Prophet Isa (Peace be upon him) said one must become like a little child. The Prophet Isa (Peace be upon him) shed light on the Way of Reality when he said this. The Murid must look at the world through the bright, open, wonderment of the child. A cynical attitude kills the spirit sight.

PRACTICE

Inhale and contemplate on the Name *Al-Muta Ali*, The Supreme Exalted. As you inhale, know that Al-Muta Ali is beyond any behavior, action or human calculation that exists. Al-Muta Ali is beyond all situations and circumstances. Say to yourself Ya Muta Ali.

Exhale and call to mind each one of your problems. Know that Al-Muta Ali is Supremely Exalted above all your difficulties. Say to yourself, as you exhale, Ya Muta Ali. Robin Becker shares her insight with us, *"The exhale should be as profound as the inhale (both directions moving into infinite space)."*

Shaykh Abdoulaye Dieye writes: *"Each and every breath of the individual is worth a golden ingot."* Repeat this exercise casually and not by rote or routine.

The beings who name the Divine Names are the vassals or devotees of those Names. In other words, it is the human being who epiphanizes a Name in the phenomenal world that has it within his or her power to name that Name, where the Name can be thought of as his or her Divine Higher Self.

"Few events can have carried such a clear cosmic message as the running of the Kentucky Derby, May 12, 1975. While two horses fought for the lead, a third came up from behind and walked away with the purse. The two horses intent only on bumping each other for the favored position were Avatar and Diabolo. Avatar means a deity. Diabolo means devil. So while the deity contended with Lucifer, who dashed home first? Foolish Pleasure. Let that be a happy lesson for us all."

- Letter to 'Time Magazine'
by Richard Goldwater

"Praise be to God, who has created the heavens and the earth and has established darkness and light."

- Ayn al-Qozat [103]

"For a tree's branches to reach to heaven,
Its roots must reach to hell."

- Medieval alchemical dictum

"Racing horses is as expressive of non-duality as sitting in meditation."
- Shaykh Nur al-Anwar
al-Jerrahi [104]

WATER YOUR BRAIN

Polarity is the nature of reality. As such, it is the reality of our psyches. The drama of life and death takes place all around us and is not just someone else's story, but our story.

Because of this polarized nature of our psyches, a need exists to adopt a spirituality that acknowledges human reality and helps humanity to make some sense of this reality. We reject old forms of spirituality that insult, ridicule and teach people to neglect their natures. If someone objects and says that humanity should be conforming to the Divine, we reply that this person does not know the nature of the Divine.

Dualistic, patriarchal religion cuts humanity off from an entire pole of being, calling it evil and devilish. This type of religion tells people that exploring this pole of the human being is sinful and will eventually lead to being completely cut off from God, the Lord of the other pole. What a terribly destructive image this is. It leads people to shun and cut themselves off from one half of their beings!

"As for the idea that one might remove the bad from the Cosmos of created being, such a thing is not possible, since the Mercy of God inheres in both the good and the bad." [105]

A Way is needed which contains a concept of Absolute Existence that includes both the Light and the Dark, and Life and Death. If, for instance, Christianity might see Lucifer as the complement and not the enemy, it might take a valuable step on the road to becoming more holistic and respectful of the human reality. If the Divine cannot partake of the Shadow, it cannot be the Divine, for the Divine cannot truly nourish humanity if it only feeds one pole of the human being. *"Have you not observed [in the case of the shadow] that it is connected to the one who casts it, and would not its becoming disconnected be absurd, since nothing can be disconnected from itself?"* [106]

We want to make it clear that our suggestions regarding the religion of Christianity is not a criticism of the Prophet Isa (Jesus), (Peace be upon him), who is known in Islam as "a Word of God." The Word that the Prophet Isa (Peace be upon him) brought to humanity has been greatly distorted by many church councils (especially the council of Nicea) in which much of the true teachings of this beloved Prophet were corrupted and lost.[107]

Sufism offers a Way. While creation, the Cosmos, is the reflection of God, it does not know what it is. Each human being contains the Essence within him or herself, but the knowledge remains latent in most people. In Sufism, this latency is the Shadow. To quote from Ibn al-'Arabi, *"This shadow extends over the essences of contingent beings in the form of the unknown Unseen."* [108] Therefore, humanity's unconsciousness of its identity, is the Shadow of the Supreme Reality.

It is only when the Murid reaches the level of spiritual maturity in which he or she faces the fact that the Living Reality is not always Benevolent, that sometimes the Living Reality is Benevolent and sometimes it is Harsh, that the Murid can finally, truly, LIVE!

Remember that Reality is not what you think it is.[109] Earthly existence is a dream within a dream.

"Indeed Zen awakening is awakening to the opposites as two valid ways of being."

- Albert Low

"Real religion should be something that liberates men. But churches don't want free men who can think for themselves and find their own divinity within. When a religion becomes organized it is no longer a religious experience but only superstition and estrangement."

- Federico Fellini

"Regarding him, say neither bad nor good,
For he is gone beyond the good and the bad."

- Jelaluddin Rumi

"It is Thou Who hast no opposite that may contend with Thee."

- Imam Zain al-Abidin

THE MYTH THAT MUST BE WEEDED OUT

Traditional religion teaches that there is a war going on between good and evil. Moreover, these teachings make it seem possible to join the good side and join the struggle against the evil that is invading our world. In this cosmogony, the good forces attempt to defeat evil rather than recognizing it as the sacred polar opposite.

The aspiring Sufi needs to root out the underlying program of "good versus evil" that is continuously running in his or her subconscious. There is no black and white. There are different tones from light to dark. Tones suggest the shadow and shape of things. We see because there exist dark tones and light tones. The Murid needs to nurture a world-view in which the light and the dark are partners in a cosmic dance. This view more accurately reflects the realities of the Spirit and the Way Spirit Expresses Itself. The sacred Yin and the Yang swirl around each other in the wheel of manifestation.

We do not believe in good and evil. We think those terms misstate the situation. There is only Reality. Sometimes cloth is rough; sometimes it is smooth, yet it is always cloth. Some things are pleasant. Some things are not.

C. G. Jung writes, *"The individual may strive after perfection but must suffer from the opposite of his intensities for the sake of his completeness."*

In coming to terms with what is called evil the Murid should shy away from linear-intellectual explanations, he or she needs to experience it as an aspect of the Divine Interplay.

It seems that most contemporary spiritual works skirt a serious analysis of the problem of evil. Spirituality is portrayed in a saccharin sweet, watered-down manner in many books. Perhaps publishers are afraid of scaring off potential readers. However, in general, people are sensitive about the subject of evil. The water does not object before it plunges over the cliff as a waterfall.

The problem of evil in the world is a frequent question that troubles the heart of the aspirant. He or she reasons, *"If God is omniscient, omnipotent, and benevolent, then why does evil exist? He would know it exists; He would be able to get rid of it; and He would want to get rid of it."*[110] Furthermore, what religions teach us is "holy" often *"does not match up in the natural occurrence of things with the right, the good, or the beautiful. We want to know why the good suffer, when they do not deserve to; and why the evil prosper, when they do not deserve to. All the polarities of value - - pleasure and pain, love and hate, right and wrong, good and bad, beauty and ugliness, holiness and pollution – are like separate rollers on a slot machine. Every pull of the arm gives us a different combination."*[111] This dilemma confronts the rational "egoic" mind of the Murid (and most serious thinking people on earth). The answer lies in self-sacrifice and surrender. Bubba Free John teaches us, *"The Way of Divine Communion is devotion, surrender of body, life, mind, self, and all circumstances, desires, and assumptions into the Presence of the Divine."*[112] The Sufi must sacrifice his or her "need for answers." This is the way Sufis die before they die. The Sufi lets go of all demands for rational explanations of existence, and allows his or her heart-petals to unfold into the Living World.
Often people's reaction toward evil is prompted from a sense of outrage that social conventions have been violated. They are angry because they perceive that their desires will be thwarted; they are like infants that get mad if they do not have the tit right away. Moreover, from that interference in their suckling schedule they invent all sorts of adult rationalizations and explanations for evil.

As a Murid, be aware of your perceptions, rather than trying to force them into the molds invented by others. Pray to Allah that He breaks you out of the molds of logic, religion and society. Simply allow yourself to experience the situation, without making judgements about God or Humanity. *"It's a gentle melting away, like mist melts away, of dualistic concerns, whether they're obsessive, selfish concerns or whether they're beautiful, noble concerns. Let it all melt away, and be established consciously on the primal ground!"* [113]

A new approach to spirituality needs to be employed in the 21st Century in which both poles are recognized without making any value judgments. This new approach acknowledges that both poles are indispensable, and while focusing on the United Totality, the Murid honors the fact that both positive and negative are eruptions of the Divine. The Murid propitiously integrates both aspects in his or her being.

When viewed from the perspective of transcendence, the world no longer appears to be a battleground between the forces of good and evil. The

Murid no longer sees a choice between doing good to "get to heaven" or being self-indulgent to "get one's needs met". In place of this dualism, appears an equilibrium in the Murid. The paradigms of spirituality, God, selfishness, and the devil disappear, and in their place appears Living Reality. *Kamal* is the equilibrium.

Kamal is a calm witnessing and observing, in other words becoming a *Shahid.* The Sufi does not do good deeds and avoid bad deeds "for a reason." The Sufi has no need to garner or steal possessions, because the Sufi realizes the Body is One. The Sufi is the best of both worlds, and transcends both worlds.

"This World Which Is Made of Our Love for Emptiness
Praise to the emptiness that blanks out existence.
Existence: this place made from our love for that emptiness!"
- Jelaluddin Rumi

"The dryness of your lips is the indication of a need for water. This thirst is
a splendid and auspicious experience, and the desire to quench it will take
care of any obstacles . . . then there would be no need for any means or
ways in the journey toward the Truth."
- Jelaluddin Rumi

TALES FROM UNDER THE OVERPASS

Sam and Mr. Khadir had made their way into Manhattan and were having lunch in a coffee shop. A waitress had been eavesdropping in on their conversation. Sam and Mr. Khadir had been chatting about money and wealth and what role spirituality has in a world that's obsessed with possessions. After the meal, Sam and Mr. Khadir were sipping tea.

The waitress leaned over and spoke to them.

"You sound like religious men. I've got a question for you. You know, it's real tough trying to survive on tips and the small salary they pay me here. Sometimes I get really down. I wonder why some people drive by in Mercedes and Acuras and I drive a beat up '87 Plymouth Colt. Sometimes I say to myself, 'Why does God allow this churchgoing gal to be such a pauper?' What would it take for Him to give me an additional $20,000 dollars a year? What do you have to say about that?"

Mr. Khadir looked up at her with his penetrating eyes and said, "Do not look for rest in any pleasure, because you were not created for pleasure: you were created for JOY. And if you do not know the difference between pleasure and spiritual JOY you have not yet begun to live."

"I'd rather ride in a limo than take the subway, that would be a real joy" she sarcastically joked. Sam was enjoying the lively conversation. Mr. Khadir continued,

"Viewed from the perspective of the Ultimate Reality, a limo and the subway are identical. Only the discerning understand this principle of the secret identity of all things."

The waitress exclaimed, "Excuse me, Mr. Philosopher, but this is the way I see it."

Mr. Khadir continued, "You say, 'This is the way I see it.' You are moving yourself into the place of the thing you see. You are connecting in a personal way with what you see. Instead of being drawn into what you see, try to develop a sense of a Reality that includes all things. You divide the world into *pleasurable and unpleasurable and then GET TOO INVOLVED!"*

"I think I'm starting to get your point. In other words you're saying that people get hypnotized by cars and bodies and clothes?" the waitress questioned.

"You are like a child who starts to think that the game he or she is playing is Reality. The game is not the Reality. It is just a game. You need to remember that there is a Reality beyond the game."

By this time the waitress had taken a seat next to Sam and was facing Mr. Khadir. She asked,

"But aren't material things necessary parts of our lives?"

"True enough. But do you realize that in the mundane world that the absence of materiality is just as important?"

"Oh now I've got to hear this! Tell me Mr. Philosopher, how can the absence of materiality be as important as having nice things?"

"Think of a bicycle wheel. Consider all the spokes in the wheel. They all meet in a central hub, right? Within this hub is a hole, emptiness. The central focus of the wheel is a hole. Nevertheless, that hole makes the bicycle move. Or, think of a pot. Someone may mold the clay into a pot, but it isn't the clay that's the most important part, it is the emptiness inside! For what good would a pot be if not for the empty space inside?"

"Wow!" the waitress exclaimed.

"When a carpenter hammers together some boards to make a house, he doesn't intend to fill the house with wooden boards. Rather, the space inside makes the house livable. At the heart of all things is emptiness."

"Does that mean that you aren't going to leave me a tip?" the waitress grinned.

"Deep within Nothing there is Something, but don't ask me what it is because I wouldn't tell you even if I knew," Mr. Khadir said with a smile.

"Know that you are an imagination, as is all that you regard as other than yourself an imagination. All earthly existence is an imagination within an imagination, the only Reality being God, as Self and the Essence," finished Mr. Khadir.

"Anyone can become angry - that is easy. But to be angry with the right person, to the right degree, at the right time, for the right purpose, and in the right way - this is not easy."

- Aristotle

"A person that does not know how to be angry does not know how to be good."   *- Henry Ward Beecher*

ARE YOU ANGRY?

If you are angry much the time, rather than trying to cut off this part of yourself, perhaps recognize it as the one, true, authentic expression of the real you. Maybe every other aspect of your personality is a sham, a capitulation to someone else's value system. Your anger may be the voice crying out in the wilderness, your hidden prophet.

Some contemporary spiritual practitioners would have you believe that spiritual masters do not get angry and do not express the dark side. This is an incorrect view of spirituality. Anger can be a potent impetus to action. When a person shouts *"I'm mad as hell and I'm not going to take this any more!"* his or her anger is rousing them out of the sleep of complacency and into action. This is not about rage. Rage is anger out of control and taking over your whole being. However, anger, expressed in appropriate ways must be acknowledged. Freud once likened anger to the smoke in an old-fashioned wood-burning stove. The normal avenue for discharge of the smoke is up the chimney; if the normal avenue is blocked, the smoke will leak out of the stove in unintended ways – around the door, through the grates, and so forth – choking everyone in the room.

Children are not taught how to deal with their anger. Parents do not talk to their children about anger. If you are a parent, take the uncomfortable step of asking your child *"Are you angry?"* Then ask your child to speak. Reassure him or her that it is okay to discuss their angry feelings with you. Feelings are not good or bad, they are just emotions. It is when people act on these feelings in non-propitious ways that moral consequences result.

The Murid must learn to manage aggression. A useful way to manage aggression is by channeling aggressive energy into causes of true importance. Do not lower yourself to outbursts of anger over inconsequential daily events. Ask yourself what are truly important causes in the world that direly need support. Then dedicate your energies to these causes. This way you ennoble your aggression and turn it into virtuous achievement.

How you express your anger and aggression is of great importance! What we espouse is being aware of your anger and then propitiously working to understand it and its roots. The Greater Jihad is to be merciful to yourself and others. At this point, the anger must be channeled into constructive assertiveness. There is a significant difference between aggression and assertiveness. Both have their origin in anger, however assertiveness is a more propitious use of anger than is aggression. Assertiveness is a marriage between aggression and politeness. Aggressive people allow their anger to rule them. They simply take and do what they want, when they want, where they want, and without regard for others. On the other hand, overly polite people (and please understand that we are not saying that politeness is bad), often become walking "doormats." They submissively allow other people to walk all over them. For instance, they will not hang up on someone who is abusing them on the telephone; they will hold the door interminably for others; and they chronically fear that they might hurt the feelings of others. Too polite people do not stand up for themselves and their needs.

You need assertiveness (an aspect of the dark shadow) when you negotiate and haggle. If you had no internal drive to acquire your goals at the best price, then you would be at the mercy of other people's greed and drives. You need assertiveness to compete in the marketplace to earn your living.

If it were not for assertiveness, you would be doomed to picking over the scraps of things people left behind. You would not enter traffic because you would be allowing others to go ahead of you; you would not enter buildings because you would be holding the door open all day for everyone. There comes a time when the individual must place him or herself first.

Others will be left behind when you place yourself first. This is an uncomfortable spiritual fact for some people. Each time you take a walk through the woods your feet trample and kill millions of microbes. No matter if you have the veneer of a great spiritual and pious person, you are still the specter of Walking Death to the microbe world.

The answer is not to cease walking, but to come to a peaceful understanding within you of the necessity for the interplay of pain and pleasure, death and life. If you want to express your United Totality, you will on occasion express it assertively. The Holy Prophet (Peace be upon him) assertively practiced Jihad. The Prophet Isa (Peace be upon him) drove the moneychangers out of the temple with a whip. Moreover, that assertiveness is Holy.

PRACTICE

The Way of the Sufi requires that the Murid seek out situations in which he or she can experience the world in a profound way. These profound situations are not always found where one would expect, as for instance in the Mosque, Tekke or Monastery.

Volunteer in your community. Various organizations can use your help. *"What is considered to be most rewarding is to love the lonely and poor ones and care for them."*[114] Helping others is essential. *"Assist any person who is oppressed - whether Muslim or non-Muslim,"* uttered our Beloved Mustafa (Peace be upon him).

Get out of the house when you come home from work. Resist the temptation to sit and watch television. This inertia will draw you down into a state of immobility. A Sufi is constantly encountering a living experience inside his or her own soul; he or she is not passively being spoon fed an artificial reality on television.

Choose vacations in which you actively engage with others for some constructive end. Travel for a purpose, not just to "sightsee." Visit places of power, such as the tombs of holy men and women that are spiritual vortexes of grace and power. Go to ancient churches and cathedrals, which they often built upon the sites of centers of worship of the indigenous European, Mediterranean and Near Eastern peoples. The native peoples would choose their areas of worship based upon the convergence of invisible energy lines (known as *ley* lines). Visit countries and areas in which worship of the Divine Feminine was the central focus, such as Ireland, Sicily, Malta, Crete, and Turkey.

"We have sent you (O Muhammad) as a mercy for all the nations."
- Qur'an 21:107

"Verily ye have a fair pattern in the Messenger of God."
- Qur'an 33:21

"God was sent down in Muhammadan form."
- Ibn al-'Arabi

"Far be it from time to bring his like to birth; Time grudges to send his equal to earth."
- 'Ain al-Qudat al-Hamadhani

THE MERCY FOR ALL THE NATIONS

The Prophet Muhammad (Peace be upon him), the possessor of Perfect Unveiling, the Master of the Praiseworthy Station, was born Friday, the 17th of Rabi-ul Awwal to Abdullah Ibn Abdu'l-Muttalib and Amina bint-e-Wahab. Allah gave him *"the knowledge of those of old and the later folk."*[115]

The Prophet of Allah (Peace be upon him) was the foremost focal point of Divine divulgence. Allah announces the fact of the uniqueness of Muhammad (Peace be upon him), *"I was a hidden treasure, and I wished to be known, so I took a handful of my light and said unto it, 'Be thou my beloved Muhammad.'"* He was the point where the rays of Absolute Being came together. Therefore, all knowledge between the east and the west, in heaven and earth, was his. Allah Most High has sent 124,000 Prophets to humankind. However, Allah revealed more to Muhammad (Peace be upon him) than any other Prophet.

The Prophet Muhammad (Peace be upon him) possessed all knowledge. *"He encompasses the knowledge of all knowers who know God, whether those who had gone before or those who would come after,"* wrote Ibn al-'Arabi. Muhammad (Peace be upon him) was of medium stature, slim, with a large head, broad shoulders, and the rest of his body perfectly proportioned. His hair and beard were thick and black, not altogether straight but slightly curled. His hair reached midway between the lobes of his ears and shoulders, and his beard was of a length to match. He had a noble breadth of forehead and the ovals of his large eyes were wide, with exceptionally long lashes and extensive brows, slightly arched but not joined. They said that his eyes were black, but other accounts say they were brown, or light brown. His nose was aquiline and his mouth was finely shaped. Although he let his beard grow, he never allowed the hair of his moustache to protrude over his upper lip. His skin was white but tanned by the sun.

He very much loved to meditate, though his meditation deepened his grief at seeing his society sunk so low in immorality, lawlessness and the absence of any sort of protection for those who were weak and oppressed.

His compassion was overwhelming, and people broke into sobs upon hearing the Prophet recite the Qur'an. However, for many years, the Blessed Prophet (Peace be upon him) met with a great deal of resistance. The people of his time believed that money was the only thing that counted, and that caravans to faraway places were worth the profit earned through such hardship. Muhammad's (Peace be upon him) voice rang clearly and true, *"The value of man is not the same which you have assessed and the object of the creation of the nomadic Arabs is not the same which you think it to be."* In addition, at that time, the heinous practice of burying daughters alive was the custom among the Arab tribes of Banu Asad and Banu Tamim. Then they heard a voice, which was expressive of deep love and sympathy for the people saying, *"Don't bury your daughters alive. Daughters are as good a creation of God as the sons are. No human being has a right to deprive others of life. It is only God who creates the people and makes them die."*

The Arabs were also always fighting at that time. They fought and shed blood for years because of trifling and insignificant things. They killed their own brothers and then rejoiced and glorified themselves about doing this. The children screamed, cried and grew up in conditions that were not conducive to the creation of love or sympathy for anyone in their minds. In these circumstances, Muhammad (Peace be upon him) spoke out, *"What are you doing? You kill one another although you are all brothers because God has created all of you. Strife is something Satanic. Peace and friendship are more beneficial for you. The blessing for which you fight can't be achieved except through peace."* However, they stoned and ridiculed him for his teachings. Yet, he said, *"I am given as the cause of mercy."*

One day, Muhammad (Peace be upon him) had an assembly at his house where he had especially gathered the heads of his family and his near kindred. He had Ali ('Alaihi Assalam) prepare a special meal: a measure of wheat, a leg of lamb and a large bowl of milk. The Prophet called them there to invite them to embrace Islam.

Imam Ali ('Alaihi Assalam) tells us what then happened: *"At that time they numbered forty men more or less, including his uncles Abu Talib, Hamzah, al-Abbas, and Abu Lahab. When they had gathered, he called me to bring the food that I had prepared. I brought it, and when I put it down, prophet took a piece of meat, broke it with his teeth, put it in the dish. Then he said, 'Take in the name of God.' They ate until they could eat no more, and yet the food was as it had been. I swear by God, in whose hand Ali's soul rests, that a single man could have eaten the amount of food that I prepared for them. Then he said,*

'Give them something to drink.' So I brought them the bowl and they drank from it until they became full, and I swear by God that one man could have drunk that amount. When the Prophet wanted to speak to them, Abu Lahab interrupted him and said, 'Your host has long since bewitched you.' Then they dispersed without the Prophet speaking to them.

On the following day he said to me 'Ali, this man interrupted what I wanted to say so that people dispersed before I could speak to them. Prepare the same food for us as you did yesterday, and invite them here.' I did this, and brought them food when he called me. He did as he had done the other day, and they ate until they could eat no more. Then he said, 'Bring the bowl,' and they drank until they could drink no more. Then he spoke to them, saying, 'Banu Abd al-Muttalib, I don't know of any young man among Arabs who has brought for his people something better than what I have brought to you. I bring the best of this world and the world after, since God has commanded me to summon you to him. Which of you will aid me in this matter, so that he will be my brother, my executor (Wasi), my successor (Khalif) among you?' They all held back, and although I was the youngest, I said, 'I will be your helper, O' prophet of God.' He put his hand on the back of my neck and said 'This is my brother, my trustee (Wasi), my successor (Khalif) among you, so listen to him and obey him.' They rose laughing and saying to Abu Talib, 'He has commanded you to obey your son and to obey him!'* "* The solemn pledge that Muhammad (Peace be upon him) made on that occasion (also narrated as follows): *"Whosoever helps me in this matter will be my brother, my testamentary trustee (Wasi), my helper, my heir, and my successor (Khalifa) after me,"* is known as the "Tradition of the House" and the "Tradition of Warning." After Muhammad (Peace be upon him) made this statement, only Ali ('Alaihi Assalam) responded and received that honor.[116]

It was only after many years that the public began to listen and adhere to Muhammad (Peace be upon him) and the Qur'an Allah revealed through him.

One day Rasulallah (Peace be upon him) awoke from sleep and informed his companions that he had a dream. He told them that he had dreamed that milk was streaming forth from his fingernails. Several times his companions had to ask him *"What is the meaning of the milk streaming from your fingernails?"* The Mercy to Humanity never lectured people, forced people or imposed his knowledge upon them. *"He was a person of great reticence and of very few words. He had to be asked a question several times for the knowledge to flow from him."*[117] He finally answered, *"It is knowledge."*[118] His character was impeccable. It was said of Muhammad (Peace be upon him) that his character was the Qur'an.

The Prophet is the most perfect of the perfect human beings, the locus of manifestation par excellence for the divine name Allah.[119] *"His is the wis-*

dom of singularity because he is the most perfect creation of this humankind, for which reason the whole affair of creation begins and ends with him." [120]

He said *"I will be the master of humankind on the Day of Resurrection."*[121] The Beloved Mercy to Humanity *"was given the all-comprehensive words (jawami' al-kalim)."*[122]

He was the Complete Human Being of preeminence, the design of all humanity. For he brought together all the Divine Names in his being. R. W. J. Austin in his introduction to Ibn al-'Arabi's "The Bezels of Wisdom" writes, *"The Perfect Man is that human individual who has perfectly realized the full spiritual potential of the human state."*[123]

They deprived the Holy Prophet of writing his will when sometime before his death he asked for writing materials to write down something whereby the Umma (the Muslim community) would be saved from going astray after him and they did not provide him with paper and pen on the excuse that he was talking nonsense. One may rightfully ask, who was the person who prevented the Prophet of Allah from making his Will? It was the Second Khalif, Umar bin al-Khattab who prevented the Holy Prophet from making his Will. This is not a matter of grief for the followers of the Ahlul Bayt alone, but the companions of the Holy Prophet also lamented over this tragic event. Bukhari, Muslim and other prominent Ulema have reported that Abdullah Bin Abbas often shed tears and said, *"Alas! That Thursday! Alas! How it was on that day of Thursday!"* Then he wept himself out, so much that the ground became wet with his tears. When the people asked him what had happened on Thursday that he wept so much, he replied that, when the Holy Prophet was lying in his death bed he asked for paper and ink, so that he might write for them a Will, which would save them from going astray after him, some of those present around him prevented him from doing so and went as far as to say that the Holy Prophet was talking nonsense. That day, Thursday, cannot be forgotten, because, besides the fact that they did not allow the Holy Prophet to write his Will, they also injured him with their words.

Imam 'Abu Hamid Muhammad Bin Muhammad Ghazali has written in his "Sirru'l Aalamin," Maqala IV, from which Yusuf Sibt Ibn Jauzi also quotes in his "Tadhkiratu'l-Khasa'isu'l-Umma," that the Holy Prophet said, *"Bring me ink and paper so that I may remove from your minds all doubts about the Khalifate and that I may repeat to you who deserves that rank (or that I may give you a writing that you may not create dissension among you in the matter)." Upon this, Umar bin al-Khattab said, "Leave this man (i.e.) the Holy Prophet, for he is really talking nonsense; the Book of Allah (Qur'an) is sufficient for us."*[124]

The companions were divided in two groups. Some of them were on Umar bin al-Khattab's side, they began to agree with him, and some agreed with the Holy Prophet. Then there was so much chaos and confusion that

Muhammad (Peace be upon him), who was an embodiment of excellent manners, felt highly indignant and said, *"Get away from me, it is not proper to get angry near me."* He then fell into a swoon because of the fatigue that he suffered. This was the first disturbance, which took place among the Muslims in the presence of the Holy Prophet in all of his twenty-three years of hard and strenuous services. The cause of all this trouble and schism was Umar bin al-Khattab, who sowed the seeds of discord among the Muslims and created two groups among them. Qutbu'd-Din Shirazi, who is one of the eminent Sunni scholars, says in this book "Kashfu'l-Ghuyub," *"It is an admitted fact that we cannot make progress on the way without a guide. We wonder at Khalif Umar Bin al-Khattab's claim that, since we have Qur'an in our midst, we do not stand in need of any guide. It is just like a man saying that, since we have got books of medicine, we do not require a physician. Obviously, it is a false assertion, because a man who cannot solve his problems by reading the books of medicine, must consult a physician. The same thing holds true in the case of the Holy Qur'an."* If the Book of Allah was sufficient why were we ordered to ask the people of "Zikr" as the Holy Qur'an says: *" Ask the followers of the Remembrance (Zikr) if ye know not!"* [125]

"When the Prophet again regained consciousness, some of his Companions said: 'O Apostle of Allah, should we not bring you a pen and shoulder blade?' 'No,' he said, 'not after what you have said! Rather, keep well my memory through kindness to the people of my Household. Treat with kindness the people of dhimmah (that is, the Jewish people and Christians), and feed the poor . . . He continued these injunctions until he could endure no longer, and turned his face away from the people." [126]

On his deathbed he called for Ali ('Alaihi Assalam). The Prophet asked Ali ('Alaihi Assalam) to come close to him, and when he did so, the Prophet embraced him. Muhammad (Peace be upon him) took off his own ring from his finger and said: *"Take it and put it on your finger!"* The Prophet then called for his sword and suit of armor and gave these to Ali ('Alaihi Assalam), along with his mule and saddle saying, *"Receive these during my life! Go to your home with Allah's blessings."*

The next day the Prophet allowed no one to come see him, Ali ('Alaihi Assalam), however, stayed beside him, not leaving except for necessary errands. On one of these errands the Prophet awoke and said: *"Call my friend back to me."* 'Aesha said: *"Call Abu Bakr."* When he came, the Prophet looked at him and turned away his face. He insisted: *"Call back for me my brother and friend!"* Hafsah said: *"Call Umar for him!"* When he came, the Prophet likewise turned his face away. Again, the Prophet demanded: *"Call back for me my brother and friend!"* Umm Salamah then said: *"Call Ali for him, for he wants no one else."* When Ali ('Alaihi Assalam) arrived, then he and the Prophet spoke for a long time.

Ali ('Alaihi Assalam) recounts that the Prophet's condition then became grave and he was near death. As his soul was about to depart, he said: *"O Ali, place my head in your lap, for Allah's command is about to be fulfilled. When my soul is released, take it in your hand and rub it on your face. Turn then my face towards the qiblah, prepare me and be the first to offer the funeral prayer over me. Do not leave me until you have put me in my tomb. Seek Allah's help."*[127] Behold Imam Ali's ('Alaihi Assalam) own words as he described that momentous event: *"Verily the soul of the Holy Prophet (S.A.) departed from this world while his head rested on my chest; he breathed his last while he was in my hands; some drops of his blood flowed down, and I then rubbed my hands on my face."*[128] Muhammad (Peace be upon him) was buried in his house adjoining the mosque at Macca (al-Mukarramah). *"He was the clearest of evidence for his Lord, having been given the totality of the divine words, which are those things named by Adam."*[129] The "Mercy for All the Nations" died at the age of sixty-three years. It was Monday, the 28th Safar 11 A.H.

To the Sufi, Muhammad (Peace be upon him) is the Sheikh. For the Sufi understands that the concept of the Complete Human is a spiritual archetype. In other words, the Sufi seeks to model him or herself on the spiritual Muhammad (Peace be upon him). *"This resplendence exists within every man and can be seen as that beauty, if one looks within."*[130] He was a clue to himself. Muhammad (Peace be upon him) is the secret of the potential of the human being.

"You are creation's gardener, flowers live only in your seeing,
By your light hangs my being or not-being;
All beauty is in you: I am the tapestry of your soul;
I am its key, but you are Love's own scroll."

- Iqbal

"The function of music is to release us from the tyranny of conscious thought."

- Thomas Beecham

"That music explores itself, examines themes, is amenable to searching the intellectual inquiry, and yet, despite its profound cerebral content, speaks to the heart, music is the true universal art form, able to find fresh expressions and interpretations of beauty whenever it is performed. Caravaggio speaks only to those before his canvas. Mozart speaks whenever and wherever people gather in his name."

- Kevin Myers, The Irish Times,
Dublin, Friday, May 23, 1997

THAT WHICH ENDURES

It is said that emotions are the thoughts of God. The spiritual aspect of the human being needs emotion as the body needs food. Unfortunately in Western Society, most people do not feed their spirits the right kind of food. Most of Western Society has a rather limited emotional repertoire. In our culture, great art, great music, and literature are not properly honored. Art answers the question, "What are we doing here?" Society at large prefers pop songs that wear out their welcome in a few weeks. Popular culture prefers "ear candy" to music of great meaning and complexity. Art speaks to the wordless part of our souls.

Our modern society is geared more toward the momentary glimpse of pleasure. A five-minute pop song cannot approach the sophistication, the subtlety and the depth of emotion that is generated by a forty-five minute symphony.

Why limit the colors on your painting palette? Why limit yourselves to experiencing only certain emotions? If you do not already do so, please go to live plays with live actors. Experience these human beings directly, and not as figures on a television screen. Television slowly corrupts people's spirits by reducing their emotions to a steady drone of mild interest. Another problem with today's society is the rapidity of images flashed before you constantly. Channel surfing with your "remotes" reduces everything to a blur of images, none of which retains any significance. Distractions take you away from the inner life of the spirit. Inner soul qualities need time to grow. Psychic qualities are like seeds that must remain undisturbed in the quiet and dark earth.

The illusion generated by the plethora of images on television is a way to distance yourselves from your feelings. Many people do not want to face their feelings. They would rather medicate their feelings through a steady stream of media noise. The Way of the Sufi is a difficult Way, difficult in that it forces you to "Know Thyself." If you are afraid to meet your self, then you might as well give up all hopes of becoming an effective Sufi.

Many people in our culture do not know what they are missing. People look for a quick rush of emotion. Sex, excitement and food form the center of people's limited palette of feeling.

We suggest that Murids seek out circumstances that move their souls to their depths. For example, a great book can transform a person's life. In a novel, the author has the time to develop in a gradual manner, emotional, psychological, social, and spiritual themes throughout many chapters. As the person reads the book, he or she becomes inspired. This inhalation of spiritual energy builds up an enormous amount of pressure inside the Murid's being. The pressure seeks an outlet, a catharsis, a gestalt. At precise moments in the novel, a given passage triggers a tremendous integration of meanings, giving the reader a new vision of humanity.

For these reasons, seek out great art, music and literature.

"The beauty and charm
Inherent in the blooms
Itself is enough to fire
The heart with Desire –
To stir it to the depths
With that exquisite thrill of life
Which springs from a due
Enjoyment of the view.
Whatever, then, the climate,
All that the eye need do
Is only to open itself!"

- Ghalib

"It is He who is revealed in every face, sought in every sign, gazed upon by
every eye, worshiped in every object of worship, and pursued in the unseen
and the visible. Not a single one of His creatures can fail to find Him
in its primordial and original nature."

- Muhyiddin Ibn 'Arabi[131]

"Only a few of the Prophet's intimates really saw him as he was, citing the
Qur'anic verse: 'And you Muhammad see them looking at you, but they do
not see.' "

- Terry Graham

"All our justice is stained in Your eyes."

- Thérése of the child of Jesus and
the Holy Face

"Knowing happens directly; where not even a thought stands between you
and the thing you know."

- Gurdjieff

SEE

See. See. See. See. See. See. See. See. See. See. See. See. See. See. See. See.
See. See. See. See. See. See. See. See. See. See. See. See. See. See. See.
See. See. See. See. See. See. See. See. See. See. See. See. See. See. See.
See. See. See. See. See. See. See. See. See. See. See. See. See. See. See.
See. See. See. See. See. See. See. See. See. See. See. See. See. See. See.
See. See. See. See. See. See. See. See. See. See. See. See. See. See. See.
See. See. See. See. See. See. See. See. See. See. See. See. See. See. See.
See. See. See. See. See. See. See. See. See. See. See. See. See. See. See.

See. See. See. See. See. See. See. See. See. See. See. See. See. See. See. See.
See. See. See. See. See. See. See. See. See. See. See. See. See. See. See. See.
See. See. See. See. See. See. See. See. See.

"Life's under no obligation to give us what we expect."
                                                    - Margaret Mitchell

"Flee from me, away from trouble;
take the path of safety, far from this danger."
                                                    -Jelaluddin Rumi

TALES FROM UNDER THE OVERPASS

*B*efore leaving Manhattan, Sam and Mr. Khadir stopped into a large mosque uptown. Inside they came upon a Pakistani man who was standing besides two pillars. They watched him post himself there for some time, as if he were waiting for someone.

"As salaam alaykum. May I ask you who you are and what you are doing here?" Mr. Khadir asked, politely.

"Alaykum as salaam. My name is Naseer," the man began, "I've heard that upon rare occasions a holy man appears here in this exact spot."

"Don't you have anything to do?" Mr. Khadir questioned him.

"No," Naseer said, annoyed.

"You should be at work," Mr. Khadir reproved. "But go to your store and I promise you that this holy man will come to your store tomorrow."

"Do you know what he looks like?" inquired Naseer.

"He looks just like me," Mr. Khadir replied.

"Oh, thank you sir," Naseer gushed, "thank you for telling me. Now I'm sure I'll recognize him when he arrives!"

The fellow left the mosque immediately. Sam had been listening intently. "What was that all about?" he said with curiosity.

"You'll see tomorrow," Mr. Khadir answered briefly.

That night, and all the next morning, Naseer was busy cleaning his shop. From top to bottom, he tidied everything, making especially sure that the floor was immaculately clean.

In the morning, Mr. Khadir took Sam a block away from the man's shop.

"Let's switch clothes," Mr. Khadir said unequivocally.

"All right. I don't know what you're up to. But you've got my curiosity up."

After they had finished switching clothes, Mr. Khadir made sure that he was as disheveled as possible and his long hair messed up. Mr. Khadir said to Sam, "Now, follow me, but at a close distance. We're going to Naseer's shop. I want you to see and hear what happens."

Mr. Khadir bought a sack of basmati rice from a merchant next door, and proceeded to walk into Naseer's shop.

"Oh, I'm so sorry, forgive me," Mr. Khadir said with feigned embarrassment as he dumped the contents of the sack on the floor. "There must have been a tear in the burlap sack."

"You fool!" Naseer said harshly, "Why did you ruin my clean store!!!" He shouted, "Get out. Get out. And take your damn sack with you!"

The next day Sam and Mr. Khadir went back to the mosque. They had switched back into their respective clothes, and Mr. Khadir had cleaned and groomed himself. Sure enough, there was Naseer, standing in wait for the holy man between the two pillars.

"Stay here and watch and listen," Mr. Khadir instructed Sam. Mr. Khadir then walked over to Naseer.

"As salaam alaykum!" Mr. Khadir greeted Naseer, "Why are you waiting here again?"

"Alaykum as salaam," Naseer said in a gruff voice. "You promised me that the holy man would show up at my shop yesterday. After you told me that, I went back to my shop and cleaned and cleaned the rest of the day and all next morning. I waited the entire day, but the holy man never came to my shop. Just some fool who spilled rice all over my floor."

Somberly, Mr. Khadir spoke, "If one does not know what one is searching for, one will not know when one finds it."

"And just what is that supposed to mean?" Naseer told Mr. Khadir, testily.

"The being that you were waiting for came to your store yesterday. The Supreme Reality is not to be searched for. The Supreme Reality was never lost!" Mr. Khadir's deep, authoritative voice observed.

Naseer just stood there, dumbfounded, frozen in astonishment and shame.

"Don't worry, my friend," Mr. Khadir began, "You may not have found the kind of holy man you were expecting, but you found me. Be more careful in the future, holy men and women don't always appear as you would expect them to appear. They have as many countenances as there are people on earth."

Mr. Khadir rejoined Sam.

"Wow!" Sam said aloud. "I can't believe he didn't recognize you in his shop!"

"Not to be as one seems, not to seem as one is. The shape of the True Guide always changes. Because of this, you need to see the inside. Even if the Greatest Guide on Earth came to a spiritual gathering, many people would not recognize him, or her. If people are not working toward beauty, they will not recognize the True Guide. The Beautiful Divine Effulgence is offering Itself each moment, but few recognize what is supremely obvious."

"Leave your caterpillar self behind O Butterfly,
For you are more grand than you can imagine."
- Anonymous

"The heart is an organ of fire."
-The English Patient

"Your secret runs in your blood, so do not let it flow anywhere other than
in your veins."
-Imam Ali ('Alaihi Assalam)[132]

"For it was He who gave me unerring knowledge of all existent being, to
know the structure of the universe and the operation of the elements."
- Prophet Solomon,
Wisdom of Solomon 7:17

"Flowing through the world,
Are four streams,They are alive; Evolving spirits all:
Minerals, plants, animals, and humans;
Each realm incorporating the preceding realm."
-Anonymous

EARTH, AIR, FIRE, AND WATER

Human Beings have fire in their blood. This is how the Absolute Existence made us. *"He has explained that He breathed into man of His spirit . . . His breathing produces a burning, because of the moisture in the body. Thus, by his makeup man's spirit is a fire."*[133] Our bodies consist of the four elements: earth, air, fire, and water. The Murid must balance these four elements.

EARTH represents: concrete manifestation; the physical body; stability; wealth; hard physical work; building; strength; establishment. Allah compared the Phrase of Declaring Oneness *(kalimat al-tawhid)* to soil because the soil gives forth much in exchange for a single seed: similarly, this phrase multiplies its return. *"Beneath the veil of each atom is hidden the soul-ravishing beauty of the face of the Beloved."*[134]

AIR represents: thought; mind; communication; speech; interpretation; wisdom; awareness; imagination; coordination of bodily motions (communication of muscles). Air is an explicit comparison for Oneness in that it is everywhere at once, available to everyone, yet one in its essential quality.

FIRE represents: energy; sex; enthusiasm; ambition; drive; assertiveness; action; idealism; change; power; life; desire; motivation. Allah compared the Phrase of Declaring Oneness *(kalimat al-tawhid)* to fire because fire burns and this phrase burns sins.

WATER represents: emotions; subconscious; feelings; love; (ki, orgone, prana, ether, cosmic mind stuff); intuition; fullness; ripening; warmth; comfort; adaptation. Allah compared the Phrase of Declaring Oneness *(kalimat al-tawhid)* to water because water cleanses: similarly, this phrase cleanses from sins.

The Murid must choose what to do with his or her miniature bodily universe. If you refine it through mercy, beautiful behavior and contemplation, then Allah will revitalize and rouse your microcosmic reality into the Reality of Light. Hadrat Shaikh Asif Hussain Farooqui writes: *"Abdullah Bin Salaam (may Allah be pleased with him) said: When the Prophet Muhammad came to Madinah and I went and examined his face, I recognized that it was not a face of a liar. The first thing he said was, 'If you people greet all whom you meet, provide food, care for the well being of your kindred, and pray at night when people are asleep, you will enter Paradise in peace' "* (Tirmidhi, Ibn Majah and Daarimi) The importance of this Hadith is the fact that when the Prophet migrated to Madina (al-Murawwarah), this was his first sermon inside the city in which resided a variety of different people. The first *Dars* (lesson) the Messenger gave them was that pertaining to *Akhlaqiaat* (manners). It was a lesson on love. It is evident that a great form of worship for a person is his or her general good conduct. Prayer and other forms of worship all have their own status and importance but the true sense of worship is that a person can become a 'proper human being' and that he or she adopts *Akhlaaq-e-Hameeda* (laudable manners). The reason for doing Dhikr and sitting in the company of the *Awliyaa* (friends of Allah) is solely to become better human beings, to diminish our bad habits and to learn from their excellent conduct. One of the biggest problems which we are facing is that we have forgotten those manners that should have been befitting of the Umma (followers of Muhammad). [135]

Considering the element of Earth, we turn to a poem by Bulleh Shah which considers the underlying reality of Earth that lies beneath the mundane, and rejoices in its all pervasiveness.

> *"The soil is in ferment, O friend,*
> *Behold the diversity.*
> *The soil is the horse, so is the rider*
> *The soil chases the soil, and we hear the clanging of soil*
> *The soil kills the soil, with weapons of the soil*
> *That soil with more on it, is arrogance*
> *The soil is the garden so is its beauty*
> *The soil admires the soil in all its wondrous forms*

After the circle of life is done it returns to the soil
Answer the riddle O Bulleh, and take this burden off my head."

The fire can be turned toward ill by acting in non-propitious ways. Then the Murid will begin to manifest all sorts of unappealing, strange and sometimes dangerous astral beings. Temper your fire of pride with the tears of humility. Balance over-emotionalism with the fire of determination. Shakespeare majestically stated the outcome of this balance in his work "Julius Caesar": *"The elements were so mixed in him that all the world said 'This is a man.'"* There is a saying of a great Sage of Persia who lived 500 years before Darwin and who gave his ideas on biology: he said that God slept in the rocks, God dreamed in the plant, God awoke in the animal, and God realized Himself in the Human Being.

PRACTICE

When two objects meet, they produce a sound. Music arises from the textures of two substances encountering each other. If there were no texture, there would not be any music. Texture is the personality of the Divine.

To achieve Realization, focus on sound. Focus on the Interplay of Sounds around you, your footsteps, the car door closing. These are the Spontaneous Arisings of Reality. Listen to your voice as you speak. Calmly listen to the panorama of Existence.

Ibrahim al-Nakha`i said concerning Allah's saying, *"There is not a thing but hymneth his praise."* (17:44): *"Everything praises Him, including the door when it squeaks."*[136] To awaken your Spirit, go out into nature and develop a real sense of awe and veneration for the natural Earth. Allah the Exalted said, *"We have placed the mountains under his dominion, they praise Allah at nightfall and at sunrise."* All creation praises the Indivisible Reality constantly. Hear the bird songs, the wind in the trees and the babbling brook. Entering into a sacred relationship with the Earth is the first step for the Aspiring Sufi - for he or she who has not realized the sacredness of the Earth will never be able to completely understand the sacredness of the Celestial!

There is a story that elaborates on this. The author of "al-Wujuh al-musfira" cited the following story, *"One of Allah's slaves sought to perform the purification from going to stool with stones. He took one stone, and Allah removed the veil from his hearing so that he was now able to hear the stone's praise. Out of shame he left it and took another one, but he heard that one praising Allah also. Moreover, every time he took another stone he heard it glorifying Allah. Seeing this, at last he turned to Allah so that He would veil from him their praise to enable him to purify himself. Allah then veiled him from hearing them. He proceeded to purify himself despite his knowledge that the stones were making tasbih, because the one who reported about their tasbih is the same Lawgiver who ordered to use them for purification. Therefore in the concealment of tasbih there is a far-reaching wisdom."*

If the Murid listens carefully, he or she can hear the resonance of The Secret One in all of everything.

"You ought to know yourself as you really are, so that you may understand of what nature you are and whence you have come to this world and for what purpose you were created and in what your happiness and misery consist. For within you are combined the qualities of the animals and the wild beasts and also the qualities of the angels, but the spirit is your real essence, and all beside it is, in fact, foreign to you. So strive for knowledge of your origin so that you may know how to attain to the Divine Presence and the contemplation of the Divine Majesty and Beauty."

- Abu Hamid Muhammad Bin
Muhammad al-Ghazali

"If you look at the beautiful one with a beautiful eye, you will look at Hak's being."

- el-Hajj el-Fakir Şerif Çatalkaya
er-Rıfa'i er-Marufi

"The dervish is a fertile field
cultivated by Divine Power.
Advancing step by step
Through seven stations of wisdom
Along the way both arduous and joyful,
Making every sacrifice,
The dervish completes this steep path,
this royal road."

- Shaykh Nur al-Anwar
al-Jerrahi

"We have indeed created man in the best of forms."

- Qur'an 95:4

"The universes in which earth appears are a psycho-physical system, (psycho-spatial and psycho-temporal), not a mere physical or material one. The same world or realm, in other of its aspects, is seen in dreams and sleeping too."

- Bubba Free John

THE SUPERSENSIBLE SEVEN BODIES

The Physical/Chemical Body

This body is made up of the physical components of our being, that is, the natural elements. It makes up the physical substance of our body. {It is most clearly seen in the rocks, sand, and minerals of the Earth}.

There exists a marvelous parallel between the highest and lowest bodies. The PHYSICAL/CHEMICAL BODY is the ultimate medium of all the other planes, in other words, the result of all these higher planes. The *"best of forms"* mentioned above can only refer to Allah's own form and nature.[137] The Earth is the apotheosis of Spirit. Unluckily, a person cannot take full advantage of one plane, until he or she has gained some wisdom and authority over the plane above that one. The PHYSICAL/CHEMICAL BODY is the finest instrument on the planet Earth. It is capable of receiving and transmitting the subtlest of messages; however to be of real use, the Murid must master the following body, the ETHERIC/LIFE/VITAL BODY. Remember: the higher levels control the lower levels. [These terms "higher" and "lower" are merely conveniences to envision all these processes, in fact, all these bodies intertwine and exist together.]

Be aware of your Physical/Chemical Body moment to moment, not only outwardly aware, but also aware of your body from the inside. Lydia Eccles writes in "The Politics of Daily Life": *"Think of your direct body experience of life. No one can lie to you about that."* Become sensitive to the way your body feels on the inside. From time to time, pause and feel what is going on in your chest, in your stomach and your legs. How does your head feel? Your shoulders? Your arms and hands? Sense your face and inside your neck. Most of all be sensitive to your chest and especially your heart.

Awareness of the body teaches you to be Consciously Present in the now. Be aware of Reality as it Arises. It is the Presence! *"Conventional meditation is inwardness, or remedy by subjectivity. Real meditation is a process of awakening from subjectivity."*[138] The sacred remembrance of the body is the highest state of spirituality. You think you know what everything is, but you do not know what anything is. *"Rest-abide in that , . . . not within what arises, but as what arises, as the body itself. . ."*[139] Leave aside all your reasoning, explanations, dogma, and opinions. Let go of definitions. *"One can only abide as the very Condition in which all conditions rise and fall."*[140]

The Etheric/Life/Vital Body

"Now the measure of life that pervades a creature is called divine, humanity being [preeminently] the locus in which the Spirit inheres."
- Ibn al-'Arabi

This body gives form to our PHYSICAL/CHEMICAL BODY, as a blueprint does to a building. Some Adepts use the metaphor of a "template." It preserves and shapes all our organs, and regulates assimilation, growth, propagation, glands, and the aging process. {It is most clearly seen in all vegetation: plants, trees, bushes, etc.}.

The ETHERIC/LIFE/VITAL BODY energizes the physical tissues and therefore cannot be separated from the physical body for long. Dislodgment of the Etheric matrix soon brings death to the overlying PHYSICAL/CHEMICAL BODY.

The moment one becomes aware of his PHYSICAL/CHEMICAL BODY from within, the second body – the ETHERIC/LIFE BODY will automatically come into view.

This second body will be known from the outside now. If you know the first body from the inside, then you will become aware of the second body from the outside. The second body is just like the first regarding shape, but it is not solid. When the first body dies, the second remains alive for about two weeks. It travels with you. Then, after about two weeks, it too is dead. It disperses, evaporates. If you come to know the second body while the first is still alive, you can be aware of this happening.

The ETHERIC/LIFE BODY is constantly transmitting life force energy into our physical organism. However, at about age thirty-five, the ETHERIC/LIFE BODY begins to lose form and congruency. This loss of congruency signals the beginning of the slow deterioration of the PHYSICAL/CHEMICAL BODY. However, there are practices, given in this book, which can help strengthen the ETHERIC/LIFE BODY and delay the onset of aging.

Compare the size of the human body with the size of trees. In the Plant World, the Etheric Force is predominant. Therefore, growth is abundant and almost unchecked. While the checking force may be invisible, it is always present. Humans do not grow to seventy meters in height. If there were no breaking force in the universe, we would grow unchecked. Our bodies would be enormous, subject to the runaway growth of our cells.

In our universe, there is Negative Space and Positive Space. When you look at a naked human body, you see a certain form, but what most people do not see is what invisibly surrounds the body; they call this the negative body. That sounds confusing, so please let us explain: there are "invisible" hands that give the body its shape. These hands are only visible through supersensible sight. These invisible hands give each part of the body its shape. The head, arms, torso, sex organs, feet, and so on, are shaped by these invisible hands. When you see a healthy naked body in front of you, you first become aware of the abundant life that is flowing forth from the body, the positive body; however, we suggest you pause and consider the deathlike, checking, breaking force that surrounds the beautiful body, giving the body shape and form.The Egyptians developed the powers of the ETHERIC/LIFE BODY to an astonishing degree.

The Astral/Desire/Astrosome Body

"The heart has no more than one aspect at a time, such that when it is occupied with a particular aspect, it is veiled from another. So take care that you are not drawn toward anything but God, lest He deprive you of the delights of intimate converse with Him."

- A. Madyan

This body is the emotional aspect of our being (divided into a darker and lighter half). This body awakens life out of unconsciousness, out of sleep. This body is most clearly seen in the animal world. The Sheikhs say that the human being possesses four trillion, ten thousand spiritual qualities of animals. The human body is the apotheosis of all the animals that have ever existed. Some Sheikhs say that we should not act like animals. Yet, animals do not commit genocide. Consider the world's greatest explorers like Cortez, who decimated native populations, raped the women, stole their gold and artifacts, and destroyed their culture. Cortez and his men murdered six thousand men, women, and children in one day in their holy temple at Cholula. Humans kill other humans by the millions out of ideology, religious fanaticism and socio-political ideas. Humans casually kill animals for sport and pleasure. Sheikh Muazaffer Ozak wrote: *"Sometimes such people look like human beings, but they are animals. They act worse than animals. Consider the most violent, carnivorous, harmful animals - the cobra, tiger, lion - after all, how much destruction can they cause? They can kill a few men and women. But a human being who becomes an animal can kill millions."*[141] We humans (if we dare call ourselves by that name) might learn more valuable lessons by clearly observing the animal world, than by studying the tawdry history of human behavior. The Prophet said, *"Revile not the world, for God – He is the world."* This is pointing to the fact that the existence of the world is God's existence without partner or like or equal. [142]

The ASTRAL BODY is concerned with emotions. It is a living polychromatic ocean of feeling, with ASTRAL "fish," in other words, emotional images, swimming through it. These are the "fish" of sentiment, nostalgia, longing, romance, regret, anger, and infatuation. The ASTRAL is an orgy of emotionally charged pictures.

Remember we mentioned a darker and a lighter half? If fear is one side of the coin, fearlessness is the other. If you hide the coin and live in denial, pretending that you have no fear, you will never be able to know fearlessness. The Murid who accepts the presence of fear within him or her and who has investigated it fully will soon reach a place where he or she will want to find out what is behind fear. The moment the Murid turns the rock of fear over he or she becomes fearless. Similarly, violence will turn into compassion.

The moment you are inside the second body you will be outside the third, the astral. There is no need even of any will power to gain entry, just the wish to be inside is enough. If you want to go in, you can go in.

THE ASTRAL/DESIRE/ASTROSOME BODY is a vapor like the second body, but it is transparent. So the moment you are outside you will be inside. You will not even know whether you are inside or outside because the boundary is transparent.

Up to the fifth body, the size of these bodies remains the same. The content will change, but the size will be the same up to the fifth. With the sixth body, the size will be cosmic. Then with the seventh, there will be no size at all, not even the cosmic.

The ASTRAL/DESIRE/ASTROSOME body is also concerned with issues of doubt and trust. If these are transformed, doubt becomes trust, and thinking becomes awareness. If doubts are repressed, you never attain trust. That is why you should leave any Murshid or Guru that does not allow you to express your doubts fully. The Murid who represses his or her doubts never attains to trust. It will creep within as a cancer and eat up your vitality.

The goal is to reach a point where you will begin to have doubt about doubt itself. The moment you begin to doubt doubt, trust begins. Awareness and clarity can be achieved through the transformation of this subtle body. Decision comes from a state of clarity that is beyond thoughts. Thoughts have no connection with decision. He or she who is always engrossed in thoughts never reaches a decision. That is why it invariably happens that those people whose lives are less dominated by thoughts are resolute, whereas those who think a great deal lack determination. These thinkers can never come to a decision, and are always finding some fault with what they are considering. No one and nothing measures up to their impossible standards. What is needed by these thinkers to allow themselves to make decisions, is: clear awareness.

Spirit/Noemasome body

"And the stupor of death will bring Truth (before His eyes)."
- Qur'an 50:19

The fourth body is wall-less. It is just a boundary, so there is no difficulty in entering and no need of any method. One who has achieved the third can achieve the fourth easily. This body is the spark of divine consciousness. Humankind has desires that transcend their everyday needs. Animals hunger and thirst and sexually desire, but only live in the moment. Humans can plan for, and sacrifice for, anticipated pleasure in the future. They recognize the permanence behind the transitory experience. Thus, the SPIRIT/NOEMASOME BODY is the "I Am" consciousness of self-awareness. A good way of understanding this principle is to realize that you can only say "I" when speaking about yourself, never for any other person, only the being uttering the word can apply it to him or her self. I am an "I" to myself only. This ability to say "I" is an important step in the evolution of the human wave. One day, animals, plants and then even minerals will be able to utter this word. Perhaps addressing this necessary, evolutionary stage of the SPIRIT/NOEMASOME BODY Shaykh Nur al-Anwar al-Jerrahi asks, *"But who says there is anything wrong with duality? If we think we are committed to non-duality, and we say, 'I hate duality,' what are we doing? We're setting up a new duality."*[143] As will be seen, the Murid must eventually transcend the SPIRIT/NOEMASOME BODY. Plutarch wrote, *"The mind is not a vessel to be filled, but a fire to be lighted."* Apart from this physical form, human beings have the power of articulation, and it is that faculty that confers distinction upon humanity. Imam Ali ('Alaihi Assalam) says, *"Man has been created with the power of speech (which is the essence of humanity). If it is adorned with knowledge and action, it will resemble the existence of the ethereal realm, which is the real origin of his recitation, and when it reaches the place of temperance and is cleared of all physical matter, it becomes one with the creation of the ethereal realm and then it leaves the animal world and reaches the highest stage of humanity."*

The Murid's job is to purify the intellect, weakening the ego's hold on it, thereby permitting the intellect to be a pure vehicle for the Lord of One's Being. To recognize clearly a true Murshid or Sheikh from the charlatan or egomaniac, *"the potential disciple must already have purified his intellect to some extent. If the disciple's ego still dominates his intellect, he will tend to be drawn to these charlatans, and their influence will help his ego to become even stronger. In contrast an individual who has already acquired some humility and made progress in virtue will be able to recognize the genuine saint."*[144]

To go beyond the fourth, the SPIRIT/NOEMASOME BODY, there is as much difficulty as there was in going beyond the first, the PHYSICAL/CHEMICAL BODY, because now the egoic self ceases. The great Yasavi Sheik Isma'il Ata gave us this instruction, *"Accept this advice from me: Imagine that the world is a green dome in which there is nothing but God and you, and remember God until the overwhelming theophany overcomes you, and frees you from yourself, and nothing remains but God."* [145]

There is a wall, but not in the same sense as there was a wall between the first body and the second. The difference is between dimensions now. SPIRIT SELF is of a different plane. In Islamic art, we depict the Prophet and Saints with their heads on fire; we never illustrate their faces. When the Murid's third eye begins to open, a great fire is created.

So to cross the fourth body there is only one technique, one method, and that is to drive the burning love that is in the heart directly into the brain. *"Let the ship of thought wander in the ocean of astonishment."*[146] The dualism of feeling and thinking must be resolved to a state of unity in which one thinks with the heart and feels with the brain. In Sufism, the story of *Majnun and*

Layla (a near-Eastern version of Romeo and Juliet or Tristan and Isolde), is often told. Majnun represents the Mind, and Layla, the Heart. The two must come together. When they achieve Unity, they become Allah.

However, initially, the first four bodies must be crossed! In the words of Sufism, the *nafs* must first be encountered. The Murid must first work on his or her PHYSICAL, ETHERIC, EMOTIONAL, and SPIRIT bodies. If the first four bodies are looking downward (in other words, not yet worked on), and the flame of your longing for Union is burning upward, then there is every possibility that physical and psychological problems will result.

The Murid should not experiment with sending the longing for Union into the brain before crossing the first four bodies. This is the case with many false Murshids, Teachers and Gurus. They have developed their spiritual bodies, but have repressed and ignored the anal, sexual, emotional, and intellectually manipulative and egotistic, aspects of themselves. They preach against sexuality, against acknowledging one's anger and against the emotions, without having themselves come to terms with these aspects of themselves. Unbeknownst to themselves, they have thereby spiritual maimed and impaired themselves and are a danger to the unsuspecting Murid. Your entire being, at this point, all four soul bodies, must be clear rivers of flowing love in order to proceed on the Way.

When a seeker sets out on this path his or her search is mainly for bliss and not truth. So one who seeks bliss may stop at the SPIRIT/NOEMASOME plane; therefore, we must tell you to seek not bliss but truth. Then you will not remain long here.

Ask yourself these questions, "I know myself, I am blissful - it is good, but from where do I arise?" "Where are my roots?" "From where have I come?" "Where are the depths of my existence?" "From which ocean has come this wave from which I arise?"

If your quest is for truth, you will go ahead of the SPIRIT/NOEMA-SOME body. Betrand Russell said, *"I am not attracted to salvation, because I hear there is nothing but bliss there. Bliss alone would be very monotonous - bliss and bliss and nothing else. If there is not a single trace of unhappiness - no anxiety, no tension in it - how long can one bear such bliss?"* However, the struggle with bliss has only just begun.

The first four steps are not so hard to cross, but the fifth is exceedingly difficult.

Spirit Self

"Self-love manipulates and dominates,
Propelling the conventional world toward blindness.
But when touched by the Shaykh, lightning of Allah,

This obscuration, this worship of the ego,
Melts into fathomless ecstasy."

- Shaykh Nur al-Anwar al-Jerrahi

This body arises when the Murid begins consciously to work with his or her astral body, in the sense of adopting a code of ethics and a chivalrous perspective.

In addition, when you work through psychotherapy or counseling to understand and embrace all your feelings, do you begin to create the Spirit Self. Psychotherapy is part of the redemption of the nafs. Thus, the SPIRIT/NOEMASOME BODY takes possession of the ASTRAL BODY by uniting itself with the latter's hidden nature. This ASTRAL BODY, overcome and transformed by the SPIRIT/NOEMASOME BODY, may be called the SPIRIT SELF.

From a deeper perspective, after going inside and understanding the SPIRIT/NOEMASOME BODY, you move into still another realm, another dimension. Thinking of moving into this body is almost nonsensical and absurd, for, in actuality, you do not have a Limited Self, so how can you lose it?

The SPIRIT SELF is the richest of the subtle bodies, the culmination of all that is possible for a human being. The fifth is the peak of love, of compassion, of everything that is worthwhile.

Therefore, from the fifth body the question is whether to have a Limited Self or to unfurl your wings and fly. The illusion of the Limited Self is the most difficult thing of all to lose. There is no method to move beyond the SPIRIT SELF because each type of method is bound with the Limited Self. The moment you use a method, the Limited Self is strengthened.

Those who are concerned with going beyond the SPIRIT SELF, talk of no-method! Here is the realm of methodlessness, or no-technique. A method or technique strengthens the Limited Self because if you use anything, the user will become stronger. Your ego will go on crystallizing; it will become a nucleus of crystallization.

To go beyond the Spirit Self, you have to pass through the Gateless Gate. There is no Gate, and yet you have to go beyond it. The question becomes, what is the solution? The answer, do not be identified with the crystallization of the Limited Self. Just be aware of this closed house of "i." Be aware of the Limitedness of the Self, do not do anything, and suddenly BOOM! You will be beyond it. So in the SPIRIT SELF BODY you must cross from the realm of method to no-method.

Do nothing but be aware of the closed house in which you live. The fifth body is non dual. It does not have two possibilities. It has only one. By the time the Murid reaches the SPIRIT/NOEMASOME BODY he or she develops so much capability and strength that it is simple to enter the SPIRIT SELF. The difference will be that he or she who has entered the SPIRIT SELF is completely rid of all unconsciousness. He or she will not actually sleep at night. That is, they sleep, but their body alone sleeps; someone within is forever awake.

Just about 99.9% of the people on Planet Earth are asleep. Sheikh Muzaffer writes, *"Don't think that everything is finished when you die. You are really asleep here. What you see here is a dream. It is at death that you will wake up and see reality."*[147] If a person puts a knife at your chest, you jump into consciousness. The point of the knife, for a moment, takes you right up to the fifth body. Except for these few moments in folk's lives, the public lives like somnambulists. You have never seen, because there must be an awakened person within you to See. The Human Being is a somnambulist before he or she enters the SPIRIT SELF, and there the quality is wakefulness.[148]

A sleeping person does not know who he or she is. This person is always striving to show others that he or she is this or that. This is the sleeping person's lifelong endeavor. This Murid tries in a thousand ways to prove him or herself. In all these efforts, the somnambulist is unknowingly trying to find out who he or she is. The sleeper knows not who he or she is.

We call the fifth body the SPIRIT SELF because there you get the answer to the quest for "Who am I?" The call of the Limited Self stops conclusively on this plane; the claim to be someone special vanishes immediately. The conflicts and problems of the Murid as a limited individual end on the fifth plane.

You have come to know yourself, and this knowing is so blissful and fulfilling that you may want to end your journey here. The hazards were, until now, all of pain and agony; now the hazards that begin are of bliss. Therefore, the Murid who enters this plane has to be alert about clinging to bliss so that it does not hinder him or her from going farther.

It is a fact that distresses and suffering do not obstruct our way as much as joy. This is why many dervishes stop at the Spirit Self, and do not go up to LIFE SPIRIT or the Cosmic Reality.

Warning: Do not become immersed in bliss! Know that this too is an experience. The Murid has not yet achieved Victory.

Words cannot go past the level of the SPIRIT SELF, so all that we can give are hints and metaphors.

Life Spirit

"God thinks through me, because I am God thinking."
- Ibn Arabi

When a person through his or her religious experiences, or through Art, divines something that persists throughout all changes, he or she develops a sense of permanence that has the effect of working upon the Etheric Body. The Dervish experiences this through the years as he or she watches with the eyes of truth the various Sheikhs end their breathing practices, family and spiritual brothers and sisters passing away, and new children being born. The ETHERIC BODY is then transformed into LIFE SPIRIT by the SPIRIT/NOE-MASOME BODY working on it

During everyday life, the SPIRIT is not active in the etheric body. However, when the Murid works consciously with his or her ETHERIC BODY he or she permeates it with the SPIRIT and by that creates the "LIFE SPIRIT." Through this work, the Murid can do such things as slow down the aging process.

At the stage of the LIFE SPIRIT, the Sufi no longer looks at life in terms of desires and attainments. In other words, the individual body-mind is no longer the point of focus. The Sufi identifies with the Omniconscious Unicity, instead of his or her limited self. The self has a cosmological context. This is the place of being the "Beholder." The Sufi is aware of the spontaneous arising of Reality, while continuing to partake in the daily activity of life.

If you look for objects then you cannot cross the sixth to the seventh, so there must be negative preparations. The Sufi needs a negative mind, a mind that is not longing for anything - not even enlightenment, not even deliverance, not even paradise, not even truth; a mind that is not waiting for anything - not even Allah. It just is, without any longing, without any desire, without any wish, just "is-ness." Nothing is of any help; everything can be a hindrance. Then it happens . . . and even the cosmos is gone!

Listen to the words of Jelaluddin Rumi from the "Mathnawi,"

"All is the Beloved and the lover is a veil
The Beloved is alive and the lover is dead."

Now, you must leave the Limitless Self behind, for even that is a limitation. It is time to disappear. The event happens instantaneously. Only one thing is to be remembered: you must not cling to the sixth. It is easy to cling to the cosmos. You can say, "I have reached!" Those who say they have reached cannot go to the seventh. Kabir Helminski, servant of Mevlana, warns us, *"Mysticism, on the other hand, can become a narcissistic obsession with higher states of consciousness."*[149] The Murid must renounce ecstasy, mysticism, and identification with the One, to attain to the level of SPIRIT HUMAN. A glimpse of this process may be found in the words of Shamsi Tabrizi. Speaking of his own teacher, Sheikh Selabaf, Shams had this to say, *"He attained intoxication but never reached sobriety!"*

Spirit Human

"This is the Sufi journey within God and beyond God through mystical annihilation."

> *- Shaykh Nur al-Anwar al-Jerrahi*

"A Sufi is not concerned with patched cloak and prayer-carpet. A Sufi is not concerned with the convention and custom of being a Sufi. A Sufi is one who is not."

> *- Abu l-Hassan Kharaqani*

"The Formless is Attributed and Unattributed,
And gone into absorption in the cosmic Void.
Himself has He made creation; Himself on it meditates.
In the cosmic Void is he absorbed,
Where plays the unstruck mystic music—
Beyond expression is this miraculous wonder."

> *- Sikhism. Adi Granth, Gauri Sukhmani*
> *21; 23.1, M.5, pp. 290, 293*

"When you give your nonexistence to God, He gives His Existence to you."

> *- Abu l-Hassan Kharaqani*

The activity of the SPIRIT is not exhausted with its work upon the ASTRAL and ETHERIC BODIES; it extends also to the PHYSICAL BODY. We can see a trace of the influence of the SPIRIT upon the PHYSICAL BODY when, for example, under certain circumstances some person blushes or turns pale. In this case, the SPIRIT is actually the cause of a process in the Physical Body. Something similar occurs in the animal kingdom. The octopus communicates through changing the color and texture of its body.

If, through the activity of the SPIRIT, s take place in the human being concerning its influence upon the PHYSICAL BODY, the SPIRIT is united with the hidden forces of this PHYSICAL BODY. We can say, then, that the SPIRIT, through this activity, works upon the PHYSICAL BODY. This activity creates the "SPIRIT HUMAN."

The Murid has completed the cycle: upward through the MINERAL, ETHERIC, ASTRAL, to the flame of indwelling SPIRIT, and then through the SPIRIT he or she (by the permission of Allah) has raised up the aforementioned bodies into the Spirit Realms.

The Murid must remember always that the "place" he or she wants to go is "nowhere" (*Nā-kojā-abād*) [150] The Murid is only a shadow, the Shadow of Allah. The Murid realizes that he or she does not exist, only Allah exists, or more specifically, only the Lord hidden within the Murid, exists. This is the Murid's hidden Self. Beyond the Unlimited.

Amiru'l-Mu'minin Ali ('Alaihi Assalam) inquires: *"Do you ponder that you are a microcosm? Contained within you is the macrocosm? And you are the Clear Book whose words manifest the inner."*

The seventh body is the ultimate body, because now You have crossed even the world of causation. You have gone to the original source, to that which was before creation and that, which will be after annihilation. From the cosmic to nothingness, there is just a happening: uncaused, unprepared for and unsought.

> *"Nonexistence*
> *within existence*
> *is my Rule*
> *getting lost*
> *in getting lost*
> *my Religion."* [151]

The Murid *"gives us all his existence and follows Ahmad in His Heavenly Ascension."*[152]

"Now know this also, that at the End of that secret Way, lieth a Garden wherein is a Rest House prepared for thee."

- Aleister Crowley

"The bird of fortune that comes from illusion will come unknown and leave unknown. A strong iman, faith, and a sincere belief will send you the Phoenix from the City of Lutfullah, Grace of God. This bird's nourishment is ashk. If you feed it Divine morsels, it will grow, become stronger, and become the Emerald Phoenix. Then this bird will fly you to the City of Guarantee."

- el-Hajj el-Fakir Şerif Çatalkaya er-Rıfa'i er-Marufi

GATES, PALACES, DEGREES AND LATIFAS

The Sufis also speak of four GATES and beyond them three PALACES, one within the other.

The first gate is the gate of the SACRED LAW (SHARIA), also known as the sweet words of the noble Messenger. It is called the SPEECH OF MUHAMMAD (Peace be upon him). Its world is the Visible World (*'ālam al-shah āda*). Its state is inclination.

Here the Sufi must confront the material appetites and certain ignorant aspects of the personality. These aspects include: unawareness, acquisitiveness, covetousness, haughtiness, insatiable desire for food, lechery, bitter jealousy, inattention, curiosity about that which does not involve it, ridicule, animosity, and harming another human being physically or emotionally.

The second gate is the gate of the MYSTIC PATH (TARIQA) also called the DEEDS OF THE MESSENGER, in other words the exemplary actions of God's beloved Prophet

Here the Sufi begins to become aware of certain of his or her behaviors that lack beauty. Inspiration commences to fill the soul. Therefore, the Sufi desires to rid him or herself of these behaviors. In the words of Shaykh Abd al-Khaliq al-Shabrawi: *"He loves to be praised and lauded for his acts, yet he detests this tendency, which he recognizes in himself, and is unable to erase it entirely from his heart. To erase it entirely would mean that he is sincere and secure; however, even sincere people are still in grave danger, since they like to know that they are sincere and this itself amounts to a secret ostentation."* 153

The third gate is the gate of REAL EXPERIENCE (HAQIQA), also known as the STATE OF THE MESSENGER and THE LEVEL OF TRUTH. REALITY consists of the states peculiar to the Prince of the two worlds. For the Sufi, Haqiqat, is but a stop for him or her.

This is the gate of the Serene Soul. The Sufi sees only Allah, for Reality has suffused him or her inwardly. This person's attributes are: generosity, surrender, heart learning, mercy, yearning, crying, uneasiness, transformation, joy in spiritual singing, disclosing communiqués of discernment, and reflective intuition. The Sufi must be vigilant at this gate because he or she is unable to differentiate between Majesty and Beauty.

The fourth gate is the gate of GNOSIS or INNER KNOWLEDGE (MA'RIFA), also known as the SECRETS OF MUHAMMAD (Peace be upon him) or the MUHAMMADAN REALITY, which consists of the secret of the most holy being, the Mercy to Humankind.

Shaykh al-Shabrawi informs us that this gate's location is secret. He tells us: *"In this station, the wayfarer is a delight to the eyes of the onlookers and to the ears of his audience. Were he to speak without cease, his words would never be boring or wearisome, since his tongue expresses that which God casts into his heart of the realities of things and the secrets of shariat. . . ."* 154

The Sufi is at the first degree of Completion at this gate and so should make time to be alone and not always in other people's company.

The first PALACE is that of the CARDINALILTY or AXIAL CENTRALITY (QUTBIYA) also known as the ANGELIC SOUL.

Shaykh al-Shabrawi informs us that the location of this PALACE is the SECRET OF THE SECRET and that its state is EXTINCTION (fanā). *"The wayfarer is extinct, neither subsistent by himself as he had been before, nor subsistent by God as he will be in the seventh station. His attributes are: a contented acceptance of everything that occurs in the universe, without so much as a quiver of the heart . . . and without objecting to anything at all."*155

However, while the Sufi should always surrender to the will of Allah, this does not mean he or she should not take action when injustice occurs. Learn from the example of our glorious Imam Hussain ('Alaihi Assalam), who did not capitulate to tyrants and had the courage to face those who would usurp the future of the Umma.

The second PALACE is that of PROXIMITY (*QURBIYA*) also known as the SECRET SOUL or the SOUL FOUND PLEASING.Shaykh al-Shabrawi reveals that this PALACE's location is THE HIDDEN and its state is PERPLEXITY (as in the hadith: *"Lord, increase my perplexity in You!"*). At this PALACE the Sufi shows the first signs of the GREATER VICEGERENCY (*al-Khilāfa al-Kubrā*). *"It is the attribute of this soul to unite [attending to] both creation and the Creator; this is a strange thing and is only for those in this sixth station. This is why, in this station, the wayfarer does not appear outwardly different from the common people. Inwardly, however, he is the very essence of secrets and the exemplar of the best of people."* 156

The Sufi manifests the qualities of gentleness and an impetus to wake up those human beings who are asleep.

The third PALACE is that of DEVOTED SERVICE ('UBUDIYA), also known as the SOUL OF THE SECRET OF THE SECRETS. Sheikh Muzaffer Ozak al-Jerrahi al-Halveti writes, *"The highest level of soul, the pure soul, is not a part of creation. It is an aspect of the Divine Attributes, al-Hai, The Ever-living. You cannot locate it either inside or outside the body. The other levels are located within the body, but the pure soul is a part of the Infinite. As such, it cannot be contained within all of creation. It is a direct manifestation of the Ever-living."*[157]

Shaykh al-Shabrawi imparts that its location is the MOST HIDDEN, the relation between it and the Hidden being similar to that of the spirit to the body. *"When people see him they are reminded of God - and how else can it be when he is God's perfect saint? The man in this station is constantly worshiping, either with his whole body, or with his tongue, or with his heart. He asks for forgiveness in abundance, and is intensely humble."* [158]

The Great Saint, Seyit Sultan, Haji Bektash Veli, may God the Most High bless his mystery, revealed the following exalted experience of the SOUL OF THE SECRET OF THE SECRETS:

> *Before the world came into being*
> *In the hidden secret of nonexistence,*
> *I was alone with Reality in his oneness.*
> *He created the world; because then*
> *I formed the picture of Him,*
> *I was the designer.*
>
> *I became folded in garments made of the elements;*
> *I made my appearance out of fire, air, earth and water.*
> *I came into the world with the best of men [Adam];*
> *I was of the same age even as Adam.*
>
> *The blessed rod I gave to Moses.*
> *I became the Holy Spirit and came to Mary.*
> *I was guide to all the saints;*
> *To Gabriel the Faithful I was the right hand companion.*
>
> *To this world of "being annihilated in God" I have often come and gone.*
> *I have rained with the rain and I have grown as grass.*
> *I have guided aright the country of Rum;*
> *I was Bektash, who came from Khurasan.*

Each of the seven levels have seven subdivisions, making a total of forty-nine. Each new level recapitulates the one before it, but on a higher plane. For example, on the level of Tariqat there is the Shariat of the Tariqat, the Tariqat of the Tariqat, the Haqiqat of the Tariqat, the Marifat of the Tariqat, followed by the Qutubyyat of the Tariqat, the Qurbiyyat of the Tariqat, and finally the Ubudiyyat of the Tariqat.

Within the word: "La ilaha ill'ALLAH" there are seven *alifs* (the first letter of the Arabic alphabet). Each exemplifies a distinct step in the journey of the human being. Molana Salaheddin Ali Nader Shah Angha ("Pir Oveyssi") writes: *"To journey through these seven stages, he must continuously be in a state of repentance which means total awareness or turning towards his centrality or the Qiblah."*[159]

"Thy face is the Kibla of the meaning of Reality, O thou best of humankind" chant the Bektashi Dervishes during the ceremony of Nevruz.

These GATES and PALACES interpenetrate one another. The Sufi may experience any of them anytime. However, it is only by the Will of Allah Most High that the Sufi may be anchored in a given station. A word of caution: do not deliberately try to live by the conditions of higher GATES or PALACES before you have perfected the preceding one, for Allah will knock you back down to the station in which you belong, and you could cause much suffering to yourself and others by attempting to live at the level of a GATE or PALACE to which you do not belong. The 13th/14th century Persian Sufi Alaoddawleh Semnani developed the doctrine of *latifs*.[160] Linking the seven Prophets of the Qur'an with the mystical physiology of seven *latifa*, Semnani referred to seven grades of being which are the ascent of the soul to the Godhead. These are:

latifah qalibiyya, the mold ("etheric body") or "Adam of one's being," black or dark-grey in color.

latifah nafsiyya, the vital senses and animal soul, the "Noah of one's being," blue in color.

latifah qalbiyya, the spiritual Heart, the "Abraham of one's being," red in color.

latifah sirriyya, the Secret, the edge of superconsciousness and stage of spiritual monologues (the Throat Chakra) or "Moses of one's being," white in color.

latifah ruhiyya, the Spirit that is the Vicegerent of Allah (Ajna chakra), the "David of one's being," yellow in color.

latifah khafiya or organ of spiritual inspiration, the "Jesus of one's being," luminous black in color.

latifah haqiqa, the Divine Center or Eternal Seal, the "Mohammed of one's being," emerald green, this being the sacred color of Khezr.

It seems that Semnani's latifa have a double meaning: they refer both to psychic centers (chakras) and to a succession of subtle bodies (Sanskrit *kosha*, Greek *okhema*) or levels of self.

PRACTICE

It is imperative that the aspiring Sufi develops both hemispheres of his or her brain. The means to accomplish this is through developing ambidexterity. We highly recommend that the Murid begin doing activities with the non-dominant hand, such as brushing his or her teeth, answering the telephone, unlocking one's front door, handwriting, and so forth.

This will send an energizing and awakening signal to the non-dominant hemisphere of the brain and stimulate it into a more active participation in your life. Some researchers suggest that the terms: Left-Brain and Right-Brain may not adequately portray the processes going on in the brain, but, this exercise will put you in touch with various forces that reside in particular areas of the brain, stimulating and awakening brain functions.

Feelings of worry and anxiety overwhelm some individuals. An effective technique to calm these feelings is to balance the blood flow and rhythmic cycles between the hemispheres of the brain.

To do so, obtain a rubber ball. Practice tossing it, over your head, from one hand to the other. The ball needs only travel a little distance over your head; the point is to be able to continue easily tossing the ball back and forth for ten to fifteen minutes. This establishes harmonic rhythmic cycles between your two brain hemispheres plus balancing the blood flow.

Ultimately Science and Spirituality will reconcile and realize that they have been climbing the same mountain, but from contrasting sides.

"Sufism is the Knowledge whereby Man can realize himself and attain permanency. Sufis can teach in any vehicle, whatever its name. Religious vehicles have throughout history taken various names."

- Rais Tchaqmaqzade

Assuredly in the creation of the heavens and of the earth; and in the alternation of night and day; and in the ships which pass through the seas with things useful to humanity; and in the rain which God sends down from Heaven, giving life thereby to the earth after it was dead, scattering over it all manner of cattle; and in the change of the winds, and in the clouds that are made to do service between the Heaven and the earth; in all these things are signs for those who understand . . . Verily God is not ashamed to set forth as well the instance of a gnat."

- Qur'an 2:27

"Remember, Caterpillars cannot understand Butterfly language. Butterflies will be grounded if they use Caterpillar language."

- Michel Foucault,
The Flower of French Philosophy

"When the star of the Real rises and enters into the servant's heart, the heart is illuminated and irradiated. Then bewilderment and fear disappear from the possessor of the heart, and he gives news of his Lord explicitly, through hints, and by means of various modes of report-giving."

- Ibn 'Arabi [161]

"Man has closed himself up, till he sees all things thro' narrow chinks of his cavern."

- William Blake

TALES FROM UNDER THE OVERPASS

One morning Sam awoke and found Mr. Khadir missing from his sleeping mat. As Sam strode outside into the morning sunlight, he found Mr. Khadir sitting among the branches of a tree, sniffing the blossoms and sunning himself. Mr. Khadir greeted Sam, "I am like the sunlight in the morning. I intensify the light of morning until you awaken."

Sam asked him what he was doing there.

"Climbing the Great Pyramid."

Sam pondered on the fact that each day he observed Mr. Khadir in some state or quality which was not there before.

Sam shouted, "You are nowhere near a pyramid. And there are four ways up a pyramid: one by each face. What you are on is called a tree!"

"Yes!" said Mr. Khadir. "But it's much more fun like this, don't you think? Birds, blossoms, zephyrs, sunshine. I hardly think I could have done better. Like a madman, I worship everything I see. But you certainly have a point about there being more than one way to the top of a pyramid. In fact, there are as many ways to the top of the pyramid as there are people on earth!"

"Are you saying what I think you're saying?" Sam said haltingly.

"If the Brahman die at the feet of an idol, according to his lights he dies for an ideal, for what he takes to be 'God'; and in the House of God, indeed he deserves to be laid to rest!"

Mr. Khadir rocked back and forth in the tree, a large smile on his face. He was a sight with his black suit and red shoes sitting in the tree.

Sam said to Mr. Khadir, "I believe in God, but I don't seem to be able to find Him."

Mr. Khadir uttered a "Hmm," then said, "Those who love God can find Him in twenty years; those that hate Him can find Him in two."

"Hate Him?" Sam inquired with amazement.

"Yes. If you can't be honest about your feelings with God, then who can you be honest with? Those people who deny that they have any negative feelings are the most in danger of a spiritual catastrophe."

"But isn't God love?"

"To think of the Indeterminate Being as love is to just confuse the issue. God is the Indwelling Divine Spirit of each soul, where true power lies. In knowing your humanity, by that I mean uniting both your loves and hates, you come to know your Divinity. The Great Work is achieved through the Unity of the Sacred and the Profane, the Unity of Conscious and Unconscious, and the Unity of Body and Spirit. It is easy to be 'spiritual', what is difficult is to be human."

"It sounds to me like you are suggesting that I give up my belief in God," Sam gruffly responded.

"There is no god but God. The belief in a personal God is not only distracting from the impersonal study of nature, but usually is degrading. Thinking of God as a person trivializes the experience of the All Pervading Life Principle, leading men and women to worship an outside deity rather than their inherent Reality."

"I've always wondered why God sometimes answers some prayers and doesn't answer others. Doesn't He feel my pain?"

"Your pure sadness that wants help is the secret God. Listen to me Sam; you are setting yourself up for disappointment if you insist on thinking of God as an external deity. They who know themselves, know the Ontos. Paradigms of God must be shattered!"

"I am feeling upset by all this," said Sam, "I was brought up to believe

in a certain way, and now you're telling me everything I was taught was wrong."

"Enlightenment is progressive disillusionment. When you start to feel angry and cheated, that's when you are beginning to grow spiritually. A person will have various reactions when the senses begin to awaken. A person may utter various sounds. He or she may experience ecstasy, confusion, pessimism, apathy, fear, loss of faith, and other feelings. These happen in the initial stages."

"So many teachers have let me down" sighed Sam.

"If you meet the Buddha on the road, slay him." Mr. Khadir shot back.

"There are a lot of caterpillars on you," Sam said, pointing to the tree. "Do you see them all dangling from their little threads?

"They are like little human beings," Mr. Khadir reflected.

These larvae are like human beings?" an astonished Sam questioned.

They are in the larval state," Mr. Khadir instructed.

"You mean that so many people seem fast asleep?" Sam began, "and that it is time for them to awake?"

"It is true that most people live a hair's breath away from illumination," Mr. Khadir explained to Sam. "However, I think it's important to distinguish between states. Many spiritual teachers and schools teach larvae as if they were butterflies. A decision has to be made. And just as many of the students of these teaches and schools want to think that they are butterflies. They aren't. Take for instance, the example of a chicken and an egg. Are we seeing humankind as an egg or as a chicken?"

"An egg which has the potential to be a chicken," Sam chirped up. "Bravo Sam! I think we have to remember that there is a period of passage of passing from one state to another. Unfortunately, spiritual aspirants strut around thinking that they are chickens. There lies the fault. First, they must accept the fact that they are only eggs which have the potential to hatch into birds. Then they must let go of their lying to themselves that they are excellent flyers. Frankly, they don't know the first thing about flying. Humility is necessary for learning; yet it is also the most difficult quality for them to cultivate in a spiritual situation. I am specifically talking about those people who have studied various spiritual paths during their lives. They need to focus on the fact that they must think with purpose, and not just regurgitate things they have read or heard.

"It is important for people to realize the enormous gulf between their daily lives and what a full human life can be. However, what might take a person a million years to do, the One Living Reality can do in an instant! Humanity is like a kind of bird with its wings all furled and contracted against the sky. I say, 'Unfurl your wings and fly!'"

"Orthodoxy to the orthodox, and heresy to the heretic, but the dust of the rose petal belongs to the heart of the perfume seller."
- Abul Fazl

"All you nobodies
OUT!
the guardian
of those
who have no one
approaches
the house
and
once the house
is vacant
of others
the mercy
will descend . . ."

- Gharib Nawāz

THE DANGER OF BELIEF

The notion that Allah is a person who must live up to certain standards and expectations, sets people up for endless disappointment. *"The Absolute in its absoluteness cannot be known."*[162] The human race has done no greater harm to itself than by inventing an anthropomorphic All-Loving Deity.

If you see the world without a mental construct of God, you see the Real. Austin Spare wrote, *"Probably Almighty is he who is unconscious of the idea of God."* Why set up that idol "God" in front of you? Whatever level or way you see "God" right now, throw it out! How can you describe the indescribable?

There is no anthropomorphic benign deity to rage against for allowing illness, disease, "ethnic cleansing," plague, death, aging, and insanity to exist in the world. These shadow elements simply are. To quote from Bhagwan Shree Rajneesh, *"God is also irrational, and it is beautiful that He is irrational – otherwise He would have been a professor of philosophy in some university, or a pope, or a priest, but not existence."* [163]

If many bad things happen to you, you become outraged that your God let you down. If you are accustomed to visualizing your God as a caring shepherd, you cannot but help to be devastated when that shepherd allows you to be repeatedly attacked by wolves. However, it is not God who is letting you down; your concept of God is letting you down.

118

Each human being has their own individual concept of God. If circumstances happen in a way that is congruent with that concept of God, then all is well for the believer. However, if something occurs which is outside his or her God-paradigm, then the believer goes through a spiritual meltdown with all sorts of disastrous effects. This is because, in traditional religion, they hand the believer a mental construct of the deity, to which he or she adds the trimmings of his or her own imagination. If something occurs which does not fit the mold they have made for their "God," it is the limitations and presumptions of their own limited beings that cannot fathom what has occurred. Their mental constructs have let them down, not Allah.

When humans pretend to understand the nature of the Divine then they run into trouble. Spiritual training consists of leaving your notions about sunlight behind you, and instead standing outside and concentrating on the Sun in front of you.

PRACTICE

Go to places where two elements meet. Choose such places as the seashore, a lava flow, a steaming geyser, or a lakeside. Gaze at a candle-flame at the exact point between where the flame ends and the air begins. Also, visit crossroads, for example, where two paths meet in the woods, two streams come together, and two oceans converge. These are the liminal places, the places where there exist doorways between the realms, doorways into the Spirit Worlds.

Contemplate at such places. Contemplation does not mean "think." Simply "be" at such places. See, watch, hear, smell, and taste. Be aware.

"How could you pursue union if you did not already feel separate?"
- Adi Da Samraj

"Everything is formed from the contemplation of unity."
- Hermes Trismegistus

UNFURL YOUR WINGS!

People feel separate from their goals. They constantly pursue their goals, seeking to achieve their objectives, and hope to find unity with what they are pursuing. Some people feel the tension of loneliness and seek a relationship, wanting to remove their feeling of separateness.

The intention of the Murid is to seek for Unity with the Beloved, yet many still insist on feeling separated. Who is seeking? The best way to find Unity is to work on your feelings of separateness. You create the separation. Unity is the natural state of Reality.

Each person has a "schema," a set of core beliefs about himself or herself, in other words, a core philosophy. Most people's schema includes the concept that on the one hand there exists themselves, and on the other hand, there exists the world. The Murid must root out, expose, and delete this concept from his or her subconscious. It is time to realize your true state, to stop separating yourself from Unity, to take responsibility for your act of separation.

"Fear not dying.
Fear not having lived."

- Old Mexican saying

GIVE UP THAT MASK OF TRAGEDY

Do not be one of those spiritual mendicants and renunciants who make their whole lives but a yearning for death. This is a great insult to the One Living Source of Divulgence who has blessed our tables with fruits and sweet meats of all kind, beautiful flowers with intoxicating perfume, and laughter, joy, and companionship. Pir-o-Murshid Inayat Khan wrote, *"Balance in all things is the greatest responsibility in the life of a mystic."* [164]

Stop suffering for your spiritual development. Continue to do the practices your Guide gives you, but give up that glum face and disposition. Some spiritual meetings look more like a wake than a celebration of living hearts that love one another.

The goal is to be a person who is involved, friendly, generous, and good. These are the beautiful manifestations of someone who has found cosmic consciousness. To develop cosmic consciousness, work on developing your interpersonal skills of involvement, friendship, generosity, and goodness. Beautiful manners and beautiful spirituality go hand in hand!

If you do not experience the Living Reality through your caring for and interaction with others, then you have missed the point completely. *"Don't worry; be happy,"* as Meher Baba stated.

"The Prophet said, 'The best of the world's women is Mary (at her life-time), and the best of the world's women is Khadija (at her lifetime).' "
> *- The Prophet Muhammad*
> *(Peace be upon him)* [165]

"She (Khadija) believed in me when all others disbelieved; she held me truthful when others called me a liar; she sheltered me when others abandoned me; she comforted me when others shunned me."
> *- The Prophet Muhammad*
> *(Peace be upon him)*

"Islam did not rise except through Ali's sword and Khadija's wealth."
> *- Arabic saying*

KHADIJA - PRINCESS OF QURAISH [166]

According to many sources, Khadija was born in 565 C.E. and died one year before the Hijra (migration of the Holy Prophet and his followers from Macca (al-Mukarramah) to Medina (al-Munawwarah) in 623 C.E. at the age of fifty-eight. Khadija's father, who died around 585 C.E., belonged to the Abd al-'Uzza clan of the tribe of Quraish and, like many other Quraishis, was a merchant, a successful businessperson whose vast wealth and business talents Khadija inherited and whom the latter succeeded in faring with the family's vast wealth. They have said that when Quraish's trade caravans gathered to embark upon their lengthy and arduous journey either to Syria during the summer or to Yemen during the winter, Khadija's caravan equaled the caravans of all other traders of Quraish put together.

Although the society in which Khadija was born was a terribly male chauvinistic one, Khadija earned two titles: *Amirat-Quraish*, Princess of Quraish, and *al-Tahira*, the Pure One, due to her impeccable personality and virtuous character, not to mention her honorable descent. She used to feed and clothe the poor, assist her relatives financially, and even provide for the marriage of those of her kin who could not otherwise have had means to marry.

Khadija had married twice before she met Muhammad (Peace be upon him), and twice she lost her husband to the ravaging wars with which Arabia was afflicted. She had no mind to marry a third time.

One particular quality in Khadija was quite interesting, probably more so than any of her other qualities mentioned above. She, unlike her people, never believed in nor worshiped idols. Macca (al-Mukarramah), also known as Becca or *Ummul-Qura* - The Mother Town, was a major commercial center at the crossroads of trade caravans linking Arabia with India, Persia, China, and Byzantium. Most important, Macca (al-Mukarramah) housed the Ka'ba, the cubic "House of God" which had been always sought for pilgrimage and used to be circled by naked polytheist "pilgrims" who kept their idols, numbering three hundred and sixty, small and big, male and female, inside it and on its rooftop. Among those idols was one for Abraham and another for Ishmael, each carrying divine arrows in his hands. Hubal, a huge idol in the shape of a man, was Macca (al-Mukarramah)'s chief idol. Two other idols of significance were those of the Lat, a gray granite image that was the deity of Thaqif in nearby Taif, and the Uzza, also a block of granite about twenty feet long. They regarded these as the wives of the Almighty [see the chapter "What's So Great About Inert Matter?]. Symbolically buried in the midst of these polytheistic practices was the vision of the Prophet Ibrahim (Peace be upon him). We will learn more of the origin of the Ka'ba in subsequent chapters.

Since Khadija did not travel with her trade caravans, she had always had to rely on someone else to act as her agent to trade on her behalf and to receive an agreed upon commission in return. In 595 C.E., Khadija needed an agent to trade in her merchandise going to Syria, and it was then that a number of agents whom she knew before and trusted, and some of her own relatives, particularly Abu Talib, suggested to her to employ her distant cousin Muhammad Ibn Abdullah (Peace be upon him) who, by then, had earned the honoring titles of *al-Sadiq*, the truthful, and *al-Amin*, the trustworthy. Her agents had seen how he traded, bartered, bought and sold and conducted business. He was only twenty-five years old. She offered him twice as much commission as she usually offered her agents to trade on her behalf. She also gave him one of her old servants, Maysarah, who was young, brilliant and talented, to assist him and be his bookkeeper. She also trusted Maysarah's account regarding her new employee's conduct, an account that was most glowing, indeed one that encouraged her to abandon her insistence never to marry again. The profits Khadija reaped from that trip were twice as much as she had anticipated. Khadija was by then convinced that she had finally found a man who was worthy of her, so much so that she initiated the marriage proposal herself.

Khadija sought the advice of a friend of hers named Nufaysa. Nufaysa came to Muhammad (Peace be upon him) and asked him why he had not married yet. *"I have no means to marry,"* he answered. *"But if you were given the means,"* she said, *"and if you were bidden to an alliance where there is beauty and wealth and nobility and abundance, would you not then consent?"* *"Who is she?"* he excitedly inquired. *"Khadija,"* said Nufaysa. *"And how could such a marriage be mine?"* he asked. *"Leave that to me!"* was her answer. *"For my part,"* he said, *"I am willing."*

The marriage was a very happy one, and it produced a lady who was one of the four perfect women in all the history of humankind: Fatima, daughter of Muhammad (Peace be upon him) and Khadija.

By the time Khadija married, she was quite a wealthy lady, so wealthy that she felt no need to keep trading and increasing her wealth; instead, she decided to retire and enjoy a comfortable life with her husband who, on his part, preferred an ascetic life to that of money making. Both Muslim and Bukhari indicate in their respective "Sahih" books that among Khadija's merits was the fact that the Lord of Dignity ordered Gabriel (Peace be upon him), to convey His regards to her. Gabriel said to Muhammad (Peace be upon him), " *'O Muhammad! Khadija is bringing you a bowl of food: when she comes to you, tell her that her Lord greets her, and convey my greeting, too, to her.' When he did so, she said: 'Allah is the Peace, and He is the source of all peace, and upon Gabriel be peace.'*"

Khadija died of an attack of fever on the tenth or eleventh day of the month of Ramadan, ten years after the start of the Prophetic mission, twenty-six years after her marriage with Muhammad (Peace be upon him), and they buried her at Hajun in the outskirts of Macca (al-Mukarramah). The Messenger of Allah (Peace be upon him) dug her grave and buried her. They report that by the time she died, her entire wealth had already been spent to promote Islam.

It is noteworthy that during the time of their marriage, Muhammad (Peace be upon him) took no other wife. He married 'Aesha at the age of fifty-four, three years after the death of Khadija. After this marriage, he took other wives, about whom non-Muslim writers have directed much unjust criticism against him. The facts are that nearly all these ladies were mature in years or widows left destitute and without protection during the repeated wars of persecution. As Head of the State at Medina (al-Munawwarah), the only proper way, according to the Arab code, in which Muhammad (Peace be upon him) could extend both protection and maintenance to them was by marriage. One young woman by the name of Maria the Copt, was presented to Muhammad (Peace be upon him) as a captive of war. He immediately freed her, but she refused to leave his kind protection and he therefore married her.

PRACTICE

When you make *dhikrullah,* do not do it for a purpose. This is the greatest misconception of the Murid. In your devotions, remember that you are not separate from Allah. Praying for a purpose, for example, to raise your level or state, is to suppose that something separates you from Allah. *"Allah is, and that there is not with Him a thing."*[167] Simply allow yourself to experience the One Self-Manifested Being.

Adi Da Samraj has put it this way, *"But the search is itself a reaction to the dilemma, an expression of this separation, this avoidance of relationship. So none of this seeking, nothing one can do, becomes or attains the Truth."* When Adi Da says there is "nothing one can do" he is referring to the Limited Self's seeking and scheming to achieve a purpose. The Limited Self cannot get to Paradise. It is only when you open up the doors of your being, loosening your spiritual contraction, that you becoming aware of the True Reality. It is then that *"whithersoever ye turn, there is the Face of God."*[168]

Ibn al-'Arabi offers this gnosis, *"Thou art not what is beside God, and that thou art thine own end and thine own object in thy search after thy Lord."*[169]

The work of the Sufi is to change his or her thinking to remove the ignorance of egoism. As Shaykh Nur al-Anwar al-Jerrahi taught, *"The main point is that beingness is not transmutable. There's nothing to transmute. But our sense of separate becomings, our sense of separate energies, needs to be transmuted. Not only our so-called negative feelings, but our so-called positive feelings need to be transmuted."*[170]

The Sufi must Watch and Listen, in other words, to become the eyes and ears of Allah. The Sufi must keep his or her being tuned to the spiritual frequency of his or her Sheikh. The Sufi always remembers that there is nothing but Allah.

"In all thoughts of man the reality of God conceals itself. And each thought is a complete figure. And when in the thinking of man at the time of his prayer an evil or alien thought arises, it comes to him in order that he may redeem it and let it ascend. But he who does not believe in this does not truly take on himself the yoke of the Kingdom of Heaven."
- Baal Shem Tov

"One who is confirmed in the station of servanthood views his acts as hypocrisy, his spiritual states as pretentiousness, and his speech as a lie."
- Abu Madyan Shu'ayb

TALES FROM UNDER THE OVERPASS

*O*ne Friday night, Sam awoke to the sound of Mr. Khadir's voice. It was the middle of the night. Mr. Khadir was speaking softly and so Sam had to strain a bit to hear what was being said. Sam realized Mr. Khadir was praying. Mr. Khadir, imploring the Divine Reality, was saying,

"O Allah! I beseech You by Your Mercy, which encompasses all things,
And by Your power, by which You overcome all things,
And by Your might by which You conquer all things,
And by Your majesty against which nothing can stand up,
And by Your grandeur which prevails upon all things,
And by Your authority which is exercised over all things,
And by Your own self that will endure forever after all things have vanished,
And by Your Names which manifest Your power over all things,
And by Your knowledge which pervades all things,
And by the light of Your contenance which illuminates everything,
O You who art the light! O You who art the most holy! O You who existed before the foremost! O You who will exist after the last!
O Allah! Forgive me my sins as would bring down calamity,
O Allah! Forgive me my sins as would change divine favors (into disfavors),
O Allah! Forgive me my sins as would hinder my supplication,
O Allah! Forgive me such sins as bring down misfortunes (or afflictions),
O Allah! Forgive my sins as would supress hope,
O Allah, Forgive every sin that I have committed and every error that I have erred,
O Allah! I endeavor to draw myself nigh to You through Your invocation,
And I pray to You to intercede on my behalf,

And I entreat You by Your benevolence to draw me nearer to You,

And grant me that I should be grateful to You and inspire me to remember and to invoke You,

O Allah! I entreat You begging You submissively, humbly and awestrickenly, to treat me with clemency and mercy, and to make me pleased and contented with what You have allotted to me,

And cause me to be modest and unassuming in all circumstances.

O Allah! I beg You as one whom is passing through extreme privation and who supplicates his needs to You and his hope has been greatly raised by that which is with You.

O Allah! Great is Your kingdom and exalted is Your greatness. Your plan is secret. Your authority is manifest. Your might is victorious, subduing. Your power is prevalent throughout, and it is not possible to escape from Your dominion.

O Allah! Except You, I do not find any one able to pardon my sins nor to conceal my loathsome acts,

Nor have I any one except You to change my evil deeds into virtues.

There is no god but You!

Glory and praise be to You!

I have made my own soul to suffer. I had the audacity to sin by my ignorance, relying upon my past remembrance of You and Your grace towards me.

O Allah! My Lord! How many of my loathsome acts have You screened from public gaze?

How many of my grievous distresses have You reduced in severity?

And how many of my stumblings have You protected? How many of my detestable acts have You averted? And how many of my undeserving praises have You spread abroad!

O Allah! My trials and sufferings have increased and my evilness has worsened, my good deeds have diminished and my yokes of misdeeds have become firm, and remote hopes restrain me to profit by good deeds. The world has deceived me with its allurements, and treachery and procrastination have affected my own self.

Therefore, my Lord! I implore You by Your greatness not to let my sins and my misdeeds shut out access to my prayers from reaching Your realm and not to disgrace me by exposing those hidden ones of which You have knowledge nor to hasten my retribution for those vices and misdeeds committed by me in secret which were due to evil-mindedness, ignorance, excessive lustfulness and my negligence

O Allah! I beg You by Your greatness to be compassionate to me in all circumstances and well disposed towards me in all matters.

My God! My Nourisher! Have I anyone except You from whom I can seek the dislodging of my evils and understanding of my problems?

My God! My Master! You decreed a law for me but instead I obeyed my own low desires, and I did not guard myself against the allurements of my enemy. He deceived me with vain hopes whereby I was led astray and fate helped him in that respect.

Thus I transgressed some of its limits set for me by You and I disobeyed some of Your commandments. You have therefore a just cause against me in all those matters and I have no plea against Your judgement passed against me.

I have therefore become justifiably liable to Your judgement and afflictions.

But now I have turned to You, my Lord, after being guilty of omissions and transgressions against my soul, apologetically, repentantly, broken heartedly, entreating earnestly for forgiveness, yieldingly confessing to my guilt as I can find no escape from that which was done by me and having no refuge to which I could turn except seeking Your acceptance of my excuse and admitting me into the realm of Your capacious mercy.

O Allah! Accept my apology, have pity on my intense sufferings, and set me free from my heavy fetters of evil deeds.

My Nourisher! Have mercy on the infirmity of my body, the delicacy of my skin and the brittleness of my bones.

O' You! Who originated my creation and accorded me my individuality, and ensured my upbringing and welfare and provided my sustenance, I beg You, to restore Your favors and blessings upon me as You did in the beginning of my life.

O' my God! My master! My Lord! And my Nourisher! What! Wilt You see me punished with the fire kindled by You despite my belief in Your unity? And despite the fact that my heart has been filled with pure knowledge of You and when my tongue has repeatedly praised You and my conscience has acknowledged Your love and despite my sincere confessions of my sins and my humble entreaties submissively made to Your divinity?

Nay, You art far too kind and generous to destroy one whom Yourself nourished and supported, or to drive away from Yourself one whom You have kept under Your protection, or to scare away one whom Your self has given shelter, or to abandon in affliction one You have maintained and to whom You have been merciful.

I wish I had known o' my Master, my God and my Lord! Wilt You inflict fire upon faces which have submissively bowed in prostration to Your greatness, or upon the tongues which have sincerely confirmed Your unity and have always expressed gratitude to You, or upon hearts which have acknowledged Your divinity with conviction, or upon the minds which accumulated so much knowledge of You until they became submissive to You, or upon the limbs which strove, at the places appointed for Your worship, to adore You willingly and seek Your forgiveness submissively?

Such sort of harshness is not expected from You, as it is remote from Your grace, O' Generous One!

O' Lord! You art aware of my weakness to bear even a minor affliction of this world and its consequence and adversity affecting the denizens of this earth, although such afflictions are momentary, short-lived and transient.

How then can I bear the retributions and the punishments of the hereafter which are enormous and of intensive sufferings, of prolonged period and perpetual duration, and which will never be alleviated for those who deserve the same as those retributions will be the result of Your wrath and Your punishment which neither the heavens nor the earth can withstand and bear!

My Lord! How can I, a weak, insignificant, humble, poor and destitute creature of You be able to bear them?

O' my God! My Lord! My King! And Master! Which of the matters will I complain to You and for which of them will I bewail and weep?

Will I bewail for the pains and pangs of the punishment and their intensity or for the length of sufferings and their duration?

Therefore my Lord! If You wilt subject me to the penalties of hell in company of Your enemies and cast me with those who merited Your punishments and tear me apart from Your friends and those who will be near to You, then my God, my Lord and my Master, though I may patiently bear Your punishments, how can I calmly accept being kept away from You?

I reckon that though I may patiently endure the scorching fire of Your hell, yet how can I resign myself to the denial of Your pity and clemency? How can I remain in the fire while I have hopes of Your forgiveness?

O' my Lord! By Your honor truly do I swear that, if You wilt allow my power of speech to be retained by me in the hell, I will among its inmates cry out bewailingly unto You like the cry of those who have faith in Your kindness and compassion.

And I will bemoan for You for being deprived of nearness to You the lamentation of those who are bereaved, and I will keep on calling unto You: 'Where art You O' Friend of the believers! O' You who are the last hope and resort of those who acknowledge You and have faith in Your clemency and kindness; O' You who art the helper of those seeking help! O' You who art dear to the hearts of those who truly believe in You!

And O' You who art the Lord of the universe.'

My Lord! Glory and praise be to You, would You wish to be seen disregarding the voice of a Muslim bondman, incarcerated in hell for his disobedience and imprisoned within its pits for his evil-doings and misdeeds, crying out to You the utterance of one who has faith in Your mercy and calling out to You in the language of those who believe in Your unity and seeking to approach You by means of Your epithet 'the Creator, the Nourisher, the Accomplisher and the Protector of the entire existence'?

131

My Lord! Then how could he remain in torments when he hopefully relies upon Your past forbearance, compassion and mercy?

And how can the fire cause him suffering when he hopes for Your grace and mercy and how can its roaring flames char him when You hear his voice and see his plight?

And how can he withstand its roaring flames when You know his frailness?

And how can he be tossed about between its layers when You know his sincerity?

And how can the guards of hell threaten him when he calls out to You?

'My Lord', and how would You abandon him in hell when he has faith in Your grace to set him free?

Alas! That is not the concept held by us of You, nor has Your grace such a reputation, nor does it resemble that which You have awarded by Your kindness and generosity to those who believe in Your unity.

I definitely conclude that had You not ordained punishment for those who disbelieved in You, and had You not decreed Your enemies to remain in hell, You would have made the hell cold and peaceful and there would never have been an abode or place for any one in it; but sanctified be Your Names, You have sworn to fill the hell with the disbelievers from amongst the jinns and mankind together and to place forever Your enemies therein.

And You, exalted be Your praises, have made manifest, out of Your generosity and kindness, that a believer is not like unto him who is an evil-liver.

My Lord! My Master! I, therefore implore You by that power which You determine, and by the decree which You have finalized and ordained, whereby You have prevailed upon whom You have imposed it, to bestow upon me this night and this very hour the forgiveness for all the transgressions that I have been guilty of, for all the sins that I have committed, for all the loathsome acts that I have kept secret and for all the evils done by me, secretly or openly, in concealment or outwardly and for every evil action that You have ordered the two noble scribes to confirm whom You have appointed to record all my actions and to be witnesses over me along with the limbs of my body, while You observe over me besides them and were witness to those acts concealed from them? Which You in Your mercy have kept secret and through Your kindness unexposed.

And I pray to You to make my share plentiful in all the good that You do bestow; in all the favors that You do grant; and in all the virtues that You do allow to be known everywhere; and in all the sustenance and livelihood that You do expand and in respect of all the sins that You do forgive and the wrongs that You do cover up

O' Lord! O' Lord! O' Lord! O' my God! My Lord! My King! O' Master of my freedom! O' You who holds my destiny and who are aware of my suffer-

ing and poverty, O' You who knows my destitution and starvation, O' my Lord! O' Lord, O' Lord!

I beseech You by Your glory and Your honor, by Your supremely high attributes and by Your names to cause me to utilize my time, day and night, in Your remembrance, by engaging myself in serving Your cause and to let my deeds be such as to be acceptable to You, so much so that all my actions and prayers may be transformed into one continuous and sustained effort and my life may take the form of constant and perpetual service to You.

O' my Master! O' You upon Whom I rely! O' You unto Whom I express my distress! O' my Lord! My Lord! My Lord!

Strengthen my limbs for Your service and sustain the strength of my hands to persevere in Your service and bestow upon me the eagerness to fear You and constantly to serve You so that I may lead myself towards You in the field with the vanguards who are in the fore rank and be swift towards You among those who hasten towards You and urge eagerly to be near You and draw myself towards You like them who sincerely draw themselves towards You and to fear You like the fear of those who believe firmly in You and thus I may join the congregation of the faithful congregated near You for protection.

O' Allah! Whosoever intends evil against me, let ill befall on him and frustrate him who plots against me and assign for me a place in Your presence with the best of Your bondsmen and nearer abode to You, for truly that position cannot be attained except through Your grace and treat me benevolently, and through Your greatness extend Your munificence towards me and through Your mercy protect me and cause my tongue to accentuate Your remembrance and my heart filled with Your love and be liberal to me by Your gracious response and cause my evils to appear fewer and forgive me my errors for verily, You have ordained for Your bondsmen Your worship and bidden them to supplicate unto You and have assured them (of Your) response.

So, my Lord! I look earnestly towards You and towards You, my Lord! I have stretched forth my hands therefore, by Your honor, respond to my supplication and let me attain my wishes and, by Your bounty, frustrate not my hopes and protect me from the evils of my enemies, from among the jinns and mankind O' You! Who readily pleased, forgive one who owns nothing but supplication for You do what You will O' You!

Whose Name is the remedy for all ills and Whose remembrance is a sure cure for all ailments and obedience to Whom makes one self sufficient; have mercy on one whose only asset is hope and whose only armor is lamentation.

O' You Who perfects all bounties and Who wards off all misfortunes! O' Light! Who illuminates those who are in bewilderment! O' Omniscient! Who knows without acquisition of learning! Bless Mohammed and the Descendants of Mohammed, do unto me in accordance with that which befits

You, and deal with me not in accordance to my worth.

May the blessings of Allah be bestowed upon His Apostle and the Rightful Imams from his Descendants and His peace be upon them plentifully. Amin." [171]

"Oak trees are more often felled by ants than by the axe."
          - Proverb

"The human soul needs actual beauty more than bread."
          - D. H. Lawrence

"Hopelessness is the final sin against the Holy Spirit: - the betrayal of the divine within - the failure to become human."
          - Hakim Bey

"The search for happiness is one of the chief sources of unhappiness."
          - Eric Hoffer

"I warn you, that if you insist on seeing everything by means of the opinions of others, what you will discover in yourself will be only the opinion of others."
          - Joseph Conrad

"I am not the soulful music
Which comes from the trembling
Chords of a living lyre;
Nor yet am I the sensitive membrane
Of an instrument wherein
Eternal melodies sleep!
For, alas, I am but
The helpless gasp of a heart
From the impact of life
Which breaks, and falls apart!"
          - Ghalib

A SUFI APPROACH TO DEPRESSION

Ghalib had no children; the ones he had, died in infancy, and he later adopted the two children of Arif, his wife's nephew who died young in 1852. Ghalib's one wish, perhaps as strong as the wish to be a great poet, that he should have a regular, secure income, never materialized. His brother Yusuf, went mad in 1826, and died, still mad, in that year of all misfortunes, 1857. The "Revolt of 1857" was a rebellion in India against the British, during which at least 27,000 persons were hanged during the summer of that one year, and Ghalib witnessed it all. During the revolt itself, Ghalib remained pretty much confined to his house, undoubtedly frightened by the wholesale massacres in the city. Many of his friends were hanged, deprived of their fortunes, exiled from the city, or detained in jails.[172]

The idea of suffering and dying for the sake of transformation permeates all of Jelaluddin Rumi's work.

> *"The soul's extravagance is endless;*
> *Spring after spring after spring . . .*
> *We are your gardens dying,*
> *blossoming."*

The Sufi seeks the treasure that can only be found in the ruins; for the heart must be broken, to find in itself the *"hidden treasure"* which is God.[173] *"I am the sound of my own breaking,"* wrote Ghalib.[174] Imam Ja'far al-Saddiq (Alaihi Assalam), the Sixth Imam, said: *"When Allah loves His servant, He drowns him in the sea of suffering."* Jelaluddin Rumi, in his inimitable and down-to earth manner writes: *"They threw the grain on the earth, then there came out branches. Next, they crushed it in the mill, and it became more expensive and useful in bread form. Next. The bread was grounded under the teeth, and after digestion, it became mind, spirit and useful thought. Again, when the mind was bewildered with love, what a surprise this cultivation had been!"*

Imam Ali ('Alaihi Assalam) in his "Nahjul Balaqah" writes: *"Although constant care is given to the garden trees, yet the deprived trees of the forest have better quality."*

Sometimes when a person becomes deeply depressed, the dark pole overwhelms the opposite pole. At these times it is vital to "water your brain" with archetypal images. Fakhruddin 'Iraqi informs:

> *"That magic spring where Khezr*
> *once drank the water of life*
> *is in your own home -*
> *but you have blocked its flow!"*[175]

The best way to do this is through stories. Stories are powerful tools of the Sufi. Through stories the Sufi journeys into the liminal and returns transformed.

Stories come in various forms. Myths, novels, fairy tales, films, plays, operas, ballets, puppet shows, performance art, modern dance, and rituals. The point of this is not to distract you from your problems, but to bathe you in the Collective Transpersonal Water-Spring of Humanity. Love, Hope, Glory, Passions, Tears, are the needs of a person's soul. They are the roots of life. You need to send down your roots into the Stream of Life. Allow yourself to convulse with tears. Tears are drops from that Sacred Stream.

The body consists of seventy-percent water. The body exists in beautiful harmony with the planet, for the planet too consists of seventy-percent water! The word Shari'a, the revealed law of Islam, derives from the word *shar'*. The original signification of the term shar' is *"to enter into the water to drink of it."*[176]

While some people may waste thousands of dollars talking about their depression with a therapist, in some cases they could be saving all that money by just feeding the neglected pole of their psyches. Talking will not connect you with the water-springs of life, while the deliberate watering of your brain with archetypal images will help your soul to sprout new growth and blossom.

As Regi De Bre, the famous French revolutionary, said, *"A person who never cries and who does not know how to cry, lacks the feelings of humanness. He is a stone, a wild, dry spirit."*

Sufis speak of an Ocean of Divine Knowledge. It comprises Grace, Wealth, Essence, Manifestations, Evil and Good, Allah's Sound, Resonance, *Adab* (rules of Sufi conduct), Explanations, this World and the Next World. The Ocean contains the Totality of Everything. The Murid must focus within. He or she must look deeply into this Ocean. There he or she will find the true manifest nature of the Human Being. The Human Being is nothing less than the attributes of the Eternal Owner of Sovereignty.

Shaykh Nur al-Anwar al-Jerrahi sheds light on how the Murid can untangle his or her "Gordian Knot" in light of the Ultimate Reality. *"The Tibetans say it's like the snake that uncoils by itself. The snake looks tangled up, but it uncoils by itself, effortlessly, in a second. Thus, apparent duality is called 'self-liberated.' Your negative feeling, by expressing itself in a conscious atmosphere of non-duality, is self-liberated . . . But the fact of non-duality reveals that there aren't any ultimate tangles, and irritation or other unpleasant feelings can be just one more opportunity for non-duality to express itself."* [177]

Another way of looking at Shaykh Nur's insights is to consider a spaceship as it approaches the speed of light. The closer the ship approaches to light speed, the more the mass of the ship increases. Scientists postulate that it is impossible to go faster than the speed of light because the mass increases to an infinite level, and therefore no amount of fuel or power can move it. The speed of light is your freedom from your problems. The mass that increases is the fact that the closer you approach to directly confronting your problems (and acting and thinking in new ways) the more internal resistance you experience. Therefore, depression can be a propitious sign in that you are directly touching upon the very reason for your depression. The only solution is to let go of the mass, that is, completely to rid yourself of your attachment to your problems. As difficult as that may be, it is the only way to shift into light speed. For you cannot carry your problems into your new life.

If you are lonely, do not despair in your loneliness. Loneliness is from

Allah Most High. It is the last step in your journey to become the Limitless Person. We learn from Abdullah Ibn Amr that the Prophet (Peace be upon him) said, " *'The people whom Allah loves best are his poor and lonely servants.'* *Somebody asked, 'What is their state, O messenger of Allah?' He answered,* *'Those are the ones who are left alone with their religion. On the Day of Last* *Judgement, they will be brought to Jesus the son of Mary.' "*

Anxiety (Qur'an 20:86) is a mystical state, and sorrow (Qur'an 9:92) is a spiritual door.[178] Ismail Ibn Abad wrote the following poem,

> *"They tell me I am plagued with difficulties*
> *and my pain became the talk of people.*
> *I said: 'leave me be with my pain and troubles*
> *Because one's pain is in proportion to one's effort.' "*

Pray to the Imam Mahdi ('Alaihi Assalam). *"He is so close to and concerned about us that our predicaments become his problems and he is readily available to rescue us."*[179] He will definitely respond to your call for he is the rescuer of every victim. In fact, the Holy Prophet (Peace be upon him) enjoins us to seek help from the Imam ('Alaihi Assalam) when in distress. We are under an obligation to invoke his aid in our needs. So, say the following supplication that the Prophet taught us in your time of need, *"Ya Sahebazzaman Agithni, Ya Sahebazzaman Adrikni."*[180] They say that the Qutub or "Pole" has this attribute, and helps to remove all obstacles from the path of the sincere seeker. Allah's is the intercession altogether, however He may permit others also to intercede, *"On that day shall no intercession avail except of him whom the Beneficent God allows and whose word He is pleased with."* [181]

Murid, remember that everybody in your life will, at sometime, let you down. Face this fact. Many people in the contemporary spiritual community are shocked when their brothers and sisters do something wrong or inconsistent. Do not be shocked. See your friends with the eyes of Allah. One must be very patient with one's brethren, and not change friends because of impatience.[182] In addition, you will at some time believe that your Sheikh has let you down. This is another kind of special lesson and you must learn why you are experiencing distress. According to the Murid's capacity, the Guide will test the Murid in a myriad of unexpected ways. It is the Sheikh's job to stretch you and to confound your version of spirituality and your opinions how a Sheikh should behave. It is all a part of the process of transformation and learning to surrender your preconceptions. *"It is the way of dissolution, in which the conventional realization of life is undermined."* [183]

Yet, the safest place for a distressed Murid to be is with his or her Sheikh and brothers and sisters of the Sufi Way. Ali Bin Isma'il b. Hirzihim stated to those in pain: *"When calamities befall you, cleave to us, for we are generous, and our guest is never distressed . . . So whenever calamities and misfortunes befall you, flee to us and be sure to seek our noble presence."*

When faced with difficult circumstances and calamities, it is wise to contemplate on the Name of the Radiant Essence, *ya Alim,* the All-Knowing. In the most desperate of circumstances, call to mind the words of Hallaj, *"As far as I am concerned, if I am forsaken it is Your abandonment that keeps me company."* [184]

By far, we have found that the best medicine for depression is to ask constantly Allah for forgiveness of our sins. Allah is Forgiving and Merciful, and if a person asks with a sincere heart for forgiveness, Allah grants the person's petition. Burdens, concerns, anxieties, and depression are thereby lifted from the soul.

"O People ! Be informed that I am Fatima, and my father is Muhammad (Peace be upon him). I say that repeatedly and initiate it continually; I say not what I say mistakenly, nor do I do what I do aimlessly."
- Fatima ar Radhia

"Because she is satisfied with Allah's rewards and grants to her, and is satisfied with Allah's will in this world, He has become well pleased with her."
- Odeh A. Muhawesh

"Fatima was called 'Muhadatheh' because the angels descended from Heaven and called her as they called Mary, daughter of Imran and said, 'O Fatima! Allah hath chosen thee above the women of all nations.' "
- Zaid Ibn Ali [185]

"Allah, The Most High, is pleased when Fatima is pleased. He is angered, whenever Fatima is angered!"
- The Prophet Muhammad
(Peace be upon him)

"May you be so blessed as to have your heart broken wide open."
- Stephen Levine

AR RADHIA (THE SATISFIED OR GRATIFIED ONE)

As the All Pervading Life Principle manifests as both the blossom and the decaying leaf in a person's life, it is imperative for the Murid to say *"Alhamdulillah"* (Praise God) whether fortune or afflictions befall him or her.

The most perfect example of this beautiful behavior was Lady Fatima Zehra, *Fatimatulzahraa* ('Alaiha Assalam), the daughter of the Prophet Muhammad (Peace be upon him). She was pleased with whatever Allah Most High decreed for her.

Hazreti Fatima ('Alaiha Assalam), The Endless Pearl from the Infinite Ocean of Bounty, was a *Semavi* woman; that is, she came to earth from the level of angelic spiritual women. We know her as Syedatun Nisa al Alamin (Leader of the Women of the Worlds).

All sorts of terrible misfortunes, disasters, mischief, and damage were done to her, and she was martyred at a young age. While she was alive, she continued to praise the All-Knowing all her days and was CONTENTED with her predestination.

Fatima ('Alaiha Assalam) was the fifth child of Muhammad and Khadijah. The date of her birth was Friday the 20th Jamad al Akhar. She was born at a time when her noble father had begun to spend long periods in the solitude of mountains around Macca (al-Mukarramah), meditating and reflecting on the great mysteries of creation. This was the time, before the Bithah, when her eldest sister Zainab was married to her cousin, al-Aas Ibn ar Rabiah. Then followed the marriage of her two other sisters, Ruqayyah and Umm Kulthum, to the sons of Abu Lahab, a paternal uncle of the Prophet. Both Abu Lahab and his wife Umm Jamil turned out to be flaming enemies of the Prophet from the very beginning of his public mission.

The little Fatima ('Alaiha Assalam) thus saw her sisters leave home one after the other to live with their husbands. She was too young to understand the meaning of marriage and the reasons why her sisters had to leave home. She loved them dearly and was sad and lonely when they left. They say that a certain silence and painful sadness came over her then.

Of course, even after the marriage of her sisters, she was not alone in the house of her parents. Barakah, the maidservant of Aminah, the Prophet's mother, who had been with the Prophet since his birth, Zayd Ibn Harithah, and Ali ('Alaihi Assalam), the young son of Abu Talib were all part of Muhammad's (Peace be upon him) household at this time. In addition, of course there was her loving mother, the lady Khadijah.

In her mother and in Barakah, Fatima ('Alaiha Assalam) found a great deal of solace and comfort. In Ali ('Alaihi Assalam), who was about two years older than she, she found a "brother" and a friend who somehow took the place of her own brother al-Qasim who had died in his infancy. Her other brother Abdullah, known as the Good and the Pure, who was born after her, also died in his infancy. However in none of the people in her father's household did Fatima ('Alaiha Assalam) find the carefree joy and happiness that she enjoyed with her sisters. She was an unusually sensitive child for her age.

When she was five, she heard that her father had become *Rasul Allah*, the Messenger of God. His first task was to convey the good news of Islam to his family and close relations. They were to worship God Almighty alone. Her mother, who was a tower of strength and support, explained to Fatima ('Alaiha Assalam) what her father had to do. From this time on, she became more closely attached to him and felt a deep and abiding love for him. Often she would be at his side walking through the narrow streets and alleys of Macca (al-Mukarramah), visiting the Ka'ba or attending secret gatherings of the early Muslims who had accepted Islam and pledged allegiance to the Prophet.

One day, when she was not yet ten, she accompanied her father to the Masjid al-Haram. He stood in the place known as al-Hijr facing the Ka'ba and began to pray. Fatima ('Alaiha Assalam) stood at his side. A group of Quraish, by no means well disposed to the Prophet, gathered about him. They included Abu Jahl Ibn Hisham, the Prophet's uncle, Uqbah Ibn Abi Muayt, Umayyah Ibn Khalaf, and Shaybah and Utbah, sons of Rabi'ah. Menacingly, the group went up to the Prophet and Abu Jahl, the ringleader, asked, *"Which of you can*

bring the entrails of a slaughtered animal and throw it on Muhammad?"
Uqbah Ibn Abi Muayt, one of the vilest of the lot, volunteered and hurried off.
He returned with the obnoxious filth and threw it on the shoulders of the
Prophet, may God bless him and grant him peace, while he was still prostrat-
ing. Abdullah Ibn Masud, a companion of the Prophet, was present but he was
powerless to do or say anything.

Imagine the feelings of Fatima ('Alaiha Assalam) as she saw her father
being treated in this fashion. What could she, a girl not ten years old, do? She
went up to her father and removed the offensive matter and then stood firmly
and angrily before the group of Quraish thugs and lashed out against them. Not
one word did they say to her. The noble Prophet raised his head on completion
of the prostration and went on to complete the Salat. He then said, *"O Lord,
may you punish the Quraish!"* and repeated this imprecation three times. Then
he continued, *"May You punish Utbah, Uqbah, Abu Jahl and Shaybah"* (these
whom he named were all killed many years later at the Battle of Badr). On
another occasion, Fatima ('Alaiha Assalam) was with the Prophet as he made
tawaf around the Ka'ba. A Quraish mob gathered around him. They seized him
and tried to strangle him with his own clothes. Fatima ('Alaiha Assalam)
screamed and shouted for help. Abu Bakr rushed to the scene and managed to
free the Prophet. While he was doing so, he pleaded, *"Would you kill a man
who says, 'My Lord is God?'"* Far from giving up, the mob turned on Abu Bakr
and began beating him until blood flowed from his head and face.

The young Fatima witnessed such scenes of vicious opposition and
harassment against her father and the early Muslims ('Alaihi Assalam). She did
not meekly stand aside but joined in the struggle in defense of her father and
his noble mission. She was still a young girl and instead of the cheerful romp-
ing, the gaiety and liveliness which children of her age are and should normally be accustomed to, Fatima ('Alaiha Assalam) had to witness and participate
in such ordeals.

Of course, she was not alone in this. The whole of the Prophet's family suffered from the violent and mindless Quraish. Her sisters, Ruqayyah and
Umm Kulthum also suffered. They were living at this time in the very nest of
hatred and intrigue against the Prophet. Their husbands were Utbah and
Utaybah, sons of Abu Lahab and Umm Jamil. Umm Jamil was known to be a
hard and harsh woman who had a sharp and evil tongue. It was mainly because
of her that Khadijah was not pleased with the marriages of her daughters to
Umm Jamil's sons in the first place. It must have been painful for Ruqayyah
and Umm Kulthum to be living in the household of such inveterate enemies
who not only joined but also led the campaign against their father.

As a mark of disgrace to Muhammad (Peace be upon him) and his family, Utbah and Utaybah were prevailed upon by their parents to divorce their
wives. This was part of the process of ostracizing the Prophet totally. The

Prophet in fact welcomed his daughters back to his home with joy, happiness and relief. Fatima ('Alaiha Assalam), no doubt, must have been happy to be with her sisters again. They all wished that her husband would also divorce their eldest sister, Zainab. In fact, the Quraish brought pressure on Abu-l Aas to do so but he refused. When the Quraish leaders came up to him and promised him the richest and most beautiful woman as a wife should he divorce Zainab, he replied, *"I love my wife deeply and passionately and I have a great and high esteem for her father even though I have not entered the religion of Islam."*

Both Ruqayyah and Umm Kulthum were happy to be back with their loving parents and to be rid of the unbearable mental torture to which they had been subjected in the house of Umm Jamil. Shortly afterwards, Ruqayyah married again, to the young and shy Al-Khalifa Othman Bin'Affan who was among the first to have accepted Islam. Both left for Abyssinia among the first *muhajirin* who sought refuge in that land and stayed there for several years. Fatima ('Alaiha Assalam) was not to see Ruqayyah again until after their mother had died.

The persecution of the Prophet, his family and his followers continued and even became worse after the migration of the first Muslims to Abyssinia. In about the seventh year of his mission, the Prophet and his family were forced to leave their homes and seek refuge in a rugged little valley enclosed by hills on all sides, which they could only enter from Macca (al-Mukarramah) by a narrow path.

To this arid valley, Muhammad (Peace be upon him) and the clans of Banu Hashim and al-Muttalib were forced to retire with limited supplies of food. Fatima ('Alaiha Assalam) was one of the youngest members of the clans - just about twelve years old - and had to undergo months of hardship and suffering. The wailing of hungry children and women in the valley could be heard from Macca (al-Mukarramah). The Quraish allowed no food and contact with the Muslims whose hardship was only relieved somewhat during the season of pilgrimage. The boycott lasted for three years. When they lifted it, the Prophet had to face even more trials and difficulties. Khadijah, the faithful and loving, died shortly afterwards. With her death, the Prophet and his family lost one of the greatest sources of comfort and strength which had sustained them through the difficult period. The year in which the noble Khadijah, and later Abu Talib, died is known as the Year of Sadness. Fatima ('Alaiha Assalam), now a young lady, was greatly distressed by her mother's death. She wept bitterly and for some time was so grief-stricken that her health deteriorated. It was even feared she might die of grief.

Although her older sister, Umm Kulthum, stayed in the same household, Fatima ('Alaiha Assalam) realized that she now had a greater responsibility with the passing away of her mother. She felt that she had to give even greater support to her father. With loving tenderness, she devoted herself to looking after his needs. So concerned was she for his welfare that she came to be called *"Umm Abi-ha* - the mother of her father."* She also provided him with solace and comfort during times of trial, difficulty and crisis. *"Amazing! My mother gave birth to her own father!"* exclaimed Fakruddin 'Iraqi.[186]

After the death of Khadija, Muhammad (Peace be upon him) married Umm Salama, an old widow, to have someone to look after the household. When Umm Salama was requested to tutor the child Fatima ('Alaiha Assalam), the wise woman replied *"How can I tutor one who is the personification of high virtues and purity? It is I who should learn from her."*

Often the trials were too much for her. Once, about this time, an insolent mob heaped dust and earth upon his gracious head. As he entered his home, Fatima ('Alaiha Assalam) wept profusely as she wiped the dust from her father's head. *"Do not cry, my daughter,"* he said, *"for God will protect your father."*

The Prophet had a special love for Fatima ('Alaiha Assalam). He once said, *"Whoever pleased Fatima has indeed pleased God and whoever has caused her to be angry has indeed angered God. Fatima is a part of me. Whatever pleases her pleases me and whatever angers her angers me."*

He also said, *"The best women in all the world are four: the Virgin Mary, Asiya the wife of Pharaoh, Khadijah Mother of the Believers, and Fatima, daughter of Muhammad."* Fatima ('Alaiha Assalam) thus found a place of love and esteem in the Prophet's heart that was only occupied by his wife Khadijah. Fatima ('Alaiha Assalam), may God be pleased with her, was given the title of *"az-Zahraa"* which means "the Resplendent One." That was because of her beaming face, which seemed to radiate light. They say that when she stood for Prayer, the mihrab would reflect the light of her countenance. She was also called *"al-Batool"* because of her asceticism. Instead of spending her time in the company of women, much of her time would be spent in Salat, in reading the Qu'ran and in other acts of *ibadah*.

Fatima ('Alaiha Assalam) had a strong resemblance to her father, the Messenger of God. 'Aesha, the wife of the Prophet, said of her, *"I have not seen any one of God's creation resemble the Messenger of God more in speech, conversation and manner of sitting than Fatima, may God be pleased with her. When the Prophet saw her approaching, he would welcome her, stand up and kiss her, take her by the hand and sit her down in the place where he was sitting."* She would do the same when the Prophet came to her. She would stand up, welcome him with joy, and kiss him.

Fatima's ('Alaiha Assalam) fine manners and gentle speech were part of her lovely and endearing personality. She was especially kind to poor and indigent folk and would often give all the food she had to those in need even if she herself remained hungry. She had no craving for the ornaments of this world nor the luxury and comforts of life. She lived simply, although on occasion, as we will see, circumstances seemed to be too much and too difficult for her.

She inherited from her father a persuasive eloquence rooted in wisdom. When she spoke, people would often be moved to tears. She had the ability and the sincerity to stir the emotions, move people to tears and fill their hearts with praise and gratitude to God for His grace and His inestimable bounties.

Fatima ('Alaiha Assalam) migrated to Medina (al-Munawwarah) a few weeks after the Prophet did. She went with Zayd Ibn Harithah whom the Prophet sent back to Macca (al-Mukarramah) to bring the rest of his family. The party included Fatima ('Alaiha Assalam) and Umm Kulthum, Sawdah, the Prophet's wife, Zayd's wife Barakah and her son Usamah. Traveling with the group also were Abdullah the son of Abu Bakr who accompanied his mother and his sisters, 'Aesha and Asthma.

In Medina (al-Munawwarah), Fatima ('Alaiha Assalam) lived with her father in the simple dwelling he had built adjoining the mosque. In the second year after the Hijrah, she received proposals of marriage through her father, two of which were turned down. Then Ali ('Alaihi Assalam), the son of Abu Talib, plucked up his courage and went to the Prophet to ask for her hand in marriage. In the presence of the Prophet, however, Ali ('Alaihi Assalam) became overawed and tongue-tied. He stared at the ground and could not say anything. The Prophet then asked, *"Why have you come? Do you need something?"* Still he could not speak and then the Prophet suggested, *"Perhaps you have come to propose marriage to Fatima."*

"Yes," replied Ali (Alaihi Assalam). At this, according to one report, the Prophet said simply, *"Marhaban wa ahlan - Welcome into the family,"* and this was taken by Ali ('Alaihi Assalam) and a group of Ansar who were waiting outside for him as indicating the Prophet's approval.

Fatima ('Alaiha Assalam) and Ali ('Alaihi Assalam) were thus married most probably at the beginning of the second year after the Hijrah. She was about nineteen years old at the time and he was about twenty-one. The Prophet himself performed the marriage ceremony. At the *walimah,* the guests were served with dates, figs and *hais* (a mixture of dates and butterfat). A leading member of the Ansar donated a ram and others made offerings of grain. All Medina rejoiced.

On her marriage, they say that the Prophet presented Fatima ('Alaiha Assalam) and Ali ('Alaihi Assalam) with a wooden bed intertwined with palm leaves, a velvet coverlet, a leather cushion filled with palm fiber, a sheepskin, a pot, a water-skin and a quern for grinding grain.

Fatima ('Alaiha Assalam) left the home of her beloved father for the first time to begin life with her husband. The Prophet was clearly anxious on her account and sent Barakah with her should she be in need of any help. And no doubt, Barakah was a source of comfort and solace to her. The Prophet prayed for them, *"O Lord, bless them both, bless their house and bless their offspring."* In Ali's humble dwelling, there was only a sheepskin for a bed. In the morning after the wedding night, the Prophet went to Ali's house and knocked on the door. Barakah came out and the Prophet said to her, *"O Umm Ayman, call my brother for me."*

"Your brother? That's the one who married your daughter?" asked Barakah somewhat incredulously as if to say, Why should the Prophet call Ali ('Alaihi Assalam) his *"brother"*? The Prophet repeated what he had said in a louder voice. Ali ('Alaihi Assalam) came and the Prophet made a *du'a*, invoking the blessings of God on him. Then he asked for Fatima ('Alaiha Assalam). She came almost cringing with a mixture of awe and shyness and the Prophet said to her, *"I have married you to the dearest of my family to me."* She was not starting life with a complete stranger but with one who had grown up in the same household, who was among the first to become a Muslim at a tender age, who was known for his courage, bravery and virtue, and whom the Prophet described as his *"brother in this world and the hereafter."*

Fatima's ('Alaiha Assalam) life with Ali ('Alaihi Assalam) was as simple and frugal as it was in her father's household. In fact, as for material comforts, it was a life of hardship and deprivation. Throughout their life together, Ali ('Alaihi Assalam) remained poor because he did not set great store by material wealth. Fatima ('Alaiha Assalam) was the only one of her sisters who was not married to a wealthy man.

In fact, we could say that Fatima's ('Alaiha Assalam) life with Ali ('Alaihi Assalam) was even more rigorous than life in her father's home. At least before marriage, there were always a number of ready helping hands in the Prophet's household. Now she had to cope virtually on her own. To relieve the extreme poverty, Ali ('Alaihi Assalam) worked as a drawer and carrier of water and she as a grinder of corn. One day she said to Ali ('Alaihi Assalam), *"I have ground until my hands are blistered."*

"I have drawn water until I have pains in my chest," said Ali ('Alaihi Assalam) and went on to suggest to Fatima ('Alaiha Assalam), *"God has given your father some captives of war, so go and ask him to give you a servant."* Reluctantly, she went to the Prophet who said, *"What has brought you here, my little daughter?"*

"I came to give you greetings of peace," she said, for in awe of him she could not bring herself to ask what she had intended. *"What did you do?"* asked Ali ('Alaihi Assalam) when she returned alone. *"I was ashamed to ask him,"* she said. So the two of them went together but the Prophet felt they were less in need than others were. *"I will not give to you,"* he said, *"and let the Ahl*

as-Suffah (poor Muslims who stayed in the mosque) be tormented with hunger. I have not enough for their keep . . . "

Ali ('Alaihi Assalam) and Fatima ('Alaiha Assalam) returned home feeling somewhat dejected but that night, after they had gone to bed, they heard the voice of the Prophet asking permission to enter. Welcoming him, both rose to their feet, but he told them, *"Stay where you are,"* and sat down beside them. *"Shall I not tell you of something better than that which you asked of me?"* he asked and when they said yes he said, *"Words which Gabriel ('Alaihi Assalam) taught me, that you should say 'Subhaan Allah- Glory be to God' ten times after every Prayer, and ten times 'Al hamdu lillah - Praise be to God,' and ten times 'Allahu Akbar - God is Great.' And that when you go to bed you should say them thirty-three times each."* Ali ('Alaihi Assalam) used to say in later years, *"I have never once failed to say them since the Messenger of God taught them to us."*

There are many reports of the hard and difficult times that Fatima ('Alaiha Assalam) had to face. Often there was no food in her house. Once the Prophet was hungry. He went to one after another of his wives' apartments but there was no food. He then went to Fatima's ('Alaiha Assalam) house and she had no food either. When he eventually got some food, he sent two loaves and a piece of meat to Fatima ('Alaiha Assalam). At another time, he went to the house of Abu Ayyub al-Ansari and from the food he was given, he saved some for her. Fatima ('Alaiha Assalam) also knew that the Prophet was without food for long periods and she in turn would take food to him when she could. Once she took a piece of barley bread and he said to her, *"This is the first food your father has eaten for three days."*

Through these acts of kindness, she showed how much she loved her father; and he loved her, really loved her in return. Once he returned from a journey outside Medina (al-Munawwarah). He went to the mosque first and prayed two rakats as was his custom. Then, as he often did, he went to Fatima's ('Alaiha Assalam) house before going to his wives. Fatima ('Alaiha Assalam) welcomed him and kissed his face, his mouth and his eyes and cried.

"Why do you cry?" the Prophet asked. *"I see you, O Rasul Allah,"* she said, *"Your color is pale and sallow and your clothes have become worn and shabby."*

"O Fatima," the Prophet replied tenderly, *"don't cry for Allah has sent your father with a mission which He would cause to affect every house on the face of the earth whether it be in towns, villages or tents (in the desert) bringing either glory or humiliation until this mission is fulfilled just as night inevitably comes."*

With such comments, Fatima ('Alaiha Assalam) was often taken from the harsh realities of daily life to get a glimpse of the vast and extensive vistas opened by the mission entrusted to her noble father.

Fatima ('Alaiha Assalam) eventually returned to live in a house close to that of the Prophet. The place was donated by an Ansari who knew that the Prophet would rejoice in having his daughter as his neighbor. Together they shared in the joys and the triumphs, the sorrows and the hardships of the crowded and momentous Medina (al-Munawwarah) days and years.

In the middle of the second year after the Hijrah, her sister Ruqayyah fell ill with fever and measles. This was shortly before the great campaign of Badr. Al-Khalifa Othman Bin'Affan, her husband, stayed by her bedside and missed the campaign. Ruqayyah died just before her father returned. On his return to Medina (al-Munawwarah), one of the first acts of the Prophet was to visit her grave.

Fatima ('Alaiha Assalam) went with him. This was the first bereavement they had suffered within their closest family since the death of Khadijah. Fatima ('Alaiha Assalam) was greatly distressed by the loss of her sister. The tears poured from her eyes as she sat beside her father at the edge of the grave, and he comforted her and sought to dry her tears with the corner of his cloak.

The Prophet had previously spoken against lamentations for the dead. Nevertheless, this had lead to a misunderstanding, and when they returned from the cemetery the voice of Umar bin al-Khattab was heard raised in anger against the women who were weeping for the martyrs of Badr and for Ruqayyah.

"Umar bin al-Khattab, let them weep," he said and then added, *"What comes from the heart and from the eye, that is from God and His mercy."* Al-Khalifa Othman Bin'Affan later married the other daughter of the Prophet, Umm Kulthum, and on this account came to be known as *Dhu-n Nurayn* - Possessor of the Two Lights.

The bereavement, which the family suffered by the death of Ruqayyah, was followed by happiness when to the great joy of all the believers Fatima ('Alaiha Assalam) gave birth to a boy in Ramadan of the third year after the Hijrah. The Prophet spoke the words of the *Athan* into the ear of the newborn babe and called him al-Hassan which means the Beautiful One.

One year later, she gave birth to another son who was called al-Hussain, which means "little Hassan" or the little beautiful one. Fatima ('Alaiha Assalam) would often bring her two sons to see their grandfather who was exceedingly fond of them. Later he would take them to the Mosque and they would climb onto his back when he prostrated. He did the same with his little granddaughter Umamah, the daughter of Zainab.

In the eighth year after the Hijrah, Fatima ('Alaiha Assalam) gave birth to a third child, a girl whom she named after her eldest sister Zainab who had died shortly before her birth. This Zainab was to grow up and become famous as the "Heroine of Karbala." Fatima's ('Alaiha Assalam) fourth child was born in the year after the Hijrah. The child was also a girl and Fatima ('Alaiha

Assalam) named her Umm Kulthum after her sister who had died.

It was only through Fatima ('Alaiha Assalam) that the progeny of the Prophet was perpetuated. All the Prophet's male children had died in their infancy and the two children of Zainab named Ali and Umamah died young. Ruqayyah's child Abdullah also died when he was not yet two years old. This is an added reason for the reverence that we accord to Fatima ('Alaiha Assalam).

Although Fatima ('Alaiha Assalam) was so often busy with pregnancies and giving birth and rearing children, she took as much part as she could in the affairs of the growing Muslim community of Medina (al-Munawwarah). Before her marriage, she acted as a sort of hostess to the poor and destitute Ahl as-Suffah. As soon as the Battle of Uhud was over, she went with other women to the battlefield, wept over the dead martyrs, and took time to dress her father's wounds. At the Battle of the Ditch, she played a major supportive role together with other women in preparing food during the long and difficult siege. In her camp, she led the Muslim women in prayer and on that place there stands a mosque named Masjid Fatima ('Alaiha Assalam), one of seven mosques where the Muslims stood guard and performed their devotions.

When the Holy Prophet returned to Medina (al-Munawwarah), Gabriel, sent by Allah Almighty, appeared and read out this verse to the Holy Prophet, *"And give to the near of kin his due and (to) the needy and the way-farer, and do not squander wastefully."*[187] Muhammad (Peace be upon him) began to think about who were the near of kin and what was their right. Angel Gabriel appeared again and informed him that Allah says, *"Let Fadak*[188] *be given to Fatima."* The Holy Prophet called Fatima ('Alaiha Assalam) and said, *"Allah has commanded me to bestow Fadak as a gift to you."*[189] So he immediately gave possession of Fadak to Fatima ('Alaiha Assalam).

Accordingly, as long as the Holy Prophet lived, Fadak remained under Fatima's ('Alaihi Assalam) possession. That exalted Lady gave it on contract and its revenue was collected in three installments. Out of this amount the Holy Lady Fatima took at the rate of one night's food for her and her children and distributed the rest to the poor people of Bani Hashim and if there was any excess money she gave it of her own will to all the destitute and needy people.

Fatima ('Alaiha Assalam) also accompanied the Prophet when he made Umrah in the sixth year after the Hijrah after the Treaty of Hudaybiyyah. In the following year, she and her sister Umm Kulthum, were among the mighty throng of Muslims who took part with the Prophet in the liberation of Macca (al-Mukarramah). They say that on this occasion, both Fatima ('Alaiha Assalam) and Umm Kulthum visited the home of their mother Khadijah and recalled memories of their childhood and memories of jihad, of long struggles in the early years of the Prophet's mission.

In Ramadan of the tenth year just before he went on his Farewell

Pilgrimage, the Prophet confided to Fatima ('Alaiha Assalam), as a secret not yet to be told to others, *"Gabriel ('Alaihi Assalam) recited the Qur'an to me and I to him once every year, but this year he has recited it with me twice. I cannot but think that my time has come."*

On his return from the Farewell Pilgrimage, the Prophet did become seriously ill. His final days were spent in the apartment of his wife 'Aesha. When Fatima ('Alaiha Assalam) came to visit him, 'Aesha would leave father and daughter together.

One day he summoned Fatima ('Alaiha Assalam). When she came, he kissed her and whispered some words in her ear. She wept. Then again, he whispered in her ear and she smiled. 'Aesha saw and asked, *"You cry and you laugh at the same time, Fatima? What did the Messenger of God say to you?"* Fatima ('Alaiha Assalam) replied, *"He first told me that he would meet his Lord after a short while and so I cried. Then he said to me, 'Don't cry for you will be the first of my household to join me.' So I laughed."*

Not long afterwards the noble Prophet passed away. Fatima ('Alaiha Assalam) was grief-stricken and she would often be seen weeping profusely. Following are the rhymes that Hazrat Zahra ('Alaihi Assalam) recited upon the mourning of Prophet's (Peace be upon him) demise.

> *"The person who smells the sweet fragrance of*
> *the grave of the Prophet (Peace be upon him) so what if he*
> *does not smell any other fragrance for long*
> *times to come?*
> *Agonies and anguishes and griefs poured upon*
> *me in such a way that had they poured upon*
> *days those would have turned into nights.*
> *(bleak, dark and bewildering).*
>
> *The dust of sorrow covered the space of sky*
> *and the sun has faded and the bright day*
> *turned bleak. The earth has become dark and*
> *gloomy after the death of the Prophet (Peace be upon him)*
> *Woe! Alas! what the earth will have much of*
> *Jolting upon being separated and parted from*
> *him (Peace be upon him).*
>
> *It is meritorious and befitting that the east and*
> *west of the world may weep upon the parting*
> *of Prophet (Peace be upon him) and the persons of Muzzir*
> *tribe and all of they rest of the Yemen tribes*
> *shed tears.*

And the great magnificent mountain of the
existence and the hidden and covered Ka'ba
(House of ALLAH) and its pillars should shed
tears.

Oh the terminator and finalizer of the (series
of) prophets! the light of whom is the source
of blessing for the worlds inhabitants, Be the
salutation and blessings of Allah the descender
of Holy Qur'an upon you." [190]

One of the companions noted that he did not see Fatima ('Alaiha Assalam), may God be pleased with her, laugh again after the death of her father.

As we have noted, before the Prophet's death, Muhammad (Peace be upon him) gifted a piece of property to Fatima ('Alaiha Assalam), called fadak. However, certain ambitious and ruthless individuals who sought power over the Muslims, tried to claim that Fatima's ('Alaiha Assalam) property was not hers. At first, she lawfully claimed and stated that it was a gift from her father. However, witnesses, from the holders and occupants of the property, were requested of her to prove her claim of ownership. She produced the witnesses, yet their evidence was rejected against the Holy Code of Islam. It was only then that she sought recourse in the law of inheritance so her rights might be established.[191]

Fatima ('Alaiha Assalam) spoke directly to these duplicitous individuals. Here are some words she said, *"You proceeded towards his (the Prophet) kin and children in swamps and forests (meaning you plot against them in deceitful ways), but we are patient with you as is we are notched with knives and stung by spearheads in our abdomens. Yet—now you claim—that there is not inheritance for us!"* She continued, *"Will my inheritance be usurped? O son of Abu Quhafeh! Where is it in the Book of Allah that you inherit your father and I do not inherit mine? Surely, you have come up with an unprecedented thing . . . You claim that I have no share! And that I do not inherit my father! What! Did Allah reveal a (Qur'anic) verse regarding you, from which He excluded my father? O you people of intellect! The strong supporters of the nation! And those who embraced Islam; What is this shortcoming in defending my right? And what is this slumber (while you see) injustice (being done towards me)? Did not the messenger of Allah (Peace be upon him), my father, used to say, 'A man is upheld (remembered) by his children'? O how quick have you violated (his orders)! How soon have you plotted against us? Allah witnesses what you do, and soon will the unjust assailants know what vicissitudes their affairs will take!! Moreover, I am the daughter of a Warner (the Prophet*

- Peace be upon him) to you against a severe punishment. So, act and so will we, and wait, and we shall wait."192

When Fatima ('Alaiha Assalam) had finished her address Ali ('Alaihi Assalam) began his remonstrance. In the public gathering of the Muslims including Muhajirs and Ansar, in the mosque of Medina (al-Munawwarah), turning toward Abu Bakr, he said, *"Why did you deprive Fatima ('Alaiha Assalam) of her father's legacy, though she was its owner and possessed it during the lifetime of her father?"* Abu Bakr replied, *"Fadak is the booty of the Muslims. If Fatima ('Alaiha Assalam) produces complete evidence that it is her own property, I will certainly give it to her; otherwise I will deprive her of it."*

When Ali ('Alaihi Assalam) and Fatima ('Alaiha Assalam) were back in their home, Fatima ('Alaiha Assalam) was depressed and dismayed. She addressed Amiru'l-Mu'minin - Ali ('Alaihi Assalam) - in these words: *"You have receded like a fetus; you have retired from the world like an accused person and have broken your hawk-like strong wings, now the weak wings of a bird do not support you. This Ibn-e-Qahafa (Abu Bakr) is forcibly snatching away from me my father's gift and my children's means of subsistence . . . In fact, these people hated me with open ill-will and railed at me."* She made a long speech. The Holy Imam ('Alaihi Assalam) continued listening to Fatima ('Alaiha Assalam) until she became silent. Then he gave her a short answer, which made her satisfied. He said, *"O' Fatima ('Alaiha Assalam)? In the matter of religion and preaching Truth, I have never been inactive as far as possible. Do you wish that this sacred Religion remain permanent and secure and your Holy Father's name is called in the mosques and 'Athan's till eternity?"* She said, *"Yes, that is my most ardent desire."* The Holy Imam ('Alaihi Assalam) said, *"Then you should be patient, as your father, the Seal of the Prophets has forewarned me about this and I know that I should be forbearing, otherwise I have such strength that I can subdue the enemy and take back your right from them. However, you should know that in that case Religion would go. So, for the sake of Allah and the security of Allah's Religion, be patient, because the recompense in the Hereafter for you is better than your right which has been usurped."*

Ibn Abi'l-Hadid writing on this occasion narrates that when the people being deeply impressed by the protests of Ali ('Alaihi Assalam) and Fatima ('Alaiha Assalam), began to make a noise, Abu Bakr, who saw that the two Holy persons (A.S.) had already left the place, went to the pulpit and said, *"O people! Why are you so disturbed? Why do you listen to everybody? Since I have rejected their evidence, they are talking nonsense. The fact is that he (meaning Ali, A.S.) is a fox, whom his own tail betrays. He creates all sorts of disturbances. He minimizes the importance of disturbances and incites the people to create agitation and uproar. He seeks help from the weak. He seeks assistance from women. He is like Ummuit-Tahal with whom the people of her own house were fond of fornicating."* It is not only we who are surprised at such behavior. Even the Sunni Ulema are amazed to learn it, as Ibn Abi'l-Hadid writes in his "Sharh Nahj al-balaghah"[193] that the utterances of the Khalif filled him with astonishment.

The essence is that the Holy Prophet said, *"He, who causes trouble to these two (i.e., Ali A.S. and Fatima A.S.), causes trouble to me and the one who causes trouble to me causes trouble to Allah."* Also, he said, *"He who vexes Ali ('Alaihi Assalam) vexes me,"* and *"He who abuses you verily, abuses me and he who abuses me, verily abuses Allah and he, who abuses Allah will be thrown straight into the Hell."*[194]

Abu Bakr, some days later at his residence, wept over the condition of Fatima ('Alaiha Assalam) and gave it in writing that he returned Fadak to her. This is when he announced *"A decree I have written for Fatima in which I assigned Fadak and her Father's inheritance to her."* Upon doing that Amr Bin Al-Khattab said, *"With what will you spend on the Muslims if the Arabs decide to fight you?!"* Umar bin al-Khattab then seized the decree and tore it up![195]

Fatima ('Alaiha Assalam) received severe injuries when Umar bin al-Khattab attacked her home in an attempt forcibly to take Ali ('Alaihi Assalam) to Abu Bakr to force Ali ('Alaihi Assalam) to swear allegiance to Abu Bakr.

Abu Bakr asked Umar bin al-Khattab, *"Go and bring these people. If they refuse to come, fight against them."*[196] Abu Ja'far Bilazuri Ahmad Bin Yahya Bin Jabir Baghdadi, who is one of the most reliable Sunni traditionists and historians, writes in his "History" that, when Abu Bakr called Ali ('Alaihi Assalam) for swearing allegiance, and he did not accept it, he sent Umar bin al-Khattab to him. Umar bin al-Khattab went there with fire to ignite his house. Fatima ('Alaiha Assalam) heard his voice and the voices of his compatriots. She cried aloud, *"O' my father, Prophet of Allah! What tortures we are being subjected to, after you, by the son of Khattab, and the son of Abi Quhafa (Umar bin al-Khattab and Abu Bakr)!"* When the compatriots heard her lamentation and cries, they went back, with their hearts broken, and tears rolling down their cheeks, but Umar bin al-Khattab remained there with some people. Umar bin al-Khattab asked them to come out and offer allegiance to Abu Bakr. He came up to the door of her house with fire in his hand. Fatima ('Alaiha Assalam) said, *"O sons of Khattab! Have you come to set my house on fire?"* Umar bin al-Khattab said, *"Yes, for whatever your father brought for us, this action is most efficacious."* Umar bin al-Khattab burst the door in, he pressed Fatima ('Alaiha Assalam) between the door and wall so heavily that she suffered severe internal hemorrhaging from a punctured lung caused by a broken rib. Fatima ('Alaiha Assalam) was also pregnant at the time with her unborn son Muhsin. Looking at Ali ('Alaihi Assalam), Umar bin al-Khattab said, *"Get hold of this dog."* Salma Bin Aslam snatched away Ali's ('Alaihi Assalam) sword and threw it against the wall. Fatima ('Alaiha Assalam) suffered a miscarriage as they dragged her husband Ali ('Alaihi Assalam) out of the house.[197]

As Ali ('Alaihi Assalam) was being dragged with force and violence to Abu Bakr, he said that he was the servant of Allah and the brother of the Holy Prophet. Nobody cared for what he said until they took him to Abu Bakr, who asked him to take the oath of allegiance to him. Ali ('Alaihi Assalam) said, *"I am the most rightful person for this position and will not pay allegiance to you. It is incumbent on you to pay allegiance to me. You took this right from the Ansar on the ground of your relationship with the Holy Prophet, and I also, on the same ground, protest against you. So do justice. If you fear Allah accept my fight, as the Ansar did yours, otherwise you should acknowledge that you are intentionally oppressing me."*

Umar bin al-Khattab said, *"We will not leave you until you swear allegiance."* Ali ('Alaihi Assalam) answered, *"You have well conspired together. Today you are supporting him, so that tomorrow he may return the Khalifate to you. I swear by Allah that I will not comply with your request, and will not take the oath of allegiance to Abu Bakr, since he should pay allegiance to me."* Then he turned his face toward the people and said, *"O' Muhajirs! Fear Allah. Do not take away the right of authority, and supremacy of Muhammad's (S.A.) family, since that right has been ordained by Allah in his family. Do not remove the rightful person from his place. By Allah, we Ahlul Bayt have better rights in this matter than you have for there should be a man among us, who has the knowledge of the Book of Allah, the Sunnah of the Prophet, and the Code of the Religion. I swear by Allah that all these things are present in us. So do not follow yourselves, lest you should be away from Truth."* After this Ali ('Alaihi Assalam) secluded himself in his house until Fatima ('Alaiha Assalam) left this world. Afterwards, he was forced to offer allegiance.

Abu Muhammad Abdullah Bin Muslim Bin Qutayba Bin Umar Al-Bahili Dinawari, who was one of the Sunni ulema and an official Qazi of the city of Dinawar, writes: *"When Abu Bakr learned that a group hostile to him had assembled in Ali's house, he sent Umar to them. When Umar shouted to Ali to come out and to swear allegiance to Abu Bakr, they all refused to come out. Umar collected wood and said 'I swear by Allah, Who has my life in His control, either you will come out, or I will set the house with all those in it on fire.' People said: 'O Abu Hafsa! Fatima is also present in the house.' He said: 'Let her be there. I will set fire to the house.' So all of them came out and offered allegiance, except Ali, who said: 'I have taken a vow that until I have compiled the Qur'an, I will neither go out of the house nor will I put on full dress.' Umar did not accept this, but the plaintive lamentation of Fatima and the snubbing by others, forced him to go back to Abu Bakr. Umar urged him to force Ali to swear allegiance. Abu Bakr sent Qanfaz several times to summon Ali, but he was always disappointed. At last Umar, with a group of people went to the door of Fatima's house. When Fatima heard their voices, she cried out 'O my father, Prophet of Allah! What tortures we are subjected to by the son of Khattab and the son of Abi Quhafa!' When the people heard Fatima's lamentation, some went back with their hearts broken, but Umar remained there with some others until finally they dragged Ali from the house. They took Ali to Abu Bakr, and told him to swear allegiance to him. Ali said: 'If I do not swear allegiance what will you do to me?' They said: 'We swear by Allah that we will break your neck.' Ali said: 'Will you kill the servant of Allah and the brother of His Prophet?' Umar said: 'You are not the brother of the Prophet of Allah.' While all this was going on, Abu Bakr kept silent. Umar then asked Abu Bakr whether he (Umar) was not following Abu Bakr's orders in this matter. Abu Bakr said that so long as Fatima was alive he would not force Ali to swear allegiance to him. Ali then managed to reach the grave of the Prophet, where, wailing and crying, he told the Prophet what Aaron had told his brother, Moses, as recorded in the Holy Qur'an: 'Son of my mother! Surely the people reckoned me weak and had well nigh slain me.' "*

The political cabal that was running things attempted to make life as difficult as possible for Fatima ('Alaiha Assalam) and her husband. Among the things banned for them was the usual *Khums,* on which so much stress has been laid in the Holy Qur'an. Since Allah had forbidden charity for the Holy Prophet and his *aal* (descendants) the door of Khums was opened to them, as He says in the Holy Qur'an, Chapter 8, "Anfal (The Accessions), *"And know that whatever thing you gain, a fifth of it is for Allah and for the Apostle and for the near of kin and the orphans and the needy and the wayfarer . . . ,"*[198] so that the Progeny of the Holy Prophet might live in peace till the Doomsday and might not need the help of their Umma. Soon after the demise of the Holy Prophet, they were deprived of this privilege also. Khalif Abu Bakr, with the concurrence of people of his fold, confiscated this compulsory right of the Ahlul Bayt and said that Khums should be used for war-materials, purchasing of arms, ammunition, and other military requirements. Fatima ('Alaiha Assalam) and Ali ('Alaihi Assalam) were thus made helpless from all sides, as charities were forbidden for them and the open right of Khums was stopped to them. Even during the Khalifate of Umar bin al-Khattab, they deprived the Progeny of the Holy Prophet of their rightful and Allah given claim on the plea that the amount of Khums was big enough and so it could not be given to the near relations of the Holy Prophet but should be spent on making war efforts.

Abu Bakr suggested to Umar bin al-Khattab that they should both go to Fatima ('Alaiha Assalam) as they had certainly enraged her. They went together to the door of Fatima ('Alaiha Assalam) but the Infallible Lady ('Alaihi Assalam) did not allow them to visit her. When they asked Ali ('Alaihi Assalam) to intervene, he kept quiet. He however, allowed them to go in. When they went in and saluted her, the oppressed Lady turned her face toward the wall. Abu Bakr said, *"O part of the Prophet's liver, by Allah, I value the relationship of the Holy Prophet with you more than my relationship with my daughter 'Aesha. I wish to Allah that I died soon after the Holy Prophet of Allah. I know your high rank and position more than anyone else. If I have deprived you of your right of heritage, it was really because of the Holy Prophet whom I myself heard saying: 'We Prophets do not leave any heritage. What we leave is charity (for the Muslims).' "* Fatima ('Alaiha Assalam) then said to Amiru'l-Mu'minin Ali ('Alaihi Assalam) that she would remind them of a tradition of the Holy Prophet and ask them to tell in the name of Allah if they had not heard the Holy Prophet saying: *"Fatima's ('Alaihi Assalam) pleasure is my pleasure, Fatima's ('Alaihi Assalam) indignation is my indignation. So one who loves my daughter Fatima ('Alaiha Assalam) loves me; one who pleases Fatima ('Alaiha Assalam) pleases me. One who offends Fatima ('Alaiha Assalam), offends me."* Both of them said, *"Yes, we heard these words from the Holy Prophet of Allah."* Then Fatima ('Alaiha Assalam) said, *"I call Allah and His angels to witness that both of you have offended me and did not treat me justly. When I meet the Holy Prophet I will certainly complain to him of you both."* Abut Bakr being vexed at these words and statements began to weep and said, *"I seek Allah's shelter from the Holy Prophet's anger."* Then Fatima Zehra ('Alaihi Assalam), wailing and lamenting, said, *"I swear by Allah that I will certainly call down curses upon you in all my prayers."* Having heard this Abu Bakr went out weeping. People gathered round him and consoled him. To them he said, *"Woe be to you! You are all happy sitting with your wives comfortably, but I am in this wretched state. I do not need your allegiance. Rid me of it. By Allah, from what I have seen and heard from Fatima ('Alaiha Assalam), I do not want any Muslim to suffer the burden of allegiance to me."* [199]

So it was. She never saw them (Abu Bakr and Umar bin al-Khattab) again and did not talk to them. When the time of her demise approached, she made her Will that none of those persons were to take part in her funeral prayers. It read: *"None of these persons, who have oppressed me and snatched away my right from me, should be allowed to join my funeral. They are certainly my and the Holy Prophet's enemies. Do not allow any one of them or their associates to offer funeral prayers for me. Bury me at night, when people are asleep."*

Fatima ('Alaiha Assalam) never recovered from her injuries sustained on the day Umar bin al-Khattab invaded her house, when she was slammed between the wall and the door. She died on 3 Jamadi Al-Thani, in Medina (al-Munawwarah), a martyr in the cause of Allah, just six months after the demise of the Prophet. She left behind two sons: al-Hassan ('Alaihi Assalam), and al-Hussain ('Alaihi Assalam). Fatima ('Alaiha Assalam) the Resplendent One, was just twenty-nine years old, when she died.

She chose to be buried in a secret place so that future generations of Muslims and Sufis would become curious about why no one knows her tomb, and therefore, investigate the reason that she chose such a interment. [200]

"Whoever has good behavior and gives his wealth to others, will always be under the protection and mercy of God. God will be with him, will be kind to him and will admit him into Paradise."

> *- Imam Musa Ibn Ja'far,*
> *the seventh Imam*

"They suppose that Woman's Love is Sin; in consequence all the Loves & Graces with them are Sin."

> *- William Blake*

GATE OF THE SOFT MYSTERY

It is generally thought that Islam treats women very unfairly and deprives them of all their rights. In practice, many examples are indeed available of such treatment meted out to women by Muslim men. Women are often put behind the veil, forbidden to leave their homes unless accompanied by a close male relative; they are often married off at an early age and have fewer opportunities for education.

The treatment of women by the Taliban in Afghanistan reinforced this image of women in Islam. However, these practices are in sharp contrast to the Qur'anic pronouncements. The Qur'an is not only fair to women, it gives them all the rights that women rally for today. However, when a religion is practiced in a conservative cultural milieu, it often loses its original thrust. This is what has happened with Islam.

What the Qur'an states about women is an ideal; the reality, as usual, is determined not by scriptural pronouncements alone, but by a combination of factors including the cultural ethos of a given society. The Taliban belonged to the extremely conservative cultural milieu of the Northwest Frontier Province and Baluchistan.

The Qur'an accepts all the fundamental rights of women. A woman must be a consenting party in marriage, and without her express consent, the *nikah* is invalid. Even her father cannot consent to a woman's marriage on her behalf. She has also been given the right to divorce in two forms: *khula'*, to liberate herself from the marital bond, is her absolute right and a *Kazi* must grant her khula' if she insists on it. Her only obligation is to return the *mahr* or dower, as she is breaking the marital contract. The other route is *mubarat* or divorce with mutual agreement.

The Qur'an permits a woman to marry after widowhood; she can also choose another marital partner after *iddah*, the period of divorce, is over (three months, if she is not pregnant, and after the delivery of a child, if she is pregnant). She is also permitted to obtain a divorce if her husband is impotent or if he has not been heard from after four years or more.

Thus, a woman in Islam is entitled to enjoy sexual pleasure as much as a man; it is not taboo for her. There is absolutely no mention of female genital excision in the Qur'an; again, this is a tribal cultural practice in certain African countries like Egypt, Sudan and so forth. Woman is also fully and absolutely entitled to property rights, as a man is. Her father or husband cannot take property away from her except by her express consent. As for inheritance, the Qur'an states that she will get half the share that her brother does. But this is more than compensated by way of the mahr she receives at the time of marriage, and she has no obligation to maintain herself. The obligation to maintain her is her father's or husband's. She can spend her inherited properties according to her own pleasure.

In case of divorce, also, she receives compensation by way of what the Qur'an calls *mata'* (provision for her maintenance until she remarries). If a woman cannot marry, the Qur'an gives her father the right to make special provisions for her through *wasiyyah,* his will, before the rest of the property is left to be inherited by other children. Thus, from whichever angle of the Qur'anic provisions, the rights of women have been taken care of by Islam in a just manner.

The Prophet of Islam also tried to combat prejudices against the girl child by stating that those who bring up girl children properly, feed and clothe them and give them the best possible education, will not be touched by hellfire. The Prophet's dearest child was his daughter Fatima. When Ali ('Alaihi Assalam), Fatima's ('Alaihi Assalam) husband, wanted to take a second wife, the Prophet showed his strong displeasure; Ali ('Alaihi Assalam) did not take another wife while Fatima ('Alaiha Assalam) was alive. This was also a message that polygamy is not a general license to marry more than one wife at one's pleasure, but is permitted only in some exceptional circumstances, to protect the interests of widows and orphans.

Muslim men have hardly been faithful in their observance of the Qu'ranic injunctions for the empowerment of women. They have even resorted to weak hadith to violate Qu'ranic injunctions. Thus, the male ego and the local cultural ethos must be held responsible for the plight of Muslim women today.

"The Sufi reaches a stage where one transcends the duality of good and bad and perceives all of the manifest dualities as part of a unitary continuum of existence. Categorizing observations or experiences into good-bad, beautiful-ugly, rich-poor, pleasure-pain disappears."
                                                    - Shafii

"But as the (Divine) Reality is inaccessible in respect (of the Essence), and there is contemplation only in a substance, the contemplation of God in women (and men) is the most intense and the most perfect; and the union which is the most intense . . . is the conjugal act."
                                    - Ibn 'Arabi, Bezels of Wisdom

"When a man and a woman become one,
that 'one' is You.
And when that one is obliterated, there You are."
                                            - Jelaluddin Rumi [201]

"The world is a mother."

                                            - Lebanese Proverb

"Come forth, o children, under the stars, & take your fill of love!"
                                            - Liber Al Vel Legis
                                            (The Book of the Law)
                                            sub figura XXXI

THE GREATEST UNION

We can encounter the Divine in every person. *"He witnesses Him as the form of all corporeal bodies and accidents which he witnesses in the cosmos, not making Him specific to one form rather than another."*[202]

Passion is the essence of existence, and can be used in a sacred manner to take one to the Heart of Reality. Hadith relates that the Prophet's bed was still warm when he returned from the *Mir'aj* (his night ascension through the levels of heaven to the throne of Allah Most High). On this night, the Prophet Muhammad (Peace be upon him) reached within *"two bow's length"* of Allah. Fakhruddin 'Iraqi explains: *"Imagine lover and Beloved as a single circle divided by a line into two bow-shaped arcs. This line but seems to exist, yet does not, and if it will be erased at the moment of the Meeting, the circle will appear again as one - as in fact it really is. This then is the secret of Two Bows' Length."*[203] The secret Sufic explanation of the fact that the Prophet's bed was still warm, is that Muhammad (Peace be upon him) was making this journey while having sexual intercourse with his wife Khadijah (although some say

160

'Aesha or Zaineb). The human beloved becomes a witness *(shahed)*, a Theophany of the Real.[204] Ibn Tamīya had   yahremarked a practice that reflected the last of these views, noting that a mystic might kiss his or her beloved and say to him or her, *"Thou art God."*[205]

Abdelwalah Bouhdiba describes the mystical approach to sexuality in Sufism, *"The body of a woman, therefore, is a microcosm of the masterly work of God. To lose oneself in it is to find oneself in God. To run over it is to continue the great book of Allah."*[206]

Ibn 'Arabi relates this account of an event in Ruzbihan Baqli's life. It reflects the spirit and nature of Sheikh Ruzbihan's ecstasy and experience of the Divine. *"The story is told of Shaykh Ruzbihan that he was afflicted with the love of a woman singer; he fell ecstatically in love with her, and he cried much in his state of ecstasy before God, confounding the pilgrims at the Ka'ba during the time he resided there. He circumambulated on the roof terraces of the sanctuary, but his state was sincere. When he was afflicted by the love of this singer, no one knew of it, but his relationship with God was transferred to her."*[207] Sufis experience Allah in various ways during their journey to the Presence. Jung asks: *"Was the urge of the unconscious perhaps only apparently reaching out towards the person, but in a deeper sense toward a god?"*[208] Who but Allah can explain why Sheikh Ruzbihan transferred his love for Allah to this woman and not another woman? Ruzbihan Baqli reinforces this point when he writes: *"But He is a secret known only to those drowned in the oceans of unity and to the knower of the secret of the actions of eternity in the station of passionate love."*[209] He behaved like a crazy man, in love with the "wrong" woman, and any "sane" person would think that he was a fool, yet he was a great *Evliya*, a Saint. The sincerest passionate love is the nest of the Bird of Paradise. Lovers "devour" one another. Ruzbihan Baqli says: *"I saw that lion when it ate me, and I became more powerful than the world from joy at that."*[210] Ruzbihan Baqli was blessed with several wives and a family of two sons and three daughters. Sadly, for a time, he suffered from depression caused by the death of a favorite wife. Because of the days he lived in, Ruzbihan Baqli could not write as openly as he would have liked about his gnosis of passionate love. However, he has left us with some hints:

"He poured me the wines of proximity; it was as though I was in that place like a bride in the presence of God. What took place after that cannot enter into expression."[211]

"He graced me in a form that I cannot tell to any of God's creatures, and he was unveiled and there manifested from him the lights of his beautiful attributes."[212]

Of course, the greatest reason that the Sufi cannot utter these mysteries is that they do not fall under the category of epistemology. Words cannot be uttered, because mentation fails us at these times of "unveiling." Also, these "secrets" are within each Murid. When we *say, "May Allah protect his (or her) secret,"* we are saying, *"We honor the fact that this human found the Ultimate Reality within him or herself."* However, even that which can be put into words has often been held back for fear of the Orthodoxy's reprobation and even their abject threats of death.

The Arabic term most widely used to describe the sexual act is *jimā'* "union."[213] Even the division between witnesser and witnessed dissolves into Beingness. Intercourse is a glyph of the Human Mystery. *"The greatest union is that between man and woman, corresponding as it does to the turning of God toward the one He has created in His own image, to make him His vice-regent, so that He might behold Himself in him."* [214]

In Islam, they do not confine the purpose of the sexual act to procreation alone. 'Aini relates that one of his companions questioned the Prophet one day concerning a concubine with whom he like to sleep on condition that there was no risk of pregnancy. Muhammad, (Peace be upon him) then recommended him to practice the *"restrictive embrace,"* adding, *"what God has decided for her will happen in any case."* [215] Abdelwahab Bouhdiba, Professor of Islamic Sociology at the University of Tunis, concludes, *"In other words there is no incompatibility between coitus reservatus and the mystery of creation."*[216]

PRACTICE

Envision a dry desert. The dry bones of the dead fill the desert. Then envision merciful rain pouring forth on the arid desert. Flowers bloom, grass grows and the dry bones become enfleshed. The people awake. Allah is the Raiser of the Dead, the Restorer, the Giver of Life; the One Whose Merciful Rain brings Life to the dry earth. Allah speaks in the Qur'an (The Holy Prophet 11:52), *"And, O my people! Ask forgiveness of your Lord, then turn to Him; He will send on you clouds pouring down abundance of rain and add strength to your strength, and do not turn back guilty."*[217]

"Where shall I look when I praise Thee? Upward or downward, inward or outward? For Thou are the place in which all things are contained; there is no other place besides Thee; all things are in Thee."

- Hermes Trismegistus

"Banish from the house of God the mumbling priest whose prayers Like a veil creation from Creator separate!"

- Iqbal

"It is a delight to discover people who are worthy of respect and admiration and love.
But it is vital to believe yourself deserving of these things!
For you cannot live in someone else.
You cannot find yourself in someone else.
You cannot be given a life by someone else.
To the questions of your life, you are the only answer.
To the problems of your life, you are the only solution."

- J. Coudert

RELIGION VS. IDENTITY

Recognize and talk with the Hidden. The Reality Itself is concealed from all understanding, except one *"who holds that the Cosmos is His form and His identity."*[218]

When religion, and even esotericism, become logical and rational you can know with certainty that something is missing. Various adherents of the exoteric side of religion think of God as a Slave who infinitely supplies their needs. They fervently believe in and pray to a God that they think exists as a kind of mail-order supply house.

Esoteric religion has nothing to do with belief. Esotericism is a mystical, personal experience in which the individual knows rather than believes. That is why, when an esoteric tradition starts to appear more like a book of rules and social conduct, than a direct line to the Divine, you can be sure that this tradition is beginning to atrophy and wither.

Yet, rules and authority figures attract some people. In childhood, children will identify themselves with their parents. This is a propitious process, unless the children introject destructive aspects of the parent's beliefs. If parents are stern disciplinarians or give strong messages that authority is to be obeyed without question, the children will often carry these messages into adulthood. When parents teach their children to be *dependent* upon them, and not *independent* individuals, frequently the children will grow up with a gnawing need for someone upon which to depend. Some Murid's come from dysfunctional homes. Often the Sheikh becomes a substitute parent-figure, even without the Murid's awareness of what is happening. When a Sheikh refers to his or her Murids as "my children" or to an individual Murid as "my son" or "my daughter," this introduces, and gradually reinforces, an unhealthy relating of the Murid to his or her Sheikh as a parent figure. To make matters worse, they often refer the Sheikh as "father" or "Baba." This only contributes to an unhealthy interrelationship with the Sheikh.

No one can say with certainty what the Murshid's work is. Following upon that, no one can say with certainty what the Murid's work is. What may appear to others as disobedience or abuse, can only be known in its true Reality by Allah. The Sheikh says, *"Nureddin, hang yourself up by your hair on a tree limb and under no circumstances untie your hair."* Then the Sheikh says, *"Nureddin, come!"* Nureddin rips his scalp off his head and runs to his Sheikh and falls prostrate before him. Did this Murshid abuse his Murid? On the other hand, what if the Sheikh says, *"Nureddin, hang yourself up by your hair on a tree limb and under no circumstances untie your hair,"* and Nureddin says *"No!"*? Is this disobedience, or the Murid's awakening? It is different for every person. That is why one person may tell the Sheikh a dream and the Sheikh gives one interpretation, and then another person may come in and tell the Sheikh the same dream, but for this person there is another interpretation.

The Murid is the Murshid of the Murshid. The child is the parent of the adult. Fakhruddin 'Iraqi knew this truth when he wrote: *"Amazing! My mother gave birth to her own father!"* A great Sheikh uttered this insight regarding the relationship of the Murid to the Murshid: *"I went to Hazur Data Dayal Ji Maharaj, my spiritual Father, and troubled him a lot with my love. I followed him everywhere like his shadow. At last he said, 'See me tomorrow.' Next day, when I went to him, he put one coconut and five [coins] in my lap and said, 'I give you an order, obey me: The Real Master shall meet you in the form of your disciples.' That is what my spiritual Father told me."* The father is always younger than the child. There comes a time when the developing chick must break through the egg shell. The chick develops strength as it breaks through the shell. If a person "helps" the chick by breaking the shell for the chick, the baby chick comes out weak and lacking in the life-force. The act of breaking out of the shell fortifies and energizes the baby bird. The breaking of the egg shell requires a type of violence by the chick inside the shell. It must chop up the very thing that sheltered, protected and nurtured it for many months. So too, the Murid's jump into spiritual adulthood, may appear to others to be harsh and tumultuous. It is Allah's aspect of Majesty that helps the chick to break out of the shell.

As Khezr ('Alaihi Assalam) chopped off the little boy's head in front of an incredulous Prophet Musa ('Alaihi Assalam), so too we, at times, may not understand the subtle work of Allah. A person's journey to Allah is both a journey and an arriving. No one can say this or that action on the part of the Murid is proof or refutation of a person's attaining the station of Marifat.

The Creator cannot exist without the Creation. Just as a father cannot call himself a "father" if he has no son, and a son cannot call himself a "son" if he has no father. As Allah's Vicegerents we each have a sacred dialogue with the Creator. Every human being establishes the existence of the Creator, as the Creator establishes IT's existence through each human being. An aspect of that sacred dialogue consists of our experiencing life in all its multitudinous forms and manifestations. The Sheikh teaches surrender and submission to Allah. Yet, the Sheikh too must show surrender and submission when the Murid manifests through works or actions, the Will of Allah. If the Sheikh teaches: *"what happens is Allah's Will,"* then perforce, a Murid's apparent disobedience is also Allah's Will.

The Sufi must examine in a more profound manner the question: who is the Sheikh? The Sheikh is our intimate dialogue with our Creator. Allah does not play hide-and-seek with you. A guide may help you in your efforts, but ultimately, you must be true to yourself. For when you are true to yourself, you are being true to Allah.

Spiritual adulthood, or Vicegerency, is feared by many on the spiritual path. Allah has made each of us His Vicegerents on the Earth. Yet people grovel and plead to Allah for help! This is a great insult to Allah. A "vicegerent" is a person appointed by a ruler or head of state to act as an administrative deputy. You are Allah's proxy. Therefore, you have authority! Learn what it means to be an "administrative deputy." First, become the "deputy" of yourself. Then use your command and leadership in the world. To do any less would be to fail in your mission as Allah's Vicegerent on Earth. Do not insult the One who has entrusted you with authority by acting helpless. For you are not helpless. You are a fool (or an ignorant person) if you believe you are incapable and powerless.

Yet, still people insist on having a spiritual "father" or "mother." Everyone is human, Murshid and Murid alike. We do not know of any Sheikh that does not need to eat and go to the toilet. The Murid must kill the Murshid, in the sense that the Murid must kill the idea that anyone or anything can stand between the Murid and Allah. This is mirrored in the act of the chick who must remove the barrier of the shell to enter the world.

Those who believe that their Murshid is perfect, in the sense of being infallible, have fallen into *shirk*. They have also shown that they would rather live in a fantasy world in which they can pretend that they have powerful and perfect parent-figures who can do no wrong. This is not spirituality. It is pathology. This attitude reveals more about a person's dysfunctional childhood, or sense of personal irresponsibility, than it does about spiritual submission or surrender. Many Sheikhs would keep all their chicks in the nest long after the time has come for them to learn to fly and leave the nest. Allah's personal relationship with you is just that, personal. It is your secret. Only Allah and you know the dialogue.

All the "parent-child" jargon in Sufism must be done away with. This kind of language only encourages the Murid to relate to the Divine and to the Sheikh as a father figure, when in fact, this disposition is a stumbling block to a Real Experience of the Divine and a hindrance to being in a proper relationship to the Sheikh. The Sheikh cannot guide you as long as you insist on making your Murshid your surrogate "parent."

Love's way is about taking responsibility, not yielding it up to an authority figure. For unless you find love within, you will never find it without.

PRACTICE

The Way of the Sufi requires one to be open to pleasure, not pleasure as the focus of the Sufi's life, but as one color on the palette of human experience. Sheikh Ahmadu Bamba said, *"Strive and work in this world in accordance to your needs and set to work for the hereafter in accordance to your fears, because life in this world should enable you to satisfy your material needs as well as those you will have in the hereafter."* The Way of the Sufi is not the Way of one who would deny his or her body at the expense of study, work, career, and so on. Pleasure is a way that the world interacts with you. Pleasure is a kind of intercourse that takes place between you and the world. You do not want to cut yourselves off from the world.

Islam and Sufism have had a long history of respect for sexual ecstasy. The Holy Prophet (Peace be upon him) instructed his community in the importance of intimate relations, and carefully outlined and emphasized the importance of kissing, beautiful speech, perfume, and fore- and afterplay. There is a distinct difference between Islam and Christianity in this matter. Christianity has taught disdain for the body. At best, Christianity has reluctantly permitted sexual intercourse to the religion's followers as either the last resort for someone who can no longer control his or her desire, or for the creation of a child.

This respect for the sacredness of sexual pleasure is made clear by Jelaluddin Rumi in the following poem,

> *"Today nature is a pleasure to the sight,*
> *Spectacle, unveiling, vision*
> *Praise be to God, creator of the rain.*
> *The earth is in flower.*
> *Its clothes are all new.*
> *Luminous with light,*
> *Flourishing with flowers.*
> *Gone all modesty.*
> *The female burns with desire for the male."* [219]

Another significant aspect of the Complete Human Being is the possession of a good sense of humor. A useful tool to accomplish this gnosis is "play." In particular, play unlocks the God-Force, for play itself is about release and freedom from the required business of the day. Play gives the Murid a taste of Total Freedom, a taste of Paradise. The Sufi is intensely committed to the Joy of Life and the Life Force.

"The ornaments of the gnostic are shyness and reverential awe."
- Abū Madyan Shu'ayb Ibn
al-Husayn al-Ansārī

TALES FROM UNDER THE OVERPASS

*T*he next morning Sam told Mr. Khadir that he heard him praying during the night.

"*Please forgive me for overhearing,*" said Sam, "*but there are many things you said which I do not understand. May I ask you about them?*"

"*Of course,*" Mr. Khadir replied, radiating a stillness that seemed to affect the area for miles in every direction. "*It is a very ancient prayer, and you must understand that it was said using the language of the time.*"

"*Well, okay. So what is sin?*" Sam began.

"*To sin is to deliberately and consciously dwell and act in duality. Sin is a withdrawal from the Real Awareness of the Oneness of God. The person becomes trapped in appearances. To sin is to place anything before or with God. Sinning is the silliest thing in the world. Sinning is like a plant deciding to jump up out of the ground, or a human deciding he or she no longer needs to breathe. You see how crazy an idea it is. It can't ever really happen, but it happens as an illusion inside the mind of the person lost in duality.*"

"*So sinning is wrong?*" Sam pressed.

"*A sin is a blink of the eyes,*" Mr. Khadir quickly replied, "*it's a momentary disbelief that the only Real Thing That Exists Is God!*"

"*Okay, next question. You spoke about your continency. What the hell were you talking about?*"

"*I was referring to maintaining a constant state of remembrance of Allah. While being immaculate is reserved for the Imams and the Prophets, humans can still achieve states that would make the earth tremble through the constant, heartfelt, moment-to-moment recollection of the One Living Personality. Now certain actions can dull this ability to recall the Truth. Such actions as getting drunk, gambling, mocking or deriding another human being, and gossiping, all have a deleterious effect on a person's ability to see the Real Truth.*"

Sam again questioned, "*You prayed that Allah would forgive you such sins as would bring down a calamity. What sins would they be?*"

"*First, breach of a covenant. You must be deeply steadfast in all your agreements, promises and contracts. Second, shameful conduct. By shameful, I mean conduct that is dishonorable and false. Third, the publication of a false-hood. Fourth, the refusal or prevention of charitable giving, and lastly, fifth, cheating someone by not giving them their full due.*"

"This is most interesting," Sam said excitedly. *"What about the sins you said could change divine favors into disfavors?"*

"Well, to begin with, we'd have to start with bias and prejudice against people. But there are many actions that can change Allah's favor into disfavor. Be grateful for Allah's grace. If Allah gives you a gift, take it with gratitude. Thank Allah for even the smallest of favors, like your morning breakfast, or the fresh air, even the blood regularly pumping through your body. Beware of displaying your poverty or making a show of it, ever. Do not utter a complaint against Allah. On a more profound level, never try to silence or oppose an Alim. As you never know who is an Alim and who isn't, I caution you never to try to silence or oppose anyone."

"What sins could hinder your supplication?"

"Ceasing to believe that Allah will answer my prayer, and hypocrisy toward human beings."

"What sins bring down misfortunes?"

"Now you bring up a very serious subject. First, you must never abandon help to those in affliction. You must call for assistance and help in any way you can those who need help, be it because of sickness, oppression or poverty. And second, and this is very terrible, do not ever stand in the way of help coming to a person."

"What about the sins in your prayer that you said would suppress hope?"

"This is the crux of the matter for the human race, Allah's Caretakers on Earth. Do not despair of the Mercy of Allah. Resist any inclination to entertain no hope of Allah's Clemency. Allah alone controls destinies, and do you doubt for a moment that He will not take care of you? Allah is the All-Sufficing and the Generous. Remember that always, especially in the time of your greatest need."

"You prayed that Allah would make you pleased and contented with what He has allotted to you. I'd like to know more about this, for it seems to me that contentment is important in a person's spiritual life."

"You are absolutely right, Sam," Mr. Khadir began. *"Our beloved Imam Ali ('Alaihi Assalam) said that 'He who is contented, is honored; and ignominious is he who yearns.' The Lion of Allah is not talking about the kind of contentment some people regard as laziness or regard as a lack of desire to further themselves. Many people stumble on this word 'contentment. They do so because they subconsciously are refusing to go to the next level which contentment brings, and so they invent all sorts of 'reasonable' explanations why they do not like the word 'contentment.' There is a great secret hidden in contentment. The Prophet (Peace be upon him) said, 'One who is contented is self-sufficient even if he is hungry and naked; one who is contented triumphs over the people of his time and one who is contented has sufficiency of means over*

his generation; he who is contented has selected self-sufficiency over disgrace and ease over hardship.' The Prophet also has said, 'Contentment is a treasure which does not exhaust.' Sam, contentment is to be pleased with whatever Allah allots for you. It is to allow yourself to experience relaxation and centeredness in the midst of daily life. People's discontent comes out of their mind's own decision that what they have is not good enough for them. But the mind often blinds people to the outstanding beauty of what is around them. The mind bursts the bubble of joy."

"But Mr. Khadir, how can a loving God allow His caretaker, as you say, to remain in torment?"

"There is a verse in the Holy Qur'an: 'Announce O' Muhammad unto my servants that verily I am Forgiving, Merciful.' Allah is not the Lord of Vengeance but of Mercy. Allah has even decided the issue for Himself, if such a thing is possible, for He also says in that Holy Book "Your Lord hath prescribed for Himself Mercy.'

"Yet, you talked about God's wrath and fear of God. You remind me of some old Christian revivalist preacher when you use words like that. Isn't all that outdated?"

"Those who know Allah by way of Love without Fear perish through pleasure and ease. Those who know the Primal State by way of Fear are only separated from this State by the mind set of servitude and avoidance. However, those who love Allah, are near to Allah, are a matter of concern to Allah, and have knowledge of Allah, and those who know Allah in Reality, are far from error. Those who give to death (as you know, Sam, death is the chief object of fear) its true significance will be mindful of it. That is, they will always bear in mind that death must bring them to the judgement of Allah and they will so live that they need not fear it. Love is not perfect without fear, nor fear without hope, nor hope without fear."

"You must tell me more. I think I know what you are saying, but it is still unclear to me. Please explain more about the person who fears."

"He or she is the person who is made to trust in Allah by those things which are rightly feared, because he or she does not let fearful things disturb his or her mind, being removed from them by his or her fear of Allah, so that such things will be removed from him or her."

"Well, what does the Sufi fear?"

"He or she fears that, at the last, the soul should be deprived forever of the vision of His Everlasting Beauty."

"Forgive me, Mr. Khadir, but I still think you are not telling me the whole story about this fear thing. Would you please reveal to me a more subtle meaning?"

"The motive of fear of punishment or hope of reward is altogether unworthy of the saint of Allah. Only Allah, the Living Reality that is Fully

Awake Within Itself, is to be feared in the sense of cultivating a reverence of Allah's Overwhelming Holiness."

"You prayed to God that He would cause you to remember Him day and night by serving His cause. What precisely did you mean by that?"

"Again I point you toward the Book of the Divine Mercy, the Holy Qur'an. 'Verily in the remembrance of Allah do hearts find rest.' Remembering Allah gives comfort to those suffering all kinds of anguish, mourning the death of a loved one, every case of poverty, and guilt about immorality. It is like a soothing balm. Yet, you remembered me saying, 'in serving Your cause.' That is very good Sam. Because not everyone realizes what Allah's 'cause' is. Service to Allah includes service to family and humanity. Sheikh Abdoulaye Dieye, the disciple of Sheikh Ahmadu Bamba of M'Backé, Senegal who founded the Muridiyya, says 'Oh! You want to attain spiritual fulfillment. Your salvation lies with the group.' That, Sam, is serving Allah's cause."

"Now I am going to ask you a question that I've been avoiding asking you. I guess because I've been afraid of your answer. What is hell?" Sam managed, his voice shaking.

Mr. Khadir was listening intently to Sam's words. "Hell is any stressful situation you may be in which you produce negative thoughts. Most people think that the stressful situations produce the negative thoughts. It is not so. It is through their response to the situation that people create these negative thoughts. For instance, if you saw your next-door neighbor drop a hammer on his toe, you would not start to think you were having a bad day; but if it were your toe the hammer dropped on, you might utter something about what a bad day you're having. Believe it or not, there is a space between an event and your response to that event. Turn your attention from your thoughts to the Presence of Life."

"But, is that it? I don't want to sound critical, but what about when someone dies? I don't think your answer has really addressed that."

"Ah, but it has, jeweled light of my eyes! For what you gain here in this life, in other words, your attitude and state of mind, you will take with you. If you gain paradise in this life, you will take paradise with you into the afterlife. If you gain hell in this life, you will take hell with you into the afterlife. How do you gain paradise? Self-sacrifice. This places responsibility squarely on your shoulders as to how you will respond to life, and thus how you will enter the life after death."

"Life is a continuing process of change."
- Camden Benares

"Sufis responded to this oppressive environment by cloaking their teachings and their activities in the outward garb of religion."
- el-Qadiri

"Allah alone creates you moment by moment, including whatever you think and whatever you do."
- Qur'an 37:96

THE SACRED FLOW

Any religion or spiritual group that resists change is unhealthy because the group is collectively denying the Process of Change, a sacred process that the Evolver has manifested. The spiritual Way is about the transformation of the mundane. As Sheikh Fakir Seyyid Burhan Edin Aktihanoglu al-Rifa'i of Izmir says, *"In perfection, there is no repetition."*

Allow the Sacred Process of Change to reveal to you the Unfolding Divinity of the Moment.

Creation is being renewed moment by moment. Moreover, the Ultimate Reality is known by various Names. Each name has one thousand doors. Make use of the Names from all the faiths. Ibn' Arabi writes, *"Let thy soul be as matter for all forms of all beliefs."*

Absolute Existence has revealed through hadith, *"I manifest in the manner in which each conscious being expects Me to manifest."* All Allah asks is that you humbly do as much as you can of your prayers and practices. To the Sufi, true religion is sincerity of heart!

Often practitioners of various religions feel that it is their responsibility to lecture, convert and give their unrequested advice to others. Part of becoming an excellent practitioner of universal religion is to learn how to leave alone whatever is not your particular spiritual responsibility.[220]

The goal is to be a Complete Person who is involved, friendly, generous, and good. These are the beautiful manifestations of someone who has found cosmic consciousness. To develop cosmic consciousness, work on developing your interpersonal skills. Beautiful manners and beautiful spirituality! Cultivate involvement, friendship, generosity, and goodness. Your behavior and conduct are important. They are the expression of the qualities of Allah.

PRACTICE

Watch and listen. These are the two most basic rules of instruction in Sufism. The Naqshbandi Order of Sufis calls this *practice* "watching your feet."[221] Gurdjieff called this *practice* "*self-observation.*" The goal is to achieve mindfulness and to pay close attention to every detail.

As you walk down the street, be sensitive to what you see and hear around you. In your daily life, attune yourself to the Manifest. If you are on the "wavelength" of the Godhead, then you will not need to struggle and work for enlightenment, you will already be an instrument of the Incomparable.

Abu Muhammad Muta'ish has written, *"The Sufi is he whose thought keeps pace with his foot, in other words he is entirely present: his soul is where his body is, and his body is where his soul is, and his soul where his foot is, and his foot where his soul is. This is the sign of presence without absence. Others say on the contrary: He is absent from himself but present with God. It is not so: he is present with himself and present with God."*

Abdullah is a Muslim name. It means "The Slave (Servant) of Allah." Slave and Servant, as it is meant here, pertains to the Murid emptying him or herself of everything that is not God. Without this emptiness, being filled with the ever-present reality of His Nearness is impossible. The Qur'an says, *"We (God) are nearer to a person than his or her jugular vein."*[222]

There is also a hidden mystery in the name "Abdullah." Ibn al-'Arabi writes: *"The slave is the Lord and the Lord is the slave; how can one tell which of the two is the debtor?"*

Abdullah is also one of the Prophet Muhammad's (Peace be upon him) secondary names, *'Abd Allāh.* The famous author, Kurt Vonnegut, Jr. writes, *"What is the Purpose of Life? To be the eyes and ears of the Creator of the Universe, you fool."* Abu l-Hassan Kharaqani declares: *"This is someone who, if he were hung in the sky by a silken thread and a wind blew up, uprooting trees and smashing down buildings, leveling mountains and whipping all the seas up in a froth, would not be stirred."*

"Like a swan, that's here and gone . . . "
> *- Simon and Garfunkel*

"May the flood of praise arising from all the minds and hearts in creation which are spontaneously overflowing, including all individual perception of all individual creatures, flow like rivers and streams into the vast ocean of Divine Radiance"
> *- Shaykh Nur*
> *al-Anwar al-Jerrahi* [223]

"How can anyone judge another, when we too will be judged.
In humility one walks behind the people
Guiding them into the light of servanthood.
O Allah, Release us from the bounds of Pride."
> *- Sheikh Salik Al Fakiriyye,*
> *New York*

"How can it then bear in itself the opposites of good and evil? In truth, there is no opposite, for the evil is the throne of the good."
> *- Baal Shem Tov*

"Because where the spirit of the Lord is, there is liberty."
> *- Robert Stone* [224]

"Isaac and Ishmael his sons buried him [Abraham] in the cave of Machpelah . . ."
> *- Genesis 25:9*

THE FLOWER OF SPONTANEOUS SPIRITUAL PRESENCE: SHAYKH NUR AL-ANWAR AL-JERRAHI (LEX HIXON) (1942 – 1995)

In 1978, Lex Hixon met Shaykh Muzaffer al-Jerrahi al-Halveti and received the name *Nur*, Divine Light. In 1980, Nur received the Green and Gold Turban of a Formal Representative, from Muzaffer Ashki. After Sheikh Muzaffer's passing in 1985, Lex was invested with the Turban again by Sayyid Sheikh Safer Dal Efendi, the new Grand Sheikh of the 300-year-old Halveti Jerrahi Order in Istanbul.

About the time Shaykh Nur received the Turban, we had just read our first book on Sufism. We had been impressed, but we were young and penniless and thought to ourselves, *"When will we ever go to the middle-east to meet these Sufis?"* That weekend we turned on WBAI-FM and immediately heard the voice of Shaykh Nur. The first words that we heard him speak were, *"I would like to introduce you to Shaykh Muzaffer, a Sufi Shaykh from Istanbul, Turkey."* Shaykh Nur was the means by which Allah brought us to Sufism.

Since 1980, he was the guide of the Masjid Al-Farah, the mosque in New York City. More than one-thousand dervishes took hand in initiation with Nur, and presently are meeting in the United States, France, England, and Mexico.

There were some that were critical of Shaykh Nur al-Anwar al-Jerrahi. A lineage holder in five different religions, Nur saw the sameness of pure Spirit at the core of them all. He was a member of several mystic, or contemplative, lineage orders including the Helveti-Jerrahi Order of Istanbul, and also branches of the Ramakrishna Lineage, and The Golden Blossom Sangha, a branch of the Soto-Rensei Lineage. He was also quite active in other expressions such as Greek Orthodox, Judaic, and Indigenous, or Natural, Mystic, or Wisdom Orders. He was, to some, a true "Non-Dualist." Ibn 'Arabi maintains that after fana an individual can recognize God's self-revelation in all religions.[225] Piro-Murshid Inayat Khan transmitted the following wisdom, *"Although there might be another flower in the same garden, under the same sun and in the same air, yet its fragrance and color are different. In the same way, spirituality expresses itself in different ways and different terms, although all mystics are inspired by one and the same truth. It is lack of understanding of this ideal of unity which has given rise to religious differences, and these have been the cause of battles fought throughout the ages."* Yet, Nur's critics wanted him to focus on only one tradition. Shaykh Nur knew that his non-dual celebration *"creates a circle that has no identification with a particular tradition."*[226]

May his critics deeply ponder the words of the Master Abū Madyan Shu'ayb Ibn al-Husayn al-Ansārī: *"When one is totally occupied in his nearness to God, the hatred of others for him quickly reaches him. Oh ego, this is a warning for you, if you would pay heed!"*[227] The Sheikh of Sheikhs, Ibn al-'Arābi:

"Consider this matter, for, as men know God [in this world], so will they see Him on the Day of Resurrection, the reason for which I have informed you of. So, beware, lest you restrict yourself to a particular tenet [concerning the Reality] and so deny any other tenet [equally reflecting Him], for you would forfeit much good, indeed you would forfeit the true knowledge of what is [the Reality]. Therefore, be completely and utterly receptive to all doctrinal forms, for God, Most High, is too All-embracing and Great to be confined within one creed rather than another, for He has said, **Wheresoever you turn, there is the face of God,** *without mentioning any particular direction. He states that there is the face of God, the face of a thing being its reality.*[228]

It is odd how, over time, the Khalifas of the great Evliyas often become close-minded, turning the beautiful vista of the Evliya's vision into a set of restrictive rules. *"Yearning should spur even those who have attained Union to aspire higher and higher still. Otherwise they are defined by what they have found and stay stuck in the station of inadequacy: 'Then they send them back to the palaces . . . therein to dwell forever, desiring no removal out of them (XVIII:108).'"*[229] These Khalifas not only lose sight of the vision, but they deny to their students the right to pursue avenues of spiritual pursuit that the Saint considered worthwhile. For example, *"Al-Ghazali was called both a Christian and a Jew . . . Al-Ghazali knew Kabbala."*[230]

As the Ashki-Jerrahi's sagaciously narrate, Shaykh Muzaffer himself, with Allah's Grace, is the founder of the Ashki-Jerrahis. Shaykh Nur was the first one to receive inspiration to put the names together, pointing to the reality that was already established by Muzaffer Efendi. "Ashki" is the dervish name of Shaykh Muzaffer, and also his spiritual quality and approach. By bringing this name out, the Ashki-Jerrahis have specified their lineage of transmission through Shaykh Muzaffer, and they acknowledge the fundamental spiritual orientation that defines their community.

Nur's proper name is Shaykh Nur al-Anwar al-Jerrahi, but the *ashk* of "Ashki" was certainly his inheritance, and his gift to us. He acknowledged that the uniqueness of this inheritance constituted a certain kind of "branching" - not substantially separate from the Jerrahi Order which flows through Istanbul, but neither synonymous.

The investiture for such a subtle "branching" was conscious and full; Muzaffer Efendi placed his turban on the head of Nur, saying, *"May everything that has come into me go into him."* Then Efendi did the same for Shaykya Fariha. Shaykh Nur himself describes some of the implications of this transmission for Masjid al-Farah: *"...Muzaffer Efendi loved the West, he loved America. He didn't want to make a situation where everything was in Istanbul: all the power, all the blessings, all the teaching, while there was a little outpost in America . . . He wanted to transfer it completely into the West, without diminishing anything in Istanbul. This meant that he didn't want a drop of possible blessings, possible power, possible transmission, missing in the West. He was totally dedicated. He loved this country, and he saw the dynamics which we see in history now: that America, for all its faults and all its hidden hypocrisies, is still an instrument of the Divine Mercy and would be an instrument of Divine Mercy for the planet."*[231]

Shaykh Nur had his own special spiritual *meshreb* - a unique way of bringing forth Shaykh Muzaffer's radical spirit, in a way that was fitting for Western seekers. However, like Shaykh Muzaffer, Nur would never make any claims or name anything after himself. Only after he passed into the realm of beauty, was his community able to understand the extent of his impression on them - that they are actually "Nur Ashki Jerrahis." This is the proper name that

Allah has inspired Shaykya Fariha to give to this community.

The great Sufi saint Al-Hallāj (whose real name was Hussain Ibn Mansur) began his training in a Hanabalite Qur'anic religious school. Later he became a disciple of the Qur'anic Sunni scholar, Sahl. Hallāj married into a family of Shi'ite Muslims. In Basra, Hallāj learned of other religious traditions. *"It was here that he felt the divisions within his own Muslim tradition that would inspire his later passionate desire for a unified Muslim community and that would ultimately lead to his own martyrdom."*[232] Al-Hallāj had many clashes with his Sufi masters. At one point, he returned to Iran to skirt additional communication with the Sufis. He was comfortable among the wealthy and well-known in society. Many of the wealthy were attracted to his teachings and became patrons. Shaykh Nur had a great love for Jesus ('Alaihi Assalam). The role of Jesus ('Alaihi Assalam) was a theme of Al-Hallāj also.

Al-Hallaj spent his last nine years in prison in Baghdad and was finally condemned as a heretic. Writing about Hallaj, Herbert Mason remarks: *"He represented in this regard a persistent recurrence in Islam of the impulse for universalism versus the fearful retrenchment and consolidation preached by so many of the ascetical and politically motivated traditionalists to the common people and literalists they influenced, if not controlled through their schools. His was the mentality of a traveler who found God as the Host of the worlds and hospitality thus as universal, not merely a cultural phenomenon among Arabs or any other single ethnic group, while many others, both Shi'ite and Sunnite, Persian and Arab, believed God was their Quranic totem exclusive to themselves: the monotheistic sin, as it has been called by modern religious universalists."*

Nur's writings stress the importance of human worth and view Islam not in terms of rigid formulas, but as an immediately available Light from Allah that rises above the heaviness and shackles of those who ceaselessly try to package spiritual gnosis in "should's" and "should not's." He taught that the practice of the Shariat was not to be done out of a sense of heavy obligation, but was a spontaneous desire to remember the Beloved in ways that please the Beloved. Robin Becker reminds us that: *"Breath cannot move through tension."* When we made prayers with Shaykh Nur, the experience was always new, always like we were gathering for the first time to make *namaz*, always a surprising and remarkable celebration of this great gift of prayer.

Molana Salaheddin Ali Nader Shah Angha says in his book "Peace," *". . . there is another way of action and belief - one not bound to custom, tradition, race, personal or social ideologies, yet capable of changing the course of human destiny."*

Shaykh Nur al-Anwar al-Jerrahi ceased his breathing practices on November 1, 1995.

"Beauty will redeem the world."

- Dostoevsky

"Stay away from lies, whether they be small or big, whether serious or in jest, because if a person tells a small lie, he will eventually have to cover it up by telling big lies."

- Imam Zainul Abedeen,
the Fourth Imam

"Following you (Prophet (Peace be upon him)) inequities (intrigues and revolts) took shape and variant voices were raised so that if you were present and supervising (things) all these differences and deviations would not have taken place. You [Muhammad (Peace be upon him)] set off (on the journey of eternity) from among us and now our condition is like the earth which becomes devoid of the beneficial rains. And your nation upset the order and discipline of matters. So be a witness and do not let their matter get out of your sight."

- Fatima ('Alaiha Assalam)

'AESHA AFTER THE PROPHET'S DEMISE [233]

Another important approach in coming to a spiritual understanding of the significance of the Ahlul Bayt is by studying the historical events that occurred after the demise of the Prophet. According to the purification sentence in Qur'an (the last sentence of Verse 33:33), the Ahlul Bayt is free from any dirt and impurity.[234] On the other hand, the documented Sunni history testifies that 'Aesha (one of the wives of the Prophet) was not righteous. If we examine her life after the death of the Prophet, we will find her misconduct more horrible than what she did during the lifetime of the Messenger of Allah (Peace be upon him). Clearly, 'Aesha was not one of the Ahlul Bayt.

Undoubtedly, one of her most terrible wrongdoings was instigating the Battle of Camel during the Khalifate of Imam Ali ('Alaihi Assalam). 'Aesha permitted the killing of innocent people, and led the first civil war against Imam Ali ('Alaihi Assalam) who people chose as Khalif. The result was the massacre of thousands of Muslims.[235] They named the battle "Camel" (Jamal) since 'Aesha was riding a Camel to lead the rebels. How can she be pure when she fought against the legitimate Khalif of his time and when she is responsible for shedding the blood of more than 10,000 Muslims? What impurity can be imagined greater than this horrible *Fitna* that caused to disunite the Muslim Umma once and forever. Let us first briefly discuss the event proceeding this strife.

'Aesha claimed that the reason for her rise against Imam Ali ('Alaihi Assalam) (which was manifested in the battle of Camel) was getting revenge

Assalam) (which was manifested in the battle of Camel) was getting revenge of the blood of Uthman. Yet, the history testifies that 'Aesha herself was one of the main figures of agitation against Uthman that ended with his murder. Once she went to Uthman and asked for her share of inheritance from the Prophet (after so many years passed from the death of the Prophet). Uthman refrained to give 'Aesha any money, and reminded her that she was one of those who counseled Abu Bakr not to pay the share of inheritance of Fatima al-Zahra ('Alaihi Assalam). So if Fatima ('Alaiha Assalam) does not have any share, then why should she? Hearing this, 'Aesha became very angry with Uthman, and came out and said to the people, *"Kill this old fool (Na'thal), for he is an unbeliever."* [236]

Some traditions in "Sahih al-Bukhari" imply to the reader that the dislike of 'Aesha toward Imam Ali ('Alaihi Assalam) was because Ali ('Alaihi Assalam) suggested that the Prophet divorce her. The Prophet was about to divorce her because he himself found her troublesome since 'Aesha and Hafsa backed each other against the Prophet to the extent that Allah sent down a revelation in this regard. She often used to offend the Prophet (Peace be upon him) and caused him distress, but the Prophet (Peace be upon him) was compassionate and kind, his character lofty, his patience deep, therefore he frequently said to her, *"Your Satan has confused you, O 'Aesha."* Nevertheless, the Prophet (Peace be upon him) did not divorce her.

She even recruited twenty thousand or more riotous and greedy Arabs to fight and depose the Commander of the Faithful. Her urging resulted in zealous discord, where they killed many people in the name of defending and aiding the mother of the believers. The historians say that when the companions of 'Aesha came to Uthman Ibn Hunaif, the governor of Basra, they took him along with seventy of his officers who were in charge of the public treasury as prisoners. They brought them to 'Aesha who ordered that they be put to death. They slaughtered them as they slaughter sheep. It is even reported there were four hundred men in all and that they were the first Muslims whose heads they cut off while they were patient.

Ibn Abi'l-Hadid, in his "Sharh," along with other historians, reported that 'Aesha sent a letter when she was in Basra to Zaid Ibn Sawhan al-'Abdi in which she said to him, *"From 'Aesha, the mother of the believers, daughter of Abu Bakr, the truthful one, wife of the Prophet. To her devoted son, Zaid Ibn Sawhan. Remain at home and make the people abandon the son of Abu Talib. I hope to hear what I would love from you, since you are the most trustworthy of my family . . . Wassalam."*

'Aesha was not content with leading the army in the battle of the Camel, but she craved for absolute control over the believers in all the corners of the land. In all matters, she would command Talha and al-Zubair, whom Umar had nominated for the Khalifate. Due to this, she made it lawful for herself to correspond with the chiefs of the tribes and with the governors, enticing them and seeking their help. If the heroes and men, famous for their courage, would abandon and flee from the lines of battle when facing Imam Ali ('Alaihi Assalam) and would not stand in front of him, she stood, inciting, screaming and arousing the people.

Why did 'Aesha hate Imam Ali ('Alaihi Assalam)? History has recorded some of her aggressive actions that could not be explained. When she was on her way back to Macca (al-Mukarramah), she heard that the plot to kill Uthman finally took place, so she became very delighted. However, when she heard that people had chosen Imam Ali ('Alaihi Assalam) to succeed him, she became very angry and said, *"I wish the sky would collapse on the earth before son of Abu Talib (i.e., Ali) could succeed the Khalifate."* Then she said, *"Take me back,"* and thus she started the civil war against Imam Ali ('Alaihi Assalam) whose name she disliked to mention. Sunni traditionalists narrated that: when Ubaydullah Ibn Utbah mentioned to Ibn Abbas that 'Aesha said *"In his death-illness the Prophet was brought to ('Aesha's) house while his shoulders were being supported by Fadhl Ibn Abbas and another person,"* Then Abdullah Ibn Abbas said, *"Do you know who this 'other man' was?"* Ibn Utbah replied, *"No."* Then Ibn Abbas said, *"He was Ali Ibn Abu Talib, but she is averse to name him in a good context."*

'Aesha's hatred for Imam Ali ('Alaihi Assalam) was so great that she always tried to distance him from the Prophet (Peace be upon him) whenever she could find the means to do so. Ibn Abi'l-Hadid also reported that one day the Prophet of Allah (Peace be upon him) was walking with Imam Ali ('Alaihi Assalam) and the conversation became prolonged. 'Aesha approached as she was walking from behind until she came between them saying, *"What is it between you two that you are taking so long?"* Upon this, the Prophet of Allah (Peace be upon him) became angry.

They have also reported that she once came upon the Prophet (Peace be upon him) while he was conversing quietly with Ali. She screamed and said, *"What is it with you and me, O son of Abu Talib? I have [just] one day with the Prophet of Allah (Peace be upon him)."* Then the Prophet (Peace be upon him) became angry.

Would the Prophet (Peace be upon him) be pleased with any believing man or woman whose heart was filled with hatred and malice toward his cousin, the leader of his progeny, about whom he said, *"He loves Allah and His Prophet, and Allah and His Prophet love him"*? He also said about him, *"Whoever loves Ali has loved me, and whoever hates Ali has hated me."* Had 'Aesha not heard the saying of the Prophet about Ali ('Alaihi Assalam) that *"None but a believer would love him, and none but a hypocrite would nurse a grudge against him"*?[237] This saying of the Prophet was so well known that some companions used to say, *"We recognized the hypocrites by their hatred of Ali.*"[238] Moreover, had 'Aesha not heard the saying of the Prophet, *"Whoever I am his master, Ali is his master. O God! Love those who love him and be hostile to those who are hostile to him?"*[239] Undoubtedly she heard all of them. Nevertheless, she did not like them, and when she heard of the assassination of Imam Ali ('Alaihi Assalam), she knelt and thanked Allah! [240]

PRACTICE

You must set aside moments each day in which you will be alone and without distraction. You need quiet time to be with yourself. The point of this exercise is to encounter yourself. Turn off the telephone and any other apparatus which may cause disturbance. There is to be no interruption in this exercise.

Before you begin this exercise, make sure you have gone to the lavatory to relieve yourself. Find a comfortable place to sit, but not so comfortable that you will fall asleep. If you choose a chair, make sure that both feet are flat on the floor. If you prefer, you may sit in the lotus or half-lotus yoga posture.

The goal of this exercise is to sit with yourself. In other words, you are simply going to be with yourself for the duration of the exercise. It does not matter what you think about or do not think about. Just sit there. We suggest beginning with fifteen minutes for the first time, and gradually working up to two or more hours.

Often spiritual seekers demand that they be given a specific set of tasks to do in a meditation. They want mantras or yantras, chakras or mandalas upon which to meditate. This exercise is not meditation in that sense. This exercise is much more powerful, for with this exercise you encounter YOURSELF. This exercise is an ancient shamanic ritual in which the Murid meets him or herself face-to-face.

In some initiations, the Murid will sit with him or herself for up to three days. Lest you think that these rigorous initiations were only done in times past, they are today practicing initiations such as this in the Yoruban syncretistic religion known as Santeria. A candidate will be bound and bandaged up in a way that limits movement and to block sensory awareness. A guide is present throughout the time, usually a weekend, to help with drinking water, elimination, and any emergencies. Through such a restriction of movement and sensory deprivation, the candidate has a profound confrontation with the spirit world.

"The man stands between life and death.
The man thinks.
The horse thinks.
The sheep thinks.
The cow thinks.
The dog thinks.
The fish doesn't think.
The fish is mute,
Expressionless.
The fish doesn't think because
The fish knows,
Everything."

> *- Goran Bregovic, soundtrack*
> *composer of "Arizona Dream"*

"What is more real, the love manifested in the Son, the Savior, for His brethren, or the essence of love that may be seen even in the vilest of passion? They are one."

> *- Edgar Cayce*

"Those who ignore the sword
shall also perish by it.
Who will teach us the path
of wholeness and balance?"

> *- Anonymous*

TALES FROM UNDER THE OVERPASS

One day Sam and Mr. Khadir witnessed a distressing sight. They were at an outdoor Fish Market and saw a thief, wielding a large knife, robbing a Fish Merchant and his wife. The thief, unhappy with the few dollars that the merchant turned over, showed his displeasure by slashing the merchant's wife.

The merchant went berserk, taking up a knife which he was using to clean fish and challenged the thief. The merchant fought valiantly, but he was not used to fighting. Gradually the thief slashed the merchant all over his body, and the merchant was losing blood and becoming faint. A powerful blow from the thief knocked the merchant to the ground. With a giant lunge, the thief unleashed a lethal thrust, but at the last second the merchant recoiled and the thief's blade lodged into the side of the fish cart.

The merchant raised his cutlery knife to the thief's neck. The thief, helpless on the ground, spat in the merchant's face.

The merchant dropped his knife, relaxed and helped the man to his feet.

The thief gasped, "Why have you spared me? How has lightening contracted back into its cloud? Speak, sir, so that my soul can begin to stir in me like an embryo."

The fish-merchant spoke these words to the thief: "I am God's servant, not the servant of passion. I have no longing except for the One. When a wind of personal reaction comes, I do not go along with it. There are many winds full of anger, and lust and greed. They move the rubbish around, but the solid mountain of our true nature stays where it's always been. There's nothing now except the divine qualities come through the opening into me. Your impudence was better than any reverence, because in this moment, I am you and you are me. I give you this opened heart as God gives gifts: the poison of your spit has become the honey of friendship."

The thief burst into tears and embraced the merchant.

"He should have killed him then and there," Sam declared.

"While a man still has life, he has the opportunity to achieve that perfection for which he was created, so that whoever tries to destroy him is seeking to prevent his achieving that for which he was made," Mr. Khadir counseled.

"But that thief could have killed the fish merchant," Sam argued back.

"There's no one to be hurt," Mr. Khadir remarked casually.

"What? Killing that thief would have prevented him from coming back and robbing someone else!" Sam exclaimed boldly.

"Shall I tell you of something much better than attacking the enemy? It is the remembrance of God."

"He's still a villain," exclaimed Sam.

"Why do you call him villain?" responded Mr. Khadir.

"What the thief did was wrong and immoral and he deserves to be punished!"

"Ah, I understand what you mean, but be careful . . . to divide the world into nice guys and bullies is to create a duality that can only bring you discouragement," Mr. Khadir suggested, "for when people act in these destructive ways they do so because they are mentally challenged, ignorant or emotionally disturbed. Yes, they do indeed harm other people, but can we blame them for being mentally challenged, ignorant or emotionally disturbed?"

"I'm listening," said Sam.

"All human beings are by their nature fallible and therefore will at some time or other act out of mental limitation, ignorance or emotional disturbance. Should we vilify them just because they are human beings?"

"No?" questioned Sam.

"If the person who is committing misdeeds is mentally challenged,

then no matter what we say or do, there is little hope to reeducate him or her, so therefore we must accept and respect this person as a human being. If a person is ignorant or disturbed in some way, our goal should be to help them out of their ignorance or faulty thinking. Truth, teachings and the whole of existence together form a hand. When an ignorant person looks at the hand he or she might see that each finger is unlike the other and will not notice the movement of the hand itself. Therefore, the task of the teacher is to speak to each person according to the level of his or her understanding. Remembering that there is a positive intention beneath every behavior is helpful."

"I think you are a bit deluded on that point, Mr. Khadir," Sam declared, "I've seen certain human beings who seem to deliberately want to hurt other people."

Mr. Khadir answered, "Oh definitely, people can behave in destructive ways, however their inner intention is positive in that they are trying to take care of themselves in the best way they know how. There is a difference between behavior and its intention. All hatred is merely a self-hatred. All resentment is only resentment of self. We are all those other conscious beings. We have to learn to respond to every stimulus out of love. Otherwise, we're just bashing ourselves. You may want to examine your thinking to weed out thinking which is irrational and illogical. Most human emotional suffering and self-destructive behavior are based on faulty thinking and old assumptions. Like other opposites of experience, good and evil are also in a sense opposites that have to be withstood and transcended. One has to rise above the duality of good and evil and accept life in its totality, in which they appear as abstractions. Life is to be seen and lived in its indivisible integrity. All beings derive from Allah; He is their Essence. Therefore, consider your opinions carefully."

"You've suddenly put new light on a problem that I've been facing for years. I blamed my guru for stealing from our ashram and for abusing the women. Yet you are teaching me a much more spiritual and constructive way to look at human behavior."

"You came like a lamb to the Ashram. But don't forget, you have a wolf within you as well. Look, can you find the force to enable these two quite opposite lives to live togther?" asked Mr. Khadir.

"I will endeavor will all my might," declared Sam.

"This approach is not just helpful in dealing with other people Sam," offered Mr. Khadir, "but apply it to yourself. When you make a mistake, do not start calling yourself a worthless shit who can't do anything right. Simply acknowledge the mistake and ask yourself how you can learn from this fumble and do better next time. Recall to yourself that every human being makes mistakes from time to time. Rather than saying bad things to yourself that make you feel removed from the human race, tell yourself that by your error you just

proved that you are a part of the experience of each man and woman on this planet."

"Oh I would feel a lot better doing that, than beating myself over the head each time I did something wrong," remarked Sam.

"Every human on the face of the earth contains within himself or herself both the forces of construction and destruction. When unpleasant things happen, just continue to breathe and remember the name ya Ahad, *the One. I do not mean to suggest that you should like evil, but you must accept it. Know that all is occurring as a spontaneous revelation of the Living Unity."*

"You know what has to be done. Why don't you do it?"
- Paul Williams

"Don't compromise yourself. You are all you've got."
- Janis Joplin

"Love, my child, is not a work
of soft politesse, but of chivalry;
& he who becomes a lover's slave
acquires the horoscope of a prince."
- Jelaluddin Rumi

THE ESSENTIAL LIFE

One goal of the daily time of contemplation is to become aware of the essential in life, to become aware of that, which does not change upon death. If you can find that which is eternal in yourselves, suddenly your lives will have attained much significance and meaning.

You have the means to direct knowledge of the spiritual worlds. You have the senses that will help you to perceive these subtle spheres. It only remains for you to develop your sleeping powers. The question should not be *"is there life after death"*; it should be *"what am I doing to awaken my faculties to perceive the spirit worlds?"*

We propose that the Sufi should be a complete human being. You need to work on yourself, in all your aspects, as much as on developing yourself spiritually. The possibility of your advancement is directly connected to the way you live your life.

You need holistically to awaken all the powers resident in your being. You must work on the body physically (get in shape), while you are learning your various spiritual practices and ceremonies. A regular daily workout regimen is as important as memorizing a *sura* from the Qur'an.

You need to develop a ruthless honesty about yourself. The last person on earth that you should deceive is yourself. You must be true to yourself and know your own "truth." You must know what you think about any given situation without obstruction in the form of denial, egotism and rationalization. The Murid must cultivate a quality of self-knowing and sincerity.

ن

PRACTICE

Try doing without your sunglasses. The Great Guides have said that sunglasses diminish your perception of the sun's light on the earth, and by that adversely affect your experience of the Inner Light. Those people who have light sensitivities or those people who are taking medications that cause light sensitivities should not practice (this exercise). Open your eyes and see the Light!

Natural light stimulates the pineal gland, the gland that we mysteriously connect to the "third eye" chakra location. The pineal gland balances the processes in the body. Ancient people knew it as the single eye. Fifty years ago the medical community in the USA had no idea what purpose the Pineal Gland served. René Descartes said that it is the place in the human body where humankind and God meet. René Descartes discovered the fundamental law of reflection in optics. He also discovered the scale of incidence of angle and the law of refraction. He paved the way for the discovery of the theory of light. In Genesis 32:30, Jacob says, *"I have seen God face to face and I will call the place Peniel."* (For those couples who are having trouble conceiving, natural light is helpful for reproduction).

The best times to do this exercise are in the morning before 10:00 A.M. and in the afternoon after 3:00 P.M. This is because the intensity of the sun's light during the middle part of the day can damage the eyes without the aid of proper sunglasses.

As humans, shiny objects, especially gold and silver have always fascinated us. The glistening reflected light reminds us of the spirit world. The Murid can also find an expression of the Divine through the computer generated images of fractals and other digitally generated shifting polychromatic presentations.

We have heard the Sheikhs say that many Murids come to them asking for a flashlight in the middle of the day. May Allah Most High protect us from spiritual blindness. Some Murids are so focused on obtaining the flashlight that they do not see that the sun is shining all around them. Kabir writes, *"I laugh when I hear that the fish in the water is thirsty."*

"You should not have your own idea when you listen to someone . . . to have nothing in your mind is naturalness. Then you will understand what he says."

- Shunryu Suzuki

"Humility is the crown of manhood."

- Medieval Arabic Proverb

DISCERNMENT

The Sufi listens with quiet esteem to someone who is speaking. Just because you do not immediately reply with your own opinion will not lower your status in the conversation. Try to let go of the need to react in an opinionated way to the position of the speaker. The Divine Presence reveals in the Book of Life, *"[Allah is] Listening, Knowing."*[242] Therefore, Divine Presence is communicating to us that It places listening before knowledge and sight.[243]

In the act of judging something, you are telling yourself that you already know this information and that someone is doing something wrong or incorrectly, or that something does not meet what you consider are the proper standards. However, ponder this: if you already know this information, why the need to repeat it to yourself constantly and reinforce it?

You are preaching to the converted (in other words – yourself) if you walk around judging everything. Why the need to repeat to yourself what you already know? There is a kind of perverse quality to being judgmental. It implies a need to reassure oneself of one's standards. Judging others comes from a place of insecurity. You know what you know. You do not need to keep calling attention to the fact (to yourself or others). Judging others comes from a need to feel secure within oneself and within one's environment.

"One judges others on grounds of that which one thinks as being right or wrong, but one does not realize that one's judgement is based on that which one has learned from others, whereas what is wrong for one person could very well be right for another. Besides, that which might be right at one time might be wrong at another time, and what is more, one's insight can change day by day in accordance with one's spiritual development," taught Pir-o-Murshid Inayat Khan.[244]

When you are with a person, attempt to quiet your mind completely and allow yourself to experience the person, in your mind's eye, standing before you in their totality. Often your judgmental thoughts are ways that you prevent yourselves from feeling your feelings for a certain person. The danger lies in judging what one does not understand. Often you dismiss something that is unusual or unconventional. Withholding judgments in such a case is far better, than to form a premature (and often mistaken) judgment.

For instance, if Bohemian and Avant-garde people subconsciously intrigue you, but because these feelings are incompatible with your political and world-views, then you might find yourself making disparaging jokes and put-downs whenever you see an eccentric person. You must search for the eternal behind the fleeting opinion. In things you do not like there is an aspect of further movement and further development. The Sufi must have a firm grip on the unchanging, and he or she must leave the opinionated rhetoric to the talk shows.

"Some of us, observing that ideals are rarely achieved, proceed to the error of considering them worthless. Such an error is greatly harmful. True north cannot be reached either, since it is an abstraction, but it is of enormous importance, as all the world's travelers can attest."
- Steve Allen

"If individuals wish to draw near to God, they must seek God in the hearts of human beings. They should speak well of all persons, whether present or absent, and if they themselves seek to be a light to guide others, then, like the sun, they must show the same face to all. To bring joy to a single heart is better then to build many shrines for worship, and to enslave one soul by kindness is worth more than the setting free of a thousand slaves.

That is the true person of God, who sits in the midst of other people, and rises up and eats and sleeps and buys and sells and gives and takes in the bazaars amongst other people, and who marries and has social intercourse with other folk, and yet is never for one moment forgetful of God."
- Abu Sa'id b. Abi 'l-Khair

THE NAME ON THE MOON

Our late father's childhood was spent in St. Charles Hospital for children with polio. The doctors told him and his three sisters they would never walk. Our father cheered them up with his sense of humor, got them all up and out of bed, and helped them to learn to walk. He taught himself how to walk without the need for braces or a cane. While he loved sports, he could never run for the rest of his life. However, he persevered and went on to play waterpolo, softball, basketball, and table tennis, using his ability to develop winning strategies. Later he won many table tennis championships. He was a brave man who continually beat the odds by refusing to let his disability keep him down. Throughout his life he had a deep devotion to the Prophet Jesus (Peace be upon him) and led his life according to high moral values.

He worked for Grumman Aerospace for more than thirty-five years. In the 1960's they gave Grumman the contract to build the Lunar Module (the spacecraft that landed on the moon). With the "race to the moon" on, Grumman built the Lunar Module twenty-four hours a day, with two shifts of workers: a day shift and a night shift. Grumman Aerospace gave our father the title of Supervisor of Quality Control and he was in charge of supervising the night crew.

When we were a young boy of about ten, our father took us into the "white room" at Grumman Aerospace to see all the Lunar Modules being built. We had to wear special "scrubs" so as not to get any dust or pollution into the spacecrafts. What we recall was the size of these vehicles. They were much larger than we had imagined from pictures in books and what we saw on television. Moreover, in this one room there must have been approximately ten of them all in various stages of completion. The moment was both awe-inspiring and a bit frightening as these huge spacecrafts took shape all around us.

The movie "Apollo XIII" dramatized how the Lunar Module, also known as the LEM because of its earlier incarnation as the Lunar Excursion Module, became a lifeboat to the three astronauts when part of the Service Module exploded. The astronauts were truly lost in space two hundred three thousand, nine hundred and eight miles from earth. They had named the LEM the "Aquarius."

The main ship's computers were out and the astronauts had no means of determining their position. The LEM's computer, when fed the coordinates of the sun, was able to calculate the location of the Apollo spacecraft in space. Designed to support two men for a day and a half while on the moon, the LEM did what the engineers never designed it to do: act as a space ship to take the astronauts around the moon and back to the earth, while carrying three men!

As Buzz Aldrin said as they made their final separation from the Lunar Module before re-entering the atmosphere of the earth, *"She sure was a good ship; farewell Aquarius and we thank you."*

One day in 1968 our father wrote his name on a piece of paper, and placed it in the first lunar lander. There were two sections of the LEM: a lower part that contained the legs of the lunar lander, and an upper part that detached and blasted off from the moon to rendezvous with the Command Module (mother ship) orbiting around the moon. It was in the lower section that our father put his name. Today our father's name is on the moon! We are proud of our father's accomplishments in helping human beings to journey to the moon.

Our Dad went on to help assemble the F-111 and the F-14 fighter jets, and become a consultant to the Navy. They sent him to Wigby Island in the state of Washington and Oceania in Virginia Beach to supervise the installation of the A-6 fighter jet simulator before retiring. While in Washington, he had the opportunity to observe the volcanic eruption of Mount Saint Helens.

However, for us, his greatest accomplishments were the changes he helped make in men who came to him for his advice. These were often troubled, broken men, some from alcohol, broken marriages, drugs, and one fellow whose wife abandoned him. Our father helped these men to repair their lives and get back on their feet. They remained devoted, lifelong friends to our father.

PRACTICE

Place a seed in front of you. **Study the seed as to its shape and color, and other characteristics. Say to yourself,** *"When I plant this seed in soil, after a while, something will occur. Out from this seed will grow a plant of great intricacy. What now only exists in my imagination, will when put into the soil, be induced from the seed by natural forces. If I placed before myself an artificial object that mimicked the appearance of the seed, the natural forces could not produce from the artificial seed a plant."*

Hear the words from the sacred Qur'an: *"O my son, consider this tiny mustard seed, which God would bring forth were it to be [hidden] in a rock, whether in heaven or earth."* [245]

After a few days of doing the above exercise begin to add this thought, *"Secretly hidden inside this seed is the entire plant. Hidden inside the* <u>artificial</u> *seed are no such forces. Yet, both appear to be the same in my consciousness. The seed then, must contain something that is not present in the artificial seed.*

"This invisible something will emerge subsequently into a visible plant. The invisible forces will become visible. If it were not for my ability to contemplate, these invisible forces would only make themselves known as a fully-grown plant. Nevertheless, because Allah has permitted humanity to ponder His Manifestation, I am aware of these hidden forces now!"

"By God, if there is a veil, it is the tariqa. As soon as a person leaves them, God grants him illumination. Our brother, Abu 'Majdhub, was one of them, then he left them and God granted him illumination. Our brother, Musa al-Majdhub, left them and God granted him illumination."
- Ibn Idris

"Trying is not the way Nature functions. The Earth doesn't try to go around the sun, nor does the seed try to sprout into a sapling. Nature functions with effortless ease, invariably taking the path of least resistance."
- Unknown

TALES FROM UNDER THE OVERPASS

*M*r. *Khadir spoke: "I want you to have more life, not less. I am painful because I am stretching you, not constricting you. My goal is not to turn you into some kind of anal-retentive robotic masochistic machine performing thousands of prayers every day. My goal is to awaken you to the full significance of who you are.*

"People erect so many barriers to ecstasy that it hurts, really hurts them to knock these barriers down. For some, it is even easier to accept the restriction of orthodoxy than to allow themselves to know their full potential. Religion is safe. I am dangerous. I am a corrosive factor.

"Many Teachers will tell you that you should submit to the Teacher-Student relationship. Nevertheless, look around you. What do you see? Everywhere you see Students dependent upon their Teachers. I say, what good is this? This dependence is no better than narcissistic independence.

"A balance must be struck. Some students who appear the most devout and submissive are secretly gloating over their 'spirituality'! Many of them develop a superior attitude. This sort of submission is only veiled egotism. After all, how can the Murid become a Complete Human Being if part of him or herself is still co-dependently attached to a Teacher? That fledgling has not reached complete maturity and eventually must leave the nest.

"It is the same way with the people who don't think they need a Teacher. They are fools, for they are like lunatics who think they can climb the Mount Everest without a guide. But those mountain-climbers are also lunatics if they think their mountain guide has the right to tell them what car to buy! The Murid must establish boundaries in his or her life. It is our capacity for individuality that makes us unique. We must cherish our individuality, rather than submerge it into the group-mind of the tekke, ashram or zendo. As Ibn 'Arabi taught, our individuality is the unique expression of our particular Lord. The Murid's first responsibility is to his or her own true self, not to any teacher or group. Beware of the group-mind. For ultimately, it is YOU who must face

Allah on the Day of Judgement; the Sheikh and other dervishes must account for their own deeds that day. The Murid's second responsibility is to find a Sheikh who will develop, nurture and encourage the Murid's relationship with his or her particular Lord, rather than strip the Murid of his or her independence and individuality. The Heart of the Murid is the Ultimate Sheikh. Disobey that, my friend, and you betray your own Reality.

"The True Guide is not a person but a process. He or she is a dissolving process. The True Guide dissolves all that keeps you from finding yourself. The False Guide dissolves all that makes you unique and independent, in order to make you dependent on him or her.

"In human individuality lies humankind's greatness. Allah has made us each of us Vice-Regents on the Earth, each with a special purpose and mission. Allah has not made us drones in a faceless collective. So, don't join or be part of a faceless collective! Find the One in your distinctive singularity."

*"The problem is, we've lost our spirituality. We've lost contact with our-
selves, and what our purpose for existence is. We've lost contact with God.
And I don't mean God as a man with a beard, a father, a punisher, but God
as a Source, a Spirit, a stream of energy and light that links all things. We
feel empty. We have a huge hole in ourselves. I don't know anyone who
doesn't have a huge emptiness in their lives."*

- Nadja [246]

*"The only courage in life
that matters is the kind
that gets you from one
minute to the next."*

- Mignon McLaughlin

*"Nobility is a matter of good intellect and good conduct, not of lineage and
descent."*

*- Imam Ali ('Alaihi
Assalam)* [247]

CLEAR THINKING ABOUT LIFE'S PROBLEMS

Allah does everything if we surrender to Him. Do not depend on your intellect, wealth or health. Be true to your word. Provide for other people. May
Allah make you a beautiful human being.

If you are agitated and distraught about a problem in your life, ask
yourself, *"Why do I believe I must be terribly upset when I have a large problem?"* Analyze what beliefs your parents, society and culture have installed in
you that tell you that you must be upset when you have a large problem.

Some folks desperately want to find answers. They become distracted
from their life goals and are redirected to seeking "answers." Wouldn't you
rather have a fulfilling life, than to have a list of "answers"?

Your "problems" can grow into a monster that steals your life, which
steals your energy and keeps you prisoner, the rest of your life. Will you sign
your life away? Some folks live a terribly sad life as a way of visibly acting out
the pain that their parents caused them. However, what is the point of this?
Why continue the pain any longer? They think that the solution is to punish
their parents. Some people think that the solution is to make the world aware
of their pain. Better to bestow upon yourself a loving functional life, than a life
lived in sadness, bewilderment and insanity.

Is this your life or your problems' life? It is time to say *"enough is enough"* and to go out and have a life for yourself.

Feeling an appropriate emotional reaction to your problems is perfectly normal; what is not helpful is when you blow your emotional reaction up into an enormous size by telling yourself that things are absolutely horrible, terrible and awful. The Sufis are aware of how and what they tell themselves; they are aware of their "self-talk."

Most important, the way to emotional health is through *tavekul*, or Trust in Allah. To make your problems so large that they take over your life is to make your set of problems into an idol. Release and surrender those problems into the Prior Unity. Have utter trust in your Source. Do not worship any god but Allah, in other words, do not fall into the error of veiling your connection to Allah by drawing a curtain of obsession with your problems between you and Allah. You will by that cut off your spiritual energy and connection to the Ultimate Reality. In addition, do not fall into the error that you must solve your problems, falsely believing (but unconsciously) that Allah cannot help you. Allahu ta'ala alone has all power. You are not alone.

PRACTICE

Place a fully-grown plant in front of yourself. Say to yourself, *"Eventually there will be nothing left of this plant in front of me. It will have withered and died. However, this plant will have produced seeds that will develop into new plants. Again I realize that within something I see - the living plant, is hidden something I do not see - the new plant. The plant that is before me will not wither away into nothingness, although that may be the appearance on the physical plane. An indwelling force continues beyond the outward death of the plant."*

Eventually you can be confident that doing exercises such as this will lead to the development of profound sensibilities that will ripen into the opening of the spiritual senses.

"I am sure that 'initiations' taught nothing but a 'key' to reading the word 'death' without a negative prefix. Like the moon, life has a face that we cannot see and that is not its opposite, but its complement, as it provides it with perfection and completeness, making it into an intact and whole sphere symbolizing being."
> *- Rainer Maria Rilke*

"Walk the path you believe in without fear."
> *- El-Hajj Şerif er-Rıfa'i*

"Please, O my Beloved Lord,
allow me a glimpse of your shadow:
Let me taste of Thy nectar.
Your fragrance, so near, intoxicates my waiting heart."
> *- Sheikh Husayn abd'ur-Rıfa'i*

"The shadow's reality is the reflection of the Essential Being. If there is no essence, there can be no shadow. That is why you should know your shadow well, so you can see your essence."
> *- El-Hajj Şerif er-Rıfa'i*

COMPLENTARITY

If you are to accept that embracing the Sacred Dark is as necessary as embracing the Sacred Light, does that mean that it does not matter if you live or die, heal or hurt, love or hate?

In this matter, you would do well to learn a lesson from Mother Nature.

Consider the anabolic and catabolic processes in the body. To function biologically you need catabolic (down-breaking) activities. The Murid dances on his or her grave. Each day a drama unfolds in which billions of your cells die and are excreted from your bodies. Many tiny deaths are taking place each moment so that you can LIVE.

This balance between the upbuilding anabolic activity and the catabolic, down-breaking activity is delicate. The body is always seeking homeostasis. The FULLEST LIFE is not possible without a constructive integration, acceptance and use of the death force.

In life, there are cycles of life and death. For instance, in a relationship, if both partners do not realize that there will be many deaths and rebirths in their relationship, then they will turn and run at the first sign of trouble, in other words: death. However, if they continue, they will realize soon enough that the relationship will be reborn and that life will return to the relationship.

Therefore, to LIVE FULLY, you must *"know your shadow well."*

ﺭ

"Our mind is capable of passing beyond the dividing line we have drawn for it. Beyond the pairs of opposites of which the world consists, other, new insights begin."

- Herman Hesse

"I realized that you have to be out of your mind to pray. That you can't rationalize with a five-billion-year-old process."

- Dr. Timothy Leary, Ph.D.

"And most surely this is a revelation from the Lord of the worlds."

- Qur'an 26:192

"The unbelievably vast and the infinitesimally small, eventually meet."

- from "The Incredible
Shrinking Man."

THE POINT OF TRANSCENDENCE

According to the French physicist Jean Charon,[248] existence should have a dual nature, and that a singular point joins these two realms. Charon calls these two universes the "Real" and the "Imaginary." The point of intersection is the dimensionless fountainhead that gives birth to the forms that inform both things and thoughts.

R. Buckminster Fuller speaks of a "vector equilibrium." He tells us, *"The center of the vector equilibrium is zero. The frequency is zero . . . the center has a value of two. The significance is that it has a concave and a convex. It has both insideness and outsideness congruently. It is as far as you can go. You turn yourself inside out and go in the other direction."*

What Fuller is saying is that as you go into the farthest reaches of space, suddenly you find yourself in the tiniest of subatomic realms, like the head and tail of the Ourobouros serpent.[249] In other words, there is a point at which the farthest limits of scale, the microcosm and the macrocosm, converge and continue into each other without hindrance. At this zero point, the finite and infinite cross paths!

The outside of everything is its inside; the end of everything is its beginning. Perhaps the guests of the Old Man of the Mountain, Hassan-I Sabbah, were given this gnosis when they ended their fasting with wine.

American scientist and inventor, Arthur M. Young distinguishes two domains of reality that he calls (after St. Basil of Caesarea) the *"intelligible world,"* which exists external to time, and the *"sensible world"* which is the world of our five senses. According to St. Basil, these two worlds share *"an intelligible matter"* that he classified as light. Various thinkers have proposed methods by which the two realms may "speak" to one another. Dennis McKenna attributes communication between the quantum level and the conscious mind to Electron Spin Resonance (ESR). Young makes the case for the photon as the quantum of action.

It is significant for Sufis that scientists are now proposing that LIGHT is the means of communication between the realms of existence. A photon is energy from an atom. Scientists destroyed, killed, a photon and it reappeared three feet away. The Associated Press stated: *"Scientists have pulled off a startling trick that looks like Beam Me Up Scotty technology of science fiction. In an Austrian laboratory scientists destroyed bits of light in one place and made perfect replicas appear about 3 feet away."* [250]

A group called "Hidden Meanings" has some interesting speculation on the nature of the photon. What comes to earth from above? Angles of light. What are angles of light? They are photons. What is a photon? A photon is a messenger particle (or as modern systems theory puts it, informational energy carriers). Thus angles of light that come from above and impact on the human brain are called messengers. An "Angel" of Light is obviously an "Angle" of Light. [251]

"When you perceive sounds, you call that light 'hearing.' When you perceive sights, you call that light 'seeing'. When you perceive objects of touch, you call that light 'touch.' So also is the case with objects of imagination . . . The faculties of smell, taste, imagination, memory, reason, reflection, form-giving, and everything through which perception takes place are all light." [252]

Photons do not have mass. They are considered both particles and waves. This shows that they 'straddle' the duality, and go BEYOND DUALITY. Photons travel at LIGHT SPEED and so do not participate in the time-line of any universe. They exist as timeless entities. Peter Lamborn Wilson writes: *"all things are sewn like pearls on threads of living light."* [253] This is one reason that doing your daily shielding practices is so important and to "send light" to those who are sick or in pain.

The presence of Light seems regularly to accompany mystical experience (although not always). Robert Anton Wilson mentions that, *"A synonym for 'illumination' appears in all the mystical writings of every language I have investigated."* Frequently frontal-lobe epileptics describe a "white light." Some academic commentators have suggested that the Prophet Muhammad's (Peace be upon him) revelations occurred during epileptic seizures. However, there is documented and corroborated evidence that when a revelation of the Holy Qur'an came to the Prophet while he was on his camel, the camel fell on his knees with the weight of the message. [254]

The *Tzaddkik*, Tzemach Tzedek related: *"The Baal Shem Tov was very fond of light, and said, 'Or' (Hebrew for 'light') is the Gematria (numerical equivalent) of 'Raz' (Hebrew for 'secret'). Therefore, whoever knows the 'secret' contained in every thing can bring about illumination."*

The initiates at the ancient Geo-Centric Mystery cult at Eleusis were called *Epoptai*, that is, one who has seen the light. When the Murid connects with the Light of Allah through the Ahlul Bayt and the Murshid, the Lights coalesce into something Unified and much more puissant than the Murid. May we all be filled with Light!

PRACTICE

The next step in the Sufi's Way of awakening is to turn your attention to two separate streams of events in the natural world. The first object of your attention should be focused on all that is flourishing and growing in the natural world. The second object of your attention should be focused on all that is dying and decaying. This exercise will focus on the first object of your attention, that is, the sprouting and growing aspect of life.

Preferably, if you have a garden or a park that you can go to, become aware of the growing plants. Notice the way the flowers bloom. It is recommended that you obtain a flowering plant from a garden center or grow one from seed or bulb. As you gaze at the beautiful blossom, allow the feelings that arise in your soul to reverberate through you. Quiet your mind and focus your attention upon the effect the flower has upon you. You want to be sensitive to the way that this scene affects your inner being.

Do not forget to use all your senses. Inhale deeply the fragrance of the blossom. Touch the petals with your hands.

First, look with total intent and attentiveness. Then close your eyes and let yourself become absorbed in the feeling that arises in your inner being.

The organs of psychic perception grow from these feelings taking place in your inner being, just as the physical organs in your body grow from the food you feed the body. The organs of spiritual sight and hearing are built up from the sensations that arise when you do this meditation, provided you allow them to develop in a gentle and slow way. You can no more force these organs to develop than you can force a seed to grow in the soil! Time and patience are the keys.

"The guru has to keep dropping-out of the guru role and shocking follow-ers out of their piety and jarring them, and he can never stay virtuously predictable."

- Dr. Timothy Leary, Ph.D.

"much madness is divinest sense—
to a discerning eye ... "

- emily dickinson

"To gain respect act insane."

- Moroccan Proverb

TALES FROM UNDER THE OVERPASS

*S*am and Mr. Khadir were walking along a residential side street and Mr. Khadir started knocking over garbage cans. After he had knocked over the tenth garbage can and was surrounded with garbage, a police patrol car stopped and a policewoman got out of the car. She approached Mr. Khadir and said, "You are obviously aware of why I stopped. Do you have anything to say?"

Mr. Khadir said, "Officer, it is known to all that a person's behavior is always taken as an index of his or her value. This has reached such a stage in our society that a person has to do no more to gain acclaim and approval than to behave in a certain manner, no matter what his inner state may be. Conversely, if a man or woman merely does something considered objection-able, he or she is regarded as objectionable."

"What's your name?" asked the officer.

"Nobody, the son of Nobody," answered Mr. Khadir.

"He's crazy," the policewoman whispered under her breath.

Sam heard what she said and responded, "He's not crazy; we are crazy."

The officer wrote Mr. Khadir a summons to appear in court.

Later, when the policewoman had left, Mr. Khadir said to Sam, "If you can't change city hall, then change yourself."

*"Your authority (wali) is God and his Apostle and those believers who per-
form the prayer and pay alms (zakat) while they are bowing (in prayer)."*
- Qur'an 5:55

"I am the city of knowledge and Ali is it's gate"
- The Prophet Muhammad (Peace
be upon him)

*"Ali is always with the Truth (haqq) and the Qur'an, and the Truth and the
Qur'an are always with him until the Day of Judgement they will not be
separated from each other."*
- The Prophet Muhammad (Peace
be upon him) [255]

*"I have been commanded by Allah to announce this to you. Know you all,
of whomsoever I am Master, Ali is his Master."*
- The Prophet Muhammad (Peace
be upon him)

*"The Commander of the Faithful Ali b. Abi Talib, had he been at leisure
from the wars to attend to us, there would have been transmitted to us from
him such secrets of this science as our hearts could not support. He was a
man to whom had been given the science divine."*
- Al-Junaid

"The mention of Ali is prayer."
- The Prophet Muhammad (Peace
be upon him)

"No one is diminished by the Truth, rather does the Truth ennoble all."
- al-Kindi

THE COMMANDER OF THE FAITHFUL [256]

Ali b. Abu Talib ('Alaihi Assalam), the Commander of the Faithful, the first
of the Imams of the believers, was born in the Sacred House (the Ka'ba)
in Macca (al-Mukarramah) Friday, the thirteenth day of the month of Rajab.
Nobody before or after him has ever been born in the House of God, the Most
High.

A serious famine hit Macca (al-Mukarramah). One day the Holy
Prophet, whom Allah had not yet declared as Prophet, told his uncle Abbas that
the latter's brother Abu Talib had too many children and his means of liveli-

hood were also narrow, so each of them should ask him to give him one child to support, so that the heavy burden on his dear uncle might be reduced. Abbas agreed, and both of them went to see Abu Talib ('Alaihi Assalam), and told him the reason of their visit. Abu Talib accepted their offer. The Holy Prophet took the responsibility of bringing up Ali ('Alaihi Assalam). Maliki goes on to say in these words, *"Ali ('Alaihi Assalam) remained continuously with the Holy Prophet till the latter was formally declared Prophet of Allah."* So Ali ('Alaihi Assalam) declared his faith in him, and followed him, and acknowledged him as Prophet of Allah, when Ali ('Alaihi Assalam) was only thirteen years old, and had not reached the age of manhood. He was the first person among the men, who accepted Islam and faith in the Holy Prophet, after the Holy Prophet's wife Khadija.

He was the son-in-law of the Prophet Muhammad (Peace be upon him), being married to the Prophet's daughter Fatima the Radiant ('Alaiha Assalam) Mistress of the Women of the Universe. The state of Ali's humbleness was such that his diet consisted of bread made of barley and clothes knitted from date leaves. He hated worldly interests and this world meant nothing to him. Khwarizami in his book "Kitabul Manaqib" has narrated the Holy Prophet (Peace be upon him) as having said *"O Ali, God adorned you with such characteristics that none other can possess them."*

Clearly, the Prophet Muhammad (Peace be upon him) loved Ali ('Alaihi Assalam) dearly and brought him up with special care. The Prophet would regularly meet with Ali ('Alaihi Assalam) to teach him mystic wisdom. The Prophet informed Ali ('Alaihi Assalam) that Allah had required him to befriend Ali ('Alaihi Assalam) and to teach him all he had received from Allah as a Prophet. *"You too should take care in learning and recording what I have taught you. Allah will certainly approve your endeavors,"* so spoke the Prophet to his beloved Ali ('Alaihi Assalam).[257] To that purpose the Prophet assigned a special hour in the night and the day when Ali ('Alaihi Assalam) used to present himself to the Prophet to learn from him.[258]

"Every book," Ali ('Alaihi Assalam) is quoted as saying, *"has its secret, and the secret of the Qur'an is in its first chapter, and the meaning of the first chapter is in the 'Bishmillah', and the meaning of that is in the 'be', its first letter, and the meaning of that letter is in the dot which makes it BE and I am that dot."* It was the function of Muhammad (Peace be upon him) to bring down the word of Allah, and of Ali ('Alaihi Assalam) to interpret it. [259]

Once, they asked Ali ('Alaihi Assalam), *"what is the reason that in comparison to other companions of the Prophet you have the most traditions?"* He replied, *"Whenever I asked the Prophet something he gave me an answer. And whenever I kept quiet he would begin the conversation."*[260] Ali ('Alaihi Assalam) shared with the Prophet all the persecutions and most of the hardships. He protected the Prophet with his own life until the day Allah Most High took Muhammad (Peace be upon him) to Heaven. On that day, the Commander of the Faithful ('Alaihi Assalam) was thirty-three years of age.

On the day of the death of the Prophet, the community differed over his Imamate, in other words, who was to be the successor. There was no doubt that Ali ('Alaihi Assalam) was the Prophet's choice. Yet, some politically minded individuals, chose to ignore this fact and pursue the leadership of the Muslim community for their personal and selfish reasons. They held a hurried gathering at Saqifa. This was a preplanned political contrivance to deprive Ali ('Alaihi Assalam) of his rightful position. No one informed Ali ('Alaihi Assalam) or other members of Bani Hashim that a gathering was taking place for the appointment of a Khalif. Umar came to the door of the Holy Prophet's house, but did not enter it, so that Ali ('Alaihi Assalam), Bani Hashim and the prominent companions of the Prophet might not be properly notified of the meeting. Umar sent a message to Abu Bakr saying, *"Come immediately, as I have an urgent business with you."* At least they should have informed Ali ('Alaihi Assalam) that they were convening a meeting at Saqifa Bani Sa'da to deliberate on the important issue of electing a Khalif but they did not do so in order to deprive him of his right of succession. At this time, Ali ('Alaihi Assalam) and members of Bani Hashim were busy with the funeral rites of the Holy Prophet. Ingeniously, they were kept uninformed of the meeting. Thus the proceedings at Saqifa were conspicuous because of the absence of such eminent and top-ranking personalities as Ali ('Alaihi Assalam), Abbas the respected uncle of the Holy Prophet, the people of Bani Umayya and the Ansar. The conspirators made so much haste, because they knew that, if they waited for all the Muslims to come, or at least for the notable people of Usama Bin Zaid's army, the prominent companions of the Prophet present in Medina (al-Munawwarah), and Bani Hashim, and others, to be present there and attend the meeting, the name of Ali ('Alaihi Assalam) among others must have been proposed. If the name of Ali ('Alaihi Assalam), and Abbas, were proposed there, the supporters of Right and Truth, with their convincing arguments, would have reversed the plot. In short, the conspirators staged an irreversible event by installing Abu Bakr into the Khalifate, with the vote of two persons!

Some Muslims believe that there was no plot, but we ask: if they had not hatched a conspiracy or plot, why did Umar go to the door of the house of the Holy Prophet but did not enter it? They could have apprized the whole Bani Hashim, and the prominent companions, of the situation, and could have asked for their help. Was Abu Bakr the only wise person they could have consulted that day? Then there are the Muslims who feel that what was done was done and it should be left alone. But we ask: where, in any part of the world is such a belief acceptable that if three persons, or a section of the people, assemble in the city, or the capital city, then it is incumbent on the intelligentsia, Ulema and intellectuals of all other cities or towns to obey them? Or even if some intelligent and learned man, whom others have not selected gives an opinion, is it necessary for the rest of the intelligentsia to follow them? In fact, the Prophet Muhammad (Peace be upon him) left the decision to the entire Muslim Community.

Even today in all the advanced countries it is customary that in order to establish a democratic State, or to select the Leader of a Nation, they make a general announcement and honor the opinion of the whole nation by accepting the vote of majority. We do not think the reader will find a single instance in the history of the world of such a bogus election of a Chief (as occurred at Saqifa), whom a handful of people voted in. The Heads of the civilized countries, and all cultured people, only scoff at such fictitious proceedings. However at Saqifa, a few persons, sitting in a corner, committed the whole Islamic nation and Umma to the mercy of one person and everyone had to (in their opinion) bow down before him.

Were Ali ('Alaihi Assalam), Abbas, the loving uncle of the Holy Prophet, and other distinguished persons of Bani Hashim not sagacious and sensible? For God's sake do tell us with justice, what kind of *ijma* it was, which was held without the presence, consultation, agreement, or acquiescence of these people?

Sheikh Suleman Balkhi Hanafi has particularized chapter fifteen of his "Yanabiu'l-Mawadda" with this topic and has narrated twenty traditions, in support of the Vicegerency of Ali ('Alaihi Assalam), from Imam Sa'lahi, Hamwaini, Hafiz Abu Nuaim, Ahmed Bin Hanbal, al-Khatib al-Khwarazmi, and Daylami.

Of course, when Ali ('Alaihi Assalam) came to know of the appointment of Abu Bakr as Khalif and after finishing the Holy Prophet's funeral rites he lodged his nonviolent protest before those responsible for this unwholesome event. His was not the only voice of opposition. The Commander of the Muslim army, Usama Bin Zaid, who was appointed as *Amir* of the army by the Holy Prophet Muhammad (Peace be upon him), and who was superior in rank to Abu Bakr and Umar, vociferously voiced his outrage. When Usama heard that through a conspiracy three persons made the Khalif, and without consulting other people, and even informing them, they swore fealty to one man, riding his horse, he came to the door of the mosque and, as written by all the historians, cried aloud! *"What is all this uproar that you have caused? With whose permission have you made your Khalif? What was the significance of a handful of people who, without consulting the Muslims and the distinguished companions and without 'ijma' appointed a Khalif?"*

Many Sunni brothers and sisters insist that they would never have appointed Ali ('Alaihi Assalam) as Khalif because of his young age. They argue that the Arabs of that time only entrusted positions of leadership to men of mature age and experience. This argument has held up for so long because there is truth to it: the Arabs did have a reluctance to entrust young and untried men with great responsibility. However, there were exceptions, and many notable ones. One of those notable exceptions was Usama Bin Zaid himself, the Commander of the Muslim Army! He was barely twenty years old at the time. Many elders resented the Prophet's decision in making Usama the Commander. The Prophet appointed him over the elder members of the Muhãjirín (the Quraish) and the Ansãr. Therefore, Muhammad (Peace be upon him) did break with the tradition of granting leadership only to elder men on at least this one occasion.

Even among the Arabs themselves, this tradition was often broken. Jafri, in "The Origin and Early Development of Shi'a Islam," relates: *"[O]ur sources do not fail to point out that, though the 'Senate' (Nadwa) of pre-Islamic Mecca was generally a council of elders only, the sons of the chieftain Qusayy were privileged to be exempted from this age restriction and were admitted to the council despite their youth. In later times more liberal concessions seem to have been in vogue; Abu Jahl was admitted despite his youth, and Hakim b. Hazm was admitted when he was only fifteen or twenty years old."* After this, Jafri cites Ibn 'Abd Rabbih, *"There are no monarchic king over the Arabs of Mecca in the Jahiliya. So whenever there was a war, they took a ballot among chieftains and elected one as 'King', were he a minor or a grown man. Thus on the day of Fijar, it was the turn of the Banu Hashim, and as a result of the ballot Al-'Abbãs, who was then a mere child, was elected, and they seated him on the shield."*[261]

When the Prophet (Peace be upon him) left for his Tabuk expedition, the hypocrites secretly planned to revolt in Medina in his absence. Therefore, he appointed an experienced man, Ali ('Alaihi Assalam), in his place to control the situation in Medina and to foil the hypocrites' plans. Were not Abu Bakr, Umar and other older companions in Medina then?

For the recitation of some of the verses of the Chapter *Al-Bara'a* (The Immunity), of the Holy Qur'an to the people of Macca, one would perhaps think an experienced man should have been appropriate. But the Holy Prophet called the older Abu Bakr back from his half-completed journey and commanded the younger Ali ('Alaihi Assalam) to perform this important task. The Prophet said that Allah had told him that the one to convey the Holy Qur'an should be him, (the Holy Prophet) or someone who was of him.

Similarly, for the guidance of the people of Yemen, why did the Holy Prophet send the Commander of the Faithful, Ali ('Alaihi Assalam) instead of the more experienced Abu Bakr, Umar or others who were present there? On many other similar occasions the Holy Prophet, in the presence of Abu Bakr, Umar and others, selected Ali ('Alaihi Assalam) to perform momentous tasks. It follows that our Sunni brothers and sisters insistence on chronological maturity is baseless. The essential condition for the Khalifate is merit.

Thus we see that this argument about Ali's ('Alaihi Assalam) age is spurious. It is only made to assuage the fears and stop the questioning of open-minded Sunnis who wonder why Ali ('Alaihi Assalam) was denied his rightful position as Khalif at this time.

Many others of the Companions of the Prophet lodged their complaints and made protests regarding Abu Bakr's artificial election. In fact, eighteen persons who were the prominent and distinguished companions of the Holy Prophet did not take the oath of allegiance to Abu Bakr.[262]

Many people ask why was not Ali ('Alaihi Assalam) more vocal and forceful in his protest regarding Abu Bakr being named to the Khalifate. These people imply that Ali's reaction was proof that he accepted the new Khalif. On the contrary, Amiru'l-Mu'minin ('Alaihi Assalam) was the lone man who, throughout his life, never looked to his person, but he was always mindful of Allah. That is, he was completely absorbed in Allah. He had resigned himself and his people to the will of Allah. He viewed the Imamate, Khalifate and authority purely for the sake of Allah and Allah's religion. Hence his patience, forbearance, silence, and abstention from confronting the opponents for obtaining his unquestionable right were simply for Allah's sake, so that there might not be discord in the ranks of the Muslims and people might not return to their previous infidelity. It was for this reason that Amiru'l-Mu'minin ('Alaihi Assalam) made patience his personal case of conduct. He assumed forbearance and silence for the safety of Islam, so that there might not appear factions among the Muslims. In many of his sermons and statements also he has referred to this point.

Ahmad Bin Muhammad Kurgi Baghdadi stated that one day Abdullah Bin Ahmad Hanbal asked his father Ahmad Bin Hanbal (the Imam of the Hanbalis) a question. Abdullah Bin Ahmad Hanbal asked about the *Sahaba* who were worthy of praise. The Imam of the Hanbalis named Abu Bakr, Umar and Uthman. His son then asked what his father thought about Ali Bin Abi Talib ('Alaihi Assalam). Ahmad Bin Hanbal said, *"He belongs to the Ahlul Bayt. The others cannot be compared with him."*

After depriving Ali ('Alaihi Assalam) of the position as Khalif and temporal head of the Muslim State, all possible steps were taken to cripple the economic and social position of Ali ('Alaihi Assalam) and other members of the Ahlul Bayt.

Every possible effort is still made today to conceal or undermine the various traditions of the Holy Prophet containing merits and distinctions of Ali ('Alaihi Assalam) or his exhortations to the Umma to follow his Ahlul Bayt ('Alaihi Assalam) after him. Several ways have been adopted to this end. In some cases parallel traditions have been forged in praise of Abu Bakr, Umar or even Uthman. Khalif Uthman gave a considerable sum of money (one hundred thousand dirhams) to Hakam Bin Abi'l- As (who was cursed and banished by the Holy Prophet[263]) to create forged hadith. In some cases less important or trivial meanings are assigned to the words used by the Holy Prophet even though such meanings might quite obviously appear to be unsuitable and off the rails. In some cases the veracity of the tradition is denied even though it is existing in the authentic books of the Sunni scholars themselves, or the narrators are alleged to be unreliable although if proper scrutiny is made they are found to have been held reliable even by just and fair-minded Sunni writers of repute. This shows that the plot against the Holy Ahlul Bayt started at Saqifa is being continued by those devote Sunni's who have pledged themselves unknowingly to following those who had engineered that plot. It is however strange that in doing so they remain unmindful of the writings and views of their own Ulema who are regarded authentic and whose works are held in great esteem.

It is important to note that Mu'awiyah Bin Abi Sufyan is responsible for the fabrication of forged *hadith*. Mu'awiyah Bin Abi Sufyan awarded Ibn Jundub and others, hundreds of thousands of dinars for coming forth with hadiths that suited him.[264] The Maliki school was the first legal center to be established in Islam. Its founder, Malik Ibn Anas (d. 795) was Medina (Al-Munawwarah) based and thus had the access to a large collection of legal hadiths with fair authenticity. Thus, he was grieved by the large number of forged hadiths that sprang from the wells of Umayyad Damascus in order to establish that dynasty or other non-Islamic features. As an inhabitant of Medina (Al-Munawwarah), Malik followed the strict Arab tradition, on the expense of the often non-Arab/Muslim legislature advocated by the Umayyads. Mu'awiyah Bin Abi Sufyan was also responsible for the introduction of the *minaret*. Let Mu'awiyah Bin Abi Sufyan and his followers have the minarets, we will take the *jami*.

The immediate result of this mischief was that the Khalifate, which should really have been a position for the protection and propagation of the Faith, soon began to be regarded as the means for securing and exercising temporal authority.

In the above quotation from the Qur'an that heads this chapter, mention is made of one who pays alms while bowing in prayer. One day the Prophet Muhammad (Peace be upon him), Ali ('Alaihi Assalam) and others were making the *Zohr* prayers in the mosque. A beggar got up and asked for alms. The beggar was the Archangel Gabriel ('Aleihi Assalam) concealed. Nobody gave him anything. Ali ('Alaihi Assalam) was bowing in the state of *Ruku*. He pointed to the ring on his finger with his hand. The beggar removed the ring from his finger.[265] We know that no one except Ali ('Alaihi Assalam) paid alms while bowing in prayer. Therefore, besides the Prophet giving Ali ('Alaihi Assalam) the right to succeed him, more importantly the Supreme Reality, in the Qur'an, specifically mentions the authority of Ali ('Alaihi

Assalam). It has been established in language that "wali" means *"the most appropriate for authority" (awla)*, without there being any opposition to this definition. If the Commander of the Faithful ('Alaihi Assalam) was, by the stipulation of the Qur'an, more appropriate for authority among the people than themselves because of his being their *wali* according to the textual nomination in the Clear Explanation (The Qur'an), it was obviously necessary for all of them to obey him.

Let us first look at a tradition occurring in the commentary of the Qur'an by Imam Abi Ishaq Ahmad Ibn Muhammad Ibn Ibrahim Nisaboori al-Tha'labi. A few comments on this respected personality: he died in 337 A.H. and Ibn Khallikan gives an account of his death saying, *"He was unique as a commentator of the Qur'an and his Tafsir al-Kabir is superior to all other interpretations."* When he reached the above verse he recorded this in his "Tafsir al-Kabir" on the authority of Abu Dharr Ghifari, who said,

"Both of my ears may turn deaf and both of my eyes may become blind if I speak a lie. I heard the Messenger of Allah, Allah's blessings and peace be upon him and his posterity, saying, 'Ali is the guide of the righteous and the slayer of the infidels. He who has helped him is victorious and he who has abandoned him is forsaken.' One day I said my prayers in the company of the Prophet. A beggar came to the mosque and begged for alms, but nobody gave him anything. Ali was in a state of kneeling in the prayer. He pointed out his ring to the beggar, who approached him and removed the ring from his finger. Thereupon the Prophet, Allah's blessings and peace be upon him and his posterity, implored Allah the Mighty and Glorious, saying: 'O Allah! My brother Moses begged you saying, "My Lord, delight my heart and make my task easy and undo the knot in my tongue so that they may understand me, and appoint from my kinsmen, Harun, my brother, as my vizier, and strengthen my back with him and make him participate in my mission so that we may glorify You and remember You more frequently. Certainly You see us." And You inspired him: "O Musa! All your requests have been granted." O Allah! I am your slave and your prophet. Delight my heart and make my task easy and appoint from among my kinsmen Ali as my vizier and strengthen my back with him.'"

Abu Dharr, then, proceeded,

"By Allah, the Messenger of Allah, Allah's blessings and peace be upon him and his posterity had not yet finished his supplication when the trustworthy Gabriel descended to him with this Verse:

'Certainly Allah is Your Master, and His Prophet and those who believe who establish prayer and give charity while they bow. And whoever takes Allah and His Messenger and those who believe as a guardian, so surely the party of

Allah will be victorious.' " [266]

Nonetheless, self-seeking individuals still chose to oppose him.

Another reason in support of Ali's ('Alaihi Assalam) right to the Imamate came from the words of the Prophet ('Alaihi Assalam) himself on the day of the assembly at his house. The Prophet had especially gathered certain individuals there to make the following solemn pledge,

"Whoever helps me in this matter will be my brother, my entrusted one (wasi) my helper (wazir), my heir and my successor after me."

Then the Commander of the Faithful ('Alaihi Assalam) stood up before the Prophet among all the gathering (on that day he was the youngest of them) and he said,

"O Apostle of God, I will help you."

Then the Prophet (Peace be upon him), said,

"Sit down, you are my brother, my trustee, my helper, my inheritor and successor after me." This was a clear statement about the succession (after the Prophet).

Ali ('Alaihi Assalam) was one of the most courageous and able men in the Muslim army. He was appointed the standard-bearer at the battles of both Badr and Khaibar. At Khaibar (A.H. 7) several Sunni and Shia histories relate the following tradition. This is the version found in a Sunni collection of Traditions, the Sahih of Muslim: *"The Apostle of God said on the day of Khaibar: 'I shall certainly give this banner to a man who loves God and His Apostle and through whom God will give victory.' Umar Ibn al-Khattab said: 'I never wished for a leadership except on that day.' And he also said: 'And so I leapt up towards it hoping to claim it as a right.' And the Apostle of God summoned Ali, the son of Abu Talib, and gave it to him and said 'Go! And do not turn aside until God gives you victory.' "* Martin Lings in his book: "Muhammad - his life based on the earliest sources" also relates this event: *"Here the garrison came out in great force, and on that day every attack made by the Muslims was repulsed. 'Tomorrow,' said the Prophet, 'will I give the standard unto a man whom God and His messenger love. God will give us the victory by his hands; he is not one who turneth back in flight.' In his previous campaigns the Prophet had used relatively small flags as standards, but to Khaibar he had brought a great black standard made from a cloak of A'isha's. They called it 'the Eagle', and this he now gave to Ali."*

When the Prophet (Peace be upon him) left to go on his longest expedition, to Tabuk, Ali ('Alaihi Assalam) was left in charge at Medina. According to some accounts, Ali ('Alaihi Assalam) felt insulted to be left with the women and children while, according to others, rumors spread that Ali ('Alaihi Assalam) had been left behind because it was feared he would bring misfortune to the expedition. In any case, Ali ('Alaihi Assalam) went to the Prophet (Peace be upon him) voicing his discontent at being left behind. It was at this time, according to numerous Sunni and Shia Traditionists, that the famous Hadith of Manzila Harun (position of Aaron) was revealed. According to this Tradition, Muhammad (Peace be upon him) said to Ali ('Alaihi Assalam): *" Are you not content to be with respect to me as Aaron was to Moses, except that after me there shall be no other Prophet."* The implication was that Ali ('Alaihi Assalam) was to be Muhammad's (Peace be upon him) chief assistant in his lifetime and his successor after him.[267]

In addition, there is also what the Prophet said on the day of *Ghadir-e-Khum.* The community had gathered to listen to the sermon in which he asked,

"Am I not more appropriate for authority (awla) over you than your-selves?"

Yes, they answered.

Then he spoke to them in an ordered manner without any interruption in his speech,

"Whomsoever I am Master over, Ali is also Master over."

At first the Prophet was reluctant to proclaim the ordinance to the peo-ple who he believed were prejudiced against it. A Qur'anic verse made the matter clear and left no room of hesitation in his mind. The verse is as follows: *"O the Prophet, deliver the message which has been revealed to you by your Lord. If you failed to do so it will mean that you have not delivered His mes-sage to the people. God will guard you against the people."* There is no sect in Islam which believe that the Prophet failed short of delivering the message of God in such matters as the performance of prayers, the payment of "zakat", the fasting or going on pilgrimage or taking part in the "jihad." We know well that he exercised his utmost in making the people offer the prayers which one can-not perform without undergoing some physical discomfort. He preached the people to pay "zakat" and the people did pay, although one does not find it easy to part with money. The people were made to fast and we know well that in fasting one has to put up with unbearable heat and thirst. He exhorted the peo-ple to go on pilgrimage which one cannot undertake without undergoing all sorts of hardships. He ordered the people to join the "jihad" and they did so at the risk of their lives.

In short, he made no hesitation in the delivering of God's message in these matters. It was only the question of "Wilayat" which worried him the most. It was the ordinance pertaining to the "Wilayat," the allegiance to Ali and the Imams from among his descendants that he was not prepared to proclaim. Finding the people burning with hatred and jealousy he hesitated to deliver this ordinance to them and he was waiting for a favorable time when the above verses were revealed to clear his doubts.

If someone were to suggest that the Prophet was not hesitant to deliver this ordinance, this stand will make the revelation of the above verse meaningless and superfluous. These verses which lay emphasis on the delivery of the ordinance prove to us that the faith in the "Wilayat" is the corner stone of our religion. Belief in the "Wilayat" of the Prophet is a pivot. On this hinges the whole system of our religious laws.

We must bear it in mind that after the death of the Prophet the belief in the wilayat of the Imams from his progeny is as important a part of our religion as the belief in the Wilayat of the Prophet in his life time. This is supported by the Tradition according to which the Prophet is reported to have said at Ghadir-e-Khum, *"Am I not more precious to you than your own-selves?"* This is an echo of the Qur'anic verse that says, *"The Prophet is more dear to the faithful than their own-selves to them."* It is said, that in response to this question by the Prophet, when the faithful said *"Yes, you are dearer to us than our own lives,"* the Prophet said, *"O God, be witness to their admission."* After this he said, *"Ali is the master of one who acknowledges me to be his master. O God love those who love Ali. Help those who help Ali. Desert those who desert Ali. Let the truth accompany Ali wherever he goes."*

"Yomul-Ghadir" is the day on which the Prophet declared Hazrat Ali to be his brother on his return from his last pilgrimage that we know in history as *"Hajjat-ul-Wida."* This took place on the 18th of *"zil-haj"* when the Prophet and his followers on the return from the pilgrimage made a halt at the Ghadir-e-Khum.

Ahmed Ahmad Bin Hanbal, one of the four Sunni Imams, has mentioned this incident in his well-known book "Musnad." He quotes Bara'a Bin Azib, one of the *"As-haab"* of the Prophet saying, *"We were in the company of the Prophet when he halted at the 'Ghadir-e-Khum' and led the congregational prayer. After finishing the prayer the Prophet took the hand of Ali and raised it up saying, 'Am I not dearer to the faithful than their own souls?' They said, 'Yes'. Again he said, "Ali is the master of the one who acknowledges me to be his master. O God love those who love Ali and hate those who hate Ali.' After hearing this, Umar bin al-Khattab went up to Ali and said, 'Congratulations to you, O the son of Abu Talib, you have become the master of every male and female Believer.' "*

Furthermore, there is the Prophet's statement to Ali ('Alaihi Assalam) at the time of setting out to Tabuk, *"You are in the same position with respect to me as Aaron (Harun) was to Moses (Musa) except that there is no prophet after me."* Moses appointed Aaron as the best individual among the Israelites to act as his Khalifa and successor, so that the mission of Prophethood might not be disturbed. Similarly the Last Holy Prophet, whose code of Religion was most perfect, whose preaching was universal and whose faultless laws will continue till the Doomsday, had greater reason not to leave the people to their own free will, and not to let them fall into chaos and confusion, so that the code of religion might not go into the hands of the ignorant, lest they should mold it according to their whims and aspirations, depend on their own conjectures, create divisions in the matter of laws and the destructive elements get an opportunity to divide the creed into seventy-three sects. Muhammad (Peace be upon him) knew humanity would need spiritual leadership in the coming centuries. Thus, Muhammad (Peace be upon him) clearly appointed Ali ('Alaihi Assalam) as his Vizier and Vice-Regent. Imam Abdullah Bin Ahmad Hanbal in "Musnad," Ibn Maghazili Faqih Shafe'iy in "Manaqib" and Tha'labi in his "Tafsir (Commentary)" have reported that the Holy Prophet said to Ali ('Alaihi Assalam), *"O' Ali! You are my brother, successor, Vice-Regent, and the payer of my debt."* The amount of hadiths reported by the most impeccable of individuals, concerning the Khalifate of Ali ('Alaihi Assalam) is astounding and wondrous. And just as the Bani Israel did not accept the Khalifate of Aaron, so too certain of the companions of the Prophet Muhammad (Peace be upon him) did not accept the Khalifate of Ali ('Alaihi Assalam).

The Prophet Muhammad (Peace be upon him) discerned that each Prophet knew who his successor and Vice-Regent would be, for Muhammad (Peace be upon him) was not only an Adept in Wisdom regarding the lives of the Prophets who came before him, he was himself the Seal of the Prophets. As Ibn' Arabi said, *"He encompasses the knowledge of all knowers who know God, whether those who had gone before or those who would come after."* Therefore, while Muhammad (Peace be upon him) knew that there would be no Prophet after him, he was keenly aware of the way Allah always provided, throughout history, a person to guide humanity on the Earth. Muhammad (Peace be upon him) would not have neglected the sacred task of alerting his followers who would be his Vice-Regent upon his death. Of course, without any doubt, Muhammad (Peace be upon him) always knew that Ali ('Alaihi Assalam) would be his Vice-Regent, and made it clear to the community on numerous occasions. This fact only seems unclear to our Sunni brothers and sisters because they are the unwitting victims of a political conspiracy that sought to deliberately erase any trace of evidence that Muhammad had clearly named Ali ('Alaihi Assalam), The Sheikh of Excellence, as his Vice-Regent. Listen to the words of the Holy Qur'an: *"Say: Is there any of your associates who guides to the truth? Say: Allah guides to the truth. Is He then Who guides to the truth more worthy to be followed, or he who himself does not go aright unless he is guided? What then is the matter with you; how do you judge?"*[268] That is, one, who possesses the best qualities of guidance, must be the supreme leader of the people and not the one, who is ignorant of the way of guidance and himself seeks guidance of others.

This Holy verse is the most valid proof to show that a superior man cannot be made subordinate to the inferior, and the question of Khalifate, Imamate, establishment of government and succession to the Holy Prophet come under the same principle. This is borne out by another verse that says: *"Are those who know equal with those who know not?"*[269] It means – never!

Should the result of the revelations of verses in praise of Ali ('Alaihi Assalam), the confirmation of his Vice-Regency, and the Holy Prophet's exhortations and pronouncements for him, be that he was to be subjected to so much torment and mental anguish that he had to reveal in his "Shiqshiqayya" sermon: *"I endured and adopted patience as if there was pricking in my eye and necrosis in my throat."* These words amply prove the Holy Imam's extreme suffering and mental anguish. He consciously and deliberately said these words: *"I swear by Allah that the son of Abu Talib is more fond of death than a suckling is of his mother's breast."*

The Commander of the Faithful ('Alaihi Assalam) lived thirty years after the Prophet's death. For twenty-four and a half of those years, they prevented him from administering his rightful position as the first Imam. During the Khalifates of Abu Bakr and his successor, Umar, not only did Ali ('Alaihi Assalam) not advance any claims to the Khalifate, he even participated in the government of Umar. Ali ('Alaihi Assalam) helped Umar on numerous occasions on which Umar made erroneous legal rulings. Umar himself said, *"If Ali ('Alaihi Assalam) had not been there, Umar would have been ruined . . . O' Abul Hassan ('Alaihi Assalam)! I wish I may not live on the day when you are not among us."* It was not until the Khalifate passed to al-Khalifa Othman Bin 'Affan, who ruled somewhat degenerately and was a member of the Umayya family, which had fiercely fought against Muhammad (Peace be upon him) during his lifetime, that Ali ('Alaihi Assalam) was provoked into accepting the Khalifate. The third Khalif, Othman Bin 'Affan's reign was particularly responsible for giving way to gross mismanagement and corruption and providing full opportunity to members of Bani Umayyah who were sworn enemies of Islam to have complete control of the state affairs, and in due course they converted Islam into a mere movement for temporal power instead of a religion aiming at a properly regulated life in this world to earn a blissful eternal life in the Hereafter. Al-Khalifa Othman Bin 'Affan placed members of his family in charge of various provinces and they ruled disgracefully; various rebel factions, seeing their grievances unredressed, attacked al-Khalifa Othman Bin 'Affan's house and assassinated him. The prominent families of Medina (al-Munawwarah) and other areas persuaded Ali ('Alaihi Assalam) to become Khalif, which he did in 656. Ali ('Alaihi Assalam) had become the fourth Khalif of Islam and the first Imam of Ahlul Bayt Islam.

However, the Umayyads in charge of the various governments and provinces would not accept this arrangement and rose up in rebellion; eventually, Ali ('Alaihi Assalam) would be forced to flee Medina (al-Munawwarah) and settle in Kufa in Iraq—as a result, central Iraq would become the axis for the followers of the Ahlul Bayt for several hundred years. Ali ('Alaihi

Assalam) would eventually have to contend with dissension in his own army while fighting the Umayyads—these dissenters called themselves the *Kharjites*. After defeating the Kharjites in battle, one of them would assassinate him a few years later in revenge for this defeat.

From this point onwards, authority was divided in the Islamic world. To support the alleged authority of the Khalifs, a pre-emptive cover-up was perpetrated through forged hadith and through the suppression and destruction of authentic hadith. [270]

They burnt and prohibited anyone from recording or narrating Hadith.[271] First, they fabricated false hadiths to support their stand to prohibit the recording of the Prophet's Sunnah and the sacred hadith. Imam Muslim, for example, records in his "Sahih" what is quoted by Haddab Ibn Khalid al-Azdi who cites Humam citing Zayd Ibn Aslam citing Ata Ibn Yasar citing Abu Sa'id al-Khudri saying that the Messenger of Allah has said, *"Do not record anything which I say, and whoever quotes what I tell you besides the Qur'an should erase what he writes, and [orally] narrate about me without any hesitation."*[272] The purpose of fabricating this alleged " hadith" is to justify what Abu Bakr and Umar did to the Prophet's hadiths written down and recorded by a number of companions of the Prophet. They fabricated this "tradition" many years after the end of the period of the "Righteous Khalifs," and the fabricators, professional liars, overlooked the following issues:

1) Had the Messenger of Allah actually said so, the *sahaba* would have acted upon his orders (not to write traditions down), and they would have erased all traditions many years before Abu Bakr and Umar had burned them.

2) Had this tradition been authentic, Abu Bakr would have first cited it, and then Umar, in order to justify their prohibition of recording hadiths, and they would have erased them, and those who had recorded them would have sought an excuse for having done so either due to their ignorance [of such a "tradition"] or to their lapse of memory.

3) Had this tradition been authentic, Abu Bakr and Umar would have had to erase all traditions, not burn them.

4) Had this "tradition" been authentic, the Muslims, who were contemporary to Umar Ibn Abd al-Aziz, till our time, would have been committing the sin of disobeying the Messenger of Allah, particularly their chief, namely Umar Ibn Abd al-Aziz who had ordered the scholars of his time to record hadith, in addition to al-Bukhari and Muslim who regarded this tradition as authentic yet they did not act upon it but wrote thousands of the Prophet's hadith.

5) Finally, had this "tradition" been authentic, it would not have been missed by the Gate of Knowledge Ali Ibn Abu Talib ('Alaihi Assalam) who compiled the hadiths of the Prophet in one *saheefa* the length of whose pieces reached seventy yards which he called *al-jami'a*, the one that includes every-

thing, and which we will discuss later by the help of Allah.

In a chapter on recording knowledge in his "Kitab al-`Ilm" (Book of Knowledge) of his "Sahih", al-Bukhari quotes Abu Hurayra saying, *"None among the companions of the Prophet narrates more hadith than me except Abdullah Ibn Umar, for he can write whereas I cannot (i.e., am illiterate)."*[273] This statement clearly shows that there were among the Prophet's sahaba those who wrote his hadiths down. Since Abu Hurayra narrated more than six thousand traditions of the Prophet orally (because he could not write), Abdullah Ibn Umar quoted more traditions of the Prophet because of his ability to write them down. Undoubtedly, there were among the sahaba those who could write the Prophet's traditions and whom Abu Hurayra did not mention because they were not famous for being so prolific. Add to the above Imam Ali Ibn Abu Talib's (`Alaihi Assalam) scroll in which he compiled all what people need of the Prophet's traditions, and which was inherited by the Imams of Ahlul Bayt who often referred to it.

Imam Ja`far al-Sadiq has said, *"We have the saheefa; it is seventy yards long: it is the dictation of the Messenger of Allah written down in the handwriting of Ali. Nothing permissible or prohibitive the knowledge thereof is needed by people, nor any other issue, except that it is in it, even the penalty for inflicting an offense as minor as a tiny scratch on one's cheek."*[274]

Al-Bukhari himself has referred to this saheefa, which was in Ali's (`Alaihi Assalam) possession, in many chapters of his book, but he, as was quite often his habit, curtailed a great deal of information about its nature and contents. In his "Kitab al-`Ilm," al-Bukhari records the following: *"Al-Sha`bi has quoted Abu Juhayfa saying, 'I asked Ali: "Do you have a book in your possession?" He said, "No, except the Book of Allah, or some knowledge bestowed upon a Muslim man, or what this saheefa quotes of the Prophet." I asked him, "And what is in this saheefa?" "It contains reason," he said, "the ransoming of the captives, and that no Muslim should kill another Muslim.'"*[275]

In another place, al-Bukhari quotes Ibrahim al-Taymi quoting his father quoting Ali (`Alaihi Assalam) saying, *"We have nothing except the Book of Allah and this saheefa which quotes the Prophet."*[276]

Elsewhere, in al-Bukhari's "Sahih," the author quotes Ibrahim al-Taymi quoting his father saying, *"Ali delivered a sermon once to us in which he said, 'We have no book to read except the Book of Allah and what is recorded in this saheefa.'"*[277] Additionally, in another place of his "Sahih," al-Bukhari quotes Ali (`Alaihi Assalam) saying, *"We did not write down from the Prophet except the Qur'an and this saheefa."*[278]

Again in his "Sahih," al-Bukhari says, *"Ibrahim al-Taymi quotes his father saying, 'Ali, may Allah be pleased with him, delivered a sermon to us once from a pulpit built of baked bricks, and he was carrying a sword from which a saheefa was draping and said, "By Allah! We do not have any book to read except the Book of Allah and what is recorded in this saheefa." ' "*[279]

Al-Bukhari, however, did not indicate that Imam Ja`far al-Sadiq had said that this saheefa was called *"al-jami'a."* Why? Because it contained all that which is permissible and prohibitive, it had all what people need (even the penalty for scratching one's cheek), and that it was dictated by the Messenger of Allah and handwritten by Imam Ali Ibn Abu Talib ('Alaihi Assalam). Incredibly, Al-Bukhari claims that on this scroll were only recorded four hadith!

Was Abu Hurayra's mind greater than that of Ali Ibn Abu Talib ('Alaihi Assalam) to the extent that he learned by heart one hundred thousand traditions from the Messenger of Allah without having written one of them down?

Strange, by Allah, is the case of those who accept one hundred thousand traditions narrated by Abu Hurayra who did not accompany the Prophet except for three years, the illiterate that he was, while claiming that Ali ('Alaihi Assalam) was the Gate of the City of Knowledge from whom the sahaba learned various branches of knowledge. Yet, according to them, Ali ('Alaihi Assalam) was carrying a scroll containing only four hadith that remained with him during the Prophet's lifetime till his own Khalifate, and he ascended the pulpit and it was draping from his sword.

The sahaba was indeed writing down the traditions of the Prophet. Abu Hurayra's statement that Abdullah Ibn Umar used to record the Prophet's traditions, in addition to the statement of Ali Ibn Abu Talib ('Alaihi Assalam) saying, according to al-Bukhari's "Sahih," *"We have not quoted of what the Prophet has said except the Qur'an and what this saheefa contains,"* irrevocably proves that the Messenger of Allah never prohibited anyone from recording his hadith; rather, it proves the opposite. The tradition recorded in al-Bukhari's "Sahih" quoting the Prophet saying, "Do not quote me, and anyone who quotes anything from me other than the Qur'an must erase it" is a false tradition fabricated by those who supported the Khalifs so that they might support them. They fabricated it to justify what Abu Bakr and Umar and Uthman had done: the burning of Prophet's hadith and the prohibition of the Sunnah from being disseminated.

What increases our conviction is the fact that not only did the Messenger of Allah refrain from prohibiting the writing of his hadith, but that he even ordered them to be recorded. Moreover, Imam Ali ('Alaihi Assalam), who was the closest person to the Prophet, said: *"We have not quoted of what the Prophet has said except the Qur'an and what this saheefa contains."* If we add to the above what Imam Ja`far al-Sadiq has said, that is, that "al-saheefa al-jami`a" was the dictation of the Messenger of Allah in the handwriting of Ali ('Alaihi Assalam), we will conclude by saying that the Prophet had ordered

Ali ('Alaihi Assalam) to quote him.

To dispel any doubt which may still linger in the mind of the reader, we would like to shed more light and state the following: Al-Hakim in his book "Al-Mustadrak," Abu Dawood in his "Sahih," Imam Ahmad in his "Musnad," and al-Darimi in his "Sunan," have all quoted a very important hadith regarding Abdullah Ibn Umar to whom Abu Hurayra referred and whom he described as having written down a larger number of the Prophet's hadith than he himself had quoted. It is as follows: *"Abdullah Ibn Umar has said: 'I used to write down whatever I heard from the Messenger of Allah, so Quraysh prohibited me from doing so saying, "Do you write everything you hear from the Messenger of Allah who is a human being talking in anger or when pleased?" 'So I stopped writing, then I told the Messenger of Allah about it, whereupon he pointed to his mouth and said, "Keep writing, for by the One Who holds my soul do I swear that nothing comes out of it except the truth." ' "* [280] This tradition clearly tells us that Abdullah Ibn Umar used to write down everything he heard from the Messenger of Allah who did not prohibit him from doing so; rather, such a prohibition came from Quraysh. Abdullah did not want to identify those who prohibited him from writing what he was writing, for their prohibition contradicted what the Messenger of Allah had told him.

It is also quite clear that his generally ambiguous reference to "Quraysh" means the leaders of Quraysh (who were then present in Medina), that is, the Meccan *Muhajirs*, immigrants, led by Abu Bakr, Umar, Uthman, Abdul-Rahman Ibn Awf, Abu Ubaydah, Talhah, al-Zubayr, and all those who followed their line. We also notice that their prohibiting Abdullah took place while the Prophet was still alive. This by itself emphasizes the depth of the conspiracy and its gravity; otherwise, why should these men prohibit Abdullah from writing hadith without first consulting with the Prophet himself in this regard?

The fact that the Prophet said the following when Abdullah Ibn Umar mentioned to him the Quraysh's prohibition and what they said about him, he pointed to his mouth and said, *"By the One Who holds my soul do I swear that nothing comes out of it except the truth"* is another proof of the Prophet's knowledge of their doubting his justice, and that they expected him to err and to utter falsehoods *(Astaghfirullah!* [We seek forgiveness of Allah]); therefore, he swore by Allah that he said nothing except the truth. This is the accurate interpretation of the verse saying, *"Surely he does not utter anything of his own desire; it is but a revelation revealed"* (Holy Qur'an, 53:3-4), and that he was protected against erring or uttering falsehoods.

Because of all the above, we emphatically state that all "traditions" fabricated during the time of the Umayyads which implied that Muhammad (Peace be upon him) was not divinely protected against erring are not authentic at all. The tradition cited above also gives us the impression that their influence on Abdullah Ibn Umar was so great that he stopped writing hadith down as he himself admitted when he said, " . . . *so I stopped writing* . . ." He remained so till an occasion came in which the Messenger of Allah interfered in person to dispel the doubts circulated against his infallibility and equity, the doubts which were quite often articulated even in his own presence such as their asking him: *"Are you really a prophet?"*[281] or: *"Are you the one who claims to be a prophet?!"*[282] or: *"By Allah, he did not seek in this distribution the Pleasure of Allah!"*[283] or 'Aesha's statement to the Prophet: *"Your God is sure swift in fulfilling your desires!"*[284] or her asking the prophet once to be fair . . . , up to the end of the list of impertinent statements which demonstrate the fact that they doubted his infallibility, believing that he was liable to be unfair, to oppress, to err, to lie . . . ; we seek Allah's protection.

He, indeed, possessed sublime morals; he was kind and compassionate as he tried to dispel such doubts by saying once, for example, *"I am only a servant receiving orders from his Master,"* and once, *"By Allah! I am kind for the sake of pleasing Allah Whom I fear,"* and at another time he said, *"By the One Who controls my life! It utters nothing except the truth."* He used quite often to say: *"May Allah have mercy on my Brother Moses! He was subjected to more afflictions than this, yet he persevered."*

Those impertinent statements which cast doubts about the Prophet's infallibility and about his Prophethood were not made by those who were outcasts or hypocritical; rather, they were unfortunately made by very prominent companions of the Prophet, and by the "Mother of the Believers," and by those who are still regarded by *"Ahl al-Sunnah wal Jama`ah"* as role models of conduct; so, there is no power nor might except in Allah, the Sublime, the Great.

What confirms our conviction that the tradition which supposedly prohibited the recording of hadith is fabricated and was baseless, and that the Prophet never said so at all, is the fact that Abu Bakr himself used to write down the traditions of the Prophet during his lifetime. Yet when he ascended to the post of Khalif, he decided to burn them for a reason with which the researchers are familiar. Here is his daughter 'Aesha saying, *"My father gathered the hadith of the Messenger of Allah, and they totaled five hundred, then he spent his night sleeplessly turning on his sides. I thought that he was upset because of someone's complaint, or because of some news that he had heard. The next morning, he said to me, 'Daughter! Bring me the hadith in your possession,' so I brought them to him, and he set them on fire."*[285]

And here is Umar Ibn al-Khattab, also upon becoming Khalif, delivering a sermon one day to people in which he said, *"Anyone who has in his possession a book must bring it to me so that I may tell him what I think of it."* People thought that he simply wanted to verify their contents to remove from them any discrepancy, so they brought him their books whereupon he set them on fire.[286] Then he dispatched his orders to Islamic lands ordering people thus:

"Anyone who has any hadith written down has to erase them."[287]

This is the greatest evidence testifying to the fact that all the sahaba, had they lived in Medina or in the rest of Muslim lands, had in their possession books in which they compiled sacred hadith of the Prophet which they had recorded during the Prophet's lifetime. They were all burnt according to the orders first of Abu Bakr then of Umar. All other books found in other lands were erased during Umar's Khalifate as he had ordered.

Based upon the above, we cannot, nor can any sane person, believe that the Messenger of Allah had prohibited them from writing the sacred hadith down, having come to know that most sahaba possessed books containing traditions especially the saheefa with which Imam Ali ('Alaihi Assalam) never parted, whose length reached seventy yards, and which he used to call "al-jami`a" [literally meaning: the university] because it contained all sorts of knowledge.

Since the interests of the ruling authority and the dominant political line dictated the obliteration and the burning of the Sunnah and the prohibition of quoting hadith, the sahaba who supported such Khalifate obeyed those orders and burnt such Sunnah and ceased quoting hadith. Thus, they left themselves and their followers no option except resorting to personal views expressed as *ijtihad*, or following the "sunnah" of Abu Bakr, Umar, Uthman, Mu'awiyah, Yazid, Marwan Ibn al-Hakam, al-Waleed Ibn Abd al-Malik, Sulayman Ibn Abd al-Malik , and so forth.

This continued till [Umayyad Khalif] Umar Ibn Abd al-Aziz came to power and asked Abu Bakr al-Hazmi to write down what he remembered of the hadith and Sunnah of the Messenger of Allah or the "sunnah" of Umar Ibn al-Khattab.[288] Thus does it become clear to us that even during the circumstances that permitted the recording of the Sunnah, a hundred years after the obliteration and prohibition of the Sunnah, we can see the moderate Umayyad Khalif whose name was added by "Ahl al-Sunnah wal Jama`ah" to the list of the "Righteous Khalifs" ordering the compilation of the Sunnah of the Messenger of Allah in addition to the "sunnah" of Umar Ibn al-Khattab, as if Umar Ibn al-Khattab was a partner of Muhammad in his Prophetic mission and prophethood!

And why did Umar Ibn Abd al-Aziz not ask the Imams from Ahlul Bayt, who were his contemporaries, to give him a copy of "al-saheefa al-jami'a"? And why did he not put them in charge of collecting the Prophet's hadith especially since they knew best what their grandfather had said? But verifiers and researchers know the secret.

Can those traditions which were compiled by "Ahl al-Sunnah wal Jama'ah" be taken for granted especially since those who compiled them belonged to Banu Umayyah and their supporters who represent Quraysh's Khalifate? Can we rely on them after having already come to know the truth about Quraysh and its attitude toward the Messenger of Allah and his purified Sunnah? It remains obvious, having come to know all of that, that the ruling authority across the centuries acted only upon the principles of ijtihad, analogy and mutual consultation. Since the said authority had expelled Imam Ali ('Alaihi Assalam) from the stage of public life and ignored him, it had nothing against him to require him to burn what he had recorded during the Prophetic Message according to the dictation of the Prophet himself.

Imam Ali ('Alaihi Assalam) remained in possession of that saheefa in which he compiled everything people need, even the penalty for scratching one's cheek. When he became Khalif, he was still letting it drape from his sword as he ascended the pulpit to deliver a sermon to people to acquaint them with its importance. Consecutive stories told by the Imams of Ahlul Bayt kept indicating that their sons inherited that saheefa from their fathers, chronologically one from another, and that they used to refer to it in order to issue religious decisions (*fatawa*) regarding questions raised to them by their contemporaries who were guided by the light of their guidance. Consequently, Imam Ja`far al-Sadiq, Imam al-Rida and many other Imams, used to repeat the same statement in its regard always. They used to say, *"We do not issue verdicts to people according to our own views; had we been issuing verdicts to people in the light of our own views and according to the dictates of our own inclinations, we would surely have been among those who perish. Rather, they are legacies of the Messenger of Allah of knowledge which sons inherit from their fathers, and which we treasure as people treasure their gold and silver."*[289]

Imam Ja`far al-Sadiq said once, *"My hadith is my father's, while my father's hadith is my grandfather's, and the hadith of my grandfather is that of Hussain; al-Husain's hadith is that of Hassan; Hassan's hadith is that of the Commander of the Faithful; the hadith of the Commander of the Faithful is the hadith of the Messenger of Allah, and the hadith of the Messenger of Allah is the speech of Allah, the Lord of Dignity and Greatness."*[290] Based on such premises, the tradition of the Two Weighty Things *(al-Thaqalain)* becomes consecutively reported *(mutawatir)*, and its text is as follows: *"I have left among you the Two Weighty Things: the Book of Allah and my Progeny; so long as you (simultaneously) uphold both of them, you shall never stray after me."*[291]

The Umayyads continued to pass the Khalifate down through the ages among their family; but there now existed in Iraq a separate Islamic community that did not recognize the authority of the Umayyad Khalifs. Rather they recognized only the successors to Ali ('Alaihi Assalam) as authorities, and they gave these successors the title Imam, or spiritual leader of Islam. This was done both to differentiate their leaders from the more worldly and secular Umayyads, and because Abu Muhammad Hassan Ibn Ali, the second Imam, ceded the Khalifate to the Umayyads. This meant, of course, that the Ahlul

Bayt could not legitimately assert themselves as Khalifs, so they invented a separate title. In Ahlul Bayt history, Ali ('Alaihi Assalam) is the first Imam (although Sunni and Western historians do not believe that he assumed this title but rather that it was retroactive). A grand total of eleven Imams succeeded Ali ('Alaihi Assalam) (ten in non-Shi'i histories), passing the Imamate down to their sons in hereditary succession. [292]

> *"The Unseen, the Forbidden*
> *when it yearned to reveal itself*
> *and raise its torches high*
> *above the hidden abyss*
> *to create in its Power*
> *through the order: 'BE!'*
> *before even the Pen*
> *and Tablet were known*
> *then Ali's heart became the Tablet*
> *Ahmad's tongue the Pen.*
> *The station of Ali, Ka'ba's lord,*
> *became the Heart itself."* [293]

The great scholar Mir Syed Ali Hamadani Shafi'i writes in his "Mawaddatu'l-Qurba" that the Holy Prophet said that the angels of the heavens look with special attention to the gathering in which the virtues and merits of Ali ('Alaihi Assalam) are narrated and they invoke Allah's blessings for those people.

To narrate the following tradition is itself a worship. The Holy Prophet of Allah said: *"I am the house of wisdom and Ali is its gate; so if somebody is desirous of gaining knowledge he should come to the gate."* [294]

PRACTICE

Inhale and contemplate on the Name *Ya Muqaddim*, The Foremost. As you inhale, know that Ya Muqaddim is Infinitely Pre-Existent and Prior to all Creation. Say to yourself, *"Ya Muqaddim."*

Exhale and release all sense of "me" and "ego." For Ya Muqaddim is the Only Reality. As you exhale, say the Name, *Ya Muqaddim* and let your pride and sense of self dissolve into the Pre-Existent. *Ya Muqaddim* is not up or down, east, west, north, or south. The Infinitely Pre-Existent is in your Heart.

"There exists a tie of kindred between all wise people. By associating with wise people you will become wise yourself."
                    - Menander

"So they went on until, when they met a boy, he slew him. (Musa) said: Have you slain an innocent person otherwise than for manslaughter? Certainly, you have done an evil thing. He said: Did I not say to you that you will not be able to have patience with me?"
                    - Qur'an 18:74-75

"Concern for humanity, and all the related beings that surround humanity, is the only meaning of human life. Maturity is greater and greater levels of this concern."

                    - Shaykh Nur al-Anwar
                    al-Jerrahi [295]

"To run from suffering is to run from Allah."
                    - Sheikh el-Hajj Şerif Çatalkaya
                    er-Rıfa'i er-Marufi

EDUCATION

Education is important. We are not just referring to our public school system; we are referring to all aspects of human existence. Education is significant. You learn to walk, to talk, you learn to ride a bicycle, to swim and to drive a car. You learn table manners, you learn how to wash, to dress, how to tie your shoes. You learn social interaction skills.

A sort of "surrender" and "submission" is required when you learn to do something. You do not tell your parents how you are going to walk, you allow them to teach you. You humble yourselves before them, allowing them to pick you up, stand you on your feet (though you would prefer the comfort of "all fours"), and then allowing them to let go of you, although you are sure you are going to fall.

This factor of the ubiquity of learning is significant. In the realm of spirituality too, you must learn. Teachers and Guides are necessary. (False teachers who seek to control and manipulate your life are not necessary). You cannot escape the fact that learning and human experience go hand in hand.

Learning is necessary to unfold our humanity. Musicians learn to play their instruments. Talents need to be cultivated. Talents are hidden or sleeping realities that exist within a person. These realities await the proper interface with an instructor combined with personal discipline to manifest. The Murid too learns to make music with his or her being.

Therefore, do not doubt the reality of your psychic abilities. They are no more a hallucination than playing the piano is a hallucination. Just because a talent is not manifest at birth does not mean it does not exist. Just because you cannot see a talent does not mean it is not there.

Playing musical instruments, painting, writing poetry, creating sculpture and all other talents (including psychic talents) are instances of an individual intensifying his or her relationship with the surrounding environment. When a bodybuilder is a child, his or her muscles await development. His or her future quietly lives in his or her body awaiting development. The faculty of Supersensible Perception also needs training and discipline to develop. Supersensible Perception is our legacy as human beings. It is a part of our intrinsic bond with the Opener. Society often looks down their noses at artists, except for the famous and successful artists. Society tends to portray artists as slightly loony people on the fringe. Artists are thus ostracized because they have a foot in each world. They bridge the threshold. So too with the Sufis. We are the liminal people.

The Sufi is a virtuoso of the music of the spheres. As Plato said, *"Music and rhythm find their way into the secret places of the soul,"* and Fakhruddin 'Iraqi informed us, *"Often Love conquers the ear before the eye."*296

There is a wisdom concerning pain and suffering. Wisdom is gained throughout mortal existence, by people who choose to reflect on life. Sometimes our mortal understanding is limited and so we see only half the picture. Folks only comprehend half the story, unless they are illuminated as to the Ultimate Reality of the events.

When an individual enters a doctoral program, he or she knows that various sacrifices must be made, great debt incurred, study must be done during long nights, a full-time job must be held down, classes attended at the expense of the person's social life, and so on. The person knows the grand scheme concerning his or her academic achievement, yet still must endure pain, sacrifice and hardships to reach his or her goal. Learning frequently involves pain and sacrifice.

Wisdom therefore comes with learning. There is also a creative and intuitive side to learning. This creativity comes from compassion and a profound understanding of human nature. Thus, there is a link between The Propitious, *An-Nāfi*, and Wisdom.

There exists a continuum of learning and wisdom. Learning leads to insight, and insight leads to wisdom. For example, one end of part of the continuum might be seen as a child's understanding of his or her surroundings, while the other end of part of the spectrum might be a mature grandparent's understanding of the world. Likewise, does that Conscious Continuum stretch beyond the wisest of human beings into the Omniconscious Unicity.

Stones, trees, birds and animals also possess parts of this wisdom, but they possess varying degrees of Explicit Consciousness in their wisdom.

"He is the guide to the Ka'ba of knowledge."
> *- The Bektashi Ceremony of New Years*
> *(Nevruz)*

"Attain to the meaning of this symbol through (mystic) knowledge;
Two buds of a hundred-leaf light
Made their appearance out of the tree of the Rose-garden of
> *Divine manifestation."*

> *- The Bektashi Ceremony of New Years*
> *(Nevruz)*

THE BOOK OF
ALI'S (ALAIHI ASSALAM) IDENTITY

There are many mysteries, mysteries within mysteries. Ali ('Alaihi Assalam) uttered seventy words, *yetmis kelime,* which defined his own identity and which became known as the *Hutbetül Beyan* or "Sermon of Explanation." The companions of the Prophet Muhammad (Peace be upon him) wrote down these words and called them "The Book of Ali's Identity," or *Kitabul enaniyeti Ali.*

Those who love the People of the House, the Ahlul Bayt, are granted through love, the wisdom to know who Ali ('Alaihi Assalam) is.

('Alaihi Assalam) is the bartender who pours the divine love-water, *kevser.* Allah created the eight thousand worlds. Allah, He is Ali!

Ali ('Alaihi Assalam) and the other Twelve Imams, [297] the Fourteen Innocents and the whole family of the Prophet, are epiphanies of Allah.

Ali ('Alaihi Assalam) is the real Ka'ba. All the ninety-nine qualities of Allah describe him except divinity, *üluhiyet.* Ali ('Alaihi Assalam) is both Muhammad el Mustafa and Ali ul Murteza.

In the Holy Qur'an is the verse, *"O Messenger! Make known that which hath been revealed unto thee from thy Lord, for if thou do it not, thou wilt not have conveyed His message. Allah will protect thee from mankind. Lo! Allah guideth not the disbelieving folk."* [298] Thirty of the Sunni Ulema have written in their most authentic books and in their own commentaries, that this verse was revealed on Ghadir-e-Khum day in respect of Amiru'l-Mu'minin Ali ('Alaihi Assalam).[299] Even Qazi Fazl Bin Rozbahan, despite all his enmity, ill-will and fanaticism writes, *"Verily, it is proved in our authentic 'Sehah' that, when this verse was revealed, the Prophet of Allah holding Ali ('Alaihi Assalam) by the hands said, 'To whomsoever I am the Mawla (Master) this Ali ('Alaihi Assalam) is also his Mawla (Master).'"* There is also a report from Razeen Bin Abdullah in "Kashful Ghummah" that is, *"In the days of the Holy Prophet (S.A.) we used to read this verse thus: 'O' our Prophet Muhammad!*

Deliver you what has been sent down to you from your Lord, that is Ali ('Alaihi Assalam) is the Master of the Believers and if you do not then you have not delivered His Message.'" [300] On the day of Ghadir-e-Khum, when the Holy Prophet appointed Ali ('Alaihi Assalam) by Divine Order, to the rank of Wilayat (Vice-Regency) and told the people whatever was ordained to say about Ali ('Alaihi Assalam) and raised him on his hand so high that the whiteness of both Ali's ('Alaihi Assalam) armpits was visible, the Prophet addressed the people thus, *"Salute Ali ('Alaihi Assalam) as he is the Ameer (Lord) of the Faithful,"* and the whole Umma complied with his order. The Holy Prophet was highly pleased with the revelation of this verse. So, addressing the people, he said, *"Allah is Great, who perfected for them their religion and completed His favor on them and was satisfied with my Prophethood and Ali's Vice-Regency after me."*[301]

Some uninformed people say that these verses mean that Muhammad (Peace be upon him) wanted the Community simply to befriend Ali ('Alaihi Assalam), or that merely Ali ('Alaihi Assalam) was their friend or helper. Yet, the reader should ponder on these facts: in that hot air, in that desert region, where there was no stage for the travelers to halt at, the Holy Prophet gathered the whole Umma, when they were sitting under the shade of the camels, with their feet covered, in the scorching heat of the sun, ordering those, who had advanced, to come back, and then he went on the pulpit and delivered that long address ordering every individual, big or small, to swear allegiance to Ali ('Alaihi Assalam). The revelation of the verse particularly at that hard and hot place with such serious instructions that the people might be put to great inconvenience and suspense could not simply mean that they should be friends of Ali ('Alaihi Assalam). And if you consider it seriously you will know that if Muhammad's (Peace be upon him) performance was not of important significance it means it was futile or frivolous, while Muhammad (Peace be upon him) is free from all futile actions.

Baba Günci wrote a *nefes* which sums up this wisdom

"Muhammad Ali established this Way.
This is the rite of the Divine Reality for him who knows Reality.
Without saying yes, Deniers cannot enter it;
The Faithful enter. It is the place of the hero."[302]

Muhammad (Peace be upon him) said, *"Whosoever would like to see Adam in his knowledge, Nuh (Noah) in his piety (or wisdom), Ibrahim (Abraham) in his love (for Allah) or submission, Musa (Moses) in his awfulness and Isa (Jesus) in his devotion to Allah, should see Ali Bin Abi Talib*

*('Alaihi Assalam)."*303

From the point of view of Light and the reality of creation, Amiru'l-Mu'minin ('Alaihi Assalam) occupied the foremost place, as many of the illustrious Sunni Ulema like Imam Ahmad Ibn Hanbal in his "Musnad," Abu'l-Hassan Faqih Shafi'i Ali Bin Muhammad Bin Tayyib al-Jalabi Ibn Maghazili in his "Mawaddatu'l-Qurba," Abu'l-Hassan Faqih Shafi'i Ali Bin Muhammad Bin Tayyib al-Jalabi Ibn Maghazili in his "Manaqib," and Ahmad Muhammad bin Talha Shafi'i in "Matalibu's-Su'ul" narrate from the Holy Prophet (S.A.) that he said, *"I and Ali Bin Abi Talib both were a Light before Allah; fourteen thousand years before the creation of Adam. When Allah created Adam, He deposited that Light in Adam's spine and we remained together as one Light, till we got separated in Abul Muttalib's spine. Then I was endowed with Prophethood and Ali with Khalifate."*

We will now relate some of these "Words."304

1. I am he who has the keys of the unknown. No one after Muhammad (Peace be upon him) knows them except me. And I know all things. 305

2. I am the owner of the two ages - the first age from when Allah first granted the Light of Saintship and the Pole of Prophecy down to the time of the Seal of Prophets, and the second age is from Muhammad's (Peace be upon him) time onward when Allah would make appear the Saintship of my descendants, Zülkarneyn mentioned in the early books.

3. I am the proof, who has the seal of Solomon.

4. I am the proof of all the prophets. It is by virtue of my light of Prophecy that all the Prophets have been able to do their deeds.306

5. I am the judge of all creatures. 307

6. I am the Preserved Tablet, the angel of death, Azrail, can do nothing without my permission.

7. I am the heart of God. 308

8. I am the place of refuge of Allah, the court, *dergâh*, of Allah. I will cause to receive the mercy of Allah whoever leans on me.

9. I am the one to whom the Prophet of Allah said, *"The Way is thine and the Station is thine."*

10. I am he who possesses the knowledge of the Book, of all that has been and of all that is to be.

11. I am the first Noah and I am the Ark of Noah. 309

12. I am the former of the clouds. 310

13. I am the one who causes people to hear the thunder and the one who makes the lightning. 311

14. I am the one who causes the rivers to flow. 312

15. I am the upholder of the heavens. 313

16. I am the friend of Job, the Tested One and the one who cured him and the friend of Jonah, of the great fish and his deliverer. I am the *Sidre* tree

in Paradise whose leaves are for the healing of all troubles of the Prophets. [314]

17. I am the light from which Moses took and by which he was granted right guidance. [315]

18. I receive my sinlessness from Allah. [316]

19. I am the revelation of Allah Most High. [317]

20. I am the one who speaks all the languages in the world. [318]

21. I am the keeper of the knowledge of Allah Most High. [319]

22. I am the evidence, or proof, of God for everything that is in the heavens and above the earth. [320]

23. I am the evidence of God for the *Jinn* and for humanity. [321]

24. I am the first and second blasts of the trumpet at the resurrection.

25. I am that book in which there is no doubt. [322]

The great Sunni Ulema have acknowledged in their authentic books that Ali ('Alaihi Assalam) possessed the knowledge of the unseen, since after the Holy Prophet, he was *"Murtaza"* (the chosen one) among the whole Umma. Abu Hamid Ghazali in his book "Bayane-e-limul-Ladunni" has reported Ali ('Alaihi Assalam) as saying: *"The Holy Prophet of Allah gave his tongue into my mouth. So from the saliva of the Holy Prophet one thousand chapters of knowledge were revealed to me and from each chapter another one thousand chapters were revealed to me."* The illustrious Sunni leader Sulayman Balkhi in his book "Yanabiu'l-Mawadda," Chapter XIV, page 77 reports from Asbagh Ibn Nabate, who quoted Amiru'l-Mu'minin ('Alaihi Assalam) as saying: *"Verily the Holy Prophet of Allah taught as one thousand chapters of knowledge, each chapter of which opened another one thousand chapters, so the total comes to a thousand thousand chapters, till I knew what has already happened and what is to happen up to the Day of Judgement and all about deaths, calamities and fair judgement."* In the same chapter he reports from Ibn Maghazili on the latter's own authority from Abus Sabah, who reported from Ibn Abbas, who quoted the Holy Prophet as saying: *"On the night of Mi'raj (ascension) when I was in the presence of Allah, He talked with me and talked in confidence. Then whatever I knew I taught it to Ali ('Alaihi Assalam), so he is the gate of my knowledge."*

The greatest Khatib 'Mu'affaq Bin Ahmad Khwarazmi narrated the same tradition from the Holy Prophet in this way: *"Gabriel ('Alaihi Assalam) brought to me a carpet from Paradise. I sat on it, till I was close to my Lord. Then He talked with me and told me secret things. Then whatever I knew was told by me to Ali ('Alaihi Assalam). So he is the Gate of my knowledge."* Then the Holy Prophet called Ali ('Alaihi Assalam) and said, *"O' Ali! Peace with you is peace with me; battle with you is battle with me and you are my sign between me and my Umma."*

He or she who says, *"I am a seeker after Muhammad Ali"* must first - it is essential - find his Murshid.

PRACTICE

Turn your attention to all that is dying and decaying. Look at dead leaves, a lifeless tree, a dead animal. Regard anything that is slowly returning to its constituent elements. Smell the pungent odor of decay. Inhale the effluvium of the dissolution process. The object of this exercise is to know the Earth, not just in its telluric aspect (flower bearing soil), but also in its chthonic aspect. Let death talk to you.

Allow the feeling to arise in your soul that this experience gives you. Again, do not force anything, or assume anything. It is of utmost importance to allow your inner self to reveal to you its reaction to these events. Do not assume ahead of time what that reaction will be. You must look and listen for the first stirrings in your inner being to these images of decay, death and decomposition. After you have looked for a while upon, for example, a decaying leaf, then close your eyes and let the experience reverberate inside your essence.

"A broken thing brings happiness."

- Bulgarian Proverb

"And set forth to them parable of the life of this world: like water which We send down from the cloud so the herbage of the earth becomes tangled on account of it, then it becomes dry broken into pieces which the winds scatter; and Allah is the holder of power over all things."

- Qur'an, The Cave, 18:45

TALES FROM UNDER THE OVERPASS

" A re you saying that harmful things can be helpful?" Sam wanted to know.

"A man or woman must rise with the aid of those things which cause his or her fall," Mr. Khadir answered.

"How can that be?"

"Have you ever heard of a surgeon amputating a limb to save a life?"

"Of course, yes."

"Well, think about it. If a passerby did not know that the person cutting off the limb was a surgeon, then he or she might think that a crime was being perpetrated. Without knowledge of the context, the action would appear to be harmful. But when the passerby is informed that this is a surgical procedure, then it takes on new meaning and significance."

"I never thought about it in that way."

"Or think about the medical science of homeopathy. They deliberately give the patient an infinitesimally small amount of a substance, which if given in large amounts would cause precisely the same symptoms from which the patient is currently suffering. In other words, they give the patient a substance that under other circumstance would be harmful. This awakens the curative forces inherent in the organism through a process homeopathic physicians term: 'therapeutic irritation,' or 'like cures like.'"

"Sorrow is the servant of the intuitive."
　　　　　　　　　　- Jelaluddin Rumi

"The nature of this Source is inconceivable; it is the Mystery of Mysteries."
　　　　　　　　　　- Murshida Amina al-Jerrahi

"Even the negative energy which He created was again for the good and beautification of people. Because when the negative and positive come together, then the beauty of Allah comes into being."
　　　　　　　　　　-el-Hajj el-Fakir Şerif Çatalkaya
　　　　　　　　　　er-Rıfa'i er-Marufi

"Adversity introduces a person to himself."
　　　　　　　　　　- Unknown

"Never give up. Never, never, never, never, never."
　　　　　　　　　　- Winston Churchill

IS PAIN NECESSARY?

Humans have an endless capacity for creativity and destruction. Often this destruction is called "evil" because it brings about the suffering of human beings. Some people are robbed, raped, tortured, and murdered. Humanity's pain is experienced by Allah Most High. When you realize the Ultimate Reality as both The Constrictor and The Expander, you come closer to understanding your involvement with the mystery of pain.

Sometimes it seems that when you are in pain and you call out to Allah in prayer, you receive a response that is seemingly alien to the situation of your humanity. First, it must be remembered that Allah is alien in that He is the Unmanifest, the Incomparable, the Impenetrable Secret, and independent of any other. *"Inasmuch as God is incomparable with all created things, He can only be understood in terms of the attributes denoting His distance, transcendence, and difference."* [323]

Yet simultaneously, Allah is the Most Intimate as He is the Manifest. In other words, He has desired to see His Own Essence by creating Adam to *"reveal to Him His own mystery."* [324] Ibn al-'Arabi elaborates further: *"When God's similarity with the creatures is affirmed, the situation appears in a different light. In respect of His similarity, God is seen as immanent and near."* [325]

The Essence of Essences does answer prayers, but Allah Most High knows best when to answer your prayers. The Sublime Reality commands, *"Call upon Me and I will answer you."* [326] How should you pray? The Prophet

Muhammad (Peace be upon hm) instructed us: *"The prayer without you is better than seventy."* As a Sufi, trust that your Beloved knows the right moment to grant your request – maybe in this life, or in the next life, for Allah tells us, *"I am here."*[327]

Also, you must deal with the danger hidden in the natural world: poisonous snakes and spiders bite people, lightning strikes a person standing in a field, and huge waves have tossed and sunk ships with all the crew drowning. Creation is Allah's Secret. It is best not to dwell on this mystery of evil with the linear mind's limitations, which are often attempts by our ego to postpone indefinitely our spiritual work. Rather than focusing on your doubts and questions, focus on The Noble, *Al-Majid*. That is, focus on your inner essence, until it becomes clear to you that Allah is the Reality, in that *"you are His form and He is your Spirit."*[328]

The Essence has revealed Itself through Its Ninety-Nine Names. The reader may wonder how One Unitary Being can have such a variety of qualities. Think of a diamond solitaire. Does it not radiate a multiplicity of colors from itself? Many colors, yet one diamond. Alternatively, think of a pen, it writes and writes many words, but there is one ink flowing from one pen.

Some of these Ninety-Nine attributes point directly to this issue of pain. Allah Most High has Ninety-Nine Names, plus one unknowable Name. Many Murids concentrate on only a few Names, like *ya Rahman* (The Merciful) and *ya Rahim* (The Compassionate). Each Name is an Attribute of Allah, and the Murid must cultivate as many Attributes as he or she has the potential to manifest. The goal of the Murid is to become a True Human Being.

We warn those who are interested in this information for reasons of garnering personal power for abusive ends, the Sufis have a saying, *"If you become its master, you also become its slave."*

There are Names that, since they represent qualities that spiritual people often do not want to explore, generally are disregarded. Examples of such Names of Allah are: *ya Khafidh* (The Abaser) or *ya Muzill* (The Degrader). Adult spirituality involves coming to terms with these Names and others like them. They are always equilibrated by other attributes. For instance, *ya Khafidh* (The Abaser) is balanced by *ya Rafi* (The Exalter); and *ya Muzill* (The Degrader) is balanced by *ya Muizz* (The Honorer). Llewellyn Vaughn-Lee reminds us, *"Deception is also a divine quality: 'They deceived and God deceived, and God is the best of deceivers'* (Qur'an 3:54)'."[329]

What was a cause of this polarity within the Divine? According to the Masters of the Qabalah, it was caused by a Divine Contraction. Gerschom Sholem has described the foundation for the initiating of the cosmogenic process. It was the wish of Ein-Sof (a Qabalistic term that refers to Allah's state prior to the act of creation) to liberate Itself from the potentiality of evil present in Its nature. These roots of evil are found in the power of Stern Judgement (or Allah's *Jalal*). The Great Sufi Saint Ruzbihan Baqli offers an astonishing vision that seems to concur with the Kabbalists: *"In the river bed of pre-eternity there are deserts and wastelands in which dwell the snakes of wrath. If one of them opened its mouth, none of creation or temporality would escape."*[330] These roots had to be made objective, to be manifested so that it became possible for Allah to emancipate Itself from them. The Absolute had to become conscious of those roots to liberate from them. Thus understood, the process of creation is the mystical purification (catharsis) of the Absolute. Creation sets into existence the powers of Stern Judgement with the potential danger of their transformation into the powers of evil. The Absolute/En-Sof contained in Itself the roots of *potential evil*, and creation was Its attempt to be liberated from them. Therefore, the created human being has a great cosmic mission.

Meher Baba taught that our rational minds cannot approach an intellectual understanding of what initiated the existence of evil: *"So let us call this initial urge to know a 'whim.' You may call this an explanation if you like or you may call it an affirmation of its inherent inexplicability. The initial whim is completely independent of reason, intellect or imagination, all of which are by-products of this whim. Reason, intellect and imagination depend upon the initial whim and not 'vice versa.' Because the whim is not dependent upon reason, intellect or imagination, it can neither be understood nor interpreted in terms of any of these faculties of the limited mind."*[331]

Ultimately, the reader must remember that Allah Most High's Mercy precedes His Wrath. The Sufis say, quoting the Qur'an, *"I seek refuge from You in You."*[332] *"Thus God, as Protector, guards against the wishes of God the Avenger, the Chastiser."*[333]

As we discussed in a previous chapter, learning requires sacrifice of some type, and sacrifice is at the least, an unpleasant experience. Pain is necessary for refinement. To create delightful spiritual wine you must crush the grapes of the Limited Self. As the sculptor chips away at the Stone with Hammer and Chisel, gradually the Divine Form is Revealed.

Another way of looking at the subject of pain is in its manifestation as negative feedback. Of all the achievements of humanity, one of the greatest was Apollo XI's trip to the moon. Most people do not know this, but Apollo XI was "off course" 70 percent of the time! Many little course corrections had to be made along the way.

They used negative and positive responses. Permit us to explain. When a modern passenger airplane is flying to a destination, they rely on the inertial guidance system. This guidance system tells the pilot when the plane is on course. Then the pilot can increase speed. The guidance system, in this case, is giving positive responses, in other words, telling the pilot "you are on the right track." Now, when the inertial guidance system signals the pilot that the plane is off course, this alerts the pilot to make a course correction. If the plane is off course, flying faster will not help.

When you are lost in a town, you tend to drive more slowly. When you begin to see familiar landmarks and roads, you then begin to speed up. Children play a game called "Hot and Cold." One person must close their eyes while the other children hide something. Then the person who has closed their eyes is told he or she can open their eyes and begin searching for the object. The children use terms like: hot, hotter, red-hot, and cold, colder, freezing. The hot terms are examples of positive responses. The cold terms are examples of negative feedback.

Negative feedback is crucial to reaching a desired goal. There is often pain associated with negative feedback, but without this pain, you may never reach your goal.

Listen to the words of Imam Ali ('Alaihi Assalam), *"Remember! Your today may be the only time left to you to hope, desire and work, and beyond today may be the biggest void-death. Whoever works during this period of expectation and hope (the span of life allocated to him) he shall reap the harvest and death will not harm him; but the person who does not care to utilize this period beneficially his time and work is wasted and death will bring calamity to him."*[334]

The most important point here is that when you UNDERSTAND that you are getting negative feedback, then you can make your own course corrections. A person may go to a coffee machine and put a quarter in it. A Styrofoam cup drops out, but no coffee is poured. This person may then try another quarter, but still he or she only gets another Styrofoam cup. The coffee is not flowing. Now, most understanding people will stop putting quarters into the machine, and maybe the considerate ones will even put an "out-of-order" sign on the machine. Yet, we all know people that metaphorically have Styrofoam cup collections! In other words, they do not know when to stop. They do not understand that by repeating the same actions over and over again, they will never reach their goal. They do not use the negative feedback to rethink their behavior.

A person trains their dog by saying the word "sit" and simultaneously pushing the dog's bottom down on the floor, at which point the dog gets a biscuit. Positive reinforcement is necessary at the time of the behavior. Our bodies are like children: they need immediate rewards. A reward is an action that results in a good feeling. Among the Sufis, having a big meal before the weekly *zikruallah* is traditional, which also includes a wonderful desert and coffee and tea. Why is this done? It is done because all humans have *nafs*. The nafs like to be fed good food. During the week after the zikr when a person is thinking, *"Do I want to go through all that again?"* the nafs say to the person, *"It wasn't all that bad, you had a delicious meal, a good desert, there were beautiful carpets to sit on, lots of decorations on the wall, it was enjoyable."* The

Sufis are wise to give respect to the nafs before the zikr, because then the nafs do not rebel about going to the *tekke* each week.

Thomas Edison, when he was working on discovering a filament for the light bulb tried hundreds of different materials. Hundreds of times he failed. He did not keep using one particular filament a hundred times if it was not working, he went on to try another filament.

When later Edison was working on developing a storage battery for Dupont, he had tried three hundred fifty configurations, and they all failed. One day a friend asked him how things were going. *"Great,"* said Edison, *"we already know three hundred fifty ways not to make it."*

Edison knew how to make constructive use of negative feedback. He did not give up in discouragement, depression and anger. Just like the Apollo XI astronauts, he used the negative feedback to keep steering himself to his goal.

There is a story about when Allah threw the Shaitan out of paradise. Allahu ta'ala took all but one of Shaitan's tools. This tool was the wedge of discouragement. Shaitan said, *"I can do all my work with just this one tool. With it I can pry all but the strongest humans away from their intended goals."*

You must take corrective action from the negative feedback you receive. It is perfectly normal to feel a reasonable and appropriate amount of sorrow when a truly difficult circumstance happens. Yet, you must remember that feeling discouraged and tearful does not change anything. You need to find constructive ways to deal with your setbacks. By that you transmute the pain into a means to achieving your goals.

Scientists will tell you that a failed experiment is a good thing. An experiment that gives the expected results only reinforces the current world view, and adds nothing new to our view of the world. Scientific experiments are not as much about "proving" a theory, as they are about "disproving" it. The scientific method is:

1) observation
[experimenting, data collecting]

2) induction
[creating a theory to describe (1) the observation]

3) deduction
[eliminating variables by testing for alternative explanations to (2) the proposed theory . . . this is where the scientist is trying to "disprove" the theory]

4) verification
[making sure the theory is testable, repeatable and predictable]

Therefore, failure is a teacher who opens new windows and who is necessary for the process of verification.

It has been said, *"The person who does not learn from his or her mistakes will be forced to repeat them."* Denial is not just a river in Egypt! Do not allow the negative to swallow you up, becoming endlessly depressed and discouraged. Give yourself kindness and self-respect.

As Ibn al'Arabi writes, *"It is for this reason that the Qur'an [the union of the two aspects] was vouchsafed to Muhammad and this Community, which is the best granted to mankind."*[335] Moreover, elsewhere he writes, *"The quotation 'There is none like unto Him' combines the two aspects."*[336] Earlier we mentioned the great cosmic mission of humankind. The understanding of this mission can be found in these teachings of Ibn al'Arabi. The union of the two aspects, the Qur'an, must become alive within the Heart of the Sufi.

Meher Baba sheds light on this process in his own terminology: *"In the infinite Beyond state of God, which transcends the categories of consciousness as well as unconsciousness, there appeared the initial urge for God to know Himself. And with the arising of this initial urge, there was an instantaneous manifestation of infinite consciousness as well as infinite unconsciousness, as simultaneous resultants. Of these two seemingly opposite but complimentary aspects, the infinite consciousness plays the part of the Avatar or Divine Incarnation. The infinite unconsciousness finds its expression through an evolution, which seeks to develop full consciousness through time processes. In the human form, the full consciousness strives to have self-knowledge and self-realization."*[337]

Let us conclude with the words of the great poet Yunus Emre:

"The Province that casts this spell
And speaks so many tongues to tell,
Transcends the earth, heaven and hell,
But is contained in this cast.
The yearning tormented my mind:
I searched the heavens and the ground;
I looked and looked, but failed to find.
I found Him inside man at last."

PRACTICE

Inhale and contemplate the Divine Name - *ya Akhir* - The Last. Allow the understanding to occur in you that after Creation has ceased to exist, only The Last, The End, The Ultimate, *ya Akhir*, will remain.

"One day Khalif Umar said to Ali Bin Abi Talib ('Alaihi Assalam) with a feeling of surprise: 'How is it that if any problem is asked of you, you give its answer without the least hesitation?' The Holy Imam ('Alaihi Assalam) replying, opened his holy hand before him and said: 'How many fingers are there in my hand?' Umar immediately said: 'Five.' Ali ('Alaihi Assalam) said: 'Why did you not ponder over it?' Umar said: 'There was no need for pondering over it since all the five fingers were before my eyes.' Then Ali ('Alaihi Assalam) said: 'Similarly all the problems, ordinances, and issues of knowledge are clearly visible to me and I give their answers without any pondering.'"

- Abul Muwaiyyid Muaffaq
Bin Ahmad Khwarazmi

THE INCOMPARABLY DEDICATED ALI'S ('ALAIHI ASSALAM) WRITINGS

It was during the Khalifate of Abu Bakr and early Khalifate of Umar that Imam Ali ('Alaihi Assalam) set to the task of registering the hadiths. Imam Ali ('Alaihi Assalam) was incomparably strict about Islam, and could foresee the need to register the hadith to be the source for future generations. Ali ('Alaihi Assalam) was fanatic about the accuracy of his writing, and in an agonizingly methodical manner he accomplished the following:

1. During Abu Bakr's Khalifate: Ali ('Alaihi Assalam) rendered in writing the following:
    a. Holy Qur'an: *Chronological* order of the Qur'an's revelations.
    b. *Tafseer* of the Holy Qur'an, 3 volumes: called *Mus'haf Fatima.*

2. During Umar's Khalifate: Ali ('Alaihi Assalam) rendered the following:
    a. Hadith of the Prophet: Voluminous writing, called *Saheefa of Ali.*
    b. *Fiqh: al-Ah'kaam* and *Mu'aamalat,* the *Halal* and *Haram.*

3. During Uthman's Khalifate: Ali ('Alaihi Assalam) rendered the following:
    a. History of the various Prophets as he learned from Prophet Muhammad (Peace be upon him), called: *The White Al-Jafr.*
    b. Islamic rules and directives of Wars, called *The Red al-Jafr.*

The books Ali rendered were called *Al-Jaami'a* ("Encyclopedia") and they were left with the Imams of Ahlul Bayt, each new Imam receiving them from the dying predecessor Imam. The Imams referred to these hadiths and books over a period of about three centuries. Notable among the Imams is Imam Ja'far Al-Sadiq, who was the teacher of great Sunni jurists such as Imam

Abu Hanifa, Yahya Bin As'id Ansari, Ibn Jarih, Muhammad Bin Ishaq, Yahya Bin Satid Qattan, Sufyan Bin 'Uyayna, Sufyan Thawri, and Malik Bin Anas. Four thousand scholars graduated from his school. As many as four hundred religious doctrines were recorded by Imam Ja'far Al-Sadiq's chief companions, which are known as *"Usul-e-Arba Mia,"* which means the *Four Hundred Verdicts.*

Hujjatul Islam Abu Hamid Ghazzali writes that there is a book written by the Chief of the Pious: Ali Bin Abi Talib ('Alaihi Assalam). Its name is "Jafr-e-Jam'u'd-Dunya wa'l-Akhira." Ghazzali writes: *"It consists of all the sciences, realities, obscurities, matters of the unseen, the essence of things and their effects, the essence of names and letters, which no one knows except Ali ('Alaihi Assalam) and his eleven descendants, who, according to the ordinance of the Holy Prophet of Allah, are the Imams and Vice-Regents. The fact is that they have inherited this thing from their fathers."*

Similarly, Sulayman Balkhi in his "Yanabiu'l-Mawadda," page 403, has reported a detailed commentary about the book from Muhammad Bin Talha Shafi'i's "Durru'l- Munazzam." He says that *"Jafr-e-Jami'a,"* having keys to knowledge, contains one thousand and seven hundred pages and exclusively belongs to Imam Ali Bin Abi Talib ('Alaihi Assalam).

The Jafr was written in secret letters and signs. The key of this secret was handed over to Ali ('Alaihi Assalam) by the Prophet, and the Prophet instructed him to pass this key down to his successors, the Holy Imams. Imam Zainul Abidin ('Alaaihi Assalam) has stated that the Imams are the countenance of Allah. Imam al-Ridha ('Alaihi Assalam) has stated that the Prophets, the Messengers and the Imams are meant by the phrase *"Countenance of Allah."*

Because of the source and chain of narration of the hadith, we rely only on the hadiths as narrated by Ahlul Bayt or those hadiths in the *Sihahu's-Sitta* (Bukhari, Muslim and others) that are *similar* to what Ahlul Bayt had quoted. We see in light of the writings of Ali ('Alaihi Assalam) that here was a man whose devotion to Islam was profound, a man whose intelligence was vast, and a man whose esoteric knowledge of the Light of Islam was complete.

"Beware of disunity and enmity."

> *- Imam Ali Ibn Abi Talib*
> *('Alaihi Assalam)*

"I advise you, and all my children, my relatives, and whosoever receives this message, to be conscious of Allah, to remove your differences, and to strengthen your ties. I heard your grandfather, peace be upon him, say, 'Reconciliation of your differences is worthier than all prayers and all fasting.'"

> *- Imam Ali Ibn Abi Talib*
> *('Alaihi Assalam)*

"And do not speak of those who are slain in the Way of Allah as dead; they are alive, but you perceive not."

> *- Qur'an 2:154*

"Call Ali! Call Ali!
Call aloud to Ali
Who is the epiphanic source of wonders
You shall surely find him helping in your troubles
All grief and anxiety will disappear
By Your power and Authority!
O Ali! O Ali! O Ali!"

> *- famous prayer to*
> *Imam Ali ('Alaihi Assalam)*

THE LION OF ALLAH

Let us listen in to Imam Ali (Alaihi Assalam) as he speaks to people assembled in the mosque: *"After the demise of the Holy Prophet we said that we were the Holy Prophet's Ahlul Bayt, his relatives, his heirs, his Progeny and his successors and the most rightful persons in the world, to receive his heritage. No one except us could be a claimant to the right of rulership after him. Nevertheless, a group of the hypocrites laid a conspiracy and snatched away our Holy Prophet's rulership and ascendancy from us and entrusted it to those, who were our opponents. By Allah our hearts and eyes wept for it. By Allah, we were full of grief and indignation. I swear by Allah that if there were no fear that the Muslims would be disintegrated and would return to their former faith of infidelity, we would have overturned the Khalifate, but we adopted silence. They continued occupying their seats until they reached their end. Now, Allah has returned the Khalifate to me. Moreover, these two men, Talha and Zubair, also swore allegiance to me. Now they have proceeded to Basra with a view to creating dissension among the people and cause civil war among you.* "338

Among the great scholars, Ibn Abi'l Hadid and Ziyad Bin Kalbi have reported that at the time of setting out to Basra, the Holy Imam ('Alaihi Assalam) addressed the people. He said, *"When the Holy Prophet of Allah passed away, the Quraish swooped down upon us and deprived us of the right, which we deserved more than anyone else. So I thought that it was better to adopt patience at that time, rather than allow the Muslims to disintegrate and their blood to be spilt as they had embraced Islam only recently."*

So the Holy Imam's ('Alaihi Assalam) silence and his abstaining from confronting the Khalifate of Abu Bakr and Umar was not due to his concurrence with it, but it was because first he wanted to prevent the differences and bloodshed among the people and secondly because he wanted to save the Religion from annihilation as it was feared that the infidels would dominate and the people of weak faith would turn apostates.

Therefore, after the Holy Imam's ('Alaihi Assalam) silence for six months and his continued disapproval of and protests against their decision when the people had understood that he was against the political supremacy, then as stated by the Sunni Ulema, he offered allegiance and cooperated with them. It really meant that he helped the religion of Islam and not that he liked or acknowledged the Khalifate. The same idea is contained in a letter, which he had sent to the people of Egypt, through Maalik-e-Ashtar. He clearly writes in it that his silence was for the sake of Islam and the help that he gave was also for the safety of Islam.

The original text of Ali's ('Alaihi Assalam) holy letter, that Ibn-Abi'l-Hadid has also recorded in his "Sharh Nahj al-balaghah" volume IV, page 164, is as follows:

"Allah Almighty sent Muhammad as a witness of the prophets to warn the people. Therefore, when the Holy Prophet passed away the Muslims created a dispute in the matter of Khalifate. I swear by Allah that I never thought and believed, nor there were the least signs of it that the people of Arabia would take away the right to Khalifate from the Ahlul Bayt and Progeny of the Holy Prophet and would give it to others after him. It was unimaginable that after the demise of the Holy Prophet, in spite of his clear decreeing and ordination, they would deprive me of that right.

"I was greatly pained and distressed that the people ran up to such and such person (Abu Bakr) and swore allegiance to him. Therefore, I withdrew myself until I saw that a group of people diverged from Islam and became apostate and were out to destroy the religion of Islam. Then I feared that if I did not help Islam and the Muslims, Islam would suffer such damage and destruction as would be more painful to me than the snatching away of the Khalifate from me, because this rulership and power could not last long. It is only to fade away like ignis fatuus and scatter like clouds. So it was under these conditions

that I had to rise, till idol-worship became weak and unstable and the religion (Islam) became firm and calm."

Now some object to the idea that the Prophet Muhammad would choose to pass his priceless wisdom down through his family. They cite the tradition (incidentally, narrated by Abu Bakr): *"We the group of Prophets, do not leave behind any legacy; whatever we leave as inheritance is charity" (i.e., the property of umma)."* First, we must say that this tradition is questionable and unacceptable. Whoever forged this tradition only uttered it without thinking over the words he used, because if he had been careful about it, he would not have used the words in such a way. For later on, the people, having wisdom and knowledge, made fun of this forger. He would never have said, *"We the Prophets do not leave any inheritance,"* because he would have known that the very wording of this concocted tradition would expose his lying. If he had used the words: *"(Only) I (who am the Last of the Prophets) have not made any inheritor"* his labored hadith would have been more credible and defendable. However, when he used the word in plural meaning *"We the Prophets . . . ,"* we are obliged to investigate the truth or otherwise of the tradition. Now we refer to the Holy Qur'an for guidance. When we compare the supposed tradition with the Holy Qur'an, we find that there are a number of verses in it, which tell us that the Prophets did leave inheritance which their successors appropriated after them. Therefore, it proves that this tradition is to be rejected outright.

Others object on the grounds that when the Prophet repeatedly uttered that Ali ('Alaihi Assalam) was to be his Vice-Regent, the Prophet Muhammad (Peace be upon him) was only meaning this in a personal or ordinary way, as in a family Will, which everyone makes for his or her successor. But if a sensible person looks at these traditions carefully and with justice, particularly those traditions which tell that Allah appointed the Prophets and the Vice-Regents and He also appointed Ali ('Alaihi Assalam) as the Holy Prophet's Vice-Regent, he or she will clearly understand that here it means succession as Khalif and the nominee or appointee who has full control over the individuals, and the society, in their affairs and that this guardianship takes the place of the office of Prophethood. Muhammad (Peace be upon him) was naming the *Qutub.*

In the 40th year of Hijri, in the small hours of the morning of the 19th Ramadan, Imam Ali ('Alaihi Assalam), the Pole of Saintship, the Cupbearer of Kevser, the Lord of the Worlds, *Ali el Mhrteza,* was struck with a poisoned sword. The weapon was wielded by a Kharijite named Abdu'r-Rahman Ibn Muljim Muradi. When Imam Ali ('Alaihi Assalam) was struck, he was offering his prayers in the Masjid of Kufa.

Ali ('Alaihi Assalam) had come out to wake the people for the dawn prayer. The assassin had been lying in wait for him from the beginning of the night. Feigning sleep, among a group of sleeping people, Ibn Muljim sprang out and struck Ali ('Alaihi Assalam) on the top of his head with his sword that was poisoned. Imam Ali ('Alaihi Assalam) exclaimed: *"By the Lord of the Ka'ba, I am victorious."* The Lion of Allah lingered through the day of the nineteenth and the night and day of the twentieth and the first third of the night of the twenty-first. Then he (Peace be upon him) died a martyr and met his Lord.

He died on the 21st day of Ramadan 40 A.H. and buried in Najaf-ul-Ashraf. His two sons, al-Hassan ('Alaihi Assalam) and al-Hussain ('Alaihi Assalam) performed the tasks of washing him and shrouding him according to his request. They removed the traces of the place of his burial, again according to his request, because the Lion of Allah knew about the regime of negativity (the Umayyads) which was to come after him and their hostile attitude toward him. His grave remained hidden until al-Sadiq Ja'far b. Muhammad ('Alaihi Assalam) pointed it out during the Abbasid regime.

The Lion of Allah was born in the House of Allah, the Ka'ba, and martyred in the House of Allah, *Masjid-e-Kufa*. Imam Ali ('Alaihi Assalam) was the first to compile and codify the Qur'an. He was the first to by styled as "brother" by the Prophet (Peace be upon him). He was the first to give burial to the Prophet (Peace be upon him). He was the first to offer to sleep in the Prophet's (Peace be upon him) bed (to protect the Prophet) on the night of the Prophet's emigration to Medina (al-Munawwarah). The honor of owning a house, which opened into the courtyard of the Prophet's mosque, was reserved for Imam Ali ('Alaihi Assalam) alone.

Hazrat Ali ('Alaihi Assalam) was never defeated in a war or a combat throughout his life. His physical strength was beyond human comprehension. He removed from the hinges the strong doors of the Khyber fort with a single jolt of his hand. Later, seven strong men with Abu Ra'fe', the famous strong-man, could not lift even an inch from the ground one of the corners of the door. When asked about his wonderful display of strength, in removing the doors, Hazrat Ali ('Alaihi Assalam) replied that it was his divine power.[339]

The Lion of Allah, the most brave and gentle Muslim after the Prophet (Peace be upon him) himself, began his glorious life with devotion to Allah and His Messenger, and ended it in the service of Islam. The Holy Prophet (Peace be upon him) is quoted as having said that, *"Knowledge has ten parts, out of which nine are mastered by Ali. The tenth portion is divided amongst wise men of the universe."*[340] Master Junaid, may Allah be please with him, has said: *"Ali, the chosen of God is our shaikh [master] in the principles of the Sufi Doctrine and also in the tolerance of calamities."* [341]

Carefully study the body of the Lion of Allah. The haunches of this Lion, Imam Ali ('Alaihi Assalam), can vault you to sublime states and levels.

PRACTICE

You will notice that a certain feeling comes over your being when you put your attention onto that which is sprouting, blossoming and flourishing. The feeling will be similar to the experience of sunrise. On the other hand, the feelings arising from the observation of dying and decaying plant life will be akin to the experience of watching the moon rise in the night sky.

One way to know The Only One is to follow the Yin and the Yang each to their extremes. At each end of the spectrum you will find The Only One. Yin is the moon rise, the decaying flower returning to its constituent parts, becoming again One with the Earth. Yang is the sun rising in the east, the shoot sprouting from the earth pointing directly to heaven, proclaiming the Oneness of Allah. Both "contrasts" express Unity.

If you assiduously practice these two simple exercises, the entire astral world will begin to open to you. After you have become familiar with the astral images that arise inside your being when you perceive these physical phenomena of nature, you are then ready to start experiencing astral forms with no counterparts in the physical world.

Do not try to grasp mentally the meaning of any of this. Let the Astral Images and Forms themselves divulge to you their mysteries.

You begin to be aware that feelings and thoughts are just as "real" as cars, hockey sticks and a new pair of pants. The Murid becomes aware of the powerful effects that thoughts can cause in the Spirit world. They are as powerful as missiles fired from a fighter-jet at a physical target, or a lover's kiss.

"My heart has become receptive of every form. It is a meadow for gazelles, a monastery for monks, an abode for idols, the Ka'ba of the pilgrim, the tables of the Torah, the Qur'an. My religion is love - wherever its camels turn, Love is my belief, my faith."

> *- Muhyiddin Ibn 'Arabi*

"The path of Sufism is the elimination of any intermediaries between the individual and God."

> *- Sheikh Muzaffer Ozak,*
> *Love is the Wine*

TALES FROM UNDER THE OVERPASS

*W*hat is Sufism?" Sam asked Mr. Khadir, "I've heard of it, and I get the feeling that you may know something about it."

"Sufism is a radical shock." Mr. Khadir said emphatically. "Sufism, or Tasawwuf as it is called in Arabic, is generally understood by scholars and Sufis to be the inner, mystical or psycho-spiritual dimension of Islam." Mr. Khadir continued. "Some say that Moses was taught it first by Yahweh in the form of the Qabalah. A river passes though many countries and each claims it for its own. Nevertheless, there is only one river. While the paths are many, the Way of Truth is single. A great Sufi Guide named 'The Great Maulani' the head of the Mevlevi Sufi Order and the twenty-first descendant of Rumi, said to me once, 'My great ancestor was just one in a chain that stretches all the way back to the beginning of time and in which Abraham, Moses and Jesus were delightful links.'

"At the time of Abraham, it was already firmly established. Abraham himself was a Sufi and employed the symbols, the legends and the practices that have ever since been the hallmark of Sufis.

"However, bear in mind the warning that Rumi himself offered, 'Know that the lover in any case is no Muslim. The religion of Love knows neither infidelity nor faith.' Often those who you least think are Sufi's are followers of this Way, for it is not advertised nor proselytized. In fact, few are invited, and even fewer respond to the invitation."

Sam was intrigued, but also confused, "Why would so few people refuse to take such an invitation?"

"The world distracts them from themselves," answered Mr. Khadir. "Instead of paying attention to the love in their hearts and truly seeing the Living Reality surrounding them, they pursue worthless goals, thinking that these toys are of great meaning."

"So," Sam questioned, "I am still a little confused as to Sufism's connection to religion. Is there a difference between Sufism and Islam?"

"While all Muslims believe that they are on the pathway to God and will become close to God in Paradise, after death and the Final Judgement, Sufis believe as well that it is possible to become close to God and to experience this closeness while one is alive. And actually, the attainment of the heart-knowledge that comes with such intimacy with God is the very purpose of the creation. Allah has said, 'I was a hidden treasure and I loved that I be known, so I created the creation in order to be known.' "

"*Sometimes God makes a command that he does not wish to be obeyed, and sometimes he wants that which he has forbidden. He ordered Eblis (Shaitan) to prostrate himself before Adam, while desiring him not to do so. He forbade Adam to eat of the tree, while desiring him to do so, whereas if he had not desired, Adam would not have eaten thereof.*"

> *- Imam Ja'far Sadiq*
> *('Alaihi Assalam)* [342]

"*I have walked behind the sky.*
We are all animals,
but, there is a better way to live.
Sometimes, at night,
I hear a voice in my head.
Who is it?
Is it you . . . ?
Is it true that the beyond,
that everything beyond,
is here in this life?"

> *- Nadja* [343]

"*Iblis was retained to watch over the door to the presence of the Almighty and was told, You are My lover. Be jealous about My threshold and keep strangers out of My presence. And continue to proclaim this,*
> *The Beloved said to me, Sit at My door,*
>> *do not allow inside anyone who is not in accord with Me.*
> *To him who desires Me, say, Be enraptured!*
>> *This state is not suitable for any man unless I find it suit able.*"

> *- 'Ain Al-Qudāt* [344]

"*Remember, there is no more empty, nor detestable creature in nature than the man who runs away from his demon.*"

> *- Joseph Conrad, Heart of Darkness*

"*Everything happens according to divine will, and it is a mistake to think that God has a rival in the form of a Devil. Accentuation of the forces for good is necessary for releasing divine life in its fullness. But evil itself often plays an important part in accentuating the forces for good; and it becomes an inevitable shadow or counterpart of the good.*"

> *- Meher Baba*

SHAITAN: THE SACRED GUARDIAN OF THE DOOR

Iblis was an angel, Azazil,[345] the most intimate angel near the throne of Allah. He worshiped seven hundred thousand years in the court of the Unity of Existence. *"If Eblis were to reveal his light to mankind, they would worship it like a God,"* wrote Hassan Basri.[346] Iblis was created of fire. Adam was created of clay, that is, earth.

When Allah created Adam, He ordered all the angels to bow down before Adam. All the angels prostrated themselves in front of the new creation, all except Iblis. Iblis refused. For his disobeying the Almighty's command, he was thrown out of the Court of Proximity, and cursed until the Final Day. It was then that Allah changed his name from Azazil to Iblis. Yet, we ask, where was he thrown out to?

How does the Sufi reconcile a Perfect, Loving, and Merciful Deity with the creation of an Evil being?

"If your slate is so clean, why did you create Satan?

You say that one should not pay attention to
Satan's wicked words;

Yet, you've given him refuge in my skin and veins,
so he can wink and encourage me to do bad deeds.

You order us to do our devotions and Satan to run
Wild in our body and soul.

You create a commotion, so the deer may flee; then
Spur on the hound to pursue the chase!

I have much to say, but I do not dare: I am so
frightened, I cannot even breathe."

So wrote the poet Naser Khosarau. Knowledge of the mysteries of the Shaitan reveals subtleties of the nature of creation Itself! We will talk more about the body later in this chapter, but first we will look at the state of Iblis after he was cursed,

"At the very moment when Eblis was cursed he
began to pray and praise. He cried,

'A curse from you is a hundred times finer than
turning from you towards anything else.' " [347]

Some Sufis are of the opinion that while Shaitan may have made a mistake, he has never stopped his devotions and love toward his Beloved Allah. In fact, they posit that Iblis refused to prostrate to Adam because of his adherence to *La illahe il ALLAH,* that is, he refused to recognize anything but Allah.

Sufis realize that all of creation must endure the wrath of the All-Pervading Life Principle. *"We know that our Beloved comes with wrath and affliction, but we have pledged ourselves to the Beloved's affliction and wrath. From the Beloved comes affliction and from us contentment, from the Beloved, wrath, from us love . . .* " so wrote Mansur Hallaj. [348]

Shaitan and Adam ('Alaihi Asslam) both knew the same things. *"Allah taught Adam the Divine Names as the fundamental nature of creation."*[349] Shaitan knew he would tempt Adam; Adam knew that Shaitan would tempt him. However, after the temptation, Shaitan said to Allah, *"You caused me to do this!"* Nevertheless, Adam ('Alaihi Asslam), bowed his head in humility. That is the difference between the two! The secret of the Sufi Way is to accept, in love and excellent etiquette, whatever Allah ordains.

"Eblis did not consider it necessary to repent; he did not seek pardon or make entreaty. Adam, however knew that repentance is the key to felicity and the means to forgiveness; hence, he considered it necessary to repent, hastening to do so and not resting until his repentance was accepted." [350]

In addition, Jelaluddin Rumi puts it this way,

> *"Satan said, 'Because You have misguided me . . . '*
> *the despicable devil covered up his act.*
> *Adam said, 'I have wronged myself'; he was not*
> *Ignorant of God's action, unlike ourselves.*
> *Out of etiquette, by accepting the responsibility for*
> *sinning, he concealed God's action; by taking the sin*
> *upon himself, he was blessed.*
> *After his repentance God asked him, 'Did I not create the sin*
> *and those tribulations within you?*
> *Was it not my ordainment and decree? Why then*
> *did you hide it when asking for forgiveness?'*
> *'I was afraid,' said Adam, 'I preserved etiquette.'*
> *God replied, 'And I, in turn, have rewarded you for*
> *this.'"* [351]

Even more significant is the fact that Shaitan said the word "I" in front of Allah. Shaitan should have known better, for to declare his existence before the One Existing Being is an unpardonable sin. The Great Pir-o-Murshid Inayat Khan wrote, *"Just as smoke obscures the brightness of the flame, in the same manner the light of the soul is dulled by the consciousness of 'I'.*[352] Moment by moment the Murid must turn attention away from him or herself: beliefs, thoughts and personal reactions to factual conditions, and turn toward *"the Divine Principle as the Power in all events . . . this must be felt attention, yielding, of the whole being, the whole of body, life, emotion, mind, knowledge, self, destiny, and circumstance."* [353]

Let us delve more deeply in the mysteries of Shaitan. In a profound sense, Shaitan separates the wheat from the chaff. In other words, he is the tester of the quality of the Murid who would knock on God's door. Shaitan is the guardian of truth. He is the gatekeeper to the throne of the Majestic One. *"Likewise the sword of this black light who reigns over the domain of La ilahe and jealously guards il ALLAH from intruders, is the sword of God's own divine power, 'By Your power, I will surely seduce them all!' "*[354] In Sufi tekkes, the dervish chosen to guard the door has the most important position in the tekke other than the Sheikh. *"God appointed Eblis the gatekeeper of His court, saying to him, 'My lover, because of the jealousy-in-love that you have for me, do not let strangers approach me.'"* [355]

Iblis is also intimately connected with the physical body. According to Dr. Javad Nurbasksh, *"Certain Sufi masters ascribe the cause of Eblis' disobedience to his consideration of the outward form (surat) of Adam and his lack of awareness of the latter's inner reality (ma'nā), which was the manifestation of the whole of the names and attributes of God."*[356] Here is a lesson for the Murid, not to be fooled by, and fall in love with, outward manifestations, and to disregard the inward Reality. Some say that the reason the Shaitan did not bow down before Adam was that the Shaitan did not realize that Adam was God! The Sufi's task is to help the Shaitan realize who the Complete Human Being is.

Therefore, this discussion must also include reference to the Lower Soul, also known as the nafs. The Sheikhs have said that the human being has "fire in the blood." *"The helper of the lower self is Satan."*[357] The Lower Soul is responsible for all sorts of terrible things that we do to others and ourselves. The Sufi's task is to spiritualize the nafs through the act of *"reforming his lower self"*[358] via Zikr. Sheikh Abu Ali Siah of Merv says, *"I saw my nafs exactly like myself; and somebody came and catching him by the hair handed him over to me. I tied him to a tree and wanted to kill him. He said, 'Abu Ali do not be angry. I am Allah's army and you cannot finish me.' "* The nafs are a special mystery of Allah. They can be the stumbling block for the Sufi, or the stepping stone to Ma'rifat. The Sufi is responsible for his or her nafs. On the Day of Judgement, it will be our nafs that will appear before Allah.

Some theologians have blamed the first poet-bards as the cause of humanity's separation from the Manifest. This is because a poet can invent an artificial reality. As some see the Shaitan as the one who bestows the ability of imagination upon humankind, these theologians hold the poets responsible for promulgating Satanic realities. 'Azizo'd-Din Nasafi illuminates this insight:

"Six persons emerged from the third heaven: Adam, Eve, Satan, Eblis, the Peacock and the Snake. Adam is the spirit, Eve the body, Satan nature, Eblis imagination, the Peacock lust, and the Snake wrath."[359] It is also said by some that just as the Shaitan refused to prostrate to Adam, so too, did the imagination refuse to bow to Allah. However, are the theologians correct when they deem the poets Satanic? Our human imagination is one of the highest gifts of Allah, the Divine Creative Power. Yet with the power comes great responsibil-

ity. *"God made the faculty of imagination the locus which brings together everything given by the sensory faculties."*360

A fascinating theory concerning Iblis' separation from proximity to Allah is that it was due to his lack of friendship with the Merciful and Compassionate One. Iblis possessed an enormous amount of esoteric wisdom, but he did not have friendship. This is a clear message to the Murid to beware of mistaking learning *about* Sufism, to actually *practicing* Sufism. Many aspirants have read hundreds of books, but feel that they do not need to make Zikruallah. The way to friendship with Allah is through being a Sufi, not through knowing about Sufism.

Duality did not appear until the creation of Adam ('Alaihi Asslam). Shaitan's refusal to prostrate suddenly created an illusory state of division. There came into existence an aspect of Allah that was pro-Adam ('Alaihi Asslam) and an aspect of Allah that was anti-Adam ('Alaihi Asslam), in other words: Shaitan.

How could this happen? Allah the Mighty is incomparable with all created things. In one sense, Adam ('Alaihi Asslam) as a created thing, must be endlessly far from Him. In other words, Adam ('Alaihi Asslam) is totally Not He. Adam ('Alaihi Asslam) cannot claim divinity, which is an unforgivable sin. Allah, in His projection as Shaitan, knew this, and so could not bow to an utterly poor creature.

Yet Allah as All Merciful realizes that He loves His creature, and Adam ('Alaihi Asslam), through Allah's love, may become Allah's "vice-regent" (Khalifa) and "friend" (wali). Humans are Allah's "Hidden Treasure" for *"He loved to be known."*

Shaitan (as the nafs, Lower Soul, "Fire in the Blood") is made aware of his annihilation in Allah and therefore no longer says "I." Adam (the Complete Human) unites God and Iblis, and restores the Primal Unity.

The Complete Human is the means that the Ever-Living Essence consummates Unity.

PRACTICE

Picture yourself off-planet. You are floating, suspended in outer space. Myriads of brilliant stars encircle you. A voice comes to you from the six directions - up, down, right, left, back, front, and you hear yourself echoing Words Spoken across the cosmos,

> *Everything I see is an Expression of the Ultimate Reality.*
> *Everything I taste is an Expression of the Ultimate Reality.*
> *Everything I smell is an Expression of the Ultimate Reality.*
> *Everything I touch is an Expression of the Ultimate Reality.*
> *Everything I hear is an Expression of the Ultimate Reality.*
> *I will interpret each phenomenon as a particular expression of the Living Reality.*

However, beware of interpreting events as particular messages to you. That is only the manipulation of your nafs, also known as the Limited Self. We can view life's happenings as the Entire Choir of Existence Chanting a Mystic Hymn declaring the Condition of the Divine.

All is the articulation of the Divine.

"The time of judging who's drunk and who's sober, who's right or wrong, who's closer to God or farther away, all that's over! This caravan is led instead by a great delight. The simple joy that sits with us. That is the grace."

- Hafiz

SERMON BETWEEN THE TWO GULFS

Before Imam Ali ('Alaihi Assalam) was martyred, he delivered an extraordinary sermon. Many Sufis readily admit that this most blessed of persons possessed incredible esoteric and mystical knowledge, but few know of this sermon. It is known as the "Sermon Between the Two Gulfs (*Khutbah Tantanjiyya*)," sometimes also called the "Sermon of the Exposition (*Khutba't'ul-Bayan*)" or "Sermon of the Climes (*Kutbah Aqalim*)" It is perhaps the most controversial yet most metaphysical and ecstatic of all his sermons.

Scholars differ on whether the sermon was delivered between Kufa and Medina before or after the Battle of Siffin. Here is a partial section of the Kutbah, as quoted in Bursi:

"O people! . . . I am hope and that which is hoped for. I preside over the twin gulfs (ana waqif 'ala tantanjayn). And my gaze beholds the two easts and the two wests (cf. Qur'an LV:17). I have seen the mercy of God and Paradise clearly through direct [physical] vision. And it is in the seventh sea . . . and in its swells are the stars and the orbits. And I saw the earth enwrapped as by a garment. I know the wonders of God's creation as no one but God knows them. And I know what was and what will be, and what has occurred at the time of the primordial covenant (adh-dharr al-awwal) [viz. yawm al-mithaq; cf. Qur'an VII:172] before the First Adam. It has been disclosed to me by my Lord . . . and this knowledge was hidden from all prophets except the Master of this Shari'a of yours (i.e., Muhammad). He taught me his knowledge and I taught him my knowledge. We are the first warning and the warning of the first and the last and the warning for all times and periods. Through us perishes him who perishes and through us is saved him who is saved. And you are incapable of what is in us. By him who breaks the seals and drives the winds! . . . Indeed, the winds and air and birds are made subservient to us. The world below was given me but I shunned it. I am the dome of the world . . . I know what is above the highest Paradise and what is below the lowest earth and what is in the highest heavens and what is between them and what is under the dust. All this is comprehensive knowledge, not related knowledge. I swear by the Lord of the Mighty Throne! If you desired I could tell you of your forefathers, where they were and what they were and where they are now and what they will be . . . If I reveal to you what was given in the first eternity and what

*is of me in the End then you would see mighty wonders and things great . . . I
am the Master of the first creation before the first Noah. And were I to tell you
what transpired between Adam and Noah, the wonders of those arts and
nations destroyed [in that time] then the truth of the statement 'evil is what they
have done' would be established. I am Master of the first two Floods [Qur'an
XXIX:14]. I am Master of the Flood [sayl al-'aram; Qur'an XXXIV:16]. I am
Master of the hidden secrets (al-asrar al-maknunat). I am Master of 'Ad and
the Gardens. And I am Master of Thamud and the Signs. And I am their
destroyer. And I am their director. I am their two gates. I am their leveler. I am
their maker to die and I am their maker to live. I am the First, I am the Last, I
am the Manifest, I am the Hidden [Qur'an LVII:3]. I was with time before time
and I was with revolution before revolution. And I was with the Pen before the
Pen and I was with the Tablet before the Tablet. And I am Master of the first
Pre-Eternity. And I am the Master of Jabalqa and Jabarsa . . . I am the director of the first world when there was no earth and heaven . . . Verily I am the
creator of the heavens and the earth . . . '*

The Safavid era authority, Muhammad Baqir Majlisi, considered the
sermon authentic. However, it was not included by the compilers of "Nahju'l-
Balagha." The sermon does appear in a few Twelver hadith collections such as
Kulayni (i.e., "Usul Kafi"). It is mentioned by Ibn Babuya, and is quoted in full
in the 9th volume of Majlisi's monumental "Bihar al-'Anwar (Oceans of
Light)." Apart from Kulayni and Majlisi, a twelfth century Syrian Isma'ili by
the name of Ibn Shahrashub refers to it in one of his treatises. The *khutbah* was
subject to numerous commentaries, the most famous of which was by the six-
teenth century Twelver follower of Ibn al-'Arabi, Rajab Bursi in his
"Mashariq'ul-Anwar al-Yaqin fi Asrar 'Amir al-Muminin (Orients of the
Lights of Certainty Regarding the Secrets of the Commander of the Faithful)."
It was also subject to numerous commentaries in the nineteenth century by
Iranian *'alims* of serious esoteric bent such as Mirza Ahmad Shirazi, Mulla
'Ali ibn Jamshid Nuri, Shaykh Ahmad Ahsai (founder of the Shaykhi school)
and his successors Siyyid Kazim Rashti and Hajj Muhammad Karim Khan
Kirmani, and Siyyid 'Ali Muhammad Shirazi (founder of the Babi sect).
Among Shia Sufis in both Iran and Iraq it is considered the highest possible
exposition of gnosis, and that from the mouth of 'Ali ('Alaihi Assalam) him-
self, and it is neither taught to nor discussed with the non-adept.

"The biggest mistake is to reveal the bad deeds of others and to hide your own bad deeds."

> *- Iman Muhammad Baqer*
> *('Alaihi Asslam)*

"The heart has no more than one aspect at a time, such that when it is occupied with a particular aspect, it is veiled from another. So take care that you are not drawn toward anything but God, lest He deprive you of the delights of intimate converse with Him."

> *- A. Madyan*

"As long as there is duality, one sees 'the other,' one hears 'the other,' one smells 'the other,' one speaks to 'the other,' one thinks of 'the other,' one knows 'the other'; but when for the illumined soul the all is dissolved in the Self, who is there to be seen by whom, who is there to be smelled by whom, who is there to be heard by whom, who is there to be spoken to by whom, who is there to be thought of by whom, who is there to be known by whom?"

> *- Bhrihadaranyaka Upanishad 4.5.15*

TALES FROM UNDER THE OVERPASS

*S*am had never walked so much in his life. Traveling such great distances was becoming hard on Sam's legs and body, so Mr. Khadir asked him if he wanted to hear another story. Sam appreciatively exclaimed, "Yes, please."

The student of a famous Sheikh came to him once and said, "Efendi, there is a man living on the small island offshore, and everyone says he is a Walyullah (Holy Man). Perhaps you should visit him."

To which the Sheikh replied, "Come, let us take this boat and you will row me to that island and I will visit this great Waliyullah."

"But Efendi," the student replied, "today is the first day of Ramadan."

"No matter," said the Sheikh, "Allah will provide." So they boarded the boat and the student rowed them to the small island.

When they arrived, they found the man sitting naked under a palm tree, unbathed and unkempt, doing absolutely nothing. "What are you doing?" demanded the Sheikh, "It is Ramadan and you don't have ablution!"

"What ablution?" asked the man.

"The prescribed washing," said the Sheikh.

"I don't know about that," replied the man, "I live simply. I only eat what I find under rocks and light a fire to keep warm after dark."

"You eat creeping things! You do not have ablution!" shrieked the Sheikh, and turning to his student said, *"This is no Waliyullah! Now you have stuck us on this island and we cannot get back to the mainland before sundown. Go and catch me a fish and cook it for our meal to break our fast."*

After sundown, the other man built a fire and used his hydaria (dervish cloak) as a table cloth for the meal. The Sheikh scolded him, *"You don't make ablution and use your haydariye to eat off!"* And turning to his student said, *"This man is no Waliyullah."*

Morning came, and the other man put his takia (dervish cap) in his pocket to use as a hankerchief and the haydariye he wrapped around this head to shield himself from the harsh sun, and the whole thing altogether wrong. *"Look! Look at what your 'Waliyullah' is doing now!"* the Sheikh shouted in disbelief. *"Not only did he use his haydariye for a table cloth, but now he puts the takke in his pocket and the haydariye on his head.... This is no Waliyullah."*

But the Sheikh was a compassionate man and took pity on the fool who was thought to be a Waliyullah, and the next morning, he undertook to instruct him on how to wear the garments of a dervish. *"You see,"* the Sheikh said, *"This piece goes on your head, not your pocket, and this piece you wear as a cloak, and not a hat."*

"Ah, I see," said the man, *"how foolish of me. Now I know better."*
Having satisfied himself that he had done what Allah Most High required of him, the Sheikh and his student left the island. However, as they were rowing back to shore, the student suddenly stopped and his mouth dropped open.

"What's the matter with you," the Sheikh asked, *"why have you stopped rowing?"*

"Look!" the student croaked, and pointed. When the Sheikh turned around, he saw the fool who did everything wrong running across the water shouting, *"Wait, Sheikh, tell me again, which goes on my shoulders and which on my head?"*

"Sam," Mr. Khadir explained, *"often Allah hides his Waliyullah from humankind. In fact, often Allah hides the station from the person him or herself!"*

"Why?" asked Sam.

"Allah often has secret missions for these men and women to perform; they can be found in the highest of places and the most common of places. Their lack of knowledge of whom they are is also a protection from Allah for these saints not to become egotistical and to fall from their station. Those special ones who know their station often deliberately hide the fact from people by behaving in outrageous ways, in order for people not to place them on pedestals. For they love only Allah. Nothing comes between them and Allah. They have no desire for fame, dervishes or tekkes. So, they play the role of fool or sinner, that their secret may be kept."

"Do not accept the witness of Ali's followers or his descendants in courts."
- Mu'awiyah Bin Abi Sufyan

THE TERROR OF MU'AWIYAH BIN ABI SUFYAN

After Imam Ali ('Alaihi Assalam) was murdered, Mu'awiyah Bin Abi Sufyan was given access to rule the whole country. Mu'awiyah assumed authority by sheer force. He did not hide this fact and put it plainly in his address at Kufa. He said, *"O people of Kufa, do you think I fought you to establish prayers or giving alms, or perform pilgrimage?"* He continued, *"I know you pray, pay alms, and perform pilgrimage. Indeed, I fought you in order to command you with contempt, and God has given me that against your wishes. You must be certain that whoever has killed any of us, then he will be killed. And the contract between us of amnesty is under these feet of mine."*

Mu'awiyah's rule caused terror in the whole Muslim land. His sending many convoys in various regions of the country spread this terrorism. It was narrated that Mu'awiyah summoned Sufyan Ibn Auf Al-Ghamidi, one of his army commanders, and said, *"This Army is under your command, proceed along the river Euphrate till Heet. Any resistance in the way should be crushed, and then invade Anbar. After that penetrate deep into Medina. O Sufyan, these invasions will frighten the Iraqis and please those who like us. Such campaigns would attract frightened people to our side. Kill whoever has different opinions from ours, loot their villages and demolish their houses. Indeed, the War against money is similar to killing but is more painful to their hearts."*

Another commander, Baser Ibn Art, was summoned and ordered to go toward Hijaz and Yemen. Mu'awiyah instructed him, *"Proceed to Medina and expel its people; meanwhile, people in the way who are not from our camp should be terrorized. When you enter Medina, let it appear as if you are going to kill them. Make it appear that your aim is to exterminate them. Then pardon them. Terrorize the people around Macca and Medina and scatter them."*

During Mu'awiyah's reign even basic human rights were denied to people. No one was free to express his opinion. Spies were employed to terrorize people, besides the army and police who spared no opportunity to crush people and silence their voices. For instance, the following letter was addressed to all judges. *"Do not accept the witness of Ali's followers or his descendants in courts."* Another letter stated, *"If you have evidence that some person likes Ali and his family, then omit his name from the rations of Zakat."* Another letter continued, *"Punish whoever is suspected to follow Ali and bring his house down."*

Such was the situation of Mu'awyiyah Bin Abi Sufyan's rule. Historians who were recording these waves of terror described them as unprecedented in history. People were so frightened that they did not mind

271

being called atheists, thieves, rather than acknowledge they were the followers of Imam Ali ('Alaihi Assalam).

Why were all these terrible things done? Outwardly, the obvious answer is that these individuals sought political power and financial wealth. However, spiritual forces were at work which sought to distort and utterly deform the spiritual message of the Mercy to All Nations: the Prophet Muhammad (Peace be upon him). Again, history shows us that those who Know the Truth are assailed and frequently killed because of the great state of denial and anger from which much of the society suffers. In short, society fears these *"uncovered lamps."*

"I find that sitting in a place where you have never sat before can be inspiring."

- Dodie Smith

"Revolution without revelation is tyranny. Revelation without revolution is slavery."

- Gurdjieff

BREAK ON THROUGH TO THE OTHER SIDE

What can people do to break out of their shells of fear? We are referring to the shields created by people's subconscious to safeguard themselves from the outside world. People only let into their consciousness information and experiences that do not frighten them.

Try the following: Go to work without combing your hair. Wear sandals to a formal dinner. Eat your dinner in a restaurant with your hands. Face the reprobation of the public. Dare to do the outrageous. Sing a song in full voice as you stroll down the street. Drive all side streets to work.

You need to disrupt your automaticities, your ways of looking at the world that have been ingrained in you, which result in actions that you do on "automatic pilot." You must tear off the blinders that culture, religion, your parents, and society have imposed on you.

There are many ways to get uptown. You can take a taxi, a bus, the subway, roller-blade, car, bike, walk, hitchhike, skateboard and so forth; yet many people, metaphorically speaking, only know of one way. Then there are others who say that their way of going uptown is the best way.

Read books that are one hundred eighty degrees different from your normal interests. People involved in metaphysics often only read books in a narrow range of genres. This selective reading is a sort of metaphysical inbreeding. Without the introduction of new elements into the system, one will eventually begin to stagnate. If you create a closed and static system, eventually things will begin to get stale and sluggish.

Often what you regard as one hundred eighty degrees dissimilar to what you are interested in, is often a secret love or interest that you have repressed. Ask yourself what would you be doing if you were not involved in your present career.

By pushing your boundaries, you can breathe new life into your spirituality. If you are the bookish type, a good hands-on class on auto mechanics or carpentry will transmute your spirituality in ways you never dreamed possible. If you are mechanically minded, a good book on haute cuisine or art appreciation will activate forces inside your being that you did not know were there. While some highly educated types look down their noses at auto mechanics, auto-mechanics are geniuses in three-dimensional spatial organization. The idea is to transcend yourself in every area of your life.

Spirituality is NOT just about reading spiritual books and doing "spiritual" things. This is a great error and misconception of many. It is not necessary to read any books on spirituality to become a puissant Sufi.

PRACTICE

Clean your dwelling space. The Great Guides say that angels are more inclined to visit a space that is clean and orderly, than a space cluttered, dirty and unhygienic. Consider if you were going to be visited by a good friend, would you not tidy up your home for them? Then consider if the person coming to visit you was someone you loved and respected dearly, would you not clean and scrub the place for your guest? Continue to contemplate on the scenario that the Prophet Himself (Peace be upon him) was going to pay a visit to you. We can imagine you would be professionally cleaning your rug, decorating with flowers, washing windows and curtains, in short, rigorously cleaning EVERYTHING! Do not stop at this point however. Now ponder on being granted a visit by the Eternal. How you would get down on your hands and knees and scrub and clean each fiber of your carpet and each nook and cranny in your entire dwelling space. You may paint your home, and you would make your space into a shining palace of light.

So too, you are the bearers of the Diamond Light of Allah Most High. Wherever you go, there God is! Clean your home. Clean your body. Prepare ye for the welcoming of the Guest!

"Spirit & Body are complete & perfect through each other. Separate from each other they do not exist."

- Haft Bab-i Baba Sayyidna

"In particular, their talking and their self-talking abilities permitted people to forget that their real needs, or necessities for human survival, were invariably of a physical or sensory nature."

- Dr. Albert Ellis

"Everyone with a mouth eats."

- Arabic Proverb

"The precious human body demands a spiritual interpretation, an esoteric hermeneutics."

- Shaykh Nur al-Anwar al-Jerrahi

SPIRITUAL FACTS OF PHYSICAL EXISTENCE

A certain "spiritual" ethic endures that would have us deny our physical selves. The reality is that the body is nothing but physical soul. Can you stop breathing, eating, drinking, and still live? Robin Becker further illuminates on the wisdom of the body, *"Our form affects and curves space. Space is our partner, and therefore we must care for it. It is the element that connects us to each other."* Physicists tell us that every body (object) distorts gravity. The body creates a "gravity well" a kind of trough in the fabric of the universe. The heavier the body, the bigger the trough. As other bodies approach the heavy body they can fall into or toward the trough.

The Prophets, Evliyas and Sheikhs are spiritual "gravity wells." They become so "heavy" because they carry Allah (the Awareness of the Entire Universe) within themselves. This is why these Holy Ones draw others toward them.

The dualistic ethos of the superiority of the soul over the body has infected all of society. You are 100 percent integrated with your physical forms. Baba Afzal Kashani writes,

> *"You must be cross-eyed not to see the Real*
> *Or lack the eyes to look at Him, I feel,*
> *To know that you, from head to toe, are HIM –*
> *The Universal Apple, core and peel."*

Our physical forms are just as much "us" as our thoughts and emotions and spiritual impressions. To think about our bodies as horses to be ridden or even temples to be occupied, is to create a duality between our thinking and our body. It is like a tourist who arrives in a wild forest in his or her Recreation Vehicle. We have all seen those campers with their televisions, and so on. Are they experiencing the nature around them? They have an insular experience, that is, camping without getting their hands dirty.

You live an insular existence, going from your soundproofed cars to your air-conditioned, insulated houses. People would not say God is dead if they only looked up at the spectacular panorama of the night sky, or had an unobstructed view of the sunset.

This is not something that we can tell to you. You have to do it. There is no way around it. Go camping in the woods for a week. Then you will know about earth wisdom. The Murid needs to connect with the energy in the natural world. Chang Tsai, an official in the Chinese administration in the twelfth century C.E., stated in the inscription that hung on the west wall of his office: *"Therefore that which extends throughout the universe I consider as my body and that which directs the universe I consider as my nature."*

It takes a while for the conditioning of the commercial world to wear off. Just an afternoon at the lake is not enough to sensitize your senses to an awareness of the subtle energies all around you. We have many armchair Sufis out there.

Where does the Life Energy come from? It radiates from the Sun, Moon and Earth, and then is translated by your Body's chakras. As much as you cut yourself off from the Sun, Moon, Earth, and your Body, to that degree will you cut yourself off from Life Energy!

Muslims make prayers five times per day. During each of these prayers, they perform a series of bodily movements. It is stated that the Prophet Muhammad (Peace be upon him) was taken up into heaven (while he was still alive) and saw angels dwelling on various heavenly levels performing specific movements. This should be a profound sign of the spiritual significance and importance of the body and its motions. It is one indication of the sacredness of the body and the truly profound meaning of certain motions and gestures of that body.

The Dervishes perform highly sophisticated, sacred movements during the ceremony of *Zikr*. The goal of the Sufi is not to destroy his or her body, but to awaken each cell to Blessed Awareness of the One Living Truth. *"The Beloved has penetrated every cell of my body."*[361] Shaykh Nur al-Anwar al-Jerrahi writes,

> *"This circle of holy recollection*
> *celebrates a spiritual wedding*
> *among hearts set sail together*
> *upon the ocean of Divine Light.*
> *During this ecstatic voyage,*

Courageous dervish dancers
Abandon the narrow ship of self
and plunge into open radiance. "362

PRACTICE

It is essential for the Murid to learn to still his or her thoughts. Bahâ ad-Dîn Naqshband wrote, *"God is silence and is most easily reached in silence."*

If at anytime in the past, you attempted to quiet your thoughts, you were aware that a ceaseless chatter goes on in your mind all day long. Many Murids find it most difficult to quiet this prattle of noise.

The solution is to become aware of your breathing. Focus on your inhalation and exhalation. When you hear any mental chatter or sound, think of it as merely a radio or television in the background. Allow this babble to go on without your participating in its flow. You will find that by just letting the thoughts drift by, and focusing on your breathing, you will gain a stationary and fixed position of calm.

Jelaluddin Rumi writes about this process as follows,

"It's like the naked man who jumped into the water,
so that he might escape from the hornets' stings:
the hornets circled above him, and whenever
he put out his head they would not spare him.
The water is recollection of God,
and the hornet is the thought, during this time,
of such-and-such a woman or man.
Hold your breath in the water of remembrance and show strength,
so you may be freed from old thoughts and temptations."[363]

Beware of drifting into reverie. Stay focused and alert.

The Murid must constantly look into his or her inner being, stilling the thoughts and peacefully sensing what is going on inside his or her being. This applies especially to the heart. Just sense what is going on. As H. Shejh Xhemali SHEHU says, *"If you want to know Allah, look inside yourself."*

Make no value judgements on any of the words or thoughts that pass through your mind. Stay detached, and just observe. As Bâyezîd Bistâmî wrote,

"All this talk and turmoil and noise and movement
is outside the veil;
inside the veil is silence and calm and peace."

For some Aspirants, merely saying the word *"Stop"* silently to yourself will quiet the cerebral babble. For other Aspirants who are still having difficulty, saying something like the following is helpful, *"Let's become aware of the sounds around us and in the room."* The latter sentence shifts the focus off of yourself and your thoughts.

"Life's waters flow from darkness.
Search the darkness, don't run from it."

- Jelaluddin Rumi [364]

"Fabric of earth and wind and wave!
Who is the secret, you or I,
Brought into light? or who the dark
world of what hides yet, you or I?"

- Iqbal

"I have seen nothing more conducive to righteousness than solitude, for he
who is alone sees nothing but God, and if he sees nothing but God, nothing
moves him but the will of God."

- Dhu 'l-Nun

TALES FROM UNDER THE OVERPASS

"*D*o you know that the Prophet Muhammad (Peace be upon him) went to college?" Mr. Khadir asked.

"*I don't really know much about Muhammad's life,*" Sam offered, "*but I'd be open to learning about him.*"

"*At the time of the Prophet Muhammad (Peace be upon him), there existed a kind of secret wisdom college in the mountains and caves around Macca (al-Mukarramah). These schools were similar to the Druid colleges found throughout the Celtic countries. Macca (al-Mukarramah) and the Arabian Peninsula as a whole seem to have been the gathering ground of ancient and contemporary religions. Esoteric schools can be traced at least as far back as Abraham; in Persia, literature, poetry and music were the source of esoteric information; in India the esoteric schools were mainly of a meditative character, and in Arabia esoteric schools were known for their metaphysical teachings.*

"*Muhammad's (Peace be upon him) wife Khadija, sent him off to study with the great wisdom teachers from all the traditions. The teachers had gathered together with the purpose of trying to decide on the best spiritual system for humanity. Muhammad (Peace be upon him) was illiterate. He could not read or write. He was educated in an oral tradition. That's why I mentioned the Druids. They never wrote anything down. It was forbidden. Everything had to be memorized.*"

"*That's remarkable,*" Sam said thoughtfully.

"*Yes, Khadija was a remarkable woman. Do you know that Muhammad (Peace be upon him) was twenty-five years old . . . a real nobody at the time, and Hazreti Khadija was forty years old when they married?*" Mr.

Khadir continued with a kind of nostalgia. "She was wealthy and successful when they met. She ran caravans through Macca (al-Mukarramah). Although he was a man of good reputation and character, he was not financially or spiritually mature when they met."

"Well, I would love to find a wife like that! How can I find one?" Sam interrupted.

"In the future, you should remember, that it is not wise to interrupt a teacher when he or she is teaching. A channel opens between the teacher and Allah . . . to interrupt the teacher is to interrupt that flow. It is as if the teacher is attuned to one branch of a tree, and suddenly the student wants to go to another branch. The original direction can get lost. However, to answer your question: to marry is to perform half of one's religion. Let me tell you a story. Allah decided to send a postcard to earth. On the way to earth, the postcard got ripped in half. The two halves long and look for one another. When they finally find each other there is much joy and ecstasy. So, how do you recognize the other half of your postcard? The quality to look for in a spouse is above all, compassion. How do you know if the potential spouse is compassionate? They will exhibit four qualities: First, they will like flowers. Second, they will like music. Third, they will like animals. Lastly, they will like children. Of course, it is understood that some people have allergies to certain flowers and animals, and that one can love children without having a child of one's own. But let me ask you a question, Sam," Mr. Khadir took Sam by surprise.

"There are two lovers in a cave. They love each other intensely and deeply and are making passionate love together. During the night, the woman dies. In the morning the man buries his deceased lover. Why?"

Sam didn't know what to say. The question was so odd.

Mr. Khadir continued, "Remember, just a few hours previously the man was making impassioned love with the woman, caressing her beautiful breasts, holding her shapely hips, and climaxing inside her sex. Yet, now he's dumping the woman he loves into the ground and covering her up with dirt. Why?"

Sam felt challenged in a way he had not expected.

Mr. Khadir explained: "He buries her because her Absolute Existence, her Essence of Essences is no longer dwelling with her body. The woman he loves continues, but not in the form of the body. So therefore he buries the body." Sam had never heard such teaching coming from a master. He was in a kind of mind-fog when Mr. Khadir's voice suddenly shocked him back to reality. "Now may I finish my story about Hazreti Khadija?"

"Oh, of course," said Sam, obviously embarrassed.

"Hazreti Khadija set Muhammad up as her partner and helped him to achieve financial success and also, as I just mentioned, sent him later to the college of wise teachers in the mountains. The Prophet Muhammad (Peace be upon him) was never interested in accumulating financial wealth, and

declared, 'I would not have the whole wealth of the world in the place of this revelation . . . ' So, Khadija, in a sense, was the True Guide to the Prophet!"

"But what if you don't have a guide?" Sam asked in a quiet voice.

"You must explore your inner self. All the Prophets and Saints were great because they focused on their spiritual goals and had the courage to go into the wilderness, into hiding, to face themselves! There is substantiation to what I am saying in the Sufi tradition . . . those Sufis who do not have a Sheikh to guide them are called Uwaysis, after the name of a man Uways al-Qarani who lived in Yemen during the time of the Prophet Muhammad (Peace be upon him). Uways never met the Prophet, but saw him in dreams and visions. The Prince of Prophets, Muhammad (Peace be upon him) once mentioned Uways by saying, 'The breath of the Merciful comes to me from Yemen.'"

"But I've heard that he who teaches himself has a fool for a master," ventured Sam.

"Each of those who enter the realm of the Imam-of-one's-own-being becomes a sultan of inverted revelation, a monarch of abrogation and apostasy."

"But don't I need a teacher to be enlightened?"

"How can you be anything but enlightened? You are already free," answered Mr. Khadir. "Whoever seeks God through another than him or herself will never attain unto God. The sage is not more evolved than the ordinary person is. They both grow from the soil of non-duality. That is why sages so often insist that they are no more special than anyone else is. There is neither Murid nor Murshid, neither information nor research, neither definition nor description! God is All in all! The Elevated is one of God's Beautiful Names; but above whom or what, since only He exists? More elevated than whom or what, since only He is and He is Elevated in Himself? In relation to existence, He is the Quintessence of existing beings. Thus, in a certain sense, relative beings are elevated in themselves, since, in truth, they are none other than He and His elevation is absolute and not relative."

"If it were always summertime,
the blazing heat would burn the garden,
soil and root, so that nothing would ever grow again.
December is grim yet kind;
summer is all laughter, and yet it burns."

- Jelaluddin Rumi [365]

"The sea
Will be a sea
Whatever the drop's philosophy."

- Attar of Neishapur

"Is this why at times, the rain refuses to fall and at times typhoons
come? We can't stop it, Only join it with a song.
The hymn of the rain is sung with a guitar,
The rhythm of the raindrops is accompanied with tears,
The song in our hearts, let it accompany the rain."

- Sugatang Langit (Wounded Sky)

PLAYING THE FLUTE IN THE RAIN

Consider two flutists: one flutist plays sweet and beautiful melodies and the other plays sad discordant noises. It is all the same to the air. Does the air care how it is vibrated?

The flutists manifest their inner feelings - the happy flutist plays jigs, and the flutist in pain plays the blues. It is all sound.

Sometimes it rains, and sometimes it is sunny. You accept the weather. You may not like the day's weather, but you do not label it "good" or "evil." Shouting at a tornado does no good. Rebuking a tidal wave has no effect.

Most people derive joy from the interplay of weather patterns and changing seasonal temperatures. Although we do not enjoy terrible storms and natural calamities (and sometimes we suffer because of them), spirituality is not about enjoyment or pleasure.

The Divine Source is the Quintessence of Existence, the Sacred Heart of Nature. *"Wherever you turn, there is the Face (the dhat) of God."* [366]

"We find a similar blending of the Waters of Life in the Cabirian Mysteries, in which the archetypal male and female, Cabirius and Cabiria, were worshiped in the form of vessels filled with water; Cabirius was identified with Dionysos and Cabiria with Demeter (who are lovers in the Orphic Tradition). Thus life is renewed by the Waters of Life."

- Kerenyi

"Be in a domain where neither good nor evil exists: both of them belong to the world of created things; in the presence of Unity there is neither command nor prohibition.

All this talk and turmoil and noise and movement is outside of the veil; within the veil is silence and calm and rest,

Dost thou hear how there comes a voice from the brooks of running water? But when they reach the sea they are quiet, and the sea is neither augmented by their incoming nor diminished by their outgoing."

- Abu Yazid al-Bistami

CLEAR THINKING

People who think most negatively about the world need to think more clearly. When a given person feels intense personal pain, frequently that person's attention begins to focus selectively on the negative aspects of his or her environment. The world becomes an increasingly inhospitable environment filled only with wars and rumors of wars, hostile races, and rampant crime.

When the Mercy and Majesty of Allah (the Yin and Yang) are not balanced within the individual, the outside world appears imbalanced. This is not to say that in some cases, a balanced person cannot have a run of bad luck or that disaster never strikes the balanced person. These things can and do happen. Spirituality is not a protection from the world.

The Balanced Person simply does not add worldly affairs to his or her "tale of woes." For instance, if a Balanced Person is fired, he or she does not list among his or her problems: wars in the Middle East and Inner City crime.

The Balanced Person feels his or her feelings, without distorting, exaggerating, or inflating the feeling to the point where he or she becomes Unbalanced. It is necessary and good to feel all your feelings; it is unhelpful to become the victim of inflated emotional reactions to your problems.

"Man is a river, woman is a lake."

- Kurdish Proverb

"A bumptious man dismissed a dervish by shouting at him: 'Nobody knows you here.'
'But I know myself,' the dervish replied. 'How sad it would be if the reverse were true.'"

- Attar of Neishapur

WHO IS WO/MAN?

In Sufism, the Prophet Muhammad (Peace be upon him) has a hidden Reality. The Sufis call this Reality *al-nur al-muhammadi*, or the Light of Muhammad. This Light is the paradigm of creation, the template of the whole natural world.

Allah calls human beings His "Vice-Regents." In the original Qur'anic Arabic, Allah is not addressing "men," but human beings (men and women). To the Sufi, Muhammad (Peace be upon him) is the Perfect Human Being, in other words, the Universal Human Being. Muhammad (Peace be upon him) is considered perfect in his hidden aspect as Archetypal Human Being and the Cosmic Template.

Once a man asked us *"If there is one God, why are there so many religions?"* Every so often, humanity needs a wake-up call from the Divine. Allah, The Mighty Splendor, says in the Qur'an to the Holy Prophet (Peace be upon him), *"Remind people, for reminding benefits them."* The message of each previous Prophet gradually degrades and is misinterpreted to the point that the message becomes confused and unclear. The sciences of physics and sociology support this idea. A given substance/entity/mass will gradually disperse over time. The Divine Message is repeated over and over again, because the Message has fallen into neglect. So, the question becomes, not why are there so many religions, but which one is the most recent which preserves the revelation most clearly. The Prophets were sent to remind humanity of their connection with the Ultimate Reality. Today, the *Qutubs* are the guardians of the message of Divine Revelations.

Allah is the Source of the Entire Universe and is also your Source. Humanity's form is drawn from twenty-eight letters. These twenty-eight letters comprise the Arabic alphabet. Each section of the human form is represented by one of these letters. When the Murid becomes the Complete Human Being, he or she becomes the eternal mother source of the Qur'an revealed to Muhammad (Peace be upon him). The inner pilgrimage to Macca (al-Mukarramah) is accomplished when the Murid becomes the Complete Human Being.

Al-Alim, The All-Knowing has said, *"My secret is humanity, and I am humanity's secret. I am humanity's wealth, and humanity is my wealth. My story is within humanity, and humanity's story is within Me. We are the progeny and God. I, the Omniconscious Unicity am the One who can understand this world, the world of the soul, and everything. Humanity will know what the angels cannot know. My royal offspring will know. But there are things that even humanity cannot understand, things that I, the Absolute Being, understand. I understand all of everything. I understand all the things which even humanity cannot understand."* [367]

In Sufism, the Ultimate Reality is the Beloved and we are the Lovers. The Sheikhs have said that all creation is Female and in search of the One Male.

The Secret of a Human Being is Allah. The Secret of Allah is the Human Being. As you enter into a sacred relationship with Muhammad (Peace be upon him) in his hidden aspect as the Light of the Ultimate Reality, in other words the Complete Human Being, you recognize that you and the One Living Being are One. Our job is to polish the rough stone from the quarry into a beautiful and radiant expression of Divine Creativity.

PRACTICE

It is reported from some of the Knowers of Allah that Zikr has seven aspects:

1. Zikr of the eyes, which consists in weeping *(buka')*
2. Zikr of the ears, which consists in listening *(isgha')*
3. Zikr of the tongue, which consists in praise *(thana')*
4. Zikr of the hands, which consists in giving *('ata')*
5. Zikr of the body, which consists in loyalty *(wafa')*
6. Zikr of the heart, which consists in fear and hope *(Kawf wa raja')*
7. Zikr of the spirit, which consists of utter surrender and acceptance *(taslim wa rida')*. [368]

When you make Zikr and contemplate on a Name of the One Living Reality, focus on your heart. Become aware that this One Living Reality exists within your heart. However, before you begin, pray to this One Living Reality beseeching forgiveness for your actions and thoughts of duality (what the traditional teachings call "sin").

As you contemplate on the Name, allow your heart to fill with this Attribute of the One Living Reality. That is all. Do not walk around thinking "God is inside me," for that is pride and dualistic behavior. You are privileged even to say the Name. Do not think you are special, for believing in a "you" is to set up partners with the One Living Reality.

This contemplation of the Beloved within the Heart is important, yet fraught with danger. This assignment is a narrow path between the spiritualization of the Murid and full-blown egoic megalomania (obsession with the illusion of a separate self). Therefore, tread carefully.

"The second stage of Sufi Training is known as 'Tariqat'. According to Sheikh Shahabu-d-Din Umar Bin Muhammad-i-Sahrwardi: 'The murid (student) attaineth power; entereth Sufism; and abandoneth the observance of religious form, exchanging outward for inward worship. Without great piety, virtue, and fortitude (based on a knowledge of the dignity of the soul of man) he cannot attain this stage.'"

- Sheikh Shahabu-d-Din Umar Bin Muhammad-i-Sahrwardi [369]

"Allah says: 'I am just as My slave thinks I am (in other words I am able to do for him what he thinks I can do for him) and I am with him if He remembers Me. If he remembers Me in himself, I too, remember him in Myself; and if he remembers Me in a group of people, I remember him in a group that is better than they; and if he comes one span nearer to Me, I go one cubit nearer to him; and if he comes one cubit nearer to Me, I go a distance of two outstretched arms nearer to him; and if he comes to Me walking, I go to him running.' "

- Hadith (Bukhari, Vol. 9 : No. 502)

TALES FROM UNDER THE OVERPASS

"*I thought spiritual realization would just happen to me someday,*" Sam was visibly disheartened and frustrated.

"*You can't receive a gift if you don't stand in the receiving line, Sam,*" Mr. Khadir softly said. "*Unless you put in an effort to develop yourself, the universe will continue to stay quiet. Each step you take toward the Divine, the Divine takes ten steps toward you.*"

"*But I shouldn't need to have to do anything; shouldn't the Divine be capable of doing all things?*" questioned Sam.

"*There's got to be a vocabulary, or how's the story told?*" answered Mr. Khadir.

"*I think I see what you're getting at,*" said Sam. "*We need to enter into some kind of context with the Divine to give the Divine a method of communicating with us. Is that what you mean?*"

"*Exactly,*" replied Mr. Khadir.

Sam thought a minute, and mulled over whether he should ask his next question. He was a bit nervous asking this question as he felt Mr. Khadir might get angry, but Sam's need for the Truth impelled him on, "*So, Mr. Khadir, does it matter what path I take - the sacred or the profane?*"

"*Why split Spirit into dualistic opposites? The world is simultaneously both the veil and the portal to enlightenment. Traditionally we have thought that only human beings have an aspect to themselves that continues after they have died. But all things have an imperishable aspect to them."*

"Yes, but things in the world decay," Sam said with a touch of sadness.

"Form and essence are like the rose and its perfume. They are so inextricably intertwined and inextricably dependent upon one another! Sam, you are someday soon going to blossom into a beautiful rose of awesome splendor and dazzling color that emanates an intoxicating perfume."

"He who is outside the door has already a good part of his journey behind him."
                                        - Dutch Proverb

"It is not wise to violate the rules until you know how to observe them."
                                        - T. S. Eliot

"Patience is one of the ways to achieve victory." [370]
                                        - Imam Ali ('Alaihi Assalam)

PROGRESS

Do not despair at your seeming lack of spiritual development even if you have done the practices for a while. None of us knows how close we are to Initiation. You may be only a hair's breadth away from a complete awakening to the Invisible World.

Await the clarion call that tells you that now is the time to awake. That call may come in a variety of ways: maybe the sound of a particular guitar solo, maybe in the words of a Guide, a crash of cymbals, perhaps it will be found in a sunset, a parent's death, an orgasm, or a hysterical fit of laughter. *"Consider the bizarre events of the 1962 outbreak of contagious laughter in Tanganyika. What began as an isolated fit of laughter (and sometimes crying) in a group of 12- to 18-year-old schoolgirls rapidly rose to epidemic proportions. Contagious laughter propagated from one individual to the next, eventually infecting adjacent communities. The epidemic was so severe that it required the closing of schools. It lasted for six months."* [371]

The moment may surprise you with its unexpectedness and the strength of its forcefulness. The outer stimulus is a trigger that is opening your spiritual faculties.

You may be making a great deal of progress though it may not be apparent to you. After all, you are developing new senses and you cannot expect to be aware of what are completely new senses to you.

IT may come upon you in such a subtle way that it may pass unnoticed at first. Your fundamental being is undergoing a great transformation. You may have expected supersensible awareness to take such and such a form, and so the new skills you have developed may not be immediately apparent to you.

People have certain preconceptions from books about what spiritual development is and how it feels and operates. However, they are just words. The truth is something different. Now you are experiencing the real thing. So give yourself much credit and be patient with yourself.

Another danger lies in believing that the budding experiences of psychic awareness are mere illusions. Remember, true spiritual sight emerges out of the imagination. *"Every thing possible to be believ'd is an image of truth,"* wrote William Blake. The Murid might be too quick to dismiss a small stirring of the psychic eye, because he or she is expecting some full-blown preconceived experience.

PRACTICE

Imagine yourself suspended in outer space with stars all shining from all directions. You see a Light resplendent in the space: a radiant luminous Light. Imagine this Ineffable Light to be a beautiful melody or song. It has both the qualities of music and light. This song gradually begins to form the outline of a human being. See and hear this Human Being shining and singing in space from out of Its Holy Person.

According to your capacity of being, you will see the form appropriate to you.

"For anyone acquainted with religious phenomenology it is an open secret that although physical and spiritual passion are deadly enemies, they are never-the-less brothers in arms, for which reason it often needs the merest touch to convert one into the other. Both are real, and together they form a pair of opposites, which is one of the most fruitful sources of energy."
- *C. G. Jung*

"And among His signs is this, that He created for you mates from among yourselves, that you may dwell in tranquility with them, and He has put love and mercy between your hearts. Undoubtedly in these are signs for those who reflect."
- *Qur'an 30:21*

THE MARRIAGE TABLET [372]

The bond that unites hearts most perfectly is loyalty. True lovers once united must show the utmost faithfulness one to another. You must dedicate your knowledge, your talents, your fortunes, your titles, your bodies and your spirits to God and to each other. Let your hearts be spacious, as spacious as the universe of God!

Allow no trace of jealousy to creep between you, for jealousy, like unto poison, vitiates the very essence of love. Let not the ephemeral incidents and accidents of this changeful life cause a rift between you. When differences present themselves, take counsel together in secret, lest others magnify a speck into a mountain. Harbor not in your hearts any grievance, but rather explain its nature to each other with such frankness and understanding that it will disappear, leaving no remembrance. Choose fellowship and amity and turn away from jealousy and hypocrisy.

Your thoughts must be lofty, your ideals luminous, your minds spiritual, so that your souls may become a dawning-place for the Sun of Reality. Let your hearts be like unto two pure mirrors reflecting the stars of the heaven of love and beauty.

Together make mention of noble aspirations and heavenly concepts. Let there be no secrets one from another. Make your home a haven of rest and peace. Be hospitable, and let the doors of your house be open to the faces of friends and strangers. Welcome every guest with radiant grace and let each feel that it is his own home.

No mortal can conceive the union and harmony that God has designed for husband and wife. Nourish continually the tree of your union with love and affection, so that it will remain evergreen and verdant throughout all seasons and bring forth luscious fruits for the healing of the nations.

O beloved of God, may your home be a vision of paradise, so that whosoever enters there may feel the essence of purity and harmony, and cry out from the heart: Here is the home of love! Here is the palace of love! Here is the nest of love! Here is the garden of love!

Be like two sweet-singing birds perched upon the highest branches of the tree of life, filling the air with songs of love and rapture.

Lay the foundation of your affection in the very center of your spiritual being, at the very heart of your consciousness, and let it not be shaken by adverse winds.

And, when God gives you sweet and lovely children, consecrate yourselves to their instruction and guidance, so that they may become imperishable flowers of the divine rose-garden, nightingales of the ideal paradise, servants of the world of humanity, and the fruit of the tree of your life.

Live in such harmony that others may take your lives for an example and may say one to another: Look how they live like two doves in one nest, in perfect love, affinity and union. It is as though God had kneaded the very essence of their beings for the love of one another.

Attain the ideal love that God has destined for you, so that you may become partakers of eternal life forthwith. Quaff deeply from the fountain of truth, and dwell all the days of your life in the paradise of glory, gathering immortal flowers from the garden of divine mysteries.

Be to each other as heavenly lovers and divine beloved ones dwelling in a paradise of love. Build your nest on the leafy branches of the tree of love. Sail upon the shoreless sea of love. Walk in the eternal rose-garden of love. Bathe in the shining rays of the sun of love. Be firm and steadfast in the path of love. Perfume your nostrils with the fragrances from the flowers of love. Attune your ears to the soul-entrancing melodies of love. Let your aims be as generous as the banquets of love, and your words as a string of white pearls from the ocean of love. Drink deeply of the elixir of love, so that you may live continually in the reality of Divine Love.

"Religion seeks grace and favor,
but those who gamble these away are God's favorites,
for they neither put God to the test
nor knock at the door of gain or loss."

- Jelaluddin Rumi [373]

"A rose's rarest essence
lives in the thorn."

- Jelaluddin Rumi

"Satan: 'And what presumption could refuse to You
Obedience? If I would not kneel to him,
The cause was Your own foreordaining will.' "
- Iqbal

"O dear friend! Don't you know what that maddened lover, whom you
called 'Eblis' in this world, was called in the divine world? If you knew his
name, you would consider yourself an unbeliever in calling him by that
name."

- Ayn al-Qozat [374]

THE QUESTION OF EVIL

Individuality involves pain. Tear ONE sheet of paper into sections and you will hear the sound of ripping. Each time you tear a piece, the paper lets out a cry. This is the pain of separation, the necessary, but unpleasant, phase of the Ultimate Reality knowing Itself. In other words, the One becomes the Many. This is the separation for the chance of union. *"Whether you assert unity or distinction, the Self is Unique. As also the Many that are and yet are not."* [375]

The Ultimate Reality is not Santa Claus. *"There is no god that is God"* writes Bubba Free John.[376] He is referring to humanity's tendency to try to classify, categorize and catalogue the Lord Who Is Without Why Or Wherefore. The Ultimate Reality should not be approached for favors or bargained with, for the *"true servant's hope is in God alone, and he hopes for nothing from God except God Himself."*[377] Do not knock on the door of advantage and benefit, for the Sufi focuses on the scent of the Singular Rose and the Sufi realizes that rose petals and thorns are both expressions of his or her Beloved. This is what we mean by The Real God.

"Whether the feet be two or four, they traverse one road, like the double shears (which) make (but) one cut . . . opposites which seem to be at strife, are of one mind and acting together in agreement."[378]

Allah does not exist to answer requests for favors. The Supreme

Reality does not exist to make you happy. The incorrect way to approach Allah is to pray to The Holy for benefit. Your heart is a compass pointing to Allah. The Beloved dwells within your heart. This is all that should concern the Sufi. When you find the Living Reality within your heart, you will find joy and bliss. Instead of worrying about the question of suffering in the world, spend your time alleviating it! Seek whose suffering you can change to happiness. You might want to start with yourself. Have you been merciful to yourself?

Instead of worrying about evil, worry about losing the power to do good! The Murid cannot become a Sufi by sitting in his or her room. Rather spiritual growth is cultivated through interaction with people and events.

Regarding the question of evil, most people cannot help falling into a linear way of analyzing the question. The Sufi abhors the idolization of rational thought, the logic of cause and effect, and realizes the might and depth of intuitive knowledge. *"This is because the intellect restricts and seeks to define the truth within a particular qualification, while in fact the Reality does not admit of such limitations."* [379]

When it states that both the good and the bad alike come from Allah, Sufism takes on a difficult issue plus a troublesome theological problem.

Sanâ'i illustrates this in the following verse,

"What do you say concerning his refusal to prostrate?
Was it predestined or was it a matter of choice?
If it was in his hands, then God is deficient;
And if his hands were tied, then God must be cruel!"

Zailan Moris writes, *"All of creation – good and evil alike – participate in the divine Desire of making the Hidden Treasure manifest."* [380] The adherent of exoteric religion must rely on faith alone that God is incomprehensible, however, the Sufi can directly experience the Unity of Opposites through coming to know the Divine Essence (dhāt) within his or her heart.

Reason cannot solve the problem of evil, but Sufism transcends reason. *"If man were able to comprehend God, that indeed is not God."* [381] Sufism travels into the realm of story, inspired analogy and esoteric understanding of the Qur'an, so that the Sufi may ultimately become the Essence.

PRACTICE

We design this exercise to unfold your powers of observation. Choose a time when you are sitting in some public place, a mall or restaurant may be a good choice. You will want to have a pen and paper in front of you. Now gaze in any particular direction for ten seconds (approximately) and then look down at your pad of paper and write down all that you saw in those ten seconds. You will find that you have remembered maybe half a dozen things.

Then again gaze up in the same direction and again give yourself ten seconds to remember what you saw. Often, you will discover that you missed a few things the first time you looked, and now you see some additional items. Write them down. Again repeat the exercise. Look at the sight for approximately ten seconds. Turn your eyes back to your pad and write down what you saw.

Repeat this exercise two more times.

Sufis will often astound people at the wealth of knowledge they have about an individual they have just met. Often this has nothing to do with supersensible insight, but relates to the highly-developed sense of observation that the Sufi has developed. The Sufi can amplify input from his or her senses. Sufis use all their senses to the fullest!

Repeat the above regularly.

"LA ILAHA IL ALLAH" (There is no reality but the Ultimate Reality)
- The Islamic Profession of Faith

"What is the mi'raj of the heavens?
Nonexistence.
the religion and creed of the lovers is nonexistence."

- Jelaluddin Rumi

TALES FROM UNDER THE OVERPASS

"Teach me," Sam startled Mr. Khadir by saying, 'out of the blue' one day.
"I have come not to teach but to awaken."

"Well, then help me to awaken," Sam said with sincerity.

"Remember God," Mr. Khadir replied.

"Remember God? I don't think I've forgotten about God," Sam was confused. "Just what do you mean?"

"It is essential that you call to mind the Ultimate Source every second of the day," Mr. Khadir explained.

"I think that's a beautiful idea," said Sam.

"Do you want to know the highest of all names by which the Ultimate Reality is remembered?" questioned Mr. Khadir.

"Please, tell me," Sam shot back

"The Blessed Name of the Sultan of sultans is LA ILAHA IL ALLAH," Mr. Khadir intoned.

"That phrase," said Sam, "it . . . it sounds like the speech of angels!"

Mr. Khadir's eyes filled with tears. "Look into yourself Sam, your heart sings with love, joy and great compassion toward all humanity."

"Dreams are sent by God."

> *- Homer*

"Indeed, the vast and dreamy world that we call imagination, or the unconscious, may merge imperceptibly into autonomously existing worlds we would call 'hyper dimensional'."

> *- Terence McKenna*

"The probability of life originating by accident is comparable to the probability of an unabridged dictionary resulting from an explosion in a printing shop."

> *- Edwin Conklin*

"Dreams are also a means of communication between the Creator and humanity."

> *- Sheikh Muzaffer Ozak*
> *al-Jerrahi al-Halveti*

"Where do you dream? Where is the place?"

> *- Bubba Free John*

A DREAM WITHIN A DREAM

The powers of imagination residing in the mind are nothing less than astounding. The subconscious decides to give us a dream. Why do we see that particular dream movie? The subconscious acts as a brilliant playwright coming up with fantastic and deeply significant scenarios. Resident within us is a deeply ingrained natural drive toward resolution, solution and the fulfillment of desires.

Some biologists feel that dreams are just the nightly garbage dump of daily neuron activity. We think their opinion belongs on the garbage dump of science. In ordinary dreams, the subconscious decides to extrapolate on given data that exist within itself.

When we were in school, if we had an important test the next day, we would usually dream that the test was over. Somehow a whole story is put together, yes even invented, to give pleasure to our wishes. We know this process as "wish-fulfillment." When our conscious mind is shut down during sleep, a level of our being (an imaginative fountain) creates a plot in which our wishes are fulfilled.

Characters that appear in our dreams often surprise us. A consciousness animates these characters; a consciousness has plotted out the surprise twists of plot during the dream. How does the dream maintain integrity and congruency if it is just the spontaneous firing of neurons? Given the presence of a "sub" consciousness in our minds, this consciousness plays on our dream minds like an expert musician improvising on his or her instrument. Humanity is nothing if not creative.

From an analysis of any person's dreams it is obvious that dreams display a story and a sub-text. "Story" is a part of whom we are as human beings. *"It's only the story of the world and what happened in it,"* as Jack Kerouac put it. Dreams maintain congruency, which flies in the face of the "scientific" position that dreams are nothing more than neural reflux. If they were just the random firing of still throbbing neurons, they could not display the congruency of theme that they do. They would be a haphazard mishmash of vocal sounds and visual impressions. Yet in dreams people speak full sentences, in congruent contexts, interacting with the dream environment. People will frequently dream of objects and situations that they never encountered during the day.

Furthermore, dreams have a presence, a force and an emotional impact that command our attention. Is a wish just like a pressure or force that beats against the unconscious, forcing it to construct a dream? A decision making process takes place. An intermediate step is missing to our view that determines the particular characteristics of the dream. A wish is more potent than we have ever imagined! The human body is a symphony of rhythms: sleep, reproductive, heart, respiratory, glandular, and so forth.

Who is awake within yourself while you are asleep? There is a witness who does not rest who is inseparable from your life. This witness watches everything that occurs in your waking state as though it were a dream. THAT witness is aware. The Way of the Sufi inspires you to see THAT.

"The waking world is not a 'place,' and 'earth,' but a realm, an indefinite dimension, just as the condition or region into which you enter in dreams is a dimensionless realm."[382] The Murid begins to realize that the world is not what he or she thinks it is.

There is THAT within us that creates dreams. There is the playwright, the cinematographer. A part of us selects which "shots" we will see. The plot and outcome of our dreams are determined. Therefore, in addition, to our waking lives, we each create our personal story, our history. We connect events and experiences to form a coherent whole. A story of our lives goes on simultaneously with our waking life. We also constantly revise our story through recurrent feedback loops, for example, during a conversation between two people, as long as the communication system is maintained. A history is accumulated over time from the impact (sending and receiving) we have on each other.

We begin this story even before we are born. The fetus in the womb, at thirty weeks of age, spends most of its time in dream sleep. Scientists tell us that during dream sleep our highest cognitive functions shut down, allowing other aspects of our brain (that evolved in much more ancient times) to express themselves. In other words, during sleep, the ego steps aside permitting humans to tap into the more ancient wisdom that predates egoic perspectives. Without sleep our beings become disturbed and a psychological crisis results. Humans must sleep. This is an important message from the Indivisible Consciousness. To be a complete human being we must allow our conscious mind to shut down every night, and allow the hidden or shadow aspect of ourselves to take over. The path to becoming a Complete Human Being lies in honoring our waking and sleeping states.

There are also the Divine Dreams. In these dreams, Allah communicates with His Servants. The Master Abū Madyan Shu'ayb Ibn al-Husayn al-Ansārī said *"One who knows God learns from Him in wakefulness and in sleep."* The Murid must take these dreams to his or her Sheikh for interpretation. The Murid must not tell them to anyone until he or she tells them to the Sheikh. If the Murid tells them before he or she relates them to the Sheikh, their energy dissipates, which sometimes results in dangerous consequences. A bridge between all the great Prophets, Imams, Saints, and the Murid exists (according to the quantum informational energy systems theory). These great beings literally live on in the Murid (through their writings and sayings), and the Murid in turn, augments their presence within his or her being. An intimate feedback loop is created, a kind of marriage. According to this theory, soul is to spirit, as information is to energy. Soul is the story of our existence. Spirit is the power and force to help our mission to be fulfilled.

The dream world teaches the Murid many lessons. As we appear in the dream world, so too do we appear in the mundane world. We think the mundane world is dense and three-dimensional, yet when we see it with the eyes of Truth, it is no more genuine, essential, established, important, or authentic than the dream world.

In Islam there is one well-known tradition of turning for advice from on high. The practice is called *istikhara*: one engages in formal worship and asks God for assistance, and then goes to sleep. The answer is revealed to one in a dream. This practice is legitimized by a saying attributed to the Prophet Muhammad (Peace be upon him). Often Muhammad (Peace be upon him) himself who appears in the dream to solve the problem. This practice is often performed in mosques, grottoes and the shrines of Sufis. Ibn Arabi spoke of the importance of benefitting from the spirits of dead mystics. There is no evidence that he had a real master to instruct him when young. He speaks of mysterious encounters with hidden "friends of God" and the enigmatic Prophet Khezr. [383]

PRACTICE

The imagination is a sacred tool of the Sufi. Each time you pray or contemplate, attempt to see and hear the Ultimate Reality with your supersensible organs of perception. If you cannot yet see the Ultimate Reality supersensibly, then using your Active Imagination, imagine the Ultimate Reality face to face with you.

The sublime Leader of the prayers for all humanity advises, *"Worship Allah Most High with the intense sincerity you would feel if you directly perceived Him. You can attain this intensity by knowing full well that He is directly perceiving you."*

Constantly renew this image throughout the time of your prayer or contemplation, always striving to represent in your imagination your intimations about the Ultimate Reality. Do not neglect the simple things, like the scent of rose oil, the feel of the prayer carpet under your feet, your heartbeat, or the air on your skin.

Continue to use your imagination as you go about your daily tasks, always remembering in a visual and sensory way that the Divine Who Is Expressed As Everything encompasses you and your surroundings. In the Holy Qur'an the Omniconscious Unicity states, *"In whatever direction of dimension you may turn, there is only the essential Face of Allah."* 384

"Sex is an expression of self-esteem . . . and a celebration of existence."
- Ayn Rand

"The prophet's power is born of the spirit's dance.
That breeds the craving flesh, the sweating palm."

- Iqbal

"This applies well to he who loves only voluptuousness, that is to say he
who loves the support of voluptuousness, the woman, but remains uncon-
scious in the spiritual sense of that which is really in question. If he knew
it, he would know by virtue of what he enjoyed it, and who (really) enjoys
the voluptuousness; then, he would be (spiritually) perfect."
- Ibn 'Arabi, Bezels of Wisdom [385]

"See how you bury the primary pain. It goes underground. It seeps into the
waters of life. You're poisoned. All your relationships are poisoned. You
must dare to dredge up the primary pain."
- Nadja [386]

THE PHYSICAL CONNECTION

Our patriarchal religions tell us that the body is something separate from us and inferior to us. Therefore, we are brought up in an environment that treats the body like an object. We take the body for granted.

We must act from a holistic philosophy of life that acknowledges the spirituality of the body, in order for people to begin to take their bodies seriously. The problem in our society is not, as the evangelical and orthodoxly religious would tell you, that society is obsessed with the body. No! The problem is that society has been conditioned to believe (by religion) that the body is not sacred, and therefore only a thing to be tolerated, looked down upon, and disciplined. Therefore, the result is pornography and the degradation of women.

Patriarchal, Fundamentalist and dualistic religion portray the body as a workhorse. The Murid must work at freeing himself or herself from the tyranny of Exoteric Authority.[387] Even those in society who do not subscribe to religious belief are nonetheless affected by the Dominator Religion and so think of the body only as something to be painted, decorated with gold and jewelry, dressed in fine garments, and used for immediate pleasure gratification. Abu Maydan said: *"One who adorns himself with the ephemeral is misled."* Priests and religions have wrecked and impoverished your relationship with your bodies. There is no comprehension by society that the body exists in an intimate interrelationship with your being.

You worry about the way your bodies look, but this is not the same thing as being in your bodies. Dieting, weight training and having facials are not the same thing as developing a real connection with the physical form. Robin Becker shares this insight, *"You create the atmosphere around you by the texture your body exudes."* One of the best ways to reawaken your primal bond to your body is through some sort of bodywork like RADIX. Begin by reading some books by Wilhelm Reich. Reich was a practicing psychoanalyst in the 1920's and 30's. He used the term *orgone* energy to describe the life force or "bioenergy." He later expanded this idea and stated that this force is present in the formation of galaxies and in nature.

Reich obtained the word orgone from "orgasm" since this energy was discovered through Reich's research into the bioelectrical nature of human sexual intercourse. Reich pointed out that this energy has been known for millennia to other cultures as Ether, Chi, Prana, Ruach, and so forth. Today, many know this energy by the name of "The Force" described in the "Star Wars" films.

Central to Reich's work was the notion of "character armoring." He taught that humans block the free flow of life force in their bodies. They do this by tensing up the muscles in various parts of the body, by that imprisoning repressed emotional energy in those muscles. The word "radix" means root or source. Through THE RADIX EDUCATION, the participant learns to release those areas of blockages.

When you were infants, you experienced and discharged your feelings fully and immediately. When you were feeling good, you laughed, when you were feeling bad, you cried. However, as you grew up you learned to block some of those feelings, perhaps because "boys don't cry" or "girls don't fight."

Most people, by the time they are grown, have blocked so many feelings that they have lost touch with themselves in ways they do not even recognize. You therefore have to resort to blatant pleasures like huge Hot Fudge Sundaes, Cocaine or Pornography. Your finer emotional responses and senses are dulled tremendously, and so you have to take your pleasure in big gulps.

Another problem with repressing bad feelings is that you thereby shut off the good feelings too! When you block yourself from pain, you block yourself from pleasure.

Think of a person who has lost a lover. He or she at first pines away because of the sad loss. However, some people decide never to trust again. They become emotionally numb, dull and unresponsive. By that, they lose the ability to be emotionally available to love and to have pleasurable feelings. Reich went further, and said that people actually stuff their pain into their muscular and nervous system, which creates physical, etheric and astral blockages to the free flow of energy.

Here is another reason that true spirituality includes the whole person and not just "so-called" spiritual thoughts and actions. If you teach your body to cut itself off from feeling, because you are afraid of experiencing your anger or sexual desires, then the body becomes so paralyzed that it cannot experience love and joy. In seeking to become "spiritual," many people end up becoming emotionally "dead."

RADIX wisely teaches that to the extent that you block pain, you cannot experience pleasure. This, on earth, is a true balance of the polarities.

"Woman is a beam of the divine Light. She is not the being whom sensual desires takes as its object. She is Creator, it should be said. She is not a creature."

- Jelaluddin Rumi

"There is no God beside me, neither in divinity nor humanity, neither in the Heavens nor on earth, outside of me, who am Fatima - Creator."

- Fatima - Fatir (the Initiator)

"The mosque may be destroyed, but the mihrab remains."

- Turkish Proverb

"The spiritual presence and essence of Fatima has inspired thousands of artists, poets, writers and artisans."

- Laleh Bakhtiar

"The womb of the mother is a manifestation of Allah Himself!"

- Hadith

"We're entering a new era, it will be the resurgence of the divine feminine spirit. We must honor that spirit, in ourselves, and in others."

- "Bliss" [388]

"I am not afraid of Allah; I love Allah."

- Nailya Beidulayeva

THE SPIRITUAL
EQUALITY OF MEN AND WOMEN

Exoteric religions tell us that we must look outside ourselves for the answers. Rather than respecting our inner responsibility, exoteric religions teach us that we should put someone else in charge of our lives, be it our rabbi, our imam, our pastor, or our priest.

The dominant religions of the Western World and the Near East have an essentially masculine orientation. They emphasize perfection, which is a masculine characteristic, rather than wholeness, which is a feminine characteristic. Males cannot give birth; therefore, patriarchal religion is centered upon pseudo-creative elements such as breath, modeling with clay (the way Yahweh constructed Adam), numbers, and words. The male-oriented religions are mental and cerebral with great emphasis on memorization of lengthy religious tracts and prayers. Since the patriarchal Gods could not give birth, as they have no wombs or vaginas, they would create by saying a "word" or breathing into a form of clay. Yet, what was that clay?

Some writers consider the matriarchy and patriarchy issue as a contest between the Sky religions and the Grounded/Nature/Earth religions, or the Machine Culture vs. the Natural Symbiotic culture. The Natural Symbiotic culture sees all of humanity as interconnected. The Machine Culture sees nature as the wild uncontrollable fury that must be controlled, just as we must control the "stranger" in us. Science has seen the world as a well-organized "machine" that they must dissect. The science of modern medicine is dehumanizing. While the intentions and actions of many scientists and doctors are noble, the paradigm behind much of their work is the notion that they can "do" something to control nature.

We fear what is uncontrollable. This "control" attitude results in an "order-fetish." People become obsessed with mowing and grooming their lawns and obsessed with neatness. People living in contemporary society are split beings divided against themselves. Our Euro-centric society is wounded. Society does not want to feel pain. Therefore, society denies history, and hides its collective head in the sand. People feed their spirits with junk food and entertainment that distracts. Television removes us from an authentic connection with nature. "I shop therefore I am," sums up people's sense of self.

We must reintegrate what we have taken apart and love the thing we fear. Our thinking must change to the consideration of long-term cycles and consequences. The Iroquois nation would think of the next seven generations before taking an action! True Islam has always accepted responsibility for the next generation's children. We are not machines, but sensitive, holistic beings. Spirituality has reached a metanoia, a turning point. This is a tyros, a moment in which things that seemed impossible become possible. We need to begin to re-appropriate compassion and give importance to fertility and nurturance. We need to care about others and ourselves. Out of the loss of the old can come the affirmation of something new. We must ask ourselves the question, *"Are we really evolving spiritually?"*

Female-oriented religions are directly connected with birth and the body, nurturing, fecundity, nonviolence, wholeness, spirals, circles and the Underworld. Perhaps this is the profound insight that the Prophet Muhammad (Upon him be peace) had when he said, *"Paradise is found at the feet of the mother."* The secret Sufi understanding of this hadith is that the Arabic word for foot is the same word for the female pubic bone, suggesting that illumination can be found through sexual intercourse between two married Sufis in the station of *Haqq*. In Sufism, Woman is the Secret. The great Sufi Sheikh, Ibn 'Arabi, *"practiced . . . the exaltation of sexual intercourse as a supreme method of realization,"*[389] and transmitted his direct knowledge from Allah to fourteen women, eight of whom received this transmission in dreams.[390]

Sheikh el-Hajj Şerif Çatalkaya er-Rıfa'i er-Marufi teaches that Sufism was first known as Theosphia. Theosophia means "knowledge of things divine." The word comes through Medieval Latin from Late Greek; that is, the type of Greek spoken from the first or second to the sixth century C.E. However, Sheikh Şerif Çatalkaya refers to the existence of a universal initiatory form, from which issued all the great religions and to which human beings can reach at the end of an inner divine search, passing to a complete metamorphosis of BEING.

The Nag Hammadi Library, a collection of thirteen ancient codices containing more than fifty texts, was discovered in upper Egypt in 1945. This immensely important discovery includes a large number of primary Gnostic scriptures. Here Eve whose mystical name is Zoe, meaning life, is shown as the daughter and messenger of the Divine Sophia, the feminine hypostasis of the supreme Godhead:

"Sophia sent Zoe, her daughter, who is called 'Eve,' as an instructor in order that she might raise up Adam, in whom there is no spiritual soul so that those whom he could beget might also become vessels of light. When Eve saw her companion, who was so much like her, in his cast down condition she pitied him, and she exclaimed: 'Adam, live! Rise up upon the earth!' Immediately her words produced a result for when Adam rose up, right away he opened his eyes. When he saw her, he said: 'You will be called "mother of the living", because you are the one who gave me life.'" [391]

The Gnostic Christians who wrote the Nag Hammadi scriptures did not read Genesis as history with a moral, but as a myth with a meaning. To them, Adam and Eve were not actual historical figures, but representatives of two intrapsychic principles within every human being. Adam was the dramatic embodiment of psyche, or soul, while Eve stood for the pneuma, or spirit. Soul, to the Gnostics, meant the embodiment of the emotional and thinking functions of the personality, while spirit represented the human capacity for spiritual consciousness. The former was the lesser self (the ego of depth psychology), the latter the transcendental function, or the "higher self," as it is sometimes known. Obviously, Eve, then, is by nature superior to Adam, rather than his inferior as implied by orthodoxy. Nowhere is Eve's superiority and numinous power more evident than in her role as Adam's awakener.[392]

Ibn 'Arabi married a holy woman by the name of Mariam al-Bajiya who introduced him to sacred sexuality. *"She certainly nourished his soul, thus enabling him, in experiences that were certainly very rare, to combine orgasm with ecstasy."* [393] She introduced him to meditation and contemplation through persuading him to learn Sufism from another pious woman, Nãna, the famous Fatma Bent Ibn El Mutanna of Cordoba. Ibn 'Arabi became her servant and Murid for two years. The Greatest Sheikh of all, Ibn 'Arabi, was taught by a woman! The concept that Eros is the fuel for the human love of God is not new. Saint Augustine said this and before him Plotinus, and before him Plato.

"The body of a woman, therefore, is a microcosm of the masterly work of God. To lose oneself in it is to find oneself in God. To run over it is to continue the great book of Allah."[394] Ibn Hazm adopts in "Tawq al-hamama" an attitude of sympathy toward love and the inclination of human nature to appreciate beauty, holding these feelings to be neither commanded nor forbidden.[395] The Prophet Muhammad (Peace be upon him) declared, *"Gazing at a comely face is an act of worship."*

Archaeologists have uncovered a wealth of evidence suggesting that before God was worshiped as a male, the Presence of Life was worshiped as a female. A nomadic hominid tribe, who predated even the Neanderthal era, has recently been carbon-dated to have existed between 232,000 and 800,000 years ago. Until the past few decades, the famous *Willendorf* goddess carved of bone 30,000 years ago was the earliest human-crafted work of art and veneration. They have recently discovered a new goddess figure, named the Acheulian goddess, in the excavation of the above-mentioned nomadic hominid tribe. It predates Willendorf by an amazing quarter-million years! They unearthed the five inch figurine at Birket Er-Ram, Golan Heights, Israel during the 1980s. Due to its extremely old age, some claimed it had to be a natural rock formation. Microscopic analysis, however, reveals the figure is not a natural rock formation. Marks left from flint tools indicate the figurine was *"deliberately sculpted and shaped."*[396] The Israel Prehistoric Society believes this sculpture may be the *"world's earliest object of art."* Woman is the secret.

Even in the sacred patriarchal traditions, we sense the presence, however repressed or denied, of the feminine aspect of Absolute Existence. In the Judaic Tradition, we find the *Shekinah* (perceived as The Holy Cloud, Holy Shadow, Holy Fire, Holy Radiance of the Divine Glory, and The Clouds of Heaven).

"The Reapers of the Field are the Comrades, masters of this wisdom, because Malkbut Shekhinab [the feminine Divine Presence], is called the Apple Field, and She grows sprouts of secrets and new flowerings of Torah. Those who constantly create new interpretations of Torah are harvesting Her." [397]

The Shekinah is a dwelling Presence of Divinity. When Muhammad (Peace be upon him) was a young boy, a cloud watched over him wherever he went. In addition, the Hebrews worshiped the Goddess Asherah, a female deity. King Solomon paid her homage. Josiah, a King of Israel, built her a sanctuary on the Mount of Olives. In Christianity, there exists the Holy Spirit, and in Islam, there exists the Sufic and Ismaili honor given to the Blessed Maryam (the mother of the Prophet Jesus), to Lady Fatima Zahra (the Prophet's daughter) and to Boraq.

During the atomic explosion at Hiroshima on August 6, 1945, a German Jesuit and seven of his colleagues were living only eight blocks from the blinding center of the nuclear flash, yet all escaped while flaming death screamed all around them. To this day, all eight occupants of that building are alive and well while others living some distance away continue to die of the radiation effects of that frightful holocaust. Over the years some two hundred scientists have examined these eight survivors, trying to discover what could have spared them from incineration or the lethal storm of radiation. Speaking on television in the United Sates, the German Jesuit, Father Hubert Shiffner, gave the startling answer. *"In that house, we were living the message of Fatima."* He was, of course, referring to the apparition that occurred to three young shepherd children in Fatima, Portugal on July 13, 1917. His words seemed to underline Sister Lucia's statement in 1977, *"Our Lady will protect all her dear ones."*

Does the reader know that before becoming a Holy Place to Catholics in honor of Our Lady of Fatima, the shrine in Portugal was a holy place to Muslims who used to make pilgrimages there in honor of Muhammad's (Peace be upon him) daughter Fatima ('Alaiha Assalam)? So then, who really is Our Lady of Fatima? The same phenomenon occurred in Nagasaki, which was hit with the second atomic bomb three days later: a Franciscan monastery, founded by Saint Maximilian Kolbe, was left standing, unharmed by the blast while everything around it was leveled to the ground.

Sufism cherishes the esoteric secret of woman, even though Sufism is the esoteric aspect of a patriarchal religion. Muslims pray five times a day facing the city of Macca (al-Mukarramah). Inside every Mosque is a niche called the "Mihrâb," a vertical rectangle curved at the top. The Sufis know this to be the vagina of the female aspect of divinity. In Sufism, woman is the secret, for woman is the soul. Toshihiko Izutsu writes, *"The wife of Adam was feminine, but the first soul from which Adam was born was also feminine."* [398]

In the words of the living Sufi Saint Habiba, *"Our culture went through the influence of many great people. The Hellenistic culture integrated with our remote cult of the Mother, the Great Mother Anahita. Along centuries, we exchanged with the Indians, the Egyptians, and the Persian cultures, the Christians and the Buddhists. When the Muslim religion appeared, it unified all these different styles and conceptions. We consider all the powerful masters of the past as Prophets, and we don't deny any other faith. Muslim is a newborn religion that originates from all the other big religions."* [399]

The Sufis say that each Prophet had a woman who made him into a Prophet. Blessed Jesus (Peace be upon him) had Mary Magdalene. She initiated him. There is biblical proof of their relationship in that Jesus (Peace be upon him) used a particular word (incorrectly translated by Biblical translators as "touch") when he met Mary in the garden. The exact translation of the word is "to touch as in fondling and sexually stimulating."

According to the Gospel of Philip 63:31, the Prophet Jesus (Peace be upon him) loved Mary Magdalene more than all the disciples and often kissed her on the mouth. *"But Christ loved her more than all the disciples and used to kiss her often on the mouth. The rest of the disciples were offended by it and expressed disapproval. They said to him, 'Why do you love her more than all of us?' "*(Philip 63. 30-35). Occasionally we have seen various Sheikhs kiss their Murids on the mouth, whether they be male or female. Mary Magdalene and the Prophet Jesus (Peace be upon him) had long and intimate conversations together, on mystical topics way above the heads of the disciples.

Each Sheikh has a woman that makes him into a Sheikh. Therefore, in this seemingly patriarchal mystery tradition, we see that woman is the Hidden Initiatrix, the Shadow Guide, the Blackness that births the Light.

However, there have been women in Islamic history whom Allah called to service of a manifest nature. These women became *Sultanas* and *Malikas* (Queens). One such famous woman was Razia Sultana, who took power in Delhi in the year 634/1236. Another Queen bearing the title of Sultana was Shajarat al-Durr, who gained power in Cairo in 648/1250 like any other military leader. In fact, she brought the Muslims a victory during the Crusades and captured the King of France, Louis IX.

Fatima tul Zehra (Fatima the Radiant, Fatima the Brightest Star, Fatima-Star of Venus, Fatima-The Evening Star), the daughter of the Prophet, is the secret in Sufism. She is the *Hujjat* of Ali ('Alaihi Assalam). In other words, she establishes the esoteric sense of his knowledge and guides those who attain to it. Through her perfume, we breathe paradise. Though she was his daughter, the Prophet Muhammad (Upon him be peace) called her *"Um Abi'ha"* (mother of her father).

What mystery was the Prophet hinting at by this statement? While Fatima Zehra ('Alaihi Assalam) was Muhammad's (Peace be upon him) daughter, the Rasulallah understood that his gnosis was bestowed upon him from the Divine Feminine. Fatima Fatir as representative of Allah's *Jamal*, saves humankind from Allah's *Jalal*. Esoterically, if it were not for Fatima (Mercy), Allah would never have sent Muhammad (Peace be upon him) and the Qur'an to humanity.

The night is the exemplification of our sovereign Fatima ('Alaiha Assalam), especially the "Night of Destiny" *(laylat al-Qadr)*. Lady Fatima ('Alaiha Assalam) was chosen from all women to be the Mother source of Muhammad's lineage, the core of the generation of Muhammad. Through her, the progeny of the Prophet multiplies – through a woman.[400]

The process of giving birth to the spirit is the feminine principle. That to which has been given birth is the masculine. *"This is why, in spiritual transformation and rebirth, only the masculine principle can be born, for the femi-*

nine principle is the process itself. Once birth is given to the spirit, this principle remains as Fatima, the Creative Feminine, the Daughter of the Prophet, in a state of potentiality within the spirit reborn."[401]

Fatima the Gracious ('Alaihi Assalam), "The Leader of all the Women of all the Worlds,"[402] is a wonderful role model for not only women in Islam, but also for men in their understanding of the importance of women in Islam.

"Fatima spent her life in struggle, resisting poverty and difficulties. We learn of Fatima as a Muslim female child who defends her father against the elders of her tribe. Fatima, the Muslim woman, who stands at the door and defends her husband and her home when usurpers try to burn it down. Fatima tells the newly elected Khalif that he has displeased God and God's Prophet by not listening to the Prophet's advice and taking his own interests to heart."[403]

Fatima ('Alaiha Assalam) is the secret within the human being. She is our ability to appreciate pleasure and beauty. Henry Corbin posits this view of Fatima's ('Alaihi Assalam) spiritual reality, *"Fatima symbolizes the essence of the feminine because she was the creator of the being (Logos) by whom she herself was created (in other words Muhammad). That is, whereas the Virgin Mary is the mother of the Logos, Word, Fatima is the daughter of the Logos, who in turn, through her marriage to Ali, gave birth to the Logos as manifested in the Imams."*[404]

Before a Sufi performs any action, he or she says, *Bismillah ir Rahman ir Rahim* (In the Name of Allah, the Compassionate, and the Merciful). We also pronounce this most sacred phrase before the recitation of any part of the Qur'an. *Rahman* is one of the Divine Names and is usually translated as "Compassion." *Rahim*, another Divine Name is translated as "Mercy." Both words are derived from the root: *rah'm* that means womb, and is an ancient name of the Goddess. *Al Rahman* is properly defined as the possessor of the womb; and *Al Rahim* is ascertained as the womb. Therefore, they might render *Bismillah ir Rahman ir Rahim* more precisely as *"In the Name of the Unknowable, the Matrix of the Womb."*[405]

Ibn al-'Arabi has a fascinating insight into the secret of the divinity of the feminine. The Mother-Father aspect of Allah is most clearly seen in the two categories: of the Names of Beauty and the Names of Majesty. As the Incomparable God of Majesty, Allah is like the strict and indifferent Father. He is the Remote Absolute, the Unknowable and Beyond Attributes. Fadlou Shehadi in his work "Ghazali's Unique Unknowable God" writes that Ghazali seems to be saying, *"that positive attribute-statements assert that God is such and such, but He is not actually so. Although we say God is just, forgiving, merciful, yet in a strict sense God is not. As descriptions of God these are false, yet they are what we should accept about Him. Such are the attributes in terms of which the believer is to characterize God, although they are not descriptively true characterizations. Man is therefore left to worship God in a human language version of Him which is descriptively inapplicable to Him.* "[406] Yet, here we are faced with a dilemma. What in a God that is wholly other and incomprehensible would prompt people to worship and pray to Him? Ghazali says: *"God is . . . an Existent who transcends all that is comprehensible by human sight or human insight . . ."* [407] D. B. Macdonald, in commenting on this "aloof" aspect of Allah declares, *"It is magnificent, but it is not - religion!"*[408] However, when we consider the Names of Beauty, as the Compassionate God of Similarity, Allah is most like a good-natured Mother who never falls short in Her duty to look out for the well-being of Her children.

The attitude that the Murid adopts in relation to the Divine will influence his or her perception of the way the Divine relates to the Murid. If the Murid acts in a certain manner because he or she believes Allah is a stern and cold deity and the Murid fears punishment, then Allah will appear to be such a deity. However, if the Murid acts out of his or her love for Allah, then Allah will manifest as a caring and loving deity to the Murid. Allah approaches us in the same manner in which we approach Allah.

Inasmuch as you are reflections of Allah's attributes, it is when you pull back from Allah, that you experience *Jalal*. If you continuously see the world with the eyes of love, beauty and compassion, then you continuously experience Allah's *Jamal*. You cannot change the world, but you can change the way you see the world.

Sara Sviri in her book "The Taste of Hidden Things: Images on the Sufi Path"[409] explains to us how creation is both the act and product of divine erotic energy, also symbolized as an act of writing or speech in the myths of the major religions. In Islamic mythology, the pen (*qalam*) represents "the thrust and outpouring" of divine male energy that writes human destinies in the Book of Creation, the Mother of Books (*Umm al-kitāb* [410]

In ancient Egyptian mythology, the hieroglyphic symbol of a Throne represents the Goddess Isis. This is because from ancient times, through the medieval age (and even beyond), people believed that the King received his power through the Goddess of the Land, represented by the Throne upon which he sat. Allah sits on the Throne of Mercy (sarir al-rahmaniyya). Mercy, in Arabic, is a feminine noun. The universe consists of the circumference of a circle (which is the Cosmos) and a point at the center of the circle (which is the Essence). Allah sits on the Throne of Mercy and governs the whole Cosmos. Hence, the masculine (Majestic) aspect of Absolute Existence draws Its power from Its feminine (Beautiful) aspect.

There is only one person buried inside the Ka'ba, the "House of God" and that is a woman, the slave Hagar, the second wife of the Prophet Abraham and the mother of Ismail.

Ibn 'Arabi speaks thus about woman, *"Woman is the highest form of earthly beauty, but earthly beauty is nothing unless it is a manifestation and reflection of the Divine Qualities."* Continuing, he says, *"Know that the Absolute cannot be contemplated independently of a concrete being, and It is more perfectly seen in a human form than in any other, and more perfectly in woman than in man."*

Whenever a religion attempts to present some one-sided, in other words, sexist view of a deity, that particular religion perforce is incomplete. Again, as in all things, balance is necessary when it comes to religion, spirituality and divinity. The body is not some donkey that we must ride through life until the rider can be united with his or her true destination. The rider, who does not realize that the "donkey" is just as much the destination, as the means to that destination, can never arrive at his or her goal.

Jelaluddin Rumi says, *"The physical form is of great importance; nothing can be done without the consociation of the form and the essence. However often you may sow a seed, stripped of the pod, it will not grow. Sow it with the pod, it will become a great tree. From this point of view, the body is fundamental and necessary for the realization of the Divine intention."*[411]

The patriarchal religious adherent is a frustrated person, for he or she can never live up to the standards that his or her God supposedly commanded. This leaves the believer feeling like a failure, down in the dumps, feeling hatred for his or her physical self. Statements such as, *". . . the spirit indeed is willing, but the flesh is weak."* (Matthew 26:41) cause the sincere devotee to experience a hopeless duality and gulf between his mind and body.

The person becomes embarrassed, wondering if anyone else has this problem of living up to the commands of his or her religion. The follower becomes unsure of him or herself and feels that he or she must hide his or her inferiority.

Adherents of these religions are generally not empowered by their religion; they are made to feel inferior. Moreover, what is the behavior of people who are made to feel inferior? Some bow down under the slave yoke of the religion, others attack people who do not believe as they do. In a desperate need to feel self-empowerment in their lives, these people resort to religious violence and terrorism. *"Indeed, solicitude in caring for God's servants is better than [killing them from an excessive] zeal for God."*[412] Some people begin to see their spiritual leaders as "Daddy" or "Mommy" while they play the role of the child. Some of these "children," after a time, will act out an adolescent rebellion against their "parents."

The Shadow side of religion must be recognized and dealt with propitiously. The spiritual Way must include the female principle in balance with the male principle, as certainly as Allah Most High created day and night! As a society, as a spiritual community and as individuals we must incorporate the contra sexual. The want of the feminine principle is keenly felt in today's spirituality.

The solution: do not pursue perfection (for that is a patriarchal and intellectual notion), rather work on developing each of your qualities and aspects into a Complete Holistic Human Being. When the Sufi uses the term *insān kāmil*, (the Perfect Human), he or she is referring to a flowering of the full potential of the Human Being. We say "perfect" in the sense that the person is a perfect reflection of his or her Lord, complete and whole, but not "perfect" by the human mind's measure of perfection (which is based on an incomplete view of reality).

The Spiritual Woman must be united to the Spiritual Man, the Sun with the Moon, Ali (May the peace of Allah be with him) united with Fatima - Al-Batool (Mother of the Succession of Epiphanies). Their house is the *living* Ka'ba.

PRACTICE

This exercise will develop your spatial acuity. Observe objects in relation to one another. Notice their spatial relationship. As you walk toward your car, for instance, observe how the perspective and proportion change. Experience dimensional space while you approach the car. See your car coming toward you in space as you move toward it. Observe how the car grows larger in your field of vision.

Do not tell yourself anything while you do this exercise. Just watch closely. Look at the distances between things. Observe how they sit near or far from each other. Notice how far, how near.

Observe the walls, ceiling and floor in the room you are sitting in right now. Watch and examine the relationship between ceiling and floor, wall to wall, wall to ceiling, and wall to floor. Sense how they interrelate with one another. Become intensely aware of the form and proportion of the room as the walls, ceiling and floor delineate it.

Sensing geometric relationships and correspondences reveals unutterably significant spiritual truths.

Arabic calligraphy and design are an example of profound truths revealed through proportion. The art in mosques and masjids is contemplative and transporting. This art requires time to enter one's being and work its spatial and abstract effect on the viewer. As Islamic art does not depict human beings, it has a kind of clearness that allows us to encounter realities beyond our ordinary, day-to-day, realities.

All the symbolism of the geometric patterns in Islamic art originates from the number one, through the concept of symmetry. It is helpful to contemplate on the revealed name of The Maker From Nothing: *Al-Bāri'*.

"If the stars should appear one night in a thousand years, how would men believe and adore."

> *- Ralph Waldo Emerson*

"I am not what the dreamer thinks I am."

> *- Adi Da Samraj*

"Night is a pregnancy."

> *- Turkish Proverb*

"The Heart of the mystic is as the full moon; his soul is as the darkness of night."

> *- Laleh Bakhtiar*

TALES FROM UNDER THE OVERPASS

Sam and Mr. Khadir walked along the bank of a stream on an exquisite moonlit evening. The moonlight shone into Sam's heart.

"I have heard that the world is like a giant elementary school," offered Sam.

"Rather than using the world as a Way to God, see it as God," replied Mr. Khadir.

"But aren't we here to learn?" questioned Sam.

"Yes, you are here to learn Who each pebble in this stream Is," answered Mr. Khadir.

"So, I see, you believe that God is incarnated in everything," concluded Sam.

"The Fact of Existence is the Condition of All Things," Mr. Khadir stated.

"I don't understand," Sam protested.

"Practice just looking around yourself, while you silently remind yourself that the Condition of everything you see expresses the Living Reality," elaborated Mr. Khadir.

"But," Sam reflected, "I thought all the activity I see around me was just nature and people going about their business."

"Truth is not what you think it is, Sam," Mr. Khadir replied.

"Then all this activity is a description of the State of the Supreme One?" Sam wondered.

"Even that One can be a stumbling block." Mr. Khadir answered.

"You cannot teach a person anything;
you can only help them to find it within themselves."
                                        - Galileo

"Know that everything is vanity except God."
                                        - Lebid

"He who has suffer'd you to impose on him, knows you."
                                        - William Blake

"Meekness and abashment are two branches of faith, and vain talking and
embellishing are two branches of hypocrisy."
                                        - Muhammad (Peace be upon him)

"Whoever is selfish and brags about himself will lose many friends and will
make many people dislike him."
                                        - Imam Hassan Askari
                                        (A.S.), the eleventh Imam

THE SUFI IN CONVERSATION

It is important to stay to the topic in a conversation. Bouncing around from topic to topic destroys spiritual power. Spiritual power derives from consistency. Consistency strengthens the subtle bodies of the human being. Carefully follow the thread of what someone is saying and add something to this conversational thread. Ouspensky informs us: *"Talking can be awakening, and it can be sleep."*[413]

It is not important to win arguments. *"Indeed Allah does not love any arrogant and boastful person."*[414] It is not your job in life to instruct everyone as to what his or her proper opinion or conduct should be. Therefore in conversation, concentrate more on the interchange between you and the other human being, rather than attempting to win them over to your point of view. Imam Sadiq ('Alaihi Assalam), the Ornament of Sainthood, has said, *"The only reason a person suffers from the disease of arrogance is due to an inferiority complex which he or she sees in him or herself."*[415] If you stay on the conversational thread and add information to the subject, perhaps your information will lead the other person to change their opinion on their own.

Never use your power of speech to wield power over another individual. The Sufi tends to be a quiet and unassuming individual who lives in the moment.

PRACTICE

Look carefully at the sunlight reflecting off trees, buildings, people, animals, garbage dumps, gardens and so forth. Thomas Fuller has stated the following insight regarding architecture, *"Light (God's eldest daughter) is a principal beauty in building."* See the light. On partly cloudy days, observe with care the subtle and dramatic changes in the intensity of the sunlight on your surroundings. For this exercise, we want you to become acutely aware of the light itself, not the objects and people.

Then observe the particular light that shines from human faces. The Light from the Human Face is the Light of the Supreme Reality. *"When you see a creature, you are seeing the First and the Last, the Outer and the Inner."* [416]

Notice how beautifully the light shines forth from the Human Face. The Human Face is Allah's beauty. Allah says, *"I am the light, the Light is I."* Each of us, in potential, is Muhammad, the Nur, the Light!

"People need joy. Quite as much as clothing. Some of them need it far more."

- Margaret Collier Graham

"Humanity is the link between God and Nature. Every person is a copy of God in His perfection; none is without the power to become a perfect human being. It is the Holy Spirit which witnesses to humanity's innate perfection, the spirit is humanity's real nature and within humanity is the secret shrine of the Divine Spirit. As God has descended in humanity, so humanity must ascend to God, and in the Perfect Human Being, the true saint, the Absolute Being, which had descended for its Absoluteness, return again to itself."

-'Abd al-Karim Jili

SOUL FOOD

The best place to carry out spiritual training is close to nature. If you can be close to a forest, river, stream, lake, mountain range, and so on, you will be in an ideal environment for the development of your psychic senses.

The city life is too frenzied. When you arrive home at the end of the day, your whole body is awash with anxiety over the evening commute. When you seek to listen to your inner voice, all you hear are the loud radios and trucks in the street.

If you cannot be out in the country, at least immerse yourself in the world of metaphysical literature and profound music each night. The body of classical music is a complete library of metaphysical knowledge just waiting to be downloaded! They call these pieces "classics" not because some stuffy old authority somewhere decided that they were great music, but because they reveal great mysteries to the soul that listens. The fact that in our society the knowledge of this fact is largely forgotten does not diminish the power of the spiritual transmission that is possible through listening to this music.

Classical music, ballet and modern dance, fine art, literature, theater, and spiritual scripture feed the soul. Do not take your soul for granted. The soul must be cultivated, watered and fertilized. Aspire to have a soul. As an aspiring Sufi, one of your tasks is to create a soul-body for yourself. Attuning yourself to Nature and discerning the message of Art help to ripen and unfold your soul-body.

However, this is not a call to judge any human being. Various human beings are here solely for the task of working on their Physical, Etheric (*Latif*) and Astral bodies. Only a few have evolved to the station where they can begin to work on the higher bodies.

"Say: I do not ask of you any reward for it but love for my near relatives; and whoever earns good, We give him more of good therein . . ."
- Qur'an 33:33

"I am the grandson of the light which shone out to the world. I am of the House, from whom God has sent away abomination and whom God has purified thoroughly."

- Imam Hassan ('Alaihi
Assalam) [417]

"Mercies are signs
  of the Mercy of Ali,
the books of the prophets
  rehearse his tale,
paradise and its fruits
  are his gifts
and the greatest gift of God
  is Ali's sacred role.
  Say yes! for THIS
  Is God's greatest favor."

-Fo'ād Kermāni [418]

"Guard your sarair [secrets] for Allah knows your zamair [minds]."
- Imam Hassan ('Alaihi Assalam)

AL-MUJTABA – HAZRAT HASSAN
('Alaihi Assalam) [419]

We tell this and other stories of the Ahlul Bayt because Imam Ali ('Alaihi Assalam) has commanded us to tell the truth. We warn the reader, that these are uncomfortable truths. The Imam after the Commander of the Faithful, The Lion of Allah, Ali ('Alaihi Assalam), was his son al-Hassan ('Alaihi Assalam), the son of the Mistress of the Women of the Worlds, Fatima, daughter of Muhammad, the Lord of Messengers, may the Pure Radiance bless him and his pure family.

Imam Hassan ('Alaihi Assalam) was born in Medina (al-Munawwarah), on the night of the middle day of the month of Ramadan, three years after the Hijra (624). His mother, Fatima ('Alaiha Assalam) brought him to the Prophet on the seventh day in a silken shawl from Heaven, which Gabriel had brought down to the Prophet. Muhammad (Peace be upon him) named the child "Hassan" and sacrificed a ram for him in the ceremony of *aqiqa*.

Al-Hassan ('Alaihi Assalam) was the most similar person to the

325

Apostle of God, in form, manner and nobility.[420] No one was more like the Apostle of God, may God bless him and his family, than al-Hassan. [421]

Fatima ('Alaiha Assalam) brought her two sons, al-Hassan and al-Hussain (Peace be upon them) to the Apostle of God, may God bless him and his family, at the time when he was suffering from the sickness from which he died. *"Apostle of God,"* she said, *"these are your two grandsons. Give them something as an inheritance."*

"As for al-Hassan," he replied, *"he has my form and my nobility. As for al-Hussain, he has my generosity and my bravery."* [422]

Years later, Hassan ('Alaihi Assalam) addressed the community toward dawn on the night in which his father, the Commander of the Faithful, Ali ('Alaihi Assalam), died. He praised and glorified the One Living Reality and blessed the Apostle of God, may God bless him and his family. He said,

"He, peace be on him, has died on this the night on which Jesus, son of Mary, was taken up to Heaven, on which Joshua, son of Nuh, the entrusted one (wasi) of Moses, peace be upon him, died." Then tears overcame him, he wept, and the people wept with him. Then he continued,

"I am the grandson of the one who brought the good news. I am the grandson of the warner. I am the grandson of the man who, with God's permission, summoned the people to God. I am the grandson of the light, which shone out to the world. I am of the House for whom God has required love in his book, when God, the Most High, said, 'Say: I do not ask you for any reward except love for my near relatives. Whoever earns good, will increase good for himself.' The good is love for us, the House." Then he sat down. [423]

Abdullah bin Abbas, may God have mercy on him, arose in front of Hassan ('Alaihi Assalam) and said, *"People, this is the grandson of your Prophet, the entrusted one (wasi) of your Imam. So pledge allegiance to him."*

The people answered him saying, *"No one is more loved by us nor has anyone more right to succession (khalifa)."*

They rushed forward to pledge allegiance to him as successor. That was Friday on the eleventh of the month of Ramadan in the year 40 A.H. (660 C.E.). Unfortunately, on earth then was a man by the name of Mu'awiyah Bin Abi Sufyan b. Abi Sufyan, a duplicitous, ambitious, deceitful, and baneful man. When Mu'awiyah Bin Abi Sufyan learnt of the death of Ali ('Alaihi Assalam), and the people's pledge of allegiance to his son, al-Hassan ('Alaihi Assalam), he sent a man secretly to Kufa, and another spy to Basra. They were to write reports to him to undermine affairs for al-Hassan ('Alaihi Assalam). As-Hassan ('Alaihi Assalam) learned of the existence of these infiltrators. He wrote to Mu'awiyah Bin Abi Sufyan:

"You sent men to use deception and to carry out assassinations and you sent out spies as if you want to meet in battle. That is something that will soon happen, so wait for it, if God wills. I have learnt that you have become

haughty in a way that no wise man would become haughty."

Mu'awiyah Bin Abi Sufyan continued to dispute Hassan's ('Alaihi Assalam) authority. Eventually, Hassan ('Alaihi Assalam) did mount an army and marched toward Iraq. Hassan ('Alaihi Assalam) knew that many people in his army were there for various ulterior motives (such as the desire for booty from the forthcoming battle, or for tribal reasons) and so he tested their resolve by saying,

"Praise belongs to God whenever a man praises Him. I testify that there is no god but God whenever a man testifies to Him. I testify that Muhammad is His servant and His apostle whom He sent with the truth and whom He entrusted with revelation, may God bless him and his family. By God, I hope that I shall always be with God's praise and kindness. I am the sincerest of God's creatures in giving advice to them. I have not become one who bears malice to any Muslims nor one who wishes evil or misfortune for him. Indeed what you dislike about unity (jama'a) is better for you than what you like about division. I see what is better for you better than you see for yourselves. Therefore do not oppose my commands and do not reject my judgement. May God forgive both me and you and may He guide me and you to that in which there is love and satisfaction."

The people began to look at one another and ask, *"What do you think he intends by what he has just said? We think that he intends to make peace with Mu'awiyah Bin Abi Sufyan and hand over the authority to him. By God the man has become an unbeliever,"* they declared and they rushed toward his tent. They plundered him to the extent that they even took his prayer mat from under him. Then Abd al-Rahman b. Abd Allah b. Ja'al al-Azdi set on him and stripped his silk cloak from his shoulder.

Hassan ('Alaihi Assalam) called his most trusted men around him. As they made their way apart from the angry crowd, a man of Banu Asad called al-Jarrah b. Sinan caught hold of the reins of his mule. He had an axe in his hand and with a thrust, stabbed Hassan ('Alaihi Assalam) in the thigh, penetrating right through to the bone. He seized Hassan ('Alaihi Assalam) by the neck and both fell to the ground. A fight followed in which they rescued and carried off Hassan ('Alaihi Assalam) in a stretcher to al-Mada'in.

While his own discomfort distracted Hassan ('Alaihi Assalam) along with treating his wound, a group of the tribal leaders wrote secretly to Mu'awiyah Bin Abi Sufyan offering to accept his authority. They urged him to come to them and they guaranteed to hand over al-Hassan ('Alaihi Assalam) when they got to his camp, or to kill him treacherously.

Moreover, the people's desertion of Hassan ('Alaihi Assalam) increased. The Kharijites (the Muhakkima) cursed him, accusing him of disbelief, and declaring that shedding his blood was lawful and plundering his property. They made the call to prayer along with an addition that cursed Imam

Hassan ('Alaihi Assalam). There remained no one to protect him from his unfortunate predicament but some close associates of his father's and his own most trusted followers.

Mu'awiyah Bin Abi Sufyan wrote to Hassan ('Alaihi Assalam) about a truce and peace treaty. He also sent him the letters of his followers in which they had guaranteed to kill him treacherously or to hand him over. Al-Hassan ('Alaihi Assalam) did not trust him. He was aware of his deception and his attempts at assassination. However he could find no escape from assenting to his demands to abandon the war and bring about a truce because of the weakness of his follower's understanding of his right, their corrupt attitude toward him and their opposition to him. Therefore, he bound himself in a treaty with Mu'awiyah Bin Abi Sufyan because he realized the desperateness of the situation. He stipulated, that the cursing of the Commander of the Faithful ('Alaihi Assalam) should be abandoned and the practice of using the personal prayer *(qunut)* in the formal prayer *(salat)* as prayer against him should be set aside. Furthermore, the treaty stipulated that Hassan's ('Alaihi Assalam) family, may God be pleased with them, should be given security, that they should expose none of them to any evil and that each of them who had certain rights should attain those rights.

Mu'awiyah Bin Abi Sufyan accepted all that and made a treaty with him to observe all of the above stipulations. He swore to him that he would fulfill it. Mu'awiyah Bin Abi Sufyan addressed the community during the mid-morning prayer *(dhua al nahar)*,

"I fought so that I might have power over you and God has given that to me when you were reluctant to obey Him. Indeed, al-Hassan has requested me, peace be on him, to give him things and I have given things to him. All of them are now under my foot, and from now on I will not fulfill anything."

Then Mu'awiyah Bin Abi Sufyan went on until he entered Kufa. At Kufa, both Al-Hassan and al-Hussain (Peace be upon them) were present. Mu'awiyah Bin Abi Sufyan was there to make the people take the pledge of allegiance to himself. He went up on the pulpit and addressed the people. He mentioned the Commander of the Faithful ('Alaihi Assalam) and that he had taken from him and from al-Hassan ('Alaihi Assalam) what he had taken.

Then al-Hassan ('Alaihi Assalam) arose and spoke,

"O you who mention Ali, I am al-Hassan and Ali was my father. You are Mu'awiyah Bin Abi Sufyan and your father was Sakhr (Abu Sufyan). My mother was Fatima and your mother was Hind. My grandfather was the Apostle of God and your grandfather was Harb. My grandmother was Khadija and your grandmother was Futayla. May God curse him who tries to reduce our reputation and to diminish our nobility, who does evil against our antiquity and yet who has been ahead of us in unbelief and hypocrisy."

Groups of the people in the mosque shouted out, *"Amen, Amen."*

Later, Mu'awiyah Bin Abi Sufyan communicated secretly with Ju'da, daughter of al-Ash'ath. She was the wife of Hassan ('Alaihi Assalam). Mu'awiyah Bin Abi Sufyan urged her to poison her husband. He offered an agreement with her that he would marry her to his son, Yazid, and he sent her a hundred thousand dirhams.

"I will arrange for you to marry my son, Yazid, if you poison al-Hassan."[424] He also gave her a hundred thousand dirhams. Ju'da gave him the poison to drink but he lingered on sick for forty days.

He spoke to his brother Hussain ('Alaihi Assalam), *"I have been given poison to drink several times but I have never been given poison like this. My brother, I am leaving you and joining my Lord, I have been given poison to drink and have spewed my liver into a basin. I am aware of the person who poisoned me and from where I have been made a subject to this deceitful action. I will oppose him before God, the Mighty and High. Therefore, by the right I have concerning you, say nothing about that and wait for what God, the Mighty and High, will decide concerning me. When I have died, shut my eyes, wash me and shroud me. Then carry me on my bier to the grave of my grandfather, the Apostle of God, may God bless him and his family, so that I may renew my covenant with him. After that take me to the grave of my mother, Fatima daughter of Asad, may God be pleased with her, and bury me there. My brother, the people will think that you intend to bury me with the Apostle of God, may God bless him and his family. For that reason, they will gather to prevent you from doing it. I swear by God that you should not shed even your blood into the cupping-glass in carrying out my command."* [425]

He passed along his final road in the month of Safar in the year 50 C.E. (670). At that time, he was forty-eight years of age. His brother and entrusted one, al-Hussain ('Alaihi Assalam) undertook the washing and shrouding of his body, and buried him with his mother, Fatima, in the cemetery of al Baqi.

Marwan and those of the Banu Umayya who were with Marwan had no doubt that they would try to bury Hassan ('Alaihi Assalam) beside the Apostle of God, may God bless him and his family. They gathered and armed themselves. When Hussain ('Alaihi Assalam) approached the tomb of the Apostle of God (Peace be upon him) with the body of al-Hassan ('Alaihi Assalam) so that he might renew his covenant with him, they came toward them with their group. 'Aesha had joined Marwan's group on a mule and she was saying, *"What is there between you and me that you should allow someone I do not want to, to enter my house?"* Abdullah bin Abbas hurried to Marwan and said, *"Go back to where you came from, Marwan. Indeed, we do not intend to bury our companion with the Apostle of God, may God bless him and his family. However, we want him to be able to renew his covenant with him by visiting him. Then we will take him back to his mother, Fatima, and bury him alongside her according to his last instructions concerning that. If he had enjoined that he should be buried alongside the Prophet, may God bless him and his family, you know that you would be the least able to deter us from that. However, he, peace be on him, was much too aware of God and His Apostle and the sacredness of his tomb to bring bloodshed to it as others have done who have entered it without his permission."*

Then Abdullah bin Abbas went to 'Aesha and said to her, *"What mischief you cause, one day on a mule and one day on a camel! Do you want to extinguish the light of God and fight the friends (awliy'a) of God? Go back! You have been given assurance against what you feared and have learned what you wanted to know. By God, victory will come to this House, even if it is after some time."*

Al-Hussain ('Alaihi Assalam) said,

"By God, if there had been no injunction to me from al-Hassan, peace be on him, to prevent bloodshed and that I should not even pour blood into a cupping-glass in carrying out his command, you would have known how the swords of God would have taken their toll from you, you have broken the agreement made between you and us, you have ignored the conditions which we made with him for ourselves."

Although Mu'awiyah Bin Abi Sufyan gave Ju'da the money, he did not marry her to Yazid. Instead, he gave her a man from the family of Talha as a substitute.

Imam Hassan (Peace be upon him) was a man of sweetness, peace, forgiveness, and love. The people of his time were not accepting of such a Love-Filled Servant of the Divine Love Radiance. They preferred war, intrigue, gossip, espionage, money, and acclaim, to being servants of the One Reality. Each of us possess the detrimental qualities that led to the murder of Imam Hassan (Peace be upon him). Each of us must look within ourselves to find Hassan ('Alaihi Assalam) and Mu'awiyah Bin Abi Sufyan. We must mercifully bring Mu'awiyah Bin Abi Sufyan into the Light and make him a servant of the Supreme Reality. As M. R. Bawa Muhaiyaddeen says, *"All the children of Adam ('Alaihi Assalam) are brothers and sisters. Where Allah does not see a difference, we must not see a difference. We must not despise anyone whom Allah loves – and Allah loves everyone."*[426] The Murid must see all lives as his or her life. Have no doubt that everything and everyone are on a spiritual path. Allah loves All because the All are Multiple Reflections of His Diamond Reality. People who apparently seem to be forgetting Allah, are participating in a mystic path of which most spiritual people are unaware. The so-called "evil" and "unspiritual" people are yet, spiritual people. Within matter is a Unifying Force with the power to Create or Destroy. Einstein described this mathematically, and the destructive force was proven in Hiroshima.

PRACTICE

You usually perceive yourself as a separate and distinct entity from the space around you. However, now become aware of the space that surrounds you and your environment. Notice how you inhere within the space. The eminent dancer-choreographer Robin Becker has stated, *"Think compassionately about the space in which you are. The energy of the space merges with the energy of your body."*

Allow yourself to play with the idea that you are one with the space. Your body is, as Pir Vilayat Inayat-Khan said, *"so inalienable from its milieu."* You are breathing, yet you cannot live without the air around you. You are standing, yet you cannot stand without gravity. Contemplate on the following question, what do air and gravity represent?

"A good world needs knowledge, kindliness and courage; it does not need a regretful hankering after the past, or a fettering of the free intelligence by the words uttered long ago by ignorant men."
- Bertrand Russell

TALES FROM UNDER THE OVERPASS

"*Which is the True Way?" Sam asked Mr. Khadir.*

"The True Way is that which brings a person knowledge."

"So if I apply the traditional methods handed down by the Masters, is that not the True Way?"

"It is not the True Way if it does not perform its function for you. A coat is no longer a coat if it does not keep a person warm."

"So the True Way changes?"

"People change and needs change. Sometimes the form of a teaching must change to suit more appropriately the psyches of another national and cultural background. So what was the True Way once is the True Way no more."

Sam felt a feeling of significance rise in him, a deeply moving sense that at last he was hearing wisdom spoken by an authentic Guide.

Mr. Khadir continued, "The True Way is the external face of internal knowledge, known as Essence. The inner factor does not change. The whole work therefore, is the Essence. What you are pleased to call the Way of the Masters is merely the record of past method."

"So the form may change but the essence remains the same?"

"Yes, and expect the Essence to arise in the most UN-expected of ways!"

"What do you mean?"

"As it is Vital and Worthwhile, the Essence appears in ways that are useful to the particular time and place. Essence is always now. Routine is the enemy of creativity, and what is the Ultimate Reality if not creative? If you are reading what someone wrote down a thousand years ago and turning that into dogma, you are like someone who is worshiping the corpse of a great Guide. The corpse is dead. The Teaching has since taken a new form. Find the new form rather than trying to make a corpse look like a living human being."

"To know and to not do, is to not yet know."
> *- Emmett Miller*

"There are people in this world who become forgetful of themselves and their reason for being here. Their example is analogous to the pilgrim who on his way to Macca stops at an oasis, tends to his camel, selects choice grass to feed it with, cools his drinking water with ice. He gets so busy with these things that the caravan leaves him behind and he doesn't notice it; he even forgets the object of his journey.

The wise pilgrim gives his camel the attention it needs and no more, for his heart is set on Macca and the pilgrimage."
> *- Mohammad Ghazali*

FOLLOW THROUGH

It is very important that you stick to your decisions. Following through on your resolutions is a potent way to develop yourself spiritually. Dismissing and disregarding your decisions can wreak havoc with your spiritual self. You must develop a sense of being able to follow through on whatever you set your mind to. Every decision is a force. If you have not applied this force to the achievement of your decision, then this force will still be operable. It will seek to expend itself in another fashion.

The Sufi does not excessively worry or plan about the future. He or she consciously does each task at hand. The Sufi lives in the present and does not dwell on the future or past.

The only thing that should stop you from completing a decided course of action is the realization that you are mistaken. Other than that follow through on EVERYTHING! This means from a decision to pick up a newspaper on the way home from work, a decision to brush one's teeth after lunch, to a decision to study toward a new profession. From the smallest to the largest of resolutions, one must be consistent.

"Our deepest fear is not that we are inadequate. Our deepest fear is that we are powerful beyond measure. It is our light, not our darkness, that most frightens us. We ask ourselves, who am I to be brilliant, gorgeous, talented, and fabulous? Actually, who are you not to be? You are a child of God. Your playing small doesn't serve the world. There's nothing enlightened about shrinking so that other people won't feel insecure around you. We were born to make manifest the glory of God that is within us. And as we let our own light shine, we unconsciously give other people permission to do the same. As we are liberate from our fear, our presence automatically liberates others."

-1994 Inaugural speech
by Nelson Mandela

THE REALITY OF YOU!

You are an epiphany. People look all over for signs of the Divine. They long for some expression of the Divine. Yet, these people need not look far for this epiphany.

"Even as a mirror stained by dust
Shines brilliantly when it has been cleansed,
So the embodied one, on seeing the nature of the Soul,
Becomes unitary, his end attained, from sorrow freed."

-Hinduism. Svetasvatara Upanishad 2.8-15

When you realize that you are an epiphany then your whole experience of "being-ness" is transformed. The Divine speaks no more directly to you than through the simple fact of whom you are.

Through knowing yourself, you know the Divine. Through knowing the Divine, you know yourself. However, as you begin to be aware of Your Presence, it is absolutely crucial that you *simultaneously* acknowledge that every other human you meet is also the mirror of Allah.

"Moses was charged with freeing God's people from the dominion of the Egyptian leader, the Pharaoh. Meanwhile the Pharaoh did everything he could to preserve his dominion over them. According to the Qur'an, Moses' adversary the Pharaoh asserted, 'I am your Lord the Most High.' (Qur'an LXXIX 24) From a metaphorical point of view, Moses represents the intellect, the Pharaoh represents the ego, and God's people represents the spirit residing in each person."

- Deb Platt

TYRANTS AND THE MERCIFUL

THE MERCIFUL

"Ask thou, 'Why this enmity for Jirbra'il?' He only imprints on thy heart what Allah permits him and that which doth confirm what is before you - tidings good - for all who would believe."
- Qur'an 2:97

"To thee comes Revelation - let not thy heart, therefore, be straitened on that count - so that, thereby, thou mayest warn and preach to those of faith."
- Qur'an 7:2

"Yes, We had given Musa a covenant to protect those who would be virtuous, and explaining in all details so that in it they may find a Guidance and a Mercy from their Lord."
- Qur'an 6:154

"When thou bringest them no revelation, they ask: 'Why dost thou not make up one?' Say thou, 'I follow only that which is revealed to me by my Lord.' These are insights bestowed by your Lord, a guidance and a blessing for those of faith."
- Qur'an 7:203

"Oh ye people! There hath come to you counsel from your Lord, balm for your hearts, guidance and grace for those who would believe."
- Qur'an 10:57

"O my sons! Return ye and inquire about Yusuf and his brother. Despair ye not of Allah's guidance. None but the heathens do despair of Allah's guidance."
- Qur'an 12:87

"Their stories only serve as lessons to those who understand. They are not invented tales. Confirmed, are they by evidence before you, giving more details, as guidance and as grace to a people who believe!"
— *Qur'an 12:111*

"We raise for every people a witness from among themselves. We have called thee as a witness against these. And We have given thee a testament, which clarifies all things, a guide, a benediction, and a harbinger, for those who submit!"
— *Qur'an 16:89*

TYRANTS

"That is only for that which you had sent ahead! By no means is Allah unjust to His servants."
— *Qur'an 8:51*

"None did acknowledge Musa - except a few among his own people - for fear that Fir'aun and his hosts would persecute them. Truly, Fir'aun was mighty in the land and one who would transgress all bounds."
— *Qur'an 10:83*

"They prayed, 'Our Lord! We fear lest he may be prejudiced against us both and himself take initiative.'"
— *Qur'an 20:45*

"And when he tried to hold him who was the enemy of both, he said, 'O Musa! Wouldst thou kill me even as thou killed a man the other night? It seems thou too would rather be a tyrant in the land than one who settles quarrels peacefully!'"
— *Qur'an 28:19*

"Verily, We entrusted to the heavens and the earth Our Trust; In awe they all fulfilled them - Man alone withheld! Verily, he is foolish (to himself) unfair."
— *Qur'an 33:72*

"He who doeth right does it for his good and he that doeth wrong does it at his cost. It is not thy Lord who forces (good or evil) upon His servants ."
— *Qur'an 41:46*

"To Fir'aun - he was, indeed, most prominent among oppressors."
- Qur'an 44:31

"There is no change in My decree; nor am I unjust to My servants."
- Qur'an 50:29

Look at the above mirror and ask yourself, *"Who has found Mercy and who has found Tyranny?"*

Who is a tyrant? The tyrant is:

1. He or she who tyrannizes his or her own *nafs*.
2. Those who tyrannize humanity.
3. Those who go astray from Allah and His Prophets.
4. Those who do not follow Allah's orders.
5. Such men as Pharaoh, Nemrud and Sedad (who tried to bring down the house of David).

Sister Mahwash Hirmendi writes in "Asthma-ul Husna": *"Justice is the opposite of tyranny. Tyranny causes pain, destruction, and disturbance. Justice secures peace, balance, order and harmony."*

In the *Qabalah*, the Divine manifests as both Justice and Tyranny. *Chesed* and *Geburah*, are balanced in polar opposites with each other.

Sister Mirmendi continues: *"Out of respect for the beautiful name of Allah, al-'Adl, we must learn to exercise shukr, tawakkul, and rida' - thankfulness, trust in God, and acceptance. We must be thankful for the good, and accept, without personal judgement or complaint, whatever falls to our lot that does not seem to be good. In so doing, perhaps the mystery of Allah's justice will be revealed to us, and we will be happy with both the joy and the pain coming from the Beloved."*[427]

Therefore, the Sufi must not regard the polar opposites of Justice and Tyranny in a simplistic "Good vs. Evil" sort of way. As difficult as it might be, the Sufi ought to regard these manifestations as the Mystery and Secret of Allah's plan. Imam Ali ('Alaihi Assalam) said: *"If you give me all of the world with everything in it, with a condition that I take a husk of barley from an ant's mouth, I will not do so!"* [428]

"I do not recognize myself. . . .
I am neither Christian nor Jew,
nor Magian, nor Muslim."

- Jelaluddin Rumi [429]

"All religions are from one God. Religion is like the vehicle which takes
you to your destination. You can become lost if you are consumed with reli-
gion, and forget God - the destination. All the religions are here for us to
choose from. The question is, what is the religion of God? The religion of
God is Divine Love. If we don't have love, we won't be able to achieve our
goal, even with the best religion. The remembrance of God is from the
heart."

- Gohar Shahi

"The path is non-existent. It causes me to run in that wilderness in which
there is no path."

- Ghalib

"If the believer understood the meaning of the saying 'the color of the
water is the color of the receptacle', he would admit the validity of all
beliefs and he would recognize God in every form and every object of
faith."

- Muhyiddin Ibn 'Arabi [430]

"The ability to simplify means to eliminate the unnecessary so that the nec-
essary may speak."   *- Hans Hofmann*

"I have learned so much.
I have learned so much from God
That I can no longer call myself
A Christian, a Hindu, a Muslim
A Buddhist, a Jew.
The Truth has shared so much of Itself
With me
That I can no longer call myself
A man, a woman, an angel,
Or even pure Soul.
Love has befriended Hafiz so completely
It has turned to ash and freed me
Of every concept and image
My mind has ever known."

- Hafiz [431]

TALES FROM UNDER THE OVERPASS

" *Just when I think I have the Divine all figured out, I seem to be kicked back to square one.*" *Sam's consternation was showing.*

"*Zeus does and does not like to be called by the name Zeus!*" *Mr. Khadir retorted.*

"*What does that suppose to mean?*" *Sam said defensively.*

"*We can approach the Divine through traditional means: prayers, church services, lighting candles and so forth, but sometimes the Divine does not respond to that sort of approach.*"

"*But isn't there one right way to follow?*"

"*The answer does not lie in being right. It lies in being real.*"

"*But many people find comfort in religion.*"

"*Religion is a device that is used to delay spirituality. I warn you . . . beware of me. I am a dangerous person,*" *remarked Mr. Khadir.*

"*Why are you so dangerous?*"

"*Because the Divine is threatening.*"

"*I'm not used to your kind of spirituality, Mr. Khadir. I'm used to reading inspirational books and performing ceremonies and rituals. But you seem to be telling me it's all different from that.*"

"*Well, first off. The Divine is obvious. One of the Ninety-Nine Names of Allah is Az-Zhahir, The Obvious, the Conspicuous and the Clear. It's not as if you have to go anywhere or do anything to find the Divine. Do you think the Divine would play hide-and-go-seek with you?*"

Sam thought for a moment and then said with a smile dawning on his face, "*I guess not. I guess that wouldn't make much sense.*"

"*Exactly! So many people will debate and argue about the nature of God, but all the philosophy books in the world are no substitute for genuine personal experience with the Real. The Real is the Radiance of Your Existence and the Expression of Everything. For Allah emanates through all Creation in Divine Resplendence and with Divine Grace.*"

"Every day is Ashura and every land is Karbala."
> - *Imam Ja'far Al-Sadiq*
> *('Alaihi Assalam)*

"O Allah, You know that what we have done was not a contest to take power, or aimed at seeking to possess the remnants of worldly trivia. We wanted, indeed, to restore the lost aspects of Your faith and revive Your laws that were being ignored, so that the oppressed may feel secure."

> - *Imam Hussain*
> *('Alaihi Assalam)*

"But weep and wail for the Imams.
However, hard one may,
God by His will since the dawn,
Had woven this woeful tale."

> - *Narain Jethanand*
> *Merani "Qalandari"*

"Their heroism challenges our admiration through all the centuries that have since passed."
> - *Percy Skyes*

"We are the people called ahli-bala (sufferers). We love bala (calamities) and feel pleased with it. We live for others and not for ourselves."
> - *Imam Hussain*
> *('Alaihi Assalam)* [432]

THE UNVEILING OF
THE COMPANY OF HEAVEN

In the month of Muharram 61 A.H. (approximately 20 October 680 C.E.), an event took place in Iraq at a place known as Karbala on the bank of the river Euphrates. It seemed in those days insignificant from the historical point of view. A large army that the Umayyad regime had mobilized besieged a group of persons numbering less than a hundred and put them under pressure to pay allegiance to the Khalif of the time and submit to his authority. The small group resisted and a severe battle took place in which, one by one, they were all killed.

It appeared then that like hundreds of similar events, they would record this battle in history and forgotten in time. However, the events that occurred on the 10th day of Muharram in Karbala were to become a beacon and an inspiration for future generations. In this chapter, we will examine briefly the principal adversaries.

The leader of the small band of seventy-two men whom they martyred in Karbala was none other than Hussain ('Alaihi Assalam), son of Ali Bin Abi Talib ('Alaihi Assalam) and a grandson of the Holy Prophet (Peace be upon him). Who was Hussain? He was the son of Fatima ('Alaiha Assalam) for whom the Holy Prophet (Peace be upon him) said, *"Hussain is from me and I am from Hussain. May God love whoever loves Hussain."* [434]

With the passing away of his brother Hassan ('Alaihi Assalam) in 50 A.H., Hussain ('Alaihi Assalam) became the leader of the household of the Holy Prophet (Peace be upon him). He respected the agreement of peace signed by Hassan ('Alaihi Assalam) and Mu'awiyah Bin Abi Sufyan, and, despite the urging of his followers, he did not undertake any activity that threatened the political status quo. He continued with the responsibility of looking after the religious needs of the people. Hussain ('Alaihi Assalam) was recognized for his knowledge, piety and generosity. We can see an example of the depth of his perception in his beautiful *du'a* on the day of Arafat, in which he begins by explaining the qualities of Allah, saying,

" (Oh Allah) How could an argument be given about Your Existence by a being whose total and complete existence is in need of you? When did you ever disappear so that you might need an evidence and logic to lead (the people) toward You? And when did You ever become away and distant so that your signs and effects made the people get in touch with you? Blind be the eye which does not see You (whereas) You are observing him. What did the one who missed You find? And what does the one who finds You lack? Certainly, the one who got pleased and inclined toward other than You, came to nothingness (failed)."

On the other hand, we have Yazid, whose father (Mu'awiyah Bin Abi Sufyan) and grandfather (Abu Sufyan - the archenemy of the Prophet) had always tried to sabotage the mission of the Holy Prophet. Yazid's family was the family of Umayyah, one of the Quraish's families. Abu Sufyan had acted as the chief adversary against Islam when it was first introduced. Mu'awiyah's mother, Hind, ate the liver of Hamza, the Uncle of the Prophet Muhammad (Peace be upon him), because of her burning hatred of Islam. The family used strategic, financial and other means in their campaign against the Muslims. Their wealth and treachery were a great burden on preventing the spread of Islam among Arab tribes. Abu Sufyan showed his true color by stating in a poem, *"Bani Hashim had staged a play to obtain kingdom, there was neither any news from God nor any revelation."* [435] By this statement he implied that Muhammad (Peace be upon him) contrived the Qur'an, and that Muhammad

(Peace be upon him) himself was a charlatan. *Astagfiruallah.*

Mas'udi writes that Yazid was a pleasure-seeking person, given to drinking. Another authority states, *"Yazid was a debauch and clothed his intentions by cruelties."*[436] It is no wonder that Imam Hussain's ('Alaihi Assalam) response to Yazid's governor, when asked to pay allegiance to Yazid was, *"We are the household of the prophethood, the source of messengership, the descending-place of the angels, through us Allah had began (showering His favors) and with us He has perfected (His favors), whereas Yazid is a sinful person, a drunkard, the killer of innocent people and one who openly indulges in sinful acts. A person like me can never pledge allegiance to a person like him . . ."*[437]

The revolution of Hussain ('Alaihi Assalam) was an Islamic movement spearheaded by one of the great leaders of Islam. The principles and laws of Islam demanded that Hussain ('Alaihi Assalam) act to warn the Umma of the evil situation that it was in, and to stand in the way of the deviating ruler. As Hussain ('Alaihi Assalam) himself remarked when he left Medina (al-Munawwarah) for the last time, *"I am not rising (against Yazid) as an insolent or an arrogant person, or a mischief-monger or tyrant. I have risen (against Yazid) as I seek to reform the Umma of my grandfather. I wish to bid the good and forbid the evil."*[438]

Under Mu'awiyah Bin Abi Sufyan, the fifth Khalif of Islam and the man responsible for the overthrow of Ali ('Alaihi Assalam), the Umayyads began publicly to decry Ali ('Alaihi Assalam) in religious ceremonies; this was too much for the partisans of Ali ('Alaihi Assalam), who were concentrated in the Iraqi city of Kufa. Mu'awiyah Bin Abi Sufyan called Amiru'l-Mu'minin Ali ('Alaihi Assalam) by ill names and also ordered the people to recite imprecations against the Holy Imam ('Alaihi Assalam) in their *Qunoots* (supplication in daily prayers) and in the sermons of Friday prayers, and so forth. The Sunni historians have acknowledged this fact. Even the historians of other nations write with one accord that this vile practice and innovation was openly pursued even on the pulpits and a big section of the people was put to death only because they did not utter the curses.

Abu'l Faraj Ispahani, Allama Samhudi in "Ta'rikhu'l-Medina", Ibn Khallikan, Ibn 'Asakir and Tabari, in their "Histories", Ibn Abi'l-Hadid in "Sharh-e-Nahju'l Balagha" volume one, and many others of the Sunni Ulema, have written that Mu'awiyah ordered Busr to take his army and launch an attack upon San'a and Yemen from Madina and Macca (al-Mukarramah). He had given a similar order to Zuhak Bin Qais Al-Fahri and others. Abu'l Faraj records the order in these words: *"Whomever from the companions and followers of Ali ('Alaihi Assalam) is found should be killed; even the women and children should not be spared."* With these strict orders, they set out with a force three-thousand strong, making havoc in Madina, San'a, Yemen, Ta'if and

Najran. They killed so many believers and Muslims, including women and children, that the pages of history are full of their guilt-stained actions.

When Mu'awiyah died in 680 C.E./60 A.H., he was succeeded by his son Yazid, who, as stated above, was a brutal, drunken and thoroughly corrupt individual. Yazid was also a deeply pragmatic and shrewd governor, and, fearing more uprisings in Kufa, sent his general, 'Ubaydu'llah Ibn Ziyad, to rule over Kufa with an autocratic and brutal hand. The Kufans sent for Hussain ('Alaihi Assalam) and promised to back him in a bid for the Khalifate and, against all the advice of his friends, Hussain ('Alaihi Assalam) agreed. With a large entourage of private citizens and soldiers, Hussain ('Alaihi Assalam) was intercepted at the Iraqi border by Hurr Bin Yazid Riyahi at Tamimi, who was leading an army of one thousand people. Hurr Bin Yazid Riyahi convinced Hussain ('Alaihi Assalam) not to go to Kufa and Hussain ('Alaihi Assalam) soon departed in another direction. Hurr Bin Yazid Riyahi followed and on the second day of Muhurram in the year 61 A.H. (October 2, 680), Hussain ('Alaihi Assalam) and his entourage entered the plain of Karbala in Iraq and set up camp. On the third of Muhurram, a new detachment of Yazid's army appeared under the command of Umar Bin Sa'd; this army numbered four thousand men. Umar had been commanded to force Hussain ('Alaihi Assalam) to declare his loyalty to Yazid or not let him leave Karbala. On 10 Muhurram, the most significant day on the Ahlul Bayt calendar, Ashura, Umar's and Hurr Bin Yazid Riyahi's men, five thousand in all, attacked Hussain's ('Alaihi Assalam) entourage. Hussain ('Alaihi Assalam) had a grand total of seventy-two fighting men. All day the fighting lasted in sporadic forays, but just about all of Hussain's ('Alaihi Assalam) soldiers were killed not by soldiers but by the continual rain of arrows shot down upon them. By the afternoon, only Hussain ('Alaihi Assalam) and his half-brother, 'Abbas, remained, but 'Abbas became separated from Hussain ('Alaihi Assalam) and the enemy surrounded Hussain ('Alaihi Assalam). Cradling his dead infant son in his arms, Hussain ('Alaihi Assalam) was cut down. Imam Hussain ('Alaihi Assalam) supplicated saying, *"O Allah! I do not die following anything which the Messenger of Allah, peace and blessings of Allah be upon him, never sanctioned nor sanctioned by Abu Bakr nor Omer."*[439] At first, no soldier wished to kill him, since he was the grandson of Muhammad, but he was soon dispatched. The Ahlul Bayt call Imam Hussain "Sayyid ash-Shuhada" or the "Prince of Martyrs," for it is his defeat and death at the hands of the Umayyads that have defined the Ahlul Bayt character.

"They knew too well that victory over the army of Yazid was impossible but they were convinced of achieving the moral and spiritual victory at any cost which they did. They fought faithfully with unparalleled courage to the bitter end."[440] Umar and Hurr Bin Yazid Riyahi's men mutilated the bodies. They carried their heads, mounted on spears, and paraded through villages and

towns, from Karbala, to Kufa and finally Damascus and presented at the feet of Yazid. The women and children were led back to Yazid in chains. Among them were Hussain's ('Alaihi Assalam) widow, Zainab, and his young son, Ali. Yazid gloated for days over the head of his dead rival. Eventually he released Zainab and Ali ('Alaihi Assalam), and the incident at Karbala came to a close.

Why is Hussain ('Alaihi Assalam) regarded as the "leader of the martyrs?" It is because he was not just the victim of an ambitious ruler. There is no doubt that the tragedy of Karbala, when ascribed to the killers, is a criminal and terrible act. The Great Poet Ghalib wrote of this, *"It is a strange occurrence that an enemy of Islam battles with Ali and is considered only to be mistaken. After Ali there is Hassan, and after Hassan there is Hussain. How can I exonerate any person who has mistreated them."* Again, we are compelled to quote Ghalib. *"The glory and jewel of faith, Hussain Ibn-e Ali, who shall be called the candle of the gathering of grandeur,"*[441] made a conscious confrontation and a courageous resistance for a sacred cause. The whole nation had failed to stand up to Yazid. They had succumbed to his will. Deviation and regression toward the pre-Islamic ways were increasing.

Passiveness by Hussain ('Alaihi Assalam) in this situation would have meant the end of Islam as we know it. Thus Hussain ('Alaihi Assalam) took upon himself the responsibility of the whole nation. The greatest tragedy was that one who stood up for the noblest of causes, the defense of Islam, was cut down in so cruel a manner.

An uprising led by the noblest and best respected personality in the entire Umma, is certainly one that is uniquely distinguished as a movement abounding with spiritual, moral and religious ideals. Due to the importance of this personality, we are honored to recount the most outstanding incidents of the dynamic Hussain movement, which stands unequaled in its greatness and fills pages upon pages of history. Characterizing the importance of Ashura for the Ahlul Bayt mind is nearly impossible, since it is so ingrained in Ahlul Bayt history, culture and religion. It is the great tragedy of Ahlul Bayt history, and is commemorated every year. It represents, in part, the Islam that a degenerate Khalifate has ruled since the beginning. However, it is also an occasion of great guilt among the followers of the Ahlul Bayt, for the death of Hussain ('Alaihi Assalam) was the direct result of the inaction of the Partisans of Ali ('Alaihi Assalam) in Kufa. While the followers of the Ahlul Bayt had called on Hussain ('Alaihi Assalam) for help, they did nothing for him when his hour of need arrived in Karbala. Therefore, the celebration of Ashura is a festival of collective guilt. Processions carry models of the Karbala tomb of Hussain ('Alaihi Assalam), but the general atmosphere is one of mourning and weeping.

Such historical events need to be studied, dissected and fully understood. Lessons should be drawn from them. It is therefore that we commemorate the sacrifice of Hussain ('Alaihi Assalam) annually throughout the Muslim world. Our sorrow never abates as we relive the tragedy. Allama Iqbal says in his "Baqiyat,"

"I am one who weeps at the plight of the Martyr of Karbala
Won't the reward be given to me by the Keeper of Kawther - Imam Ali ('Alaihi
Assalam)
We beseech the Most High and Almighty to make our effort of enduring
Benefit and to help us in disseminating benevolence and guidance."

Imam Hussain ('Alaihi Assalam) confirmed, *"My grandfather, the Prophet Muhammad (Peace be upon him) said 'I am the city of knowledge and Ali is the door.' I, Hussain, am the key."* Sufis understand this to mean that to know Muhammad (Peace be upon him) one must know Ali ('Alaihi Assalam), and to know Ali ('Alaihi Assalam) one must know Hussain ('Alaihi Assalam) and Hassan ('Alaihi Assalam). This is the importance of the chain of transmission through the Ahlul Bayt.

Each person carries the five Ahlul Bayt within him or her. Each individual has a Muhammad, Ali, Fatima, Hassan, and Hussain (Peace be upon them) inside his or her heart.

PRACTICE

Picture in your mind the DNA double helix. As you visualize this inter-twining shape, consider that a complete human being, in potential, slumbers inside this molecule. Although you cannot see the human being at this time, you know that this double helix contains all the information necessary for making a particular individual.

Ponder the fact that half this DNA came from a male parent and the other half from a female parent. Two living humans intermingled and they created this molecule. The DNA strand travels like two copulating snakes throughout the millennia. People come and go, and yet the double helix perseveres.

The Sheikhs have said that the Sufi possesses the ability to manip-ulate his or her DNA, turning on and off certain genes, to correct his or her character.

"but the duty of song
is to restore balance
and even one line can weight against
the vulgar day
so let us see how much wine
we need this night
to loosen our lips
and speak of chivalry."

- Peter Lamborn Wilson

THE LOOT

(A Poem by Noorali S. Merchant) [442]

Eerie silence hung over the battleground
Broken occasionally by drum beating sounds
The carnage, the massacre, of saintly souls
Caused a shudder, in Islam's true believers' fold.

The massacre being over, they raided their tents
To loot and destroy, they were all fiendishly bent
Helpless ladies and children, they mercilessly bashed
Young innocent babes, to the ground they dashed.

Daughters of the Prophet, simple lives had led
Coarse and patched clothes, were all they had
Woven by Fatima, they were immensely treasured
In terms of money, none could be measured.

They were shamelessly looted of even their veils
The Yazidi hordes outclassed, themselves, the devils
Earrings were snatched of the child of Hussain
She was slapped mercilessly, for crying in pain.

In stupor, lay the only surviving adult male
Ali Zainal Abedeen was flogged as in horror tales
After the looting, the tents were set on fire en masse
Hell was let loose, with a vengeance, quick and fast.

Zainab was perplexed, she was lost
Perish in flames or face still worst
This hour of trial, whom to consult
Her nephew was unconscious, lying in dust.

"Ali Zainal Abedeen, I appeal to you
As our Imam, tell us what are we to do?"
He opened his eyes, burning with fever
With utmost effort, advice he delivered.

"To save our lives is a religious duty
Go in the open and seek security."
Ladies and children, they left the tent
Salvaging what they could, as they went.

The loot, the pandemonium, was soon over
Burning embers of fire only hovered
A partially burnt tent was all that remained
A solitary witness of torture and blood stain.

The Ahl Bait cuddled together therein
Shattered in mind and body, beyond dream
The time had come almost to a standstill
The night was in sorrow; one could feel.

The mourning widows of Hussain's friends
Their anguished hearts, who could mend?
Zainab and Kulthum consulted each other
The orphaned children, they had to mother.

Zainab counted the children; one was missing
To her dismay, it was Sakina, her darling
"Tell me Sakina, where are you my child?"
In wilderness, the echo was the only reply.

Frustrated, she ran towards the battlefield
"Sakina is lost, your darling child
Hussain, where shall I look for her?"
She imploringly sobbed, in utter despair.

The silvery moon, behind the clouds was hid
The clouds dispersed, the ground was lit
Lying with her head on Hussain's chest
Little Sakina was sleeping in her usual nest.

"Sakina, my child, I have come here
After searching the desert, my dear
Your father's beheaded body, how could you find
In this dark night, with your frightened mind?"

"An irresistible urge seized me, though dampened
To tell my father all that had happened
How they snatched my earrings, after his death
The slaps I received, the treatment we met."

"Running aimlessly in the desert I cried
Tell me dearest father, where do you lie
Sakina, my darling Sakina, come here, come here!
I heard him calling and found my father dear."

"I narrated to him, all I had endured
It lightened my heart: I was re-assured
An urge to sleep on his chest, for the last time
I placed my head in the nest of mine."

With Sakina, Zainab hurried to the camp
Again it was dark; there was no lamp
All were anxiously waiting in the ghostly night
Praying silently to God, the Eternal Light.

She placed Sakina in her mother's arms
She had several other duties to perform
No, not to protect any worldly treasure
The children had suffered, beyond measure.

Advancing towards them, she saw a group
"There is nothing left, which you can loot
Pray, do not disturb the children in sorrow
If you want something, come in the morrow!"

"We do not want anything from you
We know, what you have said is true
We have brought some water and food
We know, you are in a sorrowful mood."

Zainab was surprised; so polite was the speaker
It was the widow of Hur, the truth seeker
"Soldiers of Omar Saad have deputed me
To carry food and water for thee."

"Lest you perish, due to hunger and thirst,
Before Yazid, they want to take you first
That is why they have sent water and food
Not because they have suddenly turned good."

"O, sister, we are indebted to your husband
For his precious life, in defending Hussain
He was our guest, but at a time, alas!
We had not even water; no, not a glass!"

"My lady, I am grieved, you lost not one
But eighteen members to death, were done."
They offered condolences to each other
Zainab was large hearted like her mother.

"At last there is water for you
Wake up, Sakina, see it is true
Wet your throat, sobbing will stop."
For days, she had not even a drop.

"Let Ali Asghar drink first, he is the youngest
My dear brother died of sheer maddening thirst
Now that water is available, give him first
Before I can taste it and quench my thirst."

Guarding her folks, with a half burnt pole
Alone, all alone, with no waking soul
Due to exhaustion, Zainab fell in a swoon
O' Merciful God, it was, indeed, a boon!

One person came galloping in her dream
"O' Sheikh, please go back" she screamed
"I am daughter of Hazrat Ali and Fatima
We are guardians of the holy 'Kalima'!"

The person lifted the veil from his face
It was her father Ali himself, by Divine Grace
She poured out her mutilated and bleeding heart to him
The outpourings caused convulsions, ending the dream.

Lying on the desert sand, clothes wet with tears
The dawn was breaking, time of prayer was near
Events of previous day, she recalled with pain
Ali Akbar had given Athan; prayers led by Hussain .

Finishing her prayer, she laid her head
Prostrate before God of the living and dead
To give her courage, to carry on the mission
Which, to the world, would be an everlasting lesson.

"All this takes place in superb harmony, with the cooperation of all the participants of a living system, regulated down to the smallest detail."
- Dr. Timothy Leary

"The dervish transmits Truth without egocentric bias, without any mask, never mumbling instinctively, me! me! me!"
- Shaykh Nur al-Anwar al-Jerrahi

SUPERSENSIBLE SENSE ORGANS

According to Hindu, Sufi and the Western Mystical traditions, there are seven *chakras* and seven subtle "bodies" that comprise the human being. We sometimes refer to the "bodies" as "levels." Both the chakras and the "bodies" have an intrinsic association with one another.

The seven chakras are separate sensory centers that we carry around with us that are perceptible to clairvoyance. Like the physical body, the supersensibly viewed body possesses certain organs. These subtle "organs" are the chakras. The clairvoyant may perceive them near the following parts of the body: beginning at the perineum (the area between the sex organs and the anus), then traveling up to just below the navel, the solar plexus, in the region of the heart, near the larynx, between the eyes, and finally the crown of the head.

We know these organs as wheels, *chakrams*, chakras, and lotus flowers. We use such names because of their likeness to wheels or flowers. Nevertheless, they are not wheels or flowers; they only seem similar to these things, as one would talk about the lungs appearing as two "wings". It is intuited by some that the Prophet Muhammad's (Peace be upon him) night journey, *miraç*, was a passage up through the series of chakras. During his "ascent," the Prophet Muhammad rode on a mysterious composite creature named Buraq. Buraq had the body of a horse, the head of a woman, and the wings of a bird. During this journey, guided by the Archangel Gabriel ('Alaihi Assalam), the Prophet Muhammad (Peace be upon him) traveled from his humble abode all the way to the Dome of the Rock in Jerusalem. Togther they passed through seven heavens. It is important to remember that the Archangel Gabriel ('Alaihi Assalam) took the Prophet (Peace be upon him) to the brink of the Seventh Heaven, but the Archangel could not continue past that point. The beloved Prophet (Peace be upon him) had to enter the Seventh Heaven by himself.

The Yogis call the mysterious energy that flows up the spine, and through the chakras, the *Kundalini* energy. Kundalini is considered feminine. Buraq was the way that the secret mystery of the Kundalini appeared to the Prophet Muhammad (Peace be upon him).

In people who have not developed their supersensible perception, these chakras are inert, motionless and dark in color. In the supersensibly viewed body of a Sufi however these organs are bright, movable and of polychromatic color.

When you begin the practices we have outlined in this book, your chakras will begin to glow with light. Later, they will begin to revolve. When the chakras begin revolving, then clairvoyance begins. These chakras are the sense organs of the soul. Their revolution expresses the fact that the Sufi perceives clairvoyantly.

As you penetrate within yourself, you will find two sides of each chakra. One is given to you by nature and one you have to discover.

MULADHARA

This is the Perineum Chakram. Herein awaits the Great and Holy Kundalini Energy Snake. She lies coiled, ready to spring up the spine.

This chakra is linked to survival instincts and our ability to ground us in the physical world. Blockage manifests as paranoia, territoriality and vigilance. We may liken it to the so-called "reptilian" brain. *Muladhar* means the most fundamental, and the basic, and the MULADHARA CHAKRA has a direct connection to the anus. The energy stays fixated in the anus as long as energy blockages exist. It cannot go upwards. The first great work has to happen in the MULADHARA CHAKRA.

For anal fixation: fast chaotic breathing is beneficial, because it directly affects the anal center and makes you able to ease and relax the anal mechanism. Also, try to keep the anal muscle in a relaxed state. Relax the buttocks. The energy within the MULADHARA CHAKRA has to be emancipated. Colonic treatments are helpful in this regard, as well as a proper diet, intestinal yogic cleansing and the addition of beneficial bacteria. The MULADHARA CHAKRA has to operate at a peak level, 100 percent, and then energy starts moving. The blockage of this chakra manifests as anger, greed, an obsession with the accumulation of things, or a sense of victimization. The bodily manifestation of MULADHARA blockages is constipation. Somewhat paradoxically, the result of a blockage can also be diarrhea, Irritable Bowel Syndrome, Colitis, and similar conditions. In other words, angry energy is directed *against* one's own body. These conditions are also signs of the improper use of the highest chakra's energy.

Many people never go beyond this chakra. Our culture has even developed many pejorative expressions for this type of person.

As there are seven chakras, so there are also seven bodies. Each chakra is connected in a specific way with its corresponding body. The MULADHARA CHAKRA is the chakra of the Physical/Chemical Body; it has an integral connection with the Physical/Chemical Body. All physical elements of nature lie unseeing and unaware within us. When we become conscious of them, transformation begins.

The necessity of becoming aware of these natural elements shows why it is harmful to stick to belief systems that deny or denigrate the body and concentrate only on the higher chakras and bodies. If you do not explore the PHYSICAL/CHEMICAL BODY with all its odors, liquids, sensations, and so forth, then you prevent yourself from spiritual growth. If sweat, urine, semen, menstrual blood, feces, saliva, earwax, repulse you, this shows that you need to do more work accepting your PHYSICAL/CHEMICAL BODY. To resist this work, to postpone it, will later result in an inability to spiritually transmute this most important of spiritual bodies.

In particular, if you are afraid or repulsed to become aware of your anus, then you will never become aware of your Cosmic Reality. In the words of the Hermeticists: As above; so below. In the words of the Qabalists: As Kether is to Malkuth; so is Malkuth to Kether.

The tonic that evolves this chakra is *La ilaha il ALLAH*.

SWADHISTHANA

This chakra is found two inches below the navel, and is related to our sexual and reproductive capacity. Sex energy fills this chakra, but society has damaged this chakra greatly. This society of hypocrisy has condemned sex so much, and made it so perverted, that many Murids cannot enjoy sex without guilt. Many "spiritual" teachers want you to think that today's society is sex-crazed. What has occurred is that society has become sexually perverted, because these so-called "spiritual" teachers have taken the sacredness and holiness out of sex, and have made it into a soulless activity, lacking of its truly sacred place in one's life. This sex center has to be relieved of the burden of guilt and condemnation. The Murid has to start relearning to enjoy sex - without any guilt. The tonic, which evolves this chakra, is *Allah*.

People cannot let go in this society. There are few healthy outlets for society's energy. People find themselves restricted by laws, regulations, religious taboos, parental and societal conditioning. Individuals in society feel the need to grab their pleasure quickly, and often surreptitiously. The desire to have sex is a powerful aspect of our million-year-old, biological heritage. Without this desire, the species would have died off long ago. However, since people live under the restrictive pressure of society, the result is a rush to orgasm, rather than an exploration of intimacy. Intimacy involves opening of oneself and letting go of one's defenses and personas. Yet our society discourages the process of opening-up and spontaneity. We also see this in the way people eat. Observe how most people gobble down their food, not even bothering to savor the pleasure of the meal. They grab food items from dishes in a battle with other members at the table, to make sure they have their "fill." People have become human consumption machines. A meal becomes a competitive sport. It seems it is more important to these people to swallow down their food quickly, to ensure they have a "second helping" rather than focusing on the food they have in their mouths. Blockages of this chakra manifest as emotional problems or sexual guilt. One means of unblocking this chakra is to begin paying attention to the way one eats. Slow down, chew your food, and take the time to enjoy the taste on your tongue. For sex too, has become a competitive sport, rather than a revelation of intimacy.

Human beings have been afraid of both sex and death. There is a sacred connection between the two. However, because humans fear death, they avoid the subject. That is why Sufi's go to cemeteries to contemplate - to face death. A great saint by the name of Saraha went to the cremation ground with a woman to live a life of healthy, full and optimum sex. Once you accept sex and death, and you are not afraid of them, your acceptance relaxes your two lower centers. Abdel Wahab Bouhdiba writes, *"This is because man's rootedness, even in the case of Muhammad himself, passed through the assumption of sexuality and through physical love. It was through sexuality that the fundamental unity of flesh and spirit was formed."*443

MANIPURA

The Solar Plexus chakra enables the Sufi to have a true understanding of the talents and capacities of other individuals. It also deepens the Sufi's knowledge of the roles of all the beings on earth.

The tonic of emergence is *Ya Hu.*

This chakra gives us a sense of our personal power in the world. The third center, MANIPURA is the center of all your sentiments and emotions. People repress emotions in the MANIPURA CHAKRA. The name means "The Diamond," because life is valuable because of sentiments, emotions, laughter, crying, tears and smiles.

"There is a common misperception that laughter is exclusive to human beings. From at least the time of Darwin, however, it has been known that chimpanzees and other great apes perform a laugh-like vocalization when tickled or during play . . . Breathy, panting laughter is probably the primal form that dates back to the common ancestor of all great apes and people. Human beings evolved their characteristic laughter after branching from an ancestor in common with chimpanzees (estimated to be around six million years ago, according to DNA hybridization data). It is noteworthy that chimpanzee laughter occurs almost exclusively during physical contact, or during the threat of such contact, during chasing games, wrestling or tickling. (The individual being chased laughs the most.) Although people laugh when tickled, most adult

human laughter occurs during conversation, typically in the absence of physical contact." [444] Laughter is necessary for Murids. It transmutes certain impressions that come to them. Laughter is termed: "The Best Medicine." In the human being *"the explosively voiced blasts of a laugh have a strong harmonic structure, with each harmonic being a multiple of a low (fundamental) frequency. The harmonic structure is revealed in a sound spectrogram by the evenly spaced stacks of short horizontal lines in the spectrum, the lowest of which is the fundamental frequency."* [445]Tears are another crucial dimension of the human experience. Both laughter and tears have the ability to relax the tension of contradictory impressions. The poetry of tears and the poetry of laughter are valuable to human beings in order to collapse duality and to create energy. Repress the third center and you become a soldier, not a person but a soldier - an army person, a false person.

The MANIPURA CHAKRA is the antithesis of thinking, so if the Murid cultivates and embraces the third center he or she will relax in his or her tense mind more easily and will accumulate more energy. Be authentic, sensitive, touch more, feel more, laugh more, and cry more.

ANAHATA

"Our dualistically constructed mind cannot take in the identity of opposites."
- P. D. Ouspensky

The heart is an entire world to the Sufi. Within the Heart center, the Sufi finds a number of supersensible organs. Look carefully at this form, for there is another form hidden within this form. This is the beauty of the Living Reality.

When the heart chakra opens the Murid will come to know that the suffering of each human being is his or her suffering. The Veil Over the Loving One is Lifted and the Sunshine Bursts Forth! As Bawa Muhaiyaddeen puts it, *"When that state develops inside you, that is God's love. That is God's true love because all suffering is His suffering, all sorrow is His sorrow, all hunger is His, all poverty is His, and all grief is His. Every torment is inside Him. This is how God does His duty."* [446]

The heart chakra enables the Sufi to have knowledge of the emotions, passions and sentiments of other people. Within the ANAHATA CHAKRA the Sufi has equilibrated and transcended all polar opposites into a Unity of Love.

The medicine of transformation is *Ya Haqq*. The heart chakra gives us the ability to express love. Blockages can manifest as immune system or heart problems, or a lack of compassion.

The heart is just in the middle: three centers below it, three centers above it. The heart is the door from the lower to the higher or from the higher to the lower. The heart is like a crossroads. Kabir Edmund Helminski has said, *"The Qalb (heart) is the midpoint between the Nafs (self) and Ruh (Spirit). The heart is suspended between these two equally powerful and attractive forces."*[447]

The ANAHATA CHAKRA is *Tiphareth* on the Qabalistic "Tree of Life." Unfortunately, society does not teach people to be heartful; neither do its local churches and synagogues. At best, people come out of their local place of worship with a pleasant warm feeling inside themselves, but nothing of real substance. In the heart, there is no word; it is wordless. It is not physical either. It is the place from where love arises. That is why love is not a sentiment. Sentimental love belongs to the third center, not to the fourth. Love has more depth than sentiments. Liking (infatuation) is not love. Never misunderstand liking for love. Otherwise, your whole life you will be just a driftwood . . . you will be drifting from one person to another; never will true intimacy grow.

The ANAHATA CHAKRA is significant, because it is in the heart that for the first time you were related to your mother, not through the head. In deep love, in deep orgasm, again you are related through the heart, not through the head. In contemplation, in prayer, the same happens: you are related with existence through the heart, heart-to-heart.

That is why *zikr* is so important. If you relax into the heart center; if you just become aware of your chest and what is going on inside it as you make zikr, you will sense the presence of the All Sublime One. Those who have entered the heart, they hear a continuous chanting inside their being of *La ilaha il ALLAH.* It bursts forth like a spring, suddenly it starts flowing, and it is there. According to Pir Vilayet Khan, this resonance becomes more and more vibrant until your whole being becomes vibrant with life and enhanced energy, because *La ilaha il ALLAH* has a cosmicising effect, expanding consciousness to cosmic dimensions.[448]

Many Murids want to avoid this fourth chakra. This is because it is the center out of which trust is born, faith is born. People do not want to trust their friends and mates let alone their Murshid or True Guide. Mind LIVES through doubt.

In most humans, the intellect is unable to function properly because the ego veils it. Following this mistaken identification, the intellect is unable to penetrate the outward form of those objects within its perceptual field. If it could go beyond forms to inward meaning, the intellect would discover God in all things. As an individual's ego "thins out," the intellect becomes better at fulfilling its purpose.[449]

When we appear before our *Rabb* (our Sustainer), bringing all the accomplishments of our lives, our *Rabb* will say, *"Bring me the Heart. If the Heart is pleased with you, I am pleased with you. Your relationship to your inmost Heart is your relationship to Me."*

The fourth chakra, the Anahata is connected with the fourth body - the SPIRIT/NOEMASOME BODY or the psyche. The natural qualities of this plane are imagination and dreaming. This is what the mind is always doing: imagining and dreaming. It dreams in the night and in the daytime it day-dreams. If dreaming develops fully, it is transformed into vision - psychic vision. Ibn al-'Arabi sheds further light on this matter, *"The state of sleep is the plane of the Imagination . . . The formal Self-revelation [of the Reality] on the plane of Imagination requires an additional knowledge by which to apprehend what God intends by a particular form."* [450]

If a person's ability to dream is fully developed, he or she has only to close his or her eyes and see things. The person can then see even through a wall. At first, the Murid only dreams of seeing beyond the wall; later the Murid actually sees beyond it. At first, the Murid can only guess what another is thinking, but after the transformation, the Murid sees what the other thinks. There are no more limitations of time and space for a person who develops vision. To dream is the natural quality of the SPIRIT/NOEMASOME BODY; to see the truth, to see the Real, is its ultimate possibility.

Anahata is the chakra of this fourth body, and thereby points out that the heart and mind must be connected for spiritual development to progress. We will now explore the next chakra that makes possible this connection to the mind.

VISHUDDHI

The spiritual organ near the larynx is the realm of the Shaman. In studying the *Zikruallahs* of various *tariqats*, and having studied and participated in shamanic work, we have concluded that there exists a strong shamanic influence in the Sufi practice of *Zikruallah*. Sufi sacred music, known as *illahis* are based on middle-eastern scales known as *muqams* or *maqams*. This word is derived from a word meaning "shamanic music."

John Kingsley Birge, Ph.D. in his work "The Bektashi Order of Dervishes" states that there are seven respects in which Bektashi Sufism resembles the old belief and practice of the Asiatic background:

1. Unveiled women participated in the formal worship.
2. Mystic hymns came to replace the incantations of the Shamans.
3. The *sema,* or ritual dance, resembles the ecstatic dance of the Shaman.
4. The sacrifice of the sheep or ram is reminiscent of the custom of sacrificing cattle among the Asiatic Turks.
5. The miracles performed by the saints, the metamorphosis from a human into a bird, the flying through the air, and so forth, are similar to the stories of saints in Chinese Turkestan.

6. Other legends of the saints show a type of folklore that is common to Bektashiism, and to the Buddhist influence that entered Shamanism through Tibet and Chinese Turkestan.

7. Sacred places, and particularly sacred trees are common to both. In the case of individual Bektashis as, for example, *Barak Baba*, a still further influence is apparent – in the wearing of a *tac* with two horns, the use of birds of mounts in travel, the shaved beard, and the long moustache.

Shamanistic beliefs of the Turkmen *(kyzylbashian)* rural and nomadic groups, also entered the Bektashi fraternity.[451]

We have noticed several other similarities between Shamanism and Sufism.

1. The concept of the Sacred Pole, *Qutub*, of the Universe. Shamans from all cultures speak of a Central Axis or Tree upon which they ascend to the sky world. Sufis also believe in an Exalted Spiritual Being who is the Spiritual Axis of the World.

2. The Frame Drum. Both shamanic rituals and the Sufi Zikruallah make use of repetitive rhythms played on the frame drum.

3. The use of mind-altering agents. Shamans frequently use natural hallucinogenic substances to trigger their shamanic journeys. Members of various Sufi Orders regularly consume large amounts of tobacco, caffeine (tea & coffee) and sugar, before the Zikruallah.

4. Sufis of many Orders, besides using sacred hymns, manipulate the breath in very precise and intricate ways as they vocalize the Names of Allah. Since the Vishuddhi Chakra is the spiritual organ near the larynx, it is understandable that the Sufis have developed a "science" of breath and sound.

The VISHUDDHI CHAKRA is tied to creativity and communication. Blockages manifest as problems like laryngitis, sore throats, creative blocks or general problems communicating with others. For oral freedom: howling, screaming, laughing, shouting, crying, and weeping are helpful. In fact, one Order of Dervishes is known as "The Howling Dervishes." This is not a hint to the Murid; it is a required practice. This chakra must be opened fully in order for the heart to make connection to the head.

VISHUDDI means *purity*. Only love purifies. Love is nectar. It cleanses all poisons. Therefore, VISHUDDI means absolute purity. It is the throat center. If you have come through the heart and if you have heard Allah speaking, if you have heard there the sound of Allah gushing like a waterfall, if you have heard Allah like the wind in the trees, if you have heard the sound of Allah, then you are allowed to speak, then your throat center can convey the message, then something can be poured even into words.

Repeatedly in this book, we have spoken about the necessity for the Murid to spend as much time as possible out in nature. For the Divine speaks through the wind in the trees, a gurgling stream, a thunderous waterfall, the call of birds, and the sounds of insects. Once the Murid can hear the outward sounds, he or she develops the ability to "hear" the inner sounds.

Few people come to the fifth chakra, because they do not even come to the fourth. However, the persons who have opened their VISUDDHI CHAKRA speak beautiful words and even their silence is beautiful. They speak and yet they speak not. They say the unsayable, the ineffable, the inexpressible.

When the VISUDDHI CHAKRA starts spinning, your words have God Energy in them. Then your words have a fragrance and a music to them. They dance. Then whatever you say is poetry; whatever you utter is sheer joy.

Attainment is reached through *Ya Hayy.*

AJNA CHAKRA

We also know the sixth chakra as the "Third Eye." AJNA forms the boundary between human and divine consciousness. Various powers radiate in all directions from this chakra. However, for the most part, these are still locked away and dormant in the human.

The spiritual organ in the area between the two eyes, the AJNA CHAKRA, gives the Murid knowledge of beings that exist only on the astral and other sublime worlds. Astral Travel becomes possible. The Sacred Alchemical Wedding between Sun and Moon takes place within this chakra. No duality exists now, only unity. There are no arguments, no problems or difficulties. This experience is reached through *Ya Qayyum.* Blockages manifest as sinus or eye problems.

The experience of existence, of being, becomes intense in the sixth chakra, the AJNA CHAKRA. Is-ness will be felt; "suchness" will be felt. *"In true contemplation of the Presence, the self is lost."*[452] There is no longer a sense of *my* existence, but only existence. *"Nay, the other is He, and there is no otherness."* [453]

Ajna means order. With the sixth chakra, you are in order, never before it. Ajna is the seat of intuition and awareness. With the sixth chakra, whatever you say will happen; whatever you desire will happen.

As Adi Da writes, *"The 'being' that is Awakened to the Truth may abide simply as that Identity."*[454] Many dervishes and Sheikhs will choose to remain at this station. This chakra is the seat of consciousness, intellect and discrimination, *"I am blissful, I am blissful, I am Supreme Bliss."*[455]

The AJNA CHAKRA is the center where one give commands to one's self and to others. Consequently they also call it the "Sheikh." The Sufi's goal is to find the inner Sheikh. The inner Sheikh is the Sufi's own Self, which is immortal, indescribable, immutable, clear and pure knowledge. In every heart burns the eternal divine and living light, the *Nur Muhammadi*. Seeing and recognizing this light is called Self-Actualization, Self-Knowledge, God-Realization, or Enlightenment. Seek the One within yourself, not outside. Only there can you find the Ultimate Reality. Everything that we believe in and strive for we can find only within our self and not outside.

At this time, the Murid reaches a boundary line, but on the other side of the boundary line lies NOTHING. What is to be sought? Nothing remains to be sought. You have to identify "nothing" before you can proceed to "something." To truly express Allah, the Sufi must become the nothing which is beyond any human concept of Allah. When the Sufi becomes Blackness, then the Star of Islam, Allah, the Midnight Sun, can shine on Earth. At the AJNA CHAKRA the Murid finds "the total," "the cosmic reality." There is nothing beyond. The SAHASRARA CHAKRA is the seventh chakra. There the Murid enters a different world, a separate reality. In the sixth, the Murid enjoys the sight of the Beloved, but not yet union.

From the sixth to the seventh chakras, there is not even no-method. Method is lost in the fifth, and no-method is lost in the sixth. One day you simply find that you are in the seventh. Even the cosmos has gone; only nothingness is . . . uncaused, unknown. There is no possibility of *continuity* in moving from existence to nonexistence: like the story of Enoch in the Bible. It is just a jump. Something was, and something now is - and there is no connection between the two.

"No eyes, no ears, no nose, no tongue, no body, no mind, no color, no sound, no smell, no taste, no touch, no object of mind, no realm of eyes, and so forth until no realm of mind consciousness. No ignorance and also no extinction of it, and so forth until no old age and death and also no extinction of them. No suffering, no origination, no stopping, no path, no cognition, also no attainment with nothing to attain," instructs Avalokitesvara Bodhisattva.

Various would-be Sufis do stop at the stage because death stares them in the face. Therefore, the AJNA CHAKRA is the ultimate obstacle - the last barrier in the ultimate quest of the seeker. The being, the is-ness is known, but the nonbeing has yet to be realized - that which is not, still remains to be known. The Murid must pray (as the Prophet prayed), *"O Lord, increase my bewilderment!"*

SAHASRARA

"No vision can grasp Him,
But His grasp is over all vision;
He is above all comprehension,
Yet is acquainted with all things."
                              - Qur'an 6:103

"One who knows oneself in non-existence knows one's Lord in Existence."
                    - Dr. Javad Nurbakhsh

The aim of the Murid is to develop each of the previous chakras so that he or she may symbolically give birth. Through BISMILLAHIR RAHMAN IR RAHIM, ALLAH becomes the MATRIX OF THE WOMB. Consider the following *hadith qudsi*:

"I am the rahman
(the master of the womb)
thou art rahim
(the womb itself)."

In another *hadith*, the Prophet has said, *"The womb of the mother is a manifestation of Allah Himself!"* This concept of each human being a potential "womb" is important in the context of the seventh chakra. When this chakra is developed, a beautiful Light is born from the top of the head. *"I have entered into my own womb. I have begotten myself."*[456] This is the SAHASRARA CHAKRA. Each of us is feminine (in the spiritual sense); our task is to give birth by driving the spiritual force up through the chakras and out through the top of our heads. The Sheikhs have said that the Murid's task is to connect the first and the seventh chakras.

On the initial level, we relate the SAHASRARA CHAKRA to one's personal spiritual connection to the universe. A blockage manifests as psychological problems. This is why there is often a thin line between psychosis and psychism, and why a mentally disturbed person may reveal great spiritual truths in their ravings.

The seventh chakra is the SAHASRARA, meaning "one-thousand-petalled lotus" (the "rose" in Sufi terminology). When your energy moves to the seventh, SAHASRARA, you become a lotus. Now you need not go to any other flower for honey. Other bees start coming to you. Now you attract bees from the whole earth, or even sometimes from other planets bees start coming to you. Your flower is in full bloom.

Recall that the base chakra is the MULADHARA. From the lowest stratum, life is born - life of the body and the sense. With the seventh, the SAHASRARA, life is born - life eternal, not of the body, not of the senses. We can only speak in metaphors, poetry, and song; for prosaic language is completely useless to describe these states. We say that the beautiful lotus can only grow from the mud at the bottom of the lake.

This is the journey to nonbeing, nonexistence, *Hadrat ul-gayb il-mutlaq,* absolute nonmanifestation. Existence is only half the story: there is also nonexistence. We know this in Tasawwuf as *The World of Dominion*, or the *Uncreated Universe*. Light is, but it is born out of darkness. Alogos Dhu'l-qarnen writes: *"He who is illuminated with the Darkest Shadow will shine with the Brightest Light."*[457] Therefore, knowing the remaining nonexistence, the void, is also necessary, BECAUSE WE CAN ONLY KNOW THE ULTIMATE TRUTH WHEN WE KNOW BOTH - EXISTENCE AND NONEXISTENCE. When we know Being in its entirety, and Non-Being is known in its entirety, then we know the whole. P. D. Ouspensky writes: *"So there are, as it were, two Absolutes: one begins the Ray, the other ends it. One Absolute is All, the other is Nothing. But there can be no two Absolutes, for, by its very nature, the Absolute is one. Therefore All includes Nothing and Nothing includes All."*[458] Humanity's existence is a bridge between Essence and Nothingness (*al-'adam al-mutlaq*). Regrettably, various spiritual teachers deny the importance of knowing the nothingness. Yet, there exist a few who have the courage to proclaim the truth: *"All 'idols' are to be broken, even the idol of 'liberation',"* writes Peter Lamborn Wilson and Nasrollah Pourjavady.[459]

Now it is time to go Beyond Infinity. The concepts of deity as Infinite and Limitless are no longer useful. The Dervish plunges into That Which Is Beyond The Beyond, also sometimes called The Uncreated Light. IT is beyond any conceptualization, even further than the term "Beyond." Therefore, we say: *"Beyond The Beyond."*

This is the void from where we jump from being into non-being. In the AJNA CHAKRA something yet remains unknown. That too has to be known - what it is not to be, what it is to be completely erased. Therefore, to open the seventh chakra, the SAHASRARA CHAKRA, the Murid must face ultimate death. The Murid who is ready to take the last jump knows existence and is now willing to know nonexistence. *"Say: 'Allah!' and let go of existence with all it contains, if you desire the attainment of perfection,"* said Abā Madyan Shu'ayb Ibn al-Husayn al-Ansārī . Adi Da puts it this way; *"The body-mind and world Effectively Do Not Exist."*[460] The Murid goes beyond conditional existence and beyond the cosmos. *"The price of Sufism is the total surrender of your self,"* stated Abā Madyan Shu'ayb Ibn al-Husayn al-Ansā rī Now the Murid has transcended what was once worshiped. He or she becomes "Other." The Murid is not - *(La ilaha)* - *"As I cease - so doth All - but the Design of which I speak. As I cease - so doth All - but that which I am."*[461]

If you go through the accounts of all that one Sufi has said you will say this person is mad. Sometimes the Sufi says one thing and sometimes something else. The Sufi says, *"God is"* and the Sufi also says, *"God is not."* The Sufi declares, *"I have seen him"* and in the same breath the Sufi declares, *"How can you see Him? He is not an object that the eyes can see!"* Yet, Imam Ali ('Alaihi Assalam) says, *"I will never pray to a God that I cannot see!"* Shah Ne'matollah informs us,

> *"Reality is one, but shows itself as two: subject*
> *And object, two in manifestation*
> *But not in Essence: only one Existence*
> *Though countless its attributes. The mystery*
> *Is still too deep for all to understand,*
> *For all to grasp: the supraformal Essence*
> *IS the Beloved and the formal self*
> *The lover – but if you switch the terms around*
> *The statement still remains unchanged and true.*
> *Or if you say the cup and wine are one*
> *That too is true, as true as if you claim*
> *That cup is cup and wine is wine; or if*
> *You say that one is us, the other Him.*
> *Regard these different levels of the truth*
> *As 'relative absolute' and find*
> *The subtle occult truth. Then . . . WA SALAAAM!*
> *The relativity of intellect*
> *Results in statements which must contradict*
> *Each other on the level of the mind*
> *And yet beyond the mind both are correct. "*[462]

The experience of the SAHASRARA CHAKRA is the void, the nothingness. The MANY has disappeared into darkness. *"Da tariki, tariqat"* - *"In the darkness, the Path,"* is a Sufic maxim. The Light has caused this darkness, because IT has demolished all perception of the individuality and multiplicity of things in the Murid's consciousness. This is the station of fanā in which there is no consciousness of this jump into annihilation. *"There is but one Essence, the light of the Essence being also darkness."* [463]

The void has been described as a dark cave, a shadowy mihrab, the Concealed or Secret Radiance, the Black Stone of the Ka'ba, and going back into the Womb of Fatima ('Alaiha Assalam) the Mother. The niche of the mihrab is a resonance chamber. *"The Divine words which reverberate from the niche are symbols of the Presence of God."* [464]

It is worth noting here that the Yezidis possess two scriptures: *"The*

Book of Divine Effulgence" and *"The Black Book."* Effulgence + Black = Black Light. Present is the Secret Radiance.

This is the mystery of "il ALLAH." For when all seems void, dark and subsumed into the Dark and Fathomless Ocean, *"the pre-eternity of pre-eternities"* as Ruzbihan Baqli refers to it, suddenly Muhammad (Peace be upon him) is conceived in the womb of Fatima ('Alaiha Assalam). The world is reborn into the Rainbow Ocean of Living Light. The WOMB gives birth. The rose blooms. The MANY reappears, but this time imbued with the Absolute Light of Existence, The Radiance of Existence, That Which is Expressed as Everything, the ultimate experience of the SAHASRARA CHAKRA!

In His most Hidden Aspect, Allah is a Being who has neither name, nor attribute, of whom nothing can be predicted and to whom no worship can be rendered.[466] Imam Zain al-Abidin has written, *"It is Thou Who canst not be defined for then Thou wouldst have been finite."*[456] The supreme godhead is unknowable, inaccessible, ineffable, unpredictable - *"that to which the boldest thought cannot attain."*[467] The Kadarites refused to ascribe any trait to God. Nzambi, The High God of the African Bakongo, is rendered no worship, for he has need of none and is inaccessible.[468] This is the beyond beyond state of God, therefore beyond all categories such as existence and nonexistence, knowledge and ignorance, and good and evil.

Allah has revealed Himself in the Ninety-Nine Names that He has chosen to disclose to us, that He is Al-Muta'āli, The Most High. Hadhrat Maulana Wahid Bakhsh Rabbani in his commentary to "The Kashful Mahjub" informs us that: *"Worship demands duality and duality is separation. It is when duality vanishes, that oneness with the Divine Beloved is achieved."*[469] Al-Hujweri speaks directly from the realm of Reality: *"Worship is polytheism in the realm of haqiqat, i.e. state of oneness with God, because worship demands duality which is shyrk (polytheism) because it establishes multiplicity of being."*[470] This is the correct orientation of the Sufi, for any traces of worship are veils between the Sufi and Allah. Fadlou Shehadi comments, *"What in an utterly other and unknowable God would make anyone worship and pray to Him (or It)?"*[471] Allah is beyond the most advanced thinking of humankind. *"That radically intuitive Realization has no qualities of which we can speak."*[472] Ya Qahhar is the means.

"Without the frown of clouds and lightning,
the vines would be burned by the smiling sun.
both good and bad luck become guests in your heart:
like planets traveling from sign to sign.
when something transits your sign, adapt yourself,
and be as harmonious as its ruling sign,
so that when it rejoins the Moon,
it will speak kindly to the Lord of the heart."

- Jelaluddin Rumi

"Whoever engages in travel will arrive!"

-Sheikh Muhiy'ud-Din Ibn Arabi

"If Sun & Moon lurked unmoving as solid rock
    what kind of light could they hope to bestow? . . .
And when he (Muhammad) flew upon Boraq in the Night Ascent
    reached the station of "Nearer Than Two Bows' Length . . .
Journey forth from your own self
        to God's Self – voyage without end."

- Jelaluddin Rumi [473]

TALES FROM UNDER THE OVERPASS

*S*am and Mr. Khadir continued walking and hitchhiking up through Pennsylvania and toward lower New York State.

"Travel," Mr. Khadir began, *"is mandatory for the aspiring Sufi. As a person passes through varied territories, he or she passes also through varied etheric webs and energies. These etheric forces are like keys that subtly work on the spiritual bodies of the Sufi, unlocking stored energies, reinforcing the etheric body, and manipulating the person in such a way as to cause nascent powers to blossom."*

Sam remarked, *"I've always wondered why I feel so especially good at certain locations. Sometimes they are in the middle of cities and other times out in the country with not another soul around."*

Mr. Khadir interjected, *"We need to be at certain places at certain times in our lives. There are vital energies welling up out of the ground that are essential to the well being of our bodies. Such a place is called a 'hierophany' - any geographical location or moment in time where the 'Wholly Other' is experienced. So it is that you may find yourself in some odd, out of the way spot for no apparent reason. However, the hidden fact is that you are there to soak up the energies resident in that spot. It is said of the saint: 'Through you life is brought to every land you visit, as if you were rain, falling on parcels of earth.'*

Saddle your camel, Sam. The caravan goes."

Evening was gently settling upon the two, and the stars began to twinkle above.

"You see those stars?" questioned Mr. Khadir

"Yes."

"No you don't! They're not there."

"What?"

"The light from those stars left the stars millions of years ago."

"Yes," Sam replied with some annoyance, "I'm aware of the principle of 'light-years.'"

"Therefore, the stars are now in different places then they were at the moment the light first left them. They are in different places than the way they appear to you at this moment. You are not seeing Reality. You are looking at a play of light, and you are looking at it from the point of view of the separated Limited Self."

"Well, how can I see Reality?"

"Focus your attention on the Prior Unity, the Prior Union of Allah. Breathe in yā Bāri', The Producer of Souls, The Maker From Nothing, The Creator. Center on yā Wāhid, The One Alone, The Incomparable, The Solitary One, The Singular, The Unique One. Surrender yourself to the Source!

"Do you know the story of the nightingale?" inquired Mr. Khadir.

"No, but I'd love to hear it, I mean the story . . . well, and the nightingale too . . ." Sam replied.

"The nightingale" began Mr. Khadir, becoming comfortable sitting under a tree, "sits and waits all night for the rose to bloom. The nightingale is exquisitely sensitive to the scent of the rose. The scent that I am talking about is not the chemical and physical scent that people normally associate with the rose, but rather, a rare and exquisite scent that the rose gives off just as it begins to bloom. When the Nightingale smells this perfume, it goes into a state of Wajd, or ecstasy, and begins to sing. When the red rose blooms, the nightingale becomes drunk; it's the call to intoxication."

"Continue in the good course you have taken."
                                        - Seneca

"Love is a special pleasurable pain. Whoever has this in their heart will know the secret."
                                        - Sheikh Muzaffer Ozak,
                                        Love is the Wine

"Love doesn't just sit there, like a stone; it has to be made, like bread, remade all the time, made new."
                                        - Ursula K. Le Guin

"The hands that help are holier than the lips that pray."
                                        - Robert G. Ingersoll

"Good people help, because help can't wait."
                                        - American Red Cross

"The rights that others have over you – remember them. The rights that you have over others – forget them."
                                        - Sayedna Ali

ARE YOU DONE YET?

The process of becoming a Sufi is akin to cooking a good meal. The Spiritual Murid is the meal being cooked. You are the meal. When they have cooked you, you will be a Sufi. Wine needs to ferment, cheese needs to be aged, so too the Sufi needs to mature slowly.

This is why never saying to ANYBODY that you are a Sufi is best. If you must say something, say, *"I am a student of Sufism."* Do not concern yourself with the question of whether or not you are a Sufi. Be more concerned with the process that you are undergoing. Saying *"I am a Sufi"* puts a period at the end of your experience. It stops the progress of your growth. Aspire to be a Sufi. Do not have the audacity to call yourself by that name. If you do, and you are not what you claim to be, Allah, the *Jabbar* of Heaven (The Compeller) will know it and will tear that name out of you on Judgment Day.

We give an enormous amount of credit to those followers of the Way of Sufism who act on their beliefs and go out into the streets to be of help to the people! Nothing can be of more value than to feed a hungry person. Spending hours each day reciting prayers, learning Arabic and attending Qur'an study groups is meaningless if you cannot say that you helped a single person along your way each day.

Some individuals think that saying many prayers during a day qualifies them as a spiritual person. Certain orthodox individuals make a great show of their holiness through their rigorous and demanding prayer timetable. This is not holiness. Often, it is a form of egotistical showing-off, a type of spiritual one-upmanship. Remember that the ego is subtle. Some Sheikhs make all sorts of strict rules that their students must abide by, which in their immediate circle are the requirements of saintliness, but no one is encouraged to help another human being

Pir Vilayet warns the Murid to *"beware of the obsessive quality of the being who exercises coercion upon your will, robs you of your freedom, places you in a position where your conscience is in a quandary . . ."* [474] If you feel that you are being manipulated, pressured by the Sheikh or group into doing something that in your heart you feel is not right, then you must stand up and follow the Voice of Allah in your Heart. There are many tariqats, many sheikhs, many dervishes who each have their own agendas, but there is only one Heart of Hearts. *"To thine own Self be True."* Ultimately, it is you who must face Allah on Judgement Day. Just following orders was an unacceptable defense when they brought the Nazis to trial for their crimes, and so it will be equally unacceptable in front of Allah when you are called to judgement.

We would take a person who emptied bedpans in an AID's ward as our Spiritual Guide any day over some pompous methodologist who sits around all day eating fruit and telling us long stories about how we should live our life. For us, charitableness is the gauge of spirituality.

There is a saying, *"A person never stands taller than when he or she stoops to help a child."* There is no belief involved in helping another human being. There is only action. The world does not have time for you to decide who is right who is wrong; the world needs your two hands right now! A person shows their true character in what they do, not what they say.

PRACTICE

Close your eyes. See yourself enveloped in blackness. Feel yourself moving in a certain direction. You are passing through various veils. You cannot see these veils, but you know that they are present. You experience yourself gaining in speed as you pierce through tens of thousands of veils.

Suddenly, you see an indescribably beautiful veil. You perceive light coming from the veil. Passing this veil, you come to another. You see green lights flowing and shining from behind it. These green lights are so lovely that your heart nearly bursts asunder with love. Each of these emerald green pulsating rays of light streams from this Living Reality into a soul of a human being on Earth.

Then you notice the veil is lifting. You see a globular brilliance! This is the Living Light of Lights, and from It comes a sound. The sound spreads as waves undulating throughout your body. Your body becomes the ocean and wave after wave of flooding ecstasy washes through you. You feel this rhythm inside yourself. Moreover, with each wave comes the sound, the sound that awakens each cell in your body. Each cell awakens, comes to attention, and falls prostrate before this Holy Tonal Unity.

Allow yourself to become aware of the sensation of wavelike movements in your body. Simultaneously, start humming a tone. You are part of the Cosmic Ocean and your body is now undulating and humming the Music of the Ocean of Bliss. Allow your mouth to open and permit the sound to come out more fully.

After a while, bring yourself back through the veils and into your mundane consciousness. Allow yourself to rest awhile before engaging in any other activity.

"The Koran was not delivered to Muhammad all at once. It came piecemeal according to the events and occasions, as we read in the Koran: '[It is] a Koran which we have divided [into parts from time to time], intervals; We have revealed it by stages. [Surat Al-Isra 17:106].'"
- *Sheikh Abd El-Fatah El-Kady* [475]

"It is not a sin to question traditional doctrines. It is a sin to be afraid to."
- *Bill Donahue*

THE HISTORY OF THE QUR'AN

Palm stalks, thin white stones, paper, skin, shoulders and side bones of animals, on all these objects were written sections of the first Qur'ans. The Qur'an was not collected in Muhammad's (Peace be upon him) life. It existed on the above objects, and in the hearts and memories of the close friends of the Prophet. These writings were disorganized, and further to complicate the matter, there existed seven different versions.

Allah revealed the Qur'an to Muhammad (Peace be upon him) in seven different ways. Muhammad (Peace be upon him) explained: *"The Qur'an has been revealed to be recited in seven different ways, so recite of it that which is easier for you."*[476]

After Muhammad's (Peace be upon him) death, at the time of Khalif Abu Bakr, many of those who had memorized the Qur'an died while fighting the apostates in the battle of "Yalmama." Some believe that Umar feared that the death of those men would result in the loss of a great portion of the Qur'an and suggested to Abu-Bakr that the Qur'an should be collected in one volume. Abu Bakr was reluctant to do that, because Muhammad (Peace be upon him) did not collect the Qur'an in one volume during his life. After much discussion, Umar persuaded Abu Bakr to order the collection of the Qur'an. Abu Bakr ordered Zaid Ibn Sabit to do the job.[477]

"By Allah! If they had ordered me to shift one of the mountains, it would not have been heavier for me than this ordering me to collect the Qur'an," Zaid Ibn Sabit said. Then I said to Abu Bakr, *"How will you do something which Allah's Apostle did not do?"* Abu Bakr said *"By Allah, it is a good thing."*[478]

Clearly, the collection of the Qur'an is something that Muhammad (Peace be upon him) did not do. The Muslims clearly did not write the Qur'an in one volume during Muhammad's (Peace be upon him) life. This is why Umar and Abu Bakr allegedly feared the loss of great portions of the Qur'an, if the men who memorized it should die. Therefore, Zaid Ibn Sabit agreed to collect the various pieces of the Qur'an.

The result of Zaid Ibn Sabit's work was kept privately by Abu Bakr and Umar. *"The manuscript on which the Qur'an was collected, remained with Abu Bakr till Allah took him unto Him, and then with Umar (the second successor), till Allah took him unto Him, and finally it remained with Hafsa, Umar's daughter (and wife of the Prophet)."*[479] The edition given to Hafsa was not copied nor distributed as the "Authorized Version" of the Islamic holy book, but rather appears to have been a private copy in the hands of the Khalif to safeguard against the loss of the text through incidents such as the battle in question. Other people kept their own codices, or relied on their own memorization of the text. At the time of Al-Khalifa Uthman bin 'Affan, a second "official" Sunni recension of the Qur'an took form.

When Islam became the religion of many countries, every country used the version of the Qur'an that they knew among them: the Syrians read Ubayy bin Ka'b's version, the people of Kufa read Abdullah Ibn Mas'ud's version, others read Abu Moussa Alashaby's version and so on. Muslims at the edges of the empire began arguing over what was Qur'anic scripture and what was not. An army general returning from Azerbaijan expressed his fears about sectarian controversy to the Al-Khalifa Uthman bin 'Affan (644-656), the third Islamic ruler to succeed Muhammad (Peace be upon him), and is said to have entreated him to *"overtake this people before they differ over the Qur'an the way the Jews and Christians differ over their Scripture."*

Some say that Uthman convened an editorial committee of sorts that carefully gathered the various pieces of scripture memorized or written down by Muhammad's (Peace be upon him) companions.

"Uthman ordered Zaid Ibn Sabit and three other men from Quraish, 'Abdullah bin Az-Zubair, Said bin Al-As, and Abdur Rahman bin Harith bin Hisham, to rewrite the Qur'an. It was Uthman's order to the scribes: 'If you disagree with Zaid Ibn Sabit in anything of the Qur'an, write it in the language of Quraish, because the Qur'an was revealed in the language of Quraish.' "[480]

The result was a standard written version of the Qur'an. Uthman ordered all incomplete and "imperfect" collections of the Qur'anic scripture destroyed, and they quickly distributed the new version to the major centers of the rapidly burgeoning empire. However, as we have already seen, political stratagems were going on in private which influenced Uthman's actions. The Sunni faction found it necessary to invent hadiths in which Ali ('Alaihi Assalam) was made to say that he accepted Uthman's text.[481]

After Uthman completed his Qur'an, he forced all the Islamic countries to have one Qur'an, and banned all other codices. He finished the matter by burning all other codices of the Qur'an. The Sunni position is that Al-Khalifa Uthman bin 'Affan merely corrected the variations in the Arabic dialect of the Qur'ans in existence. It is noteworthy to point out that Uthman's action, restricting the recitation of the Qur'an to the Quraish dialect, overturned the permission of the Prophet to recite the text in different dialects. In fact, Uthman went further than overturning the Prophet Muhammad's (Peace be upon him) wishes; Uthman excised references to Ali ('Alaihi Assalam) in the Qur'an. Dr. Taha Hussein, a well known author, college professor and minister of education in Egypt, wrote in his book "Al-Fitnato Al-Korba" (The Great Sedition):

"The prophet Muhammad said: 'The Qur'an was revealed in seven dialects all of them are right and perfect.' When Uthman banned whichever he banned from the Qur'an, and burned whichever he burned of it, he banned passages Allah has revealed and burned parts of the Qur'an which were given to the Muslims by the messenger of Allah. He appointed a small group of the Sahaba (close friends of Muhammad) to rewrite the Qur'an and left out those who heard the prophet and memorized what he said. This is why Ibn Mas'ud was angry, because he was one of the best men who memorized the Qur'an. He said that he took from the mouth of the prophet seventy suras of the Qur'an while Zaid Ibn Sabit was yet a young lad. When Ibn Mas'ud objected to the burning of the other codices of the Qur'an, Uthman took him out of the mosque with violence, and struck him to the ground, and broke one of his ribs."[482]

Uthman also changed the sequential order of the Qur'an. *"I heard Abu Jafar (AS) saying: 'No one (among ordinary people) claimed that he gathered the Qur'an completely in the order that was revealed by Allah except a liar; (since) no one has gathered it and memorized it completely in the order that was revealed by Allah, except Ali Ibn Abi Talib (AS) and the Imams after him (AS).' "*[483] Ali ('Alaihi Assalam) was the first to compile the Qur'an. It is significant that the Sunni scholar, Ahmad von Denffer, states that Ali wrote a copy of the Qur'an, which is held in Najaf, Iraq.[484]

If the Qur'an was inscribed in *"a tablet preserved,"* and in *"a book well-guarded,"* why was it necessary for Uthman to rewrite the Qur'an? How could he burn the other codices? Why were there other codices in the first place? These are very serious questions regarding a book said to be Allah's word.

Mr. Toby Lester, in the "Atlantic Monthly" of January 1990, wrote a highly controversial article entitled *"What is the Qur'an?"*[485] He describes how in 1972, during the restoration of the Great Mosque of Sana'a, in Yemen, laborers working in a loft between the structure's inner and outer roofs stumbled across a remarkable grave site, although they did not realize it at the time. The hoard was clearly a fabulous example of what they sometimes call a "paper grave," in this case the resting place for, among other things, tens of thousands of fragments from close to a thousand different parchment codices of the Qur'an.

Some parchment pages in the Yemeni hoard seemed to date from the seventh and eighth century C.E., or Islam's first two centuries. They were fragments, in other words, of perhaps the oldest Qur'ans in existence. What is more, some of these fragments revealed small but intriguing aberrations from the standard Qur'anic text. The first person to spend a significant amount of time examining the Yemeni fragments, in 1981, was Gerd-R. Puin, a specialist in Arabic calligraphy and Qur'anic paleography based at Saarland University, in Saarbrücken, Germany. His preliminary inspection also revealed unconventional verse orderings, minor textual variations and rare styles of orthography and artistic embellishment. Enticing, too, were the sheets of the scripture written in the rare and early Hijazi Arabic script: pieces of the earliest Qur'ans known to exist. They were also palimpsests, in other words, versions very clearly written over even earlier, washed-off versions.

What the Yemeni Qur'ans seemed to suggest, Puin began to feel, was an evolving text rather than simply the Word of God as revealed in its entirety to the Prophet Muhammad (Peace be upon him) in the seventh century C.E.

Since the early 1980's they have painstakingly flattened more than 15,000 sheets of the Yemeni Qur'ans. Cleaned, treated, sorted, and assembled, they now sit *("preserved for another thousand years,"* Puin says) in Yemen's House of Manuscripts, awaiting detailed examination. That is something the Yemeni authorities have seemed reluctant to allow. To date they have granted just two scholars extensive access to the Yemeni fragments: Puin and his colleague H. C. Graf von Bothmer, an Islamic-art historian also based at Saarland University. Von Bothmer, however, in 1997 finished taking more than 35,000 microfilm pictures of the fragments, and has recently brought the pictures back to Germany. This means that soon Von Bothmer, Puin and other scholars will finally have a chance to scrutinize the texts and to publish their findings freely.

In 1994, the journal *Jerusalem Studies in Arabic and Islam* published a posthumous study by Yehuda D. Nevo, of the Hebrew University in Jerusalem, detailing seventh and eighth-century religious inscriptions on stones in the Negev Desert that, Nevo suggested, pose *"considerable problems for the traditional Muslim account of the history of Islam."* Gerd-R. Puin's current thinking about the Qur'an's history partakes of this contemporary revisionism. *"My idea is that the Qur'an is a kind of cocktail of texts that were not all understood even at the time of Muhammad,"* he says. *"Many of them may even be a hundred years older than Islam itself. Even within the Islamic traditions there is a huge body of contradictory information, including a significant Christian substrate; one can derive a whole Islamic anti-history from them if one wants."*

The Qur'an is often extremely difficult for contemporary readers to understand. Part of the difficulty lies in the complexity involved in translating the sacred book. The Qur'an sometimes makes dramatic shifts in style, voice and subject matter from verse to verse, and it assumes a familiarity with language, stories and events that seem to have been lost even to the earliest of Muslim exegetes (typical of a text that initially evolved in an oral tradition).

"I would like to get the Qur'an out of this prison," Abu Zaid has said of the prevailing Islamic hostility to reinterpreting the Qur'an for the modern age, *"so that once more it becomes productive for the essence of our culture and the arts, which are being strangled in our society."*

Most Muslims are unaware that various conceptions of the Qur'an exist within our own historical tradition. We have shown that the prevailing version of the Qur'an is not the only one ever to have existed. The contemporary history of biblical scholarship confirms that not all critical-historical studies of a holy scripture are hostile and unfriendly.

"It seems as if heaven had sent its insane angels into our world as to an asylum, and here they will break out in their native music and utter at intervals the words they have heard in heaven . . ."

> *- Ralph Waldo Emerson*

"Heaven and Earth were born at the same time I was, and the ten thousand things are one with me."

> *- Chuang Tzu*

"I am the flame that burns in every heart of man, and in the core of every star."

> *- Liber Al Vel Legis*
> *(The Book of the Law)*
> *sub figura XXXI*

THE FIRST FRUITS

The first clue that the Sufi will have that his or her practices are bearing fruit will be noticed in the dream world. You will begin to notice that you are having dreams about things of which your five mundane senses could have no knowledge. Your inner being reveals to you in dreams the information that is starting to come in through the clairvoyant senses.

The Sufi remains awake when he or she dreams. The Sufi is just as much aware and interacting with his or her environment during the dream state as during waking life. When we dream, part of our aura body detaches and travels into the Astral World. In the deepest sleep state of total unconsciousness, it is then that we are most fully in the Spirit World. We are dipped, as it were, in the Ocean of Living Light (*Bihar al-Anwar*).

During the daytime, we cannot see the stars. They are hidden from us by the All-Powerful blazing of the Sun. It is the same with the physical senses. Their effects are so powerful that they obliterate the subtle impressions of the supersensible organs.

This is not to say that the experience of the physical senses is not spiritual. We are just declaring that there is more information available to you beyond what the five traditional senses perceive. The experience of the physical world is just as spiritual as an experience that comes to you from the etheric and astral worlds.

Here is a beautiful metaphor of the inextricable union of essence and matter: when we look at the solar system today, we see a sun surrounded by nine planets. However, as we know from science, originally the planets and the sun were all one giant swirling ball of fire. The outer parts of the swirling very gradually began to cool. As they cooled, they formed themselves into round balls of molten rock that gradually became the planets. All the atoms of the Planet Earth and all atoms that make up the beings on the face of the earth had their origin in that giant swirling ball of fire. You consist of the stuff of *stars*. "The Book of the Law," states, *"Every man and woman is a star."* [486]

With our eyes we see the sun as separate from the planets, however, at one time we were one with the sun, and previous to that, the sun was one with the primordial ball of fire. Although people experience themselves as discrete entities, originally we were All One in the Primordial Existence before the One fragmented into the Many. However, each part of the Many contains the essence of the Whole. May you reach that rare state of higher consciousness in which you are simultaneously undifferentiated from Creation and entirely unique.

". . . Fatima's book, I don't claim that it is Qur'an, rather it contains what makes people need us and makes us in need of no one."

- Imam Sadiq ('Alaihi Assalam) [487]

"There is nothing of what is permitted and what is forbidden (al-Halal and al-Haram) in this; but in it is the knowledge of what will happen."

- Abu Abdillah
('Alaihi Assalam) [488]

MUSHAF

Although this fact is little known by most contemporary Murids, Fatima al-Batool ('Alaiha Assalam) wrote a book! It has been narrated[489] that Imam Sadiq, the Spokesperson of Ma'rifat, said to Abu Basir, *". . . we also possess Fatima's book Mushaf, and had they known about the book of Fatima! ! ! It is three times the size of your Qur'an; and by Allah, it has not a letter of your Qur'an; rather it was dictated and revealed to her by Allah . . ."* Imam Abu Muhammad Ja'far Bin Muhammad as-Sadiq Bin Ali Bin Hussain (May Allah be pleased with him), was the Beauty of Islam and the Pride of Tariqat (Sufi path). He was a Spokesperson of Gnosis (ma'rifat), held in an extremely exalted position in *walayat* (friendship of God) and lived a pious life rich in inner and outer beauty. He is famous for his subtle sayings on tariqat and profound truths on *haqiqat* and is one of the greatest Sheikhs of Islam.

Mushaf refers to a collection of *Sahifa*, which is singular for "page." The literal meaning of Mushaf is "The manuscript bound between two boards." In those days, they used to write on leather and other materials. They either rolled the writings, what we know as a "scroll" in English, or kept the separable sheets and bound them together, in what could be called a "Mushaf," a book in today's terms.

Of course, the above narration requires more research and exegesis. After the Prophet's death, Fatima ('Alaiha Assalam) lived seventy-five days. During this time the Archangel Gabriel came to her and consoled her by telling her what her father was doing in the spiritual worlds, what his status was, and what would come about in the Islamic community after her death. Imam Ali ('Alaihi Assalam) wrote down what Fatima ('Alaiha Assalam) dictated to him.

Allah has not confined revelation to Prophets; but the All-Manifesting reveals IT's mystery to some chosen people, angels and even insects!

"And thy Lord taught the bee to build its cells in hills," Qur'an 16:68.

"Remember, thy Lord inspired the angels (with the message): ' I am with you: give firmness to the Believers . . .' " Qur'an 8:12.

"So We sent this inspiration to the mother of Moses: 'Suckle (thy

child),' " Qur'an 28:7.

In her book, Lady Fatima ('Alaiha Assalam) lists various facts and predictions: such as the names of rulers to come up to the day of resurrection, and descriptions of important events that will take place throughout history.

According to the traditions of the Ahlul Bayt, Fatima's Mushaf is not a Qur'an, but most definitely a revelation by Allah, to the Mistress of Women and Daughter of the Master of Prophets, just as He chose to make revelations to Moses' mother.

The book of Fatima ('Alaiha Assalam) has absolutely no connection with the Qur'an. Enemies of the Ahlul Bayt have commonly pulled out of context and used this truism against the followers of the Members of the House of the Prophet (Peace be upon him). Belief in the Mushaf is not a requirement of Islamic belief.

"Don't smite yourself to punish the ungodly."
- Unknown

One night the poet Awhadi of Kerman was sitting on his porch bent over a vessel. Shams-e Tabrizi happened to pass by.

Shams, "What are you doing?"

Awhadi, "Contemplating the moon in a bowl of water."

Shams, "Unless you have broken your neck, why don't you look at the moon in the sky?"

TALES FROM UNDER THE OVERPASS

*O*ne afternoon Sam and Mr. Khadir were having slurpees at the local 7-Eleven. Mr. Khadir spoke,

"There was a flower that lived in a nursery. The nursery owner was mean and he did not water his plants much. Consequently, the flower did not fare well. Its leaves drooped and its blossoms wilted. Then one day an old lady came into the nursery and saw the wilted flower. She took pity on the poor plant and brought it home. She watered it generously, talked to the little flower, and even fertilized it. Nevertheless, the flower continued to droop. You see this flower wanted to make a point. It wanted to tell the world how badly it had been treated in the nursery, but it did not know how. So it decided in its leafy mind to look terrible for the rest of its life, believing that by doing this people would hate the nursery owner and realize the terrible treatment the little flower received." Mr. Khadir paused a moment and then continued,

"Some people, if they were abused as children, will unconsciously live a lifestyle of pain and poverty to visibly portray their inner suffering. Sometimes it is done as a kind of public display that states: 'see what they've done to me.'

"You in your unique Divine Manifestation are infinitely more important than any need for a display of personal justice. You are more important than the need to prove that what was done to you was unjust. The Divine Essence within you and Its will take precedence over establishing the guilt of people who abused you!

"Do not throw your life away in an attempt to display your sense of justice. Hasn't enough harm been done to you? Yet, you want to harm yourself even more? There are many ways that people sabotage themselves. Sometimes, the soul of a human being deliberately sabotages the person in order to bring them back to themselves.

"The soul would rather make you fail in life, than to live out someone else's life. It's ironic but a seeming personal catastrophe, like a business going *bankrupt may be the soul's way to force a person to live his own life. The soul may be planning this for years.*

Many individuals feel a sense of incompleteness about themselves. They feel that they have fallen short of their ideals in life. These people are discontent, depressed and filled with self-loathing. They believe they have failed in life. In order to complete the missing part of themselves (the goals they have not achieved) they will often find this missing part in another person, for example by falling in love. On the other hand, they may fill the empty space with spirituality. There are people who never had a satisfactory family life, and who therefore still search for their ideal: a family who loves them. These individuals are ripe for exploitation by a spiritual system that easily lends itself to be perceived as a parent-child situation, or a family-sibling relationship. Numerous devotees of spiritual teachers are in reality only looking for their lost parents or family. The Murid should be on guard that he or she does not make the Murshid into a parent-figure, or his or her fellow dervishes into a surrogate family. Why? Because haqiqat is Reality. To live a life that is a play within a play, that is, to live a life in which you aren't authentically responding to situations as the person you are now, but as yourself as a child, causes you to live in a false contentment. This false contentment, or false construct as some people call it, will veil from you haqiqat."

"Yeah, in the ashram," said Sam, "people all had these silly smiles on their faces. Everything was joy, joy, joy. But now I know it was all bull-shit. It was like they were hypnotized."

"Well there are other actions to be conscious of, like subtle changes in one's activities because they no longer fit what you assume is the 'ideal' of the spiritual group. Did you previously enjoy poetry, exercising, reading novels, working on your car, listening to music, or going to films, but now find yourself only praying, reading devotional literature, and listening to 'sacred' music? Sometimes this is the fault of the false Murshid, but more often than not, it is an unconscious decision on the part of the Murid to replace his or her authentic experience of reality with an artificial construct. Beware my friend! True Sufism is not for those who wish to escape a painful past or to escape a sense of failure in life. True Sufism is the oftentimes brutal confrontation with reality. This is the true struggle with the nafs. This struggle with the nafs is not some fictional, albeit wonderful and dramatic war of good versus evil within yourself. Sufism is the call to know thyself. Rather than slaying 'evil' dragons, face the 'fear' dragon, the dragon of the fear of integrity that hides you from you! The only way out lies within.

"Search out your heartfelt and authentic ideals, or what some call their 'goals in life.' If you wish to have a loving family, you might choose to marry and have children, but do not substitute 'the group' and 'the teacher' for your family. If you wish to save the world, give up your naive ambitions and

join the Peace Corps, serve as a Health Care Worker, help to provide food for the starving, but do not under any circumstances talk yourself into believing that you have some special, exalted status because you are a Sufi or a special spiritual mission to save humanity. Return to pursuing your life's dreams but with the open eyes and ears of the Sufi. Sufism is not an excuse to withdraw from your world, but a Way to Complete your Full Human Potential. Sufism is what Sufism means to you. Do not be forced to agree with a group's beliefs because you fear being an outcast of the group! If you feel different from others, cultivate that difference. Resist the temptation to break down the feeling of separation by capitulating to the group's philosophy. A group is dangerous to the extent that it does not balance the process of banding together with the process of expanding, in other words, opening to other people and ideas. Beware of the group that discourages its members to be individuals. Fear is the basis of these groups, not thinking. And there can be no love where there is fear. Many Murids then decide they must conform and submit, as if to say: 'I am exactly like you, and shall be as you wish me to be, so that you will love and not hate me.' As a Murid you might ask yourself: if I have come to this group to learn about love, then why am I feeling afraid to express my opinions, doubts and questions? If you feel free to discuss openly whatever is on your mind, without fear of censure or rejection of the group, then you have found a healthy and love-oriented group. The greatest Evliyas were people whose insight was often unconventional. Their own dervishes frequently misunderstood and rejected them!"

PRACTICE

The Murid needs to immerse him or herself in the sea of thought of great initiates of the past and present. Rather than just living the entire day immersed in your own thoughts, strive to set-aside some time during the day to immerse yourself in the writings of direct spiritual transmission.

The first place to seek is in those writings that had their origin in inspirational revelation. Books such as: The Qur'an, The Tanakh (The Jewish scriptures made up of the Torah, the Prophets and the Writings), The Analects of Confucius, The Rig-Veda, The Dhammapada, The Upanishads, The Tao Te-Ching, The Bhagavad Gita, and Liber Al. These works are alive with living spiritual energy. They transmit a spiritual impulse directly to you. Textbooks are dead, lifeless entities. However, a work written in the fire of revelation is alive with spiritual power!

Next, after reading books of direct revelation, read books written by Initiates. Read works written by people who KNOW. Ignore books written by scholars that will never have the initiatory knowledge but who just choose to dissect and analyze. Stop trying to analyze the mystery. Works such as the "Discourses" of Jelaluddin Rumi, "An Outline of Occult Science" by Rudolf Steiner, "The Fourth Way" by P. D. Ouspensky, the "Equinox" of Aleister Crowley, or the books of His Holiness M. R. Bawa Muhaiyaddeen, Muhyiddin Ibn 'Arabi, Osho, Gurdjieff, and Avatar Adi Da Samraj, are all excellent vehicles to transport your essence into the spirit realms. We especially recommend the works of Abessalom Podvodny.[490]

"We hope that by manipulating matter, the physical world, we can achieve wisdom and understanding."

- Chögyam Trungpa

"The 'cosmos' consists of everything other than God. It is none other than the possible things, whether or not they exist. . . . Possibility is their neces- sary property in the state of their nonexistence as well as their existence. It is intrinsic to them, since preponderation is necessary for them. Hence [through the possible things] the Preponderator is known, and that is why the cosmos is named 'cosmos' ('ālam) – from 'mark' ('ālama) – since it is a proof of the Preponderator."

- Ibn al-'Arabi [491]

WHAT IS SO GREAT ABOUT INERT MATTER?

One way of thinking about inert matter is through those great guns they used in past wars. The great guns used for long-distance ranging had to be bed- ded in a mass of concrete. These masses of concrete, called "thrust blocks" drove the shell forward when they launched it. Action causes reaction. Some of you may remember learning in high school science class: the pressure on the breech of the gun must equal the pressure on the base of the shell when the gun goes off. In other words: every action has an equal and opposite reaction.

Energy must flow in two directions at once. Think of a rifle. When it is shot, energy is moving the bullet out the barrel, but also simultaneously, energy is shooting backwards into the shoulder of the person shooting. Inert matter is a kind of thrust block. A thrust block takes the back-pressure of a gun, just as the shoulder takes the kick of a rifle

Many contemporary spiritual teachers ignore this fact. They think they can legitimately focus on one spiritual direction, without honoring the opposite spiritual direction. They think they can have all day without night. All summer without winter. All joy without sadness. Spirituality embraces both sides of the coin. Spirit is not superior to matter; matter makes spirituality possible.

Matter and spirit are two sides of the same coin. Moreover, the Reality of the coin has subsumed them both. It is when you reverence Matter as much as Spirit that you enter a relationship with the Radiant Continuum.

"Also did heaven manifest in violent light, and in soft light."

- Abdullah the Satiricist of Shiraz

"My heart has become capable of every form:
It is a pasture for gazelles,
And a monastery for Christian monks,
And a temple for idols,
And the pilgrim's Ka'ba,
And the tablets of the Torah,
And the Book of the Qur'an.
I follow the religion of Love:
Whatever way Love's camel takes,
That is my religion and my faith."

- Ibn Arabi

"Architecture is silent music."

- J. W. von Goethe

"Saturn, however, represents a basic line of demarcation between these two opposite forces, galactic and solar. The planets inside of Saturn's orbit are mainly creatures and vassals of the Sun; while the planets beyond Saturn are what I have called many years ago ambassadors of the galaxy."

- Dane Rudhyar
"Astroview" magazine

"Of all the general meanings of Saturn, probably the most important is that Saturn represents concentrated experience which comes only through life in the physical body."

- Stephen Arroyo

"Go even unto China and search for 'Ilm."

- Nabi Muhammad Mustafā (Sal.)

SATURN'S THRONE

The Sufi precedent for the study of the mystical significance of the planets is none other than the great Sufi saint and founder of the Mevlevi Order of Dervishes, Jelaluddin Rumi, who was well-versed in astrology. With this dispensation in mind, this chapter will focus on the mystic significance of the Planet Saturn. We begin with the name of the planet. "Saturn" is the Roman name for the Greek God Cronos. The Romans added a festival to venerate him named the "Saturnalia." This was a period of misrule, around the end of the year, which emphasized the overturning of all social constraints. The Romans viewed this as a healthy renewal of the original state of nature.[492]

Saturn has a sinister quality: Saturn is the resister as well as the stabilizer and tester. He is the "God" of the most ancient form of matter. The Greeks considered him one of the Old Gods, in other words, one of the Gods who made the Gods. Theosophists connect Saturn with the basic building blocks of our mineral bodies. Our skeleton is the manifestation of our fundamental connection with Saturn. Robin Becker illuminates, *"The bones carry the energy toward the earth; meridians and other systems of the body carry the energy upward."* [493]

Saturn is throned on the most ancient rocks where no plants grow. Keats speaks of *"gray-haired Saturn, silent as a stone."* The virtue of the Dark Mother is said to be Silence. The Mother of the Qur'an is Silence. The Inner Qur'an is the Silent Qur'an. Why silence? If we are silent, then we can listen, and therefore learn. However, if we are talking, the gates of entrance to the mind are closed. This silence also refers to the silence of the soil as it quietly nurtures a seed into life, and to the silence of the mineral aspects of the Earth.

Another influence of the Saturn forces on Earth can be felt in the art of architecture. In gazing at a beautifully designed building we can see Saturnine forces at work. In structure and proportion, we find this ancient God's stamp.

Saturn, is furthermore an occult term for a previous incarnation of the Planet Earth. The beings that aided humankind during this period are called "Spirits of Wisdom," otherwise known in Christian esotericism as *"Kyriotetes."* These angelic-like beings had the power of letting life stream forth from themselves and of bestowing other beings with life. *"Know that it is a particular characteristic of the spirits that everything on which they descend becomes alive, and life begins to pervade it."* [494]

We may also connect Saturn in a mysterious way with the Nizari Isma'ili sect of Islam found at Alamut in the thirteenth century. A part of their teachings was concerned with a mysterious power called "The Lord of Time."[495] Earlier we mention that Saturn is the Roman name for the Greek God Cronos." Cronos was the God of Time. The Messenger Muhammad (Peace be upon him) relates these words directly from the exalted Creator, *"O children of Adam, how often you complain about time, yet I alone am time."*

Moreover, the Nizari Isma'ili sect, held that all power (both constructive and destructive) of the One resided in each individual. "The Lord of Time" was a being who facilitated the flow of this power. Interestingly, another name for Saturn is "The Lord of Time." It is this author's conclusion that the Nizari Isma'ili's were connecting with the Saturnine energy flow. The Nizaris actively pursued the cultivation of different branches of the Islamic sciences. Daftary observes, *"so many Muslim scholars, both Sunni and Twelver Shi'i, and even Jewish scientists, availed themselves of the Nizari libraries and patronage of learning. Some, like the celebrated philosopher, theologian, and astronomer Nasir al-Din Tusi (1201- 74) converted to Isma'ilism."*[496]

Returning to the subject of the Saturnine forces of architecture, pre-Islamic Sufi mystics spoke of the lost city "Irem of the Pillars." Irem is very important to Sufis. *"Irem Zhat al Imad* (Irem of the Pillars)" is the city's name in Arabic. The Arabs popularly believe that Irem was built by the Jinn under the direction of Shaddad, Lord of the tribe of *Ad*. The tribe of Ad, according to legend, was a race roughly equivalent to the Hebrew *"Nephlim"* (giants). Others say the people of Ad were only men and women like us, but of great physical height. They were distinguished architects and masons who had a great talent for erecting lofty buildings. Frequently cited in the Qur'an are the Ad people and their Prophet Hud.

The tomb of their Prophet Hud *(Qabr Nabi Hud)* is found in Hadramat, latitude 16 degrees north, longitude 49.5 degrees east. The Arabs sometimes call Irem: *Arabia Felix*. The place fascinates many Arabs because of its ancient ruins, places of devotion, and the fact that great treasures of historical, religious and monetary value have been found there. In the time of the accursed Mu'awiyah, a large trove of precious stones was found there. In more recent times, they have uncovered Sabaean statuary artifacts of gold, silver and bronze in Najram.[497]

In some versions of this myth, Shaddad and the Jinn built Irem before the time of Adam. The *Muqarribun*[498], pre-Islamic Sufi healers and magicians, have important beliefs about Irem and its significance. The Muqarribun believe that Irem is a locale on another level of reality, rather than a physical city like New York or Tokyo. Why Irem is important to the Muqarribun, and how they spiritually make use of the mystical city, will be more fully explained shortly. The "Pillars" in "Irem of the Pillars" has a hidden meaning. Among Arab mystics, pillar is a code name for "elder" or "old one." Thus, "Irem of the Pillars" is mystically interpreted as: "Irem of the Old Ones."

> *"Seest thou how thy God*
> *Dealt with Ad of Iram, with*
> *Lofty pillars, the like of*
> *which were not produced*
> *in All of existence?"*
>   *- The Holy Qur'an*

Modern archaeologists have identified ruins at Shisha, Oman as those of Irem, better known as the lost city of *Ubar*. This was a fortress city not of "pillars" but "towers" (which is the same word in Arabic). The city served to protect the caravans traveling the frankincense route from the gum tree groves through the land of Ad into the *Rub al Khali*. Founded five thousand years ago,

Ubar was built around a natural cistern of water that provided a unique oasis in the empty quarter. One hundred fifty people lived in the fortress surrounded by perhaps three thousand more encamped in black tents, resting before continuing their journeys. The city disappeared around the year 300 C.E. According to legend, Allah threw the buildings down as punishment for the wickedness of its ruler.[499]

In Arab legend, Irem is located in the Rub al Khali. To the Muqarribun, the Rub al Khali also has a "hidden" meaning. Rub al Khali translates as "the Empty Quarter." Here, "Empty" refers to the mystical "Void" and can be equated with the *Ain* of the Qabalistic tradition. Rub al Khali is the *"secret"* door to the Void in Arab mystical traditions. It is the exact Arab equivalent to *"Da'ath"* in the Qabalah. To the Muqarribun, the Rub al Khali is the secret gate (Daath) to the Void (Ain) in which is the "city of the Old Ones."

The Muqarribun entered the Rub al Khali (not the physical desert, but the Arab equivalent of the Qabalistic "Daath") in an altered state of consciousness (somewhere between dreams and the complete absence of thought). Irem represents that part of the "Empty Quarter" that acts as the connection to the Void. It is from this place (Irem) that the communion with the Void and that, which inhabits it, can happen.[500] The *"monsters of death"* and protective spirits are the Jinn. The Muqarribun can interact with these entities when he is in the Rub al Khali or "Irem." When the Muqarribun passes through Irem to the Void, he or she achieves Annihilation (fana). Annihilation is the supreme attainment in Sufi and Muqarribun mysticism. During Annihilation the Sufi's entire being is devoured and absorbed into the Void. The self or "soul" *(nafs i ammara)* is utterly and completely destroyed by this process. This is probably the source of stories regarding the soul eating demons (associated with Irem) in Arab legend. Irem is a type of portal to the Outside.

Some of the Prophet Muhammad's (Peace be upon him) contemporaries called him a "Mad Poet." Muhammad (Peace be upon him) was vehement in denying that he was a poet. He wanted it known that his revelation came from "God" and not the Jinn. "Mad" is usually written *majnun* in Arabic. Majnun means "mad" today. However, in the eighth century it meant "Possessed by Jinn." To be called Mad or Possessed by Demons would be highly insulting to orthodox Muslims. Yet, the Sufis and Muqarribun regard Majnun as a complimentary title. They even go so far as to call certain Sufi heroes Majnun.

Jinn were powerful creatures of Arab myth. The Jinn, according to legend, came down from heaven (the sky) in the time before Adam. Therefore, they pre-exist humankind and thus are called "Preadamites." *"Infidel pagans"* worship these incredibly powerful beings. The Jinn can *"beget young on mankind."* The Jinn are usually invisible to normal men and women. They apparently want great influence on Earth. Much of the "Islamic magic" used in

Arab countries concerns the Jinn (protection spells against them, or spells to call them up). Magic in the form of Qur'anic numerology (in relation to letters), amulets, scrolls carried on the body, and the repetition of certain Names of Allah a specific number of times, is still widely practiced by some Sheikhs and women Sufi healers throughout Eastern Europe, the Middle and Near East. For example, Allah's name has five Arabic letters, and when each letter is spelled out, there are fourteen letters in all. The same is true of the name "Muhammad." The two fourteens combined make twenty-eight which together make the Divine Word. The words *la ilaha* when each letter is written out produce fourteen letters, as do also the words *il Allah*, together making twenty-eight. We have seen how Muhammad's (Peace be upon him) name makes fourteen; the words *resul ullah* have fourteen letters in them, and so again twenty-eight is made.

It is well known in physics that when one compresses the mass of an object its potential energy increases exponentially. Coal is an example of such compression; nuclear fission another. There are several techniques in Qabalah for "compressing" a text of scripture to "increase" its "power."A book called the *Cifri Ali* is said to be one of the books used by the Bektashis. It is a book revealed to Ali ('Alaihi Assalam) and secretly handed down to his descendants. Learned Şeyh's are supposed to have learned from it and therefore to be able to practice divination.[501]

Corbin writes of Ruzebehan of Shiraz' experiences: *"In a dream . . . he mounts to the terrace of the house which is his own dwelling-place; there he finds two very beautiful personages who appear to be Sufi shaykhs and in whom he recognizes his own image . . . the three partake of a kind of mystical repast, consisting of pure wheat bread and oil so subtle it was like a pure spiritual substance. Subsequently, one of the two shaykhs ask Ruzbehan if he knows what this substance was. As he does not know, the shaykh informs him that it was 'oil from the constellation of the Bear which we gathered for you'. After emerging from the dream Ruzebehan continues to meditate on it, but it took him some time, he confesses, to realize that . . . God had admitted him to the ranks of the seven masters of initiation and intercessors who are invisibly apportioned to our world. Then [he writes] I concentrated my attention on the constellation of the Bear and I observed that it formed seven apertures through which God was showing himself to me. My God! I cried. What is this? He said to me: these are the seven apertures of the Throne."*[502] The connection of Ursa Major with celestial gateways traces back to Graeco-Egyptian magic.

Nearly all Arabic books on religion or mysticism were written as poems. The Qur'an is not poetry, but it does contain rhyme and meter. Arabic mystical poetry is a complete field of study. The Pre-Islamic prophets used the *Sadj* style of verse. This is the same style that the Qur'an is written in. The early Muqarribun poetry is in the *Ruba'i* style which is fairly simple. Later, they wrote Muqarribun and Sufi poetry in the *Mathnawi* form of verse.

The name *Cthulhu* provides an important and fascinating parallel with pre-Islamic mystical Sufi practice. Cthulhu is very close to the Arabic word *Khadhulu* (also spelled *al qhadhulu*). Khadhulu is translated as "Betrayer," "Forsaker," or "Abandoner." Many Sufis and Muqarribun writings use this term "Abandoner." In Sufi and Muqarribun writings "abandoner" refers to the power that fuels the practices of *Tajrid* "outward detachment" and *Tafrid* "interior solitude."

Tajrid and Tafrid are forms of mental "yoga," used in Arab systems of illumination, to help the mystic to free him or herself from (abandon) cultural programming. In Muqarribun texts, Khadhulu is the power that makes the practices of Tafrid and Tajrid possible for the Sufi. Khadhulu shows up in the Qur'an (in a very significant way).[503] In the Qur'an chapter 25 verse 29 it is written, *"Mankind, Shaitan is Khadhulaa."* This verse has two orthodox interpretations. The first is that Shaitan will forsake humankind. The other orthodox interpretation is that Shaitan causes humankind to forsake the "straight path of Islam" and the "good" ways of their forebears. The orthodox Muslim would view forsaking Islamic custom as sinful and ungodly. However, the Muqarribun, as do many Sufis, feel abandoning culture is vital to spiritual growth.

The identity of Shaitan of the Islamic tradition is crucial. By the time Muhammad (Peace be upon him) was reciting the Qur'an, they were calling Shaitan "the Old Serpent (Dragon)" and "Lord of the Abyss." The Old Serpent or Old Dragon is, according to experts such as E.A. Budge and S.N. Kramer, Leviathan. Leviathan is *Lotan*. Lotan traces to *Tietan*. Tietan, the authorities on Near Easter mythology tell us, is a later form of *Tiamat*. According to the experts, the Dragon of the Abyss called Shaitan is the same Dragon of the Abyss named Tiamat. Scholars specializing in Near Eastern mythology have stated this repeatedly.

What conclusions may the reader draw from this gnosis? The Murid, to reach Proximity, must pass through the mystical desert of the Abyss. In this desert are spiritual beings who can aid the Murid in his or her journey. There are also specific practices that the Murid can avail him or her self of, to help in making this crossing. These are specifically, as mentioned above: *Tajrid* and *Tafrid*. Finally, a confrontation with the Dragon of the Abyss, the Shaitan, must be undergone, to make safe passage. The Dragon is the gatekeeper to the Divine Court who lets pass only those who have stripped off all the garments of religiosity and custom, and who are ready and willing to give up their very lives. For beyond this desert, the Sufi loses him or herself and gains Allah. That is why they call it a desert. That is why it is such a frightening place, for the ego cannot pass by the Gatekeeper!

"The dragon is an abandoner for he leaves all that is sacred. The

dragon goes here and there without pause. "[504] While this line is obviously symbolic (most likely referring to the practice of Tafrid), it does serve to establish a connection between the Dragon of Near Eastern myth with Khadhulu in Arab magic.

The ancient dragon of the abyss (Tiamat) traces back to Sumeria. Sumeria was the oldest civilization known to have existed. If Khadhulu of Arab mysticism is synonymous with the Dragon of mythology (which the evidence suggests it might be), then Khadhulu has been "worshiped" for a very long time. It is becoming clear that certain centers of Sufism were settled originally by the Proto-Indian-European civilization. One of their central beliefs was that the *"ground in the midst of the waters"* was constricted by a giant serpent that prevented the expansion of the earth.

There is another interesting bit of information related to the Dragon of the Abyss (which originated in Sumeria) and Khadhulu. This data quite possibly is simple coincidence. On the other hand, it may not be coincidence; there is simply no way to tell yet. It concerns one of the titles of the Dragon, namely the "Lord of the Abyss." The title "Lord of the Abyss" translated into Sumerian is *"Kutulu."* *Kutu* means "Underworld" or "Abyss" and *Lu* is Sumerian for "Lord" or "Person of Importance." Let us consider this for a moment. The Sumerian *Kutulu* is quite similar to *Khadhulu* in Arabic.

Ruzbihan Baqli heeds us to: *"Beware one who describes the pre-eternal dominator, for in the oceans of his unicity all spirits and consciences are drowned, and they vanish in the sublimities of his greatness and might."*

There is a significant connection here and it may indicate that Kutulu and Khadhulu are the same.[505] The above information on Kutulu while accurate and very suggestive, is not conclusive. It does, however, generally support the idea that *Kutulu/Khadhulu* has been a part of the mystical traditions of the Near East for a very long time. The only thing that we can accept as proof will be the discovery, in a Sumerian text, of the direct mention of the name or word Kutulu in the context discussed. To our knowledge, this has not yet happened. Until it does (if it does), the Kutulu/Khadhulu equivalence will remain tentative. [506]

Khalil Gibran tells a tale of a woman by the name of Amena Divine, a mysterious and prophetic person.[507] Like the great saint, Bawa Muhaiyaddeen, telling her age by looking at her face was difficult. For although she looked youthful, her eyes reflected ageless wisdom and struggle. As the story goes, she was born in Damascus. Her mother died upon giving birth to Amena. Her father was Sheikh Abdul Ghany, the famous "blind prophet." They thought him to be divine and recognized him as the Imam of the time.

At age twenty three, Amena's father took her on a pilgrimage through the Damascus desert and into the wasteland. There her father became ill with fever and died. Amena buried him. For seven days and seven nights Amena sat vigil over the grave. She called out to his spirit and sought out the mysteries of his soul. On the seventh night the spirit of her father told her to stop her vigil and ordered her to go on in the direction of the south east. Amena listened to her father and resumed her journey until she reached the very heart of this desert, known as the *Rabh el Khali* or *Rub al Khali*. They said that no caravan had ever crossed this part of the desert. Pilgrims passing through this region in the early days of Islam could find no sign of Amena or her father Sheikh Abdul Ghany. They assumed that she and her father had perished and brought word back to Damascus that the two probably died of hunger and were tragically lost.

After five years had passed, something miraculous happened. Amena Divine appeared in Musil. She was radiant, dressed in long, silken robes, appearing more like one of the goddesses worshiped in ancient times, than a woman of her time and background. Perhaps it was the particular way she moved, or perhaps it was the way she would gesture. Her words were infinitely profound and immeasurable. Amena did not wear the veil. She stood with her unveiled face before the priests and teachers, and spoke of the 70,000 tears of the Angel, and the City of the Lofty Pillars.

Gradually more and more people were attracted to Amena and became her followers. The scholars became jealous and complained to the Emir. So the Emir summoned her to appear before him. When she was present, he offered her a bag of gold if she leave the city. Amena Divine refused the gold but left the city under cover that night.

She journeyed far, through Constantinople, Homs and Tripoli. Wherever she went, she spoke of the Exalted Truth. Nevertheless, the priests of each city always opposed her and she was eventually forced from each city she entered.

In each city, when the people would gather round her, she would say: *"You are here to learn about us, but you shall not know more about us than you know about yourself, and you shall hear from us only that which you hear from yourself.*

"Yes, we reached and entered the Golden City and sojourned there and filled our souls with its fragrance, and our hearts with its secrets, and our pouches with its pearls and its rubies, and our ears with its music, and our eyes with its beauty. He or she who doubts that which we have seen and heard and found there is doubting his very self."

The people always wanted to know if she entered the great City of Lofty Pillar in body or in spirit. They asked if the tribe of Ad built the city from the elements of this world or if it was an imaginary city.

Amena answered, *"All on earth, seen and unseen, is spiritual only. I entered the Golden City with my body, which is merely an earthly manifestation of my greater spirit. I entered Irem with my body concealed within my spir-*

it. He or she who endeavors to cleave the body from the spirit, or the spirit from the body is directing his or her heart away from truth. All things in this vast universe exist in you. In one atom are found all the elements of the earth. Irem of the Pillars is not far distant, but is found within you."

Amena Divine then would explain that she suffered terribly crossing the desert, enduring terrible thirst and hunger, and worst of all, the frightening silence of eternity. Yet then she would add, *"But many are those who reached the Sacred City before us without walking one cubit. They reveled in its beauty and brightness without sorrowing in body or spirit. Truly I say unto you that many have visited the Sacred City although they never left the places of their birth."*

The wisest of the people in each city would ask, *"but will that which I call myself remain?"*

Amena would answer, *"Each thing that exits remains forever, and the very existence of existence is proof of its eternity. But without that realization, which is the knowledge of perfect being, the human being would never know whether there was existence or nonexistence.*

"We each long for something. Allah has implanted this hope within us. We are empowered to hope and hope fervently, until that for which we are hoping takes the cloak of oblivion from our eyes, whereupon we will at last view our real self. Do not despair when the fulfillment of your hopes seem to fade before your eyes, for your hopes are the compass pointing to Irem. Were it not for the longing and affection within me, I would not have found the subject of my longing and affection about me in the Golden City."

"Then is there true being in all imagination, and real knowledge in every idea and fancy?" the wise asked Amena Divine.

"Verily, it is impossible for the mirror of the soul to reflect in the imagination anything which does not stand before it. It is impossible for the calm lake to show in its depth the figure of any mountain or the picture of any tree or cloud that does not exist close by the lake. So, go and say that Irem of the Pillars is a true city, existing with the same visible existence of the oceans and the mountains and the forests and the deserts, for all in eternity is real. Tell them that the giants of the ages erected the Golden City from the glittering elements of existence, and concealed it not from the people, but the people obstructed themselves from it."

It is still said today that Amena Divine has several abodes, she lives in none, yet she exists in all. She is everywhere! It is vain and wasteful to endeavor to approach Amena Divine through mere words or deeds, for she neither listens nor sees. Nevertheless, through the soul of her ear she will hear what you do not say, and through the soul of her eye she will see what you do not do. To meet her you need merely to stand in sincerity at the door of her dream. If it opens, you will reach your goal, and if it does not open, then your own self must bear blame. We are often strangers to ourselves!

"Your experience of reality depends on your inner state."
                                    - Sheikh Muzaffer
                                    Ozak al-Halveti al-Jerrahi

TALES FROM UNDER THE OVERPASS

" *I want you to meet a Real Sheikh, a True Guide,"* Mr. Khadir said late one afternoon to Sam.

"*That would be great,"* Sam answered briefly. *"When are we going to meet him?"* Sam added.

"In a few hours," Mr. Khadir explained, *"he has a tekke outside of this town."*Mr. Khadir brought Sam to a beautiful house in the country. As they walked up the driveway, they noticed a man leaning against a wooden fence.

"As salaam alaykum!" Mr. Khadir greeted the man.

"Alaykum as salaam!" the man answered.

"I would like to introduce you to my friend" Mr. Khadir said slowly. *"Sheikh Muhtar al-Rifa'i, this is my friend Sam."*

"Pleased to meet you Sam," the Sheikh warmly greeted Sam.

Sam was surprised that the Sheikh was just standing outside by himself leaning on a fence.

"I sense great strength in him," whispered Sheikh Muhtar to Mr. Khadir. Aloud, the Sheikh said to Sam, *"Do you have any questions you would like to ask me? Please don't feel shy."*

"Well," Sam awkwardly managed, *"I was wondering how one gets to be your student?"*

"Would you become the follow of a dog?"

"No!" Sam was firm in his answer.

"Then you cannot follow our path, for I myself am the follow of a dog, and you should consider my master as greater than me."

Sam stood there. *"A dog? How can you be the follower of a dog?"*

Sam's voiced trailed off vaguely. *"Because I once saw a dog deal kindly with another one which had surrendered to it. By the Lord, the Highest, the Strongest, the All-Compelling One, besides whom none is high, or strong, or powerful! This dog comprehended the essence of Sufism. But, it's time to go inside,"* announced the Sheikh.

When they entered the tekke, Sam's heart jumped into his throat, for all around him were the most beautiful carpets and prayer rugs, photographs of saints and saint's tombs, pillows, chandeliers, prayer beads of different sizes, woodwork, and examples of ornate Islamic calligraphy depicting various names of God. He wanted to say something, but his voice failed him. They sat down on some pillows near the Sheikh.

Sheikh Muhtar was speaking. *"Tonight we want to speak about the remembrance of Allah, also known as the intoxicant of lovers. The Prophet*

(Peace be upon him) said that 'the one who mentions or remembers Allah among those who forget Him is like a green tree in the midst of dry ones. The one who mentions or remembers Allah among those who forget Him, Allah shows him his seat in Paradise during his life. The one who mentions or remembers Allah among those who forget Him is like the fighter behind those who run away. The one who mentions or remembers Allah among those who forget Him, Allah looks at him with a look after which He will never punish him. The one who mentions or remembers Allah among those who forget Him is like a light inside a dark house. The one who mentions or remembers Allah in the marketplace will have light in every hair of his head on the Day of Resurrection.'

"Ahmad Ibn 'Isa Abu Sa'id al-Kharraz was an important Sufi who, according to Huwjiri, was 'the first to explain the doctrine of annihilation (fana') and subsistence (baqa').' He was the close companion of Dhul-Nun, Bishr al-Hafi, and al-Sari al-Saqati, and was renowned for the emphasis he placed on 'ishq, the passionate love of Allah, and upon the scrupulous observance of the Law. This Abdu Sa'id al-Kharraz said, 'When Allah desires to befriend a servant of His, He opens the door of dhikr for that servant. After the latter takes pleasure in dhikr, He opens the door of proximity for him. After that, He raises him to the meetings of intimacy and after that, He makes him sit on a throne of Oneness. Then He removes the veils from him and He makes him enter the abode of Singleness and unveils Majesty and Sublimity to him. When the servant beholds Majesty and Sublimity, he remains without "he." He becomes extinguished, immune to the claims and pretensions of his ego, and protected for Allah's sake.'

"The Sufis say that dhikr has a beginning which is a truthful application; it has a middle, which is a light that strikes; it has an end, which is a piercing difficulty; it has a principle, which is purity; it has a branch, which is loyalty; it has a condition, which is presence; it has a carpet, which is righteous action; it has a peculiar characteristic, which is the Manifest.

"Musa said, 'O my Lord! Are you near, so that I may speak to you intimately, or are you far, so that I may call out to you?' Allah inspired to him, 'I am sitting next to the one who remembers Me.' He said, 'O my Lord, we are sometimes in a state of major impurity and we hold You in too high regard to dare remember You at that time.' Allah replied, 'Remember me in every state.' The Great Sheikh Ghazzali mentioned this in the 'Ihya.'

"Abu Yazid al-Bistami was told by Allah, 'I have entrusted you with a secret for which you shall render Me an account under the Tree of Bliss (shajarat tuba),' whereupon al-Bistami said, 'We are under that tree as long as we remain in the remembrance of Allah.' The Prophet (Peace be upon him) said, 'No group gathers and remembers Allah seeking nothing other than Him except a caller from heaven calls out to them: "Arise forgiven, for your bad

deeds have been turned into good ones!" *'Abu al-Darda' said that the Prophet (Peace be upon him) said, 'Allah verily will raise on the Day of Resurrection people bearing light in their faces, carried aloft on pulpits of pearl, whom the people will envy. They are neither prophets nor martyrs.' Upon hearing this a Bedouin Arab fell to his knees and said, 'Show them to us (ajlihim), O Prophet of Allah!' – that is, 'describe them for us.' He replied, 'They are those who love one another for Allah's sake alone. They come from many different tribes, countries and cities. They gather together for the remembrance of Allah the Exalted, remembering Him.'*

"However, we all know that it is sometimes difficult to live as we would want. Yet, take comfort in Allah's saying, 'And speak (O Musa and Aaron) unto him (Pharaoh) a gentle word.' (20:44): Musa said, 'O Lord, how can a word be gentle?' Allah replied, 'Say to him, "Would you like a good compromise? You have followed your own self for four hundred and fifty years; follow our intent but for one year, and Allah will forgive you all your sins. If not one year, then one month; if not, one week; if not, one single day; if not, one single hour. If you do not (wish to humor us) for all of an hour, then say in a single breath, 'La illaha il ALLAH' so that I shall be able to bring peace to you."' Is not Allah the Compassionate and the Merciful? Whoever has one drop of love possesses Allah's existence.

"Permit us to tell your hearts a story. A Dervish entered a jungle and found a man remembering Allah while attended by a huge beast. (Sheikh Muhtar glanced at Sam as he said this). The Dervish asked, 'What is this?' The jungle man replied, 'I have asked Allah to empower one of His dogs to watch me in case I become heedless from remembering Him.' Whoever considers himself superior to a dog, the dog is undoubtedly better than him, for all men originate from Adam and Adam was made of clay and dust."

The splendor of the tekke had preoccupied Sam, but when the Sheikh looked at him and spoke about the dog, he caught Sam's attention. Sam leaned over to Mr. Khadir finally managing to find his voice. "But, I thought he was a True Guide." Sam was trying to keep his voice steady, "yet here material wealth and opulence surround him. He has this huge study-center, students coming and going showing him the greatest respect. He has certainly reached a higher level than looking at how dogs behave. How can he be genuine with all this stuff around?"

Sheikh Muhtar heard Sam's comment with the ears of ya Sami. He spoke aloud, directly to Sam.

"You are describing what most spiritual seekers want," said Muhtar Efendi. "They want to enter a teaching with regular ritual, with people showing respect, with a visible study-center. They do not seek to be Sufis; they seek to belong to such a community. These two are not the same thing."

"But if they have been attracted by your outward shape, it is your *fault,"* Sam said in a low, angry whisper. *"You have deliberately allowed this place to look like this. You have presented it to the world in this way."*

Sheikh Muhtar responded gently, *"What the world makes of it is one thing; what the true disciple understands by it is another. If you are seeking ritual, community, music, labor, and service, as you understand these things, you will be most in need of those who can teach you through other methods. To pander to your outward requirements is not Sufism, though everyone in the world may think so. The real Murid knows the actual reason he or she has come to the Guide. It is not that music, ritual, service, and a study-center are a waste of time. No. They have their place within the authentic context of Love, which is the core of Sufism. Sometimes Allah makes a likeness of His Beauty in shapes such as chandeliers and carpets. If the person does not ask if this is shirk, and lets go of 'how,' he or she may come to see the Presence in the most beautiful of forms. Allah yearns that those He loves become familiar with Him and love Him. In this way the Divine Reality is not unlike a woman who beautifies herself with make-up, jewelry and a beautiful dress to please her beloved. Lose sight of the core, and all the other elements become trash."*

Sheikh Muhtar then raised his hands and began making a dua, *"My Lord, give me the capability to tolerate an opposite point of view. My Lord, keep me wise and aware, so that I may not judge someone or some idea right or wrong unless I have understood him or her or it correctly and completely. My Lord, inspire me with the 'piety of rebellion' so that I may not stumble in the grandness of my responsibility; and save me from the 'piety of avoidance' so that I may not spoil in the corner of solitude. My Lord, burn me in the sacred fire of 'doubt,' so that it may burn away every 'certainty' that others have imprinted on me. Then, from its ashes raise the light of certainty, clear of every fog. My Lord, grant me success in struggle and in failure, patience in disappointment, going alone, Jihad without weapon, work without being paid, sacrifice in silence, Din in the world, Madhab without popular traditions, faith (Imam) without pretensions, nonconformity without immaturity, beauty without physical appearance, loneliness in the crowd, and loving without the beloved knowing about it. My Lord don't grant me knowledge that will not be useful to humanity. My Lord, tell to the materialists that 'human' is not the plant which grows due to a coincidence in nature, history and society. Tell my people that THE ONLY path toward you passes through THE EARTH. My Lord, inspire our religious ones that: Adam is made of dust. Tell them that a material phenomenon suggests God's existence as much as an unexplainable unseen one; that God is as much in this world as in the next. My Lord, grant me a life, such that at the deathbed, I may not be resentful of its worthlessness. And grant me a death that I may not mourn for its uselessness. Let me choose that, but in the way that pleases You the most. My Lord, You teach me how to live, I will learn how to die. Amin."*

"A man's mind, stretched by a new idea, can never go back to its original dimensions."   *- Oliver Wendell Holmes, Jr.*

"Make thyself puissant, wise, radiant in every system, and balance thyself well in thine Universe."

- Abdullah the Satiricist of Shiraz

"Re-imprinting is the process of suspending the neural synaptic routes which create 'reality' and of imprinting a new 'reality.' When the human species mastered the technique of re-imprinting and serial re-incarnation, a post-human level of evolution was attained."

- Angie Brown in
Principles of Neurogenetics

THE PRICE OF ADMISSION

How can you tell if a Chinese poem is a good poem if you do not read the kind of Chinese in which it is written? Certain realms of experience charge an entrance fee. To evaluate certain experiences a person must have encountered that realm of experience in some fashion. He or she must have access to that realm.

If your car broke down, would you take seriously the diagnosis of someone who has no experience with cars?

The physical universe is an unresolvable dilemma to the materialist because he or she insists on trying to decipher it in terms of its own makeup. Nothing can be explained in terms of itself, but only when shown in the light of a greater totality. As the saying goes, *"You cannot see the forest from the trees."* You need somehow to step out and back from some event to put it in proper perspective. Therefore, in addition, to understand the physical world, you have to take a step back. However, where do we step? All the last steps were in the physical world. There are no more steps available.

This is where Spirit becomes a feasible possibility. Spirit is the dimension you can enter to see the physical world in some perspective. Spirit is the fifth element. Earth, Air, Fire, and Water, all have their being in Spirit.

T.S. Kuhn[508] in "The Structure of Scientific Revolutions" writes, *"Each group uses its own paradigm to argue in that paradigm's defense."* To grow as a person and as a Sufi you have to step outside your paradigms. That is why it is helpful, from time to time, to put all your spiritual books and paraphernalia aside and thrust yourself into some completely different field such as: anthropology, law, air conditioner repair, fine art, computer programming, finance, or boxing. Play some touch football; study the strategy. Go out to the football stadium. Follow your favorite team.

Eventually it is best if you are able to traverse a variety of "worlds" each day. The goal is to be able to put on and take off paradigms like so much clothing. Many people feel they can only do those activities that fall in line with the list of permitted activities within their belief system. For instance, musicians do not often play contact sports, Southern Baptists do not frequent Happy Hours, Muslims do not eat ham sandwiches, mechanics do not take ballet lessons, and so on. The Sufi must break out of the artificial constraints and molds of a given belief system.

This is the true way to awakening. This is the royal Way to become awake and aware in your job and lifestyle. As far as you can break out of the stereotypical, to that degree you are awakened.

The "Way of the Sufi" is about expanding your horizons, taking in all things. Therefore, you must cultivate spiritual perceptions, intuition, shamanic experience, and extrasensory perception. Those people, who would want to exclude the spiritual from their lives, are deliberately excluding an entire realm of experience. They are denying themselves a human experience. By that, they impoverish their experience by eliminating the spiritual dimension from the smorgasbord of human experience. The goal is to view your spirituality from a variety of perspectives. In truth, by doing this exercise you will experience how the Living Reality unveils Itself in a variety of ways. The Sufi can see a given event as a Christian would, a Hindu would, an atheist would, a Shaman would, a businessperson would, an artist would, and a lunatic would. The Sufi sees all the facets of the Diamond Reality.

PRACTICE

Simple. Simple is a beautiful word. The Great Sufis throughout history lived simply, but what is more important, they had simplicity in their spiritual belief. Not simple in the sense of a lack of education, but simple in the sense that they approached all aspects of their lives in a quiet, uncomplicated and integrated way. The profound is never complicated, and the profound Ones never make a big show espousing complex and convoluted philosophies. They walk, they pray, they remember Allah, and they are charitable and kind to strangers.

The more complex your lives become with intellectual machinations, piles of paper, and social intrigue, the less you are aware of the Simplicity of the Moment. We can maintain this spirit of simplicity even in the face of today's hectic and fast paced world.

We may observe this profundity of behavior not only in Great Guides, but it is a gift that various people in all occupations display every day. Study and talk with these people and strive to take up some of their peaceful, easygoing, simple attitude.

"Remember! that extremes of right and left will lead you astray, moderation is the best course for you to adopt."

- Imam Ali ('Alaihi Assalam)

"Religion is very easy and whoever overburdens himself in his religion will not be able to continue in that way."

- The Prophet Muhammad
(Peace be upon him)

MODERATION

Religion is an inherited form. Sufism on the other hand, existed before religion. Do not make a religion out of your experience. Rather, focus on what gave birth to religion, and the rest will flow naturally. Some sincere, but frightened Murids will seek out religious form and structure (they will even join mystical groups but dwell on the form and structure of the group) as a defense against firsthand experience of Transcendental Reality.

Beware of religious obsession. The Sufi knows that everything happens within him or her self. The outside world is just a reflection of the inner. People blame God for this and that, when instead they should be facing what is inside them.

Keep everything in moderation. Do not make a burden of your spiritual practices. Your practices should gently weave throughout your daily life. You must learn how to apply mystery to your daily life.[509] Beware of making your practices so stringent that they become a hardship and eventually force you to give up out of frustration. Also, beware of building your prayers and spiritual practices into a palace for your ego that shuts out the Light of Unity.

"The wild geese do not intend to cast their reflection; the water has no mind to receive their image."

- Zenrin poem

"Observe something else with subtle understanding. Although you are asleep, who is awake within? That witness takes no rest and is inseparably one with your life. While remaining different from you, That watches everything that happens in your waking state as though it was a dream."

- Swami Muktananda

"We are the mirror as well as the face in it.
We are tasting the taste this minute of eternity.
We are pain and what cures pain, both.
We are the sweet, cold water and the jar that pours."

- Jelaluddin Rumi

THE WATCHER

When we experience a forest, laid out in front of us, we have some sort of picture formed in our minds. However, a picture requires an "eye" to perceive it. An invisible eye in our mind views the pictures that the mind creates. What is this eye? Then who perceives the image that the "eye" sees? It is as if we filmed a motion picture of a forest. (This is analogous to the physical process by which the physical sense organ called the eye processes an image through its neurons and electrical impulses). Then we develop the film and bring it into a movie theater. We show the film on the screen. We sit in the audience watching the screen, and yet we clearly realize that we are sitting in a movie theater watching a movie. So, who watches us watching the screen? A Sacred Presence watches. *"I am his hearing by which he hears and his sight by which he perceives, his hand with which he takes and his foot by which he moves along."* [510]

We are aware that we are watching a movie, and yet simultaneously also aware that we are aware of watching the movie. A kind of fun-house infinite mirror effect takes place in the mind, a repeating loop that happens. The mind seems to divide into an infinite amount of components whenever it is experiencing something. *"Man is multiple and not single of essence . . . "* [511] It is the task of the Murid to discard all his or her multiple "I's," and to create a singular "I" or essence. *"Either you control personality, or personality is controlled by thousands of different 'I's, each of whom has its own ideas, its own views and desires."* [512]

The Guide is like a photograph that shows you how the photograph inside you should be developing. Robin Becker states, *"We cannot see what we are not yet ready to see. We cannot see what we do not yet understand. The teacher prepares us to see what our next step is, to open us to new perspectives.”* You need to develop the picture inside yourself with wisdom.

There is an old teaching that a reflection shows the soul. The Hindu Gods needed their *Shaktis* or Goddess-energy aspects as their “souls.” Apollo the Sun needed the power of his sister-consort Artemis the Moon to act. In the Egyptian pantheon, his wife Isis restored the God Osiris to life. Woman gives life!

The entire universe is a mirror. As within, so without. The human being may be considered as a combination of body and soul, having a dark and light side, if you will. This physical side is dark like the back of a mirror and the soul side is light like the glass. We propose that consciousness is the silver.[513]

When we face the Abyss,[514] we stare into a mirror. In Shinto temples, there is a mirror. The purpose of this mirror is to remind the Murid of the fact that to see REALITY, it is necessary to see both oneself and the illusory nature of the self.

People look into mirrors or at their reflections in store or car windows frequently. They want to fix their hair or to judge their appearance. Mirrors are like monkeys. “Monkeying” humans, they remind us in a humorous way of the way that we are obsessed with thinking about ourselves. We must be parodied so that we can laugh at ourselves, therefore removing our pompous self-aggrandizement. Ultimately, the mirror reflects our mortality: when we gaze in the mirror, we gaze at a skeleton.

It is necessary to clean your mirrors. Otherwise, they will reflect poorly, eventually being of no use at all. How do we clean the human mirror? We have to clean our mirrors through the service that is necessary from us. Humanity will plummet into a downfall unless we give this service. Remember that actions are the qualities of Allah. There is a saying, *“Clean your face instead of blaming the mirror.”*

To paraphrase Ibn al-‘Arabi, Allah willed in respect of His Beautiful Names (Attributes), that their Essences, or you may say “His Essence,” should be seen. When Allah created humans, He created a microcosmic being. Since Allah endowed this being with existence, humanity contains the whole object of vision, and through which the inmost consciousness of Allah becomes manifest to Him. Before creation Allah’s vision of Allah consisted of seeing Allah by means of Allah. However, when Allah created humanity, Allah saw Its vision in something else, which serves, as a mirror for Allah. Allah is appearing to Allah in a form of Allah’s creation. Therefore, creation is Allah’s mirror. Earthly existence is The Exalted Truth’s epiphany to Itself.

“In Lordship is a mystery, that mystery being you, which means every being, and were it to cease, the Lordship would cease.”[515] However, Allah in

Its Essence (that which existed before Lordship) permits the universe to exist. Without humanity, Allah in Its Essence would still be.

Therefore, in addition, the Murid (in the microcosmic world) will often marry. In fact, various Sheikhs have said, that a Murid cannot begin his or her studies until he or she is married. This is because, as creation is God's mirror, your human beloved is your mirror.

Five times a day, Muslims pray in the direction of Macca (al-Mukarramah). In the center of the town of Macca (al-Mukarramah) stands the *Ka'ba*. Literally meaning, "cube" the Ka'ba is a building of approximately cubic form and an ancient sanctuary in Macca (al-Mukarramah). It is a small square building made of stones, about sixty feet long, sixty feet wide and sixty feet high. A door is fixed about seven feet above ground level facing northeast. A Black Stone (*Hajar al Aswad*) is fixed into its eastern corner. The Ka'ba is the *Baitullah*, the House of Allah.[516] Its sanctity and antiquity are older than history itself. Tradition goes that Allah ordained the Ka'ba to be built in the shape of the House in Heaven called *Baitul Ma'amoor.* Allah in His infinite Mercy ordained a similar place on earth and Prophet Adam was the first to build this place. The Torah, in the Chapter of Genesis, describes its building when God ordained Abraham to erect a Shrine for worship when Abraham was ordered to go to the Southern desert with his wife Hagar and infant son Ishmael.

It was more than four thousand years later that the last of the line of Prophets, Muhammad Ibn Abdullah (Peace be upon him) entered Macca (al-Mukarramah) triumphantly, went inside the Ka'ba and, with the help of his cousin and son-in-law Ali Ibn Abu Talib ('Alaihi Assalam) destroyed all the idols of the Ka'ba with their own hands. At one stage of this destruction of idols, the tallest idol of Hubal was brought down only after Ali ('Alaihi Assalam) stood on the shoulders of the Prophet. Muhammad (Peace be upon him) was reciting this verse from the Qur'an as they were destroying the idols, *"Truth has come and falsehood has vanished."* However, before all this occurred, the Prophet Muhammad (Peace be upon him) had a significant encounter with the Ka'ba in his younger years before he announced his ministry.

After the Prophet Ibrahim ('Alaihi Assalam) built the Ka'ba, it was rebuilt during Kusayi's time and fortified. Then, during Muhammad's (Peace be upon him) early years, floods damaged the Ka'ba and it was rebuilt again. The black stone in the Ka'ba may have been the foundation stone. This stone is possibly of meteoric origin. Arabs and the Semitic races generally, worshiped stones of this kind.[517] The secret of all human souls is within that stone. It is human, because humans give birth to humans.

> *"That black stone has*
> *known the hand*

Of all my fathers back to Adam
But this dervish swallowed
up their breath
Where shall I turn?"
  - Seemi Ghazi

When the Black Stone was to be put in its place, the residents of Macca (al-Mukarramah) quarreled among themselves who should have the honor to place it there. They had just decided that the first comer to the quadrangle should be given the task of deciding whom should have the honor. Muhammad (Peace be upon him) came in and was assigned this task. Muhammad (Peace be upon him) advised them to place the stone in a cloak and ordered the heads of each Tribe to take an end and bring the cloak nearer the corner on the eastern side. He himself then took out the stone and placed it in its position.

Opposite the northwest wall, but not connected with it, is a semi circular wall of white marble. It is three feet high and about five feet thick. This semi circular space enjoys an especial consideration and pilgrims wait in queue to find a place to pray there. The graves of Ismail and his mother Hagar are within this semi circular wall.

As Shaykh Nur al-Anwar al-Jerrahi revealed, the Ka'ba is the Six-Dimensional Mirror, the directionless direction of prayer toward which all Sufis orient themselves. Ibn 'Arabi blessed us with this divulgement: *"Thus, the six directions are manifest only through man, who is in the image of the Merciful."*[518] And Ruzbihan Baqli had this vision: *"Zulaykhā depicted her form to Joseph in all six directions, so that Joseph did not see in any direction without seeing her form there."*[519]

The brain is a mirror that reflects the One Mind. The mirror is a sacred object. For verily we are the mirror reflections of The Ancient Holy One. In looking at your mirror reflection you see The Only One.

Allah has said, *"I did not bring you a religion. I brought you a completion of the best of behavior."* Islam is not a faith. It is a beautiful behavior. As the Sultan of the Prophets, Muhammad (Peace be upon him) said, *"All things have a polish. The polish of the heart is the Remembrance of God."*[520] Therefore, who is the Watcher? *"Man's consciousness of himself is indeed God's consciousness of him."* [521]

"Do what you will, I have forgiven you."
> *- Hadith Qudsi (Hanbal, II:492)*

"Do what thou wilt shall be the whole of the Law."
> *- Aiwass*

"Know thyself and do your own."
> *- Plato*

"Dive into the plasma-pool. Drink deep or taste not the plasma-spring."
> *- The Fly*

TALES FROM UNDER THE OVERPASS

" *I* *have thought this thing through over and over again, and I can find no solution. Still, I am trying to think positively,"* Sam lamented.

"The power of positive thinking is remarkable, but nowhere as strong as the power of not thinking."

"But you are the wise one here. Tell me what to do" Sam implored.

"I am not the answer. I am only asking a few questions," Mr. Khadir declared.

"Well I need answers. You teachers are frauds. Anyone can ask questions. I don't know what's real anymore." Sam sobbed.

"Nothing is real; all is permitted. The Chains of the Law have been broken." Mr. Khadir answered.

"That's funny. You know that's the funniest thing I've heard all day. Leave it to you, my friend, to say something only a sublime madman would say. Are you trying to tell me that there shouldn't be rules and morals?"

Mr. Khadir answered, *"A wise man once said 'Let there be no difference made among you between any one thing and any other thing; for thereby there cometh hurt. But whoso availeth in this, let him be chief of all!' "*

"So, you Sufis have completely done away with all formal rules?" questioned Sam.

"By reversing the Shariah, the Sufis have in fact internalized its message, not simply abandoned it."

"As long as the word of God comes from our lips, the Last Day will not come. What is the meaning of this? As long as there is a single person who believes in God and says God's names, then the Last Day will not come. But that is not saying 'God' like saying 'Hello.' Those who say 'God' must know that humanity is divine."

> *- Sheikh Muzaffer Ashki*
> *al-Jerrahi al-Halveti* [522]

"Hell – the distance they imagined to be between them and the Reality."

> *- Ibn al-'Arabi*

"What though the corn grain of the heart be small
It is a station of the lord of both worlds to dwell therein."

> *- Mahmud Shabistari* [523]

"By Him in Whose hand the soul of Muhammad is, I do not know whether I am of the people of Paradise or of the people of Hell."

> *- Muhammad*
> *(Peace be upon him)* [524]

CAN A LOVING GOD
DAMN HIS CREATION TO HELL?

The Prophet said, *"Allah will gather the believers on the Day of Resurrection in the same way (as they are gathered in this life), and they will say, 'Let us ask someone to intercede for us with our Lord that He may relieve us from this place of ours.' Then they will go to Adam and say, 'O Adam! Don't you see the people (people's condition)? Allah created you with His Own Hands, ordered His angels to prostrate before you, and taught you the names of all the things. Please intercede for us with our Lord, so that He may relieve us from this place of ours.'*

Adam will say, 'I am not fit for this undertaking' and mention to them the mistakes he had committed, and add, 'But you'd better go to Noah as he was the first Apostle sent by Allah to the people of the Earth.'

They will go to Noah who will reply, 'I am not fit for this undertaking,' and mention the mistake which he made, and add, 'But you'd better go to Abraham, Khalil Ar-Rahman.' They will go to Abraham who will reply, ' I am not fit for this undertaking' and mention to them the mistakes he made, and add, 'But you'd better go to Moses, a slave whom Allah gave the Torah and to whom He spoke directly'.

They will go to Moses who will reply, 'I am not fit for this undertaking,' and mention to them the mistakes he made, and add, 'You'd better go to

Jesus, Allah's slave and His Apostle and His Word (Be: And it was) and a soul created by Him.'

They will go to Jesus who will say, 'I am not fit for this undertaking, but you'd better go to Muhammad whose sins of the past and the future had been forgiven (by Allah),'

So they will come to me, I will ask the permission of my Lord, and I will be permitted (to present myself) before Him.

When I see my Lord, I will fall down in (prostration) before Him and He will leave me (in prostration) as long as He wishes, and then it will be said to me, 'O Muhammad! Raise your head and speak, for you will be listened to; and ask, for you will be granted (your request); and intercede, for your intercession will be accepted.'

I will then raise my head and praise my Lord with certain praises which He has taught me, and then I will intercede. Allah will allow me to intercede (for a certain kind of people) and will fix a limit whom I will admit into Paradise.

I will come back again, and when I see my Lord (again), I will fall down in prostration before Him, and He will leave me (in prostration) as long as He wishes, and then He will say, 'O Muhammad! Raise your head and speak, for you will be listened to; and ask, for you will be granted (your request); and intercede, for your intercession will be accepted.' I will then praise my Lord with certain praises, which He has taught me (for a certain kind of people) and will fix a limit to whom I will admit into Paradise.

I will return again, and when I see my Lord, I will fall down (in prostration) and He will leave me (in prostration) as long as He wishes, and He will say, 'O Muhammad! Raise your head and speak, for you will be listened to, and ask, for you will be granted (your request); and intercede, for your intercession will be accepted.'

I will then praise my Lord with certain praises, which He has taught me, and then I will intercede. Allah will allow me to intercede (for a certain kind of people) and will fix a limit to whom I will admit into Paradise.

I will come back and say, 'O my Lord! None remains in Hell (Fire) but those whom Qur'an has imprisoned therein and for whom eternity in Hell (Fire) has become inevitable.'

There will come out of Hell (Fire) everyone who says, 'La ilaha il ALLAH,' and has in his heart good equal to the weight of a barley grain. Then there will come out of Hell (Fire) everyone who says, 'La ilaha il ALLAH,' and has in his heart good equal to the weight of a wheat grain.

Then there will come out of Hell (Fire) everyone who says, 'La ilaha il ALLAH,' and has in his heart good equal to the weight of an atom."[525]

Allah says, "*My Mercy encompasses everything.*"[526] Allah loves everything and everyone. Everything He created, He created without regard for its purpose or suitability, but only because of its Essence. Our mercy too should pour forth on everything in our environment without regard to its appropriateness or comeliness. Allah's Mercy has precedence over His wrath. *"There is no misfortune All of what God has arranged is the domain of His loving concern, because it is in the grasp of the Real. What is in His grasp is near Him, and what is near God is good and preserved; misfortune is evil and there is no evil in Him. So understand!"*[527] Consequently, even Hell fires will cool, and eventually the dwellers in the Fire will enjoy His Pleasure.

What are we discussing? Fire? Punishment? Justice? No one can understand Allah's justice. The Sufi only knows love. *"God says, 'The recompense of one evil is an evil like it,' referring to retaliation as an evil action, even though it is legal; 'but whoever forgives and does good, his reward is with God,' because he is in His image."* [528]

Some people are so sure of whom Allah will send to Hell, and exactly what Hell is. Nevertheless, they will be shocked on the final Day: *"And there is manifest to them of God what they had not expected to see."*[529] For Mercy is with Allah, and so is Providence and Divine Decree.

PRACTICE

The next step in the training of a Sufi is to focus on the world of sound. In this exercise, you will learn to differentiate psychically between a sound produced by an inanimate body, and that produced from a living, breathing being. On the one hand, there are all the sounds that are produced from inert objects: car horns, garbage trucks, rock slides, and on the other hand, there are sounds that are produced by animals and human beings.

Seek to develop awareness of the inner experience of the being within the sound that it emits. Hidden inside the cries of animals and humans are nestled the actual essence of the being emitting the sound.

During the day, listen closely to the sounds in your environment. Do not analyze the sounds, but let them enter your heart and allow your inner being to respond. Especially, listen to the voices of humans and animals. Again, permit their voices to reverberate in your being, while you still your thoughts, and await the divulgence of the sound.

In this regard, you need to ignore whether the sound is pleasant or unpleasant to yourself. There are legends in which the hero can understand the language of beasts. For example, Siegfried after he slays the dragon, can understand the language of the forest bird.

The Greatest Sufi poet of Turkey, Yunus Emre wrote,

"With the mountains, and rocks
I call out to you, my God;
With the birds as day breaks
I call out to you, my God.
With Jesus in the sky,
Moses on Mount Sinai,
Raising my scepter high,
I call out to you, my God."

Nature will begin to yield up her secrets to the Sufi who has developed his or her hearing in this fashion. Gradually you will learn to hear beyond the words of a person speaking to you and into the inner being expressed in the sound of his or her words. The more opinionated you are concerning a given conversation, the less you can perceive the hidden message contained in the speaker's words.

As with supersensible sight, after practicing these exercises with sound for a while, the apprentice will begin to be able to hear sounds that do not have a counterpart in the physical world. Purely astral sounds will become perceptible. You can listen to the "speech" of the spirits.

One must also practice with the sense of smell, and other senses. Go beyond the duality of pleasant and unpleasant. Begin to sense the inner supersensible message contained within the sensory experience.

"I am with those whose hearts are rent and whose graves are obliterated."
- Qunawi

WHAT HAPPENED TO
THE KA'BA AFTER KARBALA?

After the martyrdom of the family of the Prophet at Karbala in 61 Hijri (681 C.E.), the Ummayad Khalif Yazid Ibn Mu'awiyah did not stop there in the pursuit of his destruction. He sent a large contingent to Madina (Al-Munawwarah), under the command of Haseen Ibn Namir, which destroyed the Mosque of the Prophet. They then continued to Macca (al-Mukarramah) and demolished the four walls of the Ka'ba and killed thousands of Muslims who protested.

Yazid's rule brought disgrace and ignominy on the fair name of Islam. Because of his deeds and habits like drinking wine, murdering the son of the Holy Prophet, uttering curses on the successor of the Prophet, Ali ('Alaihi Assalam), setting fire to and demolishing the house of Allah, mass-killing (especially of the people of Medina) and his countless sins and transgressions against divine laws, all make him a tyrant. Many Muslims do not know about the mass-killings in Medina (Al-Munawwarah). Abdullah Bin Hanzala said, *"O people, we did not revolt against Yazid until we verified that he was an irre-ligious man. He killed the descendants of the Prophet, illegally associates with mothers, daughters, and sisters, drinks wine, and does not offer the ritual prayer."*

Yazid sent a large army of Syrians under Muslim Bin 'Uqba, to sup-press the Medina (al-Munawwarah) people. They carried on mass killing of the people for three continuous days. Yusuf Sibt Ibn Jauzi, Mas'udi, and others write that so many people were killed and *"so much blood was flowing in the lanes of Medina that people were submerged in it, so much so that blood had reached the grave of the Holy Prophet – the mosque and the grave of the Holy Prophet were filled with blood."* Seven hundred noble and respected men of Quraish, Muhajirs and Ansars, were put to death. Ten of thousands of the com-mon people were killed. Yusuf Sibt Ibn Jauzi, in his book "Tadhkiratu'l-Khasa'isu'l-Umma" wrote on page one sixty three, which Abu'l Hassan Mada'an has reported, *"After the mass-slaughter of the people of Madina (Al-Munawwarah) one thousand unmarried women gave birth to children."*

Most of the Sunni Ulema regard the wicked Yazid as an infidel. Even Imam Ahmad Ibn Hanbal (the Imam of the Hanbalites) and many great Sunni Ulema suggest that curses on him should be recited, particularly Abdul Rahman Abul Faraj Bin Jonzi has written a special book on this topic namely "Kitabul Rad Alal Muta'assib-al-aneed ul Mane' an-La'an-e-Yazid a'natulh." Mas'udi in his "Muruju'dh-Dhahab", Vol. II, says that the character of Yazid was like that of Pharaoh, but Pharaoh was more just to his subjects than Yazid.

Why should a dervish utter a curse at someone, no matter how terrible the person may be? The Prophet Muhammad once spoke this hadith, *"If somebody frightens the people of Madina (Al-Munawwarah) through oppression, Allah will frighten him on the Day of Judgement and curse be on him of Allah, angels, and all the humanity; and on the Day of Judgement Allah will not accept any of his deeds."*[530] Also said the Holy Prophet, *"Curse be on him who frightens my city (the people of Madina (Al-Munawwarah))."* Specifically, Muhammad Bin Jarir Tabari, one of the eminent Sunni Ulema of the third century A.H. and a great confidant of the people, wrote, *"The Holy Prophet saw Abu Sufyan riding his donkey; Mu'awiyah was pulling it from the front, and his son Yazid was pushing it from behind. The Holy Prophet said, 'Curse be upon the rider, the puller and the pusher!' "*

The Murid must remember, however, that Yazid and Mu'awiyah Bin Abi Sufyan are the shadow in all human beings. The point is not to "externalize" and hate Mu'awiyah Bin Abi Sufyan and Yazid, but to face the Mu'awiyah and Yazid inside us and to realize their destructiveness. This is the Sufi illumination of these historical persons and events. This shadow must be acknowledged and faced. Spirituality is not about running away from reality; it is about facing reality square on. Yet, why did the Prophet curse these people? The word "curse" was meant in the sense that these shadow parts of ourselves cannot be allowed to rule us. For example, as humans we are born with emotions. At times, we may become angry. It is wise to acknowledge consciously this anger. This is how we discern and face our shadow. Yet, we must not allow this emotion to tyrannize us by our becoming violent toward others. The dervish must "draw the line" when it comes to the nafs.

Yazid died and Ibn Namir returned to Damascus. Abdullah Ibn Zubair and his associates rebuilt the Ka'ba. Umawi forces came back to Macca (al-Mukarramah) and killed Abdullah Ibn Zubair, hung his body on the gates of the Ka'ba for three months for all to see the Umawi power. But eventually this arrogance of power brought its own consequences and Mukhtar became the ruler in Iraq. Under his guidance the Ka'ba was refurbished and pilgrims began to arrive in safety to perform Hajj.

The Ka'ba successfully withstood the Karamatian invasion of 317/929. Only the Black stone was carried away, but returned some twenty years later. In the year 1981, the Wahabis brought tanks inside the Ka'ba to crush the Kahtani revolution against the Saudi regime and almost demolished the South Eastern Wall. They later restored this with the help of the Maccan people.

The Ahlul Bayt were the protectors of the Ka'ba, and currently the 12th Imam from the direct descent of the Prophet of Islam is the real protector, its custodian and guardian, and will remain as such while in concealment.

*"The only courage in life
that matters is the kind
that gets you from one
minute to the next."*

> *- Mignon McLaughlin*

*" 'Seeker', said he, 'of eternal secrets! When the heart sees with clear
vision, the fates that rule earth wear no veil.' "*

> *- Iqbal*

*"An authentic guide, a true witness, will take you to your essence, dispel
your ignorance. Without that witness, you will remain where you are. If
you take a nightingale as your guide, it will lead you to roses. A crow will
lead you to garbage."*

> *- el-Hajj el-Fakir Şerif Çatalkaya
> er-Rıfa'i er-Marufi*

*"Taken captive since childhood by Allah,
tested and trained by Allah,
the Shaykh has made the long journey
to the unthinkable goal of union.
Convinced totally by Allah,
Who is the fundamental Demonstration
shining in every recess of the universe,
the Shaykh receives intimations of Divine Power
flashing in his heart, beyond names and letter."*

> *- Shaykh Nur al-Anwar al-Jerrahi*

THE DANCE OF THE 70,000 VEILS

It is said that 70,000 veils separate the human being from Perfect Freedom. These veils are not evil, below us or filthy. They are complexes that need to be dissolved, beliefs that need changing and doorways to existential core issues. God has said, *"There are seventy thousand veils between you and Me, but there are no veils between Me and you."*

This is why we so greatly stress the importance of the Murid involving him or her self in some kind of psychological and body work.

It is necessary for the Murid to have a living Guide. An intermediary is necessary for transformation. For instance, if you want to heat up some water you do not just pour the water onto the stove. You put the water into a pot. The Guide is the pot.

The breath or self of the Murshid, is the breath or self of Reality. Recognize your Murshid as Reality Itself, do not depart from his way.

"Allah gives happiness to His servants when they see His Saints," said Abu Ali al-Farmadi at-Tusi, May Allah Sanctify His Soul. This is because the Prophet said, *"Whoever sees the face of a knower of God, sees me,"* and, *"Whoever sees me, has seen Reality."* Sufi Masters have named the practice of concentrating on the face of the Sheikh *(tasawwur)*, and it is done to the end of fulfilling that state.

The Sheikh helps the student to see that the *Shariat* is only the shadow of the forest. Yet, what is that forest? The oriental master Bruce Lee indicates: *"I cannot teach you; I can only help you to explore yourselves."* Therefore, explore the forest named "Yourself." The best teachers are not those who tell you what to do, but show you how to find that answer yourself.

As Meher Baba writes: *"If any suffering comes to a Perfect Master or Avatar, it should not be interpreted as a temporary victory of evil. It happens by divine will and is a form of divine compassion. He voluntarily takes upon himself the suffering of others in order to redeem those who are engulfed in gnawing cravings, unrelieved hatred and unabated jealousies."*[531] He takes the poison and turns it into a potion.

The True Guide has few disciples, for few can handle his or her effulgence. As J. Marvin Spiegelman, Ph.D.[532] has stated, *"You may recognize a genuine master by the fact that he or she treats every person individually."* Most people prefer general platitudes and comfortable maxims, but they become frightened when personal attention is focused on them.

A "hidden" or "secret" Qur'an is written inside the Sufi. This Inner Qur'an, also known as the Silent Qur'an, is the Heart. When the Qur'an lives within the Sufi there can be no room for dogmatic disputations. Some people put great stock in Guides who know the Qur'an well. However, the Qur'an that you can see, is only a hint of the Secret Qur'an. The Guide who can read the Silent Qur'an and make it speak is the True Guide.

Three adornments are essential in the Spiritual Way: first, a True Guide (The Sheikh), second, a connection with the God Within, and third, Allah Himself. You will be lost if you try to do away with any of these three. The True Guide does not ask for money. He or she does not plunder. The True Guide also shatters the idol that others make of him or her, for to do any less would be to encourage idol-worship among his or her disciples. The Sheikhs have said, *"The Guide is without name."*

The Murid may know the True Guide:

1. From the Guide's words.

2. From the feeling the Murid has in his or her heart about the Guide.

3. From the contentment the Murid has in the Guide's presence. This is because lies give stress to people. Real Words come to your heart and will not be erased. Real Words are like *ayats* from the Qur'an; they are like the living Qur'an.

4. The True Guide's look will burn you. In him or her is the power of Allah.

5. As Shaykh Nur al-Anwar al-Jerrahi has written, *"Actions are the confirmation of the Shaykh."* And,

> *"The sure indication of a true Shaykh*
> *who divinizes the life of his times*
> *with the owner of his heart,*
> *is his similarity to the Prophets –*
> *rope-soled sandals of strength,*
> *staff of daring, sash of freedom,*
> *banner of benevolence, tambourine of praise,*
> *sword that cleanly cuts the knot of ignorance,*
> *shield of equality and impartiality.*
> *The mystic guide is known*
> *By his total submission to Allah Most Near,*
> *Conscious submersion in the ocean of Light,*
> *ascent toward Allah, and restfulness in Allah."*[533]

The True Guide removes the Murid's ignorance of his or her own nature. Many "spiritual" people prefer to hide their dark aspects from themselves, or else they become depressed by their dark side, thinking themselves as helpless sinners. The True Guide helps the Murid to bring the buried shadow into the Light and helps the Murid to make friends with the Murid's shadow, so that Murid and Shadow may come together in Unity.

However, to recognize a Real Sheikh (a True Guide) you must be a Real Human Being. This is not so easy. You have to be a jeweler to understand jewelry. Therefore, the first step to finding a True Guide is to become a True Human. Beautify your inner self. Be as a Qur'an in your own person. Then you will find the True Guide.

"The secret to listening to music is to listen to it like you were hearing it for the first time!"

- Unknown

"I can sing a prayer as well as say it."

- Baal Shem Tov

"To sing is to pray twice."

- St. Augustine

TALES FROM UNDER THE OVERPASS

" If you excite things, they start to sing," Khadir was saying, "just like a violin string when a bow is drawn across it. When an object is set into a rapidly oscillating vibration, that object begins to produce an audible sound. The Guide is like the bow and the Student is like the Violin. The Guide must determine at what frequency the Student will resonate at, and then the Guide must sing that frequency so that the Student's whole being breaks into song."

Mr. Khadir was entering a state of sublime proximity as he uttered these words, "If a violin could be aware of the sound coming forth from itself and the master which plays upon it, it would break into consciousness. I am the instrument of the Cosmos. The Cosmos sings through me."

"Through spontaneity we are reformed into ourselves. Freed from handed-down frames of reference, spontaneity becomes the moment of personal freedom when we are faced with a reality, explore it, and act accordingly."
- *Viola Spolin*

"None attains to the Degree of Truth until a thousand honest people have testified that he is a heretic."
- *Junaid of Baghdad*

GUERILLA SUFISM

In Ireland, thousands of people starved to death because a fungus destroyed their only crop – the potato. Genetically the potatoes that the Irish were growing were all the same. If they had just one different kind of potato, those people would have lived.

Being different can sometimes mean the difference between life and death!

So too, in the world of Sufism. It is often the renegade, the one who steps to the beat of his or her own drummer that channels a new spiritual current to the Earth. The various Sufi traditions have developed throughout history because diverse saints have had powerful insights and discernment granted by Allah that show them unique facets of the Diamond Reality.

There is a story about the Buddha prior to his being born as Siddhartha - where he was a merchant sailor. While on a ship with fourteen other merchants, he became aware through his precognition (even at this point, he was believed to be very "awake") that one of the sailors was planning on killing everyone else and taking the profits for himself. The evening of the planned murders, the merchant who was the "Buddha-to-be" killed the potential murderer as he was about to begin his killing spree. He did so knowing the ramifications of the killing, and out of compassion for the murderer (he would rather take on the karma, or physical and spiritual ramifications, of killing one man, than allow this man to do so for killing many) and because of his intent (compassion) this action is seen as a beneficial one, and Buddhism teaches that this action brought positive and not negative karma. There are many possible ways of looking at particular actions.[534]

PRACTICE

The concept of transcending duality, that is, of going beyond the notions of pleasing and distasteful, should be applied to the realm of rhetoric. When you are listening to someone expound on his or her ideas (or if you are reading them as a letter, e-mail or news story) endeavor to stop yourself from forming any opinion of the speaker's views. The goal is neither to agree nor to disagree. This will help you to go beyond a cerebral way of viewing the world.

In many ancient religions, one of the most important oppositions is between the clean and the unclean. The Dervish cannot afford the luxury of seeing the world in terms of this, or any other, duality.

Be quiet, and still your inner being, as you listen to someone speak. Follow the speaker's train of thought. Be still and allow there to be quiet in your mind. The Murid silences the tendency of the mind to babble incessantly throughout the day.

"When tomorrow, on Doomsday, the cry goes up: 'O men,' the first person to step forward will be Mary, the mother of Jesus."
                                        - Abbāsah Tusi

"The most beautiful book to be read is the human being."
                                        - el-Hajj el-Fakir Şerif Çatalkaya
                                        er-Rıfa'i er-Marufi

"The greatest book is this world, this life. Read it and reread it. Your past is the greater part of this book. As you keep rereading it, you will find it changed. And you will find yourself. It is a vast book, reaching from this earth to the farthest corner of the heavens."
                                        - Muzaffer Ashki al-Jerrahi
                                        al-Halveti

OFF TO THE LIBRARY

Although each person contains all the Divine Names within him or her self, each person also has a particular Name that uniquely manifests the Divine. This is his or her particular Lord *(al-rabb al-khass)*. Each person has his or her own "Lord." This "Lord" is one aspect of Allah and flows from one of His Divine Names. Each Name can be thought of as a bi-unity: first, an uncreated Lord and second, a created vassal or servant. The uncreated Lord may be thought of as the Angel or the Eternal Hexeity or the Eternal Individuality of a given individual's being. The created individual or servant is seen as an epiphanized form of the uncreated Lord.[535] As the Murid follows the way of Truth Without Form, he or she becomes aware of his or her own eternal individuality (*'ayn thabita*). However, no individualized person can manifest The Limitless.

Muhyed-Din Ibn 'Arabi, in the seventy-third chapter of his monumental opus on Sufism, "Futuhat al-Makkiyya," relates the following story,

"One of the masters was asked concerning the true number of the abdal[536] existent in the world. 'There are altogether forty,' he answered. 'Why not say: forty men?' they asked. 'Because there are women among them as well,' he replied." [537]

The Murid should study the lives of effective and influential individuals who clearly expressed their Unique Divine Name. Some recommended examples are: Viracocha, Akhenaten, Hatshepsut, Nefertiti, Mani, Zarathustra, Socrates, Cheiro, Appolonius of Tyana, Lady Wac-Chanil-Ahau, Artemesia (Queen of Halicarnassus), Rabi'a al-Adawiya, Sayyida Nafisah, Sha'wana al-Ubulliya [538], a Slave Girl of Qasim al-Dawlah [539], Bahriya al-Mausiliya [540], 'Unaida [541], Fatima bint Abi Bakr al-Kattani [542], Boadicea, Julia Domna, Wei

Furen 'mother of calligraphy", Laeta, Amalasuntha, Raziya, Avicenna (Ibn-Si'na), Mozart, Nostradamus, The Woman who was the Master of B yazid Best mi[543], Giordana Bruno, Jefferson, Rembrandt, The Sister of Hosayn Ebn Mansur Hallaj, Churchill, The Black Girl[544], Napoleon, Emily Brontë, Michelangelo, Omm Ali, Joan of Arc, Jacques DeMolay, Sha'vanah, Paracelsus, Ibn Rushd, Jacob Boehme, Goethe, Francis Bacon-Lord Verulam-Viscount St. Albans, Solomon Molkho, Pico della Mirandola, Isaac Luria, Abraham Abulafia, Baal Shem Tov, Tohfah, Madame Guashan[545], Robert Fludd, Khansa - daughter of Khaddam, Johann Valentin Andreae, Sabbatai Zevi, Khanom Moluk, Miguel de Molinos, Mme. De la Vida[546], Adam Weishaupt, Wolfgang von Goethe, Richard Wagner, Eliphas Levi, Rudolf Steiner, St. Theresa of Avila, Leonardo da Vinci, Resass Du La Chappelle[547], Frederick Douglas, George Washington Carver, Sir Aleister Crowley, G. I. Gurdjieff, Hazrat Moinydeen Chisti, Nijinsky, Rasputin, Booker T. Washington, Martha Graham, Nichola Tesla, Lady Sahinah Shirazi, Gandhi, Jesse Owens, Whilhelm Reich, El-Hajj Malik El-Shabazz - Malcolm X, Martin Luther King, Frau Hunekeh[548], Mother Theresa, and Habiba[549]. All are examples of individuals who caused change in their world through connection to the heart and a lifetime of service and self-sacrifice.

"Yesterday is but a dream, and tomorrow only a vision, but today well lived makes every yesterday a dream of happiness and every tomorrow a vision of hope. Look well therefore to this day: such is the salutation of the dawn."
- *Ancient Sanskrit Writings*

"We shall not cease from exploration,
and the end of all our exploring
will be to arrive where we started
and to know the place for
the first time."

- *T. S. Eliot*

"I am looking for Serif. I am not looking for Allah."
- *el-Hajj el-Fakir Şerif Çatalkaya*
er-Rıfa'i er-Marufi

"We bring intensive trials upon aspiring souls, carefully testing those who strive their utmost for spiritual advancement and who persevere in pure patience, so that WE can divinely demonstrate their true level."
- *Qur'an 47:31*

TALES FROM UNDER THE OVERPASS

*W*hat time is it?"
Sam was feeling impatient.

"There is only one time," Mr. Khadir informed him.

Troubled by Mr. Khadir's answer, Sam asked, "When are we going to reach our next destination?"

"Right where we are standing is our destination." Mr. Khadir gestured to the ground.

Sam was puzzled. "So . . . we're not going anywhere?"

"There is no coincidence in Allah," Mr. Khadir instructed. "You're concerned about where we are going. But to be here, at this moment, is Allah's wisdom and orders."

"If there is a God," Sam asked, "why can't we see Him?"

Mr. Khadir answered, "You ask to see Him. Who is looking?"

"I am," Sam said fervently.

"Why search for Allah? Allah was never lost. Rather than searching for what is Supremely Obvious, search for something that most of humanity has lost."

"What's that?" Sam asked intently.

"Humanity has lost its beautiful behavior," Mr. Khadir revealed.

"Look for these beauties. And then you will know your value and the value of all other humans on the planet."

"How do I begin to do that?" Sam reflected.

"You must" Mr. Khadir patiently instructed, "change your heart and your mind. Many followers of the spiritual way think that Sufism is only about the heart. However, it is also about changing your thoughts. Both the heart and mind must change."

"No child can be born except through pleasure and joy. By the same token, if one wishes his prayers to bear fruit, he must offer them with pleasure and joy."

- Baal Shem Tov

"Not with philosopher, nor with priest, my business; one lays waste The heart, and one sows discord to keep mind and soul confounded."
- Iqbal

"And when you forsake them and what they worship save Allah, betake yourselves for refuge to the cave; your Lord will extend to you largely of His mercy and provide for you a profitable course in your affair."
- Qur'an 18:16

"No prophet has ever attained prophethood without months or years of seclusion, often in caves. In the same way, the Sufis have followed the foot-steps of the prophets. They need periods of seclusion, periods of reducing the impact of the outer world on them in order to develop the inner."
- Shaykh Fadhlalla Haeri

"The longest sermon on record was delivered by Clinton Locy of West Richland, Washington, in February 1955. It lasted 48 hours, 18 minutes and ranged through texts about every book in the bible. A congregation of eight was on hand at the close."
- Anthony Rufus Isaacs
in 'Exo-Sociology'

"Nothing is better for a man than to be without anything – having no asceticism, no theory, no practice. When he is without all, he is with all."
- Bâyezîd Bistâmî

PRIESTLY ARROGANCE

Nothing is more ruinous than the priests who would take away your pleasure and joy. Life is so difficult; pleasure provides comfort and is the natural complement to pain. Pleasure is the right of every human and is an expression of a Quality of Perfect Freedom.

Priests also want us to think that they have the market on Reality cornered. They are not in awe of the Great Infinite Field of Being, because in their minds they have it all worked out. Priests create vast systems of creed and doctrine that they tell us fully explains all. Priests do not need awe, for awe presupposes a realization of ignorance. Priests are loathed to admit ignorance.

They reduce Absolute Freedom to a set of rules. They love to take what is meaningful, joyful and ecstatic and construct elaborate theologies around it. They love to make you "pay" for your spiritual experience. Priests are the toll-takers of the spirit world. They think it is their right to charge admission to the world of Spirit. There is no charge for spiritual intimacy! God does not seek to be reimbursed.

There were no priests during the first two hundred years of Christianity. The Prophet Jesus ('Alaihi Assalam) went into the desert for forty days and forty nights, but then he came back and drank wine, attended dinners and socialized with his Apostles, followers, relatives, and the lowest strata of society. The late Shaykh Nur al-Anwar al-Jerrahi reminded us: *"To appreciate non-duality is not just sitting silently and thinking, or not thinking, but actively celebrating. Celebrating should be very human. That's why it's important to have delicious food, to make joyful conversation, to wear beautiful clothes."* Muhammad (Peace be upon him) went into the cave for forty days but then came out of this supracelestial place and married eleven women, had two concubines, and said, *"Allah has placed love in my heart for three things in this lower world: women, perfume and prayer."*

The Blessed Prophets Jesus and Muhammad (Upon them be peace) understood the idea of balance in life. They perceived that physical pleasure is just as essential as making prayers. In a deeper sense, they realized that Spirit is the All Manifesting - the Pervading Life Principle That is Celebrated in the Scent of the Rose and the Warmth of Physical Affection.

Yet, there are ascetics, fundamentalists and orthodox who spend their entire lives crawling on their knees, barely eating and sleeping on straw. How misguided they are to think that their approach is more effective than the Prophet or Guide that they follow. Humans put the wild Lion of Truth into a cage of dogma, because they cannot control the wild Lion of Truth.

William Blake wrote: *"As the caterpillar chooses the fairest leaves to lay her eggs on, so the priest lays his curse on the fairest joys."* Pleasure is not our enemy! Pleasure is only an obstruction when we fail to realize that it is a sacred Expression of Existence.

"Through what do you know Allah? Through the fact that He brings the opposites together."

- Abu Sa'id al-Kharraz

"Wander in salt deserts
*   you are lost.*
And is this roaring sea
*   less than salt?"*

- 'Attar

"Don't dream this thread
*   is double-ply;*
root and branch
*   are but One.*
Look close: all is He -
*   but He is manifest through me.*
All ME, no doubt -
*   but through Him."*

- Fakhruddin 'Iraqi

TALES FROM UNDER THE OVERPASS

*S*am said, *"Since spending time in your company, I believe I am becoming confused between two completely different approaches to spiritual belief."*

Mr. Khadir replied, *"It is good to be confounded! Paradoxes are helpful to the Murid. The mind seeks to make decisions and judgments in its linear fashion. The mind is thrown into confusion and chaos when two disparate points of view are held. However, this is an advantageous thing. Because after a while the mind stops its labor and just relaxes.*

"Emotionally some people need the security of one particular set of beliefs that neatly tie up all the questions of life in a pleasant package with a pretty bow. The revelation of questions is not really in the answers, but in transcendence of the question. Your task is to transcend the dualities of the mind and to take that leap out of your familiar surroundings into the Ocean of Living Reality."

"Let go and let God, as they say, right?" Sam asked.

"Let go and let the Ocean of Love pour into your heart," Mr. Khadir said as he put his hand on Sam's heart. Then Mr. Khadir opened his arms and gave Sam such a hug that Sam snapped out of his quandary and became present in the moment.

"Every man must overcome his own obstacles, expose his own illusions. Yet others may assist him to do both, and they may enable him altogether to avoid many of the false paths, leading no whither, which tempt the weary feet of the uninitiated pilgrim. They can further insure that he is duly tried and tested, for there are many who think themselves to be masters who have not even begun to tread the way of service that leads thereto."

- Aleister Crowley

"And He it is Who has made two seas to flow freely, the one sweet that subdues thirst by its sweetness, and the other salt that burns by its saltiness; and between the two He Has made a barrier and inviolable obstruction."

- Qur'an 25:53

"... the isthmus called Mundus Imaginalis, where images appear as autonomous, or where dreams foretell the truth. In one sense neither real nor unreal ... "

- Hakim Bey

"So that righteous living
And obedience to the law
Should be freed of all possible
Taint of being inspired
By a desire for its wine,
Its honey and houries,
I wish – Oh, how I wish
That someone would fling
This Heaven of ours
Into Hell!"

- Ghalib

THE DWELLER ON THE THRESHOLD

Do you experience a chronic problem of some sort: a physical ailment, a problem in your social life, a terrible loss? The problem may be *"The Dweller on the Threshold."* There is a long-standing tradition in the esoteric community that a mighty and awful astral being guards the way into the Spectral Realm. This being is in actuality the Karma of your Life. When you dare to tread into the spectral realms, you are immediately confronted with the apparition of your life as a terrible astral being.

The Murid has to face aspects of his or her entire life, which appear in a daunting and frightening way to the Murid. These aspects are still imbued with astral life and have a quasi-human existence. The Murid's karma arises and has an effect on the present.

Have you ever felt that in spite of your greatest efforts, something was working against you? Have you ever felt that you have aspects of yourself that are out to sabotage your efforts? These aspects are often manifestations of the Dweller on the Threshold. The Dweller is the embodied karmic consequence of your past deeds, in other words, that which you should have done and did not, and that which you should not have done and did. The Dweller also embodies all your past traumas.

Your work lies before you: face these old selves or continue to be barred from crossing the Threshold. Discover what each has to say to you. For each is an aspect of you. Your work is not to destroy or conquer the Dweller. For the Dweller knows when you are ready to pass and will eagerly step aside when the time is right. Until then, the Dweller remains a formidable obstacle that you cannot circumnavigate.

In other words, the Murid has to graduate from his or her karma, to enter fully the supersensible realities. Those things which you regard as difficulties: a disability, a chronic illness, anxiety, depression, money problems and so, may be a confrontation with The Dweller on the Threshold. When you see with your spirit-eyes the threads that connect those aspects of your karma with your present, you thereby relax the hold these aspects have on you. The shedding of the light of aware understanding on these aspects causes them to disconnect from the Murid.

You must often look deeply back into your personal qualities of virtues and vices for the answers. The Sufi has much work to do on him or herself. The psychological demons of childhood and adolescence must be confronted. A great difficulty or obstacle in the life of the Murid, rather than being a hindrance to his or her spiritual development, may be the catalyst he or she needs to open new spiritual vistas. Get to the root of the problem, clear the astral support of the illusion (the astral and emotional images you have formed around your problem) and install a more useful picture of reality to replace the distorted one.

Many spiritual persons fear psychotherapy. They regard it as an anti-spiritual process that will ultimately take God away from them. Contrary to their preconceptions, there are many therapists who are intensely spiritual individuals, and they will help you to shed your fears and find your primal energy connection with the One Living Reality.

Some teachers have linked the Dweller on the Threshold with the Guardian of the Abyss. This guardian is sometimes given the name "Choronzon." Choronzon is a name of mysterious origin, related to the workings of Dr. John Dee and his Enochian system. Another name for the Guardian of the Abyss, "Khadhulu," has already been discussed in the "Saturn" chapter. Another esoteric divulgence about the Threshold is the fact that Imam Ali

('Alaihi Assalam) is the Gateway or Door of the City of knowledge. Any doorway is symbolic of Ali's spiritual significance in life. We may contemplate on the exquisite significance of Ali ('Alaihi Assalam) as being the ultimate reality of the Door.

They call the Dweller at the Threshold *"The Sultan"* in Sufism. *"Not without authority (Sultan) shall ye be able to pass."* Qur'an: Ar-Rahman, 55:33. He is also known as the Bab. The name *Bab* means "door" and "gate." Ali Rasheed writes: *"I found the word 'Bab' and its plural 'Abwaab' mentioned in the Quran twenty-seven times. In most instances, it refers to the proper way of entering into a place with permission (2:58); a place of destiny (40:76) and a passage of blessings (39:73). Symbolically, a 'bab' is the proper way to reach your desired destination. For example, in the famous tradition of the Holy Prophet (S) he said: 'I am the city of knowledge and Ali is its gate (Bab).' Meaning that if you would like to acquire the Prophet's knowledge, the proper way is through Imam Ali ('Alaihi Assalam). It also implies that to attempt to acquire by another means would be improper. In the past, people have been referred to as the 'Bab' meaning that people could find guidance through them (although it was seldom the case though)."*

A door opens to the inside of oneself. Unlike the open tent of the Bedouin, the ancient Arab house formed a sort of stronghold that could only be entered by a door, the Bab. There have been various symbolical applications of this name, some of which are pertinent in this context, for example: *"Gate of Fortune," "Sublime Porte," "Gate of the Milky Way," "Gate of Allah."* To the Sufis, this gate is the gate by which one enters the spiritual realms, in other words: the means of communication with that which is within. Bab also is defined as the forming of a relationship, a relationship with the One-and-Only Indivisible Infinitude within. It is a means needed by the Murid.

A Sheikh has said that most people envision Paradise as "above" and Hell as "below." Yet, in fact, Paradise is found in the center of Hell, and Hell protects it. The Ahlul Bayt is the line that separates Heaven from Hell.

At times in your lives, you go through crisis or change. Sometimes this crisis happens as a relationship slowly ends, or your years in college finish and it is time to graduate. This reorganization of your lives can be deliberately brought about through psychotherapy in which the therapist can guide the client through a controlled emotional breakdown. Psychotherapy can be a form of the reformation of the nafs. When the change happens slowly, feelings usually accompany it of insecurity and dread. Sometimes these changes cause a great deal of anxiety. Personal transformation is difficult and requires much courage.

Change can also happen suddenly. Abrupt shifts in one's life can be triggered through deliberate initiatory means, such as a hallucinogenic journey, an initiation and so on. We must point out that there is one step in the Mystic

Way in which some special Sufis will completely disappear into the Heart of Allah Most High. This is usually a temporary situation, for the individual must still come back into his or her body and spiritually resurrect him or herself.

There are many "quick-fixes" being offered to the spiritual aspirant. Generally, the change that takes place over time, is more effective and more permanent than the "weekend" seminar. Sudden change like an initiation is often the result of years of preparation, and the Murid must be prepared to understand the experience in some sort of context. The slow process of change is like a slow descent into sublime madness. You will get well to the degree that you are willing to lose control and break out of the cramped box your Limited Self has created for you. Each little fear of loss of control is a Dweller on the Threshold trying to frighten you to go back. Each time you dare pass, another Dweller awaits you further on. It is never easy! You must face the Dweller on the Threshold so that you can see your Transcendental Reality. There is no such thing as pretty spirituality. 'Ain al-Qudat al-Hamadhani writes in his fundamental articles of faith the following verse, *"My word is 'a decisive word; it is no merriment.'"*[550]

You can never go back once you begin this journey. You will eventually come to a state of Sanity, but it is sanity with a capital "S." In other words, you will never go back to your comfortable, little, well-ordered, and "safe" world. However, you will become oriented in a new, fluid and glimmering cosmos.

PRACTICE

Play with experiencing the world around you as a spontaneous arising of the Living One. Surrender into the moment, allowing yourself to be immersed in the Happening that is the Transcendental Reality. As the dervishes sing, *"The moment in the moment is this moment."* We are the people of the Holy Presence.

Various New Age and New Thought Guides will try to force you to believe that you are in control of your world. They want to make you think that you are responsible for the cold you had last week and that your aunt is responsible for her bad back.

Imagine that the entire world that you see around you is occurring without any effort on your part. You are not creating the world. You do not know where you came from. You do not know who or what you are. You are not controlling your breathing. You are being breathed. You are not moving. The Great Reality is Moving. Everything is Happening.

Flow into that Happening. See that Happening as a Spontaneous Expression of the Life Force arising all around you. The Divine is a Radiance that emanates from Reality, like waves of heat rising from the desert floor. The Divine Presence is being you now.

"The pomp and glory of a vicious life is to me worth less than even the sneeze of a goat."

> *- Hazrat Ali ('Alaihi Assalam)*

"O A'isha, the worst of persons is one whom you treat with respect for fear of his foul tongue."

> *- Prophet Muhammad*
> *(Peace be upon him)*

"There is a limit at which forbearance ceases to be a virtue."
> *- Edmund Burke*

"Opinion veils the heart. Opinion says, 'I know and you do not.'"
> *- Kabir Edmund Helminski*

GET OFF YOUR PODIUM!

In cases of verbal abuse, we recommend the following: If your interlocutor is taking a dominant, abusive stance in the conversation, simply say, *"Excuse me"* and walk away. Some people talk just to hear the sound of their own voice. Believe it! They are not paying you to sit there and listen to them, so just get up and walk away. They do not want a conversation; they want an audience. Remember: they are abusing you. There is no necessity in being polite to them. By their behavior, they have forfeited their right to being treated politely. *"Indeed Allah does not love any arrogant and boastful person."*[551]

Abuse happens especially in groups, when conversation is held not for mutual communication, but as a jostling for rank and position. Men frequently engage in this kind of behavior when a woman walks into the room. This kind of conversation is actually a verbal strutting around the hen house. It is only meant to show off and draw attention to oneself.

Here are several examples of how people practice verbal exhibitionism:

• Starting to speak when someone else has started speaking (as if what you have to say is more important than what they are saying).

• Speaking over someone else because you just remembered something you left out and you feel that it is important enough to interrupt another speaker (this derives from a false sense that you are the most important person there and you should be allowed to appear in the best light. If you forgot something, take your place in line like everyone else).

• Spouting forth an endless amount of factoids, and using expressions like *"Let me tell you something . . .," " "No, this is the way it is . . .", "Here's what's really happening. . . , "* or other pompous, bloated, statements to try to gain a "one-up" on your fellow interlocutor.

When someone says to you *"The problem is . . ."* or *"The reason is . . ."* he or she is implying you need him or her to explain the situation to you. If they say the above statements as a reply to a question that you have asked, then some of these responses are appropriate because you have asked the person for his or her opinion. However, if you have not asked them for their opinion, then they have "kindly" deigned to educate you out of what they perceive to be your ignorance.

Often people will feel that in a group conversation that they are the center of attention. They think that the conversation is about them. That is why they interrupt other people. They feel that they have the right to interrupt since the conversation, in their twisted view, is about their thoughts, their opinions and their lives. They will relentlessly outtalk you and constantly try to steer the conversation back to themselves. They do this because they are firmly convinced that the conversation is about them.

Do not become involved in someone's theatrical production. You can know quickly in a conversation if it is an equitable exchange of ideas between two people, or if it is merely a forum for one person to perform. For some, conversation is like a performance, accompanied by stories, faces, facts, and so forth. When approaching a group in conversation, a good way to spot this posturing is to note if all the members of the group are sitting facing one individual like they were facing a television set.

Anyone that says "No" to you in a conversation is someone that you should avoid. This is the mark of someone who is approaching the conversation as if he or she was the schoolteacher and you the Know-Nothing little school child. Now what we are saying is not meant for pompous fools, although if they are reading this maybe they will recognize themselves and rethink their behavior. It is meant more for those individuals who can guard against becoming like this. In addition, it is also meant to alert people as to some hidden dynamics that go on in conversations that you were not aware were happening. You may walk away from a conversation feeling like you just went through World War Three and you do not know why; or else you just realized that you spoke to someone for two hours and did not get one word in.

True Initiates know that they have gotten where they are by paying careful attention to the environment, rather than through forcing their own opinion onto the environment.

Here are some ways a person who seeks supremacy over others can identify himself or herself:[552]

1. He or she does not like to be equal to others in any matter.

2. He or she always wants to go ahead of others and sit at a higher place than others in a gathering.

3. He or she expects others to greet him or her first.

4. If no one accepts his or her word, he or she gets angry.

Imam Ridha insisted on eating his meal only after the entire members of the family, young and old, and the servants and grooms, were present. One day someone who was more fond of royal formalities than the fraternity of Islam, suggested that it would be better to make separate eating arrangements for the servants. The Imam replied, *"All are created by God, Adam is their father and Eve is their mother. Everyone will be dealt with by God according to his deeds; why should there be any discrimination in this world?"* [553]

*"Go beyond Reason's light: her's is the lamp
That shows the road, not marks the destination."*

- Iqbal

*"The way the Tibetans put it, there are three levels of teaching: outer
teaching, inner teaching, and secret teaching. The secret teaching is non-
duality."*

*- Shaykh Nur al-Anwar
al-Jerrahi* [554]

BEYOND THE COMPASS

The Sufi realizes that each human being is a unique Expression of the
Infinite. The Sufi is not the servant of form. He or she heeds the words
uttered by the essence of his or her heart. Have you let your desire for acceptance by your Murshid get out of hand? Is it running your life? Spiritual growth
is not about turning your Guide into a Parent figure, or trying to garner a warm
nod of approval. The Murid should have no concern with attempting to garner
his or her Guide's praise. The universe needs each of us to awake and express
our inner selves.

Some people crave answers. They go from one Teacher to another begging for the answers to life. *"The partial intellect is a denier of Love, even if it
pretends to know the mysteries. It is clever and knowledgeable, but not naughted – as long as the angle is not naughted, it is a demon."*[555] They are like vam-
pires sucking information out of the minds of their Teachers. Haji Bektash Veli
said *"For him who has perception, a mere sign is enough. For him who does
not really heed, a thousand explanations are not enough."* No amount of information will ever satisfy the intellectual mind. The Answer is beyond the compass of the linear-rational mind. Even esoteric knowledge is a waste of time to
the true Sufi. Shaykh Nur al-Anwar al-Jerrahi explains, *"All esoteric, arcane,
occult information is inner teaching, not secret teaching. Secret teaching, in a
certain sense, is absolutely not interesting to someone who's trying to gather
more information, more exoteric or esoteric maps."*[556]

The Answer is stamped onto our beings. You need to go no further than
your own face to find the guru.

We all are lions, but lions on a banner;
because of the wind they are rushing onward from moment to moment.

Their onward rush is visible, and the wind is unseen:
may that which is unseen not fail from us!

Our wind whereby we are moved and have our being are of Thy gift;
our whole existence is from Thy bringing into being."

- Jelaluddin Rumi

TALES FROM UNDER THE OVERPASS

*S*am and Mr. Khadir were enjoying a couple of slices of pizza with extra cheese and mushrooms, when Mr. Khadir looked up at Sam, and with his mouth full asked, "Sam, what's the largest number?"

Sam answered, "I think it's called a googolplex, one with a centillion zeroes after it."

Mr. Khadir replied, "It is 'one'."

"One is the smallest number?" Sam inquired.

"Do you know the word individual comes from the Latin word 'individuus' meaning undivided?"

"No, and what does that have to do with the number one?" Sam wanted to know.

Mr. Khadir continued, "Yes, of course the word has lost its meaning in today's society, but originally it stood for the Complete Human Being in Its Undivided Unity . . . the microcosmic actuality of the Creator. Every number is divisible by One."

"He who does not dance knows not what is going on."
> *- Prophet Jesus,*
> *Apocryphal Acts of John, Ch. 96*

"All that dwells upon the earth is perishing, yet still abides the Face of thy Lord, majestic, splendid."
> *- Qur'an 55:26*

"All times are the same in relation to Him as well as present with Him."
> *- al-Jami*

ISN'T TIME STRANGE?

Have you noticed that time is getting strange? In the past, people could count on time to be dependable and orderly. Today we need to be more flexible as time seems to bend and twist in strange ways.

Our plans can shift and change at a moment's notice. Change is happening so rapidly that what worked yesterday may not work today. Scientists are making discoveries by the minute; information is doubling at an ever-increasing rate. Our lives are speeding up too.

You may find that incredible opportunities are suddenly opening up which would have been unimaginable just five years ago. You may notice that you will read about a thing one day and you will see it in person the next! Sometimes it will even happen within hours, minutes or seconds.

Events will become more concentrated and profound. Time will become ever more strange in its behavior. Remain calm, buckle up and follow your intuition.

You need an anchor in the time storm. Become aware of the real motivations behind your actions. Strive to remove the rationalizations, the illusions and the deceptions from your mind. Face the facts. Examine your self. Clearing your mind of the constant stream of useless chatter that goes on inside it, cleaning out your senses and knowing yourself, these three, become the anchor.

PRACTICE

View a crystal and an animal. Your household cat would be a perfectly good candidate for such study. As you observe the crystal, you should say to yourself, *"The crystal has form. The animal has form. The crystal remains stationary in its location. The animal changes its location. The animal has emotions that cause it to change its location. In fact, the animal's body is formed according to these emotions. Yet, the 'body' of the crystal is not formed according to emotions. Rather, it is formed according to mineral forces without desire."*

Allow this realization to sink deeply into your being.

"Poetry is vocal painting, as painting is silent poetry."
- Simonides of Ceos

"My purpose in inditing it was to explain certain states claimed by the Sufis, the appearance of which depended upon the manifestation of a stage beyond the stage of reason. Philosophers deny such states because they are imprisoned in the narrow defile of reason."
- 'Ain al-Qudat al-Hamadhani [557]

BEYOND DUALITY

Words do not transcend duality, however, an image will. Aleister Crowley wrote a book of poetry called "The Book of Lies." He realized that prose often leads to duality. Prose is about definitions. It pins down all these little facts. On the other hand, poetry, story and images have the power to convey a field of experience.

Prose is subject to the polemic. The academicians can endlessly debate, defend, advance and argue over little facts. However, a tale is not so subject to debate. A story simply is. It conveys experience.

An image resists explanation. You relate to it or you do not. You cannot disagree with an image. Through identification with an image you comprehend a totality, rather than learn particular facts.

A cadaver does not yield the secret to the human experience. A bunch of dry facts does not yield the secret of *ilma la dun* hidden inside the human heart. The wise say, *"the intellect is a one-winged bird."*

Tales and images transcend duality.

"His miracles abound
in the creation
of the heavens and the earth
and in all the creatures
broadcast over them;
and as and when
He wants to garner them -
He has the power."

- Qur'an 42:49

"I am Atum, the creator of the Eldest Gods,
I am that great He-She,
I took my space in the place of my will,
Mine is the space of those who move along
like those two serpentine circles."

- Coffin Texts 558

EXTRA AND INTRA TERRESTRIALS

One evening we were driving home from work in a beautiful, blustery snowstorm. The snow was coming down heavily as we pulled into our driveway. We turned off the car and reached over to the passenger seat to retrieve our briefcase. As we sat back up, we were astonished and a bit saddened that the snow had stopped. However, something told us that this was odd that the snow could have stopped so suddenly.

On an impulse, we turned the headlights back on. There, before us, was the snow falling in all its quiet majesty. We instantly realized that without the headlights we could not see the flakes. *"What else could we not see without headlights?"* we thought. *"What worlds exist that our naked senses cannot perceive, yet must and do exist?"* we continued to muse.

The human ear can only hear sounds between sixteen and twenty thousand cycles per second. The unaided eye cannot perceive colors below red and above violet. Sitting in the car, we thought to ourselves, *"Entire choirs of existence must surround us, innumerable planes of probability extending infinitely from this moment, and yet people scoff at ideas such as angels, extraterrestrial beings, jinn, and the paranormal."* There are many probability axes in Allah's creation. Space, time and probability all have an axis on which it is possible to move. This is why they often refer to the greatest Sufi saints and Sheikhs as *Qutubs*, Poles or Axial Centralities of the Universe. But in most people's limited minds they assume the universe of which they are aware to be the only universe.

Which direction does time flow?

In your universe, or more specifically, the universe in which the uninitiated move, people move freely in three directions that you call space, and move forward in a fourth that you call time. Actually, there are more dimensions than an ordinary person can even dream of. The Sufi inhabits the entire host of dimensions and realities.

Looking back at that snowy evening, we realize that our headlights only illuminated the particular snowflakes upon which our headlights shown. In a sense, we saw only one plane of existence (that which the headlights revealed to us).

In the future, governments will officially acknowledge that civilizations have existed on the Moon and Mars and that extraterrestrial presence on this Earth has been, and continues to be, a reality. A project is going on as we write this book, entitled "The UFO Briefing Documents." They have designed these documents to convince world leaders of the reality of UFO's and to dispel and go beyond stereotypes. The documents are made up of sightings and data collected by various military witnesses, police, pilots, and other reputable authorities who have experienced contact with UFO's.

The great scholar and traditionist, Sheikh Ali Ibn Ibrahim Qummi of the 3rd century A.H. in his commentary on the sura *Saffat* (No. 37), the eminent scholar, Sheikh Fakhru'd-Din Ibn Tarih Najafi, known for his piety, in his "Kitabu'l-Lughat Ma'rafat-e-Majma'u'l-Bahrain", which was compiled about three hundred years ago, and Allama Mullah Muhammad Baqir Majlisi, in his "Biharu'l-'Anwar", v.XIV, report that Ali ('Alaihi Assalam) said: *"The stars in the skies are populated with cities as the earth is."* Now for Allah's sake, be fair. At that time there was no conception of modern astronomy. The world accepted the Ptolemaic theory that the earth was the center of the universe. If a person disclosed something new about the stellar regions and that was proved to be true a thousand years later, would not you say that he had knowledge of the unseen?

However, there were others who chose to close their minds to the truth: *"To assert that the earth revolves around the sun is as erroneous as to claim that Jesus was not born of a virgin,"* wrote Cardinal Bellarmino in 1615, during the trial of Galileo.

It would be a great error to limit the Divine Reality to only what you can see, hear, feel, touch, and smell. The great Sufi saints have said that the Ultimate Reality has created eighteen thousand worlds, and that these worlds can fit into one tiny dot!

In the distant past, humans used mantras, or words of power, to achieve remarkable feats. They lifted and manipulated heavy blocks of stone, planes flew in the sky, the oceans were crossed and they charted the continents. They produced various other astounding wonders.

For instance geologists and certain Egyptologists, like John Anthony

West have now ascertained that the great pyramids and Sphinx date back to 10,000 - 20,000 B.C.E., proving that indeed a significant and advanced civilization existed on the earth at the end of the last ice age.[559]

Science has discovered nothing new. Humanity in the past has known all that science knows today. However, at that time, no one would say, *"I am a great scientist,"* because they experienced the spirit world firsthand. They would rather say something akin to the following, *"Spirit forces flow through my being guiding me in certain matters."*

Allah has sent one hundred twenty-four-thousand Prophets to humanity since the dawn of time. We know of only a handful of these Realized Complete Human Beings. This means that more than one hundred thousand Prophets have been on earth throughout the millennia. Their names are hidden and unknown to us, but perhaps legends remain of these individuals that we know as: Viracocha in Central and South America, Math in Wales, Lugh, Dagda, Nuada, and Manannan Mac Lir in Ireland, Zarathustra in Iran, Pythagoras, Zalmoxis and Dionysos in Greece, and Ra, Atum, Osiris and Set in Egypt.

Also, there is the question that has been much debated among Sufis: can a woman be a Prophet? Let us not forget Isis, Arianrhod, Athene, Danu, Bride (Brigid), and many other great women Initiates registered in world myth.

The Murid must understand that he or she does nothing! It is Allahu *ya Qādir* working through him or her that does everything.

"Trying is not the way Nature functions. The Earth doesn't try to go around the sun, nor does the seed try to sprout into a sapling. Nature functions with effortless ease, invariably taking the path of least resistance."
- Unknown

"By God, if there is a veil, it is the tariqa. As soon as a person leaves them, God grants him illumination. Our brother, Abu 'Majdhub, was one of them, then he left them and God granted him illumination. Our brother, Musa al-Majdhub, left them and God granted him illumination."
- Ibn Idris

"Each human being is oriented toward a quest for his personal invisible guide, or . . . he entrusts himself to the collective, magisterial authority as the intermediary between himself and Revelation."
- Henry Corbin [560]

TALES FROM UNDER THE OVERPASS

*M*r. *Khadir spoke, "I want you to have more life, not less. I am painful because I am stretching you, not constricting you. My goal is not to turn you into some kind of anal-retentive robotic masochistic machine performing thousands of prayers every day. My goal is to awaken you to the full significance of who you are.*

"People erect so many barriers to ecstasy that it hurts; it is really painful for them to knock these barriers down. For some, it is even easier to accept the restriction of orthodoxy than to allow themselves to know their full potential. Religion is safe. I am dangerous. I am a corrosive factor.

"Some students who appear the most devout and submissive are secretly gloating over their 'spirituality'! Many of them develop a superior attitude. This sort of submission is only veiled egotism. The True Guide is not a person but a process. He or she is a dissolving process."

"I'd rather navigate the seas of uncertainty than be mired in the concrete of dogma."

- Patricia Livingston

"It is a mistake to assume that God is interested only, or even chiefly, in religion."

- William Temple

THE LIVING PRINCIPLE

It seems fitting to embrace a religious philosophy after having had a spiritual experience. Religion looks like the bed in which spiritual experience should lie. It seems to be the refuge of the spiritual person and it pretends to be involved in spirituality.

Spirituality consists of an immediate, Real experience of the Divine. Sharing the community of others whom the Cosmic Essence has touched is helpful. For just seeing the face of the Lovers of God removes the veils that sheath us. The mistake is willingly to put on the fetters of dogma as a response to an inner awakening. Everyone wants to either codify his or her experience, or seeks to fit it into someone else's code. It takes much courage not to run for shelter under religious doctrine.

Many people that believe that spirituality consists of going around constantly with a smile on your face and happiness in your heart always. These people are headed toward a fall. They are bound to be disappointed.

"It is not possible for the traveler to find in this journey unimpaired comfort, security, or bliss . . . We have not mentioned this to answer the people fond of comfort in this world, who strive for it and are devoted to the collection of worldly rubble." 561

A spirituality that is not organic, that does not proceed from our human natures, is a false construct. Spirituality does not need to be packaged. One cannot "act" in a spiritual fashion. Spirituality emanates from us like the sweat from our bodies.

"You are free." This statement is true, but it is also false. Each of us is covered in seventy thousand veils. You may state "I am free" and walk out the door never to think again about the things of spirit. Nevertheless, how free will you be? There are various degrees of freedom. We gather and communicate so that we can help each other gradually to strip ever more of the veils away. The process takes a lifetime.

PRACTICE

Soon you will begin to meet incorporeal beings. Shielding yourself every day is mandatory. Become used to shielding yourself upon waking and before going to sleep.

Especially during the times that we live in, protecting yourself is essential. When an animal arrives by the shore of the pond and dips its toe in the water, each creature inside the pond knows that something has entered the water. The Spirit World is akin to the pond. When you become Supersensibly Conscious and enter the Astral Worlds, all the Aware Beings know of your awakening. Some will immediately decide to attack you. Others will watch you. Some will help you.

We live in trying times and a person can collect a great deal of astral waste during a day, not to mention various slings and arrows of deliberate malicious astral intent. Therefore, it is essential that the aspiring Sufi protect him or herself through daily shielding.

We call one of the best shielding techniques "THE TOWER OF LIGHT." Visualize a large egg of electric blue light enclosing your entire body. This blue light is intense and bright. It is similar to the light you see when an electric spark jumps out of a wall socket. The blue is also comparable to the blue flame one obtains when lighting a "Sterno" canned-heat cooking flame.

This egg extends to about one to two feet beyond the surface of your body in all directions. Next, fix your attention to an area just above your head. You will see a brilliant ball of white light that is above, but not touching, your head. This ball of white light is so dazzling that you can hardly bear to look at it. The effect is similar to the white light given off by burning magnesium.

Spend a little time seeing both images: the large egg of intense blue light, and the brilliant ball of white light between your head and the top of the egg.

Then, picture the ball suddenly shattering into millions of luminous and radiant sparks that shower down all around and through you. You feel the scintillating effect on your nervous system and entire being as these silver sparkles course through your reality.

The outer shell of the blue egg remains clearly defined as you now see the interior of the egg: an intense electric blue, filled with a myriad of twinkling silver stars.

"God's prayer is seen as existentiating his creatures, whereas the devotee's prayer is seen as existentiating his personal Lord."
- Glossary of Muslim Terms

"We have unveiled you, and today your eye is sharp."
- Qur'an 50:22

THE MYSTICAL RECIPROCATION

The Murid must cultivate on a daily basis his or her devotion to The Sublime Unity. He or she does this through *teslimiat* or *taslim*, translated as "engaged surrender."[562] What is to be surrendered? The Murid must surrender every thought that *"God is absent"* or *"I am distant from God."* Every moment the Murid embraces and engages the presence of God in whatever form The Only One may appear within one's consciousness. Never lose, out of your heart and mind, the thought of the Divine Reality. Recognize all existing things as God, or Reality.

According to Ibn 'Arabi, it is the servant's devotion to his or her Lord that permits the Lord to display or manifest His attribute of Lordliness. For this reason, Ibn 'Arabi often states that the vassal holds *"the secret of his Lord's suzerainty."* There are many mysteries, mysteries within mysteries. The great mystery is that this "unveiling" (called *Mukāshafa*) is nothing less than self-unveiling.

This is the mystical reciprocation between Humanity and Its Creator. Sheikh 'Abd al-Halim Mahmud quotes his Sheikh al-Azhar as saying,

"Their expressions are manifold and Your loveliness is one
And everyone points to that beauty."

We manifest the Creator on Earth as the Creator simultaneously manifests us. Every time we speak one of the Divine Names, we manifest that Name in the world. *"The latent potentialities within the divine essence (these potentialities are usually referred to as the Divine Names) yearn to know themselves, and this knowledge is acquired via their manifestation within the created universe."*[563] God's purpose is to have knowledge of Himself. He possesses this knowledge by knowing Himself through the medium of His creatures.

The awesome responsibility of the Steward of the Planet Earth, humanity, must use this knowledge in ways that are obedient to Allah's commands. "The Force" as so beautifully depicted in the "Star Wars" movies can be used for mercy or tyranny. "The Force" is a tool that humanity wields in its hands.

"Getting rid of one's ego is the last resort of invincible egoism!"
- Alan Watts

"Do you know any name without a reality? Or have you ever plucked a rose from R.O.S.E.?
- Jelaluddin Rumi

"Every day and every instant, Allah shines forth as new spiritual states and new cosmic creations."
- Qur'an 44:29 (tafsir)

RUNNING AWAY FROM YOUR LIFE?

Ego is an outworn method of perception. Evolution brought about the ego for certain purposes, but it is time to explore other ways of comprehension that go beyond Egoic means of perception. It is time to continue our evolution and transcend our ego, not discarding it, but beginning to see the ego as another sense organ while becoming aware of our Interdimensional Reality.

This transcendence of our egos is the next evolutionary step in our development. The awareness of which we speak is to be found in a certain way of perceiving the mundane. This perception is not something that is remote and mysterious that requires crossing the Himalayas, or climbing the summit of some mountain to find a guru. Bubba Free John observes, *"Divine Communion is conscious and contemplative realization of the Real Condition of the present moment."*[564] Interdimensional Reality is found in the now. You must become a Person of the Moment!

The Realization of Spirit often comes upon us when we are intensely engaged in tasks and activities that are meaningful to us. Spirit is elusive. It is most slippery when we attempt to focus in on it and capture it. Spirit is therefore not a religious formality (although it can be the result of certain religious situations). Spirit is significant and meaningful.

So, please continue your meditations and prayers if you wish, but do not mistake the map for the territory. What about the paper the maps are drawn on? A friend may visit Holland and send you a postcard with a pretty picture of a site in Holland, but that picture is not Holland, it is only a picture of Holland, a hint of Holland.

You may want to learn how to drive a car, and so you may read a book about how to drive a car. After reading the book, you may have the opportunity to get behind the steering wheel and learn to drive a car. We ask you, how much does reading a book about driving a car resemble actually driving a car? The book can give you valuable hints and tips, but the book is truly light-years away from the experience of driving a car.

Do not allow yourself to be boxed into a web of religious words that you mistake for the Real Thing. Use the words as guidebooks, as helpful ways to process your experiences; however, do not mistake the guidebooks for the experience of being there. There comes a point in which even the guidebook must be thrown away and you fully immerse yourself into the culture you are visiting.

Stop struggling after "spiritual" experiences. Murids want to see lights, visions and spirit beings. The treasure is in your own back yard. Live your life, for spirit is Living Reality. Live your life fully and deeply. Spirit is the condition of your life, the Radiance of Your Existence. Spirit is the outline of the form of your experience and the shape of your life.

We could write many words that would anaesthetize you, make you feel pleasant and "spiritual," complete with comforting thoughts and platitudes; however, our words would take you far from the Springhead.

Dare fully to experience your "here and now." See the Mystery as it is manifesting to you this moment through all your perceptions. See it. It is in front of you. Hear it as the Music of the Earth all around you. The Divine, Who is Expressed as Everything, is manifesting in the condition of all things. Enter the Living World.

" Before the manifest came to exist there was a place of darkness - the negative existence."
> *- Ancient Myth*

"Has the black light above the Throne not been explained to you? It is the light of Eblis, which has been likened to the tresses of God; compared with the Divine Light it is darkness, but it is light just the same."
> *- Ayn al-Qozat* [565]

"Life is one part, but there is also death. Therefore, it is necessary also to know the remaining nonexistence, the void, because the ultimate truth can only be known when both are known - existence and nonexistence."
> *- Osho*

TALES FROM UNDER THE OVERPASS

*F*or the last several days, Mr. Khadir had noticed that Sam had taken to wearing white. Mr. Khadir asked Sam about this.

"I guess I am beginning to feel more spiritual," Sam explained.

"It puzzles me," Mr. Khadir laughed, "that in your culture, people equate white with good and black with bad. Yet, your own culture is not consistent on this point. What do people wear on the most solemn occasions? Black. What do people wear to the most refined social gatherings? Black. And what do they wear when they want to look important? Black. Priests and clergy wear black. Yet, if a group of self-styled spiritual seekers should all wear black they are labeled as Satanists! Incredibly inconsistent it seems to me."

"But isn't white representative of the Light?" Sam gambled.

"The Sufis often wear the color black. Black to them represents what is baffling to the Limited-Self. It is the Light of Infinite Space. To the uninitiated it appears black, for it is a mercy of Allah Most High to veil it from them. If they saw this Light and were not prepared for it, they would go mad. Contrary to popular opinion, black contains all colors. White objects reflect back the entire spectrum; black objects absorb all the colors of the spectrum. So, black is saturated with veiled polychromatic splendor."

Sam was puzzled. "Yet," he asked, choosing his words with care, "it still seems to me that there is something evil about the color black."

Mr. Khadir's deep, authoritative voice observed, "Yes, it has been associated with Iblis. The light of Iblis became black because Allah cursed him and bestowed the title of kāfir, unbeliever, upon him for all eternity. Yet this curse is paradoxically described as the chamberlain's robe of honor, for it is the insignia of Iblis' perfect obedience and his willing embrace of the role of divine instrument."

"*Perfect obedience, and a divine instrument . . . you've got to be kidding!*" *Sam was astonished.* "*Please tell me you're putting me on.*"

"*Let me tell you a story Sam,*" *Mr. Khadir began,* "*One day the Prophet Adam ('Alaihi Assalam) looked on the wretched Iblis with contempt and disdain. He manifested arrogance and conceit; he laughed at the predicament of the accursed Iblis. The jealousy of God thundered aloud, 'O upright fellow, are you not aware of the hidden secret? Were He to turn the fur inside out, He would rip the mountain from its root and base. At that moment He would tear the veil from off a hundred Adams, and bring forth a hundred Iblises newly converted to Islam.' Adam cried, 'I beg forgiveness for this look! I will never again think such presumptuous thoughts.'*"

"*I'm beginning to see that there are many mysteries in this Sufism of yours. Black is white and white is black, I don't know . . . I feel like I'm on a merry-go-round.*"

"*Black helps us to see the Light. If it weren't for darkness, we wouldn't know Radiance. All the Prophets loved to walk in the night. Therefore, don't curse the darkness, but bless it, for it is the means by which we see the light.*"

Mr. Khadir added, "*There is a state known to the Sufis as fana or annihilation. In this state, there is complete lack of consciousness of object or ego; one is moving toward darkness. There is not even any consciousness of the experience itself. There are no images. All multiplicity disappears into darkness. Thus, when light makes its full appearance, all things disappear. Light causes darkness. However, because all things lose their individuality and become obliterated from consciousness, the whole world paradoxically turns into an ocean of light!*"

"Unveiling is clarifying the veiled to the understanding, as though one sees with the eye. Its reality is the manifestation of the kingdom, the dominion, and the eternal glory of might to the eye of the gnostics. To their eye the radiance of their own glory is veiled, so that they may see with it the beauty of God's face. Then they look upon his hidden kingdom, and in gnosis they obtain an understanding of every Attribute."

- Ruzbihan Baqli

"ILM AL-GHAYB"
(THE KNOWLEDGE OF THE UNSEEN)
AND
"ILM AL-KITAB"
(THE KNOWLEDGE OF THE BOOK)

The Knowledge of the Unseen:

The original meaning of *Ghayb* in Arabic is "that which has been concealed," and it is with this meaning that is has appeared in the Holy Qur'an.[566] It signifies a meaning opposite to *Hadhir* which means, "present to the senses," and thus denotes with things to the external world (i.e., *Ma'lumat*; known things).

So it may happen that something is Ghayb in the dimension of time that does not exist now but it will be or it was; or in the dimension of place that is the knowledge of something that is elsewhere but not here.

Thus we can divide our own knowledge into two parts:

A) The knowledge of something that is present to us right here and right now (*Ilm bil Hadhir*),

B) The knowledge of something that we know but is not here now (*Ilm bil Ghayb/Gha'ib*; the knowledge of what is concealed from the senses).

The Holy Qur'an is quite specific about the fact that Allah alone has the knowledge of Ghayb (what is concealed) in the heavens and the earth. Qur'an tells us that there are keys to the Ghayb which are with Allah:

"With Him are the Keys of the Ghayb; none knows them but He."[567]

and that no one knows anything of Allah's knowledge except if He will. This shows that the keys of the Knowledge of Ghayb are with Allah, but He may release *"a news of Ghayb"* to the one He wills.

Similarly, Allah let the Prophet and Imams know whatever they needed to know. However, they do not have the whole knowledge within themselves. Allah would give them whatever they needed any time. It is important to understand that what the Prophets or the Imams wish to know is exactly what Allah wished to release to them. They do not wish to know anything that Allah does not want to release to them (among which are the keys to the knowledge of the unseen).

Based on Qur'an and the transmitted traditions by Ahlul Bayt, Allah has two types of knowledge:

1. The knowledge withheld (i.e., Ghayb). As we mentioned, nobody has control over this type of knowledge except Allah. Allah may inform *"a news from Ghayb"* to some of His servants, but this is different from *"possessing Ghayb."* In fact, there is a whole chapter in "Usul al-Kafi" that discusses this type of knowledge where it is clearly mentioned that neither the Imams nor the Prophets possess the knowledge Ghayb. *"The Will (Mashiyyah) of Allah operates on this knowledge. If He wishes He decrees it. And if He wishes He modifies it and does not carry it out."* [568]

2. The knowledge granted. *"This is the knowledge that Allah foreordained (Qadar, Taqdeer), He decrees it, and carries it out (with no modification). And this is the knowledge that has been passed down to the Prophet Muhammad, and then to the Imams."* [569]

If the Prophet or Imams possessed any knowledge about the future, it is this second type of knowledge (the knowledge of what has been foreordained), and NOT the first type of knowledge (the Knowledge of the Unseen).

Regarding the first type of knowledge, Qur'an states:

"Allah removes what He wills, and confirms what He wills, and with Him is the Essence of the Book." [570]

The Essence of the Book is the withheld knowledge (Ghayb) which Allah only possesses. The Prophet Muhammad (Peace be upon him) transferred whatever he gleaned from the news of Ghayb to those who qualified, as the following verse testifies:

"Neither doth he withhold grudgingly a knowledge of the Unseen." [571]

The Knowledge of the Book:

The Qur'an mentions this knowledge released to the Prophets and the Imams. This is the knowledge of what has been foreordained and the knowledge of the rules governing the universe. We know this type of knowledge as *"the knowledge of the Book."* Qur'an testifies that some Prophets and non-prophets had this type of knowledge by which they could perform many extraordinary things with the permission of Allah. We read in Qur'an that: *"So We did show Abraham the power and the laws of the heavens and the earth that he might (with understanding) have certitude."*[572]

According to some traditions, the Knowledge of The Book is a part of the Greatest Name of Allah. The Greatest Name of Allah consists of seventy-three units. These are not letters, but they are rather the knowledge of governing the universe. In one of the traditions in "Usul al-Kafi," Imam Muhammad al-Baqir ('Alaihi Assalam) explained this issue as well as the mystery of the action of Asaf, the Minister of Solomon. Abu Ja'far ('Alaihi Assalam) has said regarding Asaf: *"Verily, the Greatest Name of Allah consists of seventy-three units (Harf). Asaf possessed only one unit of it, and when he spoke it (i.e., used it) the ground between him and the throne of Bilqis (the Queen of Sheba/Saba)[573] folded/subsided so that he could take the throne with his hands, and then the ground opened out and returned to what it was originally in less than the twinkling of an eye. We (Ahlul Bayt) have seventy-two units of the Greatest Name, and one unit remained with Allah which is kept exclusively in His knowledge of Unseen (Ilm al-Ghayb); and there is no efficacy or power except by Allah, the High, the Great."* [574]

PROOF OF THE CLAIM THAT THE AHLUL BAYT POSSESSES ILM AL-GHAYB

The Messenger of Allah (Peace be upon him) said: *"I am the City of Knowledge, and Ali is its Gate. So whoever intends to enter the City and the Wisdom, he should enter from its Gate."*

The Messenger of Allah said: *"I am the House of Wisdom and Ali is its door."*

The Messenger said to his daughter Fatima al-Zahra ('Alaiha Assalam): *"Would it not please you that I have married you to the first Muslim in my nation, their most knowledgeable, and their greatest in Wisdom."*[575]

Similarly, Barida narrated:

The Messenger of Allah (Peace be upon him) said to Fatima ('Alaiha Assalam) that: *"I gave you in marriage to the best in my Umma, the most knowledgeable in them, the best in patience in them, and the first Muslim among them."* [576]

Ibn Abbas (RA) said: *"There were eighteen exclusive virtues for Ali which was not for any other person in the Muslim community."* [577]

Ibn Mas'ud said: *"The Holy Qur'an has outward and inward meanings, and Ali Ibn Abi Talib has the knowledge of both."* [578]

Imam Ali ('Alaihi Assalam) said: *"The Messenger of Allah at that time (before his last breath) taught me a thousand chapters of knowledge, every one of which opened for me one thousand other chapters."* [579]

Sa'id Ibn Musayyib as well as Umar Ibn al-Khattab said:

"No companion of the Prophet ever said 'Ask me' except Ali." [580]

The conclusion is that *"he who possesses the Knowledge of the Book"* in verse 13:43 refers to Imam Ali ('Alaihi Assalam) and no other companions.

Neither the Prophet nor the Imams possess the Knowledge of Ghayb with the special meaning used in the Qur'an, since this type of knowledge is something that belongs to Allah only. However, as the Qur'an mentions *"news of Ghayb"* has been transmitted to the Prophet Muhammad, and from that channel, it has been transmitted to the Imams of Ahlul Bayt. What they fully possess is the Knowledge of the Book described above.

"Oh no, an intellectual among her lovers?
                    a beauty like her? Faugh! Impossible!
Keep the brainy ones far from her door,
                    keep the bathhouse dung-smoke from the East Wind!
Sorry, no intellectual admitted here . . .
                    but a lover? Ah, a hundred salaams!
Intellect deliberates, Intellect reflects -
                    and meanwhile Love evaporates into the stratosphere.
By the time Intellect finds a camel for the Hajj,
                    Love has climbed Mt. Sinai.
Love comes and gags me: 'Scribbler!
                    Forget mere verse. The star-ship departs!' "
                                        - Jelaluddin Rumi [581]

"Thinking only begins at the point where we have come to know that reason, glorified for centuries, is the most obstinate adversary of thinking."
                                        - Heidegger

"The general rule is that a man must try always to be joyful, even if he has to resort to silly things."
                                        - Rabbi Nachman

A WORD TO ACADEMICS
(AND OTHER ARMCHAIR MYSTICS)

Some misguided scientists and professors of academe possess a kind of arrogance. By misguided we mean those who are content with the extent of their formal knowledge without being characterized by its inner meaning.[582] There is often a lack of humility in science and academia. To them, their intellectual-linear paradigms are the one true way to perceive reality.

Herein occurs an admonition to academics who delight in bursting the balloons of sincere seekers, academics who are arid wastelands completely lacking the sweet, flowing waters of spirituality. We quote from Giordano Bruno, *"There are more than many persons who, under their severe brows and subdued countenances, their profuse beards and magisterial and grave togas, studiously, to universal harm, contain ignorance no less vile than haughty and no less pernicious than the most celebrated ribaldry."*

Cynical and critical academics are like rats scurrying along besides a royal procession, criticizing the shape and color of the animal droppings because their vision does not extend farther. They cannot see the King and Queen and their Court. To these rats, the only significant aspect of the procession is the animal droppings.

They do not add anything to the discourse, they merely tear down and that unsuccessfully, for greatness can never be dented by the pebbles thrown by jealous and frustrated individuals who only seek to amass knowledge. They think that by finding some minor point to jump on and attack, everyone will admire them for their supposed genius; instead perceptive people realize that these critics do not have a clue about what is going on. Intellectual understanding has narrowness about it. We inform those who follow intellectual pursuits that they stand on shifting sand.

Molana Salaheddin Ali Nader Shah Angha (Pir Oveyssi) writes: *"One of the basic principles of Sufism is that you cannot know anything that is outside of you, because to know something in its totality requires that you be that entity. Since our recognition of things is based on contracts and our understanding of those symbols, and because our feelings keep shifting and our senses are continuously activated, we cannot know anything outside of ourselves. Therefore, the best place to look for the answers to our being is right within the unbounded reality of ourselves. In this context, each person is the researcher, the laboratory, and the subject of study."*[583]

The academician commonly is more interested in gaining information to swell his or her bag of facts, than to open him or herself up to psycho-spiritual transmutation. This wisdom would be wasted on those whose only interest is to rape wisdom for academic data.

Academicians of the arcane fall prey to the illusion that they can label and control that which will always be partially Unknowable, Fluid and Chaotic. To approach spirituality form an academic point of view may yield valuable information about the framework of the spiritual way, but never about the Alchemical Mysteries themselves.

This is because Spirit is as much the Irrational as it is the Rational. Academicians need to show some humility in the face of what will always be Irrational. They only see half the picture.

The Way does not consist of gathering more knowledge. Abū Madyan Shu'ayb Ibn al-Husayn al-Ansārī said: *"Worship saves you from the tyranny of formal knowledge."*

We would suggest that academically minded individuals make inquiries regarding the Noetic Sciences. They derive the word "Noetic" from the Greek word *nous* that means all-encompassing ways of knowing, including the rational and the transcendental.

The Noetic Sciences embrace all manners of interdisciplinary fields such as science, mind-body health, psychology, the healing arts and sciences, the social sciences, and spirituality. The stated objective of the Noetic Sciences is to study human consciousness, the mind and human potential. However, Noetic Science also includes in this study knowledge received intuitively, instinctively and spiritually.

The One Who is Expressed as Everything keeps no accounts!

Therefore strive each day to have a good laugh, to do something silly, sing a song, and to feel the joy of life. This is true spirituality. Solemn, gloomy and grim approaches to spirituality are paths that lead you away from the Glory of the Presence of Life.

PRACTICE

Picture in your mind's eye a raging forest fire. See the blaze howling all around you. Watch as the flames consume the forest and all the creatures in it. After you have pictured this powerful scene to yourself for a while, switch to another scenario.

Envision a campfire. A friendly blaze warms the chilled campers huddled around it. The campfire heats a large steaming kettle of soup that they have suspended over it. The campers gradually feed logs to the campfire to keep it going throughout the night. The fire helps to warm, protect, shed light, and feed the campers.

Consider that inside you a flame also burns. This flame is the fire of motivation and assertion. It is your job as an aspiring Sufi to tend that fire. You must be aware that the fire can flare up and consume you (turning into aggression), and yet you must also remember that without the fire your life would only be dying embers. You have an important task: tend the fire. Use the flames to light your way through your life, for it is only through fire that you can reach out for your goals, wants and desires. Use the internal spark to inflame your will.

Know that this flame, if left unattended, may start to engulf and destroy parts of your life and world. A raging, out-of-control person overflowing with aggression is like a violent forest-fire. Yet, an assertive, proactive, vibrant person is like a benevolent campfire.

Bless the internal flame, and be a wise steward of the fire!

"The unbelievably vast and the infinitesimally small, eventually meet."
        - from the film
        "The Incredible Shrinking Man"

"It is a mathematical fact that the casting of a pebble from my hand alters the center of gravity of the universe."
        - Thomas Carlyle

"Things lie hidden in their opposites . . ."
        - Al-'Alawī

THE BEGINNING AND RETURN OF EVERY THING

A new breakthrough in physics is giving new credibility to the arcane sciences. Dr. Christopher Monroe[584] and his colleagues at the National Institute of Standards and Technology in Boulder, Colorado did an interesting experiment with a single atom.

Through the results of this experiment they proved that one atom can simultaneously exist in two vastly separated places! Scientists have known for some time that in the quantum world, a single object can exist in a multiplicity of forms and places. Of great fascination is that not only can a single object exist in more than one place, but also these two manifestations of a single object can respond instantly to each other's experiences.

For many centuries, one possible sign of a Sufi saint is that he or she has the gift of bilocality, or being able to appear at two places simultaneously. There are many stories of Sufi Sheikhs performing this wonder. Yet we can go still further in our extrapolations, and posit that if there is One Ultimate Reality, then this new science is showing that ONE THING can manifest into an assortment of shapes and locations.

Dr. Monroe and his colleagues separated a single beryllium atom into different states in space. However, Dr. Monroe's true feat in this experiment is that he separated the two states of the one atom by a relatively enormous distance! Quantum events (such as what we have been speaking about) usually occur in the "micro scale" world, in other words, these events do not noticeably affect our every day, mundane world.

Nevertheless, Dr. Monroe separated the one beryllium atom so far apart that it represented a transition from the domain of quantum mechanics to the everyday "normal" world. In short, Dr. Monroe discovered a BRIDGE! *"Every atom babbles the mystery."*[585]

From the point of view of the scientific community, nothing is proven yet. A useful theory or model behind the experiment is not proof, they would point out to us. Ultimately (in the scientists' view), we can prove nothing.

Scientists do not speak of the Laws of the Universe. They speak of theories, i.e., the "theory" of relativity, the "theory" of evolution, and even the "theory" of gravity. Thorough testing is done to eliminate variables and to find an alternative explanation. If the theory is testable, and the results of these tests are shown to be repeatable and predictable, then a scientist would say it is verified. However, scientists know better than to expect a theory to be infallible, and so they keep it in the verification zone indefinitely.

Sufis now have a way to understand in a scientific sense, how by affecting the subtle realms, in other words, the quantum "micro" world, they may establish a relationship with the gross realms, in other words, the everyday "macro scale" world. This may provide some glimpse into why such tiny events such as lighting one candle, can provoke the universe into healing an entire human being.

"Oh my soul, do not aspire to immortal life, but exhaust the limits of the possible."

- Pindar

"Love, my child, is not a work
  of soft politesse, but of chivalry;
& he who becomes a lover's slave
    acquires the horoscope of a prince."
                    - Jelaluddin Rumi

A CITIZEN OF THE STATE OF REALITY

Real. Reality. Realize. All three words relate to the Infinite Existence. Becoming aware of the Infinite Existence requires attention and awareness. Robotically going about your tasks each day does not cause Realization. It is through the awareness that the Divine is the State of Infinite Existence that Realization takes place. Experience existence crystal-clearly, for the Complete Human functions with Unfiltered Perception.

It takes real practice, sometimes minute by minute. The Sufi must recall to him or herself the fact that the Divine is the Ultimate Condition of Existence. The Divine is not to be approached, but acknowledged.

Opening one's third eye is easy; it is keeping it open that is difficult. At first, the Murid must work minute by minute to be open to the Infinite Field of Being.

You must slow your mind. Find the still point at the center of the wheel. When your mind is slowed, you can do things that, in your everyday state of mind, you would find impossible.

Reality is the point; not as we commonly refer to the word in terms of that which is outside us, but Reality comprises EVERYTHING. This EVERY-THING includes our consciousness our feelings and all that makes us the COS-MOS on both subtle and gross levels. Do not section off a piece of REALITY and say, *"This is God."* Accept All of Reality. Become clear. They asked Al-Wasiti about the remembrance of Allah, may Allah have mercy on him. He said, *"It is the exiting from the battlefield of heedlessness into the outer space of direct vision (mushahada) on the mount of victory over fear and intensity of love."*[586]

"Mind your own business," said Virgil. "It is his fate to enter every door. This has been so designed that what is designed will be. Advice is fruitless. Say no more."

> *- Virgil to Mines in "The Inferno"*
> *by Dante*

"He truly knows Brahman who knows Him as beyond knowledge; he who thinks that he knows, knows not. The ignorant think that Brahman is known, but the wise know Him to be beyond knowledge."

> *- Kena Upanishad*

TALES FROM UNDER THE OVERPASS

*S*am and Mr. Khadir were staying as the guests of a young couple up in Spring Valley, New York. It was a particularly warm summer, and Mr. Khadir had placed a huge book on the floor, doing service as a doorstop, to let in a little breeze.

Sam walked in and noticed the book. Being an observant fellow, he also noticed that it was a book of sacred Islamic writings. He bent down to pick up the book.

"Let it lie there," said Mr. Khadir.

"Such disrespect toward any book is unworthy in the ranks of the Wise," countered Sam.

"Even more unworthy," said Mr. Khadir, "is to imagine that a book which is useful for some people should be forced upon others, whether it suits them or not. It is worse than unworthy if one does not know that there are means of communicating knowledge which communicate knowledge, regardless of what they look like."

"Its power is intact, if it shall have been turned toward earth."
- Hermes Trismegistus

"The way is the conscious reanimation of the entire body . . . No earthly man can perceive Spirit except in his own flesh. And this is no mere literary simile, but a most positive reality. You can only find your God by generating Him in yourself, in the darkness of your own body."
- Isha Schwaller de Lubicz

"Even our mortal clay, touched by Love's ecstasy, glows."
- Iqbal

"In all that is in the world dwell Holy Sparks, no things is empty of them; in the actions of men also, indeed even in the sins he does, dwell Holy Sparks of God."
- Baal Shem Tov

"From thy Murshid, the solution is to be found,
The Murshid will cause you to meet that city."
- Ballı Baba Baba [587]

"Our organism is very complicated. You must either change everything or nothing."
- Gurdjieff

THE ART OF PROPRIOCEPTION

By sectioning off parts of REALITY and stating: this part is gross, this part is subtle, one sabotages one's completion on the Way. The Way of the Sufi begins with the acknowledgment that one is living in a sleeping body. The sleeping body is almost a dead thing in which there lies potential but nothing more. It is as if the body has forgotten what it is.

The Murid subsequently then awakens to a sense of Consciousness, breathing in the perfume of the Omniconscious Unicity. Many Murids think that this is the conclusion of their work and stop at this point. Unfortunately, they have only finished half a day's work.

The next step consists of taking this new Consciousness and going back into the body. We must awaken all the workings of the human body to this new Consciousness. The body may be compared with an orchestra. This orchestra and its conductor are scheduled to perform at Lincoln Center in New York. During the flight, the plane hits turbulence. Unfortunately, the orchestra members are all standing around talking about music and do not have their seat belts fastened. Everything and everyone are tumbled around the aircraft. All the orchestra members bang their heads badly. Luckily, the conductor is wearing his seatbelt and does not sustain any injuries. When the plane regains its course, the conductor gets up to check on the musicians. He finds that they all have amnesia and to make matters worse, they are not even aware that they play an instrument, let alone aware that they are in an orchestra.

The Murid comes back into his or her body like this orchestra conductor and must slowly wake up all these individuals and help them to realize that they are musicians. The musicians then wander around sort of aimlessly, playing each other's instruments. Then the conductor must guide each of them to an awareness of their proper instrument. This is not an easy task. Nevertheless, once accomplished it is still not yet enough. The conductor must then tell each instrumentalist that he or she is part of an orchestra. The newly awakened orchestra must then be taught to play the symphony of "the living human being." For this reason, the BeSHT (Baal Shem Tov) said, *"one should have MERCY on the Holy Sparks,"* in other words, the body must be spiritualized.

This is the "struggle with the *nafs*" so often spoken about by the Sheikhs. However, we do not choose to use the word "struggle." The Prophet Muhammad (Peace be upon him) said, *"I have made my nafs Muslim."* The wise Murid does not struggle or tyrannize his or her *nafs*. He or she acknowledges them and then spiritualizes them. Struggle is a word that instructs wrongly, leading the Murid to incorrectly think of this process as being some kind of war, which it is not. Rather it is more like a kind of "wooing."

So either we can choose the Way of denial and negation that teaches us that the body should be despised or ridden like a horse, or we can choose the Way that gently brings our entire body to a Conscious sense of Divine Unicity. This is known as the "Divinization of Matter" and the "Enlightenment of the Cells."

PRACTICE

It is of great importance that you continue to develop a great love for the natural world. Through experiencing nature, you can most clearly see the creative power of *ya Qadir* – which is Fully Awake Within Itself and is able to do anything in the way It wills.

There is a scientific name for the love of nature: biophilia, or the yearning to be one with nature. A recent study concluded that if you must live or work in a room without windows, placing pictures on your walls of nature scenes reduces stress and boredom! Therefore, if you are in such a situation, seek out pictures of waterfalls, mountains, forests, rainbows, and hang them on your walls.

The Sufi who has disdain for the animals and trees of the natural world will become imbalanced in his or her being. He or she will be cut off from sympathy with the natural world. As we are all human, and as we are all manifesting as the human-animal, distaste for the natural kingdom is in effect a distaste of one's body.

There is a tale of an Amerindian woman who went through her entire life without wearing shoes. When asked why, she replied, *"I don't want to blindfold my feet."* You cannot escape the One Living Personality's Presence manifesting as the natural world and the human body. The angels worship around the Divine Throne in certain bodily positions; Muslims must assume certain postures as they pray five times a day; Yoga is an advanced spiritual process involving numerous sacred bodily movements and postures; Gurdjieff taught a system of intricate kinesthetic movements; Sufis and Hasidic Jewish people perform sacred postures and movements.

When you assume these sacred bodily postures, you enter a sacred relationship with the Spirit World. Spirit flows from the body, and spirit surrounds us, being manifest in each plant, tree, insect, and bird.

The Science of Alchemy is intimately linked with nature and its sacred awakening. Islam has had a notable tradition of alchemical writers. Renowned Islamic alchemists such as al-Iraqi, Rhazes, Maslamah al-Majriti, Bakr b. Bishrun, Ibn as-Samh, and Jabir Ibn Hayyan, have often performed alchemical transformations.

Islamic alchemy seeks to explode the Limited Self through bringing the Murid to an Awareness of Beauty. By gradually learning to love the beauty of nature, the beauty of music, beautiful manners, and the sight of a beautiful face, the more the soul expands. This breaks the bounds of Limitedness and unites the alchemist with the World Soul. The facade of nature is transcended and the consciousness of the Prophet Adam ('Alaihi

Asslam), the pure and harmonious interconnection of Humanity and Nature, is known.

"All work and no play makes Jack a dull boy."
                                    - John Ray

". . . when we are like babies, when we live as little children and behave as little children, what do we find? We find peace and tranquility. We find the unity and love which embraces everyone. We may totter and fall while embracing each other, but we will do so in unity and love. This is the quality of our play as God's children – we play with Him, and He understands our language, our speech, and our wisdom. This is the language we can use to converse with God, our Father. These are the qualities we must have to live in His kingdom. This is His speech, these are His qualities, and this is the state in which He lives."

                                    - His Holiness M. R. Bawa
                                    Muhaiyaddeen [588]

"Laughter is the remedy for 1001 illnesses."
                                    - Azerbaijani Proverb

"One of the signs of his [Muhammad's (Peace be upon him)] love and kindness for his people was that he joked with them. He did so that none of them would be so respectful that they would keep away."

                                    - Abdulaziz Ibn Ja-fer Hasara Ibn
                                    Jusey in Bagdad reports that
                                    Huseyn said to Ja-fer Ibn
                                    Muhammed es-Sadik

GLOOP

Recipe for Gloop:

In one bowl, mix:
        2 cups white glue
        1/2 cups water

In a separate bowl mix:
        1/3 cup water
        1 tbs. borax

Mix both bowls together and you will have a most unusual substance with which to experiment!

"Not chaos-like, together crushed and bruised,
but, as the world harmoniously confused:
where order in variety we see,
and where, though all things differ, all agree."
                              - Alexander Pope

"To James Lovelock, a British scientist and sometime collaborator of Lynn
Margulis, the planet itself is a life-form created by all this interlinking feed-
back. Lovelock has taken the notion of feedback and coevolution to dizzy-
ing heights. According to his Gaia hypothesis, the approximately four bil-
lion species on earth are coevolutionarily coordinated in such a way that
our planet itself is, in effect, an autopoetic structure, what Lewis Thomas
calls a giant 'singe cell'."
                              - John Briggs and F. David Peat

EARTH: INERT MATTER OR LIVING BEING?

The mistake that many people in today's society make is that they consider the Earth dead matter. The Earth is seen as ripe for exploitation and not as a sacred being that is to be cherished.

It is by entering into a sacred living relationship with the world that the Sufi announces his or her initiation. Initiation is a little like building a television set. You can build a powerful television, but it is of no use unless you plug it in. All your metaphysical reading, rituals and meditations are useless unless you enter into a Living Relationship with the world. Many Guides are good at giving out various practices, but curiously refrain from awakening the student to the sweetness of the Living Moment.

So many Murids wonder why their development is not proceeding more rapidly when they merely have to look at the way they regard nature for their answer.

If the world is dead to you, then you do not hold the keys to the Doorway of Divine Essence.

"The obvious face of Sufism at any given time, place or community may often vary because Sufism must present itself in a form which will be perceptible to any people."

- Tchaqmaqzade

"Love resides not in science and learning, scrolls and pages; whatever men chatter about, that way is not the lovers' way."

- Jelaluddin Rumi

TALES FROM UNDER THE OVERPASS

*O*ne *night, passing through Bath, New York, Mr. Khadir took Sam to a Sufi workshop. It was late as they walked into the lecture hall. They heard the lecturer concluding his evening talk.*

The lecturer was saying, "So hopefully you now understand what Sufism is and what it is not."

Mr. Khadir spoke up in a soft voice, inquiring of the lecturer, "So then, you are an expert in Sufism?"

"Yes, I have a Doctorate in Religious Studies with an emphasis in Islamic Sufism; I have done extensive research on the subject."

"Beware expert," Mr. Khadir intoned, "there is a knowledge beyond written transmission which is finer than the ultimate perception of sound intellects. The Sufi lives in the moment, and one-day you may walk into a Zikr and not recognize that you are in a Zikr. You think that a Sheikh who has a tekke, many disciples, ritual, music, and duties, is Sufism. This is not Sufism. You may be so sure of what Sufism is that your knowledge may blind you to the Reality of the Moment! Never say what Zikr is or is not. Beware of becoming so mired in your definition of Sufism that you forget the Heart of the Sultan."

Later, as Sam and Mr. Khadir were walking slowly, enjoying the beautiful, summer night, Mr. Khadir said to Sam, "Most of the great spiritual masters and teachers did not expect that their teachings would be given a defined and often a rigid interpretation at a later stage after their deaths, or that the Sufi Orders and schools of law would be named after them."

"You mentioned a word . . . Zikr, I think," Sam began, "am I correct?"

"Yes," answered Mr. Khadir.

"Then what is a 'Zikr'?" asked Sam.

"Allah (glorified and exalted be He) has supernumerary angels who rove about seeking out gatherings in which Allah's name is being invoked: they sit with them and fold their wings round each other, filling that which is between them and between the lowest heaven. When the people in the gathering depart, the angels ascend and rise up to heaven."

"So, it's a gathering, then?" inquired Sam.

"It's a kind of love-feast during which the people in attendance get drunk on the wine of love. Do you want to know what happens when the angels ascend and rise up to heaven?" hinted Mr. Khadir.

"Of course," Sam said.

"Then Allah (mighty and sublime is He) asks them - though He is most knowing about them: 'From where have you come?' And they say, 'We have come from some servants of Yours on Earth: they were glorifying You chanting *Subhana llah*, exalting You calling out *Allahu akbar*, witnessing that there is no god but You vocalizing *La ilaha il ALLAH*, praising You singing *Al-Hamdu lil-lah*, and asking favors of You in prayer'," Mr. Khadir detailed.

"How do you begin a Zikr?" asked Sam.

"You are learning, Sam," Mr. Khadir replied, "That is an excellent question. The Zikr begins by asking forgiveness from Allah ."

"But don't you think that it's ridiculous that Allah's creation has to ask forgiveness from Him?" Sam boldly ventured, "I mean it's like a table asking forgiveness from the carpenter for not standing properly. Isn't it the carpenter's fault?"

"Only when agitated waves cease to pass does the unlimited ocean of the intimate Divine Presence show its eternal serenity. Your agitation is your ego's contraction. Ask forgiveness for holding yourself back from a full-blown experience of the Limitless Reality. Even the Pride of the Universe, the Prophet Muhammad (Peace be upon him) asked Allah Most High for forgiveness. Now do you think he needed forgiveness? No. He asked forgiveness to show us that no matter how high our spiritual level, it is still possible to rise even higher. Each level has its sins of contraction and separation from Allah."

"I think that's enough for tonight." Sam said, "There's so much energy in my body from your words that I feel like I'm about to explode or something."

"Aywallah, ya Sami," said Mr. Khadir

"Paschal said, 'all history is one immortal man who continually learns.'
This is the immortal one whom we worship without knowing his name."
-Phillip K. Dick

"Why do you go to the forest in search of God?
He lives in all and is yet distinct;
He abides with you, too,
As a fragrance dwells in a flower,
And reflections in a mirror;
So does God dwell inside everything;
Seek Him, therefore, in your heart."

-Adi Granth, Dhanasri

"Instinctively man can know what is sour and sweet and similar things, but
instinctive knowledge ends there. So man must learn, and he must learn
from somebody who has learned before him."
-P. D. Ouspensky

EARTHWORM TO ANGEL

The universe initially appears to the student setting out on the Way as a hierarchy. The idea serves him or her only to a certain point, like training
wheels on a bicycle. Eventually the student matures and reaches that point of
transcendental awareness, in which notions such as hierarchies are of no use at
all.

From the Murid's perspective, reality may seem to have a hierarchical
structure, but from the perspective of Quiddity, reality is one. Al-Jami eluci-
dates this for us, *"Also, a difference in completeness or incompleteness in the*
same quiddity, such as a cubit or two cubits –of measure does not imply a dif-
ference in the quiddity itself."[589] In the Middle Ages, they thought of reality as
a great Chain of Being stretching from Earthworm to Archangel. To climb this
chain of being was deemed the path to enlightenment. However, those who
climb this chain discover that there is no chain! The chain only exists to those
who have not yet climbed it.

The notion of a hierarchical "chain of being" is a limited perception.
From the perspective of Spirit, hierarchy does not exist. The goal is no farther
than your backyard. There is no need to go anywhere to find enlightenment, for
Quiddity is present wherever you are.

PRACTICE

Obtain a tennis ball. Use your non-dominant hand to toss the ball against a wall and to catch it when the ball rebounds back to you. Practice throwing and catching the tennis ball with your non-dominant hand until you become proficient at it.

This exercise affects the Etheric Body. The Etheric Body starts to weaken and wear away at the age of thirty-five. As the Etheric Body is the template of our living existence, it is essential to continue to feed this body with Etheric energy as we get older.

Whenever we deliberately work on developing ambidexterity and the use of our non-dominant hand, this enlivens the Etheric Body. Other activities can also be utilized for strengthening the Etheric Body through use of the non-dominant hand, such as brushing your teeth, contending with eating utensils, handwriting, and shaving. Continue to give yourself new physical and mental tasks to learn, as you grow older. For example, learn a foreign language, renovate parts of your dwelling (anything concerning physically building something is excellent), moving to a different part of town (or a new town, state or even a new country), and so on. By doing these tasks you engage the mental planes that in turn reinforce the etheric templates for the body, thereby strengthening your physical selves.

"Patience is the key to relief."

- Imam Ali ('Alaihi Assalam) [590]

"I exist in a state
of perfect joy -
but this state is only fulfilled
through you."

- Fakhruddin 'Iraqi

MAKING WINE

When faced with oncoming spiritual ecstasy you must hold on for as long as you can. If you want truly to grow in your spirituality, do not let yourself pass out, fall down, groan, and shout when you feel the ecstasy coming over you. Fight it for as long as your mortal frame can bear. This containment of the ecstasy lets the ecstasy mature inside you as fruit ripening on the tree. It is like grape juice fermenting into fine wine.

During Zikr, resist the effects of trance - tears, tearing of clothes, cries, and fainting. If your intense love of the Divine Presence is controlled, you will be lead to higher and higher states and levels.

"In this path we say that every samā without an ecstasy possessing existence/finding is not truly a samā [591] True *fana* during Zikruallah happens without you willing it or not willing it. It is Allah's business. *"With ecstasy, which is the Absolute Proof, he can find his way to Truth. This is the way to true faith."* [592]

Ecstasy is also like splendid medicine. Let it have time to work its healing power within you.

"We must always change, renew, rejuvenate ourselves; otherwise we harden."

> *- Goethe*

"Non-duality is fluid and supremely alive."
> *- Shaykh Nur al-Anwar*
> *al-Jerrahi* [593]

GOING WITH THE FLOW

Some Sufis and esotericists of the past took great pride in having a stable, well-thought-out, model of the world.

Today's Sufi lives in a chaotic world, and accepts the fact that there are no Sufi catechism answers to the great questions of life. Today's Sufi realizes that reality is fluid and therefore does not accept stagnant dogma. He or she does not adopt a haughty, stuck-up, holier-than-thou, esoteric superiority. He or she is more developed than that. Emotional fluctuations, good times and bad times, times of faith and times of lack of faith, are all part of the life of today's Sufi.

According to modern physics, matter only has a tendency to exist. The world is made up of correlation and relationship. There are no clear demarcations between the observer and the observed. Physicist Nick Herbert[594] speaks of the *"oneness of apparently separate objects."* The mystics have spoken of this transcendental Unity. In other words, neither in science nor Sufism are there clear demarcations of "black and white."

Do not worry that you are not a Sufi just because you have times of doubt. This is a Living Way. As a Living Thing, it has its Ebb and Flow. Some people walk around in an ideological suit of armor that does not permit the penetration of the unexpected or the unusual. They do this to protect themselves from the Ebb Tide of Life. Walking around in these suits of armor is cumbersome and retards contact with your environment.

The Living Reality does not need rigid people. The anal retentive and heavily armored personality cannot truly deal with a universe that is multilayered and multifaceted. Today's Sufi readily admits that he or she does not know it all. This is the first step to true wisdom.

"We call upon Allah not as He exists in the high recesses of his secret abodes, but as he is here and now, within creation, within ourselves, within Gönül, which is the subtle heart, of bait-Allah."
> *- Seemi Ghazi*

"Listen, riffraff:
> *Do you want to be ALL?*
Then go,
> *go and become NOTHING."*
>> *- Fakhruddin 'Iraqi*

TALES FROM UNDER THE OVERPASS

*T*he Dean of the College of Theology called a meeting for all the adjunct professors in his office. Attendance was mandatory. After calling the meeting to order, he began,

"I am going to ask you three questions. If you can't answer them satisfactorily, I will be forced to let you all go."

All the adjuncts started worriedly murmuring to each other.

"Here" the Dean said emphatically, "is the first question. Does God exist?"

"Yes, of course," a chorus of voices answered.

"Second question. How do you know?"

Almost as quickly as they answered the first question, the adjunct faculty members responded by saying, "Well, He made everything. He is the Creator. He made the world and everything in it."

Slyly, the Dean had a faint smile on his lips as he said the following, "Now for the third question. What is He doing now?"

The professors were stupefied. Their mouths fell silent. Fear overcame them.

The spokesperson for the group said, trying to keep his voice steady, "We do not know."

"All right," the pompous Dean declared grimly, "I will give you one month to come up with an answer. If at the end of the month, you cannot satisfactorily answer me, you know what I must do. Nevertheless, I am after all the Dean of the College of Theology. I am a lenient man. If you can't come up with the answer, I will allow you to find someone who can come up with the answer, and let him speak in your stead."

The adjunct faculty filed out of the Dean's office. The general consensus was that since they had, in total, an enormous amount of accumulated knowledge, eventually they would come up with the answer. But their talk had a bit of the feel of people boasting about their football team, while secretly *being worried about the out-come of tomorrow's game.*

In the week that followed, they consulted with each other, but did not come up with an answer. They sought out all the wisest men and women they knew, hoping that they would have an answer for them. Still, they found no satisfactory response.

It was the third week. The adjuncts arranged a meeting among themselves to discuss their fate. The newest adjunct, a young woman by the name of Amera, who had not said a word up to this point remarked, "I saw a strange fellow camping in the woods behind the campus." Her voice was shaking, but she persisted. "I have the feeling that we should ask him."

"Well, I guess we don't have anything to lose at this point," the senior member responded. "So we might as well ask him."

Amera led them to the spot where Sam and Mr. Khadir were camped. She pointed out Mr. Khadir to her colleagues. Mr. Khadir saw them approaching and went out to meet them.

"Peace be upon you," he said.

"Yes," the senior member replied, while thinking they must be crazy to ask a homeless person these profound questions, "peace be upon you too.

"We are in quite a pickle. You see we are all adjunct professors in the College of Theology. Our Dean has asked us three questions, and told us that we would all be fired if we can't answer them. We were just curious what your answers might be to these questions. Will you help us?"

"Well, I don't know anything," Mr. Khadir said softly. "But I have a pretty good boss. So maybe I'll remember something he has said to me, and I can relate it to you."

"Thank you," Amera said.

The senior member began, "Does God . . ." Mr. Khadir cut him off and said, "Tell your Dean I will come and answer his questions."

The adjuncts thanked Mr. Khadir, but they were terribly worried that not only would they be fired, but be made fools of, in the process. They informed the Dean that they had someone who could answer the third question. The Dean called for a big assembly in the largest lecture room on campus. The word spread around the campus like wildfire. Other faculty members got wind of the meeting and cleared their calendars so to be sure they could be present on the day of the assembly. Then the students found out about the whole affair, and they too waited anxiously for the day to come.

Finally, the day the adjuncts dreaded arrived. There was standing room only in the lecture hall as throngs of people sought to get into the meeting place. Even the President of the University attended.

The adjunct faculty filed in along with Mr. Khadir and Sam. Murmurs and chuckles broke out when they saw Sam dressed in his rags, and Mr. Khadir's red shoes. Most of the adjuncts felt that bolting for the exit doors would be preferable to anything that might come next.

Finally, the Dean of the College of Theology called the assembly to order. He had taken the time to dress formally in his College robes. He was sure it was going to be a great day. The Dean spoke to Mr. Khadir, "I have heard that you can answer my three questions?"

"You are the Dean of the College of Theology and you are asking such questions?" Mr. Khadir's deep, authoritative voice boomed out across the assembly. Even the people standing out in the hallway could hear his voice just as well as those sitting in the front row.

"I was generous enough to ask you here," the Dean responded acidly, "and I expect you to answer the questions and not insult me. The fate of your comrades rests in you."

The Dean asked, "Does God exist?"

"Of course," Mr. Khadir answered.

"How do you know?"

"All Praise and Glory are due to Allah. Do you see the planets spinning in the orbits? Do you observe the sun hanging in the sky without any supports? Allah the Most High has made all these as signs for you. He has created universes upon universes. Your scientists still cannot tell how far their own universe extends, and have only begun to touch upon the existence of other realities. Look at a flower and tell me God does not exist. Stand in a field at night, look up at the infinite expanse of the stars and the moon shining over all, and say God does not exist. The Infinite Dynamism exists and has created all of nature that you see around you, including you Dean."

"Fine, fine," the Dean muttered, glancing sternly at Mr. Khadir. He felt smug that he was now going to blow this 'Mr. Khadir' out of the water. The Dean put the question bluntly to Mr. Khadir: "So, what is he doing now?"

"Well, I'm a guy just sitting in the audience," answered Mr. Khadir. "If I was up on the stage, on the podium, I can answer you."

"All right," said the Dean, "you can come up here if you think that will help you in any way."

Mr. Khadir mounted the stage, and made for the podium. He stride was so powerful and authoritative that the Dean jumped off and let Mr. Khadir step up onto the podium.

"You know Dean, it would really be better if I were in your professorial robes. Let us switch clothes." The audience roared with laughter. So Mr. Khadir took off his black jacket and handed it to the Dean, and the Dean took off his professorial robes and handed them to Mr. Khadir. Mr. Khadir put on the robes and motioned the Dean to take a seat in the audience.

Then the Dean, becoming a bit worried, and starting to sweat asked, "And what is He doing now?"

Mr. Khadir said, "He is making a total fool who sleeps in the woods in the back of the campus into a Dean of a College of Theology, and a Dean of Theology into a total fool."

The Dean said, trying to keep his voice steady, "You are right. You saved your companions' jobs." The assembled throng broke into wild applause and shouts of support for Mr. Khadir and the Adjunct Faculty. Amera smiled knowingly.

"I suggest that the anthropomorphic god-idea is not a harmless infirmity of human thought, but a very noxious fallacy, which is largely responsible for the calamities the world is at present enduring."
- William Archer

"Beware of the man whose God is in the skies."
- George Bernard Shaw

"The Soul of the World will be every man's personal Ipseity as well as his."
- H. Moore

CAN GOD BE LOVING AND OMNIPOTENT?

The philosopher Hume said, *"God is either loving but not omnipotent, or omnipotent but not loving. He cannot be both."* How can the God we were brought up to believe in, choose to "heal" some people, while letting other people scream out in anguish and despair? If we cannot hold God to a human yardstick of morality, then we are forever under the rule of an alien God. If His morality is different from ours than He is not part of our human experience.

Some people conclude that God is either a capricious or an unjust deity. Some concoct convoluted explanations that God's ways are not man's ways. Others just give up and declare that there is no God. The alternative to these explanations is to reveal that there is no traditional "God" at all! The object of the Sufi's great walk across the Abyss is to finally come to grips with the most painful realization: there is no traditional God! That is not to say however, that there is no Divine Reality. The Sufi must disabuse him or herself of the notion that there is a comprehendible deity up there sitting on some cloud who loves you in a friendly sort of way and exists to answer your prayers. What you pray for, you must look within yourself to find.

The Exalted Truth *"is not Other but Prior."*[595] Allah is Absolute Existence, the Ipseity (Essence), the Living Presence of Life that is Fully Awake Within Itself, the Radiance of your existence, the Perfect, That Which is Beyond Any Intellectual Understanding. Seek for Allah within your heart, not through any traditional orthodox means. Allah is in the heart of the believer, not in churches, mosques or synagogues.

The Walk across the Abyss consists in letting go of that last vestige of Mother-love that manifests as a belief in a traditional God. *"And there is manifest to them of God what they had not expected to see."*[596] We carry around with us all our adult lives a great reminiscence of our infant bond with our Mother. Since we as adults cannot be carried around at our mother's breast any longer, many people turn to religion as a kind of Great Mother. "Holy Mother Church" is an expression often used by clerics. Having a "God" up there who is watching out for you, is a way you can safely pretend as adults that there is still a kind of parent figure who cares about you. It is lonely to be without parents, so you invent God.

"If you are a believer, you will know that God will manifest Himself on the Day of Resurrection, initially in a recognizable form, then in a form unacceptable [to ordinary belief], and finally back into a form recognized [by belief], He alone being, [throughout], the Self-Manifesting one in every form, although it is obvious that one form is not the same as another." 597

The Sufi throws away all invented illusions. He or she faces life squarely and head-on. *"There is no God, but God,"* is the Sufi's battle cry. There is no conventional God; there is only the Reality (which is both the Praiser and the Praised). *"La ilaha il ALLAH"* is literally translated as: "There is no god but God." Many orthodox Muslims interpret this sentence literally, in other words, there are no other "gods" besides Allah. Those Muslims whose vision peers more deeply understand this beautiful phrase further, they interpret "gods" to mean anything or anyone that a person may make more important in their lives than Allah. Therefore, Muslims are careful to make Allah the central focus of their existence.

However, for those who have ears to hear, even belief in Allah, may be considered worshiping a false god. For the Ultimate Reality is Unknowable in Its Essence. When the believer begins to believe that he or she knows or understands his or her God, then the believer has committed a great error . . . he or she has put limitations on the Divine. When Allah is just another name for a well-cherished effigy, then error enters; however, on the other hand, when the sound "Allah" becomes a synonym for the Infinite Reality, then *"La ilaha il ALLAH"* kneads the Sufi like bread. This is the true meaning of having no images in Islam. Images can limit you in the sense that images are cutoff points to our complete embrace of Divinity in all Its aspects and qualities. For some, Allah can become a graven image when the believer insists on Allah being like a person. Imam Ali ('Alaihi Assalam) stated in "Nahjul Balagha, Khutba 1: *"All praise and glory is due the Lord, whose worth cannot be described even by the greatest rhetoricians of all times . . . None can fully understand or explain His Being however hard he may try. Reason and sagacity cannot visualize Him. Intelligence, understanding, and attainment cannot attain the depths of knowledge to study and scrutinize the Godhead. Human faculties of conception, perception and learning, and attributes of volition, intuition and apprehension cannot catch sight of His Person or fathom the extent of His might and glory. His attributes cannot be fixed, limited or defined. There do not exist words in any language to specify or define His qualities, peculiarities, characteristics or singularities."*

To believe in a God who you demand should answer your prayers according to your timetable, sets you up for all sorts of disappointments. Each time "God" lets you down when you need Him, you must invent all sorts of convoluted explanations for His lack of intervention. Some of these explanations are: *"It was not God's Will." "I did not have enough belief or faith."* The more you are let down, the stronger must you respond with explanations to fight back the avalanche of despair and disappointment buried inside you. Finally you are buried underneath this self-made mountain of rationalizations and the result is often madness.

We invite you to toss that mountain aside. Let the ego's machinations fall away. *"We know that the Cosmos is under the rule of a divine Name that makes all in it guarded."*[598] Having the courage to see the Expression of Everything, without attempting to pigeonhole It into neat little categories, is the Mark of the Sufi.

Heed our warning: It is dangerous to base your relationship with the Infinite on your prayers going answered or unanswered, attaining spiritual states and levels, or how well your life is going. For life is full of changes, and to base your spirituality on these criteria is to build your house on shaky ground.

Rather than becoming "servants" of Allah Most High, most people want Allah to be their servant, in other words to satisfy their egoic prayer demands.

We offer an alternative way of seeing and interacting with the Divine. When you believe in a God that is nothing more than a deified Santa Claus, then you are bound to be disappointed. However, if you believe in an Ultimate Reality that suffers when we suffer and laughs when we laugh, an Ultimate Reality that is our human essence, then we can know that the Divine never forsakes us.

When you need help, do not look outside yourself to some heavenly deity, look with your own heart.

We believe the focus of the Murid should be on praising and experiencing the Infinite. Concentrate on being aware of Allah's presence in your life. Focus on Its Presence all around and within you. They say that Allah Most High, who cannot fit into the entire universe, can fit inside your human heart!

Do not dwell on what God can do for you; focus on becoming Aware of God.

PRACTICE

Choose one day in the coming week in which you will go through the entire day without making any judgments about what is right, wrong, valuable, or invaluable. Buy any magazine, any newspaper, any drink, order any item on the menu, so forth and so on without discrimination or judgment.

When you dress, select clothes without thought for what looks good, what goes with what, or what effect your clothes may have on others. The Prophet (Peace be upon him) taught, *"There is a state in which all and everything is gathered - and it is the divine wisdom."* Hadrat Abdul-Qadir Al-Jilani tells us, *"To reach that level, one first has to abandon false appearances and the hypocrisy of doing things so that others might see or hear."*[599]

Make no value judgements on the driving habits of other people on the freeway with you. Avoid deciding what music to listen to, what movie to see, what book to read, and if you are adventurous enough: what to say.

Allow yourself to wander and travel through your world for one day without resorting to dividing the world up into pairs of opposites. The Journey Without Aim is often propitious.

The reality of the dualistic nature of the world will not change for those who are still lost in duality. However, your orientation toward that reality will change. You are just allowing that reality to arise within the TOTALITY of your being, rather than fragmenting your being by making value judgments. You will not be buying into choosing sides. In addition, when you allow your self to travel freely, the self will unerringly move and bring to you exactly those experiences, people and things that you need. A New World will be born from out of your Unicity.

"In God there is no duality. In that Presence, 'I' and 'we' and 'you' do not exist. 'I' and 'you' and 'we' and 'He' become one . . . Since in the Unity there is no distinction, the Quest and the Way and the Seeker become one."
- Mahmûd Shabistarî

"Beloved, Love and lover - three in one.
There is no place for Union here
so what's this talk of 'separation'?"
- Fakhruddin 'Iraqi

THE RETURNING HOME OF THE PILGRIM

Go beyond the duality of believing in God and the Devil. Even the duality presented by the notion of Divinity and Human is incorrect. Something is beyond any notion of God and Human.

Other dualistic traps are Teacher and Student, Body and Spirit, and Spiritual and Mundane.

When Allah manifests Itself to us as the Real, or the Cosmos, we perceive the Divine Names. The Names, due to their distinction from one another (although they all proceed from the same Essence), generate duality. The Names are the self-disclosure of the Essence. However, in knowing Allah as Essence, the dervish crosses over to Unity. *"Then the pilgrim returns home, to the home of his origin . . . that is the world of Allah's proximity, that is where the home of the inner pilgrim is, and that is where he returns. This is all that can be explained, as much as the tongue can say and the mind grasp. Beyond this no news can be given, for beyond is the unperceivable, inconceivable, indescribable."* So writes 'Abdu'l-Qâdir al-Gîlânî.

"All the different religions are only so many religious dialects."
- G.C. Lichtenberg

"To you who yet wander in the court of the profane we cannot yet reveal all; but you will easily understand that the religions of the world are but symbols and veils of the absolute truth. So also are the philosophies. To the adept, seeing all these things from above, there seems nothing to choose between Buddha and Mohammed, between atheism and theism."
- Aleister Crowley

THERE ARE AS MANY WAYS TO THE TOP OF THE MOUNTAIN AS THERE ARE PEOPLE ON EARTH

Do not shut life out; that is an insult to the Source. Do not stop up your ears when you hear a Guide from another Tradition speaking, or while listening to the opinion of a friend. You are putting limitations on the Ultimate Reality when you presuppose that revelation will only come from one person or book.

Sufism is a bridge; it is not a religion. *"Existence as a whole . . . is a barzakh, an intermediary realm between Being and nothingness."*[600] Therefore, we may call Sufism "The Way of Existence" or, more specifically, "The Way of the Adamic Being."

The human being is a living isthmus, who constitutes the all-important link or medium between the two poles of Reality.[601] The Human is part angel, part animal; part God and part Cosmos. *"That all important medium by which God perceives Himself as manifested in the Cosmos, and by which the Cosmos recognizes its source in God."* [602]

Sufism is the flame at the core of the world's religions; it is not religious dogma. Sufism is a sacred fountain from which Islam flowed. According to Ibn-'al-Arabi, *"Assuming the character traits of God - that is Sufism."*

"What? You seek followers? You would multiply yourself by ten, by a hundred, by a thousand? Seek zeroes!"

- Nietzsche

"Beware! You know he is human!"

- Maltese Proverb

TALES FROM UNDER THE OVERPASS

*S*am and Mr. Khadir found themselves at a New-Age center up in Woodstock, New York. There was a large bulletin board by the front door. Posted on the board were many notices. On the bulletin board, Sam and Mr. Khadir noticed a flyer that someone had posted. It read: "The Force is like Gaffers Tape. It has a Light Side, a Dark Side, and it holds the Universe together." Mr. Khadir said: "When you keep your eyes open, it is surprising how directly Allah speaks to us. Know the Reality and go beyond the light and the dark." There were also flyers about various workshops given by an assortment of teachers.

Sam was the first to speak, "I used to go to a lot of gurus when I was younger. I lived in various ashrams and took many weekend seminars. I did it all. But all these teachers let me down. They'd run off with all the ashram money, buy fancy clothes, drive in expensive automobiles, and so on. It seems like all these teachers have feet of clay."

Mr. Khadir continued scanning the bulletin board while speaking, "The Authentic Guide is often ordinary looking and average in appearance. He or she has no need to dress in a flashy manner, and no need to dress as a peasant either. There is no sign on his or her house, no flashy car in his or her driveway. The Authentic Guide does not advertise for students. He or she isn't a show-off and doesn't talk much in public. The student with spiritual vision recognizes the Guide. But what is this desire people have to find a Guide? Who wants to be taught?"

"No one," Sam replied.

"Praise the Divine, you are learning! Underneath the cloak of every Spiritual Guide is either a fallible human being or a Complete Human Being. Your developed spiritual sight will tell you if the human being that you see is or is not the Complete Human Being. You must trust your heart in choosing a Guide, do not base your choice on the amount of disciples he or she has, not what the disciples tell you about their Teacher, and not what the Teacher tells you that he or she is. Everyone is God incarnate, yet humans exist on many levels simultaneously and it is often difficult to determine the Truth about a person. There are many factors involved. For instance, Allah in the Qur'an speaks of only a few individuals who have been perfect. Others have achieved various *degrees of sanctity and holiness, but only those persons stated in the Qur'an were Perfect Human Beings. So you must remember there is a continuum in the excellence and capacity of the Sheikhs who you might have the opportunity to meet."*

"So what kind of yardstick do I use?"

"There is no simple answer here. Look beyond the outer shell of the Guide. Just because they wear an expensive suit, have many devotees, make their prayers, cultivate a persona of continental sophistication, or have an attractive foreign accent does not make them Guides. Many 'standards of squeaky clean' are cesspools of degradation, 'whitened sepulchers' is what Jesus, Upon him be peace, called them."

"How can that be?" Sam wanted to understand.

"Just because a person has developed his or her spiritual faculties does not mean that his or her psychological issues have been resolved! The two are not the same. Just because you can contemplate well doesn't mean that you have good muscle tone. Just because you can run ten miles doesn't mean that you have dealt with the issues of your childhood."

"I have met some Guides who were absolute monsters."

"Well, yes. I've noticed two types: there are those who have no spiritual development, but an immense intellect and much book learning. They intellectually manipulate their students. These people indeed are terrible monsters. However, the second type, the people who are spiritually developed yet who have never worked on their personal psychological issues are the most dangerous. They have real spiritual power, yet also have subconscious agendas which affect their spirituality and interactions with their students and the world around them in profoundly destructive ways."

"But truth is not a constant. Like all other aspects of the greater reality, it is cyclic. A concept emerges from the great void as heresy, grows into truth, decays into superstition and returns to the void."

- Camden Benares

". . . and that all the ways are circles. . . There is no straight line."

- Ibn al-'Arabi [603]

EXPERIENCING "IT"

An EXPERIENCE happens. Someone comes from a foreign country and for a while an experience happens. IT is about the experience, not the set of rules, laws and dogma that results from the experience.

A whirlwind appears for a while and then leaves. People then seek to copy the experience of the whirlwind by waving little fans. It is not possible to artificially preserve whirlwinds. Do not become spiritual taxidermists trying to preserve a dead animal. Do not accept the lifeless FORM for the dynamic CONTENT!

Whirlwinds often leave much devastation. This is the reality of whirlwinds. Do not be so naive as to expect that someone or something will help you to continue experiencing the whirlwind after it has passed through.

You can choose to:

1. Tell others about the Experience
2. Attempt to turn the Experience into a system
3. Try to forget the Experience and be "normal" again
4. Become a Whirlwind yourself

PRACTICE

Have a Mad Day! Plan a special day with your spiritual companions and deliberately do things during the day that are counter to society's norms.

There is a long and rich tradition to the Mad Day. In medieval times, it was known as the Feast of Fools. Traditionally held at the beginning of January, the Feast of Fools was a time in which all the rules and laws of society were stood on their head. Anyone, no matter how high their rank or privilege, could be made a target of ridicule or reproach.

Fools show us the inadequacy of intellect, of linear cognition. Fools show us that our reason and wisdom have limits, that prisons of dogma and doubt are all foolishness.

However, the time of misrule was not only for the poorer masses. The clergy, including some Church dignitaries, would join in the mirthful fun. Frequently the whole affair broke down into complete mayhem, and all sorts of activities, cavorting, dancing, and unbridled play were the order of the day.

In the summertime, nature blooms into a wild cacophony of blossoms, colors, twisting, coiling, twining shapes, and unquenchable growth. Therefore, we too, as human beings must allow ourselves periods of time when we can explode in a wild ecstatic burst of spontaneous energy. Nature is a part of the revelation of the Attributes of the Divine. Any spiritual teaching that frowns on spontaneity, celebration, diversity, and merrymaking is a dead and lifeless teaching. As we seek to become Complete Human Beings, it is wise to explore all the Aspects of Divine Revelation. There is a time to be serious and a time to be free.

Today we are left with faint reminders of this type of gaiety. Our New Year's Eve parties, Halloween and Mardi Gras are suggestions of what it must have been like in the Medieval Feast of Fools. The Carnival in Rio is still an authentic example of this antinomian impulse.

"God had two sons, an elder one, Satan, and a younger one, Christ. . . if good and evil were begotten in the same way they must be brothers."
- Jung

"Out beyond the ideas of right and wrong there is a field. Meet me there."
- Jelaluddin Rumi

"Sayedina Musa said, 'You abandoned a Command?' Iblis said, 'It was a test. Not a command.' Sayedina Musa said, 'Without sin? But your face was deformed.' Iblis replied, 'Oh Musa, that is but the ambiguity of appearances, while the spiritual state does not rely on it and does not change. Gnosis remains true even as it was at the beginning and does not change even if the individual changes.'"
- Husayn Ibn Mansur al-Hallaj,
The Tawasin[604]

"Whoever does not learn adherence to Divine Unity from Iblis, is an unbeliever."
- Ahmad al-Ghazzali

*"How strange! I am in love with his grace and his
       wrath,
I love these opposites to the fullest extent."*
- Jelaluddin Rumi [605]

PATRIARCHAL RELIGION'S ERROR

Christianity rejects the shadow - in its aspects as the Anti-Christ, The Four Horsemen of the Apocalypse, the Whore of Babylon, Satan, and Gog and Magog. Islam's shadow is represented by Iblis, Shaitan, Ta'usi-Melek ("The Peacock Angel"), and the Ad Dajjâl (a kind of "anti-Christ" or pseudo-Messiah and well-known liar who will appear at the end of the world). The Ad Dajjâl, "one who fools", will become visible before Imam Mahdi ('Alaihi Asslam). He will try to mislead the Muslims. He is described as having one eye in his forehead, red hair, broad-torso, large in his physical person, and cross-eyed. It is said that he is cross-eyed because he looks from his outer eyes, not his inner eyes. Interestingly, he will come with a musical instrument as his weapon to conquer people's hearts.[606] He will be killed by either Jesus the Messiah or Imam Mahdi ('Alaihi Asslam).

Melek Ta'us, worshiped as the principal of energy by the Yezidis, speaks,

"I was, and am now, and will continue unto eternity, ruling over all

creatures and ordering the affairs and deeds of those who are under my sway. I am presently at hand to such as trust in me and call upon me in time of need. Neither is there any place void of me where I am not present. I am concerned in all those events which strangers name evils because they are not done according to their desire. "[607]

It is important for the Sufi to understand the spiritual and social matrix from which Sufism has sprung. The great country of Azerbaijan (The World Navel) and the countries surrounding it, were the birthplaces of the Proto-Indo-European civilization. This civilization's myths form the foundation of many Sufi concepts and teachings. The Proto-Indo-Europeans believed that the Earth was surrounded by a Great Water. The Earth floated in the Water. In the waters swam a great serpent. In the center of the Earth was a "pole" which manifested above the Earth as a Tree, "Gleaming Mountain" or Mountain with a Tree on top of it. Below the Earth was a Well which connected with the Surrounding Primal Waters. Sufi's acknowledge that in each generation there is a being known as the *Qutub*, or Axial Centrality, the Spiritual "Pole" of the Age.

The Semites associated the serpent with the nature of the ocean itself.[608] This concept continued into the Islamic era. According to al-Kisa'i, a serpent surrounds the whole earth, and it will praise God until the day of judgement.[609] Ugaritic texts of the second millennium depict a struggle between God and a personification of water and the sea. Leviathan is called a many-headed monster. The waters also contain *baraka* (supernatural power and blessing). *"In parts of Morocco, he who prays on the sea-shore on forty mornings in succession at daybreak will obtain all he seeks, and he will have much baraka. In the sea there are forty saints, or the sea itself is a saint, a sultan, or a king. It prays day and night, and the waves are its prayers."*[610] Yet, these primal waters are not *"quite subdued even now; it is ill-tempered, irritable, and still shows a spirit of opposition to the divine will and the religion of the Prophet."*[611]

Therefore, it is wisdom to investigate and learn about the great Pagan[612] religions of the past. These religions honored the shadow. For instance in Greek mythology, Persephone (Kore) spends half the year with her mother Demeter and the other half with Hades. Some other deities to be considered include:

1. *Yama* or *Mara* the Lord of Death, as *Kala* or *Mahakala*. He is the baleful form of the Hindu Shiva.

2. *Mara,* a Buddhist demon that causes people to attach themselves to the Wheel of Birth, Suffering and Death. Mara is the attribute of mind that opposes enlightenment. Mara, although personified, is not viewed by the Buddhists as external to the self.

3. *Pluto* and *Dispater* (Underworld Deities), their names literally mean "wealth." One Sufi *tariqat* speaks of a great wealth and treasure under its tekke.

4. *Kali*, the Death Goddess, who is often depicted holding a decapitated head, or is decapitating the head of Shiva.

5. *Maeve*, a battle Goddess, who presided over battles urging men to fight, in the Irish Celtic Tradition.

The Greek gods were intrinsically not positive or negative, but a combination of both, like human beings. The Greek gods bestowed:

Plagues	and	Health
Ecstasies	and	Bloodbaths
Amazing and Inspiring Feats	and	Depraved Sexual Rapes
Prophecy	and	Deception
Curses	and	Advantages

What can the perceptive human conclude from these facts? The natures of these gods were similar to human natures, in other words, inconsistent. Thus, these deities were more personally meaningful to the individual, since the individual was not being asked of his or her religion to be inhumanly perfect.

Apollo offered the great esoteric insight of all time: *"Know thyself."* The above gods were personified aspects of the qualities of Allah. The divine manifests a theater of experiences. A diamond, when a bright light is shown upon it, offers up a rainbow of colors. Each color is clearly perceptible, but each has its origin in the Diamond, each only exists because of the diamond, and each has no separate existence apart from the diamond.

The pagans became mesmerized with the colors and did not realize the diamond from which the colors emerged. Nonetheless, the perceptive one can glean wisdom concerning the nature of manifestation from the pagan concepts of deity.

The rejection of the Shadow is one of the greatest failings of patriarchal religion. Life and Death are realities to our psyche. They are a package deal. Christianity tries to paint the Devil/Evil/Death as the enemy of God/Goodness/Life. Rather than giving the Devil his due, Christianity has created a bizarre and distorted image of the Shadow. C. G. Jung wrote these words of wisdom: *"With him God does not only contain love, but, on the other side*

and in the same measure, the fire of wrath, in which [Shaitan] himself dwells."
613

Even the Christian cycle of Easter recognizes that without death, nothing would be possible. It is said in the Bible that the Prophet Jesus ('Alaihi Assalam) visited the Underworld for three days after his death. In Islam it is said, *"If you let down a rope it would fall upon God [He being above and below]."*614 Regrettably, in Christian Tradition, Christ is said to have destroyed the powers of darkness, which thereby denies acknowledgment and acceptance to the other half of existence.

Christianity would have its adherents deny their shadows, and would have them believe that if they identify with the shadow they will be cut off from God and sent to Hell for eternity. Yet, in spite of all the threats of fire and brimstone, even the God of the Christians cannot sever the poles of our human psyches. Peter Ackroyd writes, *"Christ was the serpent who deceived Eve."* The Biblical Jesus tells us to forgive our enemies . . . is it not time for Him to forgive Satan, His enemy?

In Islam, Satan is known as the *Shaitan*. When Allah created humankind, He asked the angels to bow down before His creation. *Iblis*, the Shaitan, refused. For that act of refusal, he was thrown out of paradise. However, various Sufis are in sympathy with Iblis, in the sense that he refused to bow down to anyone, except Allah! The Qur'an contains at least seven levels of meaning,615 and within those levels are subtle revelations of the role of the Shaitan in creation.

Shaitan is a necessary force that is negative but absolutely essential to sustain life. In electricity there must be a positive and a negative. Without the negative there is no electricity and without electricity there is no light.

The pre-Islamic Pagan Bedouin tribes worshiped "the God, the Divinity" by the name of *Allah*. Allah was the personification of the divine world in its highest form, the creator of the universe and keeper of sworn oaths. In the *Hejaz,* three goddesses had pride of place as the "daughters of Allah." The first of these was *Allat,* mentioned by Herodotus under the name of *Alilat.* Her name means simply "the goddess," and she may have stood for one aspect of Venus, the morning star, although hellenized Arabs identified her with Athena. She was the Goddess of the Arabs of the *Nadid.* Next came *Uzza,* the All-Powerful," whom other sources identify with Venus. She was the Goddess of the Quraish confederation. The third was *Manat,* the goddess of fate, who held the shears which cut the thread of life and who was worshiped in a shrine on the seashore. She was the Goddess of the northern Arab tribes. The great god of Macca (al-Mukarramah) was *Hubal,* an idol made of red carnelian.616

The Arab leader, Kusayi, in the fifth century centralized the economic powers of Macca (al-Mukarramah). To this end, he brought together all the divinities worshiped by the Maccans into a single shrine inside the Ka'ba. The pilgrimage had already been in existence from extremely ancient times. *"The pre-Islamic version of the Hajj (Pilgrimage to Macca) was performed in the mountain wadi of 'Arafa, to the east of Macca. It took place in Autumn, and began on the afternoon of the ninth day of the "pilgrimage-month". It began at the wide, lower end of the wadi, in front of a hill called the "mountain of Beneficence" (or Rain, "Rahma")."*[617]

Allat is extremely significant for those Sufis who wish to know the quintessence and ultimate secret of Sufism. Prior to Muhammad (Peace be upon him), Hindu merchants frequently passed through Macca (al-Mukarramah). Ancient Indian *Vedic* texts refer to Macca (al-Mukarramah) as a place where *Alla* the Mother Goddess was worshiped. In Sanskrit, Alla means "mother." This name was connected to the Hindu Goddess *Ila*. She was the consort of the Hindu God *Shiva* in his form known as *Il*, and this form of Shiva was known and worshiped in pre-Islamic Macca (al-Mukarramah). There was a great deal of cultural and spiritual interchange between the merchants of Macca (al-Mukarramah) and India. Some Islamic scholars state that Allah is a contraction of *Al'llah*, which may suggest an ancient Hindu derivation.[618] *Al'lat,* "Mother of the Gods," "Goddess of Fertility," and "Goddess of War," was one of the most adored deities of the pre-Islamic pantheon. Her worship was not only confined to Macca (al-Mukarramah) but her worship spread throughout the Near East. Perhaps the reason for Her importance was that She was also the Goddess of shepherds and caravan travelers. Before the Black Stone (*Hajar al Aswad*) was placed as the cornerstone of the Ka'aba, it was worshiped at the first shrine of Al'lat. After that, it was fitted into a silver band that they had shaped in the form of the female vagina. Some scholars believe that Al'lat was the consort of Allah, taking Al'lat to be a feminine form of Allah.[619] The concept that Allah is the feminine form of the Ultimate Reality is the inner secret of the most esoteric mysteries of Islam. Ibn 'al-'Arabi pronounced: *"True divinity is female, and Mecca is the womb of the Earth."* Because he said the godhead was feminine, they accused Ibn al-'Arabi of blasphemy. To survive in a patriarchal society, Sufis disguised their mysteries in many allegorical symbols. Therefore, the Murid must be aware that there is a secret mystery hidden in the tales of the Sufis.

Later, as the Sufis entered Europe through Spain, they brought the mysteries of sacred intercourse. The *Minnesingers* and *Bards* copied the Sufi form of worship of the Goddess and of Woman. They sang in the courts of Europe about the mysteries of spiritual love. The Christian church eventually persecuted them for their musical revelation of the true nature of Allah.

The sublime and radiant Sufi saint Shemsi Tabriz took his name from the Arabic word for sun, that is, *Shams*. Interestingly, this word was derived from the Babylonian Goddess *Shamash*.

Orthodox Muslims teach that there cannot be idols in Islam. Yet listen to Ibn al'Arabi on the subject, *"Indeed, in every object of worship it is [in truth] God Who is worshiped ... for in every object of worship there is a reflection of the Reality, whether it be recognized or not."*[620] Ibn al'Arabi is not making a case for polytheism. Let those who have ears to hear, hear! He is awakening his listeners to the fact that however Allah manifests Its Reality, the Sufi must submit him or herself to that manifestation.

In Sufism, it is taught that sometimes Allah opens Its *Jalal* (Majesty) and sometimes Its *Jamal* (Beauty). Another way of describing this mystery is by stating that the characteristics of Allah can be separated into two categories: the names of gentleness *Lutf*, and the names of severity, *Qahr*.

Allah does not always open Its *Jamal*. The Murid's assignment is to unite the *Jalal* and the *Jamal*. These two are projected from, and absorbed back into, the black nothingness called Allah's *Kamal* - a state of invisible, neuter, annihilation. *Jalal* is Allah's power, force and strength. It often manifests as trials and tests for the Murid. *Jamal* is Allah's sweetness, compassion, understanding, and forgiveness. *Kamal* is the whispered breath of nonexistence.

Systems theory in modern physics proposes that all systems initially exist in a state of quasi-stationary equilibrium between "driving" and "restraining" forces.

Murids think that the world should be all *Jamal*, that is, all love and kindness. On the contrary, Allah often gives to us through Its *Jalal*, that is, through Its Wrath. *"Every rational person must know that the journey is based upon toil and the hardships of life, on afflictions and tests and the acceptance of dangers and very great terrors."*[621]

Jamal is for the next world, not this one. Ponder the lives of the Ahlul Bayt. They were the *most* beloved of Allah, yet their lives were filled with sorrow, suffering and even martyrdom. Endurance of indignities is part of the tests of Allah's *Jalal*. The Sheikhs have said that Murids should be glad when misfortune comes upon them, because that means Allah is giving to them, and that they should worry when things are going too smoothly, because Allah's wisdom does not come in comfortable placidity and satiety.

Dr. Javad Nurbakhsh describes the above approach as follows, *"The Sufi is one who loves both grace and wrath, not one who is gladdened by the grace and depressed by the wrath."* [622]

Allah has revealed to humankind Ninety-Nine names, and has kept one secret for Itself. However, according to religious scholars[623], Allah has three thousand Names. One thousand known to the angels, one thousand known by the prophets, three hundred in the Torah, three hundred in the Psalms, three hundred in the New Testament, and Ninety-Nine in the Qur'an. This does not even take into account the Names that the Primordial Source of the Universe may have chosen to reveal to beings in other parts of our galaxy or in the fathomless other galaxies of the Universe. The Sufis know that the number of Allah's names is Infinite.

Rather than approaching our spirituality with an "either/or" dualistic mind-set, we suggest that we replace the either/or with a transcendental "and". This will enable us to discover a way of relating to the universe that permits us to make some sense of pain and suffering. The fact is that there is no shelter from the storms of life. Rather than stubbornly living in denial by believing that shelter is possible, we propose that humanity embrace a Great Mystery that manifests as storm AND shelter.

It is a mistake to say that the thorn does not have anything to do with the rose, or that the thorn is the absence of the rose. *"By the mercy bestowed on pain, pain was created."*[624] The thorn is as much rose bush as the rose is. The thorn has as much validity as the rose. Let this Rose Bush be the symbol of the Heart of Real Spirituality. We are not asking you to like the thorn, but we are asking you to see it as an expression of Allah.

When we speak of the Rose Bush, we speak of a Totality, a Unity of Being. One final note: rather than speaking of right and wrong, good and bad, the Murid should concentrate on his or her actions. It is not what a person says that matters, but what he or she does.

"All the images we have for God come from images of ourselves."
                              - Meister Eckhart

"I am the mirror of thy face; through thine own eyes, I look upon my countenance."
                              - Semnani

"Nature is the immense shadow of man."
                              - Ralph Waldo Emerson

PEEK-A-BOO

When people look at a beautiful natural panorama, they enjoy it because they are looking at themselves. People intuitively sense their true knowledge of one aspect of their Reality when they look upon the natural world. Human beings are the stuff of nature, so when humans look at nature they are pleased, for they see themselves.

The "Creator" is in actuality human beings love for themselves that they have projected out onto the environment. This process is akin to the phenomena of an echo or a mirror.

We cannot love anything but the Omniconscious Unicity. Humanity has the power of imagination, the *quwwat al-khal*, as does the Omniconscious Unicity. When the Omniconscious Unicity uses this power, worlds are created. When humanity uses this power, the Omniconscious Unicity is created. In our eye, the Omniconscious Unicity sees Its eye. *"For Divinity [ulāhiyah] implies and requires that which depends on it, just as Lordship requires servanthood, since neither would have any existence or meaning otherwise."* [625]

Yet, as much as Creator and Created mutually depend upon one another, there is a more profound fact of Reality that must be always kept in mind by the Murid, *"If He were to be veiled from the world for the blink of an eye, the world would vanish at one stroke."* [626]

"Until mothers feel the pain of childbirth, the child finds no way to be born."

- Jelaluddin Rumi

"I am a great and sublime fool. But then I am God's fool, and all His work must be contemplated with respect."

- Mark Twain

"Sour godliness is the devil's religion."

- John Wesley

"The Dervish is one who know this world, but is not fooled by it, and who knows the Spirit world and does not fool people about it."

- Sufi saying

TALES FROM UNDER THE OVERPASS

*I*t was the afternoon. Sam and Mr. Khadir were in the lower region of New York State. A gentle sunlight bathed the rolling hills. Pastureland predominated in this part of the state. They noticed a man in overalls herding his sheep to a different pasture. He waved to Sam and Mr. Khadir as he passed.

Mr. Khadir remarked: "This shepherd reminds me of the Yezidis."

"The what?" Sam puzzled.

"The Yezidis, one of the oldest religions. It came from India into what is known today as Iran and Kurdisthan."

"There is something fascinating about the ancient past . . . there's so much that we don't know, so much that's been lost in the shadows of time," mused Sam.

"Once upon a time," began Mr. Khadir, "a Yezidi shepherd was bringing his flock home to the mountain cave where he lived. Suddenly the sky was torn asunder by a blinding flash of lightning whilst, almost simultaneously, there followed such a roar of thunder as would have deafened a giant. The shepherd flung himself down upon the bare rock, and hiding his face, prayed to the great Power of Life and Death that he might be spared. Then, looking up, he saw an Angel standing in the middle of the Heavens with an enormous spear in his hand. There followed another terrifying clap of thunder, and something was hurled from the sky down onto the crags below. A great gust of wind arose and swept over the mountain tops. The valley shook. Then all was quiet again. Gradually recovering from his great shock the shepherd rose from the ground and looked around. He saw that a huge cedar had been struck by the lightning and was lying across a deep ravine. On the further bank lay a beautiful peacock badly hurt but still alive. The shepherd crawled across the fallen tree *trunk and took the dying bird in his arms. After washing its wounds in a near-by stream, he carried it into the cave which was his home. Without any thought of sleep he tended it throughout the long night. When the morning came the peacock had completely recovered and spoke to the shepherd in a human voice, saying: ' Be not afraid, man, you were kind to me in my misfortune, so I will reward you and all your descendants. I am the Spirit of Evil thrown out of heaven by my twin, the Spirit of Good. But I am not conquered. On earth, as in Heaven, I shall continue the struggle. Amongst men I shall spread sorrow and instill my poison in their hearts so that the great conflict will be implanted within them. Teach your descendants to accept Evil as you have accepted me. Be compassionate toward evil both in yourselves and in others. Delight me with songs. Placate me with prayers. Tend me as you have tended me last night.' So saying, the Angel Peacock, Melek Taus as we call him, spread his wings and flew away over the inaccessible mountaintops. That is why the Yezidis, the descendants of that compassionate shepherd, sing hymns to appease and glorify the Spirit of Evil to this very day. Their hymns are scorned by the rest of the world. Both Christians and Muslims alike hate and persecute them. They call them 'Muraddun'— Infidels and Devil-Worshippers. Their priests, Qawasls, travel secretly and do not wear priestly robes. They carry with them, hidden away from Muslim and Christian eyes, the effigy of a peacock. When they pray, they do not turn toward Macca like the Muslims but toward the Polar Star, the immovable source of light in darkness, the point of the axis round which the whole universe revolves. They honor Wednesday as their day of rest, not Friday like the Muslims, nor Sunday like the Christians. A quarter of all they earn they give to the poor. Churches they have none, for if they built them they would be at once destroyed by either Muslims or Christians. But they are not angry. They do not hate their persecutors because their religion bids them to be tolerant.*

"Sam, we can lean much from the Yezidis when it comes to the issue of good and evil," advised Mr. Khadir.

"But haven't you taught me that Yazid was a terrible man? How can you praise a group that takes its name from that tyrant?" Sam was afraid that Mr. Khadir was being hypocritical.

"They do not take their name from that tyrant. The name 'Yezidi" is certainly derived from 'yezad,' meaning 'angel.' The Yezidis are one of the most ancient religions on the face of the earth. Their origins are shrouded in mystery. Later, they were influenced by Christianity and Islam, and two people, Yezid Ibn Unaisa and a Sheikh Adi strongly influenced contemporary Yezidi belief. Some think that the Yezidis were originally a Harijite sub-sect, akin to the Abadiya, bearing the name of their founder, Yezid Ibn Unaisa. Others talk about their connection to Saraf ad-Din Abu-l-Fadail 'Adi Ibn Musafir Ibn Ismael Ibn Mousa Ibn Marwan Ibn Al-Hassan Ibn Marwan. Yes, these two men *strongly influenced what we know as Yezidism today, but they were ports on a great spiritual river that stretches back into the far distant horizon. However, look within Sam! You know better than to judge a thing by its outward appearance. The inner essence of Yezidi beliefs gives us a deeper understanding of how the Sufi should honor Allah no matter how Allah manifests to the Sufi. Remember, I am dangerous, I destroy the illusion of duality and artificiality."*

Later along the road, Sam and Mr. Khadir came upon a hitchhiker. The fellow was wearing a faded tie-dyed shirt, jeans, sandals, and wore his hair long. Sam calculated that his age was about fifty-five.

Mr. Khadir in a warm and friendly voice called out to the fellow to come and say hello. They all fell to talking and soon were on the topic of spirituality. Mr. Khadir was speaking about the joy of experiencing Omniconscious Unicity.

The hitchhiker spoke, "I went to church for thirty years. Then I got into meditation and yoga. I fasted for days, weeks, and once even for three months at a time, and yet I never found any of the spiritual joy that you speak of. I took my devotion seriously and faithfully carried out my prayers and religious duties each day."

"If you had fasted and gone to church for three hundred years, you would never find IT," answered Mr. Khadir.

"Huh?" the man did a double take.

"You're selfish."

"I'm selfish?" The hitchhiker began, his voice shaking with anger. "You've got to be kidding. I could have been going out to concerts, hanging-out and getting high all that time. Instead, I spent all my time in prayer and in church."

Mr. Khadir smiled and kindly said, "You think you have been making great sacrifices and suffering for your religion. However, in reality, you have taken the chicken's way out. You truly haven't done anything that would be a real challenge. Have you ever seen those pictures of Middle Eastern women who wear the veil?"

"Yes, they are covered head to toe in fabric," the hitchhiker said impatiently.

"Well," Mr. Khadir began, "you are right. A veil separates you from their beauty."

The hitchhiker found he was being drawn into the conversation. He said, "Okay, so what conclusion am I supposed to draw from that?"

"Simply that all your praying and churchgoing has been a veil separating you from God, rather than a means to draw you closer to Him."

"Well, then what should I do?"

"You wouldn't want to know."

"Probably not. You probably want me to send in $1,500.00 to some post office box, and they will send me the secret to life."

"No, no $1,500.00, but it will still seem crazy to you.

After a moment, the hitchhiker admitted begrudgingly, "Frankly, I'm getting pretty desperate. I've searched all my life for God or the Omniconscious Unicity as you call IT, and I haven't had much success. And I don't think I have all that many years left."

Mr. Khadir looked him straight in the eye and spoke with a directness and immediacy that stood Sam's hair on end.

"Go the nearest barbershop and get a crew-cut. Buy yourself an expensive business suit. Purchase a lady's handbag and fill it with bubble-gum. Go to a shopping mall and walk around announcing, 'Anybody who gives me a whack on the head will have a free piece of bubble-gum!' Then go into a local church during Sunday service and do the same thing."

"Are you crazy? I can't do that," responded the hitchhiker, trying to keep his voice steady, "can't you give me some prayers to say, a candle to light, or perhaps another remedy?"

"Stop it!" yelled Mr. Khadir, "if you can't make a royal fool out of yourself, you are never going to attain to Absolute Freedom. You take yourself so seriously. Get rid of your mask of tragedy and let spontaneity enter your spirituality. You don't have to hand out bubble-gum, although that would be the best way for you to find God, but you do have to immediately begin to remove all vestiges of vainglorious pride, self-importance, and the sense that you are the one who must find God. It is important to get rid of all thoughts that one is chosen or special. This idea of oneself as being distinguished is subtle and insidious, especially among those who are indeed chosen. To accept the gift of 'specialness', or friendship with Allah, you must yield up all awareness of your special qualities. Become a fool, and let God find you!"

"But I need to find a wise and holy man to teach me," the hitchhiker murmured, glancing sternly at Mr. Khadir.

"If you saw him, would you recognize him?"

"I'm not sure."

"For the person who has perception, a mere sign is enough. For the person who does not really heed, a thousand explanations are not enough," Mr. Khadir murmured, glancing sternly at the hitchhiker. Mr. Khadir went over to a nearby tree and said intently, "I will tell you this. I have heard that these holy men can take a tree and bend it this way and make the entire tree prostrate itself." As he was saying this, the entire tree began to prostrate itself before Mr. Khadir.

"Well," the hitchhiker said somewhat satisfied, "at least you've given me some information on how to identify a holy man. I thank you for that much."

"There's one more thing that can help you identify a holy man."

"Please tell me so I can at last find a True Guide," the hitchhiker said plaintively.

"A True Guide will come close to you like this," as he spoke Mr. Khadir closely approached the man. *"He will then take hold of your arm like this."* At which point, Mr. Khadir grasped the man's arm. *"Then he will stretch this branch of this tree like this,"* all the while Mr. Khadir was doing exactly what he was describing. *Then he will stretch the branch, like this, and let go."* WHACK! The branch whipped up hitting the hitchhiker smack in the face!

Suddenly the hitchhiker's world began to spin around him, he felt all his intellectual moorings give loose, his everyday reality was tearing apart, and he saw Mr. Khadir standing in front of him. Splendorous Light was streaming from Mr. Khadir's face. The wind in the trees was speaking to the hitchhiker. A voice spoke, *"Look through your gaze. Remember, however you look, that is how you will receive."*

"There were six women who were given prophecy: Eve, Sarah, the mother of Moses (Yukabid), Hagar, Asiya, and Mariam."
- al-Ash'ari

"Love and beauty made a pact in pre-eternity never to be separate from one another."
- Ruzbihan Baqli

"Then we gave her the good news of Isaac, and after Isaac of Jacob."
- Qur'an 11:71

"The oceans of sainthood and prophethood interpenetrate each other."
- Ruzbihan Baqli

ABU MUHAMMAD IBN HASM AL-ANDALUCI ON NUBUWWA OF WOMEN [627]

This is a glimpse into some intellectual debates Muslim scholars had in the past about the question of the possible prophethood of certain women. Muslims debated this issue without fear of sanction, and without relying on accepted dogmas. Ibn Hazm (d. 456 Hijri) lived in the 11th century in Muslim Spain (Andalucia). This is a piece from that era. This is his position about the sensitive issue of the Prophethood of women. He has a strong argument. What follows is his view and additional views of other Muslim scholars such as Qurtubi, Ibn Hajjar al-'Asqalani, Imam al-Nawawi and others. This piece is very relevant as we try to find out the position of women in our society and understand the differences between what we have inherited as customs and what is the True Reality of Prophethood.

Abu Muhammad said, *"This is an issue we know of no debate about it except here in Cordoba and in our time. A group of people denied that Prophethood could be for women and made everyone that claims as such an innovator (Mubtadi'). Another group said that Prophethood is possible for women. A third group abstained from discussing this issue. We find no proof for those who claim that Prophethood is impossible for women other than that some of them denied it based on the Qur'anic verse, '(O Muhammad!) Whenever we sent before you Messengers to whom we have revealed Our messages, they were but men.'*

"This is a verse none can deny as nobody claimed that Allah sent women Messengers. The issue here is about Prophethood (Nubuwwa) and not Messengership. Henceforth the need to understand the meaning of the word 'Prophethood' in the language in which Allah spoke to us (i.e., Arabic). We find that this word is taken from Inba' (prophecy) which means I'lam (revela-

tion). So whomever Allah tells him about what will be before it comes to pass, or reveals to him informing him about a certain matter, then he is a Nabi (prophet) without any doubt."

This (Prophethood) should not be understood as *Ilham* (inspiration) which is natural as Allah said in Surah al-Nahl, *"And behold! Your Lord has inspired the bees with this: 'Build thy hives in the mountains, and the trees and the creepers over trellis, then drink nectar from every kind of fruit, and follow the ways made smooth by your Lord.' From its belly comes out a fluid of varying hues wherein is healing for mankind. Here is indeed a sign for those who ponder over it."*[628]

Revelation, which is *Nubuwwa* (Prophethood), is information sent from Allah to a particular being. This should be understood differently from the previous case.

This revelation can be transmitted by one of either ways: through an angel that comes to him or her, or through a message directly revealed to him or her, and this is a knowledge from Allah to whom He gives, with no transmitter or teacher. Allah revealed in the Qur'an that He sent angels to women to deliver to them truthful revelations from Allah. They gave glad tidings to the mother of Isaac (Sarah). Allah says, *". . . And his wife was standing by; hearing this, she laughed. Then we gave her the good news of Isaac, and after Isaac of Jacob. She said, 'Woe be me! Shall I bear a child now when I have grown extremely old, and this husband of mine has also become old? This is indeed a strange thing.' The angels said, 'What! Are you surprised at Allah's decree? O people of Abraham's household! Allah's mercy and blessing are upon you. Indeed, Allah is worthy of all praise and glory.'"* [629]

This is a direct address from the angels to the mother of Isaac, about the blessing Allah will bless her with - Isaac, then after Isaac – Jacob, then their testimony about the power of Allah and her astonishment concerning the matter of how Allah makes things possible.

There could not be an address from an angel to a human being, except that being was a prophet. We find also that Allah sent Gabriel to Mary mother of the Prophet *'Isa* - Jesus (Peace be upon him) with a message and told her, *" ... I am a mere messenger from your Lord and have been sent to give you a pure son."* [630]

This is a true Nubuwwa with a true revelation and a clear message from Allah. The Prophet Zacharias ('Alaihi Assalam) used to find with her *Rizq* (food) for this he asked Allah to grant him a trustworthy son.[631] We found also that Allah revealed to Yukabid, mother of Moses, that she shall throw her son into the Yam river and she shall neither worry or have grief and promised her He shall return Moses to her and make him a prophet and a messenger. With no doubt, this is a true Nubuwwa (revelation) and a logical consequence of our premises.

If she were not sure of the revelation that Allah would return her son to her, either that this was a mere vision or a feeling she had, she would be – by throwing her son in the Yam - committing a crazy act and a heinous crime against herself. If one of us did such an act, he or she would be an extreme transgressor or a crazy person that experiences the agony and the (psychological) consequences he or she has to go through - (probably) in a *bimaristan* (a mental institution).

Such logical analysis none could deny. Therefore, it becomes with assuredness, true that which came to (Yukabid) - of throwing her son in the Yam – was a revelation, like that which was revealed to the Prophet Ibrahim (Peace be upon him) in his dream. He was ordered to slaughter his son. If the Prophet Ibrahim (Peace be upon him) was not a true prophet, and had he slaughtered his son for a dream he saw or a doubt he had in himself, it would be true that whoever does such an action would not be of the Prophets but an insane person. This nobody would doubt.

Hence, their (the women's) Prophethood becomes obviously true. We find that Allah while mentioning the prophets in Surah Mariam, He mentioned Mariam among them and then said, " *These are the Prophets on whom Allah bestowed His favors. They were from the descendants of Adam, and from the seed of those whom we carried in the Ark with Noah, and from the seed of Abraham and of Israel. They were from those whom we guided aright and made our chosen ones. They were tender-hearted that whenever the Revelations of the Merciful were recited to them, they would fall down prostrate, weeping."* [632]

This is a description of all of them. One should not single her out as a special case, to be treated separately. Now the saying *"and his mother a Siddiqa"* (Qur'an) does not deny her the right to be a prophet as Allah said, *"Joseph, O Siddiq!"*[633] and as is known he is a true prophet and a messenger; and this becomes now clear. From Allah only, one seeks guidance. We can also include along with them (Yukabid and Mariam) the wife of Pharaoh, as the Prophet Muhammad (Peace be upon him) said, *"There are many persons among men who are quite perfect but there are not perfect among women except Mary, daughter of Imran, and Asiya, wife of Pharaoh."*[634] Now perfectness (*kamal*) for men can only be for some messengers-for those who are *"less than them"* are not perfect. His (the Prophet's) particularization to Mariam and Asiya (the wife of Pharaoh) was a privilege for both of them over all those to whom Prophethood was given from among women, with no doubt, as those who are a degree less than them are not perfect.

Henceforth, it is clear that these two women became perfect, more than any other women, and even if these women were prophets. From Qur'anic texts we find that Allah says, *"(O Muhammad), most surely you are of those who have been sent as Messengers. Of these Messengers, We have raised some above others in rank. "*[635]

So the perfect of one's gender is the person who excels in his or her perfection and none of this person's gender can reach him or her. They are the messengers from among humanity, of whom we find our Prophet Muhammad (Peace be upon him) and Prophet Ibrahim ('Alaihi Assalam).

After referring to Surah Tahrim, Ayah 11, Ibn Hajar al-'Asqalani[636] says, *"We can infer from this restriction of description (hasr) that they (Mariam and Asiya) were prophets as the perfection in human beings can only be for prophets (Anbiya'), then for Saints (Awliya'), then for the Truthful (Siddiqin), then Martyrs (Shuhada'). If they were not prophets then it would be necessary that there is no Waliyyah, Siddiqa, or Shahidah in the ranks of women."*

On the other hand, we find these characters are present for quite a number of them. It is as if he said, *"And there were no prophets among women except so and so."* Had he also said that *"the character of Siddiqa, Waliyya or Shahida was only for so or so,"* then we would infer that these characters cannot be for other women.

Another possibility would then be to assume that there is another type of perfection other than Prophethood. As such, the proof can no longer hold, and Allah knows best. Anyhow, the Prophet meant *"of those who came before his time."* Now he mentioned only 'Aesha of those of his time. We can hardly infer that this is a clear declaration that 'Aesha is better than other women, for *Tharid* is better than other food in the easiness of storing it, and the easiness in digesting it. It was the best food in their time. There is another addition in Tabarani after Mariam, daughter of 'Imran, and Khadija, daughter of Khuwailid, and Fatima, daughter of Muhammad.

Qurtubi said, *"The truth is that Mariam is a prophet as Allah revealed to her through an angel. But Asiya, there is no clear proof of her prophethood."*

Kirmani said, *"It should not be understood from the word perfect (kamal) a proof of her Prophethood as the word is used to describe the completeness of a certain thing and the highest point it can reach. So the meaning is: she reached the best of all qualities that women can have."* He then said *"It has been reported that there is consensus between scholars (Ijam') that there is no Prophethood (Nubuwwa) for women."*

Al-Ash'ari was reported as saying *"There were six women who were given prophecy: Eve, Sarah, the mother of Moses (Yukabid), Hagar, Asiya, and Mariam."* The condition for such a prophecy is that whoever an angel talked to about a rule of Allah or revelation of what will happen then he or she is a prophet. In addition, for him or her, it has been proven that the Angel came to them from Allah with different matters, and there are clear indications that a direct revelation was given to some of them in the Qur'an.

Ibn Hajjar then brings the above testimony of Ibn Hazm. Imam

Nawawi,[637] on the other hand says this hadith is used as a proof by those who believe in the Prophethood of women, however the majority (*Jumhur*) of Muslim scholars do not approve of the Prophethood for Mariam and Asiya. In the interpretation of this hadith, he follows the same line of reasoning as that of Kirmani.

"The exotic flavors and the vodka in which the famous 'Toasts to the Idiots' were drunk ('idiot' in this case having its original Greek meaning of private person, that which in myself I am) did not make things easier. But easiness was not the aim. The patriarchal host, massive of presence, radiating a serene power at once formidable and reassuring, dispensed this 'food' in various ways, always unexpected; sometimes in thunderclaps of rage, sometimes telling a story that only one of all the table would know was meant for himself, sometimes merely by look or gesture thrusting home the truth. Masks were mercilessly stripped off. Beneath the exacting benevolence of Gurdjieff's gaze everyone was naked." [638]

- P. Travers

SARMOUNG, SARMOUNI, SARMOUN, SARMAN

The word comes from the old Persian. It, in fact, appears in some of the *Pahlawi* texts. There are many interpretations of the word. It is the word for "bee." Bees have continually been a metaphor for those who collect the "honey." In other words, it symbolizes those who collect the ancient wisdom and safeguard it for future generations. A collection of legends exist that are well-known in Armenia and Syria. This collection is entitled: "The Bees." The legends were later revised by Mar Salamon, a Nestorian Archimandrite who lived in the thirteenth century. Possibly the collection of legends refers to a mysterious energy transmitted in symbolic design from the time of Zoroaster.

The *"man"* from "Sarman" relates to heredity, or a particular family. It also refers to the receptacle of an heirloom. The *"Sar"* of "Sarman" is defined as "head." In this sense, the "head" is meant both literally as a part of the body, and in the meaning of elder one or master. Therefore, we may tentatively conclude that "Sarman" means the "The Sovereign Receptacle of the Sacred." Or, an alternative reading would be "Those Whose Heads are Priceless."

In the ancient Armenian texts, which include the book "Merkhavat," there are references to the "Sarmoung Society." This society is described as a well-known occult school that according to tradition, dates from 2,500 B.C.E. This school is said to have fared in Mesopotamia up until the sixth or seventh century, C.E. Attributed to this school were many great occult mysteries.

Enter the infamous, George Gurdjieff [639], circa 1886, who claimed he and a friend traveled to the silent abandoned city of Ani, a former capital of the Bagratid Kings of Armenia. *"Here fate intervened. Digging irresponsibly and haphazardly in the ruins, the young men made a series of dramatic finds: an underground passage, a crumbling monastic cell, a wall niche, a pile of ancient Armenian parchments - and in one of these parchments an obscure but exhilarating reference to the 'Sarmoung Brotherhood'. Textual analysis suggested that the Brotherhood has been an Aisorian school, situated 'between Urmia and Kurdistan' in the sixth or seventh century AD. Gurdjieff's response was immediate: he 'decided to go there and try at any cost to find where the school was situated and then enter it'. "*[640]

Gurdjieff wrote that he was sworn to eternal secrecy about the matter. His story is that in 1898 or 1899 he and his companion began their journey in *Bokhara*. Bokhara is on the "Silk Road," north of Afghanistan. At the time it was under the rule of Russia. Their journey, it seems, possibly ended in *Samarkand*. Draped like an ancient shawl across the *Zarafshan* River valley, the city of Samarkand may date back as far as six thousand years, though it was then known as *Maracanda* to the Greeks. At the crossroads of history, the city was invaded by the likes of Alexander the Great (who claimed that its beauties defied his imagination), and Timur, known to the West as Tamerlane (born in nearby *Shakhrisabz*), who captured the city in 1364, dubbing it *"the Eden of the East"* and making it his capital. In modern times, artists and visionaries from John Keats to Oscar Wilde have sought to capture the romance of this ancient Silk Road oasis. Other landmarks include the *Shahi Zinda*, the 13th-15th century mausoleums, where they buried the court favorites of Tamerlane; they also say that the mausoleum entombs Qusam ibn-Abbas, cousin to the Prophet Muhammad (Peace be upon him). Tamerlane, along with his two sons and two grandsons, is buried in the less grand *Guri Amir* mausoleum.

Many great truths are told through stories and tales. "Story" is a part of whom we are as human beings. For untold centuries, occult truths were passed on orally from teacher to student, as stories. Whether these stories were true or not, did not matter. It still does not matter, as long as the message is conveyed.

There are many mythical journeys in the world's mythologies. For example, in Islam there is the crossing of the razor sharp bridge known as the *siratul mustaqim*. In Celtic mythology, Lancelot crossed a "sword bridge." The Zoroastrians crossed the *Chinvat* bridge.

Fascinatingly, Bokhara did exist. Under the *Samanid* dynasty in the tenth century it became the center of civilization, in other words, a World Navel. The great Avicenna, author of the "Canon of Medicine" came from Bohkara. Regrettably, most of the bearers of this great civilization, met their death at the hands of Genghiz Khan's "Golden Horde" in 1219 C.E.

Gurdjieff *"spent years in monasteries in Central Asia, including a spiritual community in the mountains of Bokhara, the Hindu Kush of Afghanistan; he was apparently in close contact with mystics tucked away in the esoteric circles of the Russian Orthodox orders; he studied in Tibet and India."*[641]

Many are aware of, and have studied, the works of P.D. Ouspensky. *"A student named P.D. Ouspensky introduced Gurdjieff's teachings in an intellectual form accessible to Western readers in his book 'In Search of the Miraculous.' "* [642]

Naked implies Essence. May we all know our Essence as we journey to the land of the Sarmoung.

PRACTICE

At bedtime, as you lie in bed before you fall off to sleep, review the events of the day in reverse order. Recall getting into bed, and then what you did just before getting into bed, maybe turning off the light, and then what you did before that, perhaps brushing your teeth. Continue to review the day's events in the reverse order until you reach the moment when you awakened in the morning.

This powerful exercise will awaken dormant psychic abilities. It allows you to play with time. Moreover, in addition, it will help you to become aware that time is like a great sea in which we are immersed. The clairvoyant can navigate this sea at will, heading in whatever direction he or she wishes.

This exercise will also help you to understand cause and effect in a new light. As you review your day backwards, you will become aware of certain occurrences that happened during the day. As you continue backwards in time, you will become aware of the roots or causes of those occurrences. If you met someone in the street that day with whom you had an enjoyable conversation, you will then become aware as you trace back your day's events, that many actions and decisions led up to your meeting this person. Perhaps you decided to go into town, or to take a particular shortcut or detour. Søren Kierkegaard has said, *"Life can be understood only backwards; but it must be lived forwards."*

In metaphysical training, a hidden truth is that spiritual power is released by going backwards! Looking out of the back of your head is a way that some shamans describe the shamanic experience. Anas narrates, *"The Holy Prophet himself said, 'O people! I am your Imam. Do not precede me in ruku' and sajda because in addition to seeing what is in front of me I also see what is behind me.' "* [643] The Holy Prophet could see equally during the darkness of the night and the brightness of the day. [644] When you deliberately act counter to society and the normal processing of sense perception, you open a chink in the armor of reality. A space opens in the normal space-time stream of happenstance, and you can peer between the worlds.

Spirituality has always been about turning the world on its head. Do you know there is no reason not to turn the globe upside down? Who says North America has to be above South America? There is neither up nor down, north nor south in space. The way our maps are drawn is completely arbitrary. They are based on antiquated Eurocentric geographers who considered the world from their own perspective. Uptown could just as well be downtown.

"I did not reach Allah the Exalted by standing in prayer at night, nor by fasting in the day nor by studying knowledge. I reached Allah by generosity and humility and soundness of heart."

- Sheikh Abdul-Qadir al-Gilani

"My secret is not different than my lament."

- Jelaluddin Rumi [645]

WHAT SHOULD YOU PRAY FOR?

Most people pray to God asking for favors. There is nothing wrong with this, but it is not the best way to pray. Good and bad alike are manifestations of the Divine Attributes. Al-Kharraz said, *"God cannot be known except as uniting the opposites."*[646] Desirable and undesirable things will happen to you throughout your life.

Work on accepting the fact of the polaristic nature of Manifest Reality, and realizing the Unitary Essence that pre-existed creation, instead of trying to force the universe to behave in a lopsided way.

Peter J. Awn writes, *"The essences of both Muhammad and Iblis are, therefore, grounded in the divine essence, even though they express two conflicting and opposite poles of spiritual reality."*[647]

Various people in the spiritual community have a real problem dealing with reality. The Sufi proceeds from a firm understanding of nature, and not from some pie-in-the-sky idea of a pain-free life through spirituality!

The true Sufi cannot utter any prayer beginning with the word "I," for example: *"I want to know Thee better."* For to do this presupposes that there are two beings: the Sufi and Allah. This is the greatest sin. Iblis cried, *"Ana khayrun minhu! (I am better than he is!)."*[648] The personal pronoun "I" is the classic Sufi symbol for pride in its extreme form. *"And as His existence is 'necessary,' so the nonexistence of all beside Him is necessary."*[649]

"Keep this discourse always in mind," said Iblis, *"Never say 'I', lest you end up like me. Even if you express the merest hint of existence, you are an unbeliever, not a devotee."*

As-Sami, The All-Hearing, loves to hear our voices. The best prayer is *zikruallah* (the repetition of the Divine Names) for the true dervish can only utter, *"Allah, Allah, Allah . . . "*

When Sufis say this name, often, with the utmost affection and love, they often describe this as *"calling out to Allah."* However, who is calling out to who? *Hu* is calling out to *Hu*. *"Allah, Allah, Allah . . . ,"* then is a declaration of existence, a statement. At the moment the Sufi says *"Allah,"* he or she is stating the fact of the Reality of Existence. Therefore, uttering the Name is a realization, not a begging for attention.

Remember the words of the most Great Sheikh Ibn al-'Arabi (May

Allah sanctify his mighty secret), *"Humanity is only a part of His Oneness. There is no difference between the Sender and the thing sent, for things have no existence. Thine existence is nothing. Thou are He without thou."* [650]

"The purpose of the exercise of the science of knowledge, or Sufism as it is known, is to gain an eternally durable existence."
- Al-Ghazzali

"No angel's trumpet-blast
Can bring those back to life
Whose bodies whilst they lived were void of spirit."
- Iqbal

"Man has no Body distinct from his Soul; for that called Body is a portion of Soul discerned by the five Senses, the chief inlets of Soul in this age."
- William Blake

"Morphic fields, like the known fields of physics, are non-material regions of influence extending in space and continuing in time. They are localized within and around the systems they organize. When any particular organized system ceases to exist, as when an atom splits, a snowflake melts, an animal dies, its organizing field disappears from that place. But in another sense, morphic fields do not disappear: they are potential organizing patterns of influence, and can appear again physically in other times and places, wherever and whenever the physical conditions are appropriate. When they do so they contain within themselves a memory of their previous physical existences."
- Rupert Sheldrake,
Presence of the Past

"Quanta/Wave/Vibration are the first utterances/evolutes of Witnessing Consciousness, and through entropy/tamas their vibration becomes solid matter, therefore the objective universe."
- A. Kinyon

WHY ARE WE HERE?

One of the lessons of physical incarnation is that of organizing energy. First, during our childhood and adolescence, we learn to organize the energy of our physical bodies and integrate our emotional bodies. In adulthood, we organize our minds. Then gradually we learn how to control and organize the energies of our spiritual being. Why is this necessary? It is difficult to hold matter together and even more difficult to hold astral substance and mental thought-forms together. They always want to fly off and disperse into all directions.

When we die, we need to be able to keep together the energies of our soul; or else they will disperse and return to the great ocean of souls. Just like a clay mold. If you take away the mold before the clay has a chance to harden the clay will just fall apart and return to its original undifferentiated state. The clay will return to the mud.

Do not take it for granted that you will continue past your death. Some religions have done much damage in this regard, making people think that everyone has a soul, and that we all will exist in heaven or hell after our deaths. Many people will not continue past their deaths.

We suggest that you consistently work throughout your lifetime on the creation of a coherent and integral spirit body. If your mind never turns to the spiritual in life, why do you think it will turn to the spirit in death? If you are not "at home" with things spiritual, why do you think you will be able to orient yourself when you are thrust into the spirit world? At best, you will be disoriented and uncomfortable.

However, most people on the spiritual way do not understand the relationship between body and soul. They mistakenly think that they are two separate entities. Further, they believe that soul exists on a higher "plane" than the body.

The body is nothing but coalesced soul. The soul is nothing but the mystical body. People who cut themselves off from their instincts, which are their roots in Mother Earth, cannot be open channels. These people cannot channel power from the Living World into manifestation on the physical realm. They are not rooted. Spirit is not different from Matter. The supposed "Spirit - Matter" duality is based upon a misunderstanding of the perception of the Essence.

Spirit is to matter, as ice is to water, in other words: the same substance, but in a different state. As you admire the beauty of the intricate frost lacework on a winter windowpane, you might pause to reflect that invisible lines of force existed before the frost. The cold manifests the beauty of the lines of force.

"The Adamic being . . . is the microcosmic synthesis of form and spirit, being the spirit of the form and the form of the spirit."[651]

Most people are so programmed, so myopic, that they miss the spiritual aspect of matter. They are like people who are color-blind. Color-blind people do not see all colors. They miss certain color experiences that are available to most people's sense of sight. In the body, the Complete Human Being experiences the whole range of human experiences.

Each human being has the sense organs that can experience Spirit; it is just that these organs go undeveloped in most people. The capability of perception is there, but various are the reasons it lies undeveloped. Some people are unaware that these supra-realities exist, others are aware but do not know how to develop the supersensible organs to perceive them, and finally there are those who know but who are afraid.

According to Einstein, energy never moves in a straight line, but always in a curve vast as the universe. So, picture if you will abundant streams of energy flowing out from the Source. As Einstein has shown, in this universe, things can only move in spirals and curved lines. All these streams of energy are curving around the universe. Gradually the beams begin to criss-cross, interlock and arrive at some kind of stability. As a beautiful Persian carpet is woven into being, so too is the universe woven on the Loom of Allah Most High.

"A man needs a little madness, because without it, he cannot cut the cord and become free."

- Zorba the Greek

"He is the truth that is never spoken in distinguished company."
- Nicholas R. Mann

TALES FROM UNDER THE OVERPASS

*M*r. Khadir informed Sam one day that they were going to attend a great festival.

"It's called 'Starwood'," Mr. Khadir informed Sam, "the largest festival of its kind in the country."

"Sounds fascinating," Sam responded.

"The Starwood Festival is the world's finest summer festival, featuring over one hundred and twenty classes and workshops by both locally and internationally acclaimed artists and speakers from a variety of spiritual paths, disciplines, and fields of study."

"Really, I've never heard of it."

"Starwood is known for its eclectic nature and the diversity of its offerings, as well as its fine music, dance, poetry, film, multimedia, and theatrical entertainment. I am scheduled to give three lectures."

"What are you going to talk about?"

"The believer is the mirror to the believer."

The day of the first lecture arrived and the lecture had attracted many curious people. They gathered in the largest lecture area known as the Pavilion.

Sam was thrilled and not a little proud either. He was about to see Mr. Khadir pour forth his wisdom to an entire group of people.

The time of the class arrived and Mr. Khadir took his place in the front of the assembled audience. He sat on the edge of the stage. He continued to sit in silence for a long time.

Sam started to become concerned. The audience began to fidget and murmur to themselves. Mr. Khadir just sat and said nothing. Time passed. Someone muttered, "Asshole." Another exclaimed, "This is bull-shit."

Gradually everyone got up and left the Pavilion leaving Sam and Mr. Khadir alone. Sam was the first to speak,

"You're just a phony like all the rest. You don't have anything to say."

Mr. Khadir answered "There is nothing to be explained. There is no problem. Besides, all the other lecturers here have already said it all."

"I think that's a clever cop out. I'm tired of being taken in by charlatans. I thought I could trust you. I feel like killing myself."

"You want a guru. The guru-student relationship is neurotic because it leads to dependence. It's just as bad as the person who thinks he doesn't need a guru."

"You don't make any sense. You just contradicted yourself."

Mr. Khadir, *"You want things to believe in. You would have liked it if I gave out a lot of interesting esoteric information. However, all I would have given you in that case is many ideas. The ego loves ideas. The ego masturbates itself with ideas."*

"So you think that by not saying anything you are teaching people?" Sam ventured.

"I gave them a chance to transcend ideas," Mr. Khadir softly answered.

"Well, I don't think people got the point."

"No, it does not appear that they did. They think that spirituality is an enjoyable and lovely experience."

"Isn't it? I mean why walk the spiritual path unless you want to become peaceful and loving?"

"I hate to disappoint you Sam, but spirituality has little to do with peaceful feelings, cozy platitudes, and all that stuff. Most of that is an invention on the part of people who don't want to find the Ultimate Reality. They would prefer to spend their whole lives seeking for their destination rather than arriving at their destination."

"But what about the people who spend their entire lives in ashrams or tekkes or monasteries?"

"Ego is able to convert everything to its use, even spirituality."

"What's that supposed to mean?"

"Some of the greatest egotists are found in monasteries. I don't mean to disparage them, for they are afraid deep inside. They fear transcendence. They would rather trod a hard and demanding path which keeps their Limited Selves on the throne for as long as possible, rather than braving emancipation into their Limitless Selves."

"I walked the spiritual path for many years. And I. . . ."

"There's no path!" Mr. Khadir shot back. *"The path is a trick that your mind plays on you to keep you away from enlightenment. Wake up!"*

A terrific shudder passed through Sam. His entire body shook convulsively. A waterfall of electric silver sparkles cascaded down his nervous system.

"I am an approaching thunderstorm on the horizon! I bring chaos, not sunshine! All of nature's vastness cannot contain my madness. Beware of me!" Mr. Khadir roared.

"If you cleave the heart of one drop of water
a hundred pure oceans emerge from it."
- Gulshani-Raz

"We are as the flute and the music in us is from Thee."
- Jelaluddin Rumi

ALEISTER CROWLEY: A SUFI?

"*This is The Night wherein I am lost, the Love through which I am no longer I,*" wrote Aleister Crowley. Crowley spent many years in the deserts of Egypt and Northern Africa, living with various tribes, learning the Qur'an, making prayers, and dressing and living as an Arab.

Crowley struck a balance between light and dark devotion. He did this through the glorification of his True Will, or as the Sufis would name it: his "individual Lord." Crowley saw the True Will as a pyramid *"whose summit is lost in Heaven."* In other words, his True Will was firmly anchored-up in Spirit. He declared his direct connection, and identification, with the Divine.

To Crowley, the True Will was a divine seed, borne within from eternity. The Will is the un-self-conscious instrument that channels the Divine Energy.

The Sufi knows who he or she is - the ocean in a drop of water. It is not that the Sufi disappears in the Universal Ocean; the Entire Ocean enters the Sufi. The Sufi's self is a flute upon which the Divine plays. Crowley wrote, *"I am not I; I am but an hollow tube to bring down Fire from Heaven."* As our bodies breathe in and out as we respire, so too does the Sufi respire the Divine Breath.

The Sufi is a Melody composed by the Divine. Each song is unique. Your assignment is to open your life and recognize that you Live in the Heart Continuum.

Rather than destroying the ego, discover what the ego is. A lover does not return the jewelry the Beloved has bestowed.

PRACTICE

Look at your weekly planning book or calendar. Choose one day in which you will not put on the car radio. Choose another day that you will go without watching television.

You may also consider having an electricity free day. Experience the wonderment of candlelight as it brings fluid light and contiguousness with your environment. Abruptly you are faced with your living space and your life.

This exercise will help you to live in a way that is present and cognizant with the Condition of Everything, rather than having your attention distracted by television, DVD's, home computers, and other electronic devices.

"'Fair and foul are near of kin,
and fair needs foul,' I cried . . .
'But love has pitched his mansion in
the place of excrement;
for nothing can be sole or whole
that has not been rent.'"

- W. B. Yeats

"Man needs difficulties; they are necessary for health."
- C. G. Jung

". . . an everyday mysticism underlying and giving significance to everyday
rationality, everyday tasks and duties, everyday human relationships."
- Aldous Huxley

"O son of Adam, I fell ill and you visited Me not. He will say: 'O Lord, and
how should I visit You when You are the Lord of the worlds?' He will say:
'Did you not know that My servant So-and-so had fallen ill and you visited
him not? Did you not know that had you visited him you would have found
Me with him?' "

- Hadith Qudsi

" 'Nothing . . . ,' answered Mahmud.
'And tell me, without him, is a rose garden
any better than a privy? To be with him
in the dungstore of a public bath, or a ruined house,
is that not better than paradise itself
without him?' "

- Ahmad Ghazali

TALES FROM UNDER THE OVERPASS

*M*r. *Khadir was leaning against the back of the outhouse near the Fairy*
Forest at Starwood. He was talking softly but intently with several peo-
ple.
"This entire idea of a spiritual path is all wrong. You prefer to think of
it as a path because you're afraid of arriving at your destination. This notion
of a 'path' causes you to wander around all your life, solemn and determined
but never making that great leap into the Limitless Self. This concept of a path
is an avoidance mechanism used by many 'spiritual' people. It is a way to
avoid relaxing their ego's tight grip on their limited reality. Other people use

spirituality like a hobby, dipping into spirituality here and there, every now and then."

Someone said, "I need more time to do my spiritual practices. It's so difficult to practice in today's world with all the distractions and so forth."

Mr. Khadir answered, "You always want to escape your environment into a supposedly 'spiritual' environment. What I am teaching has nothing to do with moving anywhere! I want you to be aware of the truth of your environment. In the condition of existence is found all you seek. Wake up right now! Shakespeare said: 'All the world's a stage.' I say: stop acting. Don't wait until you go on pilgrimage to Macca (al-Mukarramah) or do a thirty-day retreat. Don't search for Allah. Eternity begins here, right at this place you're sitting at this very moment. The REAL is here, and waiting to be experienced now!

"Stop looking at crystals while you meditate and start looking at shit. Rather than looking into crystal balls, look into toilet bowls! Do you think the Divine is only to be found in 'so-called' beautiful things? Don't make the mistake of entering into duality by decreeing that your God can only be found in flowers but not thorns, laughter but not screams, life but not death," Mr. Khadir exhorted.

"Shouldn't I be meditating?" someone asked.

"You should be out in the world living life, but living life in a conscious way, knowing that Life is Living You. So don't change anything. Just be aware of the Life flowing through you each moment. Allah has said, 'I was a hidden treasure longing to be known, and for this I created the Universe.' " [652]

"What is your opinion about fasting?" another person asked.

"There are so many misguided individuals who, once born on the Earth, spend their whole lives performing pious and ascetic practices. Don't they get the hint? The Divine Reality has arranged a dinner party and set this fascinating table. These misguided individuals arrive as guests and immediately start tossing away all the plates and utensils! Incredible! A meal is about to be served and yet they snub their noses at their Host and declare they'd rather fast."

"I don't want to become just part of one big Mass Mind," someone worried.

"Your individuality is so special. Do not throw it away. Cultivate it. However, know from whence it arises. Sing your unique song. Nevertheless, you do not own your breath. You do not own the atmosphere in which your voice reverberates. You do not own anything. Yet, some of you strut around acting so pompously. Know that your personality is the quintessence of Now. You are everything, that is why you are conscious."

"Why didn't you say anything at your lecture at the Pavilion?" a pretty and astute woman asked.

"Since language is arbitrary, and the sage knows it, he or she knows

that 'in saying he says nothing'. And yet paradoxically by knowing this and in fact by 'refusing to say', the sage 'says without saying' and 'refuses to say without ever failing to say'. By the way, did you know that many Taoists were women, including Lao Tzu's legendary teacher?"

The woman smiled and shook her head "no."

"In religious Taoism the deity of automatic or "spirit"-writing, Tzu-Ku-Shen, is also the goddess of the latrine—thus calling up the image of magical language as a kind of cacophony or defecatory chaos which somehow manages to convey meaning," Mr. Khadir said with a wry smile on his face.

The audience started laughing.

A rather rotund, physics graduate student in the crowd remarked, "What you just said is reminiscent of the paradox known to Information Theory in which 'noise' can be 'richer' in 'information' than certain ordered codes."

"I'm glad someone's beginning to figure me out!" exclaimed Mr. Khadir.

"Is Spirit good?" a voice asked.

"The Reality of Spirit in this world is sometimes Merciful and sometimes Harsh. It is because of the fantasy of a loving All-Powerful 'Santa-Claus' God that folks feel let down and abandoned when bad things happen. It's their own fault for creating such a childish deity. Stop looking for a 'God' to rescue you! When the Unmanifest materializes, it does so in terms of duality. The Pagan cultures of the past recognized this and even had mythology which depicted the play of Light and Dark. So many so-called 'spiritual' people today are in a state of denial. They are going around trying to make you believe that if you do what they say, you won't have any more pain in your life. Pain is simply a fact. However, it does not have to become suffering. When your awareness transcends pleasure and pain then you relate to the world with equanimity."

"Could you please speak more about this?" a young man up front requested.

"Some people choose to constrict themselves up and be violent and hateful. Others walk around filled with alcohol, drugs, or religion and are numb. Both groups are manifesting opposite poles of the same unity – life and death, although neither group is manifesting these poles in a propitious manner. The Sufi lives with his or her feelings and is conscious of his or her feelings. Feelings are neither good nor bad. They just are. Sufism is about being a Real Human Being. What must also be considered is how the Sufi then chooses to react to those feelings. For instance, he or she may get angry but choose not to commit acts of violence. He or she may feel peaceful but does not allow him or herself to walk around in a grinning and hypnotic fog. You only have to look around you to find innumerable benumbed Sufis whose lives are encased *in spiritual triviality and inanity. This is spiritual suicide. Remember: balance in all things."*

A shy fellow sitting on the side spoke up, his voice cracking with nervousness, "What about doing charitable work?"

Mr. Khadir's eyes focused on the man and a smile dawned on his face, "Blessed are you for asking that question. There are certain holy men and women: Yogis, Ministers, Sufis, Priests, and Monks who have lived blameless lives, who have spent countless hours in prayer, contemplation and self-denial; yet not one of these is greater than a nurse in a cancer ward. The Prophet Muhammad said, 'Whosoever helps any person in any form of pressing need, Allah will immediately change his destiny, both here on earth and in eternity.' The clergy and spiritual people do not have a premium on heaven. If you can recite the entire Qur'an or Bible and cannot serve soup to a hungry person, then you are not worthy to call yourself spiritual. Imam Ja'far as-Sadiq, the Ornament of Sainthood said, 'So you see, it is not sonship, but deeds which count in the eye of the Almighty.'

"So, to conclude our little talk, I give you four recommendations and a fifth: Feed those who are hungry. Quench the thirst of those who are thirsty. Help the needy. Lead people to truth. And last, but not least, have mercy on yourself."

"We are going to the sky, who wants to come with us?
We have gone to heaven, we have been the friends of the angels,
And now we will go back there, for there is our country.
We are higher than heaven, more noble than the angels,
Why not go beyond them?"

- Jelaluddin Rumi

"Thus, when the singer sings, the one worthy of sama sees God's speech
'Be!' to the thing before it comes to be."

- Ibn Arabi

"Mystical bodies of committed people who work out a coherent way of liv-
ing and a coherent way of justice among themselves, are the vessels of spir-
ituality in culture. There's no way to transmit spiritual gifts without vessels,
without organizations."

- Shaykh Nur al-Anwar
al-Jerrahi [653]

THE WOMB

Is it helpful to have spirituality nestled inside a Sacred Religious Tradition? As we have already discussed, the Murid needs to be cooked. He or she is something prepared, put in the oven, and cooked over time. Regular spiritual practice within a Sacred Religious Tradition is the shape of the dish holding the casserole. Tradition can provide a "structure" and a focus on community. *"To love the ones whom Allah loves attracts the love of Allah upon oneself."*[654] The Sufi needs a system of some sort to give him or her inspiration.

Some people ask why some Esoteric Traditions are closely tied to religions. They ask, *"Why can't we dispense with the exoteric and concentrate on the esoteric?"* A carpenter needs a ladder to ascend to the roof of a building. Although, learning to climb a ladder is fundamental and basic to learning carpentry, the master carpenter never abandons his or her ladder and attempts to leap onto the roof, or climb the sides of the building once he or she becomes a Master Craftsperson! That is why the great Esoteric Spiritual Traditions make use of the Sacred Religious Traditions. Prayers, sacred music, flowers, etiquette, song, beautiful artwork, incense, sacred movement, inspiration, and mood are powerful catalysts in developing the spiritual faculties.

Exoteric religion and esoteric religion are helpful in a spiritual context when they are used complementarily. Together they ferment the wine, they age the cheese, and they cook the dish. Many of the traditions of the past are time-proven tools.

There is a phenomenon called "sticky religious attractive matrix" also known as SRAM, or the systems of religious law and practice that are associated with systems of esoteric or mystical spiritual development. These systems are helpful for the most part, but they can become a weight holding the Murid down if they become the goal and not a means of achieving the goal.

Many spiritually-minded individuals must struggle and overcome an attraction for neat and tidy religious world views, which attraction often results in a rigid and fixed sort of fundamentalism. Even esoteric traditions are not immune from doctrinal dogmatism.

Spirituality does not develop in a vacuum. It develops in an atmosphere of stimulus and divulgence. We are not saying that the Sufi must use a religion or belief system, but he or she must mature the senses in some way: classical music, literature, theater, ballet, modern dance, fine art, and so forth. Even baseball and auto-maintenance can mature the senses if approached in the right way. A love must awaken inside the Sufi to trigger the release of the Spirit! All the ecstasy in the world is still only the vehicle and not the destination. Who would remain in his or her vehicle when the destination has been reached?

PRACTICE

It is limiting to think of the afterlife as a kind of resurrection after death. To try to fit consciousness and Essence into linear time and spatial image is to confine and limit your multidimensional, time and space Reality. Open your mind to include the possibility that you are simultaneously experiencing life as pure Essence at this moment. The hereafter is here now!

Many people see the process of enlightenment as a path to a destination. If enlightenment is a path, then it is a path that leads back to where you are at this moment.

"There is no way I can say: 'I am good' or 'I am bad'. I am human."
                                                      - Albert Ellis, Ph.D.

*"If anyone becomes a son of the bridal chamber, he will receive the Light.
If anyone does not receive it while he is in these places, he cannot receive it
in the other place."*
                                                      - Philip 86:5-7

"The constant assertion of belief is an indication of fear."
                                                      - Krishnamurti

*"When you make the two, one . . . and you say, 'Mountain, move away,' it
will move."*
                                                      - The Gospel of Thomas 11,2:106

THE GREAT DIVESTMENT OF DUALITY

A rigid adherence to law and doctrine is a sickness, not a virtue. There is no black and white in this mundane world or in the Spirit World! The Sufi surrenders to this fact and lets go of his or her security blankets, be they religious, political, societal, or scientific.

Spirituality must embrace and honor our humanity. Those who strive for perfection, in other words for an inhuman state of existence, end up frequently penning up their negative feelings and then uncontrollably these feelings discharge as some outburst.

Rather than focusing on perfection, focus on the Infinite Dynamism, and your behavior will come into harmony.

Beware of becoming too sure of your beliefs, because you run the risk of dissociation, or losing touch with parts of yourself. That is why the irrational and spontaneous are so precious to the Sufi. The "irrational" circumnavigates the rational mind and by that allows the unconscious to manifest. The spontaneous and flexible person, who is not afraid of non-rational impulses, unorthodox behaviors, poetry, and dreams, in other words, the totality of being, acquires a unitive nature.

As mature adults, we must metaphorically give birth to a child; for in children the opposites lie closer together. This child is the result of the marriage of the primordial Dark Mother (with all Her Vibrant animality) with the conscious Light Father (with all His Munificent creativity). The Prophet Isa (Peace be upon him) said: *"Bridegrooms and brides belong to the bridal chamber. No one shall be able to see the bridegroom with the bride unless one become one."*[655]

For the Gnostic, the bridal chamber represents the sacred enclosure which becomes the place of reconciliation of soul and spirit, male and female, in other words, an end to the dualisms inherent in the cosmos: *"Light and darkness, life and death, right and left...are inseparable, (but) neither are the good good, nor the evil evil . . . each one will dissolve into its original nature. But those who are exalted above the world are indissoluble, eternal."*[656]

"There can be no stable and balanced development of the mind, apart from the assumption of responsibility."

- John Dewey

"To God belongs the East and the West: wherever you turn, there is the Face of Allah; Allah is All-Embracing, All-Knowing."

- Qur'an 2:115

PSYCHOLOGICAL UNITY

Energy flows when the polarities within yourself are equilibrated. Jung conceived and theorized a process that he called "individuation" by which the human being achieves psychic wholeness by uniting anima with animus, Yin with Yang. *" The difference between the 'natural" individuation process, which runs its [own] course unconsciously, and the one which is consciously realized [by a particular individual], is tremendous. In the first case consciousness nowhere intervenes; the end remains as dark as the beginning. In the second case so much darkness comes to light that the personality is permeated with light, and consciousness necessarily gains in scope and insight. The encounter between conscious and unconscious has to ensure that the light which shines in the darkness is not only comprehended by the darkness, but comprehends it."*[657]

By assuming responsibility for all the psychological, physical and spiritual aspects of yourself (thereby assuming responsibility for your life in its totality) you grow in integrity.

The word "integrity" comes from the word: "integer," meaning UNTOUCHED OR WHOLE, and it is connected to the word "integrate." The Sufi understands the Oneness of the Body!

"1.
There is a solitude of space
A solitude of sea
A solitude of death, but these
Society shall be
Compared with that profounder site
That polar privacy
A soul admitted to itself
Finite infinity

2.
To fight aloud, is very brave -
But gallanter I know
who charge within the bosom
The Cavalry of Woe -
Who win, and nations do not see-
Who fall - and none observe -
Whose dying eyes, no Country
Regards with patriot love"

- Emily Dickinson

TALES FROM UNDER THE OVERPASS

*W*hile eating gyros at the Middle Eastern food stand, Mr. Khadir said in a muted voice to Sam, "Most Murids are still at the mercy of their inner definitions. They think they've changed their religious and spiritual convictions but deep down inside they're still operating from a childhood orientation. Throughout their lives, definitions have been seeping into their subconscious through societal and parental influences. It is time for them to become responsible for their beliefs, through careful examination and rooting out of all detrimental thinking. Remember that how society and parents define you is their definition, you have the power to reject their definitions and decide what you believe.

"Few Sufis know what real Sufism is. The true work is in the mind. The true work is to change."

"The day has eyes, the night has ears."
- Jewish Proverb

"I find that a man with no vices usually has no virtues either."
- Abraham Lincoln

"History is largely the glorification of the iniquities of the triumphant."
- Paul Eldridge

"You'll never get to be a saint if you deny the bit of the devil in you."
- Ellis Peters

"I'll ride on the devil's back if necessary, as long as I get there."
- Gurdjieff

"A dead man who never caused others to die seldom rates a statue."
- Samuel Butler

"'Ah' said Hassan, 'I don't believe in the world. There's another world where life is different.'"
- Mohammed Mrabet [658]

"Ah, why talk of abstinence
And the importance of self-control –
Empty bubbles, which only
Long to be pricked!
From a drinking party
Where passed the cup freely
Round, and deep gurgling
Flasks were emptied
Of rich, red Wine,
And quickly replaced.
That a man like me
Should have had to come
Away thirsty, is a monstrous
Sin. As no more, perhaps,
Than a mere matter of form,
I had to try to live up
To my vows: but what prevented
The Saaqee from pressing me hard
Until I yielded?"

- Ghalib

WAKE UP AND SMELL THE COFFEE

An honest and accurate analysis of the Universal Life Force results in an inescapable conclusion: the Divine Creative Presence Within Us does not always express itself in ways that we think are acceptable.

First, think upon the lives of the greatest poets, writers, artists, and musicians of all time, Sappho, Iqbal, Ibn'Arabi, Sheikh Abu Hulman al-Dimeshqi,[659] (Fakhruddin Iraqi, Awhaduddin Dermani, Abdul Rahman Jami),[660] Percy Bysshe Shelley, Samuel Taylor Coleridge, Robert Southey, Samuel Clemens, Abu Nuwas, Thomas De Quincey, Dylan Thomas, James Joyce, Oscar Wilde, Charles Baudelaire, Robert Louis Stevenson, George Sand, Jean Cocteau, Anaïs Nin, D.H. Lawrence, Algernon Swinburne, Elizabeth Barrett Browning, Dantë Gabriel Rossetti, Edgar Allan Poe, Richard Wagner, Walt Whitman, Vincent van Gogh, Ernest Hemingway, Aldous Huxley, James Joyce, Judy Garland, Ken Kesey, Dizzy Gillespie, William S. Burroughs, Leonard Bernstein, and John Lennon.

Second, consider other notable pioneers of human potential: George Washington, William James, Sigmund Freud, Aleister Crowley, English Physicist Thomas Wedgwood, Gurdijieff, English Chemist Humphrey Davy, Peter Mark Roget (Author of "Roget's Thesaurus"), Whilhem Reich, Alan W. Watts, Robert Graves, P. D. Ouspensky, Dr. John C. Lilly, Timothy Leary, Robert Anton Wilson, and Terrence McKenna.

And finally, think about these world leaders: King Solomon, Pope John VIII, Pope Alexander VI, Queen Zingua of Angolia, Charles II, Catherine the Great, King Lapetamaka of Tahiti, and Winston Churchill.

All the people in the above paragraphs experimented with one or more of the following: alcohol, sex, drugs, and alternative sexualities.

Walter Kim writing in "Time Magazine," May 4, 1998, scribes about Oscar Wilde, *"Wilde was one of his era's foremost men of letters, inordinately well-read and a master of irony. He was also a man of notoriously reckless appetites – for young men, fine things and controversy."* David Hare, an English playwright, who has written a play about Oscar Wilde entitled "The Judas Kiss" has this to say about Wilde, *"There's a heroic generosity about the man that I find enormously appealing. He literally never passed a beggar in the street without giving him money."* Honor and shame may be two sides of the same coin.

Some Sufis have been known to smoke *kif*, eat hashish, and drink alcohol. The Bektashi Order of Sufis uses the alcoholic drink *raki*, as a sacrament to attain spiritual ecstasy. Some will lace their *kif* with *Qoqa*, the pulverized dried seed of the red poppy. *"The leaves on the trees are for the healing of nations."*[661] The word *m'hashish* (equivalent in Moghrebi of "behashished" or "full of hashish") is used not only in a literal sense, but also figuratively, to describe a person whose behavior seems irrational or unexpected.[662] However, we must make it clear that some Sufi *tariqats* absolutely forbid intoxicants of any kind, as the shariat forbids this. Nonetheless, the Qur'an speaks of four rivers in Paradise. One of these rivers is of wine. This shows that the Qur'an itself is altogether broad-minded regarding alcohol. When ordinary people drink alcohol, they become uninhibited and their inner feelings come out, in other words, their lust, anger, jealousy, and so forth. It is reported however, that when certain Sufis drink alcohol, their inner Love comes out.

Peter Lamborn Wilson writes, *"I would maintain that the failure to consider entheogenesis ("birth of the god within" by ingestion of psychotropic substances) must be considered a serious flaw in any integral History of Religion."* [663]

The party line of organized religion and much of contemporary spirituality is that alcohol, sex, hard drugs, and alternative sexualities are counterproductive to true spirituality. Yet, the above-named men and women have expanded the horizons of human potential and brought untold meaning, joy and inspiration to millions of human beings. Some would say that they achieved this in spite of their use of sex, drugs and alcohol. This is incorrect. These activities are an essential aspect of their true spirituality. To quote Robert Stone in "Damascus Gate": *"His motto, alibi, guiding text, had been the words written on a scroll of Qumran, the words of the Teacher of Righteousness: Depravity is the mystery of creation. To liberate into the world the ultimate goodness of God and man, it was necessary to walk deep into the labyrinth."* [664]

Natural psychedelic substances, for example, cannabis, hashish and visionary mushrooms, have been in use for religious, recreational, spiritual, medicinal, and self-realization purposes since time immemorial.

The "darker" aspect of these towering artists' lives is nothing compared with the dark side of some all-time great world leaders - Ramses II, Alexander the Great, Caesar, Napoleon Bonaparte, Peter the Great, Richard I "Lion Heart", Caligula, Messalina, Nero, Domitian, Quintilianus, Maximinus, Constantine, Attila the Hun, Sigibert of Austrasia (France), Leo of Tripoli, England's Queen Isabelle, Zoë (Byzantine Empress), Pope Innocent, Queen Tamara, Kublai Khan, and Henry I.

These people were conquerors. They invaded other people's lands, killed hundreds of thousands and their armies committed all sorts of atrocities. Kill one person and you are a murderer, kill a hundred and you are a world leader. It is strange how provided an individual does many beneficial things for a group, nation or corporation, the members tend to forget and forgive the nasty stuff involved in achieving those gains and will instead only remember the benefits achieved.

If you gain a well-to-do account for the company, although you had to walk all over people to do it, the company will herald your praises! People will slap you on the back and admire you. They will give you a good salary, you will have a fine home, win a desirable mate, and drive an expensive car. Who remembers the fallen? No one dares speak up and say, *"But what about those people you walked all over?"* So, if barbaric behavior is your Way, realize that provided you reach your goal, no one will question your ethics or tactics. Everyone loves a success; no one has time for sob stories. In love relationships we have a hard time remembering after a few months all the terrible things our "ex" did to us, and can only fondly pine away with our memories of how sweet they were.

People have made a great mistake in deifying their heroes, pretending to themselves that these heroes have had no flaws or dark sides. The Murid's goal: to openly acknowledge his or her dark side and integrate it constructively into the fabric of his or her being. People desperately want to pretend that their heroes are perfect. However, these heroes drew an enormous amount of power from their shadow side, and they would not be heroes if they did not revel in all their shadow behavior.

Beware! The most conspicuously squeaky-clean people and situations can be hiding from your view a twisted and perverted side to themselves. We prefer at this time not to list examples of famous Sufis, Sheikhs, Gurus, Priests, Pastors, and Rabbis who, not occasionally, but consistently indulge in all sorts of abusive and destructive actions. It is enough to say that there are many who do. Jung, in his "Answer to Job" writes: *"We can, of course, hope for the undeserved grace of God who hears our prayers. But God, who also does *not* [always] hear our prayers, wants to become man, and for that purpose he has chosen, through the Holy Ghost, the creaturely man filled with darkness — the natural man who is tainted with original sin and who learnt the divine arts and sciences from the fallen angels. The guilty man is eminently suitable and is therefore chosen to become the vessel for the continuing incarnation, not the guiltless one who holds aloof from the world and refuses to pay his tribute to life, for in him, the dark God would find not room."*[665]

Instead of reveling in exposés about prominent politicians' adulterous sexual exploits, you might pause and consider that if you want dynamic, forceful, charismatic people to be your leaders than you must accept that these people will have voracious appetites in all things. Society has to stop demanding that its heroes and political leaders live up to impossible standards. Society has to allow people to be people, recognizing the shadow side in us all.

Giving expression to their dark side definitely helps the famed to be powerful and effective. Most of the time they do it unconsciously and destructively. WHAT WE ARE SUGGESTING IS THAT THIS EXPRESSION OF THE SHADOW CAN BE DONE IN A PROPITIOUS AND CONSCIOUS MANNER. The goal of the Sufi: to utilize the dark side, giving it creative and effective expression, so as not to be subconsciously manipulated and ruled by the dark side.

We, as a collective culture, pretend that we have no shadows. We ignore the facts that stare at us in the face every day. We desperately want to believe that life is a fairytale, and so we enter a state of denial when faced with Naked Reality. However, the Murid must know that life is not a matter of black and white, but life exists within a gray continuum. Furthermore, things are not always as they seem.

"Good is not necessarily something which is stamped as such. That which is good at a certain time may be very wrong at another time; and that which one considers right could very well be considered wrong by another. Nevertheless, the main thing to consider in all cases is certainly to make every effort to act rightly according to one's own conscience," divulges Pir-o-Murshid Inayat Khan.[666]

It is time to do away with religious paradigms that by their nature set up a dualistic war inside ourselves between our shadow side and our waking side, causing the religious adherents to become hypocrites, vainly attempting to hide their shadows from others. The shadow is not something to be embarrassed about. It is something to be explored and allowed propitious expression. But remember: you must pay the admission price to this Theater of Ecstasy. You must be ready to "pay the piper" if you indulge in these intense experiences. Conversely, you must be ready to "pay the piper" if you decide to cut yourself off from all expression of your dark side and try to live like a "perfect" spiritual person filled with white light and unconditional love. The price you will then pay for all your repressed anger, sexuality and passion may be even greater than if you go out and get drunk occasionally.

PRACTICE

A person who is writing with a pen or pencil will choose to shape his or her letters in a particular fashion. The writer has a certain style to his or her penmanship.

Why does a foot look like a foot? Why does the human body look like the human body? The point of these questions is not to look into the scientific and evolutionary causes of natural selection. This book goes beyond science. Ponder on the form of the human being and ask yourself, *"What does this form express?"*

The shape of things is the Divine style. There is a hidden revelation in the form of the human being. The physical form of the human being is a statement. The human being IS the face and form of the Living Reality. The Human Being is a divine form, a theomorphic entity. Allah has placed inside of the human being each one of His own attributes, just as He placed all of His attributes within the cosmos. However, in the cosmos they are scattered and dispersed, while in the human being they are gathered and concentrated. [667]

"The breath that does not repeat the name of God is a wasted breath."
- Kabīr

"For everything that lives is holy, life delights in life."
- William Blake

"Little minds are interested in the extraordinary; great minds in the commonplace."

- Elbert Hubbard

A SACRED APPROACH TO DAILY LIVING

We teach spirituality of the moment. Spirituality should not be reserved for a once a week religious service. Why set aside particular days and times for spirituality when you can transform your everyday life through a sacred approach to living? We teach a spirituality that can be useful at 7:35 A.M. on a Monday morning, spirituality that transforms the mundane, spirituality that turns the fabric of your life into a spiritual experience and not just an assortment of highlighted incidences.

We are referring to spirituality as a way of life, as opposed to an interest that you explore only occasionally. Furthermore, we are suggesting a spirituality that transforms all the little, mundane occurrences of daily life, and not just particular significant aspects of that life. *"The perfect mystic is not an ecstatic devotee lost in contemplation of Oneness, nor a saintly recluse shunning all commerce with mankind, but 'the true saint' goes in and out amongst the people and eats and sleeps with them and buys and sells in the market and marries and takes part in social intercourse, and never forgets God for a single moment."*[668]

Most of the time, your life is spent in the small situations, in mundane environments, and everyday situations. We propose a spirituality that not only concerns itself with the large issues of life, but that also transforms all those commonplace and normal events of everyday life. Spirituality is found in the here and now. *"There are different levels of remembrance and each has different ways. Some are expressed outwardly with audible voice; some felt inwardly, silently, from the center of the heart. At the beginning one should declare in words what one remembers. Then stage by stage the remembrance spreads throughout one's being – descending to the heart then rising to the soul; then still further it reaches the realm of the secrets; further to the hidden; to the most hidden of the hidden. How far the remembrance penetrates, the level it reaches, depends solely on the extent to which Allah in His bounty has guided one."* [669]

It is always helpful to work on your psychological well-being to make sure that you are emotionally balanced. Some individuals develop their spiritual or physical forms to great perfection, while neglecting to mature their psychological being. Spiritual work can put great strain on a person. In addition, society often ridicules spiritual Murids for their beliefs. It is difficult to grow up and live in our society while believing in spirits, angels, alien intelligences, nature devas, jinn, and so forth. People tell you that you are crazy. Others just think that you are hopelessly deluded, and should get down to the business of making money and watching the boob tube.

Sometimes it is helpful to have someone to talk to regularly, someone you can bounce your ideas off.

Powerful and spiritual methods for growth and change are Cognitive Therapy and Neuro-Linguistic Programming (and its development Core Transformation). We highly recommend these systems for initiating change in one's life.

"Submit, and thou conquerest; serve, and thou'lt command."
- Ovid

"Any man who bows down to no one will some day be crushed by the burden of his own weight."
- Fyodor Dostoevski

"The literal significance of the word Islam is submission, whose grammatical root is precisely Salaam. In this tradition, submission has connotations of liberty, of gentleness, of true peace, not of a blind compulsion or castigation. It is a state of positive acceptance of the divine initiative in all occurrences."
- Murshida Amina al-Jerrahi

THE FIVEFOLD SUBMISSION

What does it mean to submit? There is a deep meaning to the idea of submission. Submission serves an important function in spiritual development.

First, the ego must give up the belief that it can control life to prevent suffering.

Second, the ego must submit to the knowledge that it cannot overcome the dark side in a deliberate fashion.

Third, the ego must accept that the dark side is part of the self. The Sufi includes the dark side in the Union of the Self rather than casting it off into hell fire or the dark recesses of his or her subconscious.

Fourth, the ego submits to viewing reality as the Sacred Spontaneous Revelation of the Divine.

Fifth, the ego must allow itself to experience death, so that it may connect to a larger experience of Life.

In spite of the most exalted, mystical, unitary experiences the Murid may have, he or she must always remember that he or she is the servant of Allah. Allah covers his or her secret and the Murid must always act with beautiful behavior, etiquette and humility.

"You cannot get it by taking thought.
You cannot seek it by not taking thought."

- Zenrin poem

"Gnosis: privileged knowledge concerning nature and vouchsafed by her in ecstasy."

- Terrence McKenna

HOW TO TRIGGER A SPIRITUAL EXPERIENCE

How do you trigger a spiritual experience? Experience is the key word here. Just sitting at home doing nothing but watching television is not going to give you a spiritual experience. You need to involve yourself in something. Develop a hobby: perhaps model rocketry, horticulture, bodybuilding, haute-cuisine, remote-control airplanes, bird or dog breeding, become a connoisseur of fine wines or Middle-Eastern carpets. Join a hiking group. Explore the natural world. It is helpful, if you want to vitalize spiritual development, to get outside!

Meet new people. Read books. Take part in activities in which you must take dynamic part, activities in which you must give something of yourself, activities in which you must involve part of yourself. Yes, there is a price to pay; there is always a price to pay.

The next step is to bring two of your experiences together. Often this happens spontaneously and coincidentally, but you can do it deliberately with great benefit. For instance, if you have just read a story about two lovers, say "Romeo and Juliet," you might then choose to go to a symphony concert in which "Tristan und Isolde" is on the program. To trigger a cathartic experience, think of "Romeo and Juliet" (or Qays Ibn 'Amir and Layla, Qays Ibn Dharih and Lubna, Urwa Ibn Hizam and 'Afra, Jamil and Buthayna, Kuthayyir and 'Azza, Antony and Cleopatra, Isis and Osiris) as you listen to "Tristan und Isolde". Often a powerful flash of psychic lightning will erupt, connecting these two experiences, and creating a cathartic, point of transcendence, inside yourself. A common ground is suggested by the coming together of the two events.

Bring together an astronomical image with a spiritual ceremony and watch the results. As you walk around the sacred Circle think of the Earth orbiting the Sun, or a galaxy slowly revolving.

Marguerite Anne Biesele has given an account[670] of this moment of flux, and the resulting cathartic, point of transcendence, experienced by a South African Bushwoman named *Be*. One day in Namibia, *Be* was alone in the bush. She saw a herd of giraffes running before an advancing thunderstorm. The tumult produced by the beating hooves of the giraffes filled her ears.

Suddenly the rains fell. At that moment, a song came to her that she had never heard before. *Be* began to sing.

The Great God *Gauwa* told her that it was a medicine song. When *Be* got home she taught it to her husband, *Tike*. Together they sang and danced. Moreover, as *Gauwa* had told *Be* - it was indeed a song for trancing. In turn, *Tike* went on and taught it to others.

This method is excellent for triggering states of ecstasy. The Greek *ekstasis* means "standing aside." Ecstasy happens when the layers of our being subtly move, when the tectonic plates of our personality shift. When we are ecstatic, we are "besides ourselves." Various spiritual traditions preserve songs designed to cause these subtle shifts in one's being.

Take this technique one step farther and bring together two ideas that usually do not go together. Doing this forces your brain into unfamiliar territory, and by that you force your mind to meet with something for which the brain has not yet attached an emotional state. The brain is thrown into an unstable predicament. This state of flux allows for a true and authentic response to be produced, not just a rehashing of an old familiar response. The mind must then compute a suitable state for the new experience.

Also, undertake to bring together seemingly incompatible emotions: that is, allow yourself to become intrigued by your hatred of something or becoming excited over the fact that you are unhappy. If you are depressed, perhaps you can say to yourself that you are the best candidate on whom to try out new techniques for self-transformation. Allow your excitement to rise as you think of how helpful you could be to other people if you are successful at solving your own problems. If you are hard on yourself, abruptly become your own best friend. These are examples of the marriage of the Yin and Yang, Jachin and Boaz, thesis and antithesis, of which we have written extensively.

"Look not at the wine's bitterness, look at the joy of the drunkards! Look not at the woman's affliction, look at the hope of the midwife!"
- Jelaluddin Rumi

"I am not what the dreamer thinks I am. The dreamer thinks I must have a certain appearance, say and do certain things, have certain magical powers, produce certain magical effects. The dreamer associates all kinds of glorious and magical things with Me. But I am always performing the Awakening act, putting an end to the dream."
- Avatar Adi Da Samraj

TALES FROM UNDER THE OVERPASS

*A*t Starwood, Sam noticed that Mr. Khadir took to wearing various robes. On one day, Mr. Khadir would wear a course woolen robe that looked itchy and uncomfortable, on the next he would wear an expensive and comfortable looking silk robe. Sam asked him about this, but all Mr. Khadir would say is, "Inside my robe there is nothing but Naked Reality."

On Wednesday they had to make a run into town to buy propane for their outdoor cooking stove. One of the people hanging out with Sam and Mr. Khadir offered them a ride. Sam got into the front seat of the car, and was surprised to see Mr. Khadir climb in stark naked.

Sam said, "Ah, don't you think you should put some clothes on?"

Mr. Khadir shot back, "To cover what with what?"

"You can't go into town like that."

"A well-dressed soul in this world may be naked in the Hereafter. Cleanse your heart first, then you are qualified to wear the garb of the Sufi."

"But it's against the law to walk around naked!" Sam pleaded.

"To consider the law as necessarily good, or to see breaking the law as necessarily bad, is to live in the world of Duality."

Sam said ruefully, "You know just when I start to think that you may be a great spiritual Guide, you go and do something like this!"

"My friend, do not think of the Buddha as holy. The Buddha is only a little peephole in the latrine."

"You are blaspheming all that I hold sacred," Sam stammered out.

"The blasphemy of the Sufi is his faith," intoned Mr. Khadir, "I am never what the Murid expects me to be. I create a crisis of understanding. I do not have the qualities you prefer."

This triggered something in Sam. "I heard a saying once, 'Form is nothing but Void; Void is nothing but Form.' "

Mr. Khadir said, "You buy that garbage? Glory to Me! How great is my Majesty."

Sam uttered, "I give up."

"Good," said Mr. Khadir.

When they got into town, Mr. Khadir put on a pair of shorts. Sam was pleased that finally Mr. Khadir was clothed, but still he was uncomfortable about him only wearing shorts.

"I've never seen you in a pair of shorts, Mr. Khadir, is this a proper way for a holy man to dress?" Sam probed.

"Whatever the truthful Sufi wears is nice on him, and he will be elegant and dignified in it," answered Mr. Khadir.

Sam noticed a candy store. He walked over to the window and pressed his face against the glass looking at the lovely candies of many colors and shapes.

"Can we stop in?" Sam asked. "I love candy stores."

"Your likes and dislikes are your enemy. But why do you ask me for permission?"

"Well, I get the feeling that your type doesn't appreciate self-indulgence."

"If you want candy . . . eat! Remember though, once your outer needs are met, the inner must also be fulfilled," answered Mr. Khadir.

"Really?"

"Really," added Mr. Khadir, "If you want to do something, then do it. But remember, I am dangerous."

Sam quickly slipped into the candy shop.

Later as Sam was enjoying a large bag of sweets Sam spoke to Mr. Khadir, "You keep saying that you are dangerous. I think I understand you, but why do you keep reiterating it?"

"Flee from me, away from trouble; take the path of safety, far from this danger. I threaten your life. Make no mistake about that. I am terrible and I am dangerous."

"How do you threaten my life?"

"I change people, when they would rather just sit around and talk about change. I am a corrosive factor to your Limited Self. To be safe is to be already dead. I want you to Live."

PRACTICE

Ask yourself, *"What is my first memory?"* Examine closely this first remembrance. Write it out in detail. Then examine the story for links and clues as to your present life, lifestyle and way of looking at and relating to the world. Write out and describe each link that you uncover.

Little children have honesty about their experience. Often our first memories are our most honest, because they are the most removed from the complications of personality that we develop, as we grow older.

The stories of our lives: what stories did your parents tell you? Usually, upon reflection, you will not only be able to recall the stories they told you as you were growing up, but you can recall which stories were told repeatedly. These stories give important clues about what programming was being inputted into your psyche as you were developing your personality and world view.

After you have done the above exercise, ask yourself the following question, *"What is my favorite joke?"* Write out the joke. Then perform the same analysis as you did above. Notice all the links and similarities between the joke and your life.

Frequently our favorite joke is a stake that marks the spot of our most sensitive and frightening life issue. Let your mind play with the possibilities. Ask yourself, *"What does this joke say about what I fear the most?"*

"Even if the entire duration of the world's existence has already been exhausted and only one day is left before Doomsday (Day of Judgement), Allah will expand that day to such a length of time, as to accommodate the kingdom of a person out of my Ahlul Bayt who will be called by my name. He will then fill out the earth with peace and justice as it will have been full of injustice and tyranny before then."

> - The Holy Prophet Muhammad
> (Peace be upon him) [671]

"The Imam following me is my son Hassan. After Hassan his son is the Qa'im who will fill the earth with justice and equity just as it is filled with injustice and tyranny."

> - Imam Ali Naqi [672]

"The Proof of God and my successor was born circumcised on the 15th night of Sha'ban, year 255 (870 CE), in the early hour of dawn."

> - Imam Hassan 'Askari [673]

When al-Qa'im from the family of the Prophet will rise he will . . . guide to the secret matters (amr al-khafi) and will bring out the Torah and the other books of God from a cave in Antioch and will rule the people of the Torah according to the Torah, and the people of the Gospel according to the Gospel, and the people of the Qur'an according to the Qu'ran."

> - al-Baqir, the Fifth Imam

THE GUIDED ONE – AL-MAHDI ('ALAIHI ASSALAM) [674]

While the stories of the first eleven Imams are historical in nature, the history of the twelfth Imam is mystical and miraculous. Imam Mahdi ('Alaihi Assalam) is an obvious miracle. All the Ahlul Bayt and the Twelve Imams are beautiful miracles for the discerning. The Mahdi ('Alaihi Asslam) was the child of Imam Askari and the slave-woman Sawsan;[675] his name is Abu'l-Kasim Muhammad (which is the name of the Prophet himself).

Some Sunni brothers and sisters may wonder if Imam Askari ('Alaihi Assalam) had a son, and did the Sunni 'ulama and historians record that in their books? Indeed, there is a group of them who related the event of his birth and his history. [676]

Ja'far b. Muhammad b. Malik was among the group of the prominent members of the followers of the Ahlul Bayt. He related the following, *"We were gathered at the Imam Askari's house to find out about his successor. We were some forty people there. At that time Uthman b. Amr stood up and asked,*

'O son of the Prophet, we have come to ask you about something of which you have better knowledge.' The Imam said, 'Please be seated.' He then left the room asking everyone to remain there. He returned after an hour, having brought with him a small boy whose face was shining like the moon. He then announced, 'This is your Imam. Obey him. And also know that you will no more see him after today.' " [677]

When Hassan al-Askari ('Alaihi Assalam), the Eleventh Imam, died, the boy declared himself to be the Twelfth Imam and went into hiding. The followers of the Ahlul Bayt believed that he hid himself in a cave below a mosque in Samarra; a gate blocks this cave which the followers of the Ahlul Bayt call *Bab-al Ghayba*, or the "Gate of Occultation." This is one of the most sacred sites of the followers of the Ahlul Bayt, and the faithful gather here to pray for the return of the Twelfth Imam. However, this is not to say that Imam Mahdi ('Alaihi Assalam) stayed in the cave. No follower of the Ahlul Bayt believes in such a thing. On the contrary, many reports state that he lives among the people and associates with them.

Allah the Most High hid the Prophet Joseph (Peace be upon him) from his brothers so that his brothers could not recognize him when they came to him in Egypt. Likewise, Allah can conceal the Mahdi ('Alaihi Asslam), even though he may be walking around Presidential corridors, local malls, mosques, or visiting tekkes. And he will continue to do that until Allah permits him to introduce himself.

The central Ahlul Bayt doctrines revolving around the Hidden Imam are the doctrines of Occultation (*Ghayba*) and Return (*Raj'a*). The Doctrine of Occultation is simply the belief that the Ancient Holy One hid Muhammad al-Mahdi away from the eyes of men to preserve his life. Allah has miraculously kept him alive since the day he was hidden in 874 C.E. / 260 A.H.; eventually Allah will reveal al-Mahdi to the world and he will return to guide humanity.

The Prophet had given confidential information about the Mahdi to a few entrusted and loyal followers of Islam, namely to Ali ('Alaihi Assalam) and Fatima ('Alaiha Assalam). However, to the public, the Prophet only gave hints and general information on the subject. Why did he do this? The Prophet and the Imams were fully aware that if the unjust rulers, Khalifs and their agents knew the identity of the Mahdi with all the particulars about his parents, their names, and so on, they would not hesitate to prevent his birth even if that meant killing his parents. The Umayyads and the Abbasids were determined to hold on to their power by eliminating even the slightest threat to it. They did not pause to commit serious crimes to remain in power. In all likelihood, they would have attempted to get rid of him, even if it meant killing anyone remotely connected with a challenge to their autocratic rule. We have written elsewhere in this book how certain groups and individuals did not hesitate to kill members of the Prophet's family for purposes of riches and power.

It is important to note that even though the Umayyads and the Abbasids were not fully informed about the signs of the Mahdi's ('Alaihi Assalam) appearance, they killed thousands of the descendants of Imam Ali ('Alaihi Assalam) and Fatima ('Alaiha Assalam), to thwart the potential threat of the Mahdi's ('Alaihi Assalam) transformation of society. The case with the Imams was not very different than with the Prophet himself. They lived in fear for their lives. So, they practiced "prudential concealment" (*taqiyya*) in revealing the details about the Mahdi ('Alaihi Asslam) even to their closest associates. Abu Khalid, the close associate of Imams Baqir and Sadiq, once requested Imam Baqir to confirm the name of the Mahdi ('Alaihi Asslam) for him so that Abu Khalid would perfectly recognize the Mahdi ('Alaihi Asslam). The Imam said, *"O Abu Khalid, you have asked me something about which if the descendants of Fatima come to know anything, the authorities would cut him into pieces!"*[678] The Abbasid Khalif Mansur ordered that if the legatee of the Imam Sadiq ('Alaihi Assalam) was a specific person, he should be killed.

History records other such instances. When Pharaoh came to know that a child would be born among the Israelites who would put an end to his kingdom, he attempted to forestall the danger and so sent his spies around to keep a watch over all pregnant women and to kill all the boys and imprison all the girls that were born. With all these criminal acts he did not reach his aim, and Allah caused the birth of the Prophet Moses (Peace be upon him) to remain concealed so that the divine aim could be fulfilled. Similarly, at the time of the Prophet Jesus' (Peace be upon him) birth, the authorities acted in the same manner.

The Twelfth Imam is in occultation now. He is alive, but his whereabouts are unknown to the general population. Certain people question how this man can be helpful to humanity if he is presently in concealment. Jabir wondered the same thing and so asked the Prophet Muhammad (Peace be upon him) *"How will the people benefit from him when he will remain hidden from them?"* The Prophet (Peace be upon him) replied *"Just as they benefit from the sun when it is hidden behind the clouds."* There are many points about "The Guided One" upon which all Muslims agree, [679]

1. Mahdi ('Alaihi Asslam) is going to come in the last days to make a universal government.

2. Mahdi ('Alaihi Asslam) is from the Ahlul Bayt of the Prophet (Peace be upon him).

3. Mahdi ('Alaihi Asslam) is from the children of Fatima ('Alaiha Assalam), the daughter of the Prophet.

4. Mahdi ('Alaihi Asslam) is different from the Prophet Jesus (Peace be upon him).

5. The Prophet Jesus ('Alaihi Assalam) will be one of the followers of

Imam Mahdi ('Alaihi Asslam) and prays behind him.

The Prophet (Peace be upon him) said, *"Al-Mahdi is one of us, the members of the household (Ahlul Bayt)."*[680] It is a shame that certain people, who recognize the al-Mahdi ('Alaihi Asslam), refuse to acknowledge the rights of other members of the Ahlul Bayt. Also, Muhammad (Peace be upon him) stated, *"Al-Mahdi is one of the children of Fatima."* [681]

The Prophet (Peace be upon him) foresaw that his family would be ill treated after his death, for he said, *". . . the members of my household (Ahlul Bayt) shall suffer a great affliction and they shall be forcefully expelled from their homes after my death."* [682]

Some Holy Ones say that the Imam and his family live on a group of several islands known as the *Jaziratul Khadhra*, The Green Island. A large sea known as *Bahrul Abyadh* protects them. Haji Muhammad Jafer Sheriff Dewji describes these islands in "Imam-e-Zamana: Hazrat Mehdi ('Alaihi Assalam)." Some people wonder if these islands are so big, why are they invisible to modern technology? Once the Prophet (Peace be upon him) was sitting with a companion. An infidel enemy approached them and asked the companion if he had seen Muhammad (Peace be upon him) as he wished to assassinate him. The companion was so frightened that he denied having seen him and the enemy moved away. Absolutely bewildered, the companion asked the Prophet (Peace be upon him) how the enemy had failed to notice the Prophet (Peace be upon him) when he was sitting right there? The Prophet (Peace be upon him) explained how Allah conceals whom He chooses from the sight of the enemies. All sects of Islam accept this tradition.[683]

Muhammad (Peace be upon him), saw that before the Imam Mahdi ('Alaihi Asslam) makes his appearance, there will come people from the East carrying black flags, and they will ask for some good to be given to them, but they will be refused service; as such, they will wage war and emerge victorious, and will be offered that which they desired in the first place, but they will refuse to accept it, until a man from the family of the Prophet (al-Mahdi) appears to fill the Earth with justice, as it will have come to be filled with corruption. The Prophet (Peace be upon him) recommended that, *"So whoever reaches that time ought to come to them even if crawling on the ice or snow."* [684]

The appearance of the Mahdi ('Alaihi Asslam) will be quick, unpredicted and will enforce his appearance within a night. A small, but very efficacious *du'a* for seeing the Imam ('Alaihi Assalam) is the *salawat, "Allahumma Swalle Alaa Muhammadin Wa-ale Muhammad Wa-ajjil Farajahum."* This must be recited often each day. [685]

"One day a man from Mount Locam came to visit Sarî al-Saqatî.
'Sheikh So-and-So from Mount Locam greets you,' he said.
'He dwells in the mountains,' commented Sarî. 'So his efforts
amount to nothing. A man ought to be able to live in the midst of the mar-
ket and be so preoccupied with God that not for a single minute is he
absent from God."

- Sarī

"At judgment day everyone will have to give an account for every good
thing which he or she might have enjoyed and did not enjoy."

- Rabbi Hillel

"Everyone is a moon and has a dark side which he never shows to any-
body."

- Mark Twain

YOUR SECRET WISH

It is essential to know your Indwelling Lord and that this Expression of a Name of Allah is being manifested in your life. To uncover your Unique Expression of a Divine Name, ask yourself, *"What are my secret desires?"* Frequently, you have been taught to hide and repress the most beautiful expression of yourself. Do you secretly yearn to play in a rock band, run for political office, be a ballroom dancer, ride a motorcycle, or live in Paris? When you do any of your secret desires, you are giving LIFE and RESPECT to your shadow side. Remember that the shadow does not necessarily mean the 'evil' part of you; the shadow is that part of ourselves that we have buried, no matter what its nature.

The shadow in some cases can be spirituality. How is that you ask? Well, take for instance a person who has been brought up to be completely obsessed with earning money. This person will spend all his or her waking hours immersed in money, employment and income issues. He or she has BURIED his or her spirituality. For this person, his or her spirituality is his or her shadow side.

Not losing track of the world is necessary as you experience the Spiritual Way. If you love rock concerts, continue to go to rock concerts (although you may wish to orient yourself differently, as in not getting drunk or doing drugs during the concert). The True One does not want you to retreat into little pockets of a spiritual clan, which shuts out the world. You must be in the world, but as new individuals. Of course, keep your hobbies, loves and interests. The goal is to manifest the Complete Human, and the Complete Human lives in the world. They asked Junayd *"What is the end?"* He answered, *"To return to where one has started."*

Religion and esotericism must not be used as escapes from the world, nor should they force the adherent to give up his or her special tasks and pursuits in this universe. To quote from Hazreti Ali (May Peace be upon him), *"O you, who have been created by God! Keep in mind the purpose for which you have been created."* The Murid merely begins to see these tasks and pursuits in a complete context. Joseph Campbell said, *"Follow your bliss."* This is wisdom, as your bliss is your compass pointing to your unique and special role in this universe. Do not let yourself or anyone else talk you out of it!

PRACTICE

The Sheikhs have said not to plan your future. Of course, you must be aware of business appointments and so forth. Nevertheless, it is counterproductive to your spiritual growth to make plans for a year from now, or even five years from now.

The most desirable state of mind is to live in the present. Beware of the mind's tendency to plan out the future. Andrew Cohen writes, *"When we ultimately find the depth of courage and the strength of conviction to abandon the future once and for all, we will discover a context, a vast and infinite context where we will know beyond any doubt that we are free."* 686

The slave does not have any business knowing what his or her master intends to do. So too, the Slave of Allah, must submit to the Will of The Supreme Reality, and give up his or her schemes for the future. This is painful, as the ego wants to stay in charge and feel in control of life.

One of the ego's tricks is to tell us that something better awaits around the corner, or that when we get such-and-such then we can be happy. Lies, all lies. We must give up all hope for the future. The better moment never arrives, because *this* is the best of all moments.

Does this mean that we will not care anymore? On the contrary, we will have stopped worrying about ourselves, and have now become free to truly care about others. Again to quote Cohen, *"We are released from the hell of a morbidly self-centered existence where we only want for ourselves and where we always need more."* 687

"Oh who can cure my sickness? An outcast I have become. Family and home, where are they? No path leads back to them and none to my beloved. Broken are my name, my reputation, like glass smashed on a rock; broken is the drum which once spread the good news and my ears now only hear the drumbeat of separation. Huntress, beautiful one, whose victim I am – limping, a willing target for your arrows. I follow obediently my beloved, who owns my soul. If she says 'Get drunk,' that is what I shall do. If she orders me to be mad, that is what I shall be."

- Nizâmî

"The Merciful God must always be thanked though you may be facing hard times or encountering reverses and misfortunes."

- Imam Ali ('Alaihi Assalam)

THE ALL PERVADING LIFE PRINCIPLE

Learn a lesson from nature and apply it to your life. Presence manifests on the physical plane in terms of Polarity. The Presence in Its Inner Essence is One, in Its manifest condition It is One (appearing as) Two. Presence has decided to be known through pain and pleasure. When a tree branch breaks, it makes a cracking sound. When dogs lose their masters, they wail, whimper and often die.

When humans cry because of intense suffering, they may scream out. All creation cries out for His or Her Beloved. We are howling dogs in the street calling out for the Primordial Source of the Universe. Other living expressions of the Divine go through times of severity: we thrash wheat, violently ferment beer, pound steel, and crush grapes.

The new approach to the Divine that we suggest, requires that we completely transform our original view of the Divine. Nurture an appreciation of the ebb and flow of the manifestation of Ultimate Reality: repression balanced by expression; joy balanced by pain, life balanced by death.

Those Sufis, who realize the above, achieve a sense of balance, a sense of complete realization of their humanity, achieving a state of Unification and therefore, identification, with the Essence.

"I have bestowed on everyone a particular mode of worship, I have given everyone a peculiar form of expression. The idiom of Hindustan is excellent for Hindus; the idiom of Sind is excellent for the people of Sind. I look not at tongues and speech; I look at the spirit and the inward feeling. The religion of love is apart from all religions. The lovers of God have no religion but God alone."

- Jelaluddin Rumi

"The Self's unfolding is Life's fountainhead."

- Iqbal

"Know that the lover in any case
*   is no Moslem.*
The religion of Love
*   Knows neither infidelity nor faith.*
In love is no body, mind,
*   Heart, or spirit;*
He who has not become <u>thus</u>
*   Is not THAT."*

- Jelaluddin Rumi

TALES FROM UNDER THE OVERPASS

*S*am asked Mr. Khadir,
"How do I find Allah?"

"I have no business with Allah." He told Sam bluntly. "I am in the business of helping you to find yourself within yourself; to find your inner essence. Do not look for Allah."

"Well, then, what religion should I follow . . . you seem to be a Muslim?" Sam said thoughtfully.

"Die to all confining conceptuality, even that of religion. Allah has no religion," Mr. Khadir said fervently. "There is a Sufi saying that goes, 'Water takes on the color of the cup in which it is in.' Who you are is your religion. So first, find yourself. And then work on polishing up your cup."

"Genius is the talent for seeing things straight. It is seeing things in a straight line without any bend or break or aberration of sight, seeing them as they are, without any warping of vision."
                                                                — *Maude Adams*

"In nature there are neither rewards nor punishments - there are consequences."
                                                                — *Robert G. Ingersoll*

THE TURNING POINT

Frequently the Murid just fools him or herself into thinking that his or her greatest liabilities do not exist! If the Murid is overweight and looking for a spouse, he or she might say *"Well, I do not have the body of (insert movie star's name), but I am not bad looking."* Sure, you are not bad looking, but in this culture, a physically fit, trim body is generally regarded as sensually alluring. Friendship may abound among people who are not sexually attracted to one another, but its time to face reality, physical attraction helps romance along. Love and friendship will be the driving force that turns a romance into a lasting partnership. Still, we emphasize that Murids need to consider the respect they give to their bodies, and the exigencies of living in society if their goal is to accomplish something in that society.

Yet, people will consistently live in denial about their major habits. They walk around wondering to themselves why they are not getting their needs met. The person who does not work a forty-hour week sits around and wonders why he or she cannot afford a good apartment, making excuse after excuse for his or her laziness. The person, who cannot bring him or herself to get to one spiritual gathering once a month, sits around and wonders why he or she is not manifesting spiritual growth. The person who will not walk a mile every other day sits around and wonders why he or she feels achy and tired. The single person who will not get in the car and drive to "singles" events wonders why he or she is alone on a Saturday night! People become attached to their habits. The habits become so familiar that people feel uneasy without them. The most important and most difficult of ALL the tests that confront the Murid is to face his or her most cherished personal habits. Accept the fact that it is a habit and then work on solving the problem.

Guides will give various practices, but rarely do Murids perform them and even more rarely with any kind of consistency. Many people run around from Sheikh to Sheikh or therapist to therapist, trying to get answers. Often the problem is that these people never truly put into effect the answers they have already been given. Rather than always looking for more, more, more, they should use what they have already been given. As Andrew Cohen writes,

"Most want only to taste it and then go back. I'm speaking about never going back, and going all the way in this life." [688]

Learn how to work and then the Great Work will be revealed to you. It is not the other way around! Some Murids use spirituality as an excuse not to do any work, be it spiritual or mundane. Enlightenment can be found working as a gasoline station attendant. Clearly until the Murid commits him or herself to mastering the physical plane issues, the spiritual planes will continue to elude him or her.

PRACTICE

Contemplate on the following axiom: *"I am not I; and I am not not I."* [689] Contemplate on this statement until you begin to sense a change in your perspective. This leads to the question, *"What exists?"*

Therefore at that point, add the following predication, *"My essence is the Essence of the Supreme Reality; there is no other reality."*

Finally, allow the succeeding assertion to complete your awareness of Unity, *"The Body is One."*

"The emphasis is not upon the richness of a past tradition; the emphasis is on what is practical from the past and of immediate value for today."
> *- Fadiman and Ragib Frager al-Jerrahi*

"[True] guidance means being guided to bewilderment, that he might know that the whole affair [of God] is perplexity, which means perturbation and flux, and flux is life."
> *- Ibn al-'Arabi*

"Do not expect your children to do what you did, because they belong to a different age."
> *- Imam Ja'far as-Sadiq ('Alaihi Assalam)*

"For you to know the beautiful ones as beautiful, you have to partake either of their disposition or their essence."
> *- el-Hajj el-Fakir Şerif Çatalkaya er-Rıfa'i er-Marufi*

"He whose one day is like the next is not of us."
> *- Muhammad (Peace be upon him)*

MUTABILITY

The True Guide possesses the quality of mutability and fluidity. Fluidity is more important than rigid perfectionism. He or she encourages diversity and spontaneity. Kabir Helminski, servant of Mevlana, instructs the wise, *"Just as Sufism took a particular form beginning in the twelfth century in Khorasan and Anatolia, in the Hejaz and the Maghreb, perhaps it is taking a new form in these times and in this culture. New methods of communication, different economic structures, and different levels of human individuation necessitate change."* [690]

Stagnation equals death. A stagnant pond eventually becomes mud. A human being, whose biological system becomes stagnant, dies. There must be movement in the waters! The Waters of Life cannot flow in a clogged and stagnant human being. A Guide or Student with no sense of mutability will eventually become a stagnant pond.

The Great and Holy Naqshabandi said, *"We must speak to each person in accordance with his understanding. This is the task of the teacher. When we teach we must take into account the present concerns and obsessions, the fixed ideas of the disciples. We must, for example, use the language of Bukhara while talking to the people of Bukhara, and the language of Baghdad, in Baghdad. If a master knows what he is teaching, he must be able to adjust the form of the teachings to concrete circumstances. It does not matter where is the truth, the teacher will help them to find it. But if he uses the same method for everybody, he is not a teacher.* "[691]

The Divine does not ask the tree to grow without knots and bumps, irregularities and variations in its bark and trunk. So beware of Sheikhs and Tariqats that attempt to restrict the free, natural designs of your spiritual growth.

"Sometimes I go about pitying myself, and all the time I am being carried on great winds across the sky."

- Ojibway

". . . . I would still draw a fundamental moral distinction between two kinds of preferences: between those of the muckrakers and those of the hero-worshippers. It is the distinction between the people who, confronted by genius, are seized with a passion to ferret out flaws, real or imaginary, in other words, to find the feet of clay so as to justify their own blighted lives - as against the people who, desperate to feel admiration, want to dismiss any flaw as trivial because nothing matters to them in such a context but the sight of human greatness that inspires and awes them."

- Leonard Peikoff

SABOTAGE: A SERPENT IN EDEN

You can struggle so much, but is your goal to struggle or to make the best of the situation? Just because you cannot get all your ducks to sit in a row does not mean you should abandon your ducks.

It is easy to get into a mind set in which you become cynical and critical of spiritual communities, religious paths, guides, and so forth. After a while one must ask oneself, *"Have I been so conscientious in my high standards that I have effectively made it impossible for myself to receive any spiritual guidance within a community?"* Have you locked yourself out of the gates of paradise by demanding that everything and everyone around you be perfect?

Without a doubt, it is wise to be discriminating, but who said that a spiritual Way must be "perfect" in order for it to work? Have you ever paused to consider that a community can be just as "human" as you are? A community can explore its shadow and light sides just as you do as an individual. Just because a spiritual community (or religion) may have a shadow side, is that sufficient reason to throw the baby out with the bath water? Ideally, you will want to find a spiritual Guide and community that openly acknowledge the shadow and strive to pursue a spiritual way that transcends the light and the dark.

Ultimately if your goal is spiritual advancement, then even if a religion or philosophy does not match up exactly with your beliefs, you should still consider taking their training. Take what you need and leave the rest, as they say. The world is full of lonely, sad, resentful people waiting for the perfect thing to come along, be it the perfect mate, job, friend, or spiritual philosophy. Remember the goal of life is not to be an Inspector General who gleefully declares that nothing passes muster, the goal is to live life to the fullest. Do not get so caught up in your exacting analysis of a situation that you miss an opportunity for spiritual growth. *"Realization involves no dilemma, no strategy,"* writes Buba Free John.[692]

"Accuracy is not truth."

- Matisse

"Acquire knowledge. It enables its possessor to distinguish right from wrong; it lights the way to Heaven; it is our friend in the desert, our society in solitude, our companion when friendless; it guides us to happiness; it sustains us in misery; it is an ornament among friends and an armor against enemies."

- Muhammad (Peace be upon him)

"Let's not talk about 'spiritual' life. This sounds as if there are a few people living a spiritual life and the rest of humanity are not."

- Shaykh Nur al-Anwar al-Jerrahi [693]

TALES FROM UNDER THE OVERPASS

*O*ne of the younger students turned to Mr. Khadir and asked, "What's the most powerful form of spirituality you know?"

"The best spirituality," Mr. Khadir answered, "is to work hard in school, studying and learning as much as you can, advance to whatever grade you can achieve (a doctorate is best), to obtain the best job possible and to work steadily. The Prophet himself, when he was a young man, traded, bartered, bought, sold and conducted business with uncommon talent. In fact, on his first business trip, he reaped twice as much as his boss anticipated! It is wrong for the Sufi not to work and not to earn a livelihood. Consider it a happy occasion when someone needs help and you are able to provide it, because one doesn't know what the next moment will bring; destinies may change, life may be so short that one may not complete an act nor see a joy mature."

Mr. Khadir's answer surprised the student. The student had expected Mr. Khadir to discuss exotic spiritual practices, and yet Mr. Khadir was telling him about the most mundane practical things.

"Eat as much as you want, enjoy as much as you want, never waste. Be very honest; never kill anybody nor bring harm to anyone. God never said to deny anything for yourself or to torture your body - not in all the sacred books. He said, 'I gave everything to you so that you may enjoy them, just as long as you don't abuse anything, waste, or harm your neighbor, or commit any insult or crime.'"

Sam interrupted at this point and asked Mr. Khadir if he could speak to him privately. After Mr. Khadir politely excused himself from the crowd, Sam began to speak, "Khadir, my Friend, you always seem to go round in circles when you speak of spiritual things - one moment you are talking about Spirit *and then, before I know it, you are talking about the most commonplace of activities. This confuses me because on the one hand you seem to be telling us that there is ONE ULTIMATE REALITY and the next you seem to be talking about the necessity of doing many practical actions."*

"Who asked you to think about all that? We are the Stewards of Allah on this planet. There is work to be done, and that work is done on various levels. The Ultimate Teaching Power is teaching always. Everywhere in society, in the mundane activities of keeping one's home, a person can participate in the great teaching, and not set up a situation where he or she thinks it would be ideal if he or she could be in a monastery or some sort of retreat, where he or she could focus entirely. That would be dualistic. What we call the relative and the ultimate are never separated, so that in the midst of the struggle of our relativity we have full access to the ultimate joy. Yes there is Oneness of Being," Mr. Khadir continued with great love and affection, *"but there is also the Manyness of Reality. Existence, in its Greatest Fullness, is the One and the Many. The sound of the eternal process of transformation of singularity into diversity and diversity into singularity is heard by the fully awake consciousness. You may also call it the Absolute and the Relative. The Complete Human Being unites the One and the Many, so that the Universe depends on him for its continued existence. Love the world; do not run away from it, for It is Him. It is Him in His aspect of Multiplicity. We surrender to the world of separation for His sake, while within the heart we retain knowledge of His Oneness. Living in the world we experience His Multiplicity and offer it back to Him; thus we come to know the wonder of Oneness within Multiplicity. Love is the Tide of Essence which stems all opposite waves."*

PRACTICE

It is important for the Murid to make daily ablution. There are many reasons why this is a necessity. The Messenger of Allah taught and practiced ablution, and for Muslims, it is a prerequisite before making each of the five daily prayers. Some contemporary Sufis hold that there is no need for ablution before prayer, and feel that ablution is dispensable.

Every day the body accumulates magnetic charges that we must cleanse from the aura. Humans float in a sea of electromagnetism, gravity and other subtle force fields. Some of this energy is helpful, other energy in unhelpful.

For untold millennia, indigenous peoples (our ancestors) have practiced "grounding." Grounding consists of bringing the body into direct contact with the earth (soil) or water, in order to drain off excess and disruptive energies, and to reestablish a harmonious balance of life energy between the human and the planet.

The Prophet Muhammad (Peace be upon him) taught that when water was unavailable for making ablution, soil was absolutely appropriate. In fact, many followers of the Ahlul Bayt prostrate (while making prayers) on what is known as the *turba*, a portion of the soil of Karbala. Imam Ali ('Alaihi Assalam) took a handful of Karbala's soil when he reached that land, smelled its scent, and then cried till the ground became wet with his tears as he said, *"From this loin, seventy thousand shall be permitted to enter Paradise without being judged."* [694]

<u>Ablution is not about washing off sins.</u> It is about altering one's bio-electrical field to be in harmonious relation to the universe, and therefore in proper alignment and attunement for communion with the Divine.

"The greatest devotion, greater than learning and praying, consists in accepting the world exactly as it happens to be."
                                        - Hasidic saying

"Solve et coagula, Dissolution and condensation, emptiness and form, unmanifest and manifest, implicate and explicate. This is perhaps the most powerful dialectic of all."
                                        - François Trojani

"Before the bar of nature and fate, unconsciousness is never accepted as an excuse."
                                        - Jung

"But the thorn-pricks of the desert are the joy that he exults in."
                                        - Iqbal

"For I am divided for love's sake, for the chance of union."
                                        - Liber Al Vel Legis
                                        (The Book of the Law)
                                        sub figura XXXI

"In love there must be both rejection and acceptance, so that the lover may become mature through the grace and wrath of the Beloved; if not he remains immature and unproductive."
                                        - Ayn al-Qozat

"The wise are not fooled by miracles; they believe in the direction. Sirat ul-mustaqim, the Straight Path, is life's real bridge. The ones who cross this bridge cross it with the correct directions."
                                        - el-Hajj el-Fakir Şerif Çatalkaya
                                        er-Rıfa'i er-Marufi

"If God is unique and unknowable how can anything positive be said of Him at all?
                                        - Fadlou Shehadi [695]

EPILOGUE

Our society needs a functional mythology of the Dark. We need a spirituality that reminds us that we have to share one half of our existence with the Dark. We can do this willing or unwillingly. The paradox must be lived in our lives in order for us to be truly enlightened.

1 + (-1) = 0 is the spiritual formula of Cosmic Transcendence. In other words, to go beyond duality we have to acknowledge, accept, honor, and then marry the Light and the Dark, while always keeping our eyes and heart focused on the Essence of Essences. The formula works in both directions simultaneously.

Those who pursue the spiritual way should concentrate more on the Dark Side than the Light Side, because *"overemphasis on what is considered 'good' inevitably causes imbalance with respect to what is considered 'bad,'* ... *"*[696] The reason that one must concentrate on the Sacred Dark Side is that religion has for the last three thousand years, divorced and alienated itself from its twin sibling. We must restore balance to the spirituality of the Western populace.

"Upon the road of wayfarers and in their religion, what is unbelief? what is faith? They both become one. Yusuf 'Amiri said:
'In the alley of the tavern, who is darvish? who is king?
On the road of unity, what is obedience? what is sin?
Upon the parapet of the Throne, what is the sun? what is the moon?
Upon the countenance of a Qalendar, what is luminous? what is Black?' *"* [697]

Many priests and guides are useless because they are at the mercy of the Dark Side due to their total rejection of the idea that the Dark Side needs to be acknowledged in a sacred way. They unconsciously become egomaniacal and "control freaks." They are in complete ignorance how to balance and integrate the Dark Side. Some teach that the Fall from the Garden of Paradise is the explanation for the evil of the body. In fact, matter is the fallen angel. We can redeem this fallen angel through infusing it with Conscious Spiritual Life.

Self-righteously proclaiming that the world is an evil place and then attempting to live as much in the light as possible is not propitious for a person. That is only leaving the person vulnerable to unacknowledged and repressed darkness. Recognize that many people are at the mercy of the Dark Force precisely because spiritual traditions have not taught them to respect and integrate the Dark.

The way to become a REALIZED person does not so much lie in doing good things, which of course we all should do, but in coming to some kind of understanding with the Dark, with the Shadow.

There is an alternative to the "good" vs. "bad" duality of contemporary spirituality: The Way of the Sacred Reality of Human Life. Allah expresses Itself through both Sacred Poles of Existence. *"Every existence is poison to some and spirit-sweetness to others. Be the Friend. Then you can eat from a poison jar and taste only clear discrimination."*[698] Both Poles are the Reality's

Will and inspired by the Essence. This difficult to accept fact must be admitted for spirituality to have meaning in the new millennium. From out of the feminine Divine Blackness the masculine Divine Light is born. The In and the Out, inhalation and exhalation, "good" and "evil," are ways the Divine knows Itself in humankind.

When the Ultimate Reality folded within Itself, this resulted in a Divine In and Out, Subject and Object, God and Humanity. Hazreti Isa (Peace be upon him) said, *"Man, if indeed thou knowest and what thou doest, thou art blessed."*

To fulfill the formula of $1 + (-1) = 0$ the Murid must consciously realize what he or she conceals and keeps unrevealed within him or her self. He or she must face his or her inner demons, not in an adversarial way, but with sacred respect.

Our desire to sin is the other face of God's desire to display the tempting lures. The Baal Shem Tov states, *"In all that is in the world dwell Holy Sparks, no things is empty of them; in the actions of men also, indeed even in the sins he does, dwell Holy Sparks of God."*

The Sufi endures pain because he or she knows that his or her endurance shows his or her commitment, and the extremity of his or her passion, to the Beloved. As any True Lover will endure all suffering to get close to his or her Beloved, the Sufi wanders the wilderness of life experiencing the *"slings and arrows of outrageous fortune"* as an opportunity to experience his or her Loved One.

Giving audience to your irrational aspects accomplishes the way to approach the inner demons of your being. Give voice to the irrational aspects of your character. Experiment with being spontaneous, living in the moment, flexible, and open to new ways of living life. To paraphrase Goethe: safety is dangerous.

You must give the aggressive and hostile aspects of yourself constructive ways of expression through assertiveness, determination, self-assuredness, boldness, mental toughness, decisiveness, learning how to articulate one's feelings, speaking directly, forcefulness, and sports.[699]

In addition, the Murid must write down and reflect upon dreams. Thoughts of violence and hostility need to be honored, not by asking God to protect you from these thoughts, or to be forgiven for these thoughts, but by exploring them consciously. The Sufi does not act upon these violent thoughts, but acknowledges them as important messages from the unconscious that, when explored, will yield valuable insight into the present situation. For ultimately, our unconscious reflects the face we turn toward it. The more we become friends with our shadow side, the more friendly it becomes, thus resulting in the harmonious Alchemical marriage of Unity. If you cannot achieve a transcendent unity in yourself, how can you expect to find the Absolute Unity?

People struggle unknowingly trying to reconcile their personal demand for a Loving God with the fact that Life is both filled with Love and Malevolence. Sheikh Muzaffer calls malevolence *"heavenly afflictions."* [700] This "personal" God does exist in one sense. He is the God that came into existence when the world was created. However, as Sufis, we remember and return to the Divine which existed prior to the creation of the world, a State of Absolute Unity: God was One and his Name was One. However, that Unity was shattered (from our mundane point of view) by a rupture in the very fabric of the Ultimate Reality Itself at the moment of creation. It is humanity's role, through uniting the opposites in love, to restore the Primal State of Unity. Unfortunately, people live in fear of the world, and because of that fear they demand a God who is only loving and personal. Human beings thus feel anxiety and depression because of their failed attempts to fit a square block of cherished religious beliefs into a round hole of Holistic Completion.

People rationalize and repress, all in a vain attempt to run from the fact of the dual nature of reality. The Sufi goes beyond the pain of duality when he or she embraces both poles. Embracing both poles gives birth to the Enormous Energy of the Self in Harmony with Its Environment. The Godhead Itself must be "redeemed," that is, returned to its state of premundane unity.

"From the hand of the Friend it matters not whether it be honey or poison, sweet or sour, grace or wrath. One who is in love with the grace alone, is in love with himself, not with the Beloved." There are various "Gods." Each person has their own idea of God, and therefore, God manifests to him or her in that manner. This "God" is like a horizon of consciousness. The task of the Murid is continually to pass the limit of his or her horizon, and go to the next level. Yet at the next level, the Murid realizes that there is yet another horizon. In other words, when you enter communion with your concept of God, you then realize that you have only entered onto a new level, with a new horizon (a new consciousness of God). Each time you come to know your Lord, you realize that your knowledge is but the stepping stone to knowing a Greater Lord. Of course, there is One God, but there are various steps to the Door of the Sultan of Reality.

Who is God? Ibn al-Farid gave a glimpse of the Ultimate Reality when he wrote:

> *"Truly in form*
> > *I am Adam's son -*
> *and yet*
> *with Adam himself*
> > *lies a secret -*
> *my secret -*

that testifies:
I am his father!"

We began this chapter quoting the famous metaphysical formula: 1 + (-1) = 0. The Sufi might better understand it as (-1) + 1 = 0. When the Murid says "La ilaha" he or she is making an absolute negation, that is, there is no way to know God. This refers to the fact that Allah has had to limit Itself, an autonegation, to take form. In this first half of the *shahadat,* Allah is knowing Itself through its own limitation. However, this knowing of the negation is the pain of separation, the suffering of all life, for Allah truly does not know It is the Divinity in this limited form. Ibn al'Arabi writes thus, *"the transcendent Reality is [at the same time] the relative creature, even though the creature be distinct from the Creator."*[701] And in the same work he states (referring to Allah), *"You are both the Restricted and the All-Encompassing."*[702]

His Holiness M. R. Bawa Muhaiyaddeen illuminated this condition when he said, *". . . all suffering is His suffering, all sorrow is His sorrow, all hunger is His, all poverty is His, and all grief is His. Every torment is inside Him. This is how God does His duty."*[703] Avatar Adi Da unveils more of the mystery for us, *"Living beings are not merely the creatures or victims of God, created and set apart to suffer for some inexplicable reason. Living beings are the very Sacrifice of God. God is Alive as you. Your life is the creative ordeal to which God is eternally Submitted."*[704] Creation is renewed moment by moment through a constant act of sacrifice on the part of Allah. Therefore, we reciprocate through self-sacrifice in love, releasing all notions of the Limited Self. The Baal Shem Tov said: *"Do not pray for a thing that you lack, for your prayer will not be accepted. Rather, when you pray, pray because of the heaviness that is in the Head of the world. For the want of the thing that you lack is in the indwelling Glory. For man is a part of God, and the want that is in the part is in the Whole [which is God], and the Whole suffers the want of the part [which is man]. Therefore, let your prayer be directed to the want of [God] the Whole."* That is, the suffering of humankind is only a reflection of the suffering of Allah. Therefore prayer is effective only when it is directed toward the suffering of Allah rather than that of humankind. The important premise here, of course, is that humankind can "repair" the suffering of Allah through its own "intention" as expressed in prayer. So, the Baal Shem Tov closes with these words: *"Prayer is a high need. For man knows of his want that it comes from a higher one, and he prays that the wants of God be satisfied. And then his own wants will be satisfied at the same time."*

Following this first half of the shahadat, there is a specific positive exception, "il ALLAH," meaning "but you can know the Primordial Soul of the Universe." This illogical jump of consciousness challenges the first half of the statement, and commands that the "limited" God is also God. The second half of the shahadat is God's awakening to Its own Divinity. Moreover, when repeated by the Murid, the second half of the shahadat confirms the Living Essence of Essences within the heart of the Murid.

Ibn 'Arabi reminds us, *"Forgetfulness is a divine attribute."* This may strike some Murids as sounding very odd, but we refer them to the following verse of the Qur'an, *"They forgot God, so He forgot them."*[705] Llewellyn Vaughan-Lee, Ph.D. and author of several books on Sufism, offers this insight, *"It is His will that in us He forgets Himself, just as it is His will that He allows us to remember Him. . .He helps us to remember and then allows us to forget."*[706] Therefore, in us, Allah forgets Himself. This is the reason for the appearance of "evil" around us and in our lives. Likewise, in us, Allah remembers Himself, and thus, we see what we term "good."

This Way does not bring happiness, but it does bring joy and contentment. Each Sufi must pass over a bridge called the *Sirat ul-mustaqim*. There are many secrets on this bridge that is thinner than a hair and sharper than a sword. Over the bridge people will pass at various speeds, some like a bird in flight, some walking, and some creeping along.[707] The way to cross this bridge is through balance - just like a tightrope walker. We must perfectly balance the negative and positive poles of existence on the point of transcendence. The Dancing of the Spheres of Heaven goes on forever, despite your Ecstasies and your Tragedies. Unconditionally accept yourself in both your human aspect and in the aspect of your Ultimate Reality. Realize that ultimately both aspects are ONE.

Accept your humanity regardless if your actions seem "good" or "bad." No judgment. No self-recrimination. Accept the Divine Source regardless if your life goes well or unpleasantly. Love the thorn and the rose, but become One with the Perfume, for the Perfume is Love, and we subsume all opposites in Love.

"In me is His theater of manifestation, and we are for Him as vessels."[708]

If we have said anything wrong, our brothers and sisters, please forgive us. May the Table of the Lovers stay together. [709]

Allah knows best.

LADY FATIMA ZEHRA
('ALAIHA ASSALAM) ON THE LAST DAY

A caller - Gabriel - will call, *"Where is Fatima bint Muhammad?"* She will rise. Allah - blessed and exalted is His Name - will say,

"O people of the gathering: to whom does honor belong today?"

So Muhammad, Ali, Hassan and Hussain will say, *"To Allah, The One, The Almighty."*

Allah the Exalted will say, *"O people of the gathering: lower your heads and cast your eyes down, for this is Fatima proceeding toward Paradise."*

Gabriel will then bring her a female camel from the female camels of Paradise; its sides will be embellished, its muzzle with fresh pearls, and it will have a saddle of coral. It will kneel down in her presence; so she will ride it.

Allah will then send 100,000 angels to accompany her on her right side; and 100,000 angels to accompany her on her left side; and 100,000 angels to lift her onto their wings until they bring her to the gate of Paradise. When she is near the gate of Paradise, she will look to her side.

Allah will then say, *"Daughter of My beloved, why did you look to your side after I gave the command that you enter My Paradise?"*

She will say, *"My Lord, I wished that they would realize my position on such a Day!"*

Allah will say, *"Daughter of My Beloved! Go back and look for everyone in whose heart was love for you or for any of your progeny; take their hand and lead them into Paradise!"*

"Only within yourself exists that other reality for which you long."
- Hermann Hesse

"Bear my hand and you will be upheld in more than this."
- Charles Dickens

TALES FROM UNDER THE OVERPASS

*T*he week at "Starwood" was nearing its end. People were beginning to pack up their tents and possessions and say their good-byes. Mr. Khadir found Sam helping to clean up the outhouse.

Mr. Khadir gently took Sam by the arm. "Come. Let's take a walk." So they walked into a large field together. "Why don't we join hands and leap up over that huge tree over there?" Mr. Khadir suggested.

Sam smiled and replied, "Let's both take God's grace in hand and leap beyond the two worlds."

"Then let us begin My Friend," stated Mr. Khadir emphatically. "Start with your right foot and take one step with me."

They took the first step. "EVERYTHING," said Mr. Khadir.

Sam was taken up into the air and saw millions of believers of every faith engaging in their daily religious devotions.

"Now let us continue," continued Mr. Khadir.

And so they took a second step.

"THE TONGUE OF THE ULTIMATE REALITY," intoned Mr. Khadir, his voice beginning to rise in pitch and intensity.

Sam saw a swirling Circle of Energy from which arose a yearning so intense that was almost unbearable. In the center stood One Human Being. One word arose from this rotating wheel, "Hu."

Continuing in the same manner, they took a third step.

"THE WAY THAT IS NOT THE WAY," thundered Mr. Khadir in a wild arabesque of Divine reverberation that opened Sam's Limited-Self.

Sam saw Mr. Khadir sitting on top of a large emerald rock on the axis of the world. Sam understood Mr. Khadir was the Soul of the World. He looked closely at the face, and with a shock of realization, Sam saw his own face starring back at him. Sam said to his reflection: "Beggar! How did you get here? My God, my Friend, and my Lord! From Your Favor, Generosity, and Munificence." His last thought was, "Thy Face!" Sam blanked out in divine light and became a horizon of rays flashing from the Essence.

Finally, a fourth step.

A voice spoke coming from all directions, "THE SUBLIMELY CONSCIOUS RETURN TO LIVING LIFE!"

The One Who is Expressed as Everything saw Itself in each molecule, *atom and subatomic particle in the universe. They were all alive and whirling in Divine Ecstasy. The Merciful knew each one by name and loved the Whole, and the Whole, Who Was Expressing Itself as Sam, saw Its own reflection as Sam opened His eyes and gazed upon "Starwood."*

The Ocean of Compassion had flowed into the drop of water. Sam walked back to the outhouse and continued to help clean up.

*" He may be like Khidir, the Green One, who travels the Earth
in a variety of guises, and by means unknown to you . . .
What He says or does may seem inconsistent or even
incomprehensible to you. But it has meaning.
He does not live entirely in your world . . .
He may seem to return good for evil, or evil for good.
But what He is really doing is known only to the Few."*
- Salik

*"The Urn of Khidir is the Well of Immortality, the Graal of Blood from
whence the Seeker drinks."*
- Andrew D. Chumbley
(Alogos Dhu'l-qarnen)

*"Khidr is always there, where the two planes meet. He is there, 'where the
two seas meet', the sea of life and the sea of death, the space-bound and
the spaceless, the time-bound and the timeless."*
- Sara Sviri [711]

*"Thus the sun reaches its zenith: Reality at its most transcendent and yet at
the same time most immanent."*
- Peter Lamborn Wilson
and Nasrollah Paourjavady

KHEZR: THE GREEN MAN IN ISLAM

The character of Mr. Khadir is modeled after Hazreti Khezr (also known as: Khadir, Hizir, or Khizar), the Hidden Prophet of Sufism. As Salaam Aleikum! He is the archetypal Trickster Figure in Islam. Muslims have often known Khezr as "the Green Man" (*Khādir* literally means, "green"). He recurrently appears dressed in green, frequently with red shoes. Hazreti Khezr is the power of Allah, which reawakens the green plants in the spring from their slumber. However, he is no mere vegetation myth. Green is the most sacred color in Sufism. The supreme center, the *"mystery of mysteries,"* the *"Muhammad of thy being,"* is green.[712]

Khezr has been the immortal ruler of Hyperborea, the "King of the World," Alexander's cook, the friend/guide/servant of the Prophet Moses ('Alaihi Assalam), discoverer of the Fountain of Youth, the Prophet Elijah ('Alaihi Assalam) in the Judaic Tradition, and the initiator of Sufis who do not have a human Guide. *"Khidr {is} experienced simultaneously as a person and as an archetype . . . To have him as a master and initiand is to be obliged to be what he himself is. Khidr is the master of all those who are masterless, because*

596

he shows all those whose master he is how to be what he himself is: he who has attained the Spring of Life . . . he who has attained haqiqa, the mystic, esoteric truth which dominates the Law, and frees us from the literal religion. Khidr is the master of all these, because he shows each one how to attain the spiritual state which he himself has attained and which he typifies . . . " [713] They say that Khezr travels through the same place only once in every five hundred years. Khezr is immortal, as he is the only person to have drunk from that Well of Life - the Fountain of Youth. (He became green through diving into the spring of life). *"Yunus Emre, they say two people will remain in this world: It turns out it will be Khizir and Ilyâs, as they have drunk from Water of Eternal Life."* [714] They now estimate that he is over three-thousand years old. He lives right here on this Earth, but we cannot recognize him (to an extent similar to the case of the Imam Mahdi). Khezr has seen Kings and Queens, Kingdoms, Presidents, Czars, Czarinas, Sultans, Sultanas, Prime Ministers, and countries, pass away.

In the Qur'an, Khezr appears as the Prophet Moses' (Alaihi Assalam) guide. He reveals the mystic truth, or Haqiqat to Moses ('Alaihi Assalam), which transcends the Shariat (the literal religion) that Moses taught. This is why those who follow the spiritual path of Khezr are free from the fetters of religious law.

Khezr lived in earlier pre-Islamic myths and faiths, as is evidenced by the Islamic tradition that associates him with Moses ('Alaihi Assalam) and Alexander. Moses ('Alaihi Assalam) vowed to find the place *"where the two seas meet"* meaning the world of Spirit and the world of Earth, and there he meets Khezr. Therefore, Khezr lives at the meeting place between the opposites, the *coincidencia oppositorum*.[715] For the Sufis, this place is the Heart. The Heart is the Point of Transcendence where the Body and the Limitless Self unite. These are the two seas that manifest Khezr.

Some say he lives on an island (he may have originally been a marine being). According to Ibn 'Arabi's first-hand reports of Khezr's miracles, he walks on water and travels on the "flying carpet." He is the patron of seafaring people. *"No other holy person is associated so intimately with the sea as al-Khadir."*[716] He is Allah's Khalifa on the sea, commanding the obedience of the four quarters.

From where has this person come? Exactly, who is he? Khezr has close ties with the enigmatic being Hermes Trismegistus, otherwise known as "The Three Times Greatest Hermes." Hermes came out of early Egypt. There they regarded him as a ruler, instructor and wise man. Hermes was not exactly a god, but more like a superhuman benefactor of the human race. By the time of the second and third centuries C.E., Hermes appeared in his full glory.

By medieval times, the Muslim world recognized him as Khezr. In the book "Hermetica: The Ancient Greek and Latin Writings Which Contain Religious or Philosophical Teachings Ascribed to Hermes Trismegistus"[717] it is described how the Middle Eastern city of Harran sheltered both Hermeticists and Hermetic books into the Muslim period.

In the Muslim world Hermes Trismegistus, transformed into Hazreti Khezr (Salaam Aleikum) came to stand for a certain kind of esoteric knowledge that can only manifest in our banal everyday lives as shock, either of outrage or of laughter, or both at once. Ouspensky writes: *"A function that looks useless, such as laughter, helps to transform certain impressions which otherwise would be lost. If there were no laughter or humour on our level, this level would be even lower than it is now."*[718] That is why most of the tales about Khezr are humorous. The humor helps deliver the message to the person who hears or reads the tale. Often a person's nafs would reject this message if the information was delivered in a linear-cerebral manner. Humor can bypass the walls of dogma and close mindedness. Through humor, subtle impressions gain entry into a person, travel deeply within, and become alive. Khezr tales are often about contradictions and seeming duality. Ouspensky writings shed light on the juxtaposition of humor and contradiction. Writing about laughter and humor, he states, *"It means that a certain impression falls simultaneously on the positive and negative parts of a centre and this produces a feeling of exhilaration. It helps to see the other side, increases the capacity of seeing things."*[719] Therefore, through humor we collapse the contradiction inside ourselves, and begin to see more clearly. Khezr, the Islamic Pan or Dionysus, liberates and loosens the bonds of culture and conventionality.

Interestingly, the Staff of Hermes, the Caduceus, is the axis around which the cosmos turns. The Sufis teach that there is one spiritual being alive on earth, whom they call the Qutub or Axis. He or she is the supreme vice-regent of Allah Most High on Earth. The Caduceus has two serpents coiled around it. They represent the balance of darkness and light, the polarities of life.

Khezr is one of the *afrad*, the Unique Ones who receive light straight from God without human mediation.[720] He acts in ways that are strange and bizarre to the people around him. His purposes are often inscrutable. Often when Khezr appears, typically the narrow-minded get all upset. They ban or destroy all the writings about him or inspired by him. The revered friar Giordano Bruno, one blessed champion of Hermes, was burnt at the stake as a heretic in 1600. *"Ibn `Arabi was above all the disciple of Khidr {an invisible master} . . . such a relationship with a hidden spiritual master lends the disciple an essentially "transhistorical" dimension and presupposes an ability to experience events which are enacted in a reality other than the physical reality of daily life, events which spontaneously transmute themselves into symbols."*[721] The Islamic Orthodoxy banned Sheikh Ibn Arabi's works during his lifetime.

Hazreti Khezr as "Green Man" teaches the aspirant to return to his or her natural individuality, which is in complete harmony with the creative force of Allah Most High. *"Indeed, Khidr's "guidance" does not consist in leading all his disciples uniformly to the same goal, to one identical for all, in the manner of a theologian propagating his dogma. He leads each disciple to his own theophany, the theophany of which he personally is the witness, because that theophany corresponds to his "inner heaven," to the form of his own being, to his eternal individuality ('ayn thabita), in other words, to what Abu Yazid Bastami calls the 'part allotted' to each of the Spirituals and which, in Ibn 'Arabi's words, is that one of the which is invested in him, the name by which he knows his God and by which His God knows him . . . In Semnani's words, we should say that the Khidr's mission consists in enabling you to attain to the 'Khidr of your being,' for it is in this inner depth . . . that springs the Water of Life at the foot of the mystic Sinai . . ."* [722]

Khezr might hint at his identity through the wearing of the color green, or by revealing a knowledge of hidden things. He looks like no one and everyone, for they call him "The Shadow Man." He also seems to delight in confounding people to the point where they are not sure if the person they are seeing is some outrageous rogue or a saint drunk with the madness of Allah. Therefore, not passing judgment on the behavior of others is wise, as the person you judge may be the Green Man of Sufism.

There exist various Sufi "shrines." These are consequential holy symbols, each informing a greater level of Reality. Shrines devoted to Hazreti Khezr are frequently visited by women who are not able to bear children. In Turkey, the festival of *Hidirellez* marks the beginning of the Spring. The word Hidirellez is actually made of two words: Hizir and Ellez. Khezr is called *Hizir* in Turkish, and Ellez is a corruption of Elijah's ('Alaihi Assalam) Arabic name: *Ilyas*. Through centuries of mispronunciation and combining of the names: Khezr and Elijah ('Alaihi Assalam), the Turkish people ended up with the compound word: Hidirellez. A folk festival day, the Hidrellez, is very popular in Turkey, and is connected with both Khezr and Elijah ('Alaihi Asslam), who are thought in the Turkish tradition to be brothers (or, according to another tradition, lovers; in this legend Elijah ('Alaihi Assalam) is the young woman). They celebrate this festive day in the spring, May 5 and 6, to mark the summer's beginning, and incorporate many magical rites, among which the most prominent one is a future-revelation rite. Since Khezr means "green," he is conceptualized as connected with resumption of growth in the spring, and as a bringer of affluence, fertility and happiness. Come Hidirellez, people go out into the fields and meadows for picnicking and celebrating the rebirth of the nature and believe that whatever they wish that night before they go to bed will come true. Almost every town in Turkey has a place called Khuddur Ellez, in other words, Khezr Elijah ('Alaihi Assalam).

Khezr, not so surprisingly due to his antinomian nature, is also associated with war and has assumed at times the role of military advisor.

Another belief is that there is a chance of meeting Khezr under the central chandelier of one of the main mosques of the town on the night of Kadr, which is the 27th night of the month of Ramadan, when the Holy Qur'an started to be delivered to Muhammad (Peace be upon him). They also believe that one can recognize Khezr by checking his fingers of his right hand since one is missing. In Tajikistan, they believe that Hazrat-i-Khyzr (Khezr) walks always somewhere in the mountains of Tajikistan. One can recognize him by checking his fingers of his right hand since one is missing. So, when Tajik people see somebody walking in mountains, they run direct to him, say *"Salam-Aleikum"* and shake his hand to check, how many fingers he has. Because, it is said, that if you meet Hasrat-i-Khysr, he fulfills all your wishes!

Khezr is a customary initiation guide in the Sufi tradition. Sufi mystics would meet him in their journeys, and he would inspire them, answer their questions, save them from dangers, and in special cases even bestow on them the *khirqah*. What is more, such bestowing is thought valid initiation in the Sufi tradition, and those who pass it are considered connected to the greatest source of mystic inspiration. The great Sufi mystic Ibn al-'Arabi is one who claimed to have received his khirqah from Khezr. One of his functions is to convince doubters of the existence of the supersensible, to save those people who are disoriented in deserts of spiritual uncertainty and dry skepticism. Khezr reveals esoteric doctrines to men and women of exceptional sanctity. He sometimes appears to these individuals who are struggling along the Way. *"He . . . who is the disciple of Khidr possesses sufficient inner strength to seek freely the teaching of all masters. Of this the biography of Ibn `Arabi, who frequented all the masters of his day and welcomed their teachings, offers living proof."*[723] Hazreti Khezr is the hidden green prophet of unmediated knowledge (*'ilm al-ladun*). Therefore, he provides a direct connection with The Aware.

Whenever a Sufi comes to an empty and void place, he or she will hail and bless the place in the name of Khezr; for in speaking his name, one summons his Presence. When you say the name of Khezr in company, you should always add the greeting "Salaam Aleikum!" (*"Peace be unto you!"*) since he may be there, immortal and anonymous, going about some secret task.

Khezr also turns up as the Muslim Idries, the Egyptian Thoth and the Biblical Enoch. Some have identified Khezr with St. George, but we might more properly see him as both St. George and the dragon in one figure.[724] We philologically link the name Khezr with Elijah ('Alaihi Assalam) and with Utnapishtim of the Gilgamesh epic. We also link him with the Prophets Elijah ('Alaihi Assalam), Jesus ('Alaihi Assalam) and Idries ('Alaihi Assalam) as the three who have not tasted death. It is even possible that he may be part of the foundation for the mysterious and puzzling character in Sir Gawain and the Green Knight.

The secret Islamic name of Khezr is Ballya Ibn Malikan, according to Ibn' Arabi.[725] Although, he is open to innumerable identifications: Prophet Elijah ('Alaihi Assalam), Prophet Elishah ('Alaihi Assalam), Prophet Jermiah ('Alaihi Assalam), Khadrun Ibn Qabil, and al-Mu'ammar Ibn Malik. Al-Jahiz, poses the question: *"Tell me about Hermes, is he Idris [Enoch] and Jeremiah, is he al-Khadir, and about Yahya Ibn Zakariya [John the Baptist], is he Iliya [Elias]?"*[726]

As seen above, one of the wonderful aspects of Khezr is that he is able to bring both Muslim and Jewish concepts together. Common Arab and Jewish traditions are associated in the mystical personage of Khezr.

Khezr is Jung's anima. To the estericist, Khezr is the *latif* or life body. To the Sufi, Khezr is the Human Soul. Herein lies a great mystery. This is the revelation:

Ali ('Alaihi Assalam) is the soul and secret of Muhammad (Peace be upon him). In addition, we have earlier stated that woman is the soul. Khezr is the Soul of Luminescence that results from the Union of Ali ('Alaihi Assalam) and Fatima ('Alaiha Assalam), Jalal and Jamal, the names of gentleness Lutf and the names of severity Qahr, neither of which is in the east nor the west, but bursting into flame through their equilibration within the Sufi.

"No connection can be established between the one and the many, the luminous and the dark, without an intermediary, which in the human being's case is the soul, the locus of our individual awareness." [727]

In the words of Sohrawardi, *"If you are Khezr, you too can ascend Mt. Qaf without difficulty."*

*   *   *

In this book, Mr. Khadir's spoken words and actions are drawn first from oral transmissions of Hazreti Khezr tales told to us by Sheikhs we have met and with whom we have studied. Secondly, both Sam and Mr. Khadir's experiences together are drawn from a variety of ancient Sufi stories noted in some works we have cited in our list of sources at the end of this book. Thirdly, we have put into Sam, Mr. Khadir and Sheikh Muhtar's mouths the sacred words of various Imams, Sufi Saints and Spiritual Guides, including: al-Shaikh al-akbar Muhyiddin Ibn Al-'Arabi, Abu l-Hassan Kharaqani, Attar, Junayd, Jelaluddin Rumi, Maghribi, Ghaalib, Hassan-Ibn-Sabbah, Sa'di, Ahmed Rufa'i, Imam Malik, Abu Yazid al-Bistami, Sulaiman Halabi, Al-Ghazali, Abd al-Ra'uf al-Munawi, Fakhruddin 'Iraqi, Ismaili Pir Hassan II, Haci Bektasi Veli, Gharib Nawiz, Anis, Iqbal, Shaikh Suleyman Hayati Dede, M. b. I. al-Kalabadhi, the noble Sheikh Muzafferuddin Ashki al-Jerrahi al-Halveti, Sheikh Tosun Bayrak al-Jerrahi al-Halveti, Murshida Amina al-Jerrahi, Sheikh Mansur al-Jerrahi al-Halveti, Sheikh Salik al-Jerrahi al-Halveti, Shaykh Nur al-Anwar al-Jerrahi,

Sheikh Fadhlalla Haeri, Hakim Sana'i, H. Shejh Xhemali SHEHU, Sheikh el-Hajj el-Fakir Şerif Çatalkaya er-Rıfa'i er-Marufi, Br. Shari'ti, Mullah Nasruddin, Habiba, Suleyman Hayati Dede, Hakim Bey, and Abdullah Hicksvilli.

THE GREEN MAN IN ISLAM
by Jamshid

Mysterious one of many seekers,
the Green Man appears in the least likely places,
and the least likely of all is Islam.
It has been said
desert peoples value
three things above all else:
water, green things and great beauty.
It is al-Khidar, the Green One, salaam aliekhum!
who embodies all three.
It is the Green One:
who first tasted the waters of immortality
bringing back from Hyperborea
infinite light for all who would seek it;
he searches the universe all over
for seekers who would dare to learn the truth;
he is the teacher who appears
when the student is ready;
who is everywhere around us
constantly pouring into us
direct illumination from Divine Reality,
if we would only wake up;
it is he who shocks the mundane
to force them to acknowledge the existence
of the marvelous;
and of whose steps cause the barren soil
to spring up flowers and herbs as he walks.
May you meet the Green One soon!

"Sufism is the school of divine ethics, and the master of the Path attempts to decorate the Sufi's heart with divine attributes."
- *Dr. Javad Nurbakhsh*

"(Sufism) is a tradition of enlightenment."
- *Kabir Edmund Helminski*

"Five thousand years ago what I am saying was right. In five thousand years time what I am saying will still be right: cleanliness, honesty, decency, respect for other people, politeness, good manners, integrity - they will never be old-fashioned."
- *Charles Forte*

"According to the permutation of letters that is natural to the structure of the Arabic language and that is practiced consciously by the mystics of Judaism in Cabalistic contemplation, Sufi means fusion.
- *Shaykh Nur al-Anwar al-Jerrahi*

WHAT IS SUFISM?

Sufism *(Tasawwuf)* is the transcendental Way of Islam, the ineffable light of the Inexpressible. Some Muslim brothers and sisters ask if Sufism is an addition to Islam, and therefore, unnecessary. Therefore, we will address their question first. Many of the greatest and most renowned scholars have established the validity and usefulness of Sufism. We consider their answers to be the final word on whether or not Sufism is a true aspect of Islam.

It is mentioned in the book "Ad-Durr al-Mukhtar", vol 1. p. 43, on the explanation of Ibn 'Abidin who said, *"Abi Ali Dakkak, one of the sufi saints, received his path from Abul Qassim an-Nasarabadi, who received it from ash-Shibli, who received it from as-Sirr as-Saqati who received it from al-Ma'ruf al-Karkhi, who received it from Da'ud at-Ta'i, that he received the knowledge, both the external and the internal, from the Imam Abi Hanifa (r), who was supporting the Sufi Spiritual Path."*

Imam Malik (r) said, *"Whoever studies jurisprudence [fiqh] and didn't study Sufism will be corrupted; and whoever studied Sufism and didn't study fiqh will become a heretic; and whoever combined both will reach the Truth."* His saying are mentioned and explained in the book of the scholar 'Ali al-Adawi of the explanation of Imam Abil-Hassan, a scholar of fiqh, vol. 2, p. 195. Imam Malik was born in 95 A.H. and died in 179.

Imam Shafi'i (d, 204 A.H.) said, *"I accompanied the Sufi people and I received from them three knowledges:*
1. they made me to know how to speak;

2. they made to know how to treat people with leniency and a soft heart;

3. they made to be guided in the ways of Sufism."

This is mentioned in the books "Kashf al-Khafa" and "Muzid al-Albas" by Imam 'Ajluni, vol. 1, p 341.

Al-Imam Ahmad (r), advising his son, said *"O my son, you have to sit with the People of Sufism, because they are like a fountain of knowledge and they keep the Remembrance of Allah in their hearts. They are the ascetics and they have the most spiritual power."* This is explained in the book "Tanwir al-Qulub" p. 405, by Shaikh Amin al-Kurdi. Imam Ahmad said about the Sufis, as mentioned in the book "al-Ghiza al-Albab", vol. 1, p. 120, *"I don't know people better than them."*

Imam Ghazzali, *Hujjat ul-Islam* said about Sufism, *"I knew verily that Sufis are the seekers in Allah's Way, and their conduct is the best conduct, and their way is the best way, and their manners are the most sanctified. They have cleaned their hearts from other than Allah and they have made them as pathways for rivers to run receiving knowledge of the Divine Presence."*.[728]

Imam Nawawi said, in his Letters, "al-Maqasid", *"The specifications of the Way of the Sufis are five:*

1. to keep the Presence of Allah in your heart in public and in private;

2. to follow the Sunnah of the Prophet (s) by actions and speech;

3. to keep away from people in asking them;

4. to be happy with what Allah gave you, even if it is less;

5. to always refer your matters to Allah 'Azza wa Jall." [729]

Imam Fakhr ad-Din ar-Razi said, *"the way of Sufis for seeking Knowledge, is to disconnect themselves from this worldly life, and they keep themselves constantly busy in their mind and in their heart, with Dhikrullah, in all their actions and behaviors."* [730]

Ibn Khaldun said, *"The way of the Sufis is the way of the Salaf, the preceding Scholars between the Sahahba and Tabi'een of those who followed good guidance. Its origin is to worship Allah and to leave the ornaments of this world and its pleasures."* [731]

Tajuddin as-Subki (r) mentioned in his book "Mu'eed an-Na'am" p. 190, under the chapter entitled "Sufism", *"May Allah praise them and greet them and may Allah make us to be with them in Paradise. Too many things have been said about them and too many ignorant people have said things which are not related to them. And the truth is that those people left dunya and were busy with worship."* He said, *"There are the People of Allah, that Allah accepted their du'as and with their prayers, Allah supports human beings."*

Jalaluddin as-Suyuti said in his book "Ta'yid al-Haqiqat al-'Aliyya", p. 57, *"At-Tasawwuf in itself is the best and most honorable knowledge. It explains how to follow the Sunnah of the Prophet (s) and to leave innovation."*

The great scholar, Ibn 'Abidin in his book "Risa'il Ibn 'Abidin" p. 172 & 173: *"The Seekers in this Way don't hear except from the Divine Presence and they don't love any but Him. If they remember Him they cry, and if they thank Him they are happy; and if they find Him they are awake, if they see Him they will be relaxed; if they walk in His Divine Presence, they melt; they are drunk with His Blessings; May Allah bless them."*

Ash-Shaikh Muhammad 'Abduh: *"Tasawwuf appeared in the first century of Islam and it received a tremendous honor. It was cleansing the self and straightening the conduct and giving knowledge to people from the Wisdom and Secrets of the Divine Presence."* [732]

Ash-Shaikh Rashid Rida': *"Sufism was a unique pillar from the pillars of the religion. It was to cleanse the self and to make account of one's daily behavior and to raise the people to a high station of spirituality."* [733]

Maulana Abul Hasan 'Ali an-Nadawi is a member of the Islamic-Arabic Society of India and Muslim countries. He said in his book, "Muslims in India" p. 140-146, *"These Sufis were initiating people on Onenness and sincerity in following the Sunnah of the Prophet (s) and to repent from their sins and to be away from every disobedience of Allah 'Azza wa Jall. Their guides were encouraging them to move in the way of perfect Love to Allah 'Azza wa Jall."* He said, *"In Calcutta India, everyday more than 1,000 people were taking initiation into Sufism."* He said, *"By the influence of these Sufi people, thousands and thousands and hundreds of thousands in India found their Lord and reached a state of Perfection through the Islamic religion."*

Maulana Abul 'Ala Maudoodi said in his book "Mabadi' al-Islam li Abil 'Aala Maudoodi" p. 17, *"Sufism is a reality whose signs are the love of Allah and the love of the Prophet (s), where one absents oneself for their sake, and one is annihilated from anything other than them, and it is to know how to follow the footsteps of the Prophet (s)."* He said, *"Tasawwuf searched for the sincerity in the heart and the purity in the intention and the trustworthiness in obedience in an individual's actions."* He said, *"Sufism and Shari'ah: what is the simile of the two? They are like the body and the soul. The body is the external shari'ah knowledge and the spirit is the internal knowledge."*

Let us continue to answer the question posed by the heading of this chapter, that is, "What is Sufism?"

R. A. Nicholson: *"Sufism, the religious philosophy of Islam, is described in the oldest extant definition as 'the apprehension of divine realities.'"*

Abu 'l-Hassan: *"Sufism is neither a state nor a time; rather it is a sign which destroys, flashes which consume."*

Al-Khuldi: *"Sufism is a state in which the essence of Lordship is manifested, and the essence of servanthood is obliterated."*

Al-Muta'ish: *"Sufism is a state which a man guards jealously from both realms of being; he departs unto the Truth, and departs even out of his departing; the Great and Glorious Truth is, and he is not."*

Mahmud-I Shabustare: *"He is the one who passes quickly by the stops and burns his existence in the fiery smokless flame."*

Abu 'l-Hassan al-Aswari: *"Sufism is my forgetting myself, and my waking to my Lord."*

Abu Bakr al-Iıtlısı: *"Sufism is a state which neither heart nor reason can withstand."*

Ain al-Qudat al-Hamadhani: *"By Sufis I mean certain people who have turned with their innermost purpose to God, and have occupied themselves with following His path."*

Habashi b. Dawud: *"Sufism is the Will of the Truth in creation, without creation."*

Pir-o-Murshid Inayat Khan: *"Sufism or wisdom, related to the word 'Sophia', is acquired not only through knowledge but also by the grace of intuition. Sufism is neither a religion nor a cult, neither a doctrine nor a dogmatic institution. Perhaps one could say that Sufism has always been, ever since knowledge was knowledge. The object of worship of the Sufi is beauty, the moral of the Sufi is harmony and the goal of the Sufi is love in all its aspects, human and divine."*

"The object of Sufism has been said to be the production of saints. The saints of Islam are called awliya'. The friends of God."[734] This Way is similar to movements in other sacred traditions: Gnosticism, Rosicrucianism and Unitarianism in Christianity; the rise of Buddhism in the Hindu tradition; and Qabalah as the esoteric Way of Judaism. We have heard the Sheikhs say that Qabalah *is* Sufism, since both Ways have a mutual origin in the Prophet Moses ('Alaihi Assalam).

However, on the most profound level, the most important point of Sufism is the Oneness of the Body. *"There is Only Infinite, Unbounded Being, Indivisible, Unable To Be Differentiated From any Apparently Separate being. Indeed, There Are No conditional beings, but Only Being Itself."*[735]

According to Sheikh el-Hajj Şerif Çatalkaya er-Rıfa'i er-Marufi, Universal *Tasawwuf* began with the Prophet Idries (Elijah) who came after the Prophet Nuh (Noah), (Peace be upon them), and its first name was *theosophia*, meaning the wisdom of Allah.

It is said about Sophia that She (wisdom) is an exaltation from the power of God, a pure outpouring from the glory of the Almighty. She (wisdom) is an effulgence of everlasting light, an unblemished mirror of the active power of God. Ibn al-'Arabi met Sophia while circumambulating the Ka'ba.[736] The first book of Sufism was the twenty scrolls that Allah sent to Idries ('Alaihi Assalam). Following this, the Prophet Ibrahim (Abraham), ('Alaihi Assalam), found the Oneness of Allah inside this book and showed to all of humanity the surrender to Allah. And so, by establishing the system of Oneness, Ibrahim ('Alaihi Assalam) became the ancestor of three of the main religions of today. That is why in Islamic Tasawwuf they call him the father of *tevhid* unity. These explanations can be found in the four holy books: the Torah, the Psalms, the Gospel, and the Qur'an.

Islamic Tasawwuf traditionally has its origin in the Prophet Muhammad and Imam Ali ('Alaihi Assalam) with the Forty Companions. The forerunners of Islamic Tasawwuf are the Ahlul Bayt, the family of the Prophet Muhammad (Peace be upon him), and the *insani kamils*, the perfect human beings, who by following this road have held a light to our world and to humanity.

Some Sufi Sheikhs say that the rise of Sufism began after the first century of Islam as a struggle against the increasing distortions and misrepresentations of its teachings, especially as perpetrated by the leadership of the day.

It is true that the Islam practiced by the Prophet and his followers in Macca (al-Muharramah), before the journey to Medina (al-Munawwarah) in 622 C.E. known as the Hijra, was different from what followed the return to Macca (al-Mukarramah). It was after the return to Macca (al-Muharramah) that many of Islam's formal and ritualistic aspects originated. While before the Hijra there was no separation of men and women in the same house, the mosque was a community center in which business, social and civic exchange took place plus worship.

It was only after the return to Macca (al-Muharramah) that rules and laws became more stringent, due to the influx of many new Muslims. The mosque became a place of formal ceremonial worship and lost its primary location in the life of the community. "Islamism" - the reduction of Islam into an artificially coherent ideology, became the order of the day. [737] The Rifa'i Maruf'i Order attempts to rekindle the spirit of the first days in Macca (al-Mukarramah) before the move to Medina (al-Munawwarah). Will this approach to Islam take roots and thrive, *"Or will spirituality be hijacked by those who would offer rigid simplifications, or indoctrination into a one-dimensional reality? Such a religion, such a Din, cannot offer the human heart what it longs for."* [738]

One hundred years after the Holy Prophet's (Peace be upon him) death, Islam was codified and interpreted by the Four Imams of Sunni faith: Ibnu Mafazil Shaafi, Abu Hanifa, Ahmad Bin Hanbal, and Malik, resulting in many misinterpretations of the Words of the Qur'an and the teachings of the Prophet (Peace be upon him). These four scholars, while they were alive, had no idea that their ideas and work would be turned into religious dogma and doctrine. Unfortunately, the living Heart of Islam, was buried under the weight of this ideology. *"When Islam started getting more organized, we ended up with this mezhab, that mezhab, Shia, Sunni, Maliki, Hanbeli, and so forth. But people forget what the original purpose of all of these schools of thought was. Why did these schools come into being? All of these things were done to find out what is the right action. If it is not in the Quran and it is not in the Hadiths, you have to make a deduction. Imam Hanbeli said to do one thing, Imam Shafi said to do another. In the same area they differed from each other. But nobody has any objection about that. The important thing is that those Imams were doing it for themselves. They are not responsible for me. If they were wrong and I do the same thing, then I am wrong. I cannot say to Allah that I followed this Imam and he was wrong. I am responsible for myself. I have to make that decision. I can agree with him, but I have to take the responsibility for the action,"* writes Shaykh Taner Ansari Tarsusi er-Rifai el-Qadiri.[739]

Every passage of the Qur'an has both an outer (*zahir*) and an inner (*batin*) meaning. The Qur'an consists of *ayats* which can either mean "verses" or "signs" which are the manifestation of nature and all created reality. Everything is a "sign."

The Sufis themselves state that Sufism's origins lie in the ancient past, all the way back to the first human being. We are all the children of Adam and Eve, all one family. As Bhagwan Shree Rajneesh states, *"Sufism is not part of Islam; rather, on the contrary, Islam is part of Sufism . . . religions take form and dissolve; Sufism abides, continues, because it is not a dogma."*[740] To have the qualities of God is to be a Sufi. The Sufis are known as Friends of God. Much more to the point, to the Sufi, the Divine Essence is the Beloved, neither male nor female, and the Sufi is the Lover.

It is said that,

> *The seed of Sufism was*
> > *sown in the time of Adam*
> > *germed in the time of Noah*
> > *buddled in the time of Abraham*
> > *began to develop in the time of Moses*
> > *reached maturity in the time of Jesus*
> > *produced pure wine in the time of Muhammad.*

Throughout Islamic history, the Orthodox Muslim community has persecuted Sufis, denounced, exiled, imprisoned and sometimes even killed them. Many of the orthodoxy regarded the Sufi goal of union with God as heresy. They saw Sufis as a threat to Islam. The Islamic scholars believed that knowledge of God was obtained from the study of the Qur'an, not through personal experience. In 922 C.E., a Sufi mystic, al-Hallaj, was crucified for blasphemy for his declaration of unity with God, *"I am the Truth."* Herbert Mason in his biography on Al-Hallaj writes: *"He was accused by his enemies of dissimula-*

tion and opportunism by associating with neo-Helenists, philosophers, aesthetes, pseudo-mystics, magicians, Christians, Jews, Zoroastrians, Manichaeans, Hindus, Buddhists, the rich and the poor, indiscriminately on his travels throughout the Near East, Iran, India and possibly even China; and at home with adepts of radical Shi'ism while claiming the heritage and identity of a strict traditionalist. What kept Hallaj from syncretism was his steadfast, undeniable practice of his faith, which did not seem to him a contradiction to his universalism: because his Beloved was the source of everything to him and was free in His creativeness, His compassion, His hospitality."

The term "Sufi" is of uncertain origin. The term originates from three Arabic letters: *sa, wa* and *fa.* Some say the word came from *Ashāb-e-Suffa* (Sitters in the Shrine) - eighty or more poor men who used to stay and have religious teachings in the Prophet's mosque in Al-Medina (al-Munawwarah). These devotees sat on the "bench," a small raised platform, of the mosque. They were indigent strangers, without friends or abode, whom the Prophet Muhammad (Peace be upon him) occasionally invited to partake food with him or his Companions.

Then there were the people who stood in the first row of the faithful at prayer times; they named them *Saff Awwal.*

Another possible origin of the term "Sufi" might be an Arab "Beduin" tribe named Banu Sufa who engaged themselves in the service of the Macca (al-Mukarramah) temple. Also, feasiblely, Sufis gained their name from *soof* meaning "wool," as they wore woolen garments.

Lastly, the name most probably comes from *Safa* meaning "purity," for the Sufis are certain people who are true servants of the Ultimate Reality who walk the earth with polite and courteous bearing. They are pure because they do not see anything other than Allah.

We must remember that Sufism is a science, and that *"every science has men who devote themselves to it especially, and to whom it is necessary to have recourse if one wishes to ascertain the precise meaning of their technical terms. By the same means the Sufis also employ technical terms between themselves, the meanings of which are not known to others. Theologians are not ignorant of the fact that every department of learning has its own technical vocabulary agreed upon by those who specialize in it; the terms used in each department are only known to those who follow that path."*[741]

The most important element of Sufism is *Zikrullah,* the Remembrance of the Divine. There are various forms of this "remembrance" but the central practice consists of the repetition of certain of the Divine Names of Allah. Remembrance of God is the entrance to the Silver Palace.

Giving up your other spiritual practices to become a Sufi is not necessary (although it does make it more difficult for the Murid to juggle several practices) nor is it necessary to become a Muslim.

At his or her deepest level, the Sufi cares not for religions or mystical states (although these states and levels exist); his or her only aim is Proximity with the Beloved. The Sufi is a trumpet blast of Truth, a clarion call to all Lovers of God to gather to chant "Hu," the name of the Divine Essence.

"Friend, if you desire to be granted eternal happiness, for one moment keep the company of an 'indweller,' who is a Sufi, so that you may know what manner of being an 'indweller' is. Perchance it was of this that the shaikh spoke, 'The Sufi is God.'" [742]

PRACTICE

Visualize yourself in the midst of cosmic space. Notice the blackness of space punctuated with billions of pinpoints of brilliant starlight. In front of you is the sun. Know that there is a Sun behind the sun. This Greater Sun spiritually feeds the sun around which the planets of our solar system orbit. As Abā Ya'zā Yalannār Ibn Maymān ad-Dukkālī writes in his "Treatise on Sufism": *"The sun of the day sets by night, but the sun of the heart is never absent."* Paul Tillich has boldly referred to *"the God above God."*

This Greater Sun is the Sun at Midnight, the Night of Light, the Dark Noontide, the Black Light, and the Sun of Intimacy, which we can most clearly see shining in the Hearts of the Lovers of Allah. This Greater Sun neither has name, nor attribute, and of whom we can predict nothing, and to whom we can render no worship.

> *"That mystery, so long concealed*
> *is at last opened,*
> *the darkness of your night at last*
> *bathed in dawn.*
> *You yourself are the veil of mystery*
> *of the Unseen Heart:*
> *if it were not for you*
> *it would never have been sealed."*
> *- Fakhruddin 'Iraqi* [743]

"Each day is a little life; every waking and rising a little birth, every fresh morning a little youth, every going to rest and sleep a little death."
- Arthur Schopenhauer

"When the Yellow Emperor woke, he was delighted to have found himself."
- Lieh-Tzu

"I saw such and such, which, dreaming that I had waked, I interpreted."
- Ibn al-'Arabi

"Perhaps God is our dream, as we are His."
- Empire of the Sun

TALES FROM UNDER THE OVERPASS

*S*am stirred in bed. A strange sensation came over him. Sounds came to him *from the outside. Birds were chipping. He realized it was morning. He opened his eyes. He was in the ashram. The picture of the guru smiled at him from its frame on the wall at the end of his bed.*

"What did I just . . ." His voice trailed off. "Did I just dream all that?" HE wondered aloud.

His door opened and a pretty woman peered inside "Time to get up Sam" she said, "we must prepare for guru's breakfast."

"I'll be right there," Sam uttered half asleep. Sam's head fell back on the pillow. He felt dazed. "What happened?" He wondered to himself. This was too much. Could it be possible that he dreamed all of that with Mr. Khadir and being a homeless man? He fell back into a deep dreamless sleep.

"Samantha! Samantha!"

What's that? Samantha thought.

"Samantha!" her mother yelled. "Get up! It's time to go to school."

"School?" Samantha thought, "School? School!"

Her mother walked into the room, "I don't believe a seventeen-year-old high school junior can't get herself up on time!" The beautiful emerald jewel shown brightly around her mother's neck.

Samantha jumped out of bed and started to get dressed.

As she struggled to pull on her jeans, she looked up at a poster over her bed. It read,

"Last night I dreamed I was a butterfly. Today I believe I am a woman. And so I wonder, am I a woman who dreamed of being a butterfly, or am I a butterfly who is now dreaming she is a woman?"

The quotation was ascribed to Chuang Tzu. Samantha smiled.

"The eloquent book of Allah; The truthful Qur'an; The brilliant light; The shining beam."

> *- Lady Fatima Zehra*
> *(Peace be upon her)*

"The Holy Qur'an is not a book written in Arabic. The whole universe is the Qur'an. It is from before the before, to after the after. It is the explanation which includes everything."

> *- Sheikh Muzaffer Ozak*
> *al-Jerrahi al-Halveti* [744]

SOURCES AND FURTHER READING

Many sources quoted in this book are obscure, not available in English, and often referred to in many ways by scholars and sometimes even by authors referring to other sources. Some books are lost. Where possible, we have resolved these problems in this book, and the name of the work or author commonly used by scholars is given. In the following section, we have done our best to find citations for all the books. This has been difficult and occasionally impossible with some titles and authors because of variant Persian, Turkish and Arab transliterations. The reader will notice that occasionally, spellings of books and authors given below are different from those in the above text. This is because, in the text, we have attempted to use the most contemporary transliterations used by scholars; however, often the citations found in "WorldCat"[745] and other reference sources, give the titles and authors as the translators originally transliterated them.

To the Sufi, the Qur'an-i Karim is not a book. It is the universe. The Qur'an is alive! It is a tree whose roots are found in Paradise. The True Guides - the Sheikhs, the Holy Ones of the Ultimate Reality are the Living Qur'an, in the sense that they have become the Mother-Source of the Qur'an. The Murid seeks to find the Inner Qur'an written on his or her heart. Therefore, while we recommend reading the Qur'an, the Murid must read it with the eyes of the heart. In addition, Zikruallah is the Qur'an. The entire Qur'an is found in *"La ilaha il ALLAH."*

For Muslims, translations of the Qur'an are not the Qur'an, only the original Arabic text is the Qur'an. There is much hidden wisdom in this. The Sufi must develop the mind and the heart. Especially valuable is to have the original Arabic text explained to you by someone who is an expert (and an unbiased) interpreter of this language. For much of the subtle meanings are lost through translation. To have someone who can explain to you the various possible meanings of each word, opens new vistas and dimensions of the universal Qur'anic Reality.

Kabir Helminski points out another fact to remember in reading the *Qur'an*, *"And even when we have a revelation, such as the Qur'an, whose integrity has been preserved, there is the problem of understanding what it has to say. So much cultural distortion gets in the way, and our own selves get in the way."*[746]

The Holy Prophet (Peace be upon him) said, *"I do not speak Arabic. I speak the language of shamanism."* Muhammad (Peace be upon him) and the Qur'an brought many new words into the Arabic language. The Arabs thought that they were just new words, but they were, in actuality, shamanic language, for instance, the name Shaitan. In the Shamanic language it means to worship the material. *Sey* - means object, nonliving, it, and material. *Tan* - means to make something into an idol.

We have heard a Sheikh say that the entire Qur'an is an analogy. The reality is deeper than that. The Qur'an is a Revealed Book of Unitary Knowledge written in the language of shamanism. One must know not only Arabic, but also the vocabulary of the Shaman/Sufi to understand the Qur'an.

PRIMARY SOURCES

Abdi. *Jam'a Bainu's-Sihahu's-Sitta.*

Abdullahi'l-Haskani, Hakim Abu'l-Qasim Abdullah Bin. *Du'atu'l-Huda Ila Ada Haqqi'l-Muwala.*

Abdullahi'l-Haskani, Hakim Abu'l-Qasim Abdullah Bin. *Shawahidu't-tanzil.*

Abeekussafadi, Salahuddin Khalil Bin. *Wafi Bil Wafiyyat* (This volume of Wafi Dil Wafiyyat, In manuscript form, is present in the National Library of Haji Husain Aqa Malik, Tehran).

Abu Nu'aym, 'Abd Allah Ibn Ahmad al-'Isfahani. *Hilyat al-'awliya' wa tabaqat al-'asfiya* Cairo, 1351.

Addas, Claude. *Ibn 'Arabi, Ou La quête du Soufre Rouge* Paris, Gallimard, 1989.

Alhazred, Abdul. *The Necronomicon* New York?, Schlangekraft, 1977, Acknowledgments signed: L. K. Barnes. [Author's comment: actually written by Simon (Peter Levenda) and possibly James Wasserman.]

Ali, Hazrat. *Nahjul Balagha*, Tehran, Iran, Golshan Printing House.

Ali, Sirdar Ikbal. *Islamic Sufism* Samuel Weiser Inc., 1971.

Ali, Barkat. *Finality of The Divine Revelations of Prophethood on Muhammad* Faisalabad, Pakistan, Dar-Ul-Ehsan Publications, 1979.

Andaluci, Abu Muhammad Ali Ibn Ahmad Ibn Hazm al-. *al-Fisal fi al-Milal wa-al-Ahwa'i wa-al-Nihal.*

Angha, Molana Salaheddin Ali Nader Shah. *Sufism and Islam*, Washington, D.C. Shahmaghsoudi Publication, 1997.

Arberry, A. J. *Discourses of Rumi* New York, Samuel Weiser, 1977.

Arberry, A. J. Trans. *A Sufi Martyr: The Apologia of 'Ain al-Qudat al-Hamadhani* London, George Allen and Unwin Ltd., 1969.

Al-Askari, al-'Imam. *Tafsir al-Quran* (ascribed), Iran.

Attar, Farid al-Din. *Manteq-o't-tair* edited by Seyyed Sadeq Gauharin, Tehran, 1977

Attar, Farid al-Din. *Muslim Saints and Mystics: Episodes from the 'Tadhkiratal-Auliya' ("Memorial of the Saints")* London, Routledge and Kegan, Paul, 1979.

Attar, Farid al-Din. *Elahi-nama* edited by Nurani Wesal, Tehran, 1977.

Awn, Peter J. *Satan's Tragedy and Redemption: Iblis in Sufi Psychology*, Netherlands, Leiden E. J. Brill, 1983.

Azami, M. M. *Studies in Early Hadith Literature* American Trust Publications, 1992.

Baba, Meher. *Beams from Meher Baba on the Spiritual Panorama* Walnut Creek, Ca., Sufism Reoriented, 1958.

Baghawi, Husain Bin Mas'ud. *Masabihu's-Sunna* al-Qahirah, al-Matba'ah al-Khayriyah, 1900.

617

al-Baghdadi, Abd al-Qadi. *Al-Farq bayn al-Firaq (Moslem Sects and Schisms)* Trans. K. S. Seelye , New York, Columbia University Press, 1920.

al-Baghdadi, al-Khatib. *Tarikh Baghdad* Cairo, also al-'A'lami, Beirut.

Balkhi, Sheikh Sulayman *Yanabiu'l-Mawadda.*

Bakhtiar, Laleh. *Sufi:Expressions of the Mystic Quest*, New York, Avon Books, 1976.

Bakhtiar, Laleh. Intro. to *Fatima is Fatima* by Dr. Ali Shariati.

Baladhuri, Ahmad Ibn Yahya. *Ansab al-ashraf* vol. 5, Cairo, 1955.

Baldick, Julian. *Black God: The Afroasiatic Roots of the Jewish, Christian, and Muslim Religions* London: New York, Syracuse University Press, 1997.

Baldick, Julian. *Imaginary Muslims: The Uwaysi Sufis of Central Asia* New York, New York University Press, Washington Square, 1993

al-Barr, Ibn u'Abd. *al-Isti'ab* Ed. Hasan ibn Ahmad al-Nu'mani, 1917, 1918.

al-Barr, Ibn u'Abd. *Kitab 'al-'isti'ab fi ma'rifat 'al-'ashab* Haydar'abad, Matba'at Majlis Da'irat 'al-Ma'arif 'al-Nizamiyah, 1900.

Bayhaqi, Ahmad ibn al-Husayn. *Kitab al-da'wat al-kabir* edition: al-Tab'ah 1, al-Kuwayt, Manshurat Markaz al-Makhtutat wa-al-Turath wa-al-Watha'iq, 1993.

al-Bayhaqi, Ibrahim Ibn Muhammad. *al-Mahdsin wa al-masawi'.*

Begg, W. D. *The Holy Biography of Hazrat Khwaja Muinuddin Chishti.*

Begg, Janab W. D. and Sahizada S. M. Yunus Maharaj. *Spiritual Victory of Imama Husain: The Greatest Myrtyr* (sic) of the World Ajmer, India, Extraordinary Publications.

Bey, Hakim. *Aimless Wandering: Chuang Tzu's Chaos Linguistics.*

Bey, Hakim. *Millennium* Autonomedia and Garden of Delight, USA, 1996.

Biblioteca ambrosiana. *Manuscript. H75. Gnosis-Texte der Ismailiten: Arabische Handschrift Ambrosiana H 75,* Ed.: Strothmann, Rudolf, Gottingen, Vandenhoeck & Ruprecht, 1943.

Bill, Richard. *Introduction to the Qur'an* Edinburgh, University Press, 1953.

Birge Ph.D., John Kingsley. *The Bektashi Order of Dervishes*, London, Luzac Oriental, 1994.

Bouhdiba, Abdelwahab. *Sexuality in Islam* Trans. Alan Sheridan, Great Britain, Routledge & Kegan Paul, 1985.

Bowering, Gerhard. *The Mystical Vision of Existence in Classical Islam* Berlin; New York, Walter De Gruyter, 1980.

Bowles, Paul. *M'Hashish* Taped and Translated from the Moghrebi by Paul Bowles, San Francisco: City Light Books, 1993.

Bukhari, Khwaja Parsa. *Faslu'l-Khitab.*

Bukhari, Muhammad Bin Isma'il. *Ta'rikh.*

Chumbley, Andrew D. (Alogos Dhu'l-qarnen) *Qutub: also called The Point* Chelmsford, Essex, U.K., Xoanon, ISBN 0-9519264-2-X.

Corbin, Henry. *Cyclical Time and Ismaili Gnosis*, London, Islamic Publications, 1983.

Corbin, Henry. *The Man of Light in Iranian Sufism* Trans. Nancy Pearson, New Lebanon, Omega Publications, Inc., 1994.

Corbin, Henry. *History of Islamic Philosophy* London, Kegan Paul International, 1990.

Corbin, Henry. *Creative Imagination in the Sufism of Ibn 'Arab* , Trans. Ralph Manheim, Princeton and London, 1969.

Daftary, Farhad. *The Ismailis: Their History and Doctrines* Cambridge [England] ; New York , Cambridge University Press, 1992.

Damiri. *Hayat al-hayawan* Translator A.S.G. Jayakar, London, Luzac; Bombay, D.B. Taraporevala, 1906-1908.

Damishqi, Ibn Kathir Shafi'i. *Ta'rikh.*

Darimi, *Muqaddim*a in his *Sunan.*

Darimi, 'bd Allah Ibn 'Abd al-Rahman. *Sunan* edition: al-Tab'ah 1, Dimashq, Dar al-Qalam, 1991.

Dawud, Abu. *Sahih.*

Dhahabi, Muhammad Bin Abdu'r-Rahman. *Talkhisu'l-Al-Mustadrak 'ala al-Sahihayn.*

al-Dinawari, Abu 'Abd Allah Muhammad ibn Muslim al-Kufi al-Maruzi. (known as Ibn Qutaybah) *'Uyun al-'akhbar.*

Dinawari, Abu Muhammad Abdullah Bin Muslim Bin Qutayba Bin Umar Al-Bahili. *Ta'rikhu'l-Khulafate Raghibin* (known as: *Al-Imama wa's-Siyassa).*

Emre, Yunus. *Geldi geçti ömrüm benim, sol yel esip geçmis gibi.*

Encyclopedia of Islam: A Dictionary of the Geography, Ethnography and Biography of the Muhammadan Peoples, London, Luzac and Co., 1927.

Evradi Rifayye of Pirina Sultan Ebul Alameyn Ahmedel Kebira Rifa'i.

Friedlander, Shems with al-Hajj Shaikh Muzaffereddin *Ninety-Nine Names of Allah*, Perennial Library, New York, Harper and Row Publishers, 1978.

Ghalib. *Twenty-Five Verses: Ghalib* Trans. C. M. Naim, Calcutta, India, Writers Workshop Books, P. Lal Publishers, 1970.

Ghalib, Mirza. *Diwan-i Ghalib* Urdu, ed. Imtiaz Arshi, Aligarh: Anjuman Taraqi-e-Urdu Hind, 1958.

Al-Ghazali, 'Abu Hamid Muhammad Bin Muhammad. *Mishk t ul-Anw r* found in *al-Jawahir al-Ghawali* Cairo, 1353 A.H. (1934 C.E.).

Al-Ghazali, Abu Hamid Muhammad Bin Muhammad. *Sirru'l-Alamin.*

Al-Ghazali, 'Abu Hamid Muhammad Bin Muhammad. *Mishk t ul-Anw r* Royal Asiatic Society.

Al-Ghazali, 'Abu Hamid Muhammad Bin Muhammad. *al-Maqsad ul-Asna*

Cairo, 'Alamiyyah, (no date given).

Al-Ghazali, 'Abu Hamid Muhammad Bin Muhammad. *ma'ary ul-Quds fi Madary Ma'rifat in-Nafs* Cairo, 1346 A.H. (1927 C.E.)

Al-Ghazali, 'Abu Hamid Muhammad Bin Muhammad. *Ihya' 'Ulum id-Din* (Amiriyyah MS) Cairo, Umariyyah Press, 1352 A.H. (1933 C.E.).

Al-Ghazali, 'Abu Hamid Muhammad Bin Muhammad. *Manqul fi Ilmi'l-Usul.*

Gibran, Kahlil. *Patterns of Happiness* Kansas City, Missouri Hallmark Cards, Inc., 1971.

Gibran, Kahlil. *Thoughts and Meditations* Translated from the Arabic and Edited by Anthony R. Ferris, New York, The Citadel Press, 1969.

Günci, Baba. *Nefes in Istanbul Konservatuvari Nesriyati*, Bektasi Nefesleri, II.

Gurdjieff, George Ivanovich. *Gurdjieff: Essays and Reflections on the Man and His Teaching* edited by Needleman, Jacob and George Baker, New York, Continuum, 1996.

Haeri, Shaykh Fadhlalla. *The Elements of Sufism* Shaftesbury, Dorset, Great Britain, Element Books Limited, 1990.

Haeri, Shaykh Fadhlalla (collector). *The Sayings and Wisdom of Imam Ali* Trans. Yate, Asadullah ad-Dhaakir.

Haeri, Fadhlalla. *The Light of Iman from the House of 'Imran: Surat Al-i 'Imran:* (tafsir), Blanco, TX, Zahra Publications, 1986.

Hafez, S. M. *Teachings of Hafez (Divan)* Trans. Gertrude Bell, London, 1979.

Haidar, Asad. *Al-'Imam al-Sadiq wa al-madhahib al-'arba'ah (Al-Sadiq and the Four Madh'habs)* Vol. 1, Najaf.

Hajjaj, Muslim Bin. *Sahih* Egypt.

Hakim al-Nisaburi, Muhammad Ibn 'Abd Allah. *al-Juz' al-awwal[-al-rabi'] min al-Mustadrak 'ala al-Sahihayn fi al-hadith* Haydarabad, Matba'at Majlis Da'irat al-Ma'arif al-Nizamiyah, 1991 1915.

Halabi. *Siratu'l-Halabiyya.*

Halim, Ibn Taimiyya Ahmad Bin Abdu'l. *Minhaju's-Sunna.*

Hallaj, Hosain ebn Mansur. *Tamhidât* edited by 'Afif 'Osairân, Tehran, 1962.

al-Hallaj, Mansur. *The Tawasin of Mansur al-Hallaj* Trans. Aisha at-Tarjumana, Berkeley and London: Diwan Press, 1974.

Hamadani, Ayn al-Qozat. *The Drunken Universe: An Anthology of Persian Sufi Poetry* translations and commentary by Peter Lamborn Wilson and Nasrollah Pourjavady, Grand Rapids, Phanes Press, 1987.

Hamadani, Ayn al-Qozat. *A Sufi Martyr* Trans. A. J. Arberry, London, Allen and Unwin, 1969.

Hamawi, Muhammad Ibn al-Hasan Ibn Ahmad al-Samman. *Fayd al-mun'im min Sahih Muslim: thalath mi'at hadith wa-hadith* edition: al-Tab'ah 1,al-Kuwayt:Bayrut, Maktabat Dar al-'Urubah lil-Nashr wa-al-Tawzi;' Dar al-'Imad, 1992.

Hamidi. *Jam'i Bainu's-Sahihain.*

Hamwaini, Sheikhu'l Islam Ibrahim Bin Muhammad. *Fara'idu's-Simtain.*

al-Haraw , 'Abd Allah Ansari. *Les étapes des itinérants vers Dieu* Trans. S. de Laugier de Beaurecueil O.P., Paris 1962.

Haykal, Muhammad Husayn. *The Life of Muhammad* Trans. Ismail Ragi A. al Faruqi, American Trust Publications, 1976.

al-Haythami, Nur al-Din Ali Ibn Abi Bakr. *Majma' al-Rijal.*

al-Haythami, Nur al-Din Ali Ibn Abi Bakr. *Majma 'al-zawa'id wa manba 'al-fawa'id*

Ibn Hajar al-Haythami, Ahmad Ibn Muhammad. *Kitab al-Sawa'iq al-muhriqah fi al-radd 'ala ahl al-bida' wa-al-zandaqah* Edition:Tab'ah 1., Misr, al-Matba'ah al-'Amirah, 1891.

Ibn Hajar al-Haythami, Ahmad Ibn Muhammad. al-Sawa'iq al-muhriqah *'ala ahl al-rafd wa-al-dalal wa-al-zandaqah* edition: al-Tab'ah 1, Bayrut, Mu'assasat al-Risalah lil-Tiba'ah wa-al-Nashr wa-al-Tawzi', 1997.

Ibn Hazm, Ali b. Ahmad. *Tawq al-hamama fi 'l-ulfa wa-l-ullaf* Trans. LJon Bercher, Algiers, Editions Carbonel, 1949, p. 92.

Helminski, Kabir. *Servant of Mevlana.*

Hibban, Ibn. *Mashahir 'ulama al-amsar.*

Hilmi, Ahmet. *Awakened Dreams: Raji's Journeys with the Mirror Dede* Translators Refik Algan and Camille Helminski, Putney, Vermont, Threshold Books, 1993.

Hindi, Molvi Ali Muttaqi. *Kanzu'l-Ummal.*

Hixon, Lex (Nur al-Jerrahi). *Atom From the Sun of Knowledge* Connecticut, Pir Publications, 1993.

Hughes, Thomas Patrick. *A dictionary of Islam : being a cyclopaedia of the doctrines, rites, ceremonies, customs, with the technical and theological terms, of the Muhammadan religion* New Delhi : Ottawa, Asian Educational Services ; Laurier Publications, 1996, 1885.

al-Hujweri, Syed Ali Bin Uthman. *The Kashful Mahjub "Unveiling the Veiled": The Earliest Persian Treatise on Sufism* Trans. and commen tary by Hadhrat Maulana Wahid Bakhsh Rabbani, Malaysia, A.S. Noordeen, 1997

al-Hujw r . *Kashf al-mahjub* Trans. R. A. Nicholson, London, 1911.

Hujviri, 'Ali Ibn 'Uthman. *Stories from Hazrat Data Ganj Baksh : 101 stories selected from Kashful mahjub* Lahore, Unique Publications, 1972.

Hunekeh, Frau. *The Arab's Sun Spreads over the West.*

Husain, Ali Ibn-el. *A Part of Invocations from Saheefa-E-Kamelah (The Book of Perfection)* Kuwait, Mohammad Qabazard Charity Fund.

Ibn Abbas, Abdullah. *Hilyatu'l-Auliya.*

Ibn 'Abd Rabbih, Ahmad Ibn Muhammad. *al-'Iqd al-farid* Beirut, Librairie Sadir, 1954.

Ibn Abi'l-Hadid Mu'tazali. *Sharhe Nahul'l* Balagha Egypt, 1329.

Ibn al-'Arabi. *Futuhat al-Makkiyya* Trans. William C. Chittick in *The Sufi Path of Knowledge; Ibn al-'Arabi's Metaphysics of Imagination*; Albany, New York: SUNY Press, 1989.

Ibn al-'Arabi. Muhyiddin. *Fusfs al-Hikam* Bayrut, Lubnan, Dar al-Kittab al-Arabi, 1980.

Ibn al-'Arabi. ' *Whoso Knoweth Himself* . . . (from the *Treatise on Being, Risale-t-ul-wujudiyyah)* Oxon, 1988.

Ibn al-'Arabi. *Sufis of Andalusia: The Ruh al-quds and al-Durrat al-fakhirah of Ibn 'Arabi* Trans. R. W. Austin, London, George Allen and Unwin, 1971.

Ibn al-'Arabi. *The Bezels of Wisdom* Trans. R. W. J. Austin, New Jersey, Paulist Press, 1980.

Ibn al-'Arabi. *The Sufi Path of Knowledge; Ibn al-'Arabi's Metaphysics of Imagination* Trans. William C. Chittick, Albany, New York: SUNY Press, 1989.

Ibn al-'Arabi. *Journey to the Lord of Power: A Sufi Manual on Retreat* Trans. Rabia Terri Harris, Vermont, Inner Traditions International, 1989.

Ibn al-'Athir, 'Izz al-Din Abu al-Hassan Ali. *History.*

Ibn al-'Athir, Majd al-Din Abu al-Sa'dat al-Mubarak. *Al-Nihaya fi Gharib al-Hadith wa al-'Athar* Cairo.

Ibn 'Asakir. *Ta'rikh Dimashq* manuscript in al-Maktabat al-Zahirriyyah, Damascus.

Ibn Hajar al-'Asqalani, Ahmad Ibn Ali. *Fath al-Bari: Sharh Sahih al-Bukhari* Bayrut, Dar-al-Kutab al-'Illmiyah, 1989.

Ibn Hajar al-'Asqalani, Ahmad Ibn Ali. *Tahdhib al-Tahdhib* 10 vols. 1st ed. Hyderabad: Da'ira al-Ma'arif al-Nizamiyya, 1327H.

Ibn Hajar al-'Asqalani, Ahmad Ibn 'Ali. *Fath al-bari bi-sharh Sahih al-Bukhari* 1901 1911.

Ibn Hanbal, Ahmad Ibn Muhammad. *Musnad al-Imam al-Hafiz Abi 'Abd Allah Ahmad Ibn Hanbal al-Riyad*, Bayt al-Afkar al-Dawliyah, 1998.

Ibn Hanbal, Ahmad Ibn Muhammad. *Kitab Fada'il al-Sahabah* al-Tab'ah 1, Bayrut, Mu'assasat al-Risalah, 1983.

Ibn Hanbal, Imam Ahmad. *Manaqib.*

Ibn Hisham, 'Abd al-Malik. *The life of Muhammad: a translation of Ishaq's Sirat rasul Allah* Jubilee series ed., Karachi ; New York, Oxford University Press, 1997.

Ibn Huseyn Suleymi. *The Way of Futuwwet* Trans. Sheikh Tosun Bayrak al-Jerrahi al-Halveti, January 9, 1981, unpublished paper.

Ibn Ishaq, Muhammad. *The Making of the Last Prophet : a reconstruction of the earliest biography of Muhammad* Columbia, S.C., University of South Carolina Press, 1989.

Ibn Kathir, Isma'il Ibn Umar. *Ta'rikh (History).*

Ibn Khaldun, Abd al-Rahman Ibn Mohammad. *Muqaddimah* Trans. F. Rosenthal.

Ibn Khaldun. *Muqaddamah-i Ibn Khaldun* Chap-i 4, Tihran, Bungah-i Tarjumah va Nashr-i Kitab, 1980.

Ibn Maghazili, Abu'l-Hasan Faqih Shafi'i Ali Bin Muhammad Bin Tayyib al-Jalabi. *Manqib.*

Ibn Sa'd, Katib al-Waqidi. *Al-Tabaqat al-kubra* Leiden.

Ibn Jamak. *Musnad.*

Ibn Sin. (Avicenna). *Ode to the Human Soul* Trans. E. G. Browne.

Ibn Sulayman, Mohammad. *Fundamentals of Islam* Mecca, Islamic World League.

Iqbal. *Poems from Iqbal,* Trans. V. G. Kiernan, London, John Murray Publishers Ltd., 1955.

Ibnu'l-Iqda, Hafiz. *Kitabu'l-Wilaya.*

'Iraqi, Fakhruddin. *Fakhruddin 'Iraqi: Divine Flashes* translation and introduction by William Chittick and Peter Lamborn Wilson, New York, Paulist Press, 1982.

al-Isbahani, Abu al-Faraj. *Qutuf al-Aghani* Beirut, al-Menahil, 1950.

Isfahani, Hafiz Abu Nu'aym. *Ma Nazal Mina'l-Qur'an fi Ali.*

Isfahani, Hafiz Abu Nu'aym. *Hilyatu'l-Auliya.*

Isik, Huseyn Hilmi. *Evidences for Prophethood and Answer to a University Student,* Istanbul, Turkey 1980.

Isik, Huseyn Hilmi. *Islam and How to be True Moslem* Turkey, Isik Kitabevi, 1980.

Ivanov, Vladimir A. *Alamut and Lamasar, Two Medieval Ismaili Strongholds* Tehran, Ismaili Society, 1960.

Izutsu, Toshihiko. *The Key Philosophical Concepts in Sufism and Taoism – Ibn Arabi and Lao-Tzu, Ghuang-Tzu,* Tokyo 1966.

Jalbani, G. N. *Teachings of Shah Waliyullah of Delhi* Kashmiri Bazar, Lahore Pakistan, Sh. Muhammad Ashraf, Publisher.

Al-Jami. *The Precious Pearl Al-Jami's Al-Durrah Al-Fakhirah together with his Glosses and the Commentary of 'Abd al-Ghafur al-Lari* Trans. with an introduction, notes, and glossary by Nicholas Heer, Albany, State University of New York Press, 1979.

Jami. *Nafahat 'al-'uns* Lakhnaw, Nuval Kashawr, 1915.

Jauhari, Abu Bakr Ahmad Bin Abdu'l-Aziz. *Saqifa and Fadak.*

Jauzi, Sheikh Yusuf Sibt Ibn. *Tadhiratu'l-Khasa'isu'l-Umma.*

Jazari, Shamsu'd-din. *Asnu'l-Matalib*

Jazri, Ibn al-'Athir. *Ghayat al-nihaya.*

Jazri, Ibn al-'Athir. *Asadu'l-Ghaiba.*

Jazri, Ibn al-'Athir. *Athna'l-Matalib.*

Jeffery, Arthur, ed. *Materials for the history of the text of the Qur'an : the old*

623

codices : the Kitab al-masahif of Ibn Abi Dawud, together with a collection of the variant readings from the codices of Ibn Ma'sud, Ubai,
'Ali, Ibn 'Abbas, Anas, Abu Musa and other early Qur'anic authorities
which present a type of text anterior to that of the canonical text of
'Uthman New York, AMS Press, 1937.1975

al-Jibouri, Yasin T. *Khadija Daughter of Khuwaylid: Wife of Prophet
Muhammad (pbuh).*

al-Jilani, 'Abd al-Qadir. *The Secret of Secrets* Trans. Sheikh Tosun Bayrak al-
Jerrahi al-Halveti, Cambridge, Islamic Texts Society, 1992.

Joseph, Isya. *Devil Worship: The Sacred Books and Traditions of the Yezidiz*
Montana, Kessinger Publishing Company, 1919.

Jouzi, Abul Faraj Bin. *Kitabur Rad alal-muta'a-seebul aneed.*

Jurjani al-Sayyid al-Sharif, Ali Ibn Muhammad. *Kitab al-ta'rifat,* Misr, al-
Matba-ah al-Hamidyah al-Misriyah, 1903.

Kabir. *The Kabir Book* versions by Robert Bly, The Seventies Press/Beacon
Press, 1977.

Kermāni, Fo'ād. *The Drunken Universe: An Anthology of Persian Sufi Poetry*
translations and commentary by Peter Lamborn Wilson and Nasrollah
Pourjavady, Grand Rapids, Phanes Press, 1987.

Keshavjee, Rafique *Mysticism and the Pluarality of Meaning: the Case of the
Ismailis of Rural Iran* London: I.B.Tauris Pub., 1998.

Khan, Hazrat Inyat. *The Sufi Message of Hazrat Inyat Khan.*

Khan, Pir Vilayet *Toward the One* New York & Canada, Harper & Row,
Publishers, Inc. 1974.

al-Khani, 'Abd al-Majid Ibn Muhammad. *al-Hada'iq al-wardiyah fi haqa'iq
ajilla' al-Naqshabandiyah* 1308.

al-Khani, 'Abd al-Majid Ibn Muhammad. *al-Hada'iq al-wardiyah fi haqa'iq
ajilla' al-Naqshabandiyah* Damascus, 'Abd al-Wakil al-Darubi, 1970
1979.

Khomeini, Ayotullah Syed Ruhollah Mousavi, *A Clarification of Questions*
Trans. J. Borujerdi, London, Westview Press, 1984.

Khuwarazmi, Al-Khatid al- *Maqtalu'l Husain,* vol.1.

al-Khwarazmi, Abu'l-Mu'ayyid Muwafiq Bin Ahmad Khatib. *Al-Manaqib*
Najaf.

Kisa'i, Muhammad Ibn 'Abd Allah. *Qisas al-anbiya' (Tales of the prophets)*
Chicago, IL, distributed by KAZI Publications, 1997.

Al-Kisa'i. *Aja' ib al-malakut* Leiden MS.

Kramer, Martin. *Shi'ism Resistance and Revolution* London, Mansell
Publishing Ltd., 1987.

Al-Kulayni, Muhammad Ibn Ya'qub. *Usul-e kafi* Edited and Trans. Jawad
Mostafawi, Shiraz, 1980, I 276.

Kulayni, Muhammad Ibn Ya'qub. *Usul al-Kafi al-*Tab'ah 1, Tihran, Dar al-Uswah, 1997.

Kulayni, Muhammad Ibn Ya'qub. *Usul al-Kafi al*-Tab'ah 1, Bayrut, Dar al-Adwa', 1992.

Al-Kurdi, Shaykh Amin. *Tanwir al-qulub (Entlightenment of Hearts)*.

Lakha, Murtaza Ahmed. *The Twelfth Imam* London, R & K Tyrrell, 1993.

Lalljee, Yousuf N. *Know Your Islam* Elmhurst, N.Y., Tahrike Tarsile Qur'an, 1995.

Lings, Martin. *A Sufi Saint of the Twentieth Century: Shaikh Ahmad al-Alawi, His Spiritual Heritage and Legacy* Berkeley and Los Angeles, University of California Press, 1971.

Lings, Martin. *Muhammad: his life based on the earliest sources* New York, Inner Traditions, International, Ltd., 1983.

Lock, Steve and Jamal Khaldun. *The Muqarribun: Arab Magic and Myth*.

Madyan, Abū. *Uns al-Wahid wa Nuzhat al-Murid (The Intimacy of the Recluse and Pastime of the Seeker found in: Madyan, Abū , The Way of Abū Madyan: Doctrinal and Poetic Works of Abū Madyan Shu'ayb Ibn al-Husayn al-Ansārī* ed. and Trans. Vincent J. Cornell, Cambridge, U.K., The Islamic Texts Society, 1996.

Madyan, Abū, *The Way of Abū Madyan: Doctrinal and Poetic Works of Abū Madyan Shu'ayb Ibn al-Husayn al-Ansârī* ed. and Trans. Vincent J. Cornell, Cambridge, U.K., The Islamic Texts Society, 1996.

Maibodi, Abo'l-Fadhl Rashido'd-Din *Kashf al-asrar wa 'oddat al-abrar ma'ruf ba tafsir-e Khwaja 'Abdo'llah Ansari* 10 Vols. edited by Ali Asghar Hekmat. Tehran, 1978, III.

Majlisi, Muhammad Baqir Ibn Muhammad Taqi. *Mahdi-i maw'ud : tarjumah-i jild-i sizdahum-i Bihar al-'anwar* Qum, Masjid-i Muqaddas-i Jamkaran, 1997.

Makki, Ibn Hajar. *Sawa'iq Muhriqa*.

Makki, Shahabu'd-din Ahmad Bin Hajar. *Sawa'iq Muhriqa*.

Makki, Shahabu'd-din Ahmad Bin Hajar. *Kitabu'l-Manhu'l-Malakiyya*..

Malik, Imam. *Mawatta'*.

Maliki, Nuru'-d-Din Bin Sabbagh. *Fusulu'l-Muhimma*.

Manavi, Abdul Ra'ufu'l. *Faizu'l-Qadir fi Sharh-i-Jame'u's-Saghir*.

Maneri, Sharafuddin. *The Hundred Letters of Sharafuddin Maneri* Trans. Paul Jackson, London, S.P.C.K. 1980.

Mas'udi. *Kitab-e-Akhiru'z-Zaman* 1938.

al-Mas'udi, Ali Ibn al-Husayn. *Ausat*.

Matbaasi, Hakikat. *The Sunni Path*, Istanbul, 1980.

Maududi, Sayyid Abul Ala. *Towards Understanding Islam* Idara Tarjuman-Ul-Quran, Pakistan 1978.

Meher, Baba *Discourses* Vol. I, Vol. II, India, Sufism Reoriented, Inc., 1973.

Mernissi, Fatima. *The Forgotten Queens of Islam* Minneapolis, University of

Minnesota Press, 1993

Misri, Mohammad Bin Sabban. *Is-aafur Raghibeen.*

Misri, Munawi. *Kunuzu'd-Daqa'iq.*

Momen, Moojan. *An Introduction to Shi'i Islam: The History and Doctrines of Twelver Shi'ism* New Haven, Conn. ; London : Yale University Press, 1987.

Mrabet, Mohammed. *M'Hashish* taped and translated from the Moghrebi by Paul Bowles, San Francisco, City Light Books, 1993.

Mufid, Sheikh al-. *Kitab al Irshad (The Book of Guidance)* Trans. I. K. A. Howard, Tahrike Tarsile Quran. I.S.B.N. 0-940368-11-0.

Muhaddith of Syria. *Tafsir al-Kabir.*

Muhaiyaddeen, His Holiness M. R. Bawa. *Asma 'ul-Husna: The 99 Beautiful Names of Allah* Philadelphia, Pennsylvania, The Fellowship Press, 1979.

Muhaiyaddeen, His Holiness M. R. Bawa. *A Book of God's Love* Philadelphia, Pennsylvania, The Fellowship Press, 1981.

Muhaiyaddeen, M. R. Bawa. *The Golden Words of M. R. Bawa Muhaiyaddeen* Philadelphia, Pennsylvania, The Bawa Muhaiyaddeen Fellowship, 1991.

Muhawesh, Odeh A. *Fatima the Gracious* Qum, Iran, Shafagh Publications, 1988.

Muqibili. *Ahadithu'l-Mutawatira.*

Muslim Ibn 'al-Hajjaj 'al-Qushayri. *Sahih Muslim: being traditions of the sayings and doings of the prophet Muhammad as narrated by his companions* New Delhi, Kitab Bhavan, 1982.

Muttaqi,'Ali Ibn 'Abd al-Malik. *Kanz al-'ummal fi sunan al-aqwal wa-al-af'al* Tab'ah 1, Bayrut, Dar al-Kutub al-'Ilmiyah, 1998.

Nafzawi, Shaykh. *The Glory of the Perfumed Garden: The Missing Flowers (An English Translation from the Arabic of the Second and Hitherto Unpublished Part of Shaykh Nafzawi's Perfumed Garden)* Trans. H.E.J., London, Neville Spearman Limited, 1975.

Nahid, Babak. (review) Daftary, Farhad. *The Assassin Legends: Myths of the Ismai'ilis,* London, I. B. Tauris and Co., 1994.

Nasafi, 'Azizo'd-Din. *Ketab-e ensan-e kamel* edited by Marijan MolJ, Tehran and Paris, 1962.

Nasr, Seyyed Hossein. *Science and Civilization in Islam* New York, Barnes and Noble Books, 1968.

Nasr, Seyyed Hossein. *Ideals and Realities of Islam* London, Allen and Unwin, 1964.

al-Nawawi, Imam. *Sahih Muslim bi-Sharh al-Nawawi* Dar Ihya' al-Turath al-'Arabi, Bayrut, Lebanon, 1984.

Nazim Al-Qubrusi, Sheikh. *Mercy Oceans' Pink Pearls* Konya, Turkey, Sebat, 1988.

Newby, Gordon Darnell. *The Making of the Last Prophet : A Reconstruction of the Earliest Biography of Muhammad.*

Niaz, Sufee A. Q. *Whispers from Ghaalib* Ferozsons Ltd. Lahore.

Nisa'i, Imam Abu Abdu'r-Rahman Ahmad Bin Ali. *Khasa'isu'l-Alawi.*

Nisa'i, Imam Abu Abdu'r-Rahman Ahmad Bin Ali. *Sunan.*

Nishapuri, Abu'l-Hasan Ali Bin Ahmad Wahidi. *Asbabu'n- Nuzul.*

Nishapuri, Hafiz Abu Abdullah Muhammad Bin Abdullah Hakim. *Al-Mustadrak 'ala al-Sahihayn* Cairo.

Nishapuri, Muslim Bin Hajjaj. *Sahih.*

Norris, H. T. *Saharan Myth and Saga* Oxford, Clarendon Press, 1972.

Nurbaskhsh, Dr. Javad. *The Great Satan 'Eblis'* London, Khaniqahi-Nimatullahi Publications, 1986.

Nurbaskhsh, Dr. Javad. *Sufi Women* New York, Khaniqahi-Nimatullahi Publications, 1983.

Nurbaskhsh, Dr. Javad. *Sufi Poetry* New York, Kaniqahi-Nimatullahi Publications, 1980.

Nurbakhsh, J. *In the Tavern of Ruin: Seven Essays on Sufism* New York, Khaniqahi-Nimatull hi Publications, 1978.

Nuri, Husayn b. Muhammad Taqi. *Kash al-astar.*

Nuri, Allama. *Sharh Sahih Muslim.*

Nursi, Bediuzzaman Said. *Twenty-Third Flash, Nature: Cause or Effect? From the Risale-I Nur Collection* Trans. from the Turkish Umit Simsek, California, Risale-i Nur Institute of America, 1976.

Ouspensky, P.D. *"The Fourth Way: An Arrangement by Subject of Verbatim Extracts from the Records of Ouspensky's Meetings in London and New York, 1921-46* New York, Vintage Books, 1971.

Ozak al-Jerrahi al-Halveti, Sheikh Muzaffer. *Love is the Wine: Talks of a Sufi Master in America* Ed. Sheikh Ragip Frager, Vermont, Threshold Books, 1987.

Ozak al-Jerrahi al-Halveti, Sheikh Muzaffer. *The Unveiling of Love: Sufism and the Remembrance of God* Trans. Muhtar Holland, Inner Traditions International, 1981.

Ozak al-Jerrahi al-Halveti, Sheikh Muzaffer. *Adornment of Hearts: Zinatu-L-Qulub* Translators Muhtar Holland and Sixtina Friedrich, Connecticut, Pir Press, 1991.

al-Qari al-Harawi, 'Ali Sultan Muhammad. *Kitab jam' al-wasa'il fi sharh al-Shama'il li-'alam al-riwayah wa-'alim al-dirayah al-Imam al-Tirmidhi* al-Qahirah, Nashr Dar al-Aqsa, 1994.

Qastalani, Shahabu'd-Din. *Irshad-e-Bari.*

Qastallani, 'Ahmad Ibn Muhammad. *'al-Juz' 'al-'awwal ['al-'ashir] min* 'rshad 'al-sari 'ila sharh Sahih 'al-Bukhari. Wa-bi-hamishihi matn Sahih 'al-'Imam Muslim wa-sharh 'al-'Imam 'al-Nawawi 'alayhi edition: 'al-Tab'ah 5, Bulaq, Matba'at 'al-Kubra 'al-'Amiriyah, 1876.

Qastallani, Ahmad Ibn Muhammad. *Irshad al-sari li-sharh Sahih al-Bukhari* edition: Tab'ah jadidah bil-ufset, Bayrut, Dar al-Fikr, 1980 1992.

Qazwini, Ibn Maja. *Sunan.*

Qazwini, Ibn Maja. *Zuhd.*

Qazwini, Muhammad Bin Yazid Hafiz Ibn Maja. *Sunan.*

Qud t 'Ain Al-. *Tamhîdated.* Osseiran, 'Afif. Tehran, Chapkhana-yi danish gah, 1341 A.H.

[Qur'an] *Le Coran* Trans. From Arabic into the French by Kasimirski, Paris, Flammarion, 1970.

[Qur'an] *Qur'an* Trans. M. H. Shakir, Elmhurst, New York, Tahrike Tarsile Qur'an, Inc. 1997.

[Qur'an] *The Koran* Trans. N. J. Dawood, New York Penguin Books, 1980.

[Qur'an] *The meaning of the glorious Qur'an: text and explanatory translation* Trans. Marmaduke William Pickthall, Beltsville, Md., Amana Publications, 1996.

[Qur'an] *The Message of the Qur'an: Presented in Perspective* Trans. Hashim Amir-Ali, Rutland, Vt., C. E. Tuttle Co.,1974.

[Qur'an] *The Qur'an* Trans. Richard Bell, Edinburgh, T and T Clark, two volumes. 1937.

al-Qushayri, 'Abd al-Karim Ibn Hawazin. *al-Risalah al-Qushayriyah* 1912.

Ibn Qutayba, Abu Muhammad 'Abd Allah Ibn Muslim. *al-Ma'arif li-Ibn Qutayba, Abi Muhammad 'Abd Allah Ibn Muslim,* al-Qahirah, Matba'at Dar al-kutub, 1960.

Rajneesh, Bhagwan Shree. *Journey Toward the Heart: Discourses on the Sufi Way* San Francisco, California, Harper and Row, 1976.

Razi, Imam Fakhru'd-Din. *Tafsir-e-Kabir Mafatihu'l-Ghaib.*

Razi, Imam Fakhru'd-din. *Kitabu'l-Arba'in.*

Rifa'i, Pirina Sultan Ebul Alameyn Ahmedel Kebira. *Evradi Rifayye.*

Er-Rifâî, Ahmed. Mârifet Yolu (el-Bürhânü'l-Müeyyed, Istanbul, Erkam Yayinlari, 1416/1995.

Ross, Kelley L. Ph.D. *Shame, Beauty, and the Ambivalence of the Flesh, after Schopenhauer, C.G. Jung, Frederick Turner & Camille Paglia.*

Rodinson, Maxime. *Muhammad.* Trans. Anne Carter, New York, Pantheon Books, 1980.

Rumi, Jelaluddin. *Love is a Stranger: Selected Lyric Poetry of Jelaluddin Rumi* Trans. Kabir Edmund Helminski, Vermont, Threshold Books, 1993.

Rumi, Jelaluddin. *Open Secret: Versions of Rumi* Translators John Moyne and Coleman Barks, Putney, Vermont, Threshold Books, 1984.

Rumi, Jelaluddin. *Feeling the Shoulder of the Lion: Selected Poetry and*

Teaching Stories from the Mathnawi versions by Coleman Barks, Vermont, Threshold Books, 1991.

Rumi, Jelaluddin. *The Mathnawi of Jalaluddin Rumi* Trans. R. A. Nicholson, London, Luzac and Co., 1982.

Rumi, Jalalo'd-Din *Mathnawi-ye ma'nawi* ed. R. A. Nicholson, Tehran, 1977, Vol. I.

Rumi, Jallaludin. *Al-Majani al-haditha* vol. III.

Rumi, Maulana Jalal al-Din. *The Sufi Path of Love* Trans. William C. Chittick, Albany, State University of New York Press.

Ruzbihan Baqli, Shaikh. *The Unveiling of Secrets: Diary of a Sufi Master (original title: Kashf al-asrar)* Trans. C. W. Ernst, Chapel Hill, N.C., 1997.

Ruzhahan, Qazi Fazlullah bin. *Ibtalu'l-Batil.*

Sahih Muslim (Being traditions of the sayings and doings of the Prophet Muhammad as narrated to his companions and compiled by Imam Muslim) Trans. Abdul Hamid Siddiqi.

Samhudi, Allama. *Ta'rikhu'l-Medina.*

Samhudi, 'Ali Ibn 'Abd Allah. *Jawahir al-'iqdayn fi fadl al-sharafayn, sharaf al-'ilm al-jalii wa-al-nasab al-'alii* Baghdad, Wizarat al-Awqaf wa-al-Shu'un al-Diniyah, 1987.

Samnani, Ala'uddin. *Urwatu'l-Wuthqah.*

Al-Sarraj, Abu Nasr. *Kitab al-Luma'* Ed. Nicholson, London, Gibb Series, 1914.

Scholem, Gershom Gerhard. *Sabbatai Sevi : the mystical Messiah* Princeton, N.J., Princeton University Press, 1975 1973.

El-Shabazz, El-hajj Malik (Malcolm X) and Alex Haley. *The Autobiography of Malcolm X* New York, Ballantine Books, 1992.

Shablanji, Mu'min Ibn Hasan Ibn Mu'min. *Nur al-absar fi manaqib Al Bayt al-Nabbi al-Mikhtar* Bayrut, Dar al-Jil, 1989.

Shabistari, Mahmud Ibn 'Abd al-Karim, *The Secret Garden* Bianco, Tex., Zahra, 1982.

Al-Shabrawi, Shaykh Abd al-Khaliq. *The Degrees of the Soul: Spiritual Stations on the Sufi Path* Trans. Mostafa al-Badawi, London, The Quilliam Press, 1997.

Shabustare, Mahmud-I . *Gulshen-I Raz* Trans. Al fakir Tosun al-Jerrahi.

Shaibani, Majdu'd-Din Bin Athir Muhammad Bin Muhammad. *Jami'u'l-Usul.*

Shehadi, Fadlou. *Ghazali's Unique Unknowable God: A Philosophical Critical Analysis of some of the Problems raised by Ghazali's View of God as Utterly Unique and Unknowable* Netherlands, E. J. Brill, 1964.

Shafi'i, Abul Fath Shahristani. *Milal wa'n-Nihal.*

Shafi'i, Ali Bin Burhanu'din Halabi. compiler, *Siratu'l-Halabiyya.*

Shafi'i, Imamu'l-Haram Ahmad Makki. *Dhakha'iru'l-Uqba.*

Shafi'i, Kamalu'd-Din Abu Salim Muhammad bin Talha. *Matalibu's-Su'ul.*

Shafi'i, Mir Seyyed Ali Hamadani. *Mawaddatu'l-Qurba.*

Shafi'i, Al-Shaykh Muhammad bin Talha *Matalibu's-Su'ul.*

Shafi'i, Muhammad Bin Yusuf Ganji. *Kifayatu't-Talib.*

Shah, Idries. *The Subtleties of the Inimitable Mulla Nasrudin* New York, Mulla Nasrudin Enterprises Ltd., E. P. Dutton, 1973.

Shah, Idries. *Seeker After Truth: A Handbook of Tales and Teachings* San Francisco, Harper and Row, Publishers, 1982.

Shah, Idries. *Thinkers of the East: Teachings of the Dervishes* Tennessee, Penguin Books, 1971.

Shahrastani, Muhammad Ibn 'Abd 'al-Karim. *Kitab 'al-Milal wa-'al-nihal* Misr?, 'al-Matba'ah 'al-'Ananiyah, 1846.

Shaibani, Ibn Athir Mubarak Bin Muhammad. *Jami'u'l-Usul.*

Sharaf-Nauvi, Yahya Bin. *Tehzibu'l-Asma wa'l-Lughat.*

Sharbini, Shamsuddin Muhammad Bin Ahmad. *Siraju'l-Munir.*

Shariati, Ali. *Fatima is Fatima* Trans. L. Bakhtiar, Tehran, Iran, The Shariati Foundation.

Sharif al-Radi, Muhammad Ibn al-Husayn. *Nahjul Balagha: Peak of eloquence: sermons, letters, and sayings of Imam Ali* Elmhurst, N.Y.,Tahrike Tarsile Quran.

Shekani, Qazi. *Fathu'l-Ghadir.*

Shirazee, Sultan-ul Waezeen Aqai Syed Mohannad. *Peshawar Nights: Convincing Shia-Sunni Dialogue,* Vol. I & II, Karachi, Peermahomed Ebrahim Trust, 1977.

Shirazi, Jamaluddin. *Kitabu'l-Araba'in.*

Shirazi, Sultanu'l-Wa'izin. *Peshawar Nights* translated from the Persian by Quinlan, Hamid and Charles Ali Campbell, Palisades, NY, Pak Books, 1996.

Sijistani, Abu Sa'id. *Kitabu'd-Darayab Fi hadithi'l-Wilaya.*

Sijistani, Abu Dawud. *Sunan.*

Speeth, Kathleen Riordan. *The Gurdjieff Work* Berkeley, California, AND/OR Press, 1976.

Spiegelman, J. Marvin, Ph.D. (with Pir Vilayat Inayat Khan and Tasnim Fernandez). *Sufism, Islam and Jungian Psychology,* New Falcon Publications.

Stone, Robert. *Damascus Gate*, Boston & New York, Houghton Mifflin Company, 1998.

Stetkevych, Suzanne Pinckney. *The Mute Immortals Speak: Pre-Islamic Poetry and the Poetics of Ritual* Ithaca and London, Cornell University Press, 1993.

Suhrawardi, 'Umar Ibn Muhammad. *A Dervish textbook from the 'Awarifu-l-ma'arif* London, Octagon Press, 1980.

Suhrawardi, Yahya Ibn Habash. *Three Treatises on Mysticism* Stuttgart, W. Kohlhammer, 1935. NOTES:Contains Persian text and English translation of Suhrawardi's *Lughat-i-muran* and *Safir-i-simurgh*, and of his translation of Avicenna's *Risalat al-tair*; a Persian commentary by Umar Ibn Sahlan al- Sawaji on *Risalat al-tair* ; and a biography of Suhrawalsl, in Arable, from the *Nuzhat al-arwah* of Shahrazuri.

Sulami. *Tabaqat.*

Sulami, Muhammad Ibn al-Husayn. *The way of Sufi Chivalry: when the light of the heart is reflected in the beauty of the face, that beauty is futuwwah* Rochester, Vt., Inner Traditions International, 1991 1983.

Sulayman, Alshaykh Mohammad Ibn. *Fundamentals of Islam* Islamic University.

Suyuti. *al-Jami' al-Saghir min Hadith al-Bashir al-Nadhir* al-Tab'ah 1, Makkah al-Mukarramah, Maktabat Nizar Mustafa al-Baz, 1998.

Suyuti. *Kitab ham' 'al-hawami' : Sharh Jam' 'al-jawami' fi 'ilm 'al-'Arabiyah* 'al-Tab'ah 1, Bayrut, Dar 'al-Ma'rifah lil-Tiba'ah wa-'al-Nashr, 1970.

Suyuti. *Khulafa' Rasul Allah al-Tab'ah 1, Dimashq : Bayrut, Dar al-Rashid ; Mu'assasat al-Iman, 1997.

Suyuti, Jalalu'd-Din. *Al-LuAli'l-Masnu'a fi'l-Abadusi'l-Muzu'a.*

Suyuti, Jalalu'd-Din. *Al-Dur al- Manthur.*

Suyuti, Jalalu'd-Din. *Tarikh al-Khulafa'* Ed. Rahab Khidr 'Akkawi. Beirut: Mu'assasa 'Izz al-Din, 1992.

Suyuti, Jalalu'd-Din. *Khasa'isu'l-Kubra.*

al-Tabari, Abu Ja'far Muhammad Ibn Jarir. *Tarikh al-rusul wal muluk*, State University of New York Press.

Tabari, Muhammad Bin Jarir. *Tafsiru'l-Kabir.*

al-Tabari, Muhibu'd-din. *Riyazu'n-Nazara.*

al-Tabari, Muhibu'd-din. *Dhakha'ir al-Uqba.*

Tabarsi Nuri, Isma'il. *Kifayat al-muwahhidin* 1954.

Tabatbai, Allama Sayyid Muhammed Husayn. *A Shi'ite Anthology: A select collection of religious sayings, sermons and prayers on different subjects*, Trans. William C. Chittick, London, Muhammadi Trust, 1980.

Tabataba'i, Muhammad Husayn. *Shi'ite Islam* Houston, TX, Free Islamic Literatures, 1979.

Tabatbai, *Kitab al-Irshad (Details of lives and sayings of the twelve Imams)*, Trans. I.K.A. Howard, London, Muhammadi Trust, 1981.

Tabrani. *Mu'jim Kabir.*

Tabrani, Hafiz Sulayman Ibn Ahmad. *Ausat.*

at-Tabrisi, Abu Ali al-Fadl Ibn al-Hassan Ibn al-Fadl. *Beacons of Light (Muhammad: The Prophet and Fatimah: The Radiant)* a partial translation of *I'lamu 'l-Wara bi A'lami l'-Huda* Translators Dr. Mahmoud M. Ayoub and Mrs. Lynda G. Clarke, Tehran, World Organization for Islamic Services, 1985

Ta'us, Malek. *The Book of Divine Effulgence.*

Ta'us, Sayyid Ibn. *Maqtalu'l Husain.*

Taymiya, Ibn. *Al-Radd 'al Ibn 'Arabi wa-l-sāfiya.*

Tha'labi, Imam Ahmad. *Tafsir Kashful'l-Bayan.*

The Oxford Encyclopedia of the Modern Islamic World New York, Oxford University Press, 1995.

The Secret Shrine: Islamic Mystical Reflections edited and with photographs Catherine Hughes, The Seabury Press, New York, A Crossroads Book, 1974.

Tirmidhi, Muhammad Ibn 'Isa. *Mukhtasar Sunan al-Tirmidhi* edition: al-Tab'ah 1., Dimashq ; Bayrut, al-Yamamah lil-Tiba'ah wa-al-Nashr wa-al-Tawzi', 1997.

Tirmidhi, Muhammad Ibn 'Isa. *Sahih al-Tirmidhi* edition: al-Tab'ah 1, Cairo, al-Matba'ah al-Misriyah bi-al-Azhar, 1931 1934.

Tirmidhi, Muhammad Ibn 'Isa. *Sunan al-Tirmidhi* Homs, Maktabat Dar al-Da'wah, 1965.

Tirmidhi. *Manaqib.*

Tufail, S. Muhammad. *The Qur'an Reader: An Elementary Course in Reading the Arabic Script of the Qur'an (With Arabic text, exercises and transliteration including the Muslim prayers)* San Fernando, Trinidad, West Indies, The San Fernando Muslim Women's Association, 1974.

al-Tusi, Amali al-Shaykh. *Kitab al-Ghaybah lil-Shaykh al-Tusi* al-Tab'ah 1., Mashhad, Majma' al-Buhuth al-Islamiyah, 1989.

Urjani, Syed Sharif Hanafi. *Sharh-i-Mawaqit .*

Van Beek, Gus W. (Gus Willard). *Hajar Bin Humeid: investigations at a pre-Islamic site in South Arabia* Baltimore, Johns Hopkins Press, 1969.

Vaughan-Lee, Llewellyn. ed., *Traveling the Path of Love: Sayings of Sufi Masters* Inverness, California, The Golden Sufi Center, 1995.

Warraq, Ibn. ed., *The Origins of the Koran: Classic Essays on Islam's Holy Book* Amherst, New York, Prometheus Books, 1998.

Westermarck, E. *Ritual and Belief in Morocco* London, 1926.

Wilson, Peter Lamborn. *Divan* London : Tehran, Crescent Moon Press, 1978.

Wilson, Peter Lamborn. *Sacred Drift: Essays on the Margins of Islam* San Francisco, City Light Books, 1993.

Wilson, Peter Lamborn. *Scandal: Essays in Islamic Heresy* Brooklyn, Autonomedia, 1988.

Wird-i Sherif-i Saghir-i Hazret-i Pir Nureddin Al-Jerrahi al-Halveti Quddisa Sirrahul-Fattahi Spring Valley, New York, The Jerrahi Order of

America.

Witteveen, H. J. (Hendrikus Johannes). *Universal Sufism* Shaftesbury, Dorset: Rockport, Mass., Element, 1997.

Zamakhshari, Abdu'l-Qasim Muhammad Bin Umar Jarullah. *Rabiu'l-Abrar.*

Zarandi, Muhammad Bin Yusuf. *Kitab-e A'lam bi siratu'n Nabi*

Zorlu, Ilgaz. *Evet, Ben Selanikliyim ("Yes, I am a Salonican")* Istanbul, Belge Uluslararas, 1998.

SECONDARY SOURCES

Adams, George. *The Lemniscatory Ruled Surface in Space and Counterspace* London, Rudolf Steiner Press, 1979.

Aiwass. *Al (Liber legis) The Book of the Law,* sub figura xxxi Archive, 1970.

Aiwass. *Thelema: The Holy Books of Thelema* Maine, Samuel Weiser, 1988.

Atkinson, William Walker. *The Will: Its Nature, Power and Development* Chicago, Illinois, The Progress Company, 1909.

Avatar Adi Da Samraj. *Compulsory Dancing: Talks and Essays on the Spiritual and Evolutionary Necessity of Emotional Surrender to the Life-Principle* California, Dawn Horse Press, 1980.

Avineri, Shlomo. *Hegel's Theory of the Modern State* Cambridge University Press, 1973.

Bach, Dr. George R. And Ronald M. Deutsch. *Pairing: How to Achieve Genuine Intimacy* New York, P. H. Wyden, 1970.

Bach, Dr. George. *Creative Aggression: The Art of Assertive Living* New York, Avon, 1974.

Bach, Richard. *Illusions: The Adventures of a Reluctant Messiah* New York, Dell Publishing Co. Inc., 1977.

Bach, Richard. *One: a Novel* New York, Morrow, 1988.

Bach, Richard. *The Bridge Across Forever: a Lovestory* New York, W. Morrow, 1984.

Baigent, Michael and Richard Leigh. *The Dead Sea Scrolls Deception* Bantam, 1992.

Balog, James. *Anima* Boulder, Colorado, Arts Alternative Press, 1993.

Bandler, Richard. *Frogs into Princes: Neuro Linguistic Programming* London, Grove Editions, 1979.

Bandler, Richard. *Using Your Brain for a Change,* Utah, Real People Press, 1985.

Benares, Camden. *Zen Without Zen Masters* Arizona, New Falcon Publications, 1993.

Bertiaux, Michael. *The Voudon Gnostic Workbook* New York, Magickal Childe, Inc. 1988.

[Bible] *Master Mason edition of the Holy Bible containing the Old and New Testaments, Authorized or King James version, with study helps : words spoken by Christ printed in red, to which is added progressive steps in masonry, questions and answers relating into characters, places, words and phrases used in symbolic masonry, biblical index to freemasonry* Wichita, Kansas, Heirloom Bible Publishers, 1984.

Bittleston, Adam. *The Spirit of the Circling Stars: Human Needs and Cosmic Answers* London, The Christian Community Press, 1975.

Bonwick, James. *Irish Druids and Old Irish Religions* USA, Dorset Press,

1986.

Branden, Nathaniel. *The Disowned Self* Toronto; New York, Bantam Books, 1973.

Brigg, John and G. David Peat. *Turbulent Mirror: An Illustrated Guide to Chaos Theory and the Science of Wholeness* New York, Harper and Row, 1990.

Cabell, James Branch. *Jurgen: a Comedy of Justice* Dover, 1978.

Campbell, Joseph. *The Hero With A Thousand Faces* New Jersey, Princeton University Press, 1968.

Charon, Jean E. *The Unknown Spirit* London, Coventure, 1983.

Clark, R.T. Bundle. *Myth and Symbol in Ancient Egypt* Trans. R. T. Bundle Clark, London, 1959.

Crowley, Aleister. *Konx Om Pax: essays in the light* Kings Beach, Calif., Thelema Publications, 1975 1907.

Crowley, Aleister (Master Therion). *Magick in Theory and Practice* New York, Magickal Childe Publishing, Inc., 1990.

Crowley, Aleister. *The Law is for All* New Falcon Publications, 1991.

Crowley, Aleister. *Liber Aleph vel CXI: The Book of Wisdom or Folly* Maine, Samuel Weiser, 1991.

Crowley, Aleister. *The Book of Lies* Maine, Weiser, 1970.

Crowley, Aleister. *The Holy Books of Thelema* Maine, Samuel Weiser, 1988.

Crum, Thomas F. *The Magic of Conflict: Turning a Life of Work into a Work of Art* New York, Simon and Schuster, 1987.

Dallett, Janet O. *Saturday's Child: Encounters with the Dark Gods* Toronto, Canada, Inner City Books, 1991.

Daraul, Arkon. *A History of Secret Societies* New York, Citadel Press, 1962.

Davidson, Gustav. *A Dictionary of Angels (Including the Fallen Angels)* New York, The Free Press, 1967.

Das, Baba Ram. *Be Here Now* New Mexico, Lama Foundation, 1971.

Dick, Philip K. *A Scanner Darkly* Random, 1991.

Dick, Philip K. *Eye in the Sky* New York, Collier Books, Macmillan Publishing Co., 1989.

Dick, Philip K. *Ubik* New York, Bantam Books, 1977.

Dick, Philip K. *Valis* New York, Vintage Books, 1991.

Edwards, Flora (Layla). *Upper Hands (La Huerta)*, 1983.

Eliade, Mircea. ed., *The Encyclopedia of Religion* New York, Macmillan, 1987, vol. 12.

Ellis, Albert, Ph.D. *Reason and Emotion in Psychotherapy: A Comprehensive Method of Treating Human Disturbances* (Revised and Updated), New York, A Birch Lane Press Book, published Carol Publishing Group, 1994.

Encyclopedia Britannica.

Erickson, Milton H. *Collective Papers of Milton H. Erickson on Hypnosis - Innovative Hypnotherapy* Vol. IV, Ed. Ernest L. Rossi, New York, Irvington Publishers, 1980.

Falorio, Linda. *The Shadow Tarot,* Pittsburgh, PA, headless Press.

Feuerstein, Georg. *Holy Madness: The Shock Tactics and Radical Teachings of Crazy-Wise Adepts, Holy Fools, and Rascal Gurus* New York, Paragon House, 1991.

Fonteyn, Margot. *Margot Fonteyn Autobiography* New York, Warner Books, 1976.

Fortune, Dion. *The Mystical Qabalah* Maine, Samuel Weiser, Inc., 1984.

Galian, Laurence. *Beyond Duality: The Art of Transcendence* New Falcon Publications, 1995.

Galian, Laurence. *Isis and Osiris: An Opera Libretto* private printing.

Grant, Kenneth and Steffi Grant. *Hidden Lore: The Carfax Monographs* London, Skoob Books, 1989.

Grant, Kenneth. *Aleister Crowley and the Hidden God* London, Skoob Books, 1992.

Grant, Kenneth. *Images and Oracles of Austin Osman Spare* New York, Samuel Weiser, 1975.

Grant, Kenneth. *Nightside of Eden* London, Skoob Books, 1994.

Grant, Kenneth. *Outside the Circles of Time* London, Muller, 1980.

Grant, Kenneth. *The Magical Revival* London, Skoob Books Publishing, 1972.

Gunther, Bernard. *Neo-Tantra: Bhagwan Shree Rajneesh on Sex, Love, Prayer, and Transcendence* New York, Harper and Row, 1980.

Hall, Calvin S. and Vernon J. Nordby *A Primer of Jungian Psychology* New York, The New American Library, 1973.

Hall, Calvin S. *A Primer of Freudian Psychology* New York, New American Library, 1956.

Hamblin, William. *Cthulhu Casebook* 1990.

Hancock, Graham. *Fingerprints of the Gods: The Evidence of Earth's Lost Civilization* New York, Crown Publications, 1995.

Heindel, Max. *The Rosicrucian Cosmo-Conception* California, The Rosicrucian Fellowship, 1973.

Herbert, Nick. *Elemental Mind: Human Consciousness and the New Physics* Dutton 1993.

Herbert, Nick. *Quantum Reality: Beyond the New Physics* Garden City, N.Y., Anchor Press/Doubleday, 1987.

Herbert, Nick. *Faster than Light: Superluminal Loopholes in Physics* New York, Penguin Group, Penguin Books, 1989.

Hermetica: The Ancient Greek and Latin Writings Which Contain Religious and Philosophical Teachings Ascribed to Hermes Trismegistus edited

Walter Scott, Boston, Shambala (Random House dist.), 1985.

Hesse, Hermann. *Demian* Translators Michael Roloff and Michael Lebeck, New York, Harper and Row, 1965.

Hesse, Hermann. *Narcissus and Goldman* Trans. Ursule Molinaro, Bantam Classics, 1984.

Hesse, Hermann. *Siddhartha* Trans. Hilda Rosner, Toronto; New York, Bantam Books, 1971.

Hesse, Hermann. *Magister Ludi: The Glass Bead Game* Trans. Mervyn Savill, New York, Henry Holt, 1949.

Hesse, Hermann. *Steppenwolf* New York, Rinehart and Winston, 1964.

Hyatt Ph.D., Christopher S. and Antero Ali. *A Modern Shaman's Guide to a Pregnant Universe* Nevada, Falcon Press, 1988

I Ching Translators Rudolf Ritsema and Stephen Karcher, Shaftesbury, Dorset, Great Britain, Element 1994.

Jaynes, Julian. *The Origin of Consciousness in the Breakdown of the Bicameral Mind* Boston, Houghton Mifflin, 1976.

John, Bubba Free. *Breath and Name: The Initiation and Foundation Practices of Free Spiritual Life* San Francisco, California, The Dawn Horse Press, 1977.

John, Da Free. *The God in Every Body Book: Talks and Essays on God-Realization* U.S., The Dawn Horse Press, 1983.

Jones, Ernest *The Life and Works of Sigmund Freud* New York, Basic Books, Inc., 1961.

Jung, Carl Gustav. *Answer to Job*, Vol. 283, 1st ed., Princeton University Press, 1972.

Jung, C. G. *The Collected Works of C. G. Jung: Mysterium Coniunctionis: An inquiry into the separation and synthesis of psychic opposites in alchemy,* Volume 14, Sir Herbert Read, Michael Fordham, M.D. M.R.C.P., Gerhard Adler, Ph.D., Eds., Princeton, New Jersey, Princeton University Press, 1970.

Jung, C. G. *Jung on Evil* selected and introduced Murray Stein, Princeton, New Jersey, Princeton University Press, 1995.

Jung, C. G. *The Gnostic Jung: Including "Seven Sermons to the Dead"* Princeton, New Jersey, Princeton University Press, 1992.

Jung, C. G. *The Portable Jung* Ed. Joseph Campbell, Trans. R. F. C. Hull, New York, The Viking Press, 1971.

Kazantzakis, Niko. *The Last Temptation of Christ* Trans. P. A. Bien, New York, Simon and Schuster, 1960.

Kopp, Sheldon. *Mirror, Mask, and Shadow: the Risks and Rewards of Self Acceptance* Toronto; New York, Bantam Books, 1982.

Kramer, Joel and Diana Alstad. *The Guru Papers: Masks of Authoritarian Power* Berkeley, California, Frog, Ltd., 1993.

Kuhn, T. S. *International Encyclopedia of Unified Science* "The Structure of Scientific Revolutions" Chicago, University of Chicago Press, 1970.

Lazarsfeld, Sofie. *Woman's Experience of the Male* England, Encylopdæic Press Ltd., 1967.

Leary, Timothy. *What Does WoMan Want?* Phoenix, Arizona, Falcon Press, 1988.

Lewis, C. S. *Perelandra, a Novel* New York, Macmillan, 1944.

Lewis, C. S. *Suprised by Joy: the Shape of my Early Life* New York, Harcourt, 1956.

Lewis, C. S. *The Weight of Glory* Touchstone Books, 1996.

Lewis, C. S. *Out of the Silent Planet* New York, Macmillan Co., 1949.

Lewis, C. S. *That Hideous Strength: a Modern Fairy Tale for Grownups* New York, Macmillan, 1966.

Loehr, James E. *Take a Deep Breath* New York, Villard Books, 1986.

Lüscher, Dr. Max. *The Lüscher Color Test* New York, Pocket Books, 1971.

MacHale, Des. *Spiritual and Thought-Provoking Quotations* Mercier Press, 1997.

Machen, Arthur. *The Great God Pan* Ayer, 1977.

Maclagan, David. *Creation Myths* Thames Hudson, 1977.

Mann, Nicholas R. *The Dark God: A Personal Journey through the Underworld* St. Paul, MN, Llewellyn Publications, 1996.

Markides, Kyriacos C. *The Magus of Strovolos: The Extraordinary World of a Spiritual Healer* London, Arkana 1990.

Masters, Roy. *How Your Mind Can Keep You Well* Connecticut, Fawcett, 1976.

Math vab Mathonwy: An Inquiry into the Origins and Development of the Fourth Branch of the Mabinogi with the Text Trans. W. J. Gruffydd, Cardiff, The University of Wales Press Board, 1928.

Matthews, Caitlin. *Mabon and the Mysteries of Britain: An Exploration of the Mabinogian* New York, Routledge and Kegan Paul Inc., 1987.

McKenna, Terence. *True Hallucinations: Being an Account of the author's Extraordinary Adventures in the Devil's Paradise* San Francisco, Harper Collins, 1994.

Meera, Mother. *Answers* Ithaca, New York, Meeramma Publications, 1991.

Messadié, Gérald. *Histoire Générale du Diable,* Iditions Robert Laffont, 1993.

Moltann-Wendel, Elisabeth. *I Am My Body: A Theology of Embodiment* Continuum 1995.

Morris, Desmond. *The Naked Ape* Dell, 1980.

Mumford, Dr. John (Swami Anandakapila). *Ecstasy Through Tantra* Minnesota, Llewellyn Publications, 1988.

Neumann, Erich. *The Great Mother* Princeton: Princeton University Press, 1963.

New International Version of the Bible Grand Rapids, Michigan, Zondervan Bible Publishers.

Newman, Ernest. *Wagner as Man and Artist* New York, A. A. Knopf, 1924.

Newman, Mildred and Bernard Berkowitz. *How to Take Charge of Your Life* New York, Harcourt, Brace and Jovanovich, 1977.

Nichols, Preston B. and Peter Moon. *Montauk Revisted: Adventures in Synchronicity* New York, Sky Books, 1994.

Nijinsky, Vaslav. *The Diary of Vaslav Nijinsky* edited by Romola Nijinsky, New York, Simon and Schuster, 1936.

Nin, Anaïs. *Seduction of the Minotaur* Chicago, Swallow Press, Inc., 1973.

Nin, Anaïs. *House of Incest* Chicago, Swallow Press, Inc., 1958.

O'Kane, Françoise. *Sacred Chaos: Reflections on God's Shadow and the Dark Self,* Toronto, Canada, Inner City Books, 1994.

Original Teachings of Ch'an Buddhism (selected from "The Transmission of the Lamp") edited Chang Chung-Yuan, New York, Grove Press, 1969.

Parrot, Douglas. *"Gnostic and Orthodox Disciples"* in *Nag Hammadi, Gnosticism, and Early Christianity* Eds., Hedrick & Hodgson, Peabody, Massachusetts, Hendrickson, 1986.

Patañjali. Yoga *Philosophy of Patañjali*

Pirsig, Robert M. *Zen and the Art of Motorcycle Maintenance* New York, Morrow, 1974.

Podvodny, Abessalom. *Occultism Back: The Novel About the Subtle Seven* Trans. Iri Decent, Ed. Laurence Galian.

Pollack, Rachel. *Unquenchable Fire* Woodstock, New York, The Overlook Press, 1992.

Pollack, Rachel. *Temporary Agency* New York, St. Martin's Press, 1994.

Raffe, Marjorie. *Eurythmy and the Impulse of Dance* Rudolf Steiner Press, 1974.

Rajneesh, Bhagwan. *Tantra: The Supreme Understanding* Rajneesh Publications.

Rand, Ayn *The Fountainhead* New York, Plume, 1994.

Regardie, Israel. *The Eye in the Triangle: An Interpretation of Aleister Crowley,* Phoenix, Arizona, New Falcon Press, 1982.

Regardie, Israel. *The Tree of Life: A Study in Magic* Maine, Samuel Weiser, Inc., 1986.

Reich, Wilhelm. *The Function of the Orgasm: Discovery of the Orgone* FSandG, 1986.

Reich, Wilhelm. *Ether, God, and the Devil: Cosmic Superimposition* New York, Farrar, Straus and Giroux, 1973.

Reich, Wilhelm. *Listen, Little Man!* New York, The Noonday Press, 1965.

Reifler, Sam *I Ching: A New Interpretation for Modern Times* New York, Bantam Books, 1988.

Roberts, Jane. *The Nature of Interpersonal Reality: A Seth Book* New Jersey, Prentice-Hall, 1974.

Roberts, Susan. *The Magician of the Golden Dawn: the Story of Aleister Crowley* Chicago, Contemporary Books, 1978.

Rouget, Gilbert. *Music and Trance: A Theory of the Relations between Music and Possession* Trans. Brunhilde Biebuyck, Chicago, University of Chicago Press, 1985.

Rubinstein, Aryeh. *Hasidism* New York, Leon Amiel Publisher, 1975.

Ruether, Rosemary. *Womanguides* Boston, Beacon Press, 1935.

Schopenhauer. "The Best of Possible Worlds" from *The World as Will and Representation,* Vol. I, E.F. Payne translation, Dover Books, 1969.

Schultes, Richard Evans and Albert Hoffman. *Plants of the Gods: Their Sacred, Healing and Hallucinogenic Powers* Vermont, Healing Arts Press, 1992.

Skoob Esoterica Anthology Ed. Christopher R. Johnson, Skoob Books Publishing Ltd., 1995.

Spare, Austin Osman. *The Focus of Life: The Mutterings of Aäos* London, Askin Publishers, 1976.

Spare, Austin Osman. *Ananthema of Zos: The Sermon to the Hypocrites: an automatic writing* London, Neptune Press, 1976.

Squire, Charles. *Celtic Myth and Legend* USA, A Newcastle Book, 1975.

Steiner, Rudolf. *Knowledge of the Higher Worlds and Its Attainment* New York, Anthroposophical Press, 1947.

Steiner, Rudolf. *Reincarnation and Immortality* Steiner Books, 1970.

Steiner, Rudolf. *The Gospel of St. John* Trans. Maud B. Monges,1984.

Steiner, Rudolf. *The Philosophy of Spiritual Activity* Trans. Rita Stebbing, Anthroposophical Press, 1993.

Steiner, Rudolf. *An Outline of Occult Science* Spring Valley, New York, Anthroposophical Press, 1972.

Steiner, Rudolf. *Egyptian Myths and Mysteries* New York, Anthroposophical Press, 1971.

Steiner, Rudolf. *Guidance in Esoteric Training* London, Rudolf Steiner Press, 1972.

Steiner, Rudolf. *The Inner Nature of Music and the Experience of Tone* Spring Valley, New York, The Anthroposophical Press, 1983.

Steiner, Rudolf. *The Kingdom of Childhood* London, Rudolf Steiner Press, 1974.

Steiner, Rudolf. *The Soul's Probation: A Life Tableau in Dramatic Scenes, As Sequel to the Portal of Initiation* Translators Ruth and Hans Pusch, Toronto, Steiner Book Centre, 1973.

Steiner, Rudolf. *Verses and Meditations* London, Anthroposophical Publishing Company, 1961.

Stevens, Franklin. *Dance As Life: a Season with American Ballet Theater* Harper and Row, 1976.

Stewart, R. J. *Music and the Elemental Psyche: A Practical Guide to Music and Changing Consciousness* Vermont, Destiny Books, 1987.

Symonds, John. *The King of the Shadow Realm - Aleister Crowley: his life and magic* Great Britain, Duckworth, 1989.

The Book of the Sacred Magic of Abramelin the Mage Trans. S. L. MacGregor Mathers, New York, Dover Publications, Inc., 1975.

The Jerusalem Bible Doubleday and Company, Incorporated Garden City, New York, 1966.

The Mabinogi and Other Welsh Tales Trans. and Ed. with an Introduction Patrick K. Ford, Berkeley, University of California Press, 1977.

The Mabinogian Trans. Lady Charlotte Guest, New York, E. P. Dutton and Co., 1986.

The Soul Afire; Revelations of the Mystics edited H. A. Reinhold, New York, Meridian Books, 1960.

Three Initiates. *The Kybalian: A Study of the Hermetic Philosophy of Ancient Egypt and Greece* Chicago, The Yogi Publication Society, 1940.

Trager, James. *The Women's Chronology* Great Britain, Aurum Press, 1994.

Trismigistus, Hermes. *Hermetica: The Ancient Greek and Latin Writings which contain religious or philosophical teachings ascribed to Hermes Trismigistus* Oxford, The Clarendon Press, 1912.

Trungpa, Chögyam. *Cutting Through Materialism* Boulder, Colorado, Shamballa, 1973.

Uyeshiba, Kisshomaru. *Aikido* Translators Kazuaki Tanahashi and Roy Maurer, Jr., Japan, Kowado Publishing Co., 1973.

Van Wing Bakongo (Brussels 1921; pp. 170 ff.) Trans. Edwin W. Smith, in Smith (ed.), *African Ideas of God: A Symposium* (2nd ed: London, 1950).

Wagner, Richard. *My Life* New York, Tudor Publishing Co., 1936.

Walton, Evangeline *The Island of the Mighty* New York, A Del Rey Book, 1970.

Walton, Evangeline. *The Children of Llyr* New York, A Del Rey Book, 1971.

Walton, Evangeline. *Prince of Annwn* New York, A Del Rey Book, 1972.

Walton, Evangeline. *The Song of Rhiannon* New York, A Del Rey Book, 1972.

Ward, Milton. *You Are Enlightened Omnibeing: In Our Messianic Age* New York, Optimus Books, 1992.

Webb, Don. *The Explanation and Other Good Advice* Oregon, Wordcraft of Oregon, 1998.

Webb, Don. *Uncle Setnakt's Essential Guide to the Left Hand Path* Texas, Rûna Raven Press, 1999.

Weinberg, Dr. George and Dianne Rowe. *The Projection Principle* New York, St. Martin's Press, 1988.

West, John Anthony. *Serpent in the Sky: The High Wisdom of Ancient Egypt* Illinois, The Theosophical Publishing House, 1993.

Wilber, Ken. *Eye to Eye: The Quest for the New Paradigm* Garden City, New York, Anchor Books, 1983.

Williams, Paul. *Das Energi* Entwhistle Books, 1980.

Wilson Ph.D. , Robert Anton. *Sex and Drugs: A Journey Beyond Limits*, Phoenix, Arizona, New Falcon Publications, 1993.

Wilson, Robert Anton. *Cosmic Trigger Volume Two: Down to Earth* New Falcon Publications, 1991.

Wilson, Robert Anton. *Masks of the Illuminati* New York, A Timescape Book, 1981.

Wilson, Robert Anton. *Prometheus Rising* Arizona, Falcon Press, 1983.

Wilson, Robert Anton. *Schrödinger's Cat III: The Homing Pigeons* New York, Pocket Books, 1981.

Wilson, Robert Anton. *The Earth Will Shake: The Historical Illuminatus Chronicles,* Volume 1, New York, Lynx Books, 1988.

Winkler, Franz. *The Mythology in Wagner's 'Parsifal'.*

Winkler, Franz. *The Mythology in Wagner's 'The Twilight of the Gods'.*

Winkler, Franz Emil. *The Mythology in Richard Wagner's The Ring of the Nibelung: The Valkyrie, Siegfried* Garden City, N.Y., Myrin Institute, Inc. for Adult Education, Adelphi University, 1966.

Winkler, Franz Emil. *For Freedom Destined: Mysteries of Man's Evolution in the Mythology of Wagner's Ring Operas and Parsifal* Garden City, N.Y., Waldorf Press, 1974.

Yogananda, Paramahansa. *Autobiography of a Yogi* Los Angeles, California, Self-Realization Fellowship, 1981.

Zizek, Slavoj. *The Sublime Object of Ideology* New York, Verso Books, 1989.

Zukav, Gary. *The Dancing Wu Li Masters: An Overview of the New Physics* New York, Morrow, 1979.

PERIODICALS

Al'lat "Tantra: The Magazine", 1992.

Buck, Dorothy C. *Voicing the Inexpressible*: *The Virgin Heart of Christian/Islamic Dialogue* "Sufi" Issue 39/Autumn1998, p. 10.

Buckley, Jorunn J. *A Cult-Mystery in the Gospel of Philip* "Journal of Biblical Literature", V.99, (1980), p. 575.

Çatalkaya, Sheıkh Şerıf. *Light for Humanity* (Insanlık için Işık) "Journal of The Rıfa'i Marufi Order of America", Chapel Hill, North Carolina.

Cohen, Andrew. *Abandon the Future* "Creations Magazine" October/November 1997, p. 35.

Edmondson, Philip. *The Universal Spirit of Sufism* (review of Sara Sviri's *The Taste of Hidden Things: Images on the Sufi Path)* in "Sufi" issue no. 35/autumn 1997.

Grant, Robert. *The Mystery of Marriage in the Gospel of Philip* in "Vigiliae Christianae" # 15, 1961.

Al-Jilani, Hadrat Abdul-Qadir. *The Secret of Secrets* interpreted by Shaykh Tosun Bayrak, by permission of the Shaykh Bayrak, The Islamic Text Society, "Sufi Review" Spring, 1993.

Helminski, Kabir. *Ecstasy & Sobriety (condensed from "Parabola")* "Eye of the Heart", Vol. 2, Issue 1, p. 2, 4.

Helminski, Kabir. *Mevlana is a Wide Open Door for Humanity* "Eye of the Heart", Vol. 2, Issue 1, p. 1.

MacDonald, D. B. "Hartford Seminary Record" vol. XX, No 1.

Nepo, Mark. *Walking North* "Sufi" Issue 35, Autumn 1997, London, England, p. 35.

Rothschild, Jeffrey. *Sitting in the Circle of the Sufis: The Nature of Sama'* in "Sufi" Issue 37/Spring 1998.

Sviri, Sara. *Where the Two Seas Meet: The story of Khidr* "Sufi" Autumn 1996.

Vaughan-Lee, Llewellyn. *Forgetfulness* "Sufi" Issue 37/Spring 1998, p. 41.

DOCTORAL DISSERTATIONS

Biesele, Marguerite Anne. *Folklore and Ritual of !Kung Hunter-Gathers* thesis presented to Harvard University, Department of Anthropology, Cambridge, Massachusetts, 1975.

Elqayam, Abraham. *The Mystery of Faith in the Writings of Nathan of Gaza* thesis submitted for the Degree "Doctor of Philosophy", submitted to the Senate of the Hebrew University, December 1993.

VIDEOS

Meetings with Remarkable Men directed by Peter Brook, performers: Terence Stamp, Dragan Maksimovic, Corinth Video, 1979.

Nadja written and directed by Michael Almereyda, performers: Elina L'wensohn, Martin Donovan, Peter Fonda, Galaxy Craze, Evergreen Entertainment, 1994.

Where the Eagles Fly: Portraits of Women of Power, Habiba: A Sufi Saint from Uzbekistan video, New York, Mystic Fire Video, 1997.

WORLD WIDE WEB

It is unfortunate that due to the nature of the World Wide Web at present, many links often move to different sites, or expire and disappear. Thus, we have had to remove several citations quoted from sites that are no longer in existence.

Alchemy in Ibn Khaldun's Muqaddimah Edited and prepared by Prof. Hamed A. Ead, Cairo University, Giza
http://www.levity.com/alchemy/islam20.html
As-Sunna Foundation of America
http://www.sunnah.org/
Dhikr is the Greatest Obligation and Perpetual Divine Order
http://www.sunnah.org/ibadaat/dhikr.htm
Du'a Kumayl Trans. and commentary by Husein A. Rahim M.B.E., London
http://www.al-islam.org/kumayl/
Farooqui, Hadhrat Shaikh Asif Hussain. *Envy & Pride*
http://www.beautyofislam.org/Audio
Glossary of Muslim Terms
http://www.digiserve.com/mystic/Muslim/glossary.html
Godlas, Dr. Alan. *Sufism's Many Paths* University of Georgia
http://www.arches.uga.edu/~godlas/Sufism.html
Hidden Meanings
http://www.hiddenmeanings.com
Hixon, Lex. *A Mighty Companions Interview with Lex Hixon,*
http://www.mightycompanions.com/page6.html
Hixon, Lex. *The Core of All Kingdoms: An Exploration of Non-Duality with Lex Hixon,* hosted by Suzanne Taylor,
http://www.mightycompanions.com/page4.html
Hooker, Richard and Washington State University *"World Cultures Internet Classroom"*
http://www.wsu.edu:8080/~dee/
al-Jibouri, Yasin T. *Khadija Daughter of Khuwaylid: Wife of Prophet Muhammad (pbuh)*
http://www.al-islam.org/biographies/khadija.htm
http://home.fireplug.net/~rshand/streams/scripts/jinn.html
Merchant, Noorali S. *Sorrows & Sufferings: A Collection of Poems on the martyrdom of the grandson of Prophet Muhammad, Husayn b. Ali, peace be upon them*
http://www.al-islam.org/short/sorrows/
The New Friesian Theory of Religious Value
http://www.friesian.com/newotto.htm

Provine, Robert R. *Laughter*. "American Scientist" Jan. Feb. 1996
    http://www.amsci.org/amsci/Articles/96articles/Provine-R.html
Qadiri-Rifai Tariqa
    http://www.qadiri-rifai.org/
Qur'an English translation by M. H. Shakir,
    http://etext.virginia.edu/koran.html
Ross, Kelley L. Ph.D. *Shame, Beauty, and the Ambivalence of the Flesh, after
    Schopenhauer, C.G. Jung, Frederick Turner & Camille Paglia*
    http://www.friesian.com/shame.htm
Rogge, Michael. *Psychology of Spiritual Movement*
    http://www.xs4all.nl/~wichm/psymove.html
Rumi, Mevlâna Jalâluddîn. *Non-Existence* Translators Camille and Kabir
    Helminski,
     http://www.tue.nl/esk/rumi/rnonex.htm
School of Wisdom
    http://www.schoolofwisdom.com/index/html.
Shaykh Ahmadu Bamba
    http://micasite.org/bamba.htm.
A Shi'ite Encyclopedia
    http://www.al-islam.org/encyclopedia/newindex.html
There Is Simply The "Bright" Itself, from chapter forty-four of "The Dawn
    Horse Testament of the Ruchira Avatar"
    http://www.dabase.net/dhtchp44.htm
Wilson, Peter Lamborn. *Irish Soma.*
    http://useres.lycaeum.org/~lux/features/irshoma.htm

SOUND RECORDINGS

Andreas Ph. D., Connirae. *Advanced Language Patterns* (four audio cassettes), Colorado, NLP Comprehensive.

Chopra, Deepak. *The Path to Love* Random House, Audio Books.

Estés, Clarissa Pinkola. *How to Love a Woman: On Intimacy and the Erotic Life of Women,* (2 Cassettes), Colorado: Sounds True Recordings, Boulder, 1993.

McKenna, Terrence. *God Knows Man Thinks* [lecture given at Esalen] Big Sur, California, Dophin Tapes, 1991.

Muhaiyaddeen, His Holiness M. R. Bawa. *Hajj Discourse: Man Must Use the Seven Levels of Consciousness to Understand the Inner Form of the Qur'an* Philadelphia, Pennsylvania, 1984.

Pasic, Josip. *Anima* (two cassettes), Illinois, C. G . Jung Institute of Chicago, 1986.

Phillips, Kenneth. *Music: A Jungian Insight into the Listening Experience* (cassette) C. G. Jung Institute of Chicago, 1979.

Samraj, Avatar Adi Da. *Reality Is Not What You Think* The Adi Da Samrajya Pty Ltd., April 22, 1995.

Stein, Murray. *Stages of Masculine Development: Midlife and the Anima* (two cassettes) Illinois, C. G. Jung Institute of Chicago, 1987.

Viscott, Dr. David. *Risking* Los Angeles, California, Audio Renaissance, 1989.

Wilson, Peter Lamborn. *The Sufi Way* Boulder, CO, David Barsamian, 1989.

GLOSSARY

Abu Bakr Muhammad Ibn al-'Arabi (1165 - 1240 C.E.) - was born in Spain. He was a contemporary of Suhrawardi of Iran. Like Jelaluddin Rumi, the great Sufi poet and mystic, his theosophy is inspired by nostalgia for divine beauty and a revelation of love. Corbin gives a bibliography of his writings, which profoundly influenced Iranian Sufism.

Abdul'l-Qadir al-Gilani (1077 - 1166) - The founder of the Qadiriyya order, one of the earliest Sufi tariqas; a saint of immense prestige and spiritual grace. Multitudes of legends and stories surround him. It is said that he was brought to Sufism through a single glance of his Sheikh; he rapidly became renowned as the most moving and eloquent of speakers and addressed vast audiences: his spiritual status was such that he once stated, *"My foot is on the neck of every saint."*

Abu Sa'id Ibn Abi-l-Khayr (d. 1049) - An illustrious master-poet from Nishapur (originally from the town of Mayhana in Khurasan), who had a tremendous influence on the Sufis of his time.

Abyss - a chasm; void; the Dark Night of the Soul; the topmost veil on the Qabalistic "Tree of Life" associated with the "invisible" Sephiroth - *Da'ath,* the gulf between the phenomenal and the noumenal; the Sufi must transcend the world of subject and object, in other words the Abyss; the most acute phase of the Spiritual Way.

Adept - a person who is fully skilled in the metaphysic arts; an Initiate; a Complete Human Being.

Ahl - people.

Ahlak - a system of good behavior, beautiful conduct, good thoughts, and good intentions.

Ahli-i Haqq (People of Truth) - perhaps one of the most interesting, yet most obscure and secretive, *turuq* of Iran and eastern Turkey. In Iran they exist today as three primary subdivisions: KhAksAr, JalAli and the Ahl-i Haqq of Kurdistan. In Turkey and Muslim eastern Europe (Albania, Bosnia and parts of Bulgaria) they exist as the Bektashi Order. The original Bektashi Order sprang from the millenarian Hurufiyyah sect of Fadlullah Astarabadi which itself was a denomination of the Ahl-i Haqq. They are indeed the most persecuted Order in Iran's history, and recently after the Khomeini revolution, there was even a brief effort to eradicate them altogether. This assault has forced all the subdivisions of the Ahl-i Haqq to go even further underground. They are centered mainly in north-western Iran, in Azerbaijan, Urumiyyah, and Iranian Kurdistan. *Ali ma' Haqq wa Haqq ma' Ali* (Ali is with the Real/Truth and the Truth/Real is with Ali). Ali ('Alaihi Assalam) is understood as not just being the historical figure of Ali Ibn Abi Talib ('Alaihi Assalam) but an archetypal divine principle. The name Ali itself is derived from the word *a'lA* (high) and a'lA is symbolic of the Essence of the Real. Most Western scholars have posited Isma'ili beginnings to the Ahl-i Haqq and their Syrian counterparts, the Nusayris. Yet recent research is bringing to light information that the Ahl-i Haqq are even older than historical Islam, let alone Ismailism, and there is a possibility that they have their roots way back with the Mandaeans or other surviving Gnostic sects in Persia which were converted to Shi'ism by the Persian Shi'i kingdoms such as the Zaydis and Buyids in the mid Abbasid period.

Ahlul Bayt (Ehl-i Beyt) - the five "Companions of the Mantle"; "People of the Household"; the family of the Prophet and his descendants; narrates Aisha (in Sahih Muslim) *"One day the Prophet (Peace be upon him) came out one afternoon wearing a black cloak (upper garment or gown; long coat), then Hassan came and the Prophet accommodated him under the cloak, then Hussain came and entered the cloak, then Fatima came and the Prophet entered her under the cloak, then Ali came and the Prophet entered him to the cloak as well. Then the Prophet recited, 'Verily Allah intends to keep off from you every kind of uncleanness O' People of the House (Ehl-i Beyt), and purify you a perfect purification.'"* The Prophet Muhammad stated, *"My family is like the Noah's Ark, whosoever boards it, is divinely blessed; those who avoid it, are drowned in the waters and misled."*

Alawi, Ahmad al-' (d. 1934) - A modern Sufi who founded a Sufi order in Algiers.

Alchemy - the work of alchemy is the spiritual synthesis and assimilation of nature. Meister Eckhart: *"the nature which is in God seeks nothing but the image of God."* For some alchemists the goal is nothing less than the recovering of the "fallen" state of all matter. [The "fall" of nature means the ignorance of nature as to its True Reality.]

Aleister Crowley - (1875 - 1947) - Poet, author, mountain climber, magickian, and one of the greatest initiates of this century. He founded several occult movements. Member of the "Golden Dawn." His teachings drew on Golden Dawn Teachings, higher Yoga, the sex techniques of the "Ordo Templi

Orientis," and "The Book of the Law" a channeled book that Crowley received from Aiwass, the messenger of an unknown alien intelligence, in Cairo in 1904. Author of many works on the occult. Publisher of "The Equinox." Followers of "The Book of the Law" are known as Thelemites. Crowley also founded the esoteric organization "Argentum Astrum" (The Silver Star) which replaced the earlier "Golden Dawn."

Al-Fatiha - "The Opening", the name of the traditional first sura of the Qur'an.

Alexander the Great - King of Macedonia 336 - 323 B.C.E.; conqueror of Greek city-states and of the Persian Empire from Asia Minor to Egypt to India.

Hazreti Ali (Ali Ibn Abi Tālib) - a cousin of Muhammad (Peace be upon him); he married the Prophet's daughter Fatima ('Alaiha Assalam); the father of Hassan and Hussain; the fourth Khalif from 656 to 661; the noble leader of the mystic path; the son-in-law of the Prophet; Muhammad (Peace be upon him) brought the Qur'an and Shariah, but Ali ('Alaihi Assalam) embodied their secret significance;[747] the wali or guardian of believers; Ali ('Alaihi Assalam) is the Pir of all Tariqats; Ali ('Alaihi Assalam) is the door to the state of Muhammadiya.

Molana Salaheddin Ali Nader Shah Angha - Molana Salaheddin Ali Nader Shah Angha, known as Hazrat Pir, is the 42nd Sufi in this continuous succession of Sufi Masters dating back fourteen hundred years to the time of the Holy Prophet Muhammad (peace and blessings upon him). Hazrat Pir was born in Tehran, Iran, Sunday noon, the 30th of September 1945, which also coincided with one of the holiest days for Muslims, *Eid al-Qurban*, which celebrates the Hajj. His spiritual journey began in childhood, when special signs were seen in him. For eleven years, he was under the tutelage of his grandfather, who was the 40th Sufi Master of the Oveyssi Order. Hazrat Pir's training continued under the guidance of his father, Molana Shah Maghsoud Sadegh Angha (Professor Angha), the 41st Sufi Master of the Oveyssi Order (Maktab Tarighat Oveyssi Shahmaghsoudi). Professor Angha was world-renowned for his in-depth and expansive knowledge. His works reflect not only his knowledge of the sacred, but also his facility in the sciences, including physics, astrophysics, nuclear physics, physical chemistry, and biochemistry. He also operated his own astronomy laboratory near Tehran. At the age of twenty-three, he wrote: *"My soul is in harmony with the forces commanding the galaxies and those commanding the atoms."* In the year one thousand, three hundred and fifty-two S.H. [September 4, 1970], in one of the guiding sessions held in the presence of Hazrat Shah Maghsoud, with the attendance of a great number of devotees; and with the confirmation of Benevolent Allah, he was blessed by receiving the

Robe of Faqr from the hand of his father. Hazrat Shah Maghsoud, with a speech, handed over his Robe to him.

Anthroposophy - the wisdom of humanity; the study of the Cosmic Human Being, the Primordial Human Being; a brilliant Way of realization articulated by Rudolf Steiner which offers a comprehensive view of the spirit worlds (or subtle realms); Steiner describes a world invisible to the senses but central to the human condition, a spiritual world of subtle bodies, angelic beings, reincarnating souls, planetary and galactic development, Lemuria, Atlantis, and the workings of karma.

Antithesis - an opposition or contrast ; also the direct opposite.

Antinomian - a person who believes that due to Jesus Christ's sacrificial death, he or she is not obligated under any religious law - faith alone being necessary for salvation; opposed to or denying the fixed meaning or universal application of moral law; one who rejects the herd mentality.

Apotheosis - deification; glorification; embodiment; quintessence.

Archetypes – according to Jungian theory, universally meaningful symbolic images and ideas that emerge from the collective unconsciousness. In spiritual terms, archetypes are living powers which represent the essence of anything. By way of illustration, there are many different types of chairs yet we always recognize a chair when we see one, therefore, in the spirit world there exists an "ultimate chair" from which all chairs obtain their "chairness."

'Arsh al-A'la (arshu-ala) - the highest heavens; the holy dimension of space.

Ashk - the love of Divine Reality.

A.S. (aleihissalam) - Peace be upon him or her; this phrase does not mean that we human beings are wishing Peace to the person named, for Peace (As Salām) is a Name of Allah, the phrase is more of an acknowledgment that the Source of Peace is with the person named. *"Allah is Salam."* - Prophet Muhammad (Peace be upon him).

Asthma' (esma) - names; Divine Names.

Astral - the supersensible world of emotions, above the Etheric world, and below the world of the Divine Spark.

Atavism - a physical reappearance in an organism of a form typical of its evolutionary past; an energy-form of the above appearing in the psyche or personality of the individual.

Athan (Adhân) - the call to five-times-a-day prayer.

Autopoetic - "automatic writing," that is, writing produced without conscious intention and sometimes without awareness. Some people consider the phenomena of "automatic writing" to come from the spirit worlds (telepathic or spiritualistic in origin). All sorts of results are produced: word fragments, unrelated words, poetry, obscenities, stories, and complete books. Some well-known esoteric books were produced in this way, such as the following: "The Book of the Law," the Seth material, and "A Course in Miracles." Other experts consider "automatic writing" to be of subconscious or unconscious origin and therefore completely internal.

Avatar Adi Da Samraj - is a truly Free Adept, and his work is a spontaneous revelation to his devotees, day by day, in all that he does. He has been described as, *"a religious genius of the ultimate degree."* – James Steinberg. Adi Da has taken many names, each indicative of his mode of working during a particular time: Bubba Free John, Da Free John, Da Love-Ananda, Da Avabhasa (The "Bright"), and Adi Da (The Da Avatar). In 1997, he took the name of Ruchira Avatar Adi Da Samraj. His devotees regard him as The Divine Person. Regardless, in this author's opinion, many of his works are Sufic and helpful for the advanced Murid. To quote Avatar Adi Da Samraj, *"It has nothing whatsoever to do with this world or any world, even though these present conditions and other conditions may appear to arise. The Realization is prior to all arising."* The renunciant Hermitage Residence of Avatar Adi Da Samraj is located on the tropical island of Naitauba.

Avicenna (Ibn-Si'na) - (980 - 1037), Arab physician and philosopher who wrote the most important book in medicine that was in use for more than three hundred years in Europe.

Awallah - "as Allah wishes."

Awareness - unbiased looking.

Ayn al-Qozat Hamadani - taught and initiated by Ahmad Ghazzali, imprisoned in Baghdad and executed in his hometown of Hamadan (in northwest Iran) in 1131 C.E. at the age of thirty-three.

Azazel - (Azael, Hazazel, *"God strengthens"*). In Enoch, Azazel is one of the chiefs of the 200 fallen angels. Azazel *"taught men to fashion swords and shields"* while women learned from him *"finery and the art of beautifying the eyelids."* He is the scapegoat in rabbinic literature, Targum, and in Leviticus 16:8, although in the latter they do not name him. In "The Zohar" (Vayeze 153a) the rider on the serpent is symbolized by *"the evil Azazel."* Irenaeus calls Azazel *"that fallen and yet mighty angel."* In "The Apocalypse of Abraham" he is *"lord of hell, seducer of mankind,"* and here his aspect, when revealed in its true form, shows him to be a demon with seven serpent heads, fourteen faces, and twelve wings. Milton in "Paradise Lost" (I, 534) describes Azazel as *"a cherub tall,"* but also as a fallen angel and Satan's standard bearer. Originally, according to Maurice Bouisson in "Magic; It's History and Principal Rites," Azazel was an ancient Semitic god of the flocks whom they later degraded to the level of a demon. [Rf. Trevor Ling, "The Significance of Satan in New Testament Demonology"]. Bamberger in "Fallen Angel" inclines to the notion that the first star that fell (star here having the meaning of angel) was Azazel.[748]

Ismailism - The practices and beliefs in "Ismailism" that became contrary to the Islamic Shari'a as a whole began on 17 Ramadhan 559 A.H. (8 August 1164) when an Ismaili leader, Imam Hassan the II declared that he was the *hujjah* (divine proof) on the earth; and that he was the *Qaim* (the living Imam or master of the time). In the capacity as an Imam and the Hujjat he declared that he was freeing his followers from: *"all rules of the Sharia and had brought to them the Qiyama Kubra (Great Resurrection). Also, as the master of the time and the culmination of spiritual authority of the Imams who had preceded him he had ushered in a new religious order in which his followers were absolved from following Islamic law and enjoined instead (of Shari'a) to emphasize the mystical experience of the inner life and moral perfection, by following (his example) as the only reality."*[749]

Israel ben Eliezer, the Baal Shem Tov, or BeSHT ("Master of the Divine Name") - was born in the Ukraine in 1700 and died in Podolia in 1760. He was the founder of mystical Hasidism that was, largely, a reaction to and legitimization of the Sabbatian events of 1665-1666. Like Sabbatai Zevi (called AMIRAH by his Believers), the BeSHT had clear antinomian tendencies which were, however, unlike those of Sabbatai, more acceptable to mainstream Judaism.

Baha ad-Din Naqshband (d. 1390) - one of the most revered masters in the Sufi tradition; a follower in spirit of 'Abd'l-Khaliq Ghijduwani; Naqshband re-instituted the "silent zikr" and, consequently, the tariqa of the Khwajagan

("Masters") became known as the Naqshbandiyya.

Barzakh – interval; any intermediate state between two degrees of existence; especially the world of subtle forms between the physical and supraformal worlds.

Batin - esoteric truth.

Bektash Veli, Haji – *"The birth of the Patron Saint, generosity of soul. He came from Khorasan to Rum. The length of his life is the beauty of Muhammad. The Bektashi date of death, very true."*[750] Haji Bektash's ancestry is traced back to the Prophet Muhammad (Peace be upon him). The name "Bektash" means "companion in rank" or "an equal with a prince." It was from Ali ('Alaihi Assalam) that Bektash received the power to work miracles. Also from Ali ('Alaihi Assalam), Haji Bektash was granted the "sign," a luminous green spot in the palm of his hand and a similar spot on his forehead. One day when young Bektash's teacher, Lokman, asked for some water with which to perform ablution, Bektash prayed and immediately water began to flow from his hand. By miracles he proved his superiority to all his fellow students and later to all the dervishes and Sheikhs of his time.

Bayezid Bistami (d. 874) - An ecstatic Sufi from Iran who has become known for his intoxicated exclamations uttered in the state of "oneness," to cite an instance, *"Glory be to me! How great is my majesty!"*

Abdelwahab Boudhiba – Professor of Islamic sociology at the University at Tunis, where he is also Director of the *Centre d'Etudes et de Recherches Economique et Sociales*. He is an adviser to international organizations such as UNESCO and the UN, and to the Tunisian government, on issues dealing with development and human rights.

Bulleh Shah 1680 – 1758, was born in Uch Gilaniyan in Bahawalpur (Pakistan). Bulleh's earlier name was Abdullah Shah, later changed to Bulleh. His family background was religious, his father being a highly religious person. Bulleh Shah was the disciple of Inayat Shah, a Qadiri Sufi. Bulleh composed much poetry in Punjabi, the local spoken language. His style of poetry is called *Qafi*, which was already an established style with Sufis who preceded him. The tomb of Bulleh Shah is in Qasur (Pakistan) and all Punjabis hold him in reverence.

Chakra or Chakram - one of a series of seven energy centers connected with the human being; their task is to channel or "step-down" the energy of the cosmos so that it can be used in a constructive way by the individual; when properly energized the chakras enable the individual to experience all sorts of paranormal phenomena. To the clairvoyant the chakras appear to be akin to flowers or disks

Catechism - a study-book of doctrine and dogma that each student of Christianity had to learn in the past; a body of fundamental principles or beliefs, especially when accepted uncritically.

Chthonic – deathlike; from the earth; irrational and destructive forces; used in this book to point out that these forces belong to God, and are expressions of God's attributes, as much as do light and benevolent powers.

Clairvoyance - "clear seeing"; mental pictures or images received psychically.

Collective Unconscious - a collection of primeval images passed down through our ancestors, these images include the experience of not only our human ancestors, but also of our pre-human and animal ancestors; a bipolar phenomena; the interconnected Web of Life: all of humanity is interconnected, this interconnection is known as the Collective Unconscious.

The Complete Human (The Universal Human Being, insān kāmil) - One who has fully evolved all the Names of Allah resident in his or her being; one who recognizes his or her Oneness with the Divine and has in turn awakened his or her entire body to spiritual life; One who has made Allah as his or her only wealth; the Fully Awakened One; The Total Human. [also, see Limitless Self]

Conscious - (etymologically: to look through knowledge); bias; distortion; seeing through certain filters.

Consciousness - consciousness is its own content.

Continuum - anything continuous in which a basic common quality is discernible.

Contradiction - a discrepancy; incongruence; inconsistency; variance.

Corbin, Henry (d. 1978) - A French scholar and philosopher who had dedicated his life to the study of Muslim *wilaya* in Sufism and in Shi'ism. Among his many writings, the best-known books are "Creative Imagination in the

Sufism of Ibn'Arabi"and "The Man of Light in Iranian Sufism."

Dervish - from the Turkish *dervish* and Persian *darvish*, originally meaning beggar, but now used as another term for a Sufi.

Devil - Satan, or the Chief Enemy of God; largely a creation of Christianity based on a composite of the nature gods of the indigenous peoples of Europe that the conquering Roman Christians defeated. [See also "Shaitan" and "Iblis"]

Dhat (or Zat) – that from which all springs, the basis of all phenomena.

Dionysus - Lord of Grain, Leaf, and Vine; this God played a central role in the Eleusinian mystery cult. They partook of his flesh and blood as bread and wine. The *Maenad* priestesses (often in wine-induced frenzy) escort him. He is the primal archetype of self-sacrificing, masculine Divinity. Dionysus is depicted carrying the *thrysus* or phallic wand.

Druid - a member of an ancient pre-Christian Celtic religious order; Druids had to complete a twenty-two-year course of study; Druid colleges were scattered throughout Ireland and Great Britain and other Celtic settlements; science, poetry, magic, and the Fine Arts were various disciplines in which the Druid could specialize.

Duality - the state of being two; doubled; coupled; twofold.

Dhu-l-Nun, Thauban Ibn Ibrahim (d. 859) - an early Sufi from Upper Egypt who had acquired an aura of great holiness in the Sufi tradition; known for his deep piety, wisdom and love poetry. Because of his mystical theories the Orthodox authorities persecuted him, but his life was spared.

Ecstasy Breathing - a method that employs extreme hyperventilation to achieve ecstatic experiences, and to break through emotional blockages.

Emre, Yunus (d. 1321) - Considered by some the greatest Turkish poet of all time, his life is shrouded in legend. In his poems, written in the simple spoken language, he combines elements of three categories into which Western Turkish poetry was later divided. His impact upon succeeding generations of mystics was such that many identified themselves with him, using the same name. His work has been the main source of inspiration for many modern poets who, in the years leading to the Republic, achieved the renaissance of Turkish poetry.

Enantiodrama - from the Greek *enantios*, meaning opposite or antagonistic; in this sense an "antagonistic drama." There is a tendency of any characteristic to turn into its opposite in the course of time. Where one area or characteristic is overvalued, dominant and overt, its opposite characteristic is unconscious, but that may change.

Entheogens - Shamanic visionary plants and cacti; shamanic inebriants; such as the following: Sacred Mushroom, Peyote, Mescaline, Ayahuasca.

Epiphany - a Divine manifestation or realization.

Esoteric - secret knowledge; knowledge withheld from the masses and only revealed to the initiated.

Etheric Body – a subtle body through which life-energy flows, similar in shape to the Physical Body. The Etheric Body interpenetrates every atom of the Physical Body and is visible to supersensible perception as a network of energy streams.

Evangelical - any school of Protestant Christianity that teaches that humans are in a sinful condition and have need of salvation.

Exoteric - the external teachings of a religion, meant primarily for the uninitiated masses; only suitable to be disseminated to the public.

Fana - ego death.

Fatima ('Alaiha Assalam) – the daughter of Muhammad (Peace be upon him) and Khadija; born in Macca (al-Mukarramah); the Mahdi ('Alaihi Asslam) will be born from her posterity.

Fundamentalist - a Christian movement that believes that the Biblical scriptures are infallible, in other words free from mistake.

Ghalib, Mirza Asadullah Beg Khan (1796-1869) – "Ghalib" was his "nom de plume"; Indian poet, philosopher, author.

Ghazzali, Abu Hamid al- (d. 1111) - one of the most celebrated Sufi writers and teachers. In his late forties he left a thriving career as a theologian in the great religious academy of Baghdad, went into solitude and wandered for several years to taste mystical truth through immediate experience. His greatest literary work is his "The Revival of the Religious Sciences" in which he strove to reconcile Sufism with Orthodox Islam.

Glyph - a mark or symbol.

Gnosis - a profound knowledge of the universe, of God and humankind: usually of secret or initiatory nature.

Gnostic - as used in this book refers to a person who seeks to find God in his or her Heart. Shaqiq said, *"When they are denied, they render thanks, and when they are given anything, they prefer others to enjoy it."*

Gnostics - those who claim to have a positive knowledge of spiritual truth; a Pagan and Christian philosophicoreligious movement with a doctrine that stated that humans could be saved from Matter through direct knowledge of the Divine.

George Ivanovich Gurdjieff (1872 - 1949) - a gifted Russian spiritual teacher who revolutionized Western psychological thought in the 1920's. A great traveler and student, Gurdjieff gathered insights from various wisdom traditions and synthesized these with his own experience. He called his teaching system the "Fourth Way" - a unique contribution to the evolution of human consciousness. Much of his practice focused on what he called Movements or Sacred Dances which he had forged out of his initiatic experience in monasteries and special schools in Asia and the Levant. Much of Gurdjieff's legacy stemmed from the power of his personality, *"involving ways of behaving with his pupils that were, in turn, shocking, mysterious, frightening, magical, delicately gentle, and omniscient."*[751] Some believe that Gurdjieff received his most important training in the fabled Yezidi "Sarmoung" monastery (branches of which are reported to be scattered between Mesopotamia and the Northen Himalayas).

Hadith – (also known as "the Traditions"); a saying of the Prophet Muhammad (Peace be upon him) corroborated by various reputable witnesses. Full advantage of Islam cannot be derived without both the Qur'an and the Hadith. Some misguided individuals say that one must study only hadith one's entire life to make statements about the hadith knowledgeably, or to base one's actions upon them. Yet, human life is brief. It is the responsibility of every person to exercise his or her God-given reason with respect to what he or she thinks, and how he or she conducts his or her actions. A person should not postpone the living of his or her religion because he or she has not devoted fifty years to the study of hadith. Would any citizen delegate his or her right to vote to another person, because the citizen had not studied everything a candidate has said and written, and all that has been written about him or her? Of course not. A man or woman should look at the Traditions carefully and with justice, consult those whom he or she respects, and then come to his or her own conclusions. The Believers are not fools who cannot think for themselves. It is hard to think clearly when everything you know is filtered through other people. A person should think on his or her own.

Hadith Qudsi – "a celestial tradition"; sacred account; a saying of the Prophet Muhammad (Peace be upon him) through which Allahu t'ala speaks to humanity; a Divine hadith (saying of God) conveyed by the Prophet Muhammad (Peace be upon him); a non-Qur'anic Word revealed through the Prophet (Peace be upon him).

Hadrat (Hazreti) - saint; a term of respect denoting the attribute of sainthood.

Hafez - the most beloved poet of Persia. Born in Shiraz; he lived at about the same time as Chaucer and about one hundred years after Jelaluddin Rumi. He spent nearly all his life in Shiraz, where he became a Sufi master. When he died he was thought to have written an estimated 5,000 poems of which 500 to 700 have survived. His *Divan* (collected poems) is a classic in the literature of Sufism.

Hajj - the Pilgrimage to the Ka'ba and surrounding holy places in Macca (al-Mukarramah); first Pagan, then Muslim.

Hallaj, Hussain Ibn Mansur al- (d. 922) - a famous Sufi from Baghdad. He expressed openly the mystical truth *"ana 'l Haqq (I am Truth, I am God)"* which is equivalent to proclaiming oneself the deity. This shook the orthodox Muslims. They accused him of heresy and witchcraft, brutally tortured and crucified him in front of cheering crowds in Baghdad. At his death, he uttered words of forgiveness for his torturers. Many later apologists have attributed his statements to a loss of control due to ecstasy in zikr, sema or prayer. However, careful review of what is known of Hallaj's life and writings show this not to be the case. The subsequent apologetics may have evolved either as a form of Sufi taqqiya, or as a deliberate attempt to sweep Hallaj's exegesis of the Qur'an and theosophy under the carpet of obscurity. Hallaj, far from being an ecstatic mystic unable to refrain from speaking ineffable truths in a state of *fana fi 'llah*, annihilation in Allah, was in fact a sober erudite scholar who formulated a deliberate school of thought and practice. Central to his doctrine is the concept of *anniyat*, or isolate intelligence, a consciousness which does not acknowledge a deity other than itself. In his writings, Hallaj engages a personal equation with two Qur'anic anti-heros, Iblis and Pharaoh, individuals who like himself have proclaimed their own anniyyat despite the seeming approbation of Allah himself. Hallaj writes in his "Kitab al-Tawasin": *"If ye do not recognize God, at least recognize his signs. I am that Sign; I am the Creative Truth, because through the Truth I am a Truth eternally. My friends and teachers are Iblis and Pharaoh. Iblis was threatened with Hellfire, yet he did not recant. Pharaoh was drowned in the sea, yet he did not recant, for he would not acknowledge anything between him and God. And I, though I am killed and crucified, and though my hands and feet are cut off, I do not recant!"* The conventional Muslim has suppressed this left-hand doctrine in Islam, calling it *shirk* (which means to associate partners with Allah), considered the highest sin in Islam. Yet Hallaj's mysticism is internally consistent, straightforward and simpler than the mental gymnastics of later apologists who try to convince the reader that Hallaj was a dervish intoxicated with the love of Allah and unable to control his utterances.

Hallucinogen/Plant Hallucinogen - a substance that when ingested gives the taker an intense and often profound experience of existence and consciousness.

Haqiqat (Hakikat) - the world of Reality.

Haqq (Hak) - Truth; one of the Ninety-Nine Names or Attributes of Allah (*". . . And He taught Adam the Names, all of them . . ."* Qur'an 2:30); the known invisible values and realities that Allah has created, and everything that is deserved through working with loyalty.

Heresy/Heretic - a heresy is a religious or spiritual opinion that goes against mainstream doctrine; the heretic is a person who deliberately upholds a concept or doctrine that varies from that of his or her church or religion.

Hu - the symbol of Allah's Being or Essence; the ineffable Divine Identity; God Himself transcending attribute or description.

Huzur - peace and tranquility in harmony.

Iblis (also Eblis) - the personal name of the devil (Shaitan); it is said that he has both male and female organs and that he impregnates himself; the essences of both Muhammed and Iblis are grounded in the divine essence; declared his existence before the One Existing Being.

Ijtihad - is to endeavor to understand the hidden meanings in the Qur'an and Hadith.

Initiate - a person who is about to undergo the elementary rite of entry into an occult / esoteric / mystical tradition.

al-insān al-kāmil - the True Human Being; a God-Realized Being; One who has the completeness (wholeness) of the form of Allah's qualities, actions, conduct, behavior, and virtue. [See Limitless Self]

Insha-Allah - "If God So Wills"; God willing.

Interdimensional - that which exists, or can exist, on various dimensions simultaneously.

Ipseity - [f. L. ipse + ITY] ; personal identity and individuality; selfhood. *"The quality of God as a wholly independent being who is complete in Himself. The term gives emphasis to the paradox that God, without any need to do so, creates and draws creatures to Him through love and knowledge."*[752]

Iqbal, Allama – "The National Poet of Pakistan." Sir Allama Muhammad Iqbal was born in Sialkot on November the 9th, 1877. He acquired his school and college education from Sialkot. He obtained his B.A. and M.A. from Government College Lahore. He also received an M.A. in philosophy from University of the Punjab, winning the Gold Medal. Iqbal stayed in Europe from 1903 to 1907 for higher studies. He studied at Cambridge (England) and Munich (Germany). Finally, he earned his Ph.D. degree from Munich University. The title of his thesis was "The Development of Metaphysics in Persia." He also did barristery during his stay in Europe. After his return to Lahore, he was an advocate at Lahore High Court. By this time, he was a very popular poet. Iqbal died in Lahore on April the 21st, 1938, after an illness of about four months. He is buried near the footsteps of the Badshahi Mosque Lahore. His desire was that his age should not be more than the age of Hazrat Muhammad (Peace be upon him). His poetry books are: Urdu — Baal-e Jibreel, Baang-e Dara, Zarb-e Kaleem, and Armaghan-e Hijaz (this book is both in Urdu and Persian). Persian — Asrar-e Khudi, Ramooz-e Be-khudi, Piyaam-e Mashriq, P'as Cheh Baa-eyad Kard ai Aqwaam-e Sharq, Javed Nameh, and Armaghan-e Hijaz. [753]

Islam - from the Arabic word Islam meaning submission or "total self-abandonment to God"; Muslims (the adherents of the religion of Islam) acknowledge One Ultimate Reality - the qualities of this Ultimate Reality may be seen in the world around us; Islam also teaches that the Prophet Muhammad (Peace be upon him) is the last and greatest of the prophets sent by Allah (God); Islam is the infinitive of the verb of which "Muslim" is the active participle.

Ismailis - a Shia group which originated during the Ninth century and developed in some provinces of Iraq, Syria and Iran. They belong to the Sevener branch of the Shia (as opposed to the majority Shia branch of the Twelvers) and recognize the authority of a series of seven imams, the last of whom is - according to the majority Nizari branch, the present Aga Khan Karim, the 49th in the line of Nizari Ismaili imams. The total number of Ismailis today is uncertain, varying according to different sources, from one million to twenty million. They are distributed in several countries in the Middle East and in Asia and Africa; in the present century, because of political and economic emigration, they also settled in America, especially Canada, and Europe. [754]

Jinn (also known as genii) - Jinn are said to have come to the Earth ages before man existed. They were the first of Earth's masters. They built huge cities whose ruins still stand in forgotten places. Aeons later many Jinn were forced to flee Earth while other were imprisoned. Still other roam desolate places to this day. The Jinn are said to be invisible to normal men. They are, however able to interbreed with humans but the human parent may suffer when the dark offspring is born.[755] Belief in Jinn was common in early Arabia, where they were thought to inspire poets and soothsayers. Their existence was further acknowledged in official Islam, which indicate that they, like human beings, would have to face eventual salvation or damnation. Jinn, especially through their association with magic and healing have always been favorite figures in North African, Egyptian, Syrian, Persian, and Turkish folklore. [756]

Ka'ba - The Ka'ba is a building located within the court of the Great Mosque at Mecca. Muslims all over the world face in the direction of the Ka'ba while praying. Pilgrims at Mecca are supposed to circumambulate the Ka'ba. The Ka'ba contains a sacred black stone.

Kabir - (1440-1518): a great poet-saint who lived his life as a weaver in Benares. His followers were both Hindus and Muslims, and his influence was a strong force in overcoming religious factionalism.

Abd al-Rahman Ibn Mohammad Ibn Khaldun - Ibn Khaldun's chief contribution lies in philosophy of history and sociology. He sought to write a world history preambled by a first volume aimed at an analysis of historical events. This volume, commonly known as "Muqaddimah" or "Prolegomena," was based on Ibn Khaldun's unique approach and original contribution and became a masterpiece in literature on philosophy of history and sociology. The chief concern of this monumental work was to identify psychological, economic, environmental and social facts that contribute to the advancement of human civilization and the currents of history. In this context, he analyzed the dynamics of group relationships and showed how group feelings, *al-'Asabiyya*, cause the ascent of a new civilization and political power and how, later, its diffusion into a more general civilization invites the advent of a still new 'Asabiyya in its pristine form. He identified an almost rhythmic repetition of rise and fall in human civilization, and analyzed factors contributing to it.[757]

Karma - the inherited qualities formed at the time of conception; the qualities of mind; the qualities of action; the qualities of the essences of the five elements; the qualities of the degree of separation from the Ultimate Reality.

Kemal – perfection beyond polarization.

Krishna - Eighth incarnation of the beneficent, earth-preserving God Vishnu. He is worshiped through *bhakti*, that is, love. His devotees liken themselves to his flute, played upon by the breath of God.

Limen - threshold.

Liminal - pertaining to the threshold.

Limited Self - the concept of our potential and nature conveyed to us by conventional society, our parents and culture; this concept consists of believing in the notion that our being stops at the edge of our physical bodies; we are asleep to the wholeness of our being; made up of our likes and dislikes, in other words our biases; our mask.

Limitless Self - the activation of your totality; awareness of the All-Pervading Life Principle; the Luminous Radiance of your Existence; a state of clear sensing without distortion.

Isaac Luria (1534-1572) - also known as the "Ari Zaal," or "Divine Rabbi Isaac,"- was, and remains to this day, unarguably the greatest Kabbalist in world history.

Lutfullah - the Grace of Allah.

Macrocosm – the "Great World," the wider universe.

Hazreti Marufi - lived in the 1700's in Istanbul. He was a member of the Rifa'i Order and incorporated elements of the Bektasi Order's spiritual practices into the Rifa'i's teachings. He formed a new branch of the Rifa'i's which today is called the "Rifa'i Ma'rufi Order."

Maestro - a master of any art, especially music.

Mage - from the Latin *Magus* meaning a magician.

Magick - The word magick is sometimes spelled with a "K" in this book. This is to discriminate between sleight-of-hand stage magic, and magic as a spiritual way. "Magick" was a common spelling of the word in the Elizabethan period. John Dee's diaries spell the word with a K. These diaries date from the 1580's. The -ick ending began to change to -ic in English print about 1700, although -ick can still be found in American print until about 1840. We define Magick as the art of arising in perfect harmony with the universe. The Western Magickal Tradition is a means of personal transformation, the Way of the Complete Human. Magick is the discovery within the ordinary of the extraordinary. [See Occult]

Mahavira - a Prophet; also known as Vardhamana.

Mandala - a sacred schematized representation of the cosmos, characterized by a concentric configuration of geometric shapes; in Jungian psychology, a symbol representing the effort to reunify the self.

Manifest - to reveal; to make real on the physical plane.

Mandelbrot Set - known as the "Thumb Print of God" and the "Semaphore of Nature"; discovered in 1980, the Mandelbrot Set is the most famous fractal; it is a geometrical equation that when generated as a picture by a computer produces an astounding effect: if the "camera" zooms-out, the observer will see mini-replicas of the first fractal, but these replicas are continually and subtly different. The contrary is also true: if the "camera" zooms-in to a portion of the picture, the details continue to be infinitely new and distinct. This "picture" represents infinite complexity. Jonathan Swift in 1733 captured the essence of the fractal in the following verse:

> *So, Nat'ralists observe, a Flea*
> *Hath smaller Fleas that on him prey,*
> *And these have smaller fleas to bit 'em,*
> *And so proceed ad infinitum.*

The Mandlebrot Set can be demonstrated in the physical world by the example of looking at the coastline of the continent of North America from outer space. The closer the viewer gets to the earth, the more detail he or she sees. "Details" are new visual information, in other words, the viewer is seeing forms he or she had not seen before. Moreover, this process of seeing ever more detail continues infinitely as the viewer gets nearer to the earth. All of creation has features similar to the Mandelbrot Set.

Mantra - a sacred word repeated without ceasing that brings the individual into an awareness of the Infinite Reality which dwells within him or herself; a sacred sound symbolizing a particular divine energy.

Marifat - the word *ma'rifat* (recognition of God) has special significance. It is used only when you see a person for the second time and remember that you had met him before. Since the origin of man is Godhead, the word recognition is most appropriate for meeting Him again.[758]

Matrix - the womb; a place in which something originates; that which gives form to something enclosed or embedded in it; a frame; a mold; an environment.

Melek Taus (also Ta'usi-Melek) - is as fire with two dualistic elementary abilities: fire as light, but also fire to burn: the good and the evil are one and the same Person. Simultaneously is a human being itself a mixture of two powers: good and evil, that is, every Yezidi has a part of Ta'usi-Melek in him or herself.

Metanoia – unfragmented consciousness.

Metaphysics/Metaphysician - pertaining to the preternatural or super natural; that which concerns Real Being or the essential nature of Reality.

Microcosm – the human being as a miniature model of the Macrocosm.

Mihrab - the niche at the east end of the mosque that gives the direction of Macca (al-Mukarramah); an established place where the beloved turns toward the lover.

Mi'raj (mirac) - Muhammad's (Peace be upon him) ascent to *'arsh al-a'la*; a spiritual ladder.

Mithra - a Persian God of Light, defender of truth and enemy of the powers of darkness.

Murid (Mutasawwif) – comes from the Arabic word *iradah* meaning a strong will, that is, a desire to devote oneself totally to one's Lord; first used eight centuries ago when Sheikh Abdul Qadir Jilani, Imam Ghazali, among others denoted their disciples as murids; the student of a Murshid; a novice; or one who "wills" to follow a spiritual teacher.

Murshid - spiritual master or guide; *"The master of the Path is like a mirror reflecting the disciple's devotion to God and transmitting God's favor to the disciple."* [759]

Mystical - having a spiritual reality that is neither apparent to the five senses nor obvious to the intelligence.

Nabi - a Prophet.

Nafs (nefs) - the immature system within the human that is a part of the Divine. The nafs are not lifeless aspects of our being. In fact, while they need to be "tamed," they are the very Essence of Allah in the human being. When we appear before Allah on Judgement Day, our nafs will appear, not us. The Arabic term is related to words for "breath," "soul," "essence" "self," and "nature"; it refers to a process which comes about from the interaction of body and soul.

Divine Name (Ninety-Nine Names) - Each Name can be thought of as a bi-unity: an uncreated Lord and a created vassal or servant. These two roles are forever distinct. The uncreated Lord may be thought of as the Angel or the eternal hexeity or the eternal individuality of a given individual's being. The created individual or servant is seen as an epiphanized form of the uncreated Lord. As God is indivisible, all of the divine Names are said to be in sympathetic union with one another, yet each Name embodies a unique attribute of the Godhead. Unlike other divine Names, Al-Lah is the Name which is invested with the sum of all the divine Attributes.

Nesimi – a famous poet from a district called Nesim, near Baghdad, partly of Turkish blood. He made the acquaintance of Fazlullah, a Sheikh who proclaimed himself divine, in the sense that *"Whoso knoweth himself knoweth his Lord."* Nesimi became an enthusiastic missionary of this new mystical stream. Finally, in Aleppo he was convicted from his own poems of heresy, and was flayed alive. To posterity he left two Divan's, or collections of poems, one in Persian and the other in Turkish. While they flayed him alive he was reported to have said, *"The God whom you worship is under my foot."*

New Testament - the Christian holy scriptures consisting of: the life of Jesus Christ traditionally ascribed to be written by the Apostles Matthew, Mark, Luke, and John, the Acts of the Apostles (an account of the early years of the church), several letters from the Apostles to various communities and friends, and finally the Apocalypse (a prophetic account of the eschaton).

The Nur Ashki Jerrahi Sufi Order - is a community of dervishes within the Halveti-Jerrahi Tariqat in the lineage and leadership of Sheikh Muzaffer Ashki al-Jerrahi, Shaykh Nur al-Anwar al-Jerrahi, and Sheikha Fariha al-Jerrahi. They are based at Masjid al-Farah in New York City, with circles in various cities in the United States and Mexico.

Dr. Javad Nurbakhsh – was born in Kerman, Iran. Prior to his retirement he was professor and head of the Department of Psychiatry at the University of Tehran. He has written numerous books on psychiatry and written and published extensively on the subject of Sufism. Dr. Nurbakhsh, currently residing in London, is the Sufi Master of the Nimatullahi Order of Sufis, a position that he has held since he was twenty-six years old.

Occult - that which is hidden; having to do with astrology and the magickal arts; beyond the scope of the understanding; occultists believe in hidden or mysterious powers and the potentiality of human mastery of them; a system of mystical wisdom kept secret by those who practice it.

Ontos [from the Greek Onto] - the Essence of Essences; the essential nature of anything; being; existence; individual living thing.

Orthodox - the approved practice of a standardized religious doctrine.

Osho   (December 11, 1931 - January 19, 1990) - an enlightened master whose work, in all its depth and color, continues to unfold. Tom Robbins, one of America's greatest living novelists, describes him as *"the most dangerous man since Jesus Christ"* and Jean Lyell in Vogue Magazine as *"a gentle and compassionate man of complete integrity . . . the most inspired, the most literate, and the most profoundly informed speaker I have ever heard anywhere."* ; born in Kuchwada, Madhya Pradesh, India; at the age of twenty-one, Osho became enlightened; on March 21, 1953, Osho graduated from the University of Saugar with first class honors in philosophy; while a student he won the All-India Debating Championship; he served as professor of philosophy at the University of Jabalpur for nine years.

Osiris - the Great God of Egypt who co-reigned with his sister and wife Isis; Osiris was noted for bringing civilization to the peoples of Egypt.

Ouspensky, Piotr Demianovich - Born in 1878 in Moscow, Russia, P. D.

Ouspensky was already a well-known mathematician, author and journalist before becoming a pupil of G. I. Gurdjieff in 1915 in Tsarist, and later revolutionary, Russia. He put the system into what was then (early 20th century) contemporary Russian language and organized the fragments of knowledge into a form suitable for the Western mind. Later, P. D. Ouspensky founded "The Society for the Study of Normal Man," and its publishing arm the "Historico-Psychological Society," in London, England, and in Lyne Place near Virginia Water, where, except for the years of the Second World War when he was in the United States at Franklin Farms, he taught from the 1920s until his death in 1947.

Pagan - L. "paganus," a peasant or civilian. A European (by birth or culture) who actively practices a religion not based on Judaic scriptures, usually a polytheistic cultus pre-existing or reconstructed from those pre-existing the Christian conversion of Europe.[760]

Passive-Aggression - a psychological term concerning individuals, who when they get angry, cannot state it explicitly but say and do things that indirectly convey their anger.

Pir - One; Qutub; the One Living Human Spiritual Master of the World.

Polemic - involving controversy; a controversialist.

Pranayama - a method of bringing into the body the Vital Force through special breathing practices.

Preponderator - The Prevailer; The Predominator.

Propitious - auspicious; advantageous, beneficial.

Qibla - the direction, faced during prayer, toward the Ka'ba.

Quantum - a step or unit of energy; subatomic; quantum theory holds that the flow of energy in the universe is not continuous but takes place through packets of energy.

Quiddity - the essence of a thing; quiddity is the answer when you ask yourself the question: "What is it?"

Quintessence - the ancient peoples of Greece and Pre-Christian Europe recognized four elements: Earth, Air, Fire, and Water. The fifth and last element, proposed by the Pythagoreans and Aristotle, is the power and essence of the body.

Qutb – axis or pivot; Nurturer; the highest station in the Sufi hierarchy of saints. The *Qutb* is directly responsible for the welfare of the entire world. The Qutb is said to be the spiritual successor of the Prophet Muhammad (Peace be upon him).

Qur'an (also Koran) - "recitation"; a word derived from its Syriac counterpart, used first for the particular revelations transmitted by the Archangel Gabriel (Jibraeel) from Allah Most High to Muhammad (Peace be upon him), which he then recited and invited his followers to recite; they later gave the name to the book containing those revelations, the Qur'an.

Radix - a neo-Reichian form of therapy which uses the breath to break through muscular armoring (see Reichian growth work).

Rahim - The All Beneficent, All Compassionate; one of the Ninety-Nine Names or Attributes of Allah.

Rahman - The All Merciful; one of the Ninety-Nine Names or Attributes of Allah.

Rak'a - bending the body in prayer.

Re-birthing - an individual is regressed back to the birth experience through certain techniques such a breathing and laying in warm water or in the arms of caring facilitators.

Reichian Growth Work - a form of therapy based on the work of Wilhelm Reich; it is designed to free the individual from areas of trapped emotional-energy locked in his or her muscles, permitting the free flow of *orgone* energy throughout the body.

Rifa'i Marufi - a Sufi path that works inside the existence and unity of Islam. One of the branches of Tasawwuf, Sufism, is the Rifa'i. This name was given because the Order was begun by Ahmet er-Rifa'i, who lived in the thirteenth century in the town of Basra, which is in today's Iraq. In this branch the second Pir or founder, Mohammad Fethel Marufi, expanded the teachings, knowledge and cultural scope in the seventeenth century. The tomb of Marufi is in Istanbul, Turkey. So by adding the Marufi to the Rifa'i this branch became the Rifa'i Marufi.

Jeffrey Rothschild – holds a Ph.D. in English Education from New York University. He is Assistant Professor at the City University of New York where he teaches writing. He has edited a number of books for Khaniqahi Nimatullahi Publications.

Rumi - Jelaluddin Rumi (1207 - 1273), the great Persian poet of the Sufi or mystical tradition; the greatest mystical poet of Islam; founder of the Mevlevi Order of Dervishes (The Whirling Dervishes); Jelaluddin Rumi represents the highest possible reach of inspiration or insight.

Salat - prayer.

Santeria - a Yoruban African religion brought over to the West by slaves; it is a syncretistic religion because of the ban by white slave owners on the slaves to practice their indigenous African religious traditions.

Shaman – a spiritual traveler between our world and the world of spirits, with whom the Shaman can communicate, often for healing purposes and purposes of obtaining esoteric information.

Shamanism - an ancient religion of the peoples of northern Europe and Asia which include animism, possession, soul (or astral) travel, and shape shifting.

Sheikh - (Persian *Shah* and Turkish *Shayk*), a spiritual master or guide, an Arab chief; now used as a title of respect; also known as a Murshid.

Sheikh Ahmad Ibn Ali al-Rifa'i - born in Basra in 1182 C.E. The Rifa'i Order has spread to Egypt, Syria, Anatolia in Turkey, Eastern Europe and the Caucasus, and more recently to North America.

Sirat al-Mustaqim - the Straight Path that must be walked on with delicacy, care and balance.

Soul - our Divine Essence; the Divine Reality uniquely manifested as the Human Being.

Sufi/Sufism - a system of Islamic mysticism developed especially in Persia. Today a wide spectrum of Sufi groups exist, some completely devoid of all Islamic attachments, while others continue to be deeply tied to Islam; personally experienced religion (as distinct from formal theology or ritual).

Rudolf Steiner - born an Austrian on February 27, 1861. He went through grammar school in Neudorfl and high school in Winer Neustadt, after which he attended the Technical Institute in Vienna from 1897 to 1883. From 1890 to 1896, he was on the staff of scholars at the Goethe-Schiller Archives in Weimar. Steiner founded the esoteric science of Anthroposophy (The Study of the Human Being). He gave information concerning the evolution and future of humankind as well as the spiritual forces working in humankind and in the universe. He was an architect (designed the Goetheanum 1 and 2, among other buildings); painter; playwright (four mystery dramas); author of numerous books, and sculptor. He created a system of agriculture named "Bio-Dynamic Agriculture"; an internationally known form of pedagogy known as "The Waldorf School"; he introduced Speech Formation; made suggestions for the healing arts; and created the system of movement known as "Eurythmy" practiced around the world. He gave more than six thousand lectures. Rudolf Steiner died on March 30, 1925. *"Anthroposophy is a path of knowledge aiming to lead the spiritual in man to the spiritual in the cosmos."* - Rudolf Steiner.

Supersensible - that which is cognizable through senses which are normally dormant in most human beings.

Sura - a chapter of the Qur'an.

Synthesis - the combination of separate elements into a whole.

Tafsir – an exploration of the hidden meanings of the Qur'an through intuitive awareness and interpretation; a study of the hidden Qur'an in light of economic, social, moral and political spheres; also an external philological exegesis of the Qur'an.

Tantra - a Yogic practice which involves awakening of the Kundalini energy at the base of the spine and sending it up the seven chakras; a Hindu Way in which the practitioner explores the sexual energies of his or her being, and transforms them into subtler, spiritual energies.

Tariqa (tarike) - spiritual path.

Ta'wil (also see Tafsir) - hermeneutic exegesis; esoteric interpretation; the science of allegorical interpretation; the word occurs in the Qur'an itself referring to the revelation delivered by Muhammad (Peace be upon him); exposition of the Qur'an.

Tekke (Arabic: *Zawiyyah*; Persian: *Khanaqah*) – literally "corner"; a special place or retreat where Sufi groups gather and worship; a lodge. In the Middle

Ages, tekkes were often significant social centers where many dervishes lived and worked. In Turkey, Kemal Ataturk closed the tekkes in the mid-1920's as part of his modernizing revolution following the collapse of the Ottoman Empire. However, certain Sufis maintain that Ataturk was himself a dervish, and his hidden purpose in closing the tekkes was because many of them were turning into social-clubs and forgetting their original purpose. Particular tekkes continued to operate under the name of "Music and Cultural Centers."

Taoism - Tao means "Way"; based on the teachings of the Chinese philosopher Lao-tse who lived, along with Buddha, in the 6th century B.C.E.

Tariqat (tariqah) - (from Arabic "path" or "way"); the spiritual path; a Sufi Order; the social organization and devotional practices that are the basis of the order's ritual and structure.

Tasawwuf – gerund form, literally "being a Sufi" or "Sufism."

Tavern – the place where Divine Love is dispensed. It is not an ordinary bar or cocktail lounge, but for example, a Tekke, Mosque, or anywhere the Sufis gather.

Theophanic Vision - Theophanic vision is mediated by *himma*, the power of the heart. An individual with theophanic vision doesn't just process sensory data. Instead he sees through things, gaining an intimation of what the thing symbolizes on a spiritual level. It's as if the each object of theophanic vision were a window into paradise. Viewed in this way, material things are spiritualized. This is often referred to in Sufi literature as ascent or return.

Third Eye - the Chakra which, when activated, permits a person to have supersensible experiences.

Transcendent - surpassing; going beyond what is given or presented in experience; to go beyond knowledge itself; beyond the rational; going beyond the limits of all possible experience.

Tree of Life - the central focus of the Western Magickal Tradition's study of Qabalah. The "Tree" represents creation in all its invisible and visible processes.

True Guide - a process that dissolves the artificial self.

Abu Ali al-Farmadi at-Tusi (d. 447 H.) – he is called the Knower of the

Merciful and the Custodian of Divine Love. He was a scholar of the Shafi'i school of jurisprudence and a unique *arif* (endowed with spiritual knowledge). He was deeply involved in both the School of the Salaf (scholars of the First and Second Centuries) and that of the Khalaf (later scholars), but he made his mark in the Science of Tasawwuf. From it he extracted some of the heavenly knowledge which is mention in the Qur'an in reference to al-Khidr (s), *"and We have taught him from our Heavenly Knowledge"* [18:65]. Sparks of the light of *jihad an-nafs* (self-struggle) were opened to his heart. He was known everywhere in his time until he became a very famous Sheikh in Islamic Divine Law and theology. Al-Ghazali al-Kabir said of him, *"He was the shaikh of his time and he had a unique way of reminding people."* No one surpassed him in his eloquence, delicacy, ethics, good manners, morality, nor his ways of approaching people. He said, *"Who prefers the company of the rich over the company of the poor, Allah will send him the death of the heart."* [761]

Umma - the community, body of believers, of a Prophet.

Unconscious - that which dissolves the fixed and narrow; undoing "looking through knowledge"; presence of tremendous awareness; everything that consciousness has rejected.

The Underworld – a region or realm conceived to be below the surface of the earth; the dwelling of Hades; the opposite side of the earth, in other words: the antipodes; the subconscious; in mythology, the place visited by Orpheus when he sought to save Eurydice; the world of the dead.

Undifferentiated - not to distinguish between one thing and another; not expressing differences; not becoming a distinct character.

Unmanifest - not yet evident to the senses; nor obvious to understanding; the Divine disrobed of all attributes. [see Void]

Upanishads - Hindu treatises composed between 8th and 6th century B.C.E. representing a philosophical development beyond the Vedas having as their principal message the Unity of Brahman and Atman.

Usûl - methodology or fundamentals of a religious science.

Uwaysis - Uwyasis are not instructed by a Sheikh in the phenomenal world. This path is reserved for those who are called to a direct unmediated relationship with the Divine World. True Uwaysi initiation does not necessarily take place in the temporal realm of physicality. If it has happened to you, you would know it. More than this we cannot say. Those who claim to transmit Uwaysi knowledge in an established tariqat are really carriers of transmission from a past Uwaysi master. Whether these individuals have actual Uwaysi transmission themselves is dubious given their own lack of insight into the matter. Uwaysis do not seek justification in a historical succession of Sheikhs. Uwaysi initiation is quite close to the concept of the Imam in Hiding, or the Hidden Imam. All those among the Sufis who had no visible murshid (guide), that is, an earthly man like themselves and a contemporary, called themselves Uwaysis. One of the most famous was Abu'l-Hassan Kharraqani (d. 425/1034), an Iranian Sufi, who left us the following saying: *"I am amazed at those disciples who declare that they require this or that master. You are perfectly well aware that I have never been taught by any man. God was my guide, though I have the greatest respect for all the masters."*

Llewelly Vaughan-Lee, Ph.D. – is the author of several books on Sufism including: Sufism, the Transformation of the Heart, The Paradoxes of Love and The Face Before I Was Born, A Spritual Autobiography. Born in 1953, he has followed the Naqshbandi Sufi Path since he was nineteen. In 1991 he moved from London to northern California where he lives with his wife and two children.

Vector - a quantity possessing both magnitude and direction.

Vector Field - a region or domain with a vector assigned at each point.

Void - the state of nothingness experienced in deep sleep; the state of the formless Absolute, which according to the Buddhists is a state of nonexistence; in Kashmir Shaivism the Void has the nature of being, consciousness and bliss.

Wajd - ecstasy, finding.

Wali – saint, one who possesses a direct experience of the reality of God demonstrated through extraordinary spiritual knowledge or miracles. A Wali often becomes a spiritual guide (Sheikh), however sometimes Allah chooses to keep his or her sainthood hidden. Now and then, Allah even keeps it a secret from the saint.

Wicca - A.S. "wicce," to turn or bend; also "willow." A twentieth century pagan cultus reconstructed from fragments of classical Greek and Roman fertility rites and Neolithic artifacts. Wiccans seek to attune themselves to the rhythms and cycles of nature. They do not engage in any form of ritual slaughter, drinking blood and putting hexes on people.[762]

675

Wine – In Sufi terminology, wine is a metaphor for Divine Love. It does not refer the intoxicating alcoholic beverage known to drunkards and alcoholics.

Yantra – symbolic visual diagrams upon which one meditates in Eastern mysticism which are specifically designed to trigger enlightenment; often constructed from intricately arranged triangles or geometric figures, enabling the meditator to contemplate various spiritual realities.

Yezidi [also spelled Yazidi, Azidi, Zedi, or Izdi] - those who worship the angel Ta'usi-Melek. The Yezidi religion is one of the oldest controversial religions of the world, going back to at least 2000 B.C.E. The sect is found primarily in the districts of Mosul, Irqa; Diyarbakir, Turkey; Aleppo, Syria; Armenia and the Caucasus region; and in parts of Iran. They pray five times a day. Their two chief prayers are the morning prayers during which they face toward the sun and the evening prayer during which they face the sunset. The Yezidis regard the snake (especially the black snake) as holy, in fact as a saint. The Christian Easter, in fact the names of Mary and Jesus were expressly mentioned in the Yezid religious texts, where they have a place of honorable saints. The Christians also took over some customs from the Yezidis: such as the coloring of Easter-eggs. The Ayatollah Khomeini of Iran recently put thousands of Yezidi to death, perhaps all of them. Originally they were said to summon the lower demons and elements, fully acknowledging the evil of the King of the "Black Powers," who opposes Allah. However, their rationale is that one day Allah and Shaitan will reconcile their differences and those who have shown disrespect for Shaitan will then suffer for it, bringing both God and Devil after them. Modern Yezidism is a mixture of unorthodox Islam and Christianity. The real name of the God of the ancient Yezidis is unknown as they were forbidden to utter it.

Yin/Yang - the universal interplay of polarity, such as the following: light and dark, male and female, active and passive, and hot and cold, within the context of One Reality; the ebb and flow of life creating a state of dynamic balance. Legend tells us that Chinese philosophers realized the concept as they meditated upon a hill on which they could clearly see the shadow side and the light side; Yin is feminine, negative and dark, Yang is masculine, positive and light. *"The Great Primal Beginning (t'ai chi) generates . . . the two primary forces [yang and yin]."*[763]

Zikr (Zikruallah/Dhikru'llah) - Divine Remembrance; repetition of Allah's names; intimate dialogue; a meeting of dervishes at which phrases containing the names of God are chanted rhythmically to induce a state of ecstasy, which also consists of sacred movement, prayer, chanting of the Qur'an, the playing of flutes, cymbals and drums, and spontaneous utterances and calling out to Allah; it is a truthful inspiration which stirs the heart toward truth, so he or she who listens truthfully will realize the truth. The Zikr is like a bridge that may lead some to the loftiest heights and throw others to the lowest depths. It is a slippery bridge on which only the feet of sincere individuals can stand firmly.

ABOUT THE AUTHOR

Laurence Galian is an initiate of two Sufi Orders: the Rifa'i-Marufi and the Halveti-Jerrahi. He has been a student of Sufism for more than two decades. The author is a faculty member of the *Hofstra University Hofstra College of Continuing Education* (Hempstead, New York) where he has taught since 1992.

In 1980, after a series of extraordinary "coincidences" (although coincidences are merely Allah's orders), Galian became interested in Sufism and Islam and eventually made the profession of faith making him a Muslim, taking the name "Abdullah" (The Servant of God). He "took hand" (became initiated as a Sufi Dervish) with the Grand Sheikh Muzafferuddin "Ashki" Ozak of the *Halveti-Jerrahi Order of Dervishes* from Istanbul, Turkey. He continued his studies with Sheikh Tosun Bayrak al-Jerrahi al-Halveti, Shaykh Nur al-Anwar al-Jerrahi (Lex Hixon), and Sheikh Salik Schwartz al-Jerrahi al-Halveti, at the *Halveti-Jerrahi tekke* (Spring Valley, New York) and the *Masjid al-Farah* (Manhattan, New York).

Galian subsequently studied with Sheikh Mansur al-Jerrahi al-Halveti (from Greece and Australia) in the 1990's. Abdullah renewed his "hand" (also known as *Bai'at*) in the *Halveti-Jerrahi Order* with Grand Sheikh Sayyid Safer Dal Efendi in 1996, and the same year he "took hand" with a representative of Seyyid Burhaneddin Aktihanoglu. He was bestowed the name "Muzaffer" by Sheikh Hydar of the *Nur Ashki Jerrahi Sufi Order*, in honor of the memory of Sheikh Muzafferuddin "Ashki" Ozak.

Galian has traveled widely, making spiritual pilgrimages to Azerbaijan, Bulgaria, Colombia, England, France, Ireland, Israel, Malta, Mexico, Palestine, and Turkey. In Bulgaria, he visited holy sites in Sofia, Bankia, Plovdiv, Melnik, and Koprivshtitsa. Laurence has visited the tomb of Hazreti Pir Nureddin al- Jerrahi al-Halveti in the tekke in Istanbul, Turkey and the tombs of various other Pirs and saints in Baku, Azerbaijan; Istanbul, Manissa, Turkey; and throughout Israel and Palestine. While in Baku, Laurence Galian received the *khirqah* (cloak) from Khezr which Khezr himself fastened on him.

The New York Times ran an article about Galian's lectures at the *Hofstra College of Continuing Education*, and he is a regular lecturer at New Age Centers, bookstores and festivals both nationally and internationally. He has been a frequent columnist for *Long Island Voices*.

Since the age of six, Galian studied western classical piano music with James Gerard DeMartini, a professor at *Brooklyn College* and noted Abstract Fine Artist. Today, Galian holds the full-time position of *Administrator* in the *Hofstra University Department of Drama and Dance* (Hempstead, New York) serving as Senior Dance Accompanist. He has accompanied many of the greatest dancers and companies in the world including Natalia Makarova, *Jennifer Muller and The Works, Joyce Trisler Danscompany,* and *The San Francisco Ballet.*

Galian has recorded a solo piano album of ballet music entitled *Ballet Music for Barre and Center Floor,* available as a double-length CD from *Roper Records, Inc. National Public Radio* aired his original Sufi ballet, *Zemzem,* on the program *"New Sounds with John Schaefer."* In 1999, *The John F. Kennedy Center for the Performing Arts* awarded him a "Regional Certificate of Merit" for his work as *Musical Director* at *Hofstra University.* Laurence Galian is listed in the fifteenth edition of *International Who's Who in Music* (Cambridge, England) as well as *Outstanding People of the 20th Century*

In 2003, Galian was admitted into the membership of the *American Oriental Society* (Hatcher Graduate Library, University of Michigan).

END NOTES

[1] Rumi, Jelaluddin. Open Secret: Versions of Rumi Trans. Moyne, John and Coleman Barks, Putney, Vermont, Threshold Books, 1984, p.1.

[2] Habiba. Where the Eagles Fly: Portraits of Women of Power, Habiba: A Sufi Saint from Uzbekistan video, New York, Mystic Fire Video, 1997.

[3] *"It* [Ta'wil] *means, to cause to return, to lead back to the origin, and thus return to the true and original meaning of a written text. It is to cause something to arrive at its origin. He who practices ta'wil, therefore, makes something revert to is truth, to its haqiqah."* – Corbin, Henry. History of Islamic Philosophy London, Kegan Paul International, 1990.

[4] Ibn 'Omar reported that the Prophet related that he heard a servant of Allah say this prayer; narrated by Ibn Majah.

[5] A prayer taught by the Prophet Muhammad (Peace be upon him) to Juwayriyya bint al-Harith, one of his wives; Muslim and Abu Dawud, authorities.

[6] If a person recites this one hundred times a day, all his or her sins will be wiped off even if they were as numerous as the foam on the surface of the sea, so revealed the Prophet Muhammad (Peace be upon him); Muslim, Tirmidhi and Nasa'i, authorities.

[7] Narrated 'Aesha (in Sahih Muslim) *"One day the Prophet (Peace be upon him) came out one afternoon wearing a black cloak, then Hassan came and the Prophet accommodated him under the cloak, then Hussain came and entered the cloak, then Fatima came and the Prophet entered her under the cloak, then Ali came and the Prophet entered him to the cloak as well. Then the Prophet recited: 'Verily Allah intends to keep off from you every kind of uncleanness O' People of the House (Ahlul Bayt), and purify you a perfect purification.'"* (the last sentence of Verse 33:33). Additionally: *"The messenger of Allah (Peace be upon him) said: 'I am leaving for you two precious and weighty Symbols that if you adhere to both of them you shall not go astray after me. They are the Book of Allah, and my progeny, that is my Ahlul Bayt. The Merciful has informed me that these two shall not separate from each other till they come to me by the Pool (of Paradise)."* Sahih al-Tirmidhi. This second hadith has been reported in various forms by both the Shi'a and Sunni sources. Moreover, it has been regarded as an authentic tradition. More than twenty close companions of the Prophet have related it. Lastly, another tradition, which is widely acknowledged in all Sunni and Shi'a sources is related by Ibn'Abbas who heard the Prophet declare: *"The likeness of my family is the Ark of Noah. Whoever embarks upon it is saved; and whoever stays away from it will perish."*

[8] Rumi, Jelaluddin. Love is a Stranger: Selected Lyric Poetry of Jelaluddin Rumi Vermont, Threshold Books, 1993, p. 61.

[9] Al-Ghazali, 'Abu Hamid Muhammad Bin Muhammad. Miskat ul-Anwar found in al-Jawahir al-Ghawali Cairo, 1353 A.H. (1934 C.E.) p. 96.

[10] Al-Ghazali, 'Abu Hamid Muhammad Bin Muhammad. al-Maqsad ul-Asna Cairo, 'Alamiyyah, (no date given), p. 23.

[11] Al-Ghazali, 'Abu Hamid Muhammad Bin Muhammad. Ma'ary ul-Quds fi Madary Ma'rifat in-Nafs Cairo, 1346 A.H. (1927 C.E.) p. 197.

[12] Al-Kurdi, Shaykh Amin. Tanwir al-qulub (Enlightenment of Hearts) p. 522.

[13] 'Arabi, Ibn al-. The Sufi Path of Knowledge; Ibn al-'Arabi's Metaphysics of Imagination Trans. William C. Chittick, Albany, New York: SUNY Press, 1989, p. 108.

[14] 'Arabi, Ibn al-. The Sufi Path of Knowledge; Ibn al-'Arabi's Metaphysics of Imagination Trans. William C. Chittick, Albany, New York: SUNY Press, 1989, p. 108.

[15] Qur'an 17:110 and 'Arabi, Ibn al-. Muqaddima III 129.17, Trans. William C. Chittick, in The Sufi Path of Knowledge; Ibn al-'Arabi's Metaphysics of Imagination; Albany, New York: SUNY

Press, 1989, p. 107.

[16] Al-Ghazali, 'Abu Hamid Muhammad Bin Muhammad, Ihya' 'Ulum id-Din (Amiriyyah MS) Cairo, Al-Khalifa Othman Bin'Affaniyyah Press, 1352 A.H. (1933 C.E.) p. 165.

[17] Nur al-Jerrahi, Sheikh. Juma prayers, *Khutba*, Tekke as-Safa, Nashville, Tennessee 9/23/94.

[18] Evidence of this Fresh Vision can been seen in the fact that, over time, many Dervish Orders were established, and from these Orders many new "branches" were (and are being) established by those special "Friends of Allah" who bring a Fresh Vision (a particular brand of mysticism) to Earth. People are creatures of habit and they do not like change. Those saints who attempt to establish a new Sufi Order have always met with resistance and ridicule, even from certain well-respected dervishes.

[19] Gleick, James. Chaos: Making a New Science London, Minerva, 1997.

[20] School of Wisdom http://www.primasounds.com/fractal/paradigm.html#paradigm

[21] Qur'an 4:175.

[22] Qur'an 3:138, Trans. Shakir, M. H., Elmhurst, New York, Tahrike Tarsile Qur'an, Inc. 1997.

[23] Birge, John Kingsley. The Bektashi Order of Dervishes London, Luzac Oriental, 1994, p. 33.

[24] Rumi, Jelaluddin. Open Secret: Versions of Rumi Trans. Moyne, John and Coleman Barks, Putney, Vermont, Threshold Books, 1984, p. 1.

[25] Khan, Pir-o-Murshid Inayat. The Object and Moral of Worship of the Sufi.

[26] Schopenhauer. "The best of possible worlds" from The World as Will and Representation, Vol. I, p. 325, E. F. Payne translation, Dover Books, 1969.

[27] Ross, Kelley L. Ph.D. Shame, Beauty, and the Ambivalence of the Flesh, after Schopenhauer, C.G. Jung, Frederick Turner & Camille Paglia http://www.friesian.com/shame.htm

[28] Nepo, Mark. Walking North "Sufi" Issue 35, Autumn 1997, London, England, p. 35.

[29] Jami. The Precious Pearl Trans. Heer, N., Albany, State University of New York Press, 1979, p.37.

[30] Hixon, Lex. A Mighty Companions Interview with Lex Hixon, http://www.mightycompanions.com/page6.html

[31] Helminski, Kabir. Servant of Mevlana.

[32] Rumi, Jelaluddin. Feeling the Shoulder of the Lion: Selected Poetry and Teaching Stories from the Mathnawi versions by Coleman Barks, Vermont, Threshold Books, 1991, p. 18.

[33] Rogge, Michael. Psychology of Spiritual Sects, Religion, Prediction http://www.xs4all.nl/~wichm/psymove.html

[34] Kabir. The Kabir Book versions by Robert Bly, The Seventies Press/Beacon Press, 1977.

[35] Estés, Clarissa Pinkola. How to Love a Woman: On Intimacy and the Erotic Life of Women, (2 Cassettes), Colorado: Sounds True Recordings, Boulder, 1993.

[36] Hixon, Lex. A Mighty Companions Interview with Lex Hixon, http://www.mightycompanions.com/page6.html

[37] Arberry, A. J. Trans. A Sufi Martyr: The Apologia of 'Ain al-Qudat al-Hamadhani London, George Allen and Unwin Ltd., 1969, p.83.

[38] Hixon, Lex. The Core of All Kingdoms: An Exploration of Non-Duality with Lex Hixon hosted by Suzanne Taylor, http://www.mightycompanions.com/page4.html

[39] 'Arabi, Ibn al-. The Bezels of Wisdom Mahwah, New Jersey, Paulist Press, 1980, p.56.

[40] Qur'an 12:6.

[41] Wilson, Peter Lamborn. Sacred Drift: Essays on the Margins of Islam San Francisco: City Light Books, 1993, p. 63.

[42] Ouspensky, P. D. The Fourth Way New York, Vintage Books, 1971, p. 206.

[43] 'Arabi, Ibn al-. The Sufi Path of Knowledge; Ibn al-'Arabi's Metaphysics of Imagination Trans. William C. Chittick, Albany, New York: SUNY Press, 1989, p. 127.

[44] Qur'an 31:27.

[45] Lings, Martin. A Sufi Saint of the Twentieth Century: Shaikh Ahmad al-Alawî: his spiritual

heritage and legacy California, University of California Press, 1973.

[46] Traditionally , a dervish never uses the personal pronoun "I" out of respect for the Singularity of the Indivisible Consciousness. It is used here, merely as a teaching tool.

[47] Samraj, Avatar Adi Da. Reality Is Not What You Think cassette lecture, The Adi Da Samrajya Pty Ltd., April 22, 1995.

[48] John, Bubba Free. Breath and Name: The Initiation and Foundation Practices of Free Spiritual Life San Francisco, California, The Dawn Horse Press, 1977, p. 77, 4.7.

[49] Vaughn-Lee, Llewellyn, ed. Traveling the Path of Love: Sayings of Sufi Masters Inverness California, The Golden Sufi Center, 1995, p. 167.

[50] Samraj, Avatar Adi Da. Reality Is Not What You Think cassette lecture, The Adi Da Samrajya Pty Ltd., April 22, 1995.

[51] Wilson, Peter Lamborn. Sacred Drift: Essays on the Margins of Islam San Francisco: City Light Books, 1993, p. 59.

[52] Khan, Pir-o-Murshid Inayat. The Object and Moral of Worship of the Sufi.

[53] Qur'an, The Cow 2:116, Trans. Shakir, M. H., Elmhurst, New York, Tahrike Tarsile Qur'an, Inc. 1997.

[54] Hixon, Lex. A Mighty Companions Interview with Lex Hixon
http://www.mightycompanions.com/page6.html

[55] 'Arabi, Ibn al-. The Bezels of Wisdom Mahwah, New Jersey, Paulist Press, 1980.

[56] 'Arabi, Ibn al-. The Bezels of Wisdom Mahwah, New Jersey, Paulist Press, 1980

[57] Modern Dance Class, Hofstra University, April 7, 1998.

[58] 'Arabi, Ibn al-. "Whoso Knoweth Himself . . ." from the Treatise on Being Abingdon, Oxon, Great Britain, Beshara Publications, 1976, p. 10.

[59] al-Hujweri, Syed Ali Bin Al-Khalifa Othman Bin'Affan. The Kashful Mahjub: Unveiling the Veiled translator and commentator Hadhrat Maulana Wahid Bakhsh Rabbani (r.a.).

[60] Bamba, Shaykh Ahmadu. http://vzone.virgin.net/ismael.essop/bamba.htm

[61] Attar, Farid al-Din. Muslim Saints and Mystics: Episodes from the 'Tadhkiratal-Auliya' ("Memorial of the Saints") London, Routledge and Kegan, Paul, 1979.

[62] Helminski, Kabir. Ecstasy & Sobriety (condensed from "Parabola") "Eye of the Heart", Vol. 2, Issue 1, p. 2, 4.

[63] Nurbakhsh, J. In the Tavern of Ruin:Seven Essays on Sufism New York, Khaniqahi-Nimatullahi Publications, 1978, p. 32.

[64] We acknowledge the work of Jeffrey Rothschild Sitting in the Circle of the Sufis: The Nature of Sama' in "Sufi" Issue 37/Spring 1998, for the vision of this practice.

[65] Narrated by Tirmidhi (book of da'awat #102, Hassan sahih), Ibn Majah (Du'a #2), and Ahmad (1:227) with a strong chain.

[66] Narrated by Tirmidhi (Hassan gharib) and Ahamad.

[67] Qur'an 2:152.

[68] Related in the Malik's Muwatta', the Musnad of Ahmad, the Sunan of Tirmidhi, Ibn Majah, and the Mustadrak of Nishapuri. Al-Bayhaqi, Hakim and others declared it sahih.

[69] Dhikr is the Greatest Obligation and Perpetual Divine Order
http://www.sunnah.org/ibadaat/dhikr.htm

[70] In Tirmidhi and Ibn Majah from Ibn Jubayr.

[71] Ibn Hajar al-'Asqalani, Ahmad Ibn Ali. Fath al-Bari: Sharh Sahih al-Bukhari Bayrut, Dar-al-Kutab al-'Illmiyah, 1989, 11:250.

[72] Qur'an 2:255.

[73] http://www.geocities.com/Athens/Oracle/7319/hadiths.htm

[74] We have this on the authority of Muhammad Ibn Hatib Jumahi, that Nasa'i related that the Prophet said this. This Tradition is recorded by Tirmidhi who declares it "good;" others pronounce it "sound."

75'Arabi, Ibn al-. Journey to the Lord of Power: A Sufi Manual on Retreat Trans. Harris, Rabia Terri, Vermont, Inner Traditions International, 1989, p. 28.

It is related that a certain Companion [Anas B. Malik, according to Al-Qushairi, al-Risala (Cairo, 1330/1912), 108.] entered the presence of Uthman, and heard him attest to this hadith.

Jurjani al-Sayyid al-Sharif, Ali Ibn Muhammad. Kitab al-ta'rifat Misr, al-Matba-ah al-Hamidyah al-Misriyah, 1903.

8 Wilber, Ken. Eye to Eye: The Quest for the New Paradigm Garden City, New York, Anchor Books, 1983.

9 Arberry, A. J. Trans. A Sufi Martyr: The Apologia of 'Ain al-Qudat al-Hamadhani London, George Allen and Unwin Ltd., 1969, p. 59.

80Arberry, A. J. Trans. A Sufi Martyr: The Apologia of 'Ain al-Qudat al-Hamadhani London, George Allen and Unwin Ltd., 1969, p. 31.

81Qur'an 20:114 (tafsir).

82Glossary of Muslim Terms http://www.digiserve.com/mystic/Muslim/glossary.html

83Arberry, A. J. Trans. A Sufi Martyr: The Apologia of 'Ain al-Qudat al-Hamadhani London, George Allen and Unwin Ltd., 1969, pp. 32-33.

84Al-Qurtubi as quoted by Ibn Hajar al-'Asqalani, Ahmad Ibn Ali. Fath al-Bari: Sharh Sahih al-Bukhari Bayrut, Dar-al-Kutab al-'Illmiyah, 1989, 12:449.

85Ruzbihan Baqli, Shaikh. The Unveiling of Secrets: Diary of a Sufi Master (original title: Kashf al-asrar) Trans. Ernst, C. W., Chapel Hill, N.C., 1997, p. 7.

86Sarraj Al-Qari, Ja'far Ibn Ahmad. Masari'al-'ushshaq Cairo, Maktabet al-Anjlu al-Misriyah, 1956, p. 209.

87Al-Qari. Jam' al-wasa'il (Cairo, 1317 H) p. 209.

88Qur'an 27:40.

89Bukhari narrates it in the book of knowledge of his Sahih.

90From a sobhet given by Sheikh el-Hajj Şerif Çatalkaya er-Rlfa'i er-Marufi on the 'esma Ya Wadud.

91Khan, Pir-o-Murshid Inayat. The Object and Moral of Worship of the Sufi.

92Wison, Peter Lamborn. Divan London : Tehran, Crescent Moon Press, 1978.

93This contemplation is not only a powerful image for the awakening of the soul-powers, but it lends credence to our conviction that practices for supersensible development are appropriate for the Murid. This imagery is taken directly from the Qur'an al-Karim, Sura Nur 24:35. We have used the translations of Hashim Amir-Ali The Message of the Qur'an: Presented in Perspective; and of Shaykh Nur al-Jerrahi given in Atom From The Sun Of Knowledge.

94Hixon, Lex. The Core of All Kingdoms: An Exploration of Non-Duality with Lex Hixon, hosted by Suzanne Taylor, http://www.mightycompanions.com/page4.html

95We hear through Ibrahim Ibn Ahmed al Bazari.

96We hear through Abdul Wahid Ibn Bekr al Weresani-Kannad Ebu Musa ad-Dabili.

97Kabir. The Kabîr Book versions by Robert Bly, The Seventies Press/ Beacon Press, 1977.

98Qur'an, Chapter Luqman 31:18.

99Messadié, Gerald. Histoire Général du Diable Éditions Robert Laffont, 1993.

100Ibrahim Ad'ham, mentioned in, Love is the Wine: Talks of a Sufi Master in America by Sheikh Muzaffer al-Jerrahi al-Halveti, edited and compiled by Sheikh Ragip Frager, Vermont: Threshold Books, 1987.

101 The believers are those who, when they hear Allah mentioned, their hearts tremble. (al-Anfal).

102Rumi, Jelaluddin. Open Secret: Versions of Rumi Trans. Moyne, John and Coleman Barks, Putney, Vermont, Threshold Books, 1984.

103Hamadani, Ayn al-Qozat. A Sufi Martyr Trans. Arberry, A. J., London, Allen and Unwin, 1969.

[104] Hixon, Lex. The Core of All Kingdoms: An Exploration of Non-Duality with Lex Hixon, hosted by Suzanne Taylor, http://www.mightycompanions.com/page4.html

[105] 'Arabi, Ibn al-. The Bezels of Wisdom Mahwah, New Jersey, Paulist Press, 1980, p. 279.

[106] 'Arabi, Ibn al-. The Bezels of Wisdom Mahwah, New Jersey, Paulist Press, 1980, p. 124.

[107] It has been established that early Christian Councils distorted and deliberately deleted the words of the Prophet Isa (Peace be upon him). Some of the words of the Mercy to the Worlds, the Prophet Muhammad (Peace be upon him), were also manipulated and effaced by certain of his followers. For example, we have numerous hadith from 'Aesha, but where are the hadith from Fatima ('Alaiha Assalam)? Is this not strange and a bit suspicious? We shall see that this was, and continues to be, a deliberate attempt on the part of certain individuals to control Islamic thought and the knowledge of the life and sayings of the Prophet. It is said that Muslims accept two thirds of their faith from 'Aesha, because a large number of the Traditions concerning Muhammad (Peace be upon him), on which Muslims rely, were derived from this wife of the Prophet.

[108] 'Arabi, Ibn al-. The Bezels of Wisdom Mahwah, New Jersey, Paulist Press, 1980, p.123.

[109] Samraj, Avatar Adi Da. Reality Is Not What You Think cassette lecture, The Adi Da Samrajya Pty Ltd., April 22, 1995.

[110] The New Friesian Theory of Religious Value http://www.friesian.com/newotto.htm

[111] The New Friesian Theory of Religious Value http://www.friesian.com/newotto.htm

[112] John, Bubba Free. Breath and Name: The Initiation and Foundation Practices of Free Spiritual Life San Francisco, California, The Dawn Horse Press, 1977, p. 130.

[113] Hixon, Lex. The Core of All Kingdoms: An Exploration of Non-Duality with Lex Hixon, hosted by Suzanne Taylor, http://www.mightycompanions.com/page4.html

[114] Ibn Huseyn Suleymi: The Way of Futuwwet Trans. from Turkish: Bayrak al-Jerrahi al-Halveti, Sheikh Tosun, January 9, 1981, unpublished paper.

[115] Tirmidhi. Manaqib 1; Qazwini, Ibn Maja. Zuhd 37; Darimi. Muqaddima 8. Ahmad I 281, 295; III 144.

[116] Besides the Shia and Sunni ulema of Islam, many impartial historians of other nations have given the details of this feast. They had no religious bias, being neither Shias nor Sunnis. One of these writers is the nineteenth-century British historian and philosopher, Thomas Carlyle. In his Heroes and Hero-worship he described the details of the feast at Abu Talib's house. After the Prophet's statements, Ali stood and proclaimed his faith in the Prophet. Therefore, the Khalifate was bestowed on him. Other European writers have confirmed this fact, including George Sale of England and Hashim, a Christian of Syria, in his Maqalatu'l-Islam, and Mr. John Davenport in his Muhammad and the Qur'an. All agree that the Prophet, immediately after the proclamation of his prophethood, called Ali his brother, helper, successor, and Khalif. Moreover, several hadith confirm that the Prophet emphasized this fact on many other occasions.

[117] Nur al-Anwar al-Jerrahi, Sheikh. Juma prayers, Khutba, Tekke as-Safa, Nashville, Tennessee 9/23/94.

[118] *"By this knowledge he means knowledge of God. Knowledge of other than God is a waste of time."* 'Arabi, Ibn al-. The Sufi Path of Knowledge; Ibn al-'Arabi's Metaphysics of Imagination Trans. William C. Chittick, Albany, New York: SUNY Press, 1989, p. 150.

[119] 'Arabi, Ibn al-. The Sufi Path of Knowledge; Ibn al-'Arabi's Metaphysics of Imagination Trans. William C. Chittick, Albany, New York: SUNY Press, 1989, p. 241.

[120] Arabi, Ibn al-. The Bezels of Wisdom Mahwah, New Jersey, Paulist Press, 1980, p. 272.

[121] Bukhari, Anbiya 3; Muslim, Iman 327, 328, etc. Some versions add, *"without boasting"* (Tirmidhi, Tafsir Sura 17, 18; Ahmad I 281, 195, etc.).

[122] Bukhari, Jihad 122, Ta'bir 22, I'tisam 1; Nasa'i, Jihad 1, Tatbiq 100.

[123] 'Arabi, Ibn al-. The Bezels of Wisdom Mahwah, New Jersey, Paulist Press, 1980, p. 37.

[124] Imam Ghazali has written in his Sirru'l-Alamin, Maqala IV, from which Yusuf Sibt Ibn Jauzi

also quotes in his Tadhkiratu'l-Khasa'isu'l-Umma, p. 36, and many others of the eminent Sunni ulema.

[125] Qur'an, Trans. Pickthall, 16:43.

[126] at-Tabrisi, Abu Ali al-Fadl Ibn al-Hassan Ibn al-Fadl. Beacons of Light (Muhammad: The Prophet and Fatimah: The Radiant) a partial translation of I'lamu 'l-Wara bi A'lami l'-Huda Trans. Ayoub, Dr. Mahmoud M., and Mrs. Lynda G. Clarke, Tehran, World Organization for Islamic Services, 1985. p. 211.

[127] at-Tabrisi, Abu Ali al-Fadl Ibn al-Hassan Ibn al-Fadl. Beacons of Light (Muhammad: The Prophet and Fatimah: The Radiant) a partial translation of I'lamu 'l-Wara bi A'lami l'-Huda Trans. Ayoub, Dr. Mahmoud M., and Mrs. Lynda G. Clarke, Tehran, World Organization for Islamic Services, 1985, p. 212.

[128] Recorded by Ali ('Alaihi Assalam) himself in his Nahju'l-Balagha and by Ibn Abi'l-Hadid in his Sharh Nahj al-balaghah Egypt, 1329, vol. II, p. 561-562.

[129] 'Arabi, Ibn al-. The Bezels of Wisdom Mahwah, New Jersey, Paulist Press, 1980, p. 37.

[130] Muhaiyaddeen, His Holiness M. R. Bawa. Asma'ul-Husna: The 99 Beautiful Names of Allah Philadelphia, The Fellowship Press, 1979, p. 136.

[131] Arabi, Ibn. Futuhat al-Makkiyya Trans. William C. Chittick, in The Sufi Path of Knowledge; Ibn al-'Arabi's Metaphysics of Imagination; Albany, New York: SUNY Press, 1989.

[132] Haeri, Shaykh Fadhlalla (collector). The Sayings and Wisdom of Imam Ali Trans. Yate, Asadullah ad-Dhaakir.

[133] 'Arabi, Ibn al-. The Bezels of Wisdom Mahwah, New Jersey, Paulist Press, 1980, pp. 273-274.

[134] Shabistari, Mahmud Ibn 'Abd al-Karim, The Secret Garden Bianco, Tex., Zahra, 1982.

[135] Farooqui, Hadhrat Shaikh Asif Hussain. Envy & Pride
http://www.geocities.com/Athens/7253/Issue1/EnvyPride.html

[136] Abd al-Hakim Murad: I. Ibn Yazid al-Nakha'i (d. c96/714-5) was a devout and learned scholar of Kufa. He studied under al-Hassan al-Basri and Anas Ibn Malik, and taught Abu Hanifa, who may have been influenced by his extensive use of personal judgment (ra'y) in matters of jurisprudence. Sources: Ibn Hibban, Mashahir 'ulama al-amsar 101; M.M. Azami, Studies in Early Hadith Literature 65-66; Ibn al-Jazari, Ghayat al-nihaya 1:29.

[137] Birge, John Kingsley. The Bektashi Order of Dervishes London, Luzac Oriental, 1994, p. 150.

[138] John, Bubba Free. Breath and Name: The Initiation and Foundation Practices of Free Spiritual Life San Francisco, California, The Dawn Horse Press, 1977, p. 147.

[139] John, Bubba Free. Breath and Name: The Initiation and Foundation Practices of Free Spiritual Life San Francisco, California, The Dawn Horse Press, 1977, p. 146.

[140] John, Bubba Free. Breath and Name: The Initiation and Foundation Practices of Free Spiritual Life San Francisco, California, The Dawn Horse Press, 1977, p. 143.

[141] Ozak, Sheikh Muzaffer al-Jerrahi al-Halveti. Love is the Wine: Talks of a Sufi Master in America by edited and compiled by Sheikh Ragip Frager, Vermont: Threshold Books, 1987, p. 76.

[142] 'Arabi, Ibn al-. "Whoso Knoweth Himself . . ." from the Treatise on Being Abingdon, Oxon, Great Britain, Beshara Publications, 1976, p. 10.

[143] Hixon, Lex. The Core of All Kingdoms: An Exploration of Non-Duality with Lex Hixon, hosted by Suzanne Taylor, http://www.mightycompanions.com/page4.html

[144] Glossary of Muslim Terms http://www.digiserve.com/mystic/Muslim/glossary.html

[145] Al-Khani. Hada'iq al-wardiya p. 109. The Yasavi Order is named after Khwajah Ahmad Yasavi (d. 562 AH/ 1166 C.E.) from the city of Yasi, where his tomb is located. Today it is called Turkestan and is situated in Kazakhstan, about a six hour drive northwest from Tashkent, the capital of Uzbekistan.

[146] Birge, John Kingsley. The Bektashi Order of Dervishes London, Luzac Oriental, 1994, p. 225.

[147] Muzaffer al-Jerrahi al-Halveti, Sheikh. Love is the Wine: Talks of a Sufi Master in America edited and compiled by Sheikh Ragip Frager, Vermont: Threshold Books, 1987, p. 48.

[148] It should be remembered that the ASTRAL BODY awakens life out of unconsciousness, out of the sleep of the plant world. The SPIRIT SELF process is the grace of the SPIRIT/NOEMA-SOME BODY working on the ASTRAL BODY to awaken to Spirit Realities.

[149] Helminski, Kabir. Ecstasy & Sobriety (condensed from "Parabola") "Eye of the Heart", Vol. 2, Issue 1, p. 4.

[150] Hamadani, Ayn al-Qozat. The Drunken Universe: An Anthology of Persian Sufi Poetry translations and commentary by Peter Lamborn Wilson and Nasrollah Pourjavady, Grand Rapids, Phanes Press, 1987, p. 54.

[151] Hamadani, Ayn al-Qozat. The Drunken Universe: An Anthology of Persian Sufi Poetry translations and commentary by Peter Lamborn Wilson and Nasrollah Pourjavady, Grand Rapids, Phanes Press, 1987, p. 44.

[152] Mahmud-I Shabustare. Gulshen-I Raz Trans. Al fakir Tosun al Jerrahi.

[153] al-Shabrawi, Shaykh Abd al-Khaliq. The Degrees of the Soul: Spiritual Stations on the Sufi Path London, The Quilliam Press, 1997, pp. 29-30.

[154] al-Shabrawi, Shaykh Abd al-Khaliq. The Degrees of the Soul: Spiritual Stations on the Sufi Path London, The Quilliam Press, 1997, pp. 48-49.

[155] al-Shabrawi, Shaykh Abd al-Khaliq. The Degrees of the Soul: Spiritual Stations on the Sufi Path London, The Quilliam Press, 1997, pp. 53-54.

[156] al-Shabrawi, Shaykh Abd al-Khaliq. The Degrees of the Soul: Spiritual Stations on the Sufi Path London, The Quilliam Press, 1997, pp. 56-57.

[157] Muzaffer al-Jerrahi al-Halveti, Sheikh. Love is the Wine: Talks of a Sufi Master in America edited and compiled by Sheikh Ragip Frager, Vermont: Threshold Books, 1987, p. 32.

[158] al-Shabrawi, Shaykh Abd al-Khaliq. The Degrees of the Soul: Spiritual Stations on the Sufi Path London, The Quilliam Press, 1997, p. 59.

[159] Angha, Molana Salaheddin Ali Nader Shah. Sufism and Islam ISBN: 0-910735-97-2, Shahmaghsoudi Publication pp. 39-40.

[160] The Sheikhs often refer to several subtle organs or centers, called *latifa*, each of which is associated with a particular color and psychospiritual faculty

[161] 'Arabi, Ibn. Futuhat al-Makkiyya Trans. William C. Chittick in The Sufi Path of Knowledge: Ibn al-'Arabi's Metaphysics of Imagination; Albany, New York: SUNY Press, 1989.

[162] The Drunken Universe: An Anthology of Persian Sufi Poetry translations and commentary by Peter Lamborn Wilson and Nasrollah Pourjavady, Grand Rapids, Phanes Press, 1987, p. 54.

[163] Rajneesh, Bhagwan Shree. Journey Toward the Heart: Discourses on the Sufi Way San Francisco, Harper and Row, Publishers, 1976, p.4.

[164] Khan, Pir-o-Murshid Inayat. The Object and Moral of Worship of the Sufi.

[165] Translation of Sahih Bukhari, Book 58: Volume 5, Book 58, Number 163: Narrated by Ali.

[166]   Al-Majlisi. Bihar al-Anwar.
            Al-Sayyuti. Tarikh al Khulafa.
            Abul-Faraj al-Isfahani. Aghani.
            Ibn Hisham. Seera.
            Muhammad Ibn Ishaq. Seerat Rasool-Allah.
            Abu Ja'far Muhammad Ibn Jarir al-Tabari. Tarikh al-rusul wal muluk, State University of New York Press.
            Yasin T. al-Jibouri. Khadija Daughter of Khuwaylid: Wife of Prophet Muhammad (pbuh), http://www.as-islam.org/biographies/khadija.htm, May 12, 1994.

167 'Arabi, Ibn al-. "Whoso Knoweth Himself . . ." from the Treatise on Being Abingdon, Oxon, Great Britain, Beshara Publications, 1976, p. 7.

168 Qur'an 28:88.

169 'Arabi, Ibn al-. "Whoso Knoweth Himself . . ." from the Treatise on Being Abingdon, Oxon, Great Britain, Beshara Publications, 1976, p. 8.

170 Hixon, Lex. The Core of All Kingdoms: An Exploration of Non-Duality with Lex Hixon, hosted by Suzanne Taylor, http://www.mightycompanions.com/page4.html

171 Du'a Kumayl Trans. and commentary by Rahim M B F London, Husein A., http://www.al-islam.org/kumayl/
Kumayl Ibn Ziyad Nakha'i was a confidant among the companions of Amir al Muminin, Imam Ali Ibn Abi Talib ('Alaihi Assalam) and this sublime Du'a was first heard from the beautiful, though anguished, voice of Imam Ali. According to Allama Majlisi (on whom be Allah's Mercy) Kumayl had attended an assembly in the Mosque at Basra which was addressed by Imam Ali in the course of which the night of the 15th of Shaban was mentioned. Imam Ali said, *"Whosoever keeps awake in devoutness on this night and recites the Du'a of Prophet Khizr, undoubtedly that person's supplication will be responded to and granted."* When the assembly at the Mosque had dispersed, Kumayl called at the house where Imam Ali was staying, and requested him to acquaint him with Prophet Khizr's "Du'a." Imam Ali asked Kumayl to sit down, record and memorize the "Du'a" which Imam Ali dictated to Kumayl. Imam Ali then advised Kumayl to recite this "Du'a" on the eve of (i.e., evening preceding) every Friday, or once a month or at least once in every year so that, added Imam Ali ('Alaihi Assalam), *"Allah may protect thee from the evils of the enemies and the plots contrived by impostors. O' Kumayl! In consideration of thy companionship and understanding, I grant thee this honor of entrusting this Du'a to thee."*

172 Mr. Rajiv Chakravarti from the University of Texas, Austin.

173 The Encyclopedia of Religion ed. by Eliade, Mircea, New York, Macmillan, 1987, vol. 12, p. 484.

174 "Ghazal XII" by Mirza Ghalib.

175 'Iraqi, Fakhruddin. Divine Flashes translation and introduction by William Chittick and Peter Lamborn Wilson, New York, Paulist Press, 1982, p. 119.

176 'Arabi, Ibn al-. The Sufi Path of Knowledge; Ibn al-'Arabi's Metaphysics of Imagination Trans. William C. Chittick, Albany, New York: SUNY Press, 1989, p. 27.

177 Hixon, Lex. The Core of All Kingdoms: An Exploration of Non-Duality with Lex Hixon, hosted by Suzanne Taylor, http://www.mightycompanions.com/page4.html

178 Ansari al-Harawi, 'Abd Allah. Les Etapes Des itinérants vers Dieu Trans. S. de Laugier de Beaurecueil O.P., Paris 1962.

179 Lakha, Murtaza Ahmed. The Twelfth Imam London, R & K Tyrrell, 1993, p. 47.

180 See "Pir" in glossary.

181 Qur'an 20:109.

182 Sulami, Muhammad Ibn al-Husayn. The way of Sufi Chivalry: when the light of the heart is reflected in the beauty of the face, that beauty is futuwwah Trans. Bayrak al-Halveti al-Jerrahi, Sheikh Tosun, Rochester, Vt., Inner Traditions International, 1991 1983.

183 John, Bubba Free. Breath and Name: The Initiation and Foundation Practices of Free Spiritual Life San Francisco, California, The Dawn Horse Press, 1977, p. 31.

184 Quoted by Massignon 1982, vol. 3, p. 353.

185 Sheikh Sadeuq narrated in Ilal Ash Sharaea that Zaid Ibn Ali made this statement.

186 'Iraqi, Fakhruddin. Divine Flashes translation and introduction by William Chittick and Peter Lamborn Wilson, New York, Paulist Press, 1982, p. 91.

187 Qur'an 7:26, Trans. Shakir, M. H., Elmhurst, New York, Tahrike Tarsile Qur'an, Inc. 1997.

188 Fadak was an area in the valley of the Medina (al-Munawwarah) hills. It contained seven villages which extended as far as the sea-coast. Many were very fertile and there were oases there.

The area of land was very vast. There was a peace treaty with the people stating that half of the whole of Fadak was to be in their possession and the other half would be the property of the Holy Prophet.

[189] The chief of the commentators testifying to the authenticity of this Holy verse is Ahmad Tha'labi in his Kashfu'l-Bayan; the verse is also verified by Jalalu'd-din Suyuti in his Tafsir, vol. IV, reporting from Hafiz Ibn Mardawiyya, and numerous others.

[190] Contributed by Br. Ali Abbas, abbas@seas.gwu.edu

[191] It is written in Siratu'l-Halabiyya, p. 39, compiled by Ali Bin Burhanu'd-din Halabi Shafi'i (died 1044 A.H.) that at first, Fatima ('Alaiha Assalam) remonstrated with Abu Bakr that she had the owner's possession of Fadak and it was gifted to her by the Holy Prophet of Allah but since religious witnesses could not be available she was forced to claim her right according to the law of inheritance. Hence, the claim of heritage was after the claim of gift.

[192] The great scholar and traditionist Abu Bakr Ahmad Bin Abdul Aziz Jauhari, about whom Ibn Abi'l-Hadid says in his Sharh Nahj al-balaghah Egypt, 1329, that he was one of the eminent Ulema and traditionists of the Sunnis and was a pious and upright man, in his Kitab-e-Saqifa; Ibn-e-Aseer in his Nahaya; Mas'udi in Kitab-e-Akhiru'z-Zaman and in Ausat; Ibn Abi'l-Hadid in his Sharh Nahj al-balaghah vol. IV, page 78, quoting from Abu Bakr Ahmad Jauhari's book Saqifa and Fadak in different ways and from a number of sources some of which refer to the fifth Imam Muhammad Baqir ('Alaihi Assalam) through Siddiqai Sughra Zainab-e-Kubra ('Alaiha Assalam) and some refer to Abdullah Ibn-e-Hassan from the authority of Siddiqai Kubra Fatima Zehra ('Alaiha Assalam) and on page 93 from the authority of Ummul Momineen Ayesha and also on page 94 from Muhammad Bin Imran Marzbani, he from Zaid Bin Ali Bin Hussain ('Alaihi Assalam); he from his father and he from his father Imam Hussain ('Alaihi Assalam) and he from his illustrious mother, Fatima Zehra ('Alaiha Assalam); and many other Sunni Ulema have narrated the speech of Fatima ('Alaiha Assalam) the oppressed one, inside the mosque before a large gathering of the Muslims.

[193] Hadid, Ibn Abi'l. Sharh-e-Nahjul Balabha Volume IV, p.80.

[194] Muhammad Bin Yusuf Ganji Shafi'i, in his book Kifayatu't-Talib chapt. 10, narrates this detailed tradition on the authority of Ibn-e-Abbas, who told a section of the Syrians, who were imprecating and cursing Ali ('Alaihi Assalam) that he had heard the Holy Prophet say this about Ali ('Alaihi Assalam).

[195] When he became Khalif, Umar Bin al-Khattab was feared rather than loved: he had a harsh disposition and carried a whip while walking in order to chastise those who broke the law. He congratulated himself that he was responsible for the inroduction of the veil.

[196] Reported by Abu Umar Ahmad Bin Abd Rabbih, writing in his Iqdu'l-Farid Part III, p. 63.

[197] Salahuddin Khalil Bin Abeekussafadi in his Wafi Bil Wafiyyat in connection with the letter "alif" (A) has reported the beliefs of Ibrahim Bin Sayyar Bin Hani Basari (popularly known as Nazzam-e-Motazali), and quotes Nazzam as saying, *"On the day of allegiance Umar bin al-Khattab cause such a serious injury on Fatima ('Alaiha Assalam) that she miscarried her son Muhsin."* (This volume of Wafi Bil Wafiyyat, in manuscript form, is present in the National Library of Haji Hussain Aqa Malik, Tehran).

[198] Qur'an 8:41, Trans. Shakir, M. H., Elmhurst, New York, Tahrike Tarsile Qur'an, Inc. 1997.

[199] Abu Muhammad Abdullah Bin Muslim Bin Qutayba Bin Umar Al-Bahili Dinawari (died 276 A.H.) in his Ta'rikh-e-Khilafa'i'r-Rashidin, known as Al-Imama wa's-Siyasa, Volume I, page 14, relates the above events.

[200] Hazreti Hassan and Hazreti Hussain also chose to be martyred in order that the true message of Muhammad (Peace be upon him) might be persevered and known by those who take the time to question and learn about their deaths.

[201] Rumi, Jelaluddin. Love is a Stranger: Selected Lyric Poetry of Jelaluddin Rumi Vermont, Threshold Books, 1993, p. 54.

202 'Arabi, Ibn al-. The Sufi Path of Knowledge; Ibn al-'Arabi's Metaphysics of Imagination; Trans. William C. Chittick, Albany, New York: SUNY Press, 1989, p. 185.

203 'Iraqi, Fakhruddin. Divine Flashes translation and introduction by William Chittick and Peter Lamborn Wilson, New York, Paulist Press, 1982, p. 98.

204 Wilson, Peter Lamborn. Sacred Drift: Essays on the Margins of Islam San Franciso: City Light Books, 1993, 60-61.

205 Taymīya, Ibn. Al-Radd 'alā Ibn 'Arabî wa-l-sūfîya p. 56; cited by Ritter (Meer, pp. 476-77).

206 Bouhdiba, Abdelwahab. Sexuality in Islam London, Routledge & Kegan Paul plc, 1985, p. 135.

207 Baqli, Shaikh Ruzbihan. The Unveiling of Secrets: Diary of a Sufi Master (original title: Kashf al-asrar) Trans. Ernst, C. W., Chapel Hill, N.C., 1997, pp. 3-4.

208 Jung. The Portable Jung Ed. Joseph Campbell, Trans. R.F.C. Hull, New York, Viking Penguin Inc., 1971, p. 78.

209 Baqli, Shaikh Ruzbihan. The Unveiling of Secrets: Diary of a Sufi Master (original title: Kashf al-asrar) Trans. Ernst, C. W., Chapel Hill, N.C., 1997, p. 43.

210 Baqli, Shaikh Ruzbihan. The Unveiling of Secrets: Diary of a Sufi Master (original title: Kashf al-asrar) Trans. Ernst, C. W., Chapel Hill, N.C., 1997, p. 65.

211 Baqli, Shaikh Ruzbihan. The Unveiling of Secrets: Diary of a Sufi Master (original title: Kashf al-asrar) Trans. Ernst, C. W., Chapel Hill, N.C, 1997, p. 71.

212 Baqli, Shaikh Ruzbihan. The Unveiling of Secrets: Diary of a Sufi Master (original title: Kashf al-asrar) Trans. Ernst, C. W., Chapel Hill, N.C., 1997, p. 54.

213 Nafzawi, Shaykh. The Glory of the Perfumed Garden: The Missing Flowers (An English Translation from the Arabic of the Second and Hitherto Unpublished Part of Shaykh Nafzawi's Perfumed Garden Trans. H.E.J., London, Neville Spearman Limited, 1975, p. 214.

214 'Arabi, Ibn al-. The Bezels of Wisdom Mahwah, New Jersey, Paulist Press, 1980, p. 275.

215 'Aini, vol. IX, p. 494ff; vol. V, p. 597.

216 Bouhdiba, Abdelwahab. Sexuality in Islam London, Routledge & Kegan Paul plc, 1985, p. 125.

217 Qur'an 11:52, Trans. M. H. Shakir, http://etext.virginia.edu/koran.html.

218 'Arabi, Ibn al-. The Bezels of Wisdom Mahwah, New Jersey, Paulist Press, 1980.

219 Rumi, Jallaludin. Al-Majani al-haditha vol. III, p. 126, Ibn Rumi p. 33ff. To read Rumi and the other Sufi poets as speaking only in metaphor in this and many other instances, is to undermine the reverence they give to sacred sexuality.

220 Hixon, Lex (Nur al-Jerrahi). Atom From The Sun Of Knowledge Westport, Connecticut: Pir Publications, Inc., 1993.

221 Wilson, Peter Lamborn. Sacred Drift: Essays on the Margins of Islam San Franciso: City Light Books, 1993, p. 148.

222 Qur'an 50:16.

223 Juma prayers, *Khutba*, Tekke as-Safa, Nashville, Tennessee 9/23/94.

224 Stone, Robert. Damascus Gate Boston, Houghton Mifflin Company, 1998, p. 170

225 Glossary of Muslim Terms http://www.digiserve.com/mystic/Muslim/glossary.html

226 Hixon, Lex. The Core of All Kingdoms: An Exploration of Non-Duality with Lex Hixon, hosted by Suzanne Taylor, http://www.mightycompanions.com/page4.html

227 Madyan, Abā Uns al-Wahid wa Nuzhat al-Murid (The Intimacy of the Recluse and Pastime of the Seeker) found in: Madyan, Aba, The Way of Aba Madyan: Doctrinal and Poetic Works of Abā Madyan Shu'ayb Ibn al-Husayn al-Ansārī Ed. and Trans. Vincent J. Cornell, Cambridge, U.K., The Islamic Texts Society, 1996, p. 136.

228 'Arabi, Ibn al-. The Bezels of Wisdom Mahwah, New Jersey, Paulist Press, 1980, p. 137.

229 'Iraqi, Rakhruddin. Divine Flashes translation and introduction by William C. Chittick and Peter Lamborn Wilson, New York, Paulist Press, 1982, p. 107.

[230] Stone, Robert. Damascus Gate Boston, Houghton Mifflin Company, 1998, p. 117.

[231] Shaykh Nur al-Jerrahi, from sohbet 10/20/94.

[232] Buck, Dorothy C. Voicing the Inexpressible: The Virgin Heart of Christian/Islamic Dialogue "Sufi" Issue 39/Autumn1998, p. 10.

[233] A Shi'ite Encycolpedia http://www.al-islam.org/encyclopedia/

[234] " *And stay quietly in your houses, and make not a dazzling display, like that of the former Times of Ignorance; and establish regular Prayer, and give regular Charity; and obey God and His Apostle. And God only wishes to remove all abomination from you, ye members of the Family, and to make you pure and spotless.* " Yusufali.

[235] See the History of al-Tabari and the History of Ibn al-'Athir on the events of the year 36 A.H.

[236] Sunni references:

·   History Ibn al-'Athir, v3. p. 206.

·   Lisan al-Arab, v14, p. 141.

·   Iqdu'l-Farid, v4, p. 290.

    Sharh Ibn Abi'l-Hadid pp. 220-223.

[237] Sahih Musilm, English version, Chapter XXXIV, p. 46, Tradition #141; Sahih al-Tirmidhi, v5, p. 643; Qazwini, Ibn Maja. Sunan, v1, p. 142; Musnad Ahmad Ibn Hanbal v1, pp. 84,95,128; Tarikh al-Kabir, by al-Bukhari, v1, part 1, p. 202; Hilyat al-'awliya' wa tabaqat al-'asfiya, by Abu Nu'aym, v4, p. 185; Tarikh, by al-Khatib al-Baghdadi, v14, p. 462.

[238] Fadha'il al-Sahaba, by Ahmad Ibn Hanbal, v2, p.639, Tradition #1086; al-Isti'ab, by Ibn Abdul'l-Birr, v3, p. 47; al-Riyadh al-Nadhirah, by Muhibu'd-din Tabari, v3, p. 242; Dhakha'ir al-Uqba, by Muhibu'd-din Tabari, p. 91.

[239] Sahih al-Tirmidhi, v2, p. 298, v5, p. 63; Qazwini, Ibn Maja. Sunan, v1, pp. 12,43.

[240] See the History of al-Tabari and the History of Ibn al-'Athir on the events of the year 40 AH.

[241] Kabîr. The Kabir Book versions by Robert Bly, The Seventies Press/ Beacon Press, 1977.

[242] Qur'an 9:98.

[243] 'Arabi, Ibn al-. The Sufi Path of Knowledge: Ibn al-'Arabi's Metaphysics of Imagination; Trans. William C. Chittick, Albany, New York: SUNY Press, 1989, p. 213.

[244] Khan, Pir-o-Murshid Inayat. The Object and Moral of Worship of the Sufi.

[245] Qur'an 31:16.

[246] Nadja written and directed by Michael Almereyda, performers: Elina L'wensohn, Martin Donovan, Peter Fonda, Galaxy Craze, Evergreen Entertainment, 1994.

[247] Haeri, Shaykh Fadhlalla (collector). The Sayings and Wisdom of Imam Ali Trans. Yate, Asadullah ad-Dhaakir.

[248] Charon, Jean E. The Unknown Spirit London, Coventure, 1983.

[249] Wilson, Peter Lamborn. Sacred Drift: Essays on the Margins of Islam San Franciso: City Light Books, 1993, p. 140.

[250] Associated Press release dated December 11, 1997.

[251] Hidden Meanings http://www.hiddenmeanings.com

[252] 'Arabi, Ibn al-. The Sufi Path of Knowledge: Ibn al-'Arabi's Metaphysics of Imagination; Trans. William C. Chittick, Albany, New York: SUNY Press, 1989, p. 214.

[253] Wilson, Peter Lamborn. Divan London : Tehran, Crescent Moon Press, 1978.

[254] Muzaffer al-Jerrahi al-Halveti, Sheikh. Love is the Wine: Talks of a Sufi Master in America edited and compiled by Sheikh Ragip Frager, Vermont: Threshold Books, 1987, p. 36.

[255] Umm Salamah quotes on the authority of the Holy Prophet. According to S. H. Nasr this hadith has been transmitted through fifteen channels in Sunni sources and eleven in Shia sources. (Tabatab'I, Shi'ah, Tr. S. H. Nasr, Chapter I, Note 4; with slight difference in Mizan al-Hikmah, Hadiths 980, 981 & 982).

[256] Mufid, Sheikh al-. Kitab al Irshad (The Book of Guidance) Trans. I. K. A. Howard, Tahrike Tarsile Quran. I.S.B.N. 0-940368-11-0, pp. 1-6.

257 See al-Khwarazmi. Manaqib Khwarazmi, p. 199, Kulayni. Usul al-Kafi, Vol. 1, p. 64.

258 Yanabi' al-mawadda Vol. 1, p. 77.

259 Birge, John Kingsley. The Bektashi Order of Dervishes London, Luzac Oriental, 1994, p. 155.

260 Hanafi, Yanabi' al-mawadda Vol. 2, p. 36; Ibn Sa'd. Tabaqat Vol. 2, Part II, p. 101.

261 Jafri, S.H.M., The Origin and Early Developments of Shí'a Islam p. 22.

262   1. Salman Farsi
       2. Abu Dharr Ghifari
       3. Miqdad Bin Aswad Kindi
       4. Buraida Ammar Bin Yasir
       5. Khalid Bin Sa'id Bin As
       6. Buraida Aslami
       7. Ubai Bin Ka'b
       8. Khuzaima Bin Thabit
       9. Abu'l-Hathama Bin Tihan Dhu'sh-Shahadatain
       10. Sahl Bin Hunaif
       11. Uthman Bin Hunaif Aslami
       12. Abu Ayyub Ansari
       13. Jabir Ibn Abdullah Ansari
       14. Hudhaifa Bin Yaman
       15. Sa'd Bin Ubaida
       16. Qais Bin Sa'd
       17. Abdullah Bin Abbas
       18. Zaid Bin-Arqam

263 Imam Fakhru'd-Din Razi narrates from Ibn-e-Abbas to the authenticity of this curse. Furthermore, Ibn Hajar, after one tradition, relates from Umar Bin Murratu'l-Jihni; Halabi in Siratu'l-Halabiyya, vol. I, p. 337; Baladhuri in Ansab al-ashraf, vol. 5, p. 126; Sheikh Sulayman Balkhi in Yanabiu'l-Mawadda.; Hakim Nishapuri in Al-Mustadrak 'ala al-Sahihayn, vol. 4, p. 481; Damiri in Hayat-ul Haiwan, vol. II, p. 291; Ibn 'Asakir in his Ta'rikh; Imamu'l-Haram Muhyi'd-Din Tabari in Zakr a'iru'l-Uqba; and others too have narrated from Umar Bin Murra that Hakam Bin Abi'l-As sought permission of the Holy Prophet for an interview. The Holy Prophet recognizing his voice said, *"Let him come in. Curse be on him and on his descendants excepting those who are believers, and they will be few."*

264 Haidar, Asad. Al-Sadiq and the Four Madh'habs Vol. 1, p. 218.

265 This event is reported Ibn Maghazili Faqih Shafii by in his Manqib, Jalalu'd-Din Suyuti in Durr-e-Mansur, the renowned theologian Ahmad Tha'labi in Kashfu'l-Bayan, and others, including Asma Bint Umais (the wife of Abu Bakr).

266 Sunni reference: Tafsir al-Kabir, by al-Tha'labi under the commentary of verses 5:55-56 of Qur'an.

267 Momen, Moojan. An Introduction to Shi'i Islam: The History and Doctrines of Twelver Shi'ism New Haven, Conn. ; London : Yale University Press, 1987.

268 Qur'an 10:35.

269 Qur'an 39:9 Pickthall.

270 The author is indebted to Dr. Muhammad Tijani al-Samawi and his book The Shi'ah are (the real) Ahl al-Sunnah translated from the Arabic by Yasin T. al-Jibouri, New Jersey, Pyam-e-Aman, for the information contained in the following chapters concerning the destruction of hadith.

271 al-Samawi, Dr. Muhammad Tijani. Ask Those Who Know Trans. Yasin T. al-Jibouri pp. 200 ff .

272 Muslim. Sahih, Vol. 8, p. 229, Kitab al-Zuhd (Book of Asceticism) in a chapter dealing with

verification of hadith and the injunction regarding the recording of knowledge.

273 Bukhari, Sahih. Vol. 1, p. 36, Kitab al-'Ilm (Book of Knowledge).

274 Usul al-Kafi Vol. 1, p. 239, and also on p. 143 of Basair al-Darajat.

275 Al-Bukhari, Sahih Vol. 1, p. 36, [original Arabic text].

276 Al-Bukhari, Sahih Vol. 2, p. 221.

277 Al-Bukhari, Sahih,Vol. 4, p. 67, and Muslim, Sahih, Vol. 4, p. 115.

278 Al-Bukhari, Sahih Vol. 4, p. 69.

279 Al-Bukhari, Sahih Vol. 8, p. 144.

280 Al-Hakim, Mustadrak Vol. 1, p. 105. Also Abu Dawud, Sunan Vol. 2, p. 126. Also al-Darimi, Sunan, Vol. 1, p. 125, and Imam Ahmad Ibn Hanbal, Musnad Vol. 2, p. 162.

281 This statement was made by Umar Ibn al-Khattab during the Treaty of Hudaybiya, and it is recorded on p. 122, Vol. 2, of al-Bukhari's Sahih.

282 This statement was made by 'Aesha, daughter of Abu Bakr; see p. 29, Vol. 2, of al-Ghazali's book Ihya al-'Ulum.

283 This was the statement made to the Prophet by an Ansar companion as recorded on p. 47, Vol. 4, of al-Bukhari's Sahih.

284 Al-Bukhari, Sahih Vol. 6, p. 24, and also Vol. 6, p. 128, of the same reference.

285 See p. 237, Vol. 5, of Kanz al-'Ummal. Refer also to Ibn Kathir's book Al-Bidaya wal-Nihaya as well as p. 5, Vol. 1, of al-Dhahabi's Tadhkirat al-Huffaz.

286 Ibn Sa'ad. Al-Tabaqat al-Kubra Vol. 5, p. 188. It is also recorded in Taqyeed al-'Ilm by al-Khateeb al-Baghdadi.

287 Refer to Ibn Abd al-Birr's book Jamai' Bayan al-'Ilm.

288 Malik. Al-Muwatta' Vol. 1, p. 5.

289 'Allama al-'Askari. Ma'alim al-Madrasatayn Vol. 2, p. 302.

290.Al-Kulayni. Al-Kafi Vol. 1, p. 53.

291.Muslim. Sahih. Vol. 5, p. 122, also al-Tirmidhi, Sahih, Vol. 5, p. 637.

292 The original source for the material in the above three paragraphs is Richard Hooker and Washington State University "World Cultures Internet Classroom," http://www.wsu.edu: 8000/~dee/.

293 Kermāni, Fo'ād. The Drunken Universe: An Anthology of Persian Sufi Poetry translations and commentary by Peter Lamborn Wilson and Nasrollah Pourjavady, Grand Rapids, Phanes Press, 1987, pp. 111-112.

294 The traditionists of both sects (Sunni and Shia) have narrated it. Among the Sunni Ulema, who have reported it, include Imam Ahmad Bin Hanbal Manaqib, Musnad; Hafiz Abu Abdullah Muhammad Bin Abdullah Hakim Nishapuri Al-Mustadrak 'ala al-Sahihayn; Molvi Ali Muttaqi Kanzu'l-Ummal, part VI, p. 401; Hafiz Abu Nu'aym Isfahani Hilyatul Aulya, vol. I, p. 64; Muhammad Bin Sabban Misri Is-aafur Raghibeen; Abu'l-Hassan Faqih Shafi'i Ali Bin Muhammad Bin Tayyib al-Jalabi Ibn Maghazili Manaqib; Jalalu'd-Din Suyuti Al-Jami' al-saghir min hadith al-bashir al-nadhir, Kitab ham' 'al-hawami': Sharh Jam' 'al-jawami' fi 'ilm 'al-'Arabiyah and La-aali-ul Masnoo-ah; Abu Isa Tirmidhi Sahih, Vol. II, p. 214; Ahmad Muhammad bin Talha Shafi'i Matalibu's-Su'ul; Sheikh Sulayman Qanduzi Hanafi Yanbiu'l-Mawadda; Muhammad Bin Yusuf Ganji Shafi'i Kifayat-ut Talib; Yusuf Sibt Ibn Jauzi Tadhkiratu'l-Khasa'isu-Umma; Muhibu'd-Din Tabari Riyadh al-Nadhirah; Ibrahim bin Muhammad Hamwaini Fara'idu's Simtain; Nuru'-d-Din Bin Sabbagh Maliki [known as Ibn Sabbagh] Fusulu'l-Muhimma; and a host of others, confirm the authenticity of this tradition.

295Hixon, Lex. A Mighy Companions Interview with Lex Hixon, http://www.mightycompan-ions.com/page6.html

296.'Iraqi, Fakhruddin. Divine Flashes translation and introduction by William Chittick and Peter Lamborn Wilson, New York, Paulist Press, 1982, p. 108.

297 Many Sufis who follow the Sunni path are unaware that some of the great Sunni jurists and

distinguished Sunni Imams were among the pupils of Imam Ja'far Sadiq ('Alaihi Assalam). For instance, Abu Hanifa, Malik Bin Anas, Yahya Bin Sa'id Ansari, Ibn Jarih, Muhmmad Bin Ishaq, Yahya Bin Satiq Qattan, Sufyan bin 'Uyayna, Sufyan Thawri, and others received benefit from his knowledge according to their capacities. Imam Abu Hanifa (ra), (85 H. - 150 H) said, *"If it were not for two years, I would have perished."* He said, *"For two years I accompanied Sayyidina Ja'far as-Sadiq and I acquired the spiritual knowledge that made me a gnostic in the Way."* Imam Yafe'ey Yamani in his history, commending the merits of the Holy Imam, says that, in the vast expanse of knowledge Ja'far Sadiq ('Alaihi Assalam) had no equal and his versabil-ity had no bounds. One of his pupils Jabir Ibn Hayyan Sufi has written a thousand page book and compiled as many as five hundred booklets based on the teachings of the Holy Imam ('Alaihi Assalam). But it is a matter of great regret – that although his excellence in knowledge and per-fection in all merits, were recognized by all friends and enemies, certain Sunnis refused to treat him as the most learned theologian and perfect man of his age. They were not even prepared to include his name in the four Imams, and as he possessed the most exalted position in all learn-ing, ability, piety and devotion as admitted by the Sunni Ulema and belonged to the Progeny of the Holy Prophet (S.A.), he had a right to receive preference over others. If we consider this mat-ter from the point of view of his followers even then there is not the least doubt that the number of followers of any of the four Imams would not equal that of Imam Ja'far Sadiq ('Alaihi Assalam). In spite of such pre-eminent factors, the Sunnis have shown such callous disregard for this great man's wisdom that high ranking theologians like Bukhari and Muslim could not even tolerate to record traditions from this *Faqih* (Jurist) of the Ahlul Bayt in their books. Not only that, they did not quote any traditions from any of the Imams.

298 Qur'an 5:67, Pickthall.

299 Shirazee, Sultan-ul Waezeen Aqai Syed Mohannad. Peshawar Nights: Convincing Shi-Sunni Dialogue, Vol. I & II, Karachi, Peermahomed Ebrahim Trust, 1977. pp. 425-6.

300 Also Jalalu'd-Din Suyuti in his Tafsir-e-Durru'l-Manthur from Ibn-e-Mardaviyah, Ibn 'Asakir and Ibn-e-Abi Hatim from Abu Sa'id Khadri. Abdullah Ibn-e-Masod (one of the writers of Wahi (Revelations) and Qazi Shekani in Fathu'l-Ghadir narrate that in the day of the Holy Prophet they also recited that verse in that very way.

301 Imam Haskani and Imam Ahmad Ibn Hanbal have given full details of this event.

302 Nefes by Baba Günci, in Istanbul Konservatuvari Nesriyati, Bektasi Nefesleri, II, 200.

303 Reported by ibn Abi'l-Hadid Mutazali in his Sharh Nahj al-balaghah Vol. II, p. 449, Imam Ahmad Ibn Hanbal in Musnad, and numerous other Sunni authorities.

304 The source of the translation of "The Book of Ali's Identity" comes from: Birge, John Kingsley. The Bektashi Order of Dervishes London, Luzac Oriental, 1994, pp. 143-5.

305 According to a tradition from Ibn Abbas the Prophet said that Allah gave knowledge in six portions. One portion was given to the people of the world. Five portions were placed in Ali ('Alaihi Assalam).

306 The Prophet Muhammad himself bore this testimony: *"I and Ali are one Light."*

307 The Prophet Muhammad himself bore this testimony: *"Ali, the son of Abu Talip, is the one who will apportion the Fire and Paradise."*

308 The Prophet Muhammad himself bore this testimony: *"The heart of the believer is the House of God."*

309 The Prophet Muhammad himself bore this testimony: *"The Ark of Noah is a parable of the love of the People of My House."* As salvation came to the Prophet Noah (Peace be upon him) by the Ark, so it comes to humanity by Ali ('Alaihi Assalam).

310 The Prophet Muhammad himself bore this testimony: *"The hand of saintship or sovereignty, vilayet eli, is Ali's. He is appointed to watch over the clouds."*

311 The Prophet Muhammad himself bore this testimony: *"The voice of Ali in battle is like the sound of thunder."*

312 The Prophet Muhammad himself bore this testimony: *"Ali is the one who cause the fountains to pour forth and the rivers to flow."* Related by Abdullah ibni Abbas.

313 Ibni Abbas has quoted the Prophet's saying that in every heaven as he ascended on his midnight journey, *miraç*, he heard the name of Ali ('Alaihi Assalam) being praised. In answer to the question as to what language he talked with Allah on this journey the Prophet of Allah replied: *"My Lord addressed me in the language of Ibni Abu Talib."*

314 Around this tree are *houris* and young men bearing on their banners the words: *"There is no god but God; Muhammad is the Prophet of God and Ali is the Saint, Veli, of God."*

315 A tradition from the Prophet says that the Prophet Moses (Peace be upon him) received various kinds of learning from the light of Ali's ('Alaihi Assalam) saintship.

316 *"O apostle, proclaim all that hath been sent down to thee from thy Lord."* Qur'an 5:71.

317 *"I am the point under the letter be,"* said Imam Ali ('Alaihi Assalam).

318 Ali ('Alaihi Assalam) knows the seventy-two languages.

319 Muhammad is the City of knowledge and Ali is its Gateway.

320 The Prophet Muhammad himself bore this testimony: *"The Imams and the Evidence of God after me shall be twelve from the Quraish; the first of them shall be Ali and the last of them Mehdi."* Reported by Ibni Abbas.

321 The Prophet Muhammad himself bore this testimony: *"Ali the son of Abu Talib, he is the Imam and the Evidence after me, and my child Hüseyin is the evidence of God and his brother, and they are the fathers of the nine evidences, and the ninth of them endures permanently, Kaimdir."*

322 The Prophet Muhammad (Peace be upon him) called Ali ('Alaihi Assalam) the *"vocal Qur'an."*

323 'Arabi, Ibn al-. The Sufi Path of Knowledge; Ibn al-'Arabi's Metaphysics of Imagination; Trans. William C. Chittick, Albany, New York: SUNY Press, 1989, p. 23.

324 'Arabi, Ibn al-. The Bezels of Wisdom Mahwah, New Jersey, Paulist Press, 1980.

325 'Arabi, Ibn al-. The Sufi Path of Knowledge; Ibn al-'Arabi's Metaphysics of Imagination, Trans. William C. Chittick, Albany, New York: SUNY Press, 1989, p. 24.

326 Qur'an 40:60.

327 Qur'an 2:186.

328 'Arabi, Ibn al-. The Bezels of Wisdom Mahwah, New Jersey, Paulist Press, 1980.

329 Vaughan-Lee, Llewellyn. Forgetfulness "Sufi" Issue 37/Spring 1998, p. 41.

330 Ruzbihan Baqli, Shaikh. The Unveiling of Secrets: Diary of a Sufi Master (original title: Kashf al-asrar) Trans. Ernst, C. W., Chapel Hill, N.C., 1997, p. 37.

331 Meher Baba, Beams from Meher Baba on the Spiritual Panorama pp. 7-11 Copyright 1958 Sufism Reoriented, Inc.

332 Qur'an 9:118.

333 'Arabi, Ibn al-. The Bezels of Wisdom Mahwah, New Jersey, Paulist Press, 1980, p. 185.

334 Husain, Ali Ibn-el. A Part of Invocations from Saheefa-E-Kamelah (The Book of Perfection). Kuwait, Mohammad Qabazard Charity Fund.

335 'Arabi, Ibn al-. The Bezels of Wisdom Mahwah, New Jersey, Paulist Press, 1980, p. 76.

336 'Arabi, Ibn al-. The Bezels of Wisdom Mahwah, New Jersey, Paulist Press, 1980, p. 76.

337 Baba, Meher. Beams From Meher Baba - Sufism Reoriented 1958, pp. 27-28.

338 Ibrahim Bin Sa'd Saqafi, who is one of the trustworthy Ulema of the Sunnis, Ibn Abi'l-Hadid Mu'tazali and Ali Ibn Muhammad Hamdani report that, when Talha and Zubair broke off their allegiences and left for Basra, Ali ('Alaihi Assalam) preached the above sermon.

339 Sayyidul Ausiya, p. 65.

340 Shahryar.

341 al-Hujweri, Syed Ali Bin Uthman. The Kashful Mahjub "Unveiling the Veiled": The Earliest Persian Treatise on Sufism Malaysia, A.S. Noordeen, 1997, p. 82.

342 Kolayni, Muhammad ibn Ya'qub. Usul-e kâfi Edited and Trans. Jawad Mostafawi, Shiraz, 1980, I 276.

343 Nadja written and directed by Michael Almereyda, performers: Elina L'wensohn, Martin Donovan, Peter Fonda, Galaxy Craze, Evergreen Entertainment, 1994.

344 Qudāt, 'Ain Al-. Tamhîdât ed. Osseiran, 'Afif. Tehran: Chapkhana-yi danishgah, 1341 A.H. solar, pp. 228-229 #296.

345Also known as "Haris" while still in angelic state.

346 Hallai, Hosain ebn Mansur Tamhidât edited by 'Afif 'Osairân, Tehran, 1962, p. 211.

347 Attar, Farido'd-Din. Elâhi-nâma edited by Nurani Wesal, Tehran, 1977, p. 108.

348 Hallaj, Hosain ebn Mansur. Tamhidât edited by 'Afif 'Osairân, Tehran, 1962, pp. 221-9.

349 Qur'an 2:31.

350 Maibodi, Abo'l-Fadhl Rashido'd-Din. Kashf al-asrar wa'oddat al-abrar ma'ruf ba tafsir-e Khwaja 'Abdo'llah Ansari 10 Vols. edited by Ali Asghar Hekmat. Tehran, 1978, III p. 573.

351 Rumi, Jalalo'd-Din. Mathnawi-ye ma'nawi edited by R. A. Nicholson, Tehran, 1977, I p. 1488-93.

352 Khan, Pir-o-Murshid Inayat. The Object and Moral of Worship of the Sufi.

353 John, Bubba Free. Breath and Name: The Initiation and Foundation Practices of Free Spiritual Life San Francisco, California, The Dawn Horse Press, 1977, pp. 130 – 131.

354 Awn, Peter J. Satan's Tragedy and Redemption: Iblis in Sufi Psychology Netherlands, Leiden E. J. Brill, 1983, p. 137; and Qur'an 38:82.

355 Hallaj, Hosain ebn Mansur. Tamhidāt edited by 'Afif 'Osairan, Tehran, 1962, pp. 221-9.

356 Nurbakhsh, Dr. Javad The Great Satan 'Eblis' London, Khaniqahi-Nimatullahi Publications, 1986, p. 50.

357 Ozak al-Jerrahi, Sheikh Muzaffer. Adornment of Hearts: Zinatu-l-Qulub Trans. Muhtar Holland and Sixtina Friedrich, Westport, Connecticut, Pir Publications, Inc., 1991, p. 27.

358 Ozak al-Jerrahi, Sheikh Muzaffer. Adornment of Hearts: Zinatu-l-Qulub Trans. Muhtar Holland and Sixtina Friedrich, Westport, Connecticut, Pir Publications, Inc., 1991, p. 27.

359 Nasafi, 'Azizo'd-Din. Ketâb-e ensân-e kâmel edited by Marijan MolJ, Tehran and Paris, 1962, p. 301.

360 'Arabi, Ibn al-. The Sufi Path of Knowledge; Ibn al-'Arabi's Metaphysics of Imagination; Trans. William C. Chittick, Albany, New York: SUNY Press, 1989, p. 162-163.

361 Jelaluddin Rumi.

362 Hixon, Lex (Nur al-Jerrahi). Atom From The Sun Of Knowledge Westport, Connecticut: Pir Publications, Inc., 1993.

363 Rumi, Mevlâna Jalâluddîn. Non-Existence Trans. Camille and Kabir Helminski, http://www.sufism.org/books/jewels/rnonex.html

364 Rumi, Jelaluddin. Love is a Stranger: Selected lyric Poetry of Jelaluddin Rumi Vermont, Threshold Books, 1993, p.37.

365 Rumi, Jelaluddin. Love is a Stranger: Selected lyric Poetry of Jelaluddin Rumi Vermont, Threshold Books, 1993, pp. 42-43.

366 Qur'an II:115.

367 Muhaiyaddeen, His Holiness M. R. Bawa. A Book of God's Love Philadelphia, Pennsylvania, Bawa Muhaiyaddeen Fellowship, 1981.

368 As-Sunna Foundation of America http://www.sunnah.org/ibadaat/dhikr.htm

369 Suhrawardi, 'Umar Ibn Muhammad. A Dervish textbook from the 'Awarifu-l-ma'arif London, Octagon Press, 1980.

370 Haeri, Shaykh Fadhlalla (collector). The Sayings and Wisdom of Imam Ali Trans. Yate, Asadullah ad-Dhaakir.

371 Provine, Robert R. "Laughter." American Scientist Jan. Feb. 1996 http://www.amsci.org/amsci/Articles/96articles/Provine-R.html

[372] Attributed to Ahmad Sohrab in the style of 'Abdu'l-Bahá.

[373] Rumi, Jelaluddin. Love is a Stranger: Selected lyric Poetry of Jelaluddin Rumi Vermont, Threshold Books, 1993, p. 53.

[374] Hamadani, Ayn al-Qozat. A Sufi Martyr Trans. A. J. Arberry, London, Allen and Unwin, 1969.

[375] 'Arabi, Ibn al-. The Bezels of Wisdom Mahwah, New Jersey, Paulist Press, 1980, p. 88.

[376] John, Bubba Free. Breath and Name: The Initiation and Foundation Practices of Free Spiritual Life San Francisco, California, The Dawn Horse Press, 1977, p. 58, 3.3.

[377] Al-Sarraj, Abu Nasr. Kitab al-Luma' Ed. Nicholson, London, Gibb Series, 1914.

[378] Rumi, Jelaluddin. The Mathnawi of Jalaluddin Rumi Trans. R. A. Nicholson, London, Luzac and Co., 1982.

[379] 'Arabi, Ibn al-. The Bezels of Wisdom Mahwah, New Jersey, Paulist Press, 1980, p. 88.

[380] Moris, Zailan. Rumi's View of Evil in "Sufi" issue # 36, London, England. J345

[381] Rumi, Jelaluddin. The Mathnawi of Jalaluddin Rumi Trans. R. A. Nicholson, London, Luzac and Co., 1982.

[382] John, Bubba Free. Breath and Name: The Initiation and Foundation Practices of Free Spiritual Life San Francisco, California, The Dawn Horse Press, 1977, p. 52, 2.14.

[383] Baldick, Julian. Imaginary Muslims: The Uwaysi Sufis of Central Asia New York, New York University Press, Washington Square, 1993, pp. 28-29.

[384] Qur'an 2:115.

[385] 'Arabi, Ibn al-. The Bezels of Wisdom Mahwah, New Jersey, Paulist Press, 1980.

[386] Nadja written and directed by Michael Almereyda, performers: Elina L'wensohn, Martin Donovan, Peter Fonda, Galaxy Craze, Evergreen Entertainment, 1994.

[387] Wilson, Peter Lamborn. Sacred Drift: Essays on the Margins of Islam San Francisco, City Light Books, 1993.

[388] Bliss directed by Lance Young, performers: Craig Sheffer, Sheryl Lee, Terence Stamp, Casey Siemaszko, Spalding Gray, Triumph Films, 1997.

[389] Wilson, Peter Lamborn. Sacred Drift: Essays on the Margins of Islam. San Franciso: City Light Books, 1993.

[390] Addas, Claude. Ibn 'Arabi, ou La qête du Soufre Rouge Paris, Gallimard, 1989.

[391] On the Origin of the World Translated Bethge, Hans-Gebhard and Bentley Layton, http://www.gnosis.org/naghamm/origin.html

[392] Hoeller, Stephan A. The Genesis Factor published in Quest, September 1997.

[393] Bouhdiba, Abdelwahab. Sexuality in Islam London, Routledge & Kegan Paul plc, 1985, p. 121.

[394] Bouhdiba, Abdelwahab. Sexuality in Islam London, Routledge & Kegan Paul plc, 1985, p. 135.

[395] Ibn Hazm, Ali b. Ahmad. Tawq al-hamama fi 'l-ulfa wa-l-ullaf Trans. Bercher, LJon, Algiers, Editions Carbonel, 1949, p. 92.

[396] Biblical Archaeological Review S/O 97.

[397] Moses Cordovero, Or ha-Hammab.

[398] Izutsu, Toshihiko. The Key Philosophical Concepts in Sufism and Taoism – Ibn Arabī and Lao-Tzu, Ghuang-Tzu, Tokyo 1966.

[399] Habiba. Where the Eagles Fly: Portraits of Women of Power, Habiba: A Sufi Saint from Uzbekistan video, New York, Mystic Fire Video, 1997.

[400] Bakhtiar, Laleh. Intro. to Fatima is Fatima by Dr. Ali Shariati.

[401] Bakhtiar, Laleh. Sufi: Expressions of the Mystic Quest New York, Avon Books, 1976, p. 23.

[402] One of several honorable titles the Holy Prophet gave Fatima.

[403] Bakhtiar, Laleh. Sufi: Expressions of the Mystic Quest New York, Avon Books, 1976.

[404] Corbin, Henry. Creative Imagination in the Sufism of Ibn 'Arabi Trans. Manheim, Ralph,

Princeton and London, 1969.

[405] Allah Most High transcends both masculine and feminine, and in Its most sublime gnosis cannot be considered as male or female. However, much more examination must be given to this most revealing and mystical divulgence: *Bismillah ir Rahman ir Rahim*. Are Rahman and Rahim proper names of the Ultimate Reality which are sacred and holy in themselves, and therefore should not be translated into common adjectives which have no venerable associations, or even understood as common nouns? Yes, they are proper names which are sacred and holy, but "womb" is no common adjective and this word is filled with mystic meaning, and has a deep significance that is recently been re-taught to us by the women's spirituality movement. Another point which should be mentioned is that *Rahman* and *Rahim* were names of God used by the Nestorian Christians and the Jewish people respectively. In this light, *Bismillah ir Rahman ir Rahim*, affirms the singular remembrance of the Supreme Being by other monotheistic religions.

[406] Shehadi, Fadlou. Ghazali's Unique Unknowable God: A Philosophical Critical Analysis of Some of the Problems Raised by Ghazali's View of God as Utterly Unique and Unknowable Netherlands, E. J. Brill, 1964. p. 115.

[407] Ghazali. Mishkât ul-Anwâr Royal Asiatic Society, p. 96.

[408] Macdonald, D. B. Hartford Seminary Record vol. Xx, No 1, p. 36.

[409] Inverness, California: The Golden Sufi Center 'Arabi, Ibn al-. The Sufi Path of Knowledge; Ibn al-'Arabi's Metaphysics of Imagination; Trans. William C. Chittick, Albany, New York: SUNY Press r, 1997.

[410] Edmondson, Philip. The Universal Spirit of Sufism (review of Sara Sviri's The Taste of Hidden Things: Images on the Sufi Path) in "Sufi" issue no. 35/autumn 1997.

[411] Rumi, Jelaluddin. The Mathnawi of Jalaluddin Rumi Trans. R. A. Nicholson, London, Luzac and Co., 1982.

[412] 'Arabi, Ibn al-. The Bezels of Wisdom Mahwah, New Jersey, Paulist Press, 1980, p. 208.

[413] Ouspensky, P. D. The Fourth Way New York, Vintage Books, 1971, p. 58.

[414] Qur'an Chapter Luqman 31:18.

[415] 3rd Quality To The 5th Door Of Heaven in "Friday Supplement" http://www.world-federation.org/europe/cujfri27.htm

[416] 'Arabi, Ibn al-. The Bezels of Wisdom Mahwah, New Jersey, Paulist Press, 1980, p. 189.

[417] Abu Mikhnaf Lut b. Yahya al-Azdi reported: *"Ashath b. Suwar told me on the authority of Abu Ishaq al-Sabi'I and others, who said: [the above quote]"*.

[418] The Drunken Universe: An Anthology of Persian Sufi Poetry translations and commentary by Peter Lamborn Wilson and Nasrollah Pourjavady, Grand Rapids, Phanes Press, 1987, pp. 112-113.

[419] Mufid, Sheikh al-. Kitab al Irshad (The Book of Guidance) Trans. I.K.A. Howard, Tahrike Tarsile Quran, pp. 279-289.

[420] This is reported by a group of authorities including Ahmad b. Salih. Al-Tamimi on the authority of Abd Allah B. Isa, on the authority of Ja'far al-Sadiq b. Muhammad.

[421] This is reported by a group of authorities including Ma'mar, on the authority of al-Zuhri, on the authority of Anas b. Malik.

[422] Ibrahim b. Ali al-Rafi'i reported on the authority of his father, on the authority of his grandmother Zainab, daugther of Abu Rafi'- and Shabib b. Abi Rafi' al-Rafi'i on the authority of those who told him: [the above quote].

[423] Abu Mikhnaf Lut b. Yahya al-Azdi reported: *"Ashath b. Suwar told me on the authority of Abu Ishaq al-Sabi'i and others, who said: [the above quote]."*

[424] Isa b. Mihran reported: Ubayd Allah b. al-Sabb'ah told us: *"Jarir told us on the authority of Mughira, who said: [the above quote]."*

[425] Abd Allah b. Ibrahim reported on the authority of Ziyad al-Makhariqi, who said: [the above quote].

426 Muhaiyaddeen, M. R. Bawa. The Golden Words of M. R. Bawa Muhaiyaddeen Philadelphia, Pennsylvania, The Bawa Muhaiyaddeen Fellowship, 1991.

427 Hirmendi, Sister Mahwash. Asthma-ul Husna mhirmend@opal.tufts.edu

428 Ali, Hazrat. Nahjul Balagha Tehran, Iran, Golshan Printing House.

429 Rumi, Jelaluddin. Love is a Stranger: Selected lyric Poetry of Jelaluddin Rumi Vermont, Threshold Books, 1993, p. 56.

430 'Arabi, Ibn al-. Muhyiddin. Fusūs al-Hikam Bayrut, Lubnan, Dar al-Kittab al-Arabi, 1980.

431 Translated by Daniel Ladinsky.

432 al-Hujweri, Syed Ali Bin Uthman. The Kashful Mahjub "Unveiling the Veiled": The Earliest Persian Treatise on Sufism Malaysia, A.S. Noordeen, 1997, p. 88.

433 Sources:
Sharif, Adel; and Imam Hussein on the Day of Ashura Al-Huda Foundation, 1992; and Richard Hooker and Washington State University "World Cultures Internet Classroom," http://www.wsu.edu:8000/~dee/

434 Qazwini, Ibn Maja. Sunan, Hadith 144.

435 Ibn Jarir Tarikhu'l Umam wa'l Muluk, vol.13, p. 2174.

436 Begg, Janab W. D. and Sahizada S. M. Yunus Maharaj. Spiritual Victory of Imama Husain: The Greatest Myrtyr (sic) of the World Ajmer, India, Extraordinary Publications, p. 3.

437 Ta'us, Sayyid ibn. Maqtalu'l Husain, pp.10-11.

438 Khuwarazmi, Al-Khatid al-. Maqtalu'l Husain ,vol.1, p. 88.

439 Ibn Sa'd tells us in his Tabaqat Vol. 6, Chapter 2, p. 35.

440 Begg, Janab W. D. and Sahizada S. M. Yunus Maharaj. Spiritual Victory of Imama Husain: The Greatest Myrtyr (sic) of the World Ajmer, India, Extraordinary Publications, p. 3.

441 Ghalib, Mirza. Diwan-i Ghalib Urdu, ed. Imtiaz Arshi (Aligarh: Anjuman Taraqi-e-Urdu Hind, 1958), pp.285-286.

442 Merchant, Noorali S. Sorrows & Sufferings: A Collection of Poems on the martyrdom of the grandson of Prophet Muhammad, Husayn b. Ali, peace be upon them
http://www.al-islam.org/short/sorrows/

443 Bouhdiba, Abdelwahab. Sexuality in Islam London, Routledge & Kegan Paul plc, 1985, p. 124.

444. Provine, Robert R. "Laughter." American Scientist Jan. Feb. 1996
http://www.amsci.org/amsci/Articles/96articles/Provine-R.html

445. Provine, Robert R. "Laughter." American Scientist Jan. Feb. 1996
http://www.amsci.org/amsci/Articles/96articles/Provine-R.html

446. Muhaiyaddeen, His Holiness M. R. Bawa. A Book of God's Love Philadelphia, Pennsylvania, Bawa Muhaiyaddeen Fellowship, 1981.

447 Helminski, Kabir Edmund. A talk delivered at the conference: Sufism and The Attractiveness of Islam, Casablanca, Morocco, April 1997.

448 Khan, Pir Vilayet. Toward the One New York & Canada, Harper & Row, Publishers, Inc. 1974, p.232.

449 Glossary of Muslim Terms http://www.digiserve.com/mystic/Muslim/glossary.html

450 'Arabi, Ibn al-. The Bezels of Wisdom Mahwah, New Jersey, Paulist Press, 1980 p.99.

451. Professor Evgueny Torchinov, University of St.Petersburg, Russia.

452 John, Bubba Free. Breath and Name: The Initiation and Foundation Practices of Free Spiritual Life San Francisco, California, The Dawn Horse Press, 1977, p. 58, 3.3.

453 'Arabi, Ibn al-. "Whoso Knoweth Himself . . ." from the Treatise on Being Abingdon, Oxon, Great Britain, Beshara Publications, 1976.

454 What Is to Be Realized? from Scientific Proof of the Existence of God Will Soon Be Announced by the White House! http://www.adidam.org/wisdom/Nov97/whatis.htm

455 Madhavananda, Sri Deep. International Sri Deep Madhavananda Ashram Fellowship, 1040

Vienna,Schikanedergasse,12/13,Austria/Europe.Publisher: Paramhans Swami Maheshwarananda.
[456]Tukaram (a Perfect Master of Maharastra) in J. Nelson Fraser and K. B. Marate- The Poems of Tukaram Delhi: Motilal Banarsidass, 1909, 1991 reprint, p. 260.
[457] Chumbley, Andrew (Alogos Dhu'l-qarnen). Qutub: also called The Point Chelmsford, Essex, U.K., Xoanon.
[458] Ouspensky, P.D. The Fourth Way New York, Vintage Books, 1971, p. 211.
[459] The Drunken Universe: An Anthology of Persian Sufi Poetry translations and commentary by Peter Lamborn Wilson and Nasrollah Pourjavady, Grand Rapids, Phanes Press, 1987, p. 85.
[460] There Is Simply The "Bright" Itself from chapter forty-four of The Dawn Horse Testament Of Adi Da
http://www.adidam.org/wisdom/Nov97/simply.htm
[461] Chumbley, Andrew (Alogos Dhu'l-qarnen). Qutub: also called The Point Chelmsford, Essex, U.K., Xoanon, p. 64.
[462] The Drunken Universe: An Anthology of Persian Sufi Poetry translations and commentary by Peter Lamborn Wilson and Nasrollah Pourjavady, Grand Rapids, Phanes Press, 1987, pp. 97-98.
[463] 'Arabi, Ibn al-. The Bezels of Wisdom Mahwah, New Jersey, Paulist Press, 1980 p. 150.
[464] Bakhtiar, Laleh. Sufi: Expressions of the Mystic Quest New York, Avon Books, 1976, p.47.
[465] Strothmann, Rudolf. Gnosis-Texte Ismailiten (G'ttingen, 1943).
[466] Al-Abidin, Imam Zain. Al-Sahifah Al-Sajjadilyyah Trans. Sayyid Ahmad Muhani, ed. Bakhtiar, Laleh and Dr. Ziya' Sa'adi, Tehran, Islamic Propogation Organization, 1984-1405, p. 461.
[467] Strothmann, Rudolf. Gnosis-Texte Ismailiten (Göttingen, 1943).
[468] Van Wing Bakongo (Brussels 1921; pp. 170 ff.) Trans. Edwin W. Smith in Smith (ed.), African Ideas of God: A Symposium (2nd ed: London, 1950) p.159.
[469] Rabbani, Hadhrat Maulana Wahid Bakhsh, in his commentary in: al-Hujweri, Syed Ali Bin Uthman. The Kashful Mahjub "Unveiling the Veiled": The Earliest Persian Treatise on Sufism Malaysia, A.S. Noordeen, 1997, p. 22.
[470] al-Hujweri, Syed Ali Bin Uthman. The Kashful Mahjub "Unveiling the Veiled": The Earliest Persian Treatise on Sufism Malaysia, A.S. Noordeen, 1997, p. 22.
[471] Shehadi, Fadlou. Ghazali's Unique Unknowable God: A Philosophical Critical Analysis of some of the Problms raised by Ghazali's View of God as Utterly Unique and Unknowable Netherlands, E. J. Brill, 1964, p. 23.
[472] John, Bubba Free. Breath and Name: The Initiation and Foundation Practices of Free Spiritual Life San Francisco, California, The Dawn Horse Press, 1977, p. 22.
[473] Chittick, William. Trans.
[474] Khan, Pir Vilayet Toward the One New York & Canada, Harper & Row, Publishers, Inc. 1974, p. 457 & 459.
[475] El-Kady, Sheikh Abd El-Fatah. Al Mushaf Al-Shareef (The Koran - Its History and Tests) pp. 14 and 55.
[476] Sahih-al-Bukhari, Vol. 6, p. 510.
[477] Al-Mush Al-Shareef, page 59,60
[478] Sahih-al-Bukhari Part 6, page 477.
[479] Bukhari, 6.201.
[480] Al-Mushaf Al-Shareef Pages 66,70.
[481] Jeffery, Arthur. The Qur'án Readings of Zaid b. 'Alí Rivista degli Studi Orientali, 16, 1936, p. 249.
[482] Hussein, Dr. Taha. Al- Fitnato Al-Korba (The Great Sedition) pages 160,161,181,182.
[483] Usul al-Kafi, Tradition 607.
[484] von Denffer, Ahmad. 'Ulum al-Qur'an Leicester, Islamic Foundation, 1983.

[485] Lester, Toby. "What is the Koran?" The Atlantic Monthly January 1998; pp. 43-56.

[486] Aiwass. Liber Al Vel Legis (The Book of the Law) sub figura XXXI, Archive, 1970.

[487] Related by Hussein Ibn Alala.

[488] Usul Kafi, Tradition # 636.

[489] V. 10 of Al-Bihar.

[490] Podvodny, Abessalom. Return of Occultism: The Novel About the Subtle Seven Trans. Iri Decent, Ed. Laurence Galian.

[491] 'Arabi, Ibn al-. The Sufi Path of Knowledge; Ibn al-'Arabi's Metaphysics of Imagination; Trans. William C. Chittick, Albany, New York: SUNY Press, 1989, p 83.

[492] Mann, Nicholas R. The Dark God: A Personal Journey through the Underworld St. Paul, MN, Llewellyn Publications, 1996.

[493] Becker, Robin.

[494] 'Arabi, Ibn al-. The Bezels of Wisdom Mahwah, New Jersey, Paulist Press, 1980 p. 175.

[495] Daraul, Arkon. A History of Secret Societies New York, Citadel Press, 1962.

[496] Nahid, Babak. (review) Daftary, Farhad. The Assassin Legends: Myths of the Ismai'ilis London, I. B. Tauris and Co., 1994.

[497] British Museum Quarterly Volume 4, September 1937.

[498] *"Excavations in central Yemen suggest that the Sabaean civilization began as early as the 10th-12th century BC. By the 7th-5th century BC, besides "kings of Saba' there were individuals styling themselves 'mukarribs of Saba', who apparently either were high priest-princes or exercised some function parallel to the kingly function."* - Encyclopaedia Britannica Online

[499] Jinn and the City of the Pillars, http://home.fireplug.net/~rshand/streams/scripts/jinn.html

[500] See "Dweller on the Threshold Chapter".

[501] Birge, John Kingsley. The Bektashi Order of Dervishes London, Luzac Oriental, 1994, p. 258.

[502] Corbin, Henry. The Man of Light in Iranian Sufism Trans. Nancy Pearson, New Lebanon, Omega Publications, Inc., 1994.

[503] Hamblin, William. Cthulhu Casebook 1990.

[504] The connection of the "Abandoner" with the Dragon is strengthened somewhat by a line from The Book of Annihilation an Arabic text on magic.

[505] Alhazred, Abdul. The Necronomicon New York?, Schlangekraft, 1977, Acknowledgements signed: L. K. Barnes. [Author's comment: written by Simon (Peter Levenda) and possibly James Wasserman.]

[506] For those who want to research how Irem fits into Arab magick and Mysticism should locate the following books: The Muqarribun: Arab Magic and Myth by Steve Lock and Jamal Khaldun, it discusses the "hidden" meaning of Irem etc., and is a good source on Arab magick; Tales of the Prophets of al-Kisai by Muhammad Ibn abd Allah Kisai 11th century is good for its data on pre-Islamic prophets; Making of the Last Prophet by Mohammad Ibn Ishaq [Newby, Gordon Darnell.] The Making of the Last Prophet: A Reconstruction of the Earliest Biography of Muhammad has some interesting material on Pre-Islamic prophets. Hajar Bin Humeid by Gus Willa VanBeek is a good source on Pre-Islamic culture in general.

[507] Wolf, Martin L. ed. A Treasury of Kahlil Gibran New York, The Citadel Press, 1963 pp. 124-151.

[508] Kuhn, T. S. International Encycolpedia of Unified Science "The Structure of Scientific Revolutions" Chicago, University of Chicago Press, 1970.

[509] Habiba. Where the Eagles Fly: Portraits of Women of Power, Habiba: A Sufi Saint from Uzbekistan video, New York, Mystic Fire Video, 1997.

[510] Bukhārî 81:38.

[511] 'Arabi, Ibn al-. The Bezels of Wisdom Mahwah, New Jersey, Paulist Press, 1980 p. 210.

[512] Ouspensky, P. D. The Fourth Way New York, Vintage Books, 1971, p. 81.

513 This combination is fascinatingly similar to Sigmund Freud's concept of the Id, Ego and SuperEgo. In this case we may draw the following comparisons:
- Id: the dark physical creation;
- Ego: the mediating spark of divinity - consciousness - in the human being;
- SuperEgo: Allah's Nur.

Furthermore, according to Freud, the Ego is ruled by the reality principle, and it should be remembered that the task of the Sufi is to know reality! The point of many Sufi tales is that the "buried treasure" is in your own backyard, or plain as the nose on your face. It is quite clear that the most obvious thing in life is Reality. The world is as plain as the nose on your face. Reality is the Sacred Expression of the Divine Unfoldment in the Moment. Therefore, Reality is the how and where you find the Divine.

514 See 'Abyss' in glossary.

515 Sahl.

516 The Real *Baitullah*, house of Allah, is the Heart of the Complete Human Being. The Real *Kible*, the direction of prayer, is the face of the human being.

517 Rodinson, Maxine. Muhammad Trans. from the French by Anne Carter, New York: Pantheon Books, 1980.

518 'Arabi, Ibn al-. The Bezels of Wisdom Mahwah, New Jersey, Paulist Press, 1980 p. 214.

519 Ruzbihan Baqli, Shaikh. The Unveiling of Secrets: Diary of a Sufi Master (original title: Kashf al-asrar) Trans. Ernst, C. W., Chapel Hill, N.C., 1997, p. 42.

520 'Abd Allah ibn Umar said that the Prophet used to say the above. Bayhaqi narrated it in Kitab al-da'awat al-kabir as well as in his Shu'ab al-masawi, at the end of the book of Supplications.

521 'Arabi, Ibn al-. The Bezels of Wisdom Mahwah, New Jersey, Paulist Press, 1980, p. 184.

522 Muzaffer al-Jerrahi al-Halveti, Sheikh. Love is the Wine: Talks of a Sufi Master in America edited and compliled by Sheikh Ragip Frager, Vermont: Threshold Books, 1987, p. 28.

523 Shabistari, Mahmud Ibn 'Abd al-Karim, The Secret Garden Bianco, Tex., Zahra, 1982.

524 Stated in two Sahih: Bukhari and Muslim.

525 Bukhārî Vol. 9 No. 507.

526 Qur'an 7:156.

527 'Arabi, Ibn al-. Journey to the Lord of Power: A Sufi Manual on Retreat Trans. Rabia Terri Harris, Vermont, Inner Traditions International, 1989, p. 86-87,

528 'Arabi, Ibn al-. The Bezels of Wisdom Mahwah, New Jersey, Paulist Press, 1980, p. 209.

529 Qur'an 39:47.

530 Bukhari and Muslim in the Sahih, Allama Samhudi in Ta'rikhu'l-Medina, Abu'l-Faraj Bin Jawzi in Kitabu'r-Radd Ala'l-Muta'asibu'l-Anid, Yusuf Sibt Ibn Jauzi in Tadhkiratu'l-Khasa'isu'l-Umma, Imam Ahmad Ibn Hanbal in Musnad and others quote the Holy Prophet as saying the above hadith.

531 Baba, Meher. Beams From Meher Baba Sufism Reoriented, Inc., 1958, pp. 55-58.

532 Spiegelman, J. Marvin Ph.D. Sufism, Islam and Jungian Psychology Scottsdale, Arizona, New Falcon Publications, 1991.

533 Hixon, Lex (Nur al-Jerrahi). Atom From The Sun Of Knowledge Westport, Connecticut: Pir Publications, Inc., 1993.

534 We thank A Buddhist Bible for this tale.

535 Glossary of Muslim Terms http://www.digiserve.com/mystic/Muslim/glossary.html

536 Literally, the "substitutes". One of the categories of the hierarchy of saints.

537 Nurbaskhsh, Dr. Javad. Sufi Women New York, Khaniqahi-Nimatullahi Publications, 1983, p. 22.

538 She discoursed to the devotees. Her fear of God reached such extremes that she was power-less to worship. Then she saw a dream by which the burden was removed from her, and she resumed her religious practices.

[539] *"She belonged to our master the Prince of the Faithful. She lived in the neighborhood of Macca (al-Mukarramah) and died there. She was unique in her time and had attained the power to cover great distances quickly. When she was away on her wanderings she would commune with the mountains, rocks and trees, saying to them, 'Welcome, welcome!' Her spiritual state was strong and she served the Fold and followed the Way with unswerving sincerity. She had the virtues of chivalry and was most strenuous in self-discipline, frequently practicing day-and-night fasting. Despite this she was strong and her exertions seemed to suit her well. I have never seen one more chivalrous than her in our time. Dedicated to the exaltation of God's majesty, she attached no worth to herself."* - Ibn al-'Arabi. Sufis of Andalusia: The Ruh al-quds and al-Durrat al-fakhirah of Ibn 'Arabi Trans. R. W. Austin, London, George Allen and Unwin, 1971, p. 154.

[540] She wept unitl she went blind.

[541] Grandmother of Abu 'l-Klhailr al-Tinati al-Aqta'. She had five hundred pupils, men and women.

[542] She died in the presence of Summun while he was discoursing on love. Three men died with her.

[543] 'Attār. Tadhkerat al-awliā.

[544] Jāmi. Nafahāt al-ons.

[545] Madame Guashan spent her entire life studying and finding the roots of the philosophical ideas and the wisdom of Avicenna, Ibn Rushd, Mulla Sadra, and Haji Mulla Hadi Sabzevari and compared them to the works of Aristotle. She corrected that which had been badly translated and incorrectly understood for the 1000 years of Islamic civilization.

[546] Mme. De la Vida edited and completed the Science of the Soul of Avicenna from the ancient Greek manuscript of Aristotle on the soul.

[547] Resass Du La Chappelle, a Swedish woman, about whom Ali Shariati writes: *"She knew more about the sanctity of Ali than all the Islamic scientists and even all the Shi'ites who claim today to be aware of Ali and the Alavis."*

[548] Frau Hunekeh has written a very comprehensive study of Islam and its influence upon European civilization which has been translated into Arabic and is entitled The Arab's Sun Spreads over the West.

[549] Habiba is a living Sufi Saint from Uzbekistan. She is a *Tabib*, a Muslim healer, who belongs to the earliest Sufi "Chain of Mystic Transmission," a lineage of teachers whose main representative is the great master Bahaudin Nacksband.

[550] Qur'an 86: 13-14.

[551] Qur'an chapter Luqman 31:18.

[552] Friday Supplement, Friday Supplement Issue #27 | 20 Muharram 1417 | June 1996, published by Coucil of European Jamaats in conjunction with Tabligh Sub-Committee, Car-Es Salaam.

[553] al-Majlisi, Allama. Bihar al-'Anwar p. 101, Vol. 49.

[554] Hixon, Lex. The Core of All Kingdoms: An Exploration of Non-Duality with Lex Hixon, hosted by Suzanne Taylor, http://www.mightycompanions.com/page4.html

[555] Jalal al-Din Rumi, Maulana. The Sufi Path of Love Trans. William C. Chittick, Albany, State University of New York Press, p. 223.

[556] Hixon, Lex. The Core of All Kingdoms: An Exploration of Non-Duality with Lex Hixon, hosted by Suzanne Taylor, http://www.mightycompanions.com/page4.html

[557] Arberry, A. J. Trans. A Sufi Martyr: The Apologia of 'Ain al-Qudat al-Hamadhani London, George Allen and Unwin Ltd., 1969, p. 30.

[558] Clark, R.T. Bundle. Myth and Symbol in Ancient Egypt Trans. R.T. Bundle Clark, London, 1959. p. 80.

[559] Geologists: Schoch, Dr. Robert. Professor Geology at Boston University, "Conde Nast Traveller," February 1993, p. 176. and West, John Anthony. Serpent in the Sky, pp. 184-242.

[560] Corbin, Henry. Creative Imagination in the Sūfism of Ibn 'Arabi New Jersey, Princeton

University Press, 1969, p.33.

561 'Arabi, Ibn al-. Journey to the Lord of Power: A Sufi Manual on Retreat Trans. Rabia Terri Harris, Vermont, Inner Traditions International, 1989, p. 29.

562 Godlas, Dr. Alan. Sufism's Many Paths University of Georgia http://www.arches.uga.edu/~godlas/Sufism.html

563 Glossary of Muslim Terms http://digiserve.com/mystic/Muslim/glossary.html

564 John, Bubba Free. Breath and Name: The Initiation and Foundation Practices of Free Spiritual Life San Francisco, California, The Dawn Horse Press, 1977, p. 40.

565 Hamadani, Ayn al-Qozat. A Sufi Martyr Trans. A. J. Arberry, London, Allen and Unwin, 1969.

566 Qur'an: 4:34, 12:52, etc.

567 Qur'an 6:59.

568 See Usul al-Kafi, Kitab al-Hujjah, Tradition #664

569 See Usul al-Kafi, Kitab al-Hujjah, Tradition #664.

570 Qur'an 13:39.

571 Qur'an 81:24.

572 Qur'an 6:75.

573 No evidence has been found so far of the Queen of Saba ; nor is any reference made to her in Sabaic inscriptions. It is, however , worth mentioning that it was by no means unusual for a woman to sit on the throne in ancient Arabia. Inscriptions of Assyrian rulers in the 18th century B.C.E. contain many references to "Queens of the Arabs" who brought tribute or were defeated in battle. Think of the Yemen and you will think of Bilqis, the Queen of Saba, — but less well known in Europe is the fact that Yemen had a Queen who really did exist – Queen Arwa, who reigned for over half a century (from 1074 or 1086 C.E.) her contemporaries called her "Bilqis the Younger". She is mentioned here not as a curiosity but because she is remembered for her long and, for the most part, peaceful reign, for the many monuments she built, and for the political stability she gave to the country.- From the Queen of Saba to a Modern State: 3,000 years of civilization in southern Arabia http://www.gpc.org.ye/Ancient0.htm [The author would like to point out that archaeologists have discovered ruins called: "The Marib,"a temple of the god II muqah (also called "throne of Bilqis, Queen of Saba").]

574 Usul al-Kafi, Kitab al-Hujjah, Tradition #613.

575 Sunni reference: Musnad Ahmad Ibn Hanbal, v. 3, p. 136; v. 5, p. 26.

576 Sunni reference: Kanz al-Ummal, by al-Muttaqi al-Hindi, v. 6, p. 398.

577 Sunni Reference: al-Awsat, by al-Tabarani

578 Sunni references: Hilyat al-'awliya' wa tabaqat al-'asfiya, by Abu Nu'aym, v. 1, p. 65.

579 Sunni references:
   Kanz al-Ummal, by al-Muttaqi al-Hindi, v. 1, p. 392
   Hilyat al-'awliya' wa tabaqat al-'asfiya, by al-Hafidh Abu Nu'aym
   Nuskhatah, by Abu Ahmad al-Faradi)

580 Sunni References:
   Fadha'il al-Sahaba Ahmad Ibn Hanbal, v. 2, p. 647, Tradition #1098
   al-Isabah Ibn Hajar al-Asqalani, v. 2, p. 509
   Sawa'iq Muhriqa Ibn Hajar Haythami, Ch. 9, section 3, p.196
   al-Faqih wal Mutafaqih al-Khatib al-Baghdadi, v. 2, p.167
   Tarikh al-Khulafaa Jalaluddin al-Suyuti, p. 171
   al-Tabaqat Ibn Sa'd, v. 2, p.338
   al-Isti'ab Ibn Abdul'l-Birr, v. 3, p.40
   al-Riyadh al-Nadhirah Muhibu'd-din Tabari, v. 3, p. 212
   Khakh'irul'-Uqba Muhibu'd-din Tabari, p. 83

581 William C. Chittick translation.

582 Madyan, Abū, The Way of Abū Madyan: Doctrinal and Poetic Works of Abū Madyan Shu'ayb Ibn al-Husayn al-Ansārī ed. and Trans. Cornell, Vincent J., Cambridge, U.K., The Islamic Texts Society, 1996, p. 146.

583 Angha, Molana Salaheddin Ali Nader Shah, Sufism and Wisdom Shahmaghsoudi Publication, ISBN: 0-910735-95-6, p. 18.

584 Monroe, Dr. Christopher. National Institute of Standards, Colorado.

585'Iraqi, Fakhruddin. Divine Flashes translation and introduction by William Chittick and Peter Lamborn Wilson, New York, Paulist Press, 1982, p. 71.

586 Muhammad Ibn Musa al-Wasiti (d. 320/932): A Sufi who associated with al-Junayd and al-Nuri in Baghdad and who later moved to Merv where he died. He was also an authority on *fiqh*. Sources: Qushayri, Risala 1:174; Sulami, Tabaqat 302-307.

587 The totality of existence is reflected in the body.

588 Muhaiyaddeen, His Holiness M. R. Bawa. A Book of God's Love Philadelphia, Pennsylvania, Bawa Muhaiyaddeen Fellowship, 1981.

589 Al-Jami. The Precious Pearl Al-Jami's Al-Durrah Al-Fakhirah together with his Glosses and the Commentary of 'Abd al-Ghafur al-Lari Trans. with an introduction, notes, and glossary by Heer, Nicholas, Albany, State University of New York Press, 1979.

590 Haeri, Shaykh Fadhlalla (collector). The Sayings and Wisdom of Imam Ali Trans. Yate, Asadullah ad-Dhaakir.

591 William C. Chittick Ibn al-'Arabi's Metaphysics of Imagination: The Sufi Path of Knowledge Albany, New York, State University of New York Press, 1989, p. 213.

592 Mahmud-I Shabustare. Gulshen-I Raz Trans. Al-fakir Tosun al-Jerrahi.

593 Hixon, Lex. The Core of All Kingdoms: An Exploration of Non-Duality with Lex Hixon, hosted by Suzanne Taylor, http://www.mightycompanions.com/page4.html

594 Herbert, Nick. Elemental Mind: Human Consciousness and the New Physics Dutton 1993 (Nick Herbert is the author of three books: Quantum Reality, Faster-Than-Light and Elemental Mind.)

595 John, Bubba Free. Breath and Name: The Initiation and Foundation Practices of Free Spiritual Life San Francisco, California, The Dawn Horse Press, 1977, p. 43.

596 Qur'an 39:47.

597 'Arabi, Ibn al-. The Bezels of Wisdom Mahwah, New Jersey, Paulist Press, 1980 p. 232.

598 'Arabi, Ibn al-. The Bezels of Wisdom Mahwah, New Jersey, Paulist Press, 1980, p 78.

599 Hadrat Abdul-Qadir Al-Jilani. The Secret of Secrets interpreted by Shaykh Tosun Bayrak, by permission of the Shaykh Bayrak, The Islamic Text Society, "Sufi Review" Spring, 1993.

600 'Arabi, Ibn al-. The Sufi Path of Knowledge; Ibn al-'Arabi's Metaphysics of Imagination; Trans. William C. Chittick, Albany, New York: SUNY Press, 1989, p 15.

601 'Arabi, Ibn al-. The Bezels of Wisdom Mahwah, New Jersey, Paulist Press, 1980, p. 34.

602 'Arabi, Ibn al-. The Bezels of Wisdom Mahwah, New Jersey, Paulist Press, 1980, p. 206.

603 'Arabi, Ibn al-. Journey to the Lord of Power: A Sufi Manual on Retreat Trans. Rabia Terri Harris, Vermont, Inner Traditions International, 1989, p. 40.

604 The Tawasin of Mansur al-Hallaj, Trans. Aisha at-Tarjumana, Berkeley and London: Diwan Press, 1974.

605 Rumi, Jalalo'd-Din Mathnawi-ye ma'nawi Edited by R. A. Nicholson, Tehran, 1977, I p. 1570.

606 The Murid must be careful in regard to what music he or she listens to, as music (being an aspect of the One Power) can be helpful or destructive.

607 Ta'us, Malek. The Book of Divine Effulgence

608 Norris, H. T. Saharan Myth and Saga Oxford, Clarendon Press, 1972, pp. 10, 11.

609 Al-Kisa'i. Aja' ib al-malakut Leiden MS.

610 Norris, H. T. Saharan Myth and Saga Oxford, Clarendon Press, 1972, p. 12.

[611] Westermarck, E. Ritual and Belief in Morocco London, 1926, pp. 90-3 and 256.

[612] See "Pagan" in Glossary.

[613] Jung, C. G. The Collected Works of C. G. Jung: Mysterium Coniunctionis: An inquiry into the separation and synthesis of psychic opposites in alchemy, Volume 14, Eds. Sir Herbert Read, Michael Fordham, M.D. M.R.C.P., Gerhard Adler, Ph.D., Princeton, New Jersey, Princeton University Press, 1970, (vol. 18, p. 1654).

[614] Tirmidhî, V:58.

[615] Wilson, Peter Lamborn. Sacred Drift: Essays on the Margins of Islam San Francisco: City Light Books, 1993, p. 88.

[616] Rodinson, Maxime. Muhammad, Trans. from the French by Anne Carter, New York, Pantheon Books, 1980.

[617] Baldick, Julian. Black God: The Afroasiatic Roots of the Jewish, Christian, and Muslim Religions London: New York, Syracuse University Press, 1997.

[618] "AL'LAT" Tantra: The Magazine, 1992.

[619] "AL'LAT" Tantra: The Magazine, 1992.

[620] 'Arabi, Ibn al-. The Bezels of Wisdom Mahwah, New Jersey, Paulist Press, 1980, p. 78.

[621] 'Arabi, Ibn al-. Journey to the Lord of Power: A Sufi Manual on Retreat Trans. Rabia Terri Harris, Vermont, Inner Traditions International, 1989, p. 27.

[622] Nurbakhsh, Dr. Javad The Great Satan 'Eblis' London, Khaniqahi-Nimatullahi Publications, 1986, p. 30.

[623] Friedlander, Shems. with Al-Hajj Shaikh Muzafferiddin, Ninety-Nine Name of Allah: The Beautiful Names, by Perennial Library, Harper and Row Publishers, New York, 1978, p. 7.

[624] 'Arabi, Ibn al-. The Bezels of Wisdom Mahwah, New Jersey, Paulist Press, 1980, p. 224.

[625] 'Arabi, Ibn al-. The Bezels of Wisdom Mahwah, New Jersey, Paulist Press, 1980, p. 148.

[626] 'Arabi Ibn al-. Journey to the Lord of Power Into by Sheikh Muzaffer Ozak al-Jerrahi, Trans. Rabia Terri Harris, Vermont, Inner Traditions International, 1989, p. 25.

[627] Nubuwwa (Prophethood) of Women, Volume V, pp 17-19, al-Fisal fi al-Milal wa-al-Ahwa'i wa-al-Nihal, by Abu Muhammad Ali Ibn Ahmad Ibn Hazm al-Andaluci.

[628] Qur'an, al-Nahl 16:68.

[629] Qur'an, Hud 11:72.

[630] Qur'an, Mariam 19:19.

[631] This is in reference to the verses in Surah Al 'Imran 3:37-38. It reads:
" *Whenever Zacharias entered the sanctuary to see her, he found some eatables (Rizq) with her. He would ask, 'O Mary, whence have these come to you?' She would answer, 'It is from Allah, Allah provides without stint for whom he wills.' Thereupon, Zacharias invoked his Lord and said, 'Lord, bestow upon me from Thyself righteous offspring for Thou alone hearest prayers.' "*

[632] Qur'an, Mariam 19: 58.

[633] Siddiq (M) or Siddiqa(F) (Ar.): An embodiment of truth and righteousness.

[634] This is a part of a Sahih hadith reported by both Bukhari and Muslim. The hadith, as it appears in Sahih Muslim looks as follows:
Abu Musa reported Allah's messenger saying: *"There are many persons amongst men who are quite perfect. But there are not perfect amongst women except Mary, daughter of Imran, and Asiya wife of Pharaoh. And the excellence of 'Aisha as compared to women is that of Tharid (some type of food) over all foods."*

[635] Qur'an, al-Baqarah 2:253.

[636] Ibn Hajjar al-'Asqalani, Fath al-Bari bi-Sharh Sahih al-Bukhari, Vol. 6, pp. 514-516, Dar al-Rayyan lil-Turath. Cairo, 1986

[637] Imam al-Nawawi, Sahih Muslim bi-Sharh al-Nawawi, Vol. 15, pp. 198-199, Dar Ihya' al-Turath al-'Arabi, Bayrut, Lebanon, 1984.

[638] P. Travers, "Gurdjieff", Man, Myth & Magic, An Illustrated Encyclopedia of the

Supernatural.

[639] *"Original name George S. Georgiades (b. 1872?, Alexandropol, Armenia, Russian Empire—d. Oct. 29, 1949, Neuilly, near Paris), Greco-Armenian mystic and philosopher who founded an influentialquasi-religious movement. Details of Gurdjieff's early life are uncertain, but he is thought to have spent his early adult years traveling in northeast Africa, the Middle East, India, and especially Central Asia, learning about various spiritual traditions."* Encyclopaedia Britannica

[640] James Moore, Gurdjieff- Anatomy of a Myth.

[641] John Shirley, The Shadows of Ideas - A Distant Glimpse of Gurdjieff

[642] Richard Hodges

[643] Muslim.

[644] Bukhārī.

[645] Rumi, Jelaluddin. Love is a Stranger: Selected Lyric Poetry of Jelaluddin Rumi Vermont, Threshold Books, 1993, p. 50.

[646] Abu Sa'id al-Kharraz died in A. D. 899. Cf. Hujwîrî, Al'. Kashf al-mahjub Trans. R. A. Nicholson, London, 1911.

[647] Awn, Peter J. Satan's Tragedy and Redemption: Iblis in Sufi Psychology Netherlands, Leiden E. J. Brill, 1983, p. 138.

[648] Qur'an 7:12 and 38:76.

[649] 'Arabi, Ibn al-. "Whoso Knoweth Himself . . ." from the Treatise on Being Abingdon, Oxon, Great Britain, Beshara Publications, 1976, p. 11.

[650] 'Arabi, Ibn al-. "Whoso Knoweth Himself . . ." from the Treatise on Being Abingdon, Oxon, Great Britain, Beshara Publications, 1976, pp. 4, 5, 6, 16.

[651] 'Arabi, Ibn al-. The Bezels of Wisdom Mahwah, New Jersey, Paulist Press, 1980, p. 72.

[652] Hadith Qudsi

[653] Hixon, Lex. A Mighty Companions Interview with Lex Hixon, http://www.mightycompanions.com/page6.html

[654] Ibn Huseyn Suleymi. The Way of the Futuwwet Trans. from Turkish: Sheikh Tosun Bayrak al-Jerrahi al-Halveti, unpublished paper, January 9, 1981.

[655] The Gospel of Philip 82: 20-25.

[656] The Gospel of Philip 53:10-25.

[657] Jung, Carl Gustav. Answer to Job, Vol. 283, 1st ed., Princeton University Press, 1972, Para. 756.

[658] Bowles, Paul. M'Hashish taped and trans. from the Moghrebi by Paul Bowles, San Francisco: City Light Books, 1993

[659] Abd al-Qadi al-Baghdadi. Al-Farq bayn al-Firaq, Trans. as Moslem Sects and Schisms by K. S. Seelye , New York, Columbia University Press, 1920.

[660] Practitioners of the "Witness Game" which uses "gazing" chastely at beautiful boys (also known as "Contemplation of the Beardless"), musical improvisation, and dance.

[661] Bible.

[662] Bowles, Paul. M'Hashish taped and trans. from the Moghrebi by Paul Bowles, San Francisco: City Light Books, 1993.

[663] Wilson, Peter Lamborn. Irish Soma http://www.t0.or.at/hakimbey/soma.htm

[664] Stone, Robert. Damascus Gate Boston & New York, Houghton Mifflin Company, 1998, p. 373.

[665] Jung, Carl Gustav. Answer to Job, Vol. 283, 1st ed., Princeton University Press, 1972 Par. 746.

[666] Khan, Pir-o-Murshid Inayat. The Object and Moral of Worship of the Sufi.

[667] 'Arabi, Ibn al-. The Sufi Path of Knowledge; Ibn al-'Arabi's Metaphysics of Imagination; Trans. William C. Chittick, Albany, New York: SUNY Press, 1989, p 17.

668 Abû Sa'îd Ibn Abî-l- Khayr.

669 'Abdu'l-Q'âdir al-Gîlânî.

670 Biesele, Marguerite Anne. Folklore and Ritual of !Kung Hunter-Gathers, thesis presented to Harvard University, Department of Anthropology, Cambridge, Massachusetts, 1975.

671 Sunni Reference: Sahih Tirmidhi, V. 2, P. 86, V. 9, P. 74-75.

672 Saqr b. Abi Dalf relates that he heard this statement made by Imam Ali Naqi (Ithbat al-hudat, Vol. 6, p. 275).

673 Fadl b. Shadhan, who died after the birth of the twelfth Imam and before the death of Imam Hassan 'Askari, wrote in his book on *Ghayba*, relating from Muhammad b. Ali b. Hamza who said that he heard Imam Hassan 'Askari make this statement. (Muntakhab al-athar, p. 320).

674 Lalljee, Yousuf N. Know Your Islam Elmhurst, N.Y., Tahrike Tarsile Qur'an, 1995.

675 Other sources give various names: Narjis, Sayqal, Rayhana, Khumt, Hukayma, and Maryam. The seeming confusion regarding the name of the mother may have been a deliberate stratagem in order to protect the identity of the mother.

676 Muhammad b. Talha Shafi'i, Muhammad b. Yusuf, Nuru'd-din Bin Sabbagh Maliki, Yusuf b. Qazughli, Shablanji, Ibn Hajar, Muhammad Amin Baghdadi, Ibn Khallikan, Mir Khwand, Sha'rani, Skwaja Parsa, Abut al-Falah Hanbali, Dhahabi, and Muhammad b. Ali Hamawi. Besides all these above mentioned Sunni scholars there are numerous others who have recorded the birth of Imam Hassan Askari's son (see the references complied in the volume Kash al-astar, by Husayn b. Muhammad Taqi Nuri and Kifayat al-muwahhidin by Tabarsi, especially volume 2).

677 Ithbat al-hudat Vol. 6, p. 311.

678 Al-tusi, Sheikh. Kitab al-ghayba p. 202

679 For our respected Sunni brothers and sisters, there are six authentic collections of tradions based on the Sunni standards for verifying the authenticity of a tradition. These six books are: Sahih al-Bukhari; Sahih Muslim; Sahih al-Tirmidhi; Qazwini, Ibn Maja. Sunan; Sunan Abu Dawud; and Sahih al-Nisa'i.

   Sunni References:

   a. Sahih Tirmidhi, V. 2, P. 86, V9, pp. 74-75.

   b. Sunan Abu Dawud, V. .2, P. 7.

   c. Musnad Ahmad Ibn Hanbal, V. 1, p. 376 and V. 3, p. 63.

   d. Al-Mustadrak 'ala al-Sahihayn al-Hakim al-Nishaburi, V. 4, p. 557.

   e. Al-Majma' Tabarani, p. 217.

   f. Tahdhib al-Thabit Ibn Hajar al-Asqalani, V. 9, p. 144.

   g. Sawaiq al-Muhraqa Ibn Hajar Makki, p. 167.

[and many others]

680 Qazwini, Ibn Maja. Sunan, V. 2, Tradition #4085.

681 Qazwini, Ibn Maja. Sunan, V. 2, Tradition #4086.

682 Qazwini, Ibn Maja. Sunan, V. 2 Tradition #4082.

683 Lakha, Murtaza Ahmed. The Twelfth Imam, London, R & K Tyrrell, 1993, p. 9.

684 Qazwini, Ibn Maja. Sunan, V. 2 Tradition # 4082.

685 Lakha, Murtaza Ahmed. The Twelfth Imam London, R & K Tyrrell, 1993, p. 54.

686 Cohen, Andrew. Abandon the Future "Creations Magazine" October/November 1997, p. 35.

687 Cohen, Andrew. Abandon the Future "Creations Magazine" October/November 1997, p. 35.

688 Cohen, Andrew. Abandon the Future "Creations Magazine" October/November 1997, p. 35.

689 For those who understand, this axiom is a tawil rendition of: La illahe il ALLAH.

690 Helminski, Kabir. Mevlana is a Wide Open Door for Humanity "Eye of the Heart", Vol. 2, Issue 1, p. 1.

691 Habiba. Where the Eagles Fly: Portraits of Women of Power, Habiba: A Sufi Saint from

Uzbekistan video, New York, Mystic Fire Video, 1997.

[692] John, Bubba Free. Breath and Name: The Initiation and Foundation Practices of Free Spiritual Life San Francisco, California, The Dawn Horse Press, 1977, p. 42.

[693] Hixon, Lex. A Mighty Companions Interview with Lex Hixon, http://www.mightycompanions.com/page6.html

[694] This incident is transmitted by al-Tabrani and is recorded on p. 191, Vol. 9, of al-Haythami's book Majma' al-Rijal, a concordance of trusted transmitters of hadith.

[695] Shehadi, Fadlou. Ghazali's Unique Unkowable God: A Philosophical Critical Analysis of some of the Problems raised by Ghazali's View of God as Utterly Unique and Unknowable Netherlands, E. J. Brill, 1964, p. 93.

[696] Austin, R. W. J. in his introduction to chapter XIX of The Bezels of Wisdom.

[697] Qud't, 'Ain Al-, quoted in: Awn, Peter J. Satan's Tragedy and Redemption: Iblis in Sufi Psychology Netherlands, Leiden E. J. Brill, 1983.

[698] Rumi, Jelaluddin. Open Secret: Versions of Rumi Trans. Moyne, John and Coleman Barks, Putney, Vermont, Threshold Books, 1984, p. 81.

[699] See our book Beyond Duality: The Art of Transcendence (New Falcon Publications, 1995) for more information on how to achieve constructive equilibration with the Sacred Dark Side.

[700] Ozak, Sheikh Muzaffer al-Jerrahi al-Halveti Love is the Wine: Talks of a Sufi Master in America Ed. and Compiler Sheikh Ragip Frager, Vermont: Threshold Books, 1987.

[701] 'Arabi, Ibn al-. The Bezels of Wisdom Mahwah, New Jersey, Paulist Press, 1980, p. 87.

[702] 'Arabi, Ibn al-. The Bezels of Wisdom Mahwah, New Jersey, Paulist Press, 1980, p. 102.

[703] Muhaiyaddeen, His Holiness M. R. Bawa. A Book of God's Love Philadelphia, Pennsylvania, Bawa Muhaiyaddeen Fellowship, 1981.

[704] What Is to Be Realized? from Scientific Proof of the Existence of God Will Soon Be Announced by the White House! http://www.adidam.org/wisdom/Nov97/whatis.htm

[705] Qur'an 9:67.

[706] Vaughan-Lee, Llewellyn. Forgetfulness "Sufi" Issue 37/Spring 1998, p. 35.

[705] Qur'an 9:67.

[708] 'Arabi, Ibn al-. The Bezels of Wisdom Mahwah, New Jersey, Paulist Press, 1980, p. 95.

[707] Qur'an 22:32.

[709] *"The men and women who remember Allah abundantly."* Qur'an 33:35.

[710] Abu Ja'far ('Alaihi Assalam) reported that his father told him that his grandfather reported that Allah's Messenger (Peace be upon him) made this statement.

[711] Sviri, Sara. Where the Two Seas Meet: The story of Khidr "Sufi" Autumn 1996.

[712] Corbin, Henry. Creative Imagination in the Sufism of Ibn 'Arabi New Jersey, Princeton University Press, 1969, pp. 56-57.

[713] Corbin, Henry. Creative Imagination in the Sufism of Ibn 'Arabi New Jersey, Princeton University Press, 1969, pp. 60-61.

[714] Emre, Yunus. Geldi geçti ömrüm benim, sol yel esip geçmis gibi.

[715] This topic is explained in greater detail in our first book Beyond Duality: The Art of Transcendence New Falcon Publications, 1995.

[716] See al-Tha'labi, Qia al-anbiya Cairo, 1920, p. 120 and I. Friedländer, Die Chadirlegende und der Alexanderroman Leipzig, 1913.

[717] Trismigistus, Hermes. Hermetica: The Ancient Greek and Latin Writings which containa religious or phiolosophical techings ascribed to Hermes Trismigistus Oxford, The Clarendon Press, 1912.

[718] Ouspensky, P. D. The Fourth Way New York, Vintage Books, 1971, p. 224.

[719] Ouspensky, P. D. The Fourth Way New York, Vintage Books, 1971, p. 224.

[720] Wilson, Peter Lamborn. Sacred Drift: Essays on the Margins of Islam San Franciso: City

Light Books, 1993, p. 139.

[721] Corbin, Henry. Creative Imagination in the Sufism of Ibn 'Arabi New Jersey, Princeton University Press, 1969, p. 32.

[722] Corbin, Henry. Creative Imagination in the Sufism of Ibn 'Arabi New Jersey, Princeton University Press, 1969, p. 60-61.

[723] Corbin, Henry. Creative Imagination in the Sufism of Ibn 'Arabi New Jersey, Princeton University Press, 1969, p. 67.

[724] Wilson, Peter Lamborn. Sacred Drift: Essays on the Margins of Islam San Francisco. City Light Books, 1993, p. 140.

[725] Wilson, Peter Lamborn. Sacred Drift: Essays on the Margins of Islam San Franciso: City Light Books, 1993, p. 141.

[726] Pellat, Charles. Kitab al-Tabari' wa'l-Tadwir.

[727] 'Arabi, Ibn al-. The Sufi Path of Knowledge; Ibn al-'Arabi's Metaphysics of Imagination; Trans. William C. Chittick, Albany, New York: SUNY Press, 1989, p 17.

[728] al-Munqidh min ad-Daallal, p. 131.

[729] Maqasid at-Tawhid, p. 20.

[730] Itiqadaat Furaq al-Muslimeen, pp. 72, 73.

[731] Muqaddimat ibn al-Khaldun, p. 328.

[732] The magazine "al-Muslim," 6th ed. 1378 H, p. 24.

[733] "Majallat al-Manar," 1st year, p. 726.

[734] 'Arabi, Ibn al-. Journey to the Lord of Power Intro by Sheikh Muzaffer Ozak al-Jerrahi, Trans. Rabia Terri Harris, Vermont, Inner Traditions International, 1989, p.5.

[735] There Is Simply The "Bright" Itself from chapter forty-four of The Dawn Horse Testament Of Adi Da http://www.adidam.org/wisdom/Nov97/simply.htm

[736] Corbin, Henry. Creative Imagination in the Sufism of Ibn 'Arabi New Jersey, Princeton University Press, 1969, p. 278.

[737] Bey, Hakim Millennium, New York: Automedia and Garden of Delight, 1996

[738] Helminski, Kabir Edmund. A talk delivered at the conference: Sufism and The Attractiveness of Islam Casablanca, Morocco, April 1997.

[739] Shaykh Taner Ansari Tarsusi er-Rifai el-Qadiri. Qadiri Rifai Tariqa Statement of Purpose http://www.qadiri-rifai.org/purpose.html

[740] Rajneesh, Bhagwan Shree. Journey Toward the Heart: Discourses on the Sufi Way San Francisco, Harper and Row, Publishers, 1976.

[741] Arberry, A. J. Trans. A Sufi Martyr: The Apologia of 'Ain al-Qudat al-Hamadhani London, George Allen and Unwin Ltd., 1969, pp. 40-41.

[742] Arberry, A. J. Trans. A Sufi Martyr: The Apologia of 'Ain al-Qudat al-Hamadhani London, George Allen and Unwin Ltd., 1969, p. 101.

[743] 'Iraqi, Fakhruddin. Divine Flashes translation and introduction by William Chittick and Peter Lamborn Wilson, New York, Paulist Press, 1982, p.123.

[744] Ozak, Sheikh Muzaffer al-Jerrahi al-Halveti. Love is the Wine: Talks of a Sufi Master in America edited and compliled by Sheikh Ragip Frager, Vermont: Threshold Books, 1987, p. 37.

[745] OCLC (Online Computer Library Center). "WorldCat" is the OCLC "Online Union Catalog,"containing more than thirty five million records.

[746] Helminski, Kabir Edmund. A talk delivered at the conference: Sufism and The Attractiveness of Islam Casablanca, Morocco, April 1997.

[747] Wilson, Peter Lamborn. Sacred Drift: Essays on the Margins of Islam San Franciso: City Light Books, 1993, p.62.

[748] Davidson, Gustav. A Dictionary of Angels (Including the Fallen Angels) New York, The Free Press,1967, pp. 63 - 64.

[749] Moosa, Matti. Extremist Shiites:The Ghulat Sects pp.186-187.

[750] Birge, John Kingsley. The Bektashi Order of Dervishes London, Luzac Oriental, 1994, p. 34 –5.

[751] Gurdjieff: Essays and Reflections on the Man and His Teaching edited by Needleman, Jacob and George Baker, New York, Continuum, 1996, pp. 433-4.

[752] Definition couresty of G. Thursby.

[753] Shah, Amjad. Allama Iqbal
http://www.cis.ohio-state.edu/hypertext/faq/usenet/pakistan-faq/faq-doc-15.html

[754] Calderini, Simonetta. Cosmology and authority in medieval Ismailism "Internet Journal of Religion" 1997, pp. 11-12. http://www.uni-marburg.de/fb03/religionswissenschaft/journal/

[755] A Dictionary of Islam.

[756] Encyclopedia Britannica.

[757] Alchemy in Ibn Khaldun's Muqaddimah Edited and prepared by Prof. Hamed A. Ead, Cairo University, Giza http://www.levity.com/alchemy/islam20.html

[758] Rabbani, Hadhrat Maulana Wahid Bakhsh, in his commentary in: al-Hujweri, Syed Ali Bin Uthman. The Kashful Mahjub "Unveiling the Veiled": The Earliest Persian Treatise on Sufism Malaysia, A.S. Noordeen, 1997, p. 20.

[759] Nurbakhsh, Dr. Javad. A Selfless Master "Sufi", Issue 37/Spring 1998, p. 28 (reprinted from Discourses on the Sufi Path).

[760] Definition courtesy of Cynndara.

[761] Naqshbandi Sufi Way, http://www.naqshbandi.org/chain/8.htm

[762] Definition courtesy of Cynndara.

[763] Confucianism. I Ching, Great Commentary 1.11.5-6.

[764] 'Attar, Farido'd-Din Manteq-o't-tair edited by Seyyed Sadeq Gauharin, Tehran, 1977, p. 183.

INDEX

"If you distinguish between a gem and a stone
received from the King, you are not a person of the path!
If you're pleased with a gem and disappointed
by a Stone, you have not interest, then, in the King.
Neither like the gem, nor dislike the stone; consider Only that both are from the hand of the King.
If the drunken Beloved throws a stone at you, it is Better than receiving a gem from another." 764

"If the sword of your anger puts me to death,
My soul will find comfort in it.
If you impose the cup of poison upon me,
My spirit will drink the cup.
When on the day of Resurrection
I rise from the dust of my tomb,
The perfume of your love
Will still impregnate the garment of my soul.
For even though you refused me your love,
You have given me a vision of You
Which has been the confidant of my hidden secrets."

- Sa'dî

"Be!"

"My Mercy encompasses everything."

Ya Ali Madad